ISBN 978-1-5280-8241-9
PIBN 10927154

C000010541

1 MONTH OF
FREE
READING

at

www.ForgottenBooks.com

By purchasing this book you are eligible for one month membership to ForgottenBooks.com, giving you unlimited access to our entire collection of over 1,000,000 titles via our web site and mobile apps.

To claim your free month visit:

www.forgottenbooks.com/free927154

SUMMER SESSION

Bulletin of

MONTCLAIR
STATE TEACHERS COLLEGE

JULY 1 to AUGUST 10

1940

UPPER MONTCLAIR, NEW JERSEY

SUMMER SESSION

Bulletin of
MONTCLAIR
STATE TEACHERS COLLEGE

1940
July 1 to August 10

UPPER MONTCLAIR, NEW JERSEY

Officers of Administration

STATE BOARD OF EDUCATION

D. Stewart Craven, *President*..Sal

Oscar W. Jeffery, *Vice-President*..Englewo

Mrs. Edward L. Katzenbach...Trent

Gustave A. Hunziker ....Little Fa

D. Howard Moreau..Flemingt

Joseph W. Mott..Atlantic Ci

Miss May M. Carty..Jersey Ci

Mrs. William F. Little..Rahw

Carl R. Woodward...New Brunswi

Miss Mary Merchant ....Dov

COMMISSIONER OF EDUCATION

Charles H. Elliot..Trenton Trust Bldg., Trent

DIRECTOR OF TEACHER EDUCATION

Robert H. Morrison...Trenton Trust Bldg., Trent

OFFICERS OF ADMINISTRATION
NEW JERSEY STATE TEACHERS COLLEGE
UPPER MONTCLAIR SUMMER SESSION

Harry A. Sprague..Director of Summer Sess

Charles W. Finley..Dean of Instruct

Elizabeth S. Favor...Secretary of Summer Sess

Charlotte G. Marshall...Regist

Maude L. Carter..Dean of Wor

Zaidee Brown...Libra

Donald A. DeWitt..Business Man

FACULTY

rles William Finley, Ph.D. .... Dean of Instruction; Biology
via Block, A.B. .... Applied Arts
old C. Bohn, A.M. .... English
derick H. Brunswick, A.M. .... Integration
gar C. Bye, A.M. .... Social Studies
ise B. Cason, A.M. .... Psychology
l C. Clifford, A.M. .... Mathematics
vrence H. Conrad, A.M. .... English
Winifred Crawford, A.M. .... Multi-Sensory Aids
maine Poreau Cressey, A.M. .... French
l G. Cressey, A.M. .... Sociology
vid R. Davis, Ph.D. .... Mathematics
ome Pennington DeWitt, A.A.A. .... Fine Arts
ward Franklin Fehr, A.M. .... Mathematics
lter H. Freeman, Ph.D. .... Acting Head, Dept. of Foreign Languages
ncis R. Geigle, A.M. .... Business Education
rl Rouse Glenn, A.M. .... Head of the Department of Science
arles E. Hadley, Ph.D. .... Biology
lliam Paul Hamilton, A. M. .... English
y Winthrop Hatch, A.M. .... Head of the Department of Social Studies
anuel H. C. Hildebrandt, Ph.D. .... Mathematics
on Crist Hood, A.M. .... Radio
is C. Ingebritsen, Ph.D. .... Psychology
aude E. Jackson, A.M. .... Research
enry Johnson, A.M. .... History
ussell Krauss, Ph.D. .... English
rdinand Meyer Labastille, A.M. .... Economics
rant Leman, Ph.D. .... Multi-Sensory Aids
hel F. Littlefield, A. M. .... Languages
irgil S. Mallory, Ph.D. .... Head of the Department of Mathematics
lna McEachern, Ph.D. .... Director of the Department of Music
bert W. McLachlan, Ph.D. .... Science
arley P. Milstead, Ph.D. .... Geography
nest DeAlton Partridge, Ph.D. .... Sociology
hn R. Patterson, Ph.D. .... Administration
mes Parker Pettegrove, A.M. .... English
hester M. Pittser, A.M. .... Physical Education
homas Clark Pollock, Ph.D. .... Head of the Department of English
ed M. Raubinger, A.M. .... Public Relations
hn J. Rellahan, A.M. .... Social Studies
eber Hinds Ryan, Ph.D. .... Head of the Department of Integration
rthur M. Seybold, A.M. .... Director, College H.S.; Integration
nneth Orville Smith, Ph.D. .... Science
. cott Smith, Ph.D. .... Integration
i ard Voliva, A.M. .... Physical Education
arry A. Wann, Ph.D. .... Administration
live G. Williams, A.M. .... Supervision
lix Wittmer, Ph.D. .... Social Studies
oy R. Zimmerman, A.M. .... Administration

SUMMER SESSION 1940

Visiting Teachers

Sylvia Block, A.B.: Director of the Puppet Center of New York, which is under the spon: ship and supervision of the Board of Education of that city.

Frederick H. Brunswick, A.M.: Supervising Principal, Public Schools of Fairlawn, N. J.

Eloise B. Cason, A.M.: Formerly psychologist in Rochester, N. Y., Public Schools, and rece Instructor of Psychology at Syracuse University.

E. Winifred Crawford, A.M.: Supervisor of Visual Education, Public Schools of Montcl N. J.

Jerome Pennington DeWitt: Member of the American Association of Artists. New Y studio. Has exhibited in New York, Boston, and Philadelphia.

Leon Crist Hood, A. M.: Teacher of English in Clifford J. Scott High School, East Orar N. J. Chairman of Radio Committee for New Jersey Association of Teachers of Eng and New Jersey Education Association.

Henry Johnson, A.M.: "Dean of history teachers of the United States"; Head of the Dep ment of History at Teachers College, Columbia University. Author of our best-knc textbook on "The Teaching of History," and nationally well-known lecturer in his chc field.

Grant Leman, Ph.D.: Supervising Principal, Bogota, N. J. President, New Jersey Visual / Association.

John R. Patterson, Ph.D.: Supervising Principal, Public Schools of Millburn, N. J.

Fred M. Raubinger, A.M.: Principal-elect, Passaic County Regional High School, Li Falls, N. J.

Harry A. Wann, Ph.D.: County Superintendent of Schools, Morris County, New Jersey.

Olive G. Williams, A.M.: Principal, Green Avenue School, Madison, New Jersey.

Roy R. Zimmerman, A.M.: County Superintendent of Schools, Bergen County, New Jerse:

SUMMER SESSION OF THE
EW JERSEY STATE TEACHERS COLLEGE AT MONTCLAIR

LOCATION AND GROUNDS

Located about three and one-half miles from the center of Montclair, on the jrst range of the Watchung mountains, with a campus of about seventy acres,)f which thirty are undeveloped .and wooded or rocky and precipitous and forty re beautifully developed with roadways, walks, shrubbery, trees, and lawns, with n amphitheatre, tennis courts, athletic fields, and college buildings, the State Teachers College at Montclair offers an admirable opportunity to pursue intellectual vork and to enjoy recreational activities while doing so.

Because of the elevation and abundant shade, the campus has been considered generally comfortable and attractive throughout the summer session.

Eighteen miles away on the horizon rise the towers of the buildings and bridges)f the city of New York, with its World's Fair beyond. Still nearer, the city of Newark, New Jersey, can be seen.

Within a few miles of the college are the wooded reservations that afford ielightful walks, horseback rides, and picnics. Lakes Mohawk, Hopatcong, Green-vood, and many smaller lakes are easily reached by car over beautiful roads through he mountains of .northern New Jersey. To the south, the shore resorts of Asbury ?ark, Ocean Grove, Atlantic City, and other beaches invite one to the sea.

RESIDENCE HALLS FOR MEN AND WOMEN

Edward Russ Hall and Chapin Hall are Montclair's two well-appointed resi-ences. In summer, Chapin is reserved as living quarters for all students. The main lining room is in Edward Russ Hall. The charge for living on campus is reasonable —$10.00 per week, including room, breakfast, and dinner. A la carte luncheons ire served in the college cafeteria. For one student in a double room, an extra charge of $10.00 is made. The college provides all furnishings, with the exception)f towels, blankets, and desk lamps. The fee must be paid on or before the first lay of the summer session. No rebate is made for occasional absence or voluntary withdrawal during the session. Students who are absent on account of illness for two weeks or more will receive a rebate of $5.00 per week during the illness.

The elevation of the residence halls on the campus hill assures a cool breeze lay and night, and also a magnificent view of the gardens and small farms in he valley and the jagged New York skyline just beyond.

The summer recreational activities include baseball, tennis, archery, swim-ming, riding, and hiking. These activities and others are easily planned and also easily accessible. The Dean of Women, athletic directors, and hostesses of he residence halls make a special effort to provide social and recreational activities for the men and women living on the campus.

For reservations in the college residence hall, address Mrs. Maude L. Carter; State Teachers College, Upper Montclair, New Jersey.

PURPOSE OF THE SUMMER SESSION AT MONTCLAIR

All courses have been organized and selected primarily for men and wom
engaged in or preparing for professional service in junior and senior high schoo
This includes:

1. Candidates for a bachelor's degree in the field of secondary education;

2. Teachers holding a bachelor's degree who are candidates for gradua
   credit or master's degree;

3. Junior and senior high school principals and supervisors seeking spec
   courses or higher certificates and degrees;

4. Graduates of non-professional colleges who wish to take certificate cour:
   or a master's degree in special teaching fields;

5. Graduates of high schools, junior colleges, and four-year colleges w.
   wish to take subject-matter courses for general culture.

FOR NON-MATRICULATED STUDENTS

The College feels a special responsibility to those who are interested in pr
moting the profession of teaching. It also serves laymen and women who des
to take courses for cultural, vocational, or avocational purposes, in which case t
work may be taken with or without credit. High school graduates, or studer
who have not pursued college courses for credit, may take for credit cour:
numbered 100 to 299 inclusive. Students who have credit for at least two ye:
of work on college level may take for credit courses numbered 300 to 4:
inclusive. Courses numbered 500 and above may be taken for credit only l
those who have had three or more years of college work.

AUDITORS

Those who desire merely to audit courses should indicate on their regist:
tions that they are taking the work for no credit and have a clear understandi
with their instructors at the beginning of the summer session to that effe
Failure to do this may result in the student's receiving a failing mark for i
course.

MATRICULATION

Those who wish to become candidates for the A.B. or the A.M. deg
at Montclair must matriculate. Registration for courses does not constit
matriculation. Students should make application for matriculation on the fc
provided for that purpose. This may be obtained from the office of the Dean
Instruction. The request for it should make clear which degree the studen'
interested in obtaining. When submitting the application, properly filled in,
student must send his official transcripts of all previous work of college grade.
letter should be addressed to the Registrar. When an applicant has been accep
as a candidate for a degree, a definite statement will be furnished him, show
the requirements to be fulfilled in order to obtain the degree desired.

COURSES LEADING TO THE A.B. DEGREE

Candidates for the A.B. degree at Montclair should consult the complete atalogue of the college for the general requirements and for the details of the quirements in their particular major and minor fields. Also, they should confer ith the Dean of Instruction regarding the general program of their work and ith the Head of the Department in which they are majoring regarding the lection of their courses. Matriculated students should not take courses without his guidance.

COURSES LEADING TO THE A.M. DEGREE

Candidates for the A.M. degree at Montclair should consult the graduate ulletin of the college for the general requirements for that degree and for the etails of the requirements in their major field. Also, they should confer with he Dean of Instruction regarding the general program of their work and with he Head of the Department in which they are majoring regarding the selection f their courses. Matriculated students should not take courses without this uidance.

A graduate student may not take a course on the 100 or 200 level for credit.

A student matriculated for the A.M. degree at Montclair may not take a ourse on the 300 level for credit unless the Head of the Department in which he student is majoring so requests in writing to the Dean of Instruction. Only ne such course may be offered for credit toward the A.M. degree.

Courses numbered 400 and above may be taken for graduate credit.

Courses numbered 500 and above are designed for students holding baccalaureate degrees.

STUDENTS MATRICULATED AT OTHER COLLEGES

Graduate and undergraduate students matriculated at colleges other than Montclair who desire to take courses here this summer for credit to be presented at such other colleges should obtain in advance the approval of their own Deans of their selection of courses.

TEACHING CERTIFICATES

Anyone desiring information regarding the requirements for New Jersey teaching certificates should write to the State Board of Education at Trenton for the booklet entitled: "Rules Concerning Teachers Certificates."

Students definitely seeking New Jersey teaching certificates should submit official transcripts of all previous work on college level to the Secretary of the State Board of Examiners, State Department of Public Instruction, Trenton, N. J. No one working for a teaching certificate should select his courses until he has received a statement showing the evaluation of his previous work and the further courses needed to qualify him for the certificate he desires. As this requires time, the student who decides at the last minute to work for a teaching certificate will need to take his transcripts to Trenton, rather than to wait to mail them and receive a reply by mail.

LIST OF COURSE OFFERINGS FOR THE NEW JERSEY LIMITED
SECONDARY CERTIFICATE

This is not an official statement. It does not emanate from the State Depart
ment which issues the certificate. It is furnished the student merely for hi
convenience in selecting his courses. It shows where the courses of this colleg
fit into the plan outlined by the State Department.

I Health Education—3 semester-hours required
   Biology 409 Human Physiology—3 s.h.
   Physical Education 301B—Health and Health Teaching, Part I—2 s.h.
   Physical Education 302B Health and Health Teaching, Part II—2 s.h

II Educational Psychology—3 semester-hours required
   Integration 200A Introduction to Educational Psychology and Ment
                     Testing—2 s.h.
   Integration 200B Adolescent Psychology and Mental Hygiene—2 s.h
   Integration 500B Advanced Education Psychology—3 s.h.

III Aims and Organization (Principles) of Secondary Education—3 s.h. require
   Integration 300A Aims and Organization of Secondary Education—2 s.h
   Integration 400A Principles and Philosophy of Secondary Education-
                     2 s.h.
   Integration 405   Principles of Junior High School Teaching—2 s.h.
   Integration 500A History and Principles of Secondary Education—3 s.h
   Integration 502A Organization and Administration of the Modern Hig
                     School, Part I—2 s.h.
   Integration 502B Organization and Administration of the Modern Hig
                     School, Part II—2 s.h.

IV Principles and Techniques of Teaching in the High School—3 s.h. require
   Integration 300B Principles and Techniques of Teaching in the Second
                     ary School—2 s.h.
   Integration 500C Teaching Procedures in Secondary Education—3 s.h

V Curriculum Organization and Courses of Study (Methods) in One Endorse
   Teaching Field—3 semester-hours required.
   Business Education 401 The Teaching of Business Education in th
                           Secondary School—3 s.h.
   English 401 The Teaching of English in the Secondary School—3 s.h
   Language 401 The Teaching of Foreign Languages in the Secondar
                 School—3 s.h.
   Mathematics 401—The teaching of Mathematics in the Secondary Scho
                 —3 s.h.
   Music 401 The Teaching of High School Music—3 s.h.
   Science 401 The Teaching of Science in the Secondary School—3 s.h
   Science 505 Survey of Curricula and Science Courses in State and Cit
                Systems—3 s.h.
   Biology 501 The Teaching of Biology—3 s.h.
   Chemistry 501 The Teaching of Chemistry—3 s.h.
   Physics 501 The Teaching of Physics—3 s.h.
   Social Studies 401 The Teaching of the Social Studies in the Seconda
                       School—3 s.h.

VI Elective—3 semester-hours required
   Courses in the Department of Integration that are definitely in the fie
   of Secondary Education and that have not been taken to satisfy one
   the above requirements.

The student will note that either an undergraduate or a graduate course m
be applied toward the certificate. Not all the above courses are offered duri
any one semester or summer session.

CONFERENCES

Students are urged not to wait until the opening of the summer session to consult their advisers. Between the date of publication of the bulletin and the close of the spring semester, students may arrange to confer with both the Dean of Instruction and the Department Heads relative to matriculation, courses, credit, etc., by writing directly to the particular official concerned for an appointment. For those who have found it impossible to make an earlier appointment, the Dean of Instruction and the Heads of Departments will hold office hours on July 1. The Secretary of the State Board of Examiners also will be at the college on July 1, between the hours of 10 A.M. and 3 P.M., to see students who desire a last word of advice. He cannot, however, undertake at this time to evaluate all the previous work of a student, as the interviews are but five minutes long. (See instructions on page 7, under "Teaching Certificates.") The Secretary of the Summer Session will receive requests for appointments with this State Official and will notify the student of the exact time of the appointment.

REGISTRATION

There is no advance registration, except for the Field Study courses.* In all other courses, registration takes place on July 1, in the individual classes. Unless there are 10 students present, the course is discontinued immediately. Students from such discontinued courses register in other classes on July 2. Registration is completed by calling at the Business Office, in the basement of the college, in the late afternoon or on the day following registration in class, to obtain the Class Admission Card. This must be delivered to the instructor not later than July 3 or no credit will be granted for the course. The mail clerk in the college bookstore will, if requested, place the Class Admission Card in the postbox of the instructor for the student.

Training Teachers, taking a course without charge, follow these same procedures. The Class Admission Card will be audited without payment of fees, upon presentation to the Business Manager of evidence that the teacher is entitled to this credit.

FEES

There is a registration fee of $1.00 for the summer session. This fee will not be refunded in case of withdrawal.

Legal residents of New Jersey are required to pay a tuition fee of $6.00 per point or semester-hour credit. Non-residents of New Jersey are required to pay $8.00 per point. Courses taken for no credit cost the same as those for credit.

Laboratory Fee: A fee of $1.50 will be charged in connection with each of the following courses: Biology S407, Biology S408, Physics S102A and Physics S304.

Deferred payment fee: Students taking two or more courses may arrange in the Business Office for payment on a deferred basis; for this privilege, there is an extra charge of $1.00 per course. No deferred payment is permitted for a single course.

*Because of the necessity for knowing in advance how many students will take these two courses, students may register for them at any time, provided the fees accompany the registration. If interested, write for registration blanks.

WITHDRAWAL FROM COURSES

A student who finds it necessary to withdraw from any course after havi completed his registration for it must so notify the Secretary of the Summ Session in writing immediately; otherwise the registration stands as a char against the student and the fees for it are not refunded. No refunds of tuiti fees are made except in cases of illness.

CREDITS AND TRANSCRIPTS

The total amount of credit which may be earned in one summer is 8 semest hours.

Each course is in session at least thirty hours and receives credits as designat Official transcripts of the summer's work are mailed directly to students within week or ten days of the close of the summer session. This first transcript is fu nished to the student without charge. The cost of a second transcript depen upon the amount of work which the student has completed at this college, rangi from 25c for one semester or summer session to $1.00 for four or more. The colle cannot provide a second transcript that covers less than all the work complet by the student. Stamps cannot be accepted as payment for transcripts; check post-office money order should be used when remitting fees by mail.

The mark of "D" when earned in summer, part-time, or extension cours is not accepted for credit at Montclair, but will be given when earned, for possi use elsewhere.

Courses that carry a credit of 4 semester-hours in the regular curriculum the college are usually given in the summer session in two parts, each half cou carrying a credit of 2 semester-hours. Occasionally, the nature of the course such that the two parts must be taken in a designated sequence, in which c attention is drawn to that fact in the course description.

INCOMPLETE WORK

A student who has made an earnest endeavor to meet all requirements, t has failed in one particular, on account of illness, may see the instructor in cha of the course, and, if he thinks it advisable, the student may be granted t months' time in which to complete the work. If the work has not been finisl by the end of this time, the mark for the course shall be "F." The responsibil regarding incomplete work rests with the student.

THE COLLEGE HIGH SCHOOL

The College High School will be continued this summer. Opportunities thus be afforded students to observe demonstration lessons. College students desire to place their own children in the demonstration school should make quiries as early as possible. Families who desire to live in the residence hall, att college, and place their children in the high school will be given special c sideration.

SUPERVISED STUDENT TEACHING

The opportunity to do supervised student teaching is not offered during summer session. Students desiring to do this work during the fall semester sh write to Dr. Robert H. Morrison, Director of Teacher Education, State Departn of Public Instruction, Trenton, New Jersey.

10

ROOM NUMBERS

Room numbers followed by the letters CHS indicate rooms in the College High School building. All other room numbers refer to rooms in College Hall, the main building on the campus. Meetings and conferences that take place in the living rooms of the residence halls are indicated by ERH for Edward Russ Hall and CH for Chapin Hall.

SCHEDULE

Classes are so scheduled that all courses that meet daily are held in the morning, and that no afternoon class meets on either Wednesday or Saturday, thus leaving Wednesday and Saturday afternoons free each week for all students. Furthermore, no classes are held on Saturday, July 13, or on Saturday, July 27. This may be kept in mind in planning for afternoons and week-ends in New York, at the World's Fair, or at shore or mountain resorts.

THE SCHOOLMEN'S CONFERENCE
July 11 and 12
"FACING YOUTH PROBLEMS"

The aim of this conference is to bring together administrators and other leaders for discussion of the problems that confront youth today. It is desired that this should be a conference out of which will come definite action. It is hoped, therefore, that administrators, principals, and supervisors of high schools and junior high schools will come with suggestions of a practical nature to present to each other.

CALENDAR

Monday, July 1
 8:00 A.M.—Summer Session opens

Thursday, July 11
 10:00 A.M.—Schoolmen's Conference begins

Friday, July 12
 4:00 P.M.—Schoolmen's Conference ends

Saturday, July 13
 No classes

Saturday, July 27
 No classes

Tuesday, August 6
 8:00 A.M. - 12:25 P.M. and 1:00 - 2:25 P.M.—Examinations
 in classes receiving 2 semester-hours credit

Thursday, August 8
 8:00 A.M. - 12:25 P.M. and 1:00 - 2:25 P.M.—Examinations
 in classes receiving 3 semester-hours credit
 3:00 P.M.—Summer Session ends

CURRICULUM OF COURSES COVERING CURRENT PROBLEMS IN SECONDARY SCHOOL ADMINISTRATION, GUIDANCE, CURRICULUM, AND TEACHING

Supplementing a full program of summer courses, the College offers a curriculum of relate courses. The eight courses that are linked in this program are organized solely for dealing wit the current problems and the new movements and materials on the secondary school level. Th "workshop" plan, as developed in the "summer workshops" of the Progressive Educatio Association, is used.

Courses are arranged in two groups:

GROUP I

Director: Dr. H. H. Ryan

Section I—*Managing the School*   Credit: 4 semester hours
Problems in administration, guidance programs, curriculum construction, extra-curricu lar activities, finance, educational philosophy

Section II—*Directing Instruction*   Credit: 4 semester-hours
Problems in supervision, teaching techniques, curriculum experimentation, evaluatio corrective reading, multi-sensory aids

Section III—*Understanding Youth*   Credit: 4 semester-hours
Problems in adolescent psychology, "human relations," mental hygiene, the teacher i guidance, educational sociology, community relations, the visiting teacher

GROUP II

Directors: Heads of Departments

Current Problems in the Teaching of English
Current Problems in the Teaching of Foreign Languages
Current Problems in the Teaching of Mathematics
Current Problems in the Teaching of Science
Current Problems in the Teaching of the Social Studies
Credit: 4 semester-hours each

Each of the above five courses in this group is based on current movements in th fields represented, individual professional problems, and an examination of the new materials and methods recently developed or now in the course of development.

Each course, both in Group I and Group II, is conducted as follows:

1. Under the supervision of the Director, general conference periods are held ea week as arranged.
2. Conferences between the individual student and a special consultant are he by appointment.
3. Free unassigned time for individual study is allowed.

The course includes the definition, study, evaluation, and report on each individu problem.

The Workshop Plan

Under this plan, teachers, deans, principals, supervisors, and superintendents bring to t college their own current problems and receive credit for research, study, and planning that carried forward under a qualified leader, with the direct assistance of a special consultant whom the student is assigned by the Director, and with a group of people who have simi interests.

Individual Problems

Reports on individual problems by members of the group comprise a large part of subject matter of the course. Each individual works upon his own problem. Individuals wh problems are closely related may work also as small committees, pooling such parts of th findings as would prove of mutual benefit.

Courses May Be Taken in Pairs

The courses are arranged in two groups: a group of three courses organized to deal w administrative and guidance problems, and a group of five courses organized to deal with major fields of instruction. Most of the problems upon which individuals wish to work requ membership in two courses, one in each of these groups, making a program of 8 semester-ho

DESCRIPTION OF COURSES

LEISURE TIME ACTIVITY COURSES

Applied Art S413   Puppetry and Related Crafts   Dr. Partridge and Miss Block

This course constitutes a complete experience in the construction, manipulation, and utilization of puppets in teaching. All phases of puppet construction, including hand puppets, marionettes, and shadow puppets, are studied, as well as the construction of stages, stage properties, and models from discarded materials. Stress is placed upon keeping cost at a minimum and utilizing the facilities that are to be found in any classroom. Demonstrations show how puppets can be used to motivate various types of subject-matter. Meets Mondays, Tuesdays, Thursdays, and Fridays for one and one-half hours.
Begins Monday, July 1; 8:00 A. M. - 30 hours - Credit: 2 S. H.   Room: Shop

Fine Art S409   Outdoor Sketching   Mr. DeWitt

This course pertains to art in the open. It includes the fundamentals of drawing and painting from nature; the structure and character of different motifs used in landscape painting, such as trees, buildings, mountains, the sky, water, animals, and men at work; the effect of light and the lack of light on things painted and its application to art; and the study of nature as a whole and as it is used to create a result of art. The class is held on a farm not far from the college campus, where the conditions and materials at hand are ideal for the work. On rainy days, a large barn is used for a studio. Any medium may be studied and its technique developed. Both beginners and advanced students may enter the class, because the instruction is mostly individual. Meets Tuesdays, Wednesdays, and Thursdays, for three hours. Credited on a laboratory basis.
Begins Monday, July 1, 9:30 A. M. - 45 hours - Credit: 2 S. H.   Room 11 CHS

Note: Students may earn credits in the above courses toward a college degree or they may work solely for their own enjoyment and for the purpose of developing a hobby. In addition to these courses, students will find in other departments one or more courses which may be taken with a view to their possibilities for the enrichment of leisure time. The following list is suggestive:

> *English S 312—Acting, Directing, and Make-up*
> *English S 408—Creative Writing*
> *Physical Education S 406—Games and Game Skills*
> *Physics S 304—Photography for High School Teachers*
> *Social Studies S 512—Old Virginia, Maryland, West Virginia, Pennsylvania*

DEPARTMENT OF BUSINESS EDUCATION

Business Education S401   The Teaching of Business Education in the Secondary School   Mr. Geigle

The history and development of business education, aims or objectives, laws of learning, lesson plans, teaching procedures, tests and measurements, and special helps for the teacher of business education are studied in this course. Consideration is given to the current trend in teaching in these fields, with emphasis on the viewpoint of the consumer as well as the social and vocational objectives. Meets daily for one and one-half hours.
Begins Monday, July 1; 1:00 P. M. - 45 hours - Credit: 3 S. H.   Room D

Business Education S411A   Cost Accounting   Mr. Geigle

A thorough knowledge of bookkeeping is a prerequisite to a profitable study of this course. The course deals with the basic principles of modern cost finding and cost keeping, and endeavors to give a practical application of these principles to present-day conditions. The practical application consists of a laboratory budget containing business papers, vouchers, etc., together with full instructions for writing up a practice set of cost books. Meets Mondays, Tuesdays, Thursdays, and Fridays for one and one-half hours.
Begins Monday, July 1; 9:30 A. M. - 30 hours - Credit: 2 S. H.   Room D

DEPARTMENT OF ENGLISH

English S100A   World Literature, Part I   Dr. Kraus

This course surveys the main contributions of Egyptian, Babylonian, Persian, Hebrew, Greek and Roman Literature to world thinking. The specific contributions of such renowned writer as Homer, Sappho, Aeschylus, Sophocles, Euripides, Plato, Aristotle, Cicero, Virgil, Horace Livy, and Tacitus are considered in detail. The objective of the course is three-fold: to increase literary appreciation, to trace the influence of a body of literature or a single author upon late writers, and to examine the thought of the past in relation to that of the present. Meets Mon days, Tuesdays, Thursdays, and Fridays for one and one-half hours.

Begins Monday, July 1; 9:30 A. M. - 30 hours - Credit: 2 S. H.   Room

English S312   Acting, Directing, and Make-up   Mr. Bohr

The various steps from the choosing of a play, through rehearsal techniques, to final perform ance are taken up in their proper order. Fundamentals in acting are studied on the stage b practice and exercise. The study of make-up is of laboratory type, involving actual make-up by members of the class. A play is directed by the instructor before the class and presented at a college assembly. Students also interview actors, designers, directors, and others actively engaged in theatre work on Broadway. Meets Mondays, Tuesdays, Thursdays, and Fridays fo one and one-half hours.

Begins Monday, July 1; 1:00 P. M. - 30 hours - Credit: 2 S. H.   Room

English S401   The Teaching of English in the Secondary School
                                                                                Mr. Hamilton

This course deals with the methods of teaching composition and literature in the high school It aims to unify and organize the professional training and practical experience of all student in the course, and to provide new points of view for their active English teaching by setting up objectives and indicating concrete methods of obtaining those objectives. The require work in composition and literature, as outlined in city and state courses of study, receive attention. Demonstrations of composition, grammar, and literature teaching are given in th College High School classes for observation and criticism. (This course satisfies the require ment of Curriculum Organization and Courses of Study in the field of English for the Limite Secondary Certificate.) Meets daily for one and one-half hours.

Begins Monday, July 1; 11:00 A. M. - 45 hours - Credit: 3 S. H.   Room 13, CH

English S402A   Survey of English Literature, Part I   Dr. Kraus

The survey of English literature draws together into a systematic narrative the story of th development of literature in the English language. The course enables students to secure sound background in English literature as an historical development, to become acquainte with a number of great masterpieces, and to fill in gaps in their reading. Part One carries th study to 1660. Meets Mondays, Tuesdays, Thursdays, and Fridays for one and one-half hour

Begins Monday, July 1; 8:00 A. M. - 30 hours - Credit: 2 S. H.   Room

English S406   The Modern Novel   Mr. Conra

Particular emphasis is given to British and American novels since 1870, and all importa tendencies of present-day prose fiction are explored. Students are taught how to read a nov with profit, and how to guide and direct the reading of others. Meets Mondays, Tuesday Thursdays, and Fridays for one and one-half hours.

Begins Monday, July 1; 1:00 P. M. - 30 hours - Credit: 2 S. H.   Room

English S408   Creative Writing   Mr. Conra

Students in this course attempt seriously the standard literary forms in prose and verse. Ea student is assisted in finding his own best field of writing, and is given further training in th field. The course is based entirely upon the needs of the class as revealed in student-writt manuscripts. Much time is devoted to criticism and to discussion of mutual problems. Where possible, the course is made to reflect methods of creative teaching in the field of compositio Meets Mondays, Tuesdays, Thursdays, and Fridays for one and one-half hours.

Begins Monday, July 1; 9:30 A. M. - 30 hours - Credit: 2 S. H.   Room

14

English S426   The Victorian Novel   Mr. Pettegrove

This is an intensive unit of work on the novel in Victorian England. A review of the development of the English novel before this period is followed by studies in the works of Dickens, Thackeray, Austen, Eliot, Trollope, Meredith, and Hardy. Novels studied in the high school are treated professionally in class. Meets Mondays, Tuesdays, Thursdays, and Fridays for one and one-half hours.

Begins Monday, July 1; 8:00 A. M. - 30 hours - Credit: 2 S. H.   Room 1

English S431A   Shakespeare and the English Drama, Part I   Mr. Hamilton

The main emphasis of this course is upon eight Shakespearean tragedies and chronicle plays: Hamlet, Othello, King Lear, Macbeth, Richard II, Henry IV (part one), Henry V, and Richard III. The topics studied include Shakespeare's conception of tragedy; his dramatic art; his poetry; the sources of his plays; staging in Shakespeare's theatre and in our own; typical textual problems; and aids for the teaching of Shakespeare in the secondary school. Meets Mondays, Tuesdays, Thursdays, and Fridays for one and one-half hours.

Begins Monday, July 1; 8:00 A. M. - 30 hours - Credit: 2 S. H.   Room 13, CHS

English S442B   American Literature from Walt Whitman to the Contemporary Period   Mr. Conrad

This course surveys the development of American literature from the Civil War to the contemporary period. The writers studied include Walt Whitman, Sidney Lanier, Emily Dickinson, William Dean Howells, Mark Twain, Henry James, Henry Adams, Hamlin Garland, Stephen Crane, Frank Norris, O. Henry, Vachel Lindsay, E. A. Robinson, Carl Sandburg, and Robert Frost. Meets Mondays, Tuesdays, Thursdays, and Fridays for one and one-half hours.

Begins Monday, July 1; 8:00 A. M. - 30 hours - Credit: 2 S. H.   Room C

English S443   Modern Drama   Mr. Bohn

This course is intended to stimulate interest in one of the most powerful expressions of contemporary life—the theatre. An historical survey of trends, dramatists, plays, and accomplishments from Ibsen to the latest prize plays on Broadway provides background. An examination of the structure and content of plays to determine what constitutes a good play stimulates appreciation. Students are encouraged to read widely and to see many of the current productions on Broadway. Meets Mondays, Tuesdays, Thursdays, and Fridays for one and one-half hours.

Begins Monday, July 1; 11:00 A. M. - 30 hours - Credit: 2 S. H.   Room A

English S446   The One-Act Play   Mr. Bohn

This course studies the one-act play as an art form, devoting special attention to plays which are suitable for high school production. The student is given an opportunity to enrich his knowledge of a type of drama which, though frequently neglected in courses in literature, is of great professional value to the teacher in the secondary school. Meets Mondays Tuesdays, Thursdays, and Fridays, for one and one-half hours.

Begins Monday, July 1; 9:30 A. M. - 30 hours - Credit: 2 S. H.   Room A

English S503   Geoffrey Chaucer and His Times   Dr. Krauss

Some of the works of Chaucer are read rapidly, others studied intensively, so that the student may acquire a broad general understanding of Chaucer's place in the history of English literature, as well as facility in reading and interpreting the mediaeval text of his stories. Meets Mondays, Tuesdays, Thursdays, and Fridays, for one and one-half hours.

Begins Monday, July 1; 11:00 A. M. - 30 hours - Credit: 2 S. H.   Room 2

English S506   John Milton   Mr. Hamilton

This course has for its primary aim the thorough understanding and true evaluation of Milton's poetry. Contributory to this end are the following topics: the Puritan struggle for civil and religious liberty; the growth of science in the seventeenth century; the life, personality, and prose writings of Milton; his literary heritage and influence; and a comparison of Milton with the Cavalier and Metaphysical poets. Meets Mondays, Tuesdays, Thursdays, and Fridays, for one and one-half hours.

Begins Monday, July 1; 9:30 A. M. - 30 hours - Credit: 2 S. H.   Room 13, CHS

English S514   The Origin and Development of the Arthurian Legend

Dr. Kraus

This course deals with the vague and tentative beginning of the Arthur story, in early chronicl and legend; with Geoffrey of Monmouth's pseudo-historical and Chretien de Troyes's romanti treatments; with the great mediaeval recapitulations of Gottfried von Strassburg, Wolfram vo Eschenbach, and Sir Thomas Malory; with the Victorian retellings of Tennyson, Arnold, an Morris; with the musical adaptations of Wagner; and with the modern versions of E. / Robinson. It includes a detailed history of the development of the legend in its divers form. Meets Mondays, Tuesdays, Thursdays, and Fridays, for one and one-half hours.
Begins Monday, July 1; 1:00 P. M. - 30 hours - Credit: 2 S. H.   Room

English S517   Recent Research and Experiment in the Teaching of Englis

Dr. Polloc

This course analyzes and evaluates current research in the fields of language, literature, an composition relevant to the teaching of English in the high school, and examines crit250ll recent experimentation in methods of teaching English. The aim of the course is to mak available to the student any recent knowledge and experience which may throw light on th problems of English teaching in secondary schools and to evaluate tendencies in this fiel< The course is conducted as a seminar. Meets Mondays, Tuesdays, Thursdays, and Fridays, fc one and one-half hours.
Begins Monday, July 1; 9:30 A. M. - 30 hours - Credit: 2 S. H.   Room:

English S601   Workshop: Current Problems in the Teaching of English

Dr. Pollock and the English Sta

This course is designed to give the secondary school teacher of English an opportunity to wor under expert direction on a professional problem which he has met in his teaching. The worl shop method is used. Working in close cooperation with others interested in similar problem the teacher is helped to analyze and approach a solution of his problem in the light of the be modern knowledge concerning materials and methods for the teaching of English.*
Begins Monday, July 1; 11:00 A. M. - 60 hours - Credit: 4 S. H.   Room

DEPARTMENT OF FOREIGN LANGUAGES

French S102B   Modern French Civilization From 1871 to 1940   Mrs. Cresse

This course presents a picture of modern France from 1871 to today. The form and structu: of the French government and modern industrial and commercial life are surveyed. Speci; emphasis is placed on a study of modern social institutions and other trends of present-d French civilization. French newspapers and magazines are read and discussed. The course conducted in French with due regard to the language ability of the students. Prerequisite: o year of college French or the ability to understand oral French. Meets Mondays, Tuesday Thursdays, and Fridays for one and one-half hours.
Begins Monday, July 1; 9:30 A. M. - 30 hours - Credit: 2 S. H.   Room

French S407A   Survey of French Drama From Its Beginning to 1887

Mrs. Cress<

This course traces the development of the French theatre from the early religious and secul plays to the formation of the "theatre libre." The influence of the imitation of the Greek a Roman theatres in the sixteenth century on the formation of the classical ideals is considere It includes a study of the decadence of tragedy, the influence of Shakespeare, the beginning the drama in the 18th century. It studies the development of comedy from the mediaeval fa to Labiche, and shows the influence of the different literary movements on the 19th centu theatre. The course is conducted in French. Meets Mondays, Tuesdays, Thursdays, and Frid for one and one-half hours.
Begins Monday, July 1; 11:00 A. M. - 30 hours - Credit: 2 S. H.   Room

French S415   The French Club and Other Extra-Curricular Activities

Mrs. Cress

This course, designed particularly for teachers of French, surveys briefly the aims of ext curricular activities in modern language work and emphasizes especially: the organization

For complete information as to the conduct of the Workshops, see page 12.

16

extra-curricular activities, the preparation of materials, and the procedures. The course is conducted on the model of a forum with general discussion. The actual conduct of an extra-curricular activity is required as a laboratory feature. Meets Mondays, Tuesdays, Thursdays, and Fridays for one and one-half hours.
Begins Monday, July 1; 1:00 P. M. - 30 hours - Credit: 2 S. H.   Room 9

Language S300   Foundations of Language   Miss Littlefield

This course is required of all candidates for the A.B. degree regardless of their major subjects. A comprehensive survey is made of the background, growth, and structure of the English language, traced from its remote Indo-European ancestry down through the changes wrought by foreign additions and influences. By a systematic and comparative study of the main elements of Greek, Latin, French, Anglo-Saxon, and English, and of the phonetic phenomena recurring in language development, the course presents and augments the important diction values derived from foreign language study. It aims especially to train teachers of general language or of exploratory courses in foreign language. Meets Mondays, Tuesdays, Thursdays, and Fridays for one and one-half hours.
Begins Monday, July 1; 8:00 A. M. - 30 hours - Credit: 2 S. H.   Room 10

Language S401   The Teaching of Foreign Languages in the Secondary School
Miss Littlefield

This course is open to seniors and graduates majoring or minoring in foreign languages and satisfies the requirement in Curriculum Organization and Courses of Study in the foreign language field for the Limited Secondary Certificate. The work is focused on such topics as the following: ultimate and immediate aims in foreign language teaching; new fields opening up for the foreign language teacher; survey of outstanding methods, with emphasis on oral work; new methods of reading and of developing grammar; new realia; reports on new textbooks; review, tests, and supervised study. A unit on Comparative Phonetics is included. Special attention is given to the city and state courses of study in New Jersey. General language teachers find this course helpful to them also. Meets daily for one and one-half hours.
Begins Monday, July 1; 11:00 A. M. - 45 hours - Credit: 3 S. H.   Room 10

Language S414   Language Relationships   Miss Littlefield

An investigation of the way languages behave and the formulae derived from such behaviour. This develops into an introduction to language study in general and to the most economical attack for acquiring another language. Meets Mondays, Tuesdays, Thursdays, and Fridays for one and one-half hours.
Begins Monday, July 1; 1:00 P. M. - 30 hours - Credit: 2 S. H.   Room 10

Language S601   Workshop: Current Problems in the Teaching of Foreign
Languages   Dr. Freeman and Foreign Language Staff

This course is designed to give the secondary school teacher an opportunity to work under expert direction on individual professional problems related to present curriculum requirements and specific interests in language teaching methods based on current movements in language teaching. The workshop method is used.*
Begins Monday, July 1; 11:00 A. M. - 60 hours - Credit: 4 S. H.   Room 10

DEPARTMENT OF GEOGRAPHY

Geography S202B   Geography of the Western Hemisphere, Part II: South
America   Dr. Milstead

A detailed regional study is made of the activities of the people of South America in relation to their natural environment. The commercial relations and possibilities for future development are emphasized. Part I of this course, dealing with North America, will be given at a later date, but is not prerequisite to this part. Meets Mondays, Tuesdays, Thursdays, and Fridays for one and one-half hours.
Begins Monday, July 1; 9:30 A. M. - 30 hours - Credit: 2 S. H.   Room 26

*For complete information as to the conduct of the Workshops, see page 12.

Geography S411   Geographic Influences in American History   Dr. Milstead

A study is made of the geographic factors influencing the development of social, economic, and political life in America. It is recommended especially to students of history and related subjects. Meets Mondays, Tuesdays, Thursdays, and Fridays for one and one-half hours.

Begins Monday, July 1; 11:00 A. M. - 30 hours - Credit: 2 S. H.   Room 2

Geography S503   Economic Geography of the United States   Dr. Milstead

This course constitutes a study of the economic geography of the United States in relation to the growth and development of this nation. Meets Mondays, Tuesdays, Thursdays, and Friday for one and one-half hours.

Begins Monday, July 1; 1:00 P. M. - 30 hours - Credit: 2 S. H.   Room 2

Geography S504   Economic Geography of Europe   Dr. Milstead

This is a study of the economic and commercial development of the countries of Europe in relation to their environment. Meets Mondays, Tuesdays, Thursdays, and Fridays for one and one-half hours.

Begins Monday, July 1; 8:00 A. M. - 30 hours - Credit: 2 S. H.   Room 2

DEPARTMENT OF INTEGRATION

Integration S200A   Introduction to Educational Psychology and Mental Testing
Mrs. Caso

This course covers the psychology of classroom procedure. Growth and development of child and adolescent personality are studied from the physical, intellectual, social, and emotional aspects of individual pupils and their adjustment to the group. The relation of testing to th problems of understanding children as learners and to the problem of treating individual differences is studied through testing projects. Meets Mondays, Tuesdays, Thursdays, and Fridays for one and one-half hours.

Begins Monday, July 1; 11:00 A. M. - 30 hours - Credit: 2 S. H.   Room 3, CH

Integration S300A   Aims and Organization of Secondary Education
Dr. W. Scott Smith

The content of this course may be summarized by the topics included, which are as follows (1) nature and function of the American secondary school; (2) historical development of secondary education in the United States; (3) organization of the administrative units; (4) secondary education in other lands; (5) the students; (6) the program of studies and activities (7) the staff; (8) buildings, grounds, and equipment; (9) cost and support of education; and (10) the secondary school as a social and economic instrument. Meets Mondays, Tuesday Thursdays, and Fridays for one and one-half hours.

Begins Monday, July 1; 1:00 P. M. - 30 hours - Credit: 2 S. H.   Room

Integration S300B   Principles and Techniques of Teaching in the Secondary
School   Mr. Brunswic

After having established the fundamental principles underlying the teaching process, the following techniques and procedures are presented and evaluated: the question, the lesson plan the assignment, testing and marking systems, classroom management and routine; and speci procedures, such as supervised study. In addition to the above topics, based on subject-matt organization and administration, various types of classroom procedure are considered. T course seeks to develop a critical attitude with sound principles as bases. Meets Monday Tuesdays, Thursdays, and Fridays for one and one-half hours.

Begins Monday, July 1; 9:30 A. M. - 30 hours - Credit: 2 S. H.   Room 3, CH

Integration S400A   Principles and Philosophy of Secondary Education
Dr. Ry

This course evaluates educational objectives, techniques, procedures, and organizations in re tion to the needs and demands made upon the school by society and by the developing personality. It involves a discussion of the meaning of philosophy and an interpretation of hum values. Fundamental principles of education are evolved from previous work in the vario fields of thought contributing to educational philosophy. Meets Mondays, Tuesdays, Thursda and Fridays for one and one-half hours.

Begins Monday, July 1; 8:00 A. M. - 30 hours - Credit: 2 S. H.   Room

18

Integration S406   Educational Sociology   Dr. Partridge

This course deals with the application of sociological principles to educational problems. The school is treated as a part of the community, and the various social forces that affect the school and its administration are considered. The following topics are included: family backgrounds; community organization; social breakdown; socialized classroom methods; the social approach to individual behavior difficulties. Meets Mondays, Tuesdays, Thursdays, and Fridays for one and one-half hours.

Begins Monday, July 1; 9:30 A. M. - 30 hours - Credit: 2 S. H.   Room 29

Integration S408   Multi-Sensory Aids   Miss Crawford and Dr. Leman

Sources, principles of selection, standards of evaluation, and methods of use of the various multi-sensory aids are studied in relation to all phases of school-work: the utilization of field trips, specimens, models, exhibits, and experiments; prints, stereopticon slides, film slides, silent and sound motion pictures; photoplay appreciation; maps, graphs, charts, diagrams, cartoons; and puppets and marionettes. Instruction is given in making many of the above aids and in the operation and care of the various projectors. Meets Mondays, Tuesdays, Thursdays, and Fridays for one and one-half hours.

Begins Monday, July 1; 8:00 A. M. - 30 hours - Credit: 2 S. H.   Room 4

Integration S409   Radio and Sound Equipment in the Classroom   Mr. Hood

This course studies the ways in which radio programs and sound equipment may be used to achieve the recognized objectives of high school teaching. The desirable aims and procedures of classroom practice are analyzed briefly. The class is given practice in the handling of radios, amplifying systems, and recording equipment as teaching aids. Problems of script writing, microphone and recording techniques, and simple production are considered. As a practical integration of the work of the course, each student develops a teaching unit involving the use of radio or of sound equipment in the classroom. Students who have taken English 444 for credit may not receive credit for this course. Meets Mondays, Tuesdays, Thursdays, and Fridays for one and one-half hours.

Begins Monday, July 1; 1:00 P. M. - 30 hours - Credit: 2 S. H.   Room 13, CHS

Integration S500A   History and Principles of Secondary Education
Dr. Patterson

This course traces the development of secondary education. Consideration is given to the meaning of liberal education as it was conceived by earlier civilizations. Special attention is given to organizations, curricula and methods of instruction, and to the social conditions affecting the development of secondary schools in England, Germany, France, and the United States. Meets daily for one and one-half hours.

Begins Monday, July 1; 8:00 A. M. - 45 hours - Credit: 3 S. H.   Room 24

Integration S500B   Advanced Educational Psychology   Dr. Ingebritsen

Prerequisite: Integration 200A or its equivalent. In this course, a comparative study is made of contemporary schools of psychology with emphasis on their direct application to education. Practical applications are made to classroom problems and the work of guidance departments. Meets daily for one and one-half hours.

Begins Monday, July 1; 9:30 A. M. - 45 hours - Credit: 3 S. H.   Room 30

Integration S500C   Teaching Procedures in Secondary Education   Mr. Seybold

This course emphasizes the fundamental principles underlying the technique of teaching on the secondary school level. Some of the topics considered are: organization of knowledge; the logical and psychological aspects of method; developing appreciations; social-moral education; teaching motor control; fixing motor responses; books and verbalism; meeting individual differences; guidance in study; tests and examinations; marks and marking. Meets daily for one and one-half hours.

Begins Monday, July 1; 11:00 A. M. - 45 hours - Credit: 3 S. H.   Auditorium, CHS

Integration S501   Tests and Measurements in Secondary Education
Mr. Jackson

The purpose of this course is to develop an appreciation of the meaning and importance of measurement in education and to give a working knowledge of instruments of measurement.

19

The topics covered are: historical sketch of the development of educational tests and measurements; limitations of traditional types of examinations; newer types of examinations; standardized tests for teachers of English, mathematics, social studies, science, and the languages; criteria for the choice of tests; and applications of statistics in interpreting tests and measurements Meets Mondays, Tuesdays, Thursdays, and Fridays for one and one-half hours.
Begins Monday, July 1; 11:00 A. M. - 30 hours - Credit: 2 S. H. Room C

Integration S502A   Organization and Administration of the Modern High School, Part I   **Dr. Wann**
The problems considered are: the student personnel; building and revising the high school curriculum; providing for individual differences; making the school schedule; records; the guidance program; pupil participation in government; the extra-curricular program; the health program; the safety program; discipline; library and study hall; cafeteria; the principal's office and evaluating results. Meets Mondays, Tuesdays, Thursdays, and Fridays for one and one-half hours.
Begins Monday, July 1; 9:30 A. M. - 30 hours - Credit: 2 S. H. Room 2

Integration S503   Methods and Instruments of Research   Mr. Jackson
This course is required of all candidates for the Master's degree without regard to their field of major interest. Its purpose is to introduce students of education to research and its practical application to immediate problems. The course treats: the nature and types of educational research; methods and techniques of educational research; and the tools used in interpreting statistical data. During the course, the student sets up a problem and plans and carries out its solution. Meets Mondays, Tuesdays, Thursdays, and Fridays for one and one-half hours.
Begins Monday, July 1; 1:00 P. M. - 30 hours - Credit: 2 S. H. Room 2

Integration S504A   Curriculum Construction in the Secondary School
                                                                Mr. Seybold
This course purposes to introduce the student to constructive criticism of American culture, to consider the extent to which the secondary school curriculum meets the needs of a changing civilization, and to consider effective means of curriculum construction. Meets Mondays, Tuesdays, Thursdays, and Fridays for one and one-half hours.
Begins Monday, July 1; 9:30 A. M. - 30 hours - Credit: 2 S. H. Auditorium, CHS

Integration S505   Organization and Administration of Extra-Curricular Activities   **Dr. W. Scott Smith**
The first part of this course considers such general problems of extra-curricular activities as their growing importance; their relation to the curriculum; the principles underlying their organization, administration, and supervision; and methods of financing. In the second part an intensive study is made of the home room, the assembly, the student council, clubs, athletics, school publications, and other activities in which the class is especially interested. Meets Mondays, Tuesdays, Thursdays, and Fridays for one and one-half hours.
Begins Monday, July 1; 11:00 A. M. - 30 hours - Credit: 2 S. H. Room

Integration S507   Organization and Administration of Guidance Programs
                                                                Dr. Wann
The purpose of this course is to acquaint the student with the various agencies and methods for the guidance of students in school work, with certain implications in the choice of and the preparation for a vocation. Among the topics are: the abilities of students as related to guidance; the exploration of special interests; the organization of the guidance program; and the integration of the entire high school program for purposes of guidance. Meets Mondays, Tuesdays, Thursdays, and Fridays for one and one-half hours.
Begins Monday, July 1; 8:00 A. M. - 30 hours - Credit: 2 S. H. Room 3

Integration S508A   Supervision and Criticism of Teaching, Part I
                                                                Dr. Patterson
This course emphasizes the more practical phases of supervision which are met most frequently by those engaged in it. Among the topics are: the set-up for adequate supervision; supervision as encouraging and guiding the growth of teachers and the improvement of educational procedures; the supervisory functions of teachers' meetings; discussion groups; general and pr

fessional reading; the writing of articles; cooperative curriculum modification; utilization of community resources; and teacher inter-visitation. Meets Mondays, Tuesdays, Thursdays, and Fridays for one and one-half hours.
Begins Monday, July 1; 11:00 A. M. - 30 hours - Credit: 2 S. H.   Room 27

Integration S515   Guidance and Personnel Problems of Classroom Teachers
Mr. Seybold

This course considers all types of personnel problems with which the classroom teacher deals. It is concerned with the growth of pupils and seeks to point out the ways by which proper growth may be attained. Classroom, health, social, and personal activities are analyzed in terms of the needs of present-day social life. The course seeks to show how the teacher may effectively direct pupils into worthwhile channels. The teacher's own personal problem of adjustment, as it affects dynamic guidance, is considered. Meets Mondays, Tuesdays, Thursdays, and Fridays for one and one-half hours.
Begins Monday, July 1; 1:00 P. M. - 30 hours - Credit: 2 S. H.   Auditorium, CHS

Integration S516   School Finance   Dr. Patterson

This course is of special interest to school administrators, since it acquaints them with the field of finance in relation to a well-ordered school program. The topics considered are: basic problems of school support; systems of taxation; allocation of costs; computing school costs: sources of information; techniques; comparative costs; purchasing; and standards. Meets Mondays, Tuesdays, Thursdays, and Fridays for one and one-half hours.
Begins Monday, July 1; 1:00 P. M. - 30 hours - Credit: 2 S. H.   Room 27

Integration S517   Administration of the Elementary School*   Mr. Zimmerman

This course analyzes and evaluates the administrative duties and relationships of the elementary school principal. Particular consideration is given to: building management; effective use of the school plant; sanitation; health service; the library; personnel management; the administration of the curriculum; community relationships; publicity. Meets Mondays, Tuesdays, Thursdays, and Fridays for one and one-half hours.
Begins Monday, July 1; 8:00 A. M. - 30 hours - Credit: 2 S. H.   Room 27

Integration S518   Supervision of Instruction in the Elementary School*
Mr. Zimmerman

This course is planned for those engaged in the supervision of the elementary school and those who are preparing for such responsibilities. Principles of classroom supervision are developed and applied to learning situations. Among the more important topics are: the nature and function of supervision; the organization necessary for effective supervision; the nature and significance of the teacher's purposes; the methods and techniques of group and individual supervision; the technique of observation; and the supervisory conference. Meets Mondays, Tuesdays, Thursdays, and Fridays for one and one-half hours.
Begins Monday, July 1; 9:30 A. M. - 30 hours - Credit: 2 S. H.   Room 27

Integration S521   Psychological Tests in Guidance Programs   Dr. Ingebritsen

This course is designed to familiarize the student with various psychological tests and scales that may be used in guidance programs in the secondary school. The student is given practice in administering many types of group tests. This includes scoring the tests and evaluating the results, with a discussion of ways in which these results may be used. Much time is spent in actual laboratory demonstration of tests, giving students an opportunity to serve as subjects and as examiners. Class discussion is based upon first-hand information gained through use of the tests, on readings, and on class reports. Meets Mondays, Tuesdays, Thursdays, and Fridays for one and one-half hours.
Begins Monday, July 1; 11:00 A. M. - 30 hours - Credit: 2 S. H.   Room 30

*The three courses offered in the field of the supervision and administration of Elementary Education are given as a part of the graduate major in Administration and Supervision.

21

Integration S524   The Study of the Failing Pupil   Dr. Ry:

The first part of the course is devoted to the "disparity technique," a method of evaluating t pupil's achievement in relation to his ability. The second part treats of procedures to be us in finding the causes of failure, and in planning treatment. Meets Mondays, Tuesdays, Thu: days, and Fridays for one and one-half hours.

Begins Monday, July 1; 11:00 A. M. - 30 hours - Credit: 2 S. H.   Room :

Integration S531   The High School Teacher and the Community
                                                        Dr. Partrid

Based on the assumption that the school is only one of many agencies dealing with you: people, this course presents the community as an integrated whole, showing the position of t high school in this scheme. Among other things, the course deals with community organizatio supplementary agencies such as the Boy Scouts, Girl Scouts, the Y.M.C.A. and the Y.W.C./ school financing; juvenile courts and probationary forces; relief agencies, etc. Experts fr New Jersey communities in the various fields listed above describe the work of their agenci and lead discussions. Several field trips to outstanding community projects are offered. Mei Mondays, Tuesdays, Thursdays, and Fridays for one and one-half hours.

Begins Monday, July 1; 1:00 P. M. - 30 hours - Credit: 2 S. H.   Room :

Integration S532   The Teaching and Supervision of Reading in Elementa:
Schools*   •   **Miss Willian**

The place of reading in the entire elementary school program is analyzed. Attention is given necessary remedial work for junior high school students. Materials and their use in instrt tional programs are studied with a view toward increasing power. All growth levels are cc sidered. Good first teaching is of primary concern; however, the analysis and correction certain reading difficulties constitute an important portion of the course. Meets Monda' Tuesdays, Thursdays, and Fridays for one and one-half hours.

Begins Monday, July 1; 11:00 A. M. - 30 hours - Credit: 2 S. H.   Room

Integration S540   Recreational and Activity Leadership   Dr. Partrid

It is the aim of the course to furnish each student with practical skills that will be of servi in dealing with young people of high school age. The practical side is supplemented by thorough consideration of source material and theory. A partial list of the areas covered the course follows: how to organize and handle groups; the use of leaders from within t group; indoor games, stunts, mixers; outdoor games, special hikes, outdoor cooking, camp-f leadership. Special field trips are provided so that those who care to can observe camps a playgrounds in operation. Meets Mondays, Tuesdays, Thursdays, and Fridays for one a one-half hours.

Begins Monday, July 1; 8:00 A. M. - 30 hours - Credit: 2 S. H. ·   Room

Integration S542   The High School and the New Leisure   Dr. Partrid

This course surveys the amount and nature of leisure in the modern world and directs attenti to what can and is being done to meet the problem. The content of the course deals specifica with what the secondary school can do. Consideration is given to the types of courses of stt being used throughout the country and an evaluation is made of such things as photograp dramatics, music, crafts, science and similar hobby activities in the high school curriculu Meets Mondays, Tuesdays, Thursdays, and Fridays for one and one-half hours.

Begins Monday, July 1; 11:00 A. M. - 30 hours - Credit: 2 S. H.   Room

Integration S545   Interpreting the Schools to the Public   Mr. Raubin

The aim of this course is to equip school heads and teacher-leaders to organize a balan program of educational interpretation. It includes an analysis of the publics to be found any given community; a study of the devices—press, meetings, organizational contacts, sch papers, superintendents' reports, pictures, graphs, cartoons, leaflets, posters, radio, and so o which affect the thinking of these publics; and projects in setting up and executing a progi to meet the public relations problems posed by the students. Meets Mondays, Tuesdays, Thi days, and Fridays for one and one-half hours.

Begins Monday, July 1; 9:30 A. M. - 30 hours - Credit: 2 S. H.   Roor

*The three courses offered in the field of the supervision and administration of Elemeni Education are given as a part of the graduate major in Administration and Supervision.

22

**Integration S601A   Workshop, Section I: Current Problems in Managing the
School   Dr. Ryan and Staff**
Problems in administration, guidance programs, curriculum construction, extra-curricular activities, finance, educational philosophy.*
Begins Monday, July 1; 9:30 A. M. - 60 hours - Credit: 4 S. H.   Room 4

**Integration S601B   Workshop, Section II: Current Problems in Directing
Instruction   Dr. Ryan and Staff**
Problems in supervision, teaching techniques, curriculum experimentation, evaluation, corrective reading, multi-sensory aids.*
Begins Monday, July 1; 9:30 A. M. - 60 hours - Credit: 4 S. H.   Room 4

Integration S601C   Workshop, Section III: Current Problems in Understanding Youth   Dr. Ryan and Staff
Problems in adolescent psychology, "human relations," mental hygiene, the teacher in guidance, educational sociology, community relations, the visiting teacher.*
Begins Monday, July 1; 9:30 A. M. - 60 hours - Credit: 4 S. H.   Room 4

DEPARTMENT OF MATHEMATICS

**Mathematics S101A   Mathematical Analysis, Part I: College Algebra
                                                          Mr. Clifford**
This course contains the usual topics found in a beginning course in college algebra, such as: study of functional relationships; graphing of functions; solution of equations; rational and irrational functions; permutations; combinations; probability; and the use of increments in finding rate of change. Meets Mondays, Tuesdays, Thursdays, and Fridays for one and one-half hours.
Begins Monday, July 1; 8:00 A. M. - 30 hours - Credit: 2 S. H.   Room 3

**Mathematics S101B   Mathematical Analysis, Part II: Trigonometry
                                                          Mr. Clifford**
This course treats the following topics: functions and their graphical representation; functions of an acute angle; relationship of trigonometric functions; functions of any angle; reduction of functions; solution of triangles; complex numbers; trigonometric analysis; logarithms; slide rule; practical solution of triangles. When time permits, a study is made of Demoivre's theorem and its extension, the construction of trigonometric tables. Meets Mondays, Tuesdays, Thursdays, and Fridays for one and one-half hours.
Begins Monday, July 1; 9:30 A. M. - 30 hours - Credit: 2 S. H.   Room 3

**Mathematics S102A   Mathematical Analysis, Part III: Analytical Geometry
                                                          Dr. Hildebrandt**
This course is recommended particularly to those students seeking a minor in mathematics or those in need of a review course in analytic geometry. The topics include: rectangular and polar coordinate systems; loci and their equations; the straight line; the conics—circle, parabola, ellipse, and hyperbola; parametric equations; transformation of coordinates; and the general equation of the second degree. Meets Mondays, Tuesdays, Thursdays, and Fridays for one and one-half hours.
Begins Monday, July 1; 11:00 A. M. - 30 hours - Credit: 2 S. H.   Room 4, CHS

**Mathematics S102B   Mathematical Analysis, Part IV: Introduction to the
Calculus   Mr. Fehr**
This course treats the following topics: function and functional notation; average rate of change; the derivative of algebraic functions; applications to maxima and minima; velocity and acceleration; integration as the inverse operation of differentiation; applications to area, volume, and force problems; and applications of polar coordinates, parametric equations and trigonometric analysis in the Calculus. Meets Mondays, Tuesdays, Thursdays, and Fridays for one and one-half hours.
Begins Monday, July 1; 1:00 P. M. - 30 hours - Credit: 2 S. H.   Room 14, CHS

*For complete information as to the conduct of the Workshops, see page 12.

Mathematics S201A   Differential Calculus   **Dr. Da**

The chief purpose of this course is to give the student a clear understanding of the process
differentiation and its applications. The ordinary formulas for differentiating algebraic a
transcendental functions are carefully developed and applied in practical problems. The us
topics of a first course in calculus, such as: parametric equations, curvature, Theorem of Me
Value, indeterminate forms, maxima and minima, etc., are included. This course is designed
meet the needs of teachers-in-service who expect to introduce elements of the calculus in hi
school mathematics, and of students seeking further preparation in mathematics. Me
Mondays, Tuesdays, Thursdays, and Fridays for one and one-half hours.
Begins Monday, July 1; 1:00 P. M.   -   30 hours   -   Credit: 2 S. H.   Room

Mathematics S300   Social and Commercial Uses of Mathematics   Mr. Cliffo

This course is required of all candidates for the A.B. degree, regardless of their major subjec
A consideration of the economic problems met by the intelligent citizen, independent of i
vocation, forms the basis for selection of material for it. The mathematics is mostly arithmei
and includes the problems met in home and civic life. Some of the topics are: budgeting a
wise expenditure of income; providing for future independence through wise investments a
insurance; taxation; cost of installment purchases; the operation of personal finance compani
cost of living versus the buying power of income; etc. Meets Mondays, Tuesdays, Thursda
and Fridays for one and one-half hours.
Begins Monday, July 1; 11:00 A. M.   -   30 hours   -   Credit: 2 S. H.   Room

Mathematics S400   Educational Statistics   **Mr. Fe**

The aim of this course is to provide a sufficient background to enable the student to comprehe
and criticize articles of statistical nature in current educational literature, to apply statisti
methods in testing and rating pupils, and to carry on the simpler types of educational resear
Among the topics treated are: graphical and tabular representation; measures of central tend
cies; measures of variability; linear correlation; the normal distribution; sampling; and rel
bility of measures. The application of the subject provides natural integration with psycholo
tests and measurements, and procedures in secondary education. The methods are equa
applicable to physical and social data. Meets Mondays, Tuesdays, Thursdays, and Fridays f
one and one-half hours.
Begins Monday, July 1; 9:30 A. M.   -   30 hours   -   Credit: 2 S. H.   Room 14, Cl

Mathematics S401   The Teaching of Mathematics in the Secondary School
                                                      Dr. Mallory and Mr. Fe

This course is required of all candidates for the A.B. degree with a major in mathematics a
meets the requirements for a course in Curriculum Organization and Courses of Study in
field of mathematics for the limited secondary certificate. In this course, special consideratior
given to specific problems which arise in the teaching of junior and senior high school mat
matics. These include the following: adaptation of material to students of varying abiliti
selection and treatment of subject matter; use of texts and supplementary material; importa
of the fundamental concepts; use of special methods and devices; how to treat the more diffic
phases of the subject matter; and the preparation of students for college entrance examinatic
Daily demonstrations in the College High School illustrate units in enriched teaching. M
daily for one and one-half hours.
Begins Monday, July 1; 8:00 A. M.   -   45 hours   -   Credit: 3 S. H.   Room 14, C

Mathematics S410   Mathematics of Finance   **Instructor to be Assigr**

A course introducing the student to the elementary theory of simple and compound inte
and leading to the solution of practical problems in annuities, sinking funds, amortizat
depreciation, stocks and bonds, installment buying, and building and loan associations; an
the mathematics of life insurance covering the subjects: the theory of probability as rel
to life insurance, the theory and calculation of mortality tables, various types of life annui
and insurance policies, and reserves. This course is designed to give a helpful backgroun
the mathematics teacher as well as to be an aid to the student of economics and insura
Meets Mondays, Tuesdays, Thursdays, and Fridays for one and one-half hours.
Begins Monday, July 1; 1:00 P. M.   -   30 hours   -   Credit: 2 S. H.   Roo

24

Mathematics S507   General or Integrated Mathematics in the Junior High School   Dr. Mallory and Mr. Fehr

The seventh, eighth, and ninth grades afford an excellent opportunity to develop an integrated program in mathematics. The fundamental arithmetical processes require repeated and frequent drill. At the same time, the junior high school student may be made conscious of the importance of mathematics in everyday life and in its relation to the various fields of knowledge. This course considers some of the problems arising in the development of such a program and includes demonstrations in the College High School on methods of presenting some of the material discussed. Meets daily for one and one-half hours.

Begins Monday, July 1; 8:00 A. M.   -   45 hours   -   Credit: 3 S. H.   Room 7, CHS

Mathematics S509C   Fundamental Concepts of Secondary Mathematics, Part III: The Junior High School   Mr. Fehr

This course treats the following topics: the mathematical nature of graphs and their construction; intuition and experimentalism in geometry; approximate measurement and computation; applications of social arithmetic to current problems of business and government. Meets Mondays, Tuesdays, Thursdays, and Fridays for one and one-half hours.

Begins Monday, July 1; 11:00 A. M.   -   30 hours   -   Credit: 2 S. H.   Room 14, CHS

Mathematics S513   Synthetic Projective Geometry   Dr. Hildebrandt

Those properties of geometric figures which remain invariant under projection and section are studied. The student gains experience in viewing geometric figures in perspective position. In particular, a study is made of such topics as: primitive forms; the principle of duality; projectively related forms; Desargue's Theorem; harmonic ranges and harmonic pencils; Pascal's and Brianchon's Theorems; poles and polars; etc. As a part of the professional equipment of the teacher of secondary school mathematics, a knowledge of projective geometry is found useful. Prerequisite: at least one year of college mathematics. Meets Mondays, Tuesdays, Thursdays, and Fridays for one and one-half hours.

Begins Monday, July 1; 8:00 A. M.   -   30 hours   -   Credit: 2 S. H.   Room 4, CHS

Mathematics S516A   The Theory of Functions   Dr. Davis

The major part of this course deals with the properties of functions of a complex variable. The underlying theory forms a natural extension of the calculus and includes such topics as: continuity; differentiability; integrability; line-integrals; Green's Theorem, Cauchy's Integral Theorem; the Cauchy-Riemann and Laplace's differential equations; etc. The fundamental concepts of the theory of functions form an essential part of the equipment of every student and teacher of mathematics. Prerequisite: differential and integral calculus. Meets Mondays, Tuesdays, Thursdays, and Fridays for one and one-half hours.

Begins Monday, July 1; 9:30 A. M.   -   30 hours   -   Credit: 2 S. H.   Room 5

Mathematics S517   The Theory of Numbers   Dr. Davis

This course offers a systematic treatment of certain fundamental properties of numbers. It includes such topics as: properties of integers; prime numbers; composite numbers; factorization; relatively prime numbers; properties of congruences and their solutions; fundamental theorems of Fermat, Euler, Wilson, Gauss, etc.; primitive roots of a congruence; quadratic residues; and certain types of Diophantine equations. From the theory of numbers, the student of mathematics obtains a far better understanding of the fundamental structure of arithmetic and of algebra, as well as an interesting view of a comparatively recent field of mathematics which is still rapidly growing. Teachers find here a large number of topics which have numerous applications to secondary school mathematics. Prerequisite: two years of college mathematics. Meets Mondays, Tuesdays, Thursdays, and Fridays for one and one-half hours.

Begins Monday, July 1; 11:00 A. M.   -   30 hours   -   Credit: 2 S. H.   Room 5

Mathematics S522   The Correlation and Application of Secondary School Mathematics   Dr. Davis

An investigation is made of ways and means of correlating the material taught in the different branches of secondary school mathematics, giving special attention to applications of this material to other subjects. Leading texts in the field are analyzed and compared with respect to

selection, organization, presentation, correlation, and application of subject matter. Sp
consideration is given to the use of these texts and supplementary material in order to
the requirements of the college entrance examinations. Meets Mondays, Tuesdays, Thursc
and Fridays for one and one-half hours.
Begins Monday, July 1; 8:00 A. M. - 30 hours - Credit: 2 S. H.   Roo

Mathematics S531   Survey of Higher Mathematics   Dr. Hildebra

This is a course planned to introduce the student to the major fields of mathematics. It aff
him an opportunity to decide which branches are of interest for additional intensive grad
study, as well as acquainting him with some other fields which are usually not treated
separate course. Fundamentals of the following fields are considered: theory of numb
higher algebra; theory of groups; foundations of logic; synthetic projective geometry;
Euclidean geometry; N-dimensional geometry; topology; theory of functions; Fourier se
calculus of variations; vector analysis; theory of relativity; and differential and integral e
tions. Meets Mondays, Tuesdays, Thursdays, and Fridays for one and one-half hours.
Begins Monday, July 1; 9:30 A. M. - 30 hours - Credit: 2 S. H.   Room 4, (

**Mathematics S601   Workshop: Current Problems in the Teaching of Mat
matics   Dr. Mallory and Mathematics S**

This course is conducted as a workshop for the solution of such actual problems in the teach
of mathematics as: courses in mathematics for the general and for the specializing stud
integration of mathematics with other courses; revision of subject-matter in particular fi
such as in plane geometry; and research problems in specific units of work.*
Begins Monday, July 1; 11:00 A. M. - 60 hours - Credit: 4 S. H.   Room 7, (

DEPARTMENT OF MUSIC

Music S202A   Harmony, Part I   Dr. McEach

This course aims to give a practical treatment of harmony as related to the classroom.
includes a study of scales, intervals, primary and secondary triads, seventh chords, enharm
tones and modulation. The above theory is presented first as musical experience; analy
defined, and used as a basis for ear training, dictation, and melody writing. Special atten
is given to the functional aspects of harmony as applied to the piano keyboard in transposit
chording, and harmonization of melodies. Prerequisite: Music sightreading ability satisfac
to the instructor. Meets Mondays, Tuesdays, Thursdays, and Fridays for one and one-half h
Begins Monday, July 1; 11:00 A. M. - 30 hours - Credit: 2 S. H.   Roo

Music S302   Epochs in Music Development   Dr. McEach

This course makes an intensive study of great epochs in music making, including media
polyphonic, classic, romantic, and modern periods. Special attention is given to related m
ments in other fields of artistic endeavor, and to the social aspects of music as reflecting s
ficant forces in the various periods studied. A feature of this course is the making
chronological index showing parallel developments in the fields of music, art, literature,
history. Because of integration possibilities, this course is particularly recommended to m
in English, social studies, and modern languages. Meets Mondays, Tuesdays, Thursdays,
Fridays for one and one-half hours.
Begins Monday, July 1; 9:30 A. M. - 30 hours - Credit: 2 S. H.   Ro

Music S401   The Teaching of High School Music   Dr. McEac

This course deals with the aims, content, and procedure in the teaching of music in the j
and senior high school (grades seven to twelve inclusive). It is organized on the unit
and includes a study of the adolescent voice; music for boys; assembly music; materi
special programs; song dramatizations; integration of music with other subjects in the s
curriculum; music appreciation; and extra-curricular music activities. Opportunity is
students to work out special problems confronting them in the teaching of music in
respective high schools. Meets daily for one and one-half hours.
Begins Monday, July 1; 8:00 A. M. - 45 hours - Credit: 3 S. H.   Rc

For complete information as to the conduct of the Workshops, see page 12.

26

DEPARTMENT OF PHYSICAL EDUCATION

Note: With the exception of "The Coaching of Football," which is open only to men, all of the courses that follow are open to men and women alike.

Physical Education S201A   The Coaching of Football   Mr. Voliva

A careful study of the fundamentals of the several positions is made. The various systems of offense and defense are studied and coaching methods explained. The last week of the summer session is devoted to the study of the coaching of basketball. Meets Mondays, Tuesdays, Thursdays, and Fridays for one and one-half hours.
Begins Monday, July 1; 9:30 A. M. - 30 hours - Credit: 2 S. H.   Room 5, CHS

Physical Education S201B   Organization of Physical Education   Mr. Pittser

In this course the student is made aware of the breadth of the field of physical education. The field is broken up into its integral parts, showing how each part is a unit in itself and how these units when combined form the physical education unit which in turn is a unit of the general education program. The following subjects are discussed: required physical examination; required program; restricted program; games and activities; elective program; intramural program; and interscholastic athletics program. Meets Mondays, Tuesdays, Thursdays, and Fridays for one and one-half hours.
Begins Monday, July 1; 11:00 A. M. - 30 hours - Credit: 2 S. H.   Room 6, CHS

Physical Education S202B   Management of Athletic Activities   Mr. Pittser

In this course information is provided which will enable the young teacher or director of physical education to avoid many of the common errors of management. Emphasis is placed upon: making schedules; care of equipment; care of playground; care of locker rooms; purchasing equipment; handling finances; budgeting; conduct of students while on trips; etc. Meets Mondays, Tuesdays, Thursdays, and Fridays for one and one-half hours.
Begins Monday, July 1; 1:00 P. M. - 30 hours - Credit: 2 S. H.   Room 6, CHS

Physical Education S302A   Methods and Practice in Physical Education
Mr. Voliva

Various methods used in assembling and handling classes on the field or gymnasium floor are discussed. The student is required to take charge of physical education activities of the fellow members of his class under the supervision of the instructor. Reports of systems used in nearby high schoos are required. Meets Mondays, Tuesdays, Thursdays, and Fridays for one and one-half hours.1
Begins Monday, July 1; 1:00 P. M. - 30 hours - Credit: 2 S. H.   Room 5, CHS

Physical Education S302B   Health and Health Teaching, Part II   Mr. Pittser

This course is a continuation of S301B—Health and Health Teaching, Part I, which was given in the summer of 1939, but which is not, however, necessarily prerequisite to this part. Some fields of subject-matter are considered intensively, the choice being governed by the needs of the group. Criteria for judging materials and procedures are developed. Meets Mondays, Tuesdays, Thursdays, and Fridays for one and one-half hours.
Begins Monday, July 1; 9:30 A. M. - 30 hours - Credit: 2 S. H.   Room 6, CHS

Physical Education S406   Games and Game Skills   Mr. Voliva

In recent years, much impetus has been given the physical education program in our high schools by the substitution of interesting games and contests for the calisthenics of yesterday. This course gives consideration to the rules of the games, methods of supervision, and to the acquiring of techniques by much practice and by individual and class competitions. Among the games and sports studied are archery, badminton, paddle tennis, shuffle board, horseshoes, indoor baseball, golf, and volley ball. Meets Mondays, Tuesdays, Thursdays, and Fridays for one and one-half hours.
Begins Monday, July 1; 11:00 A. M. - 30 hours - Credit: 2 S. H.   Room 5, CHS

Physical Education S407   Safety Education   Mr. Pittser

In this course, a study is made of a number of safety controls which will have an influence upon the health and happiness of the individual throughout his entire life span. The subject matter is derived from the following sources: the study of anatomy, physiology, biology, growth of the child, hygiene; and from psychology, sociology, physical education, and athletics. The

safety controls are discussed in chronological order, showing how it is possible for the teacl in the field of physical education to contribute to the welfare of each individual. Safety fi and first aid on the playground and in the gymnasium are stressed. Meets Mondays, Tuesda Thursdays, and Fridays for one and one-half hours.
Begins Monday, July 1; 8:00 A. M.   -   30 hours   -   Credit: 2 S. H.   Room 6, Cl

DEPARTMENT OF SCIENCE

Biology S407   Comparative Embryology   Dr. Hadl
A study is made of the stages in development and factors influencing the development of diff ent types, particularly the vertebrates. Students in this course follow carefully the developm of the chick through the earlier stages. Serial sections of entire chick embryos in differ stages of development are prepared by individual students and used as a basis for the st of the development of tissues and organs of the animal. Applications of these details of ver brate development to the development of the mammal are based on observations made throu the dissection of pig embryos. Prerequisite: Biology 406, Animal Histology, or its equivale Meets Mondays, Tuesdays, Thursdays, and Fridays for one and one-half hours of lecture a classroom work, and Monday and Tuesday afternoons for laboratory work.
Begins Monday, July 1; 11:00 A. M.   -   90 hours   -   Credit: 4 S. H.   Room

Biology S408   Biological Technique   Dr. Hadl
This course is designed to furnish the prospective teacher of biology with the technical det necessary to enable him, as a secondary school teacher, to handle successfully biological ma rials and experiments and demonstrations in which these materials are employed. Students trained in methods of collecting and preserving plants and animals for use in the laborat and classroom. Study is made of the proper methods of preparing illustrative materials w special emphasis laid upon the purpose of these materials. Prerequisites: Biology 201 and 2 Zoology. Meets Mondays, Thursdays, and Fridays for one and one-half hours of lecture a classroom work and Thursday and Friday afternoons for laboratory work.
Begins Monday, July 1; 9:30 A. M.   -   67½ hours   -   Credit: 3 S. H.   Room

Biology S409   Human Physiology   Dr. Finl
This course meets the State requirement in Health Education for the limited secondary cert cate. A careful study of human anatomy is used as basis for discussion of both normal a abnormal physiology. In addition to an analysis of the part played by organs and tissues carrying out the essential functions of the body, attention is given to problems of hygiene a sanitation. Applications of the above problems are made in reference to children of sch age. Meets daily for one and one-half hours.
Begins Monday, July 1; 8:00 A. M.   -   45 hours   -   Credit: 3 S. H.   Room

Physics S102A   General College Physics, Part III—Sound and Light
**   Dr. McLachl**
This is an elementary course consisting of lectures, demonstrations, and laboratory experime pertaining to the nature and transmission of sound, properties of musical sounds, nature propagation of light, image formation, color phenomena, diffraction, polarization, and ot topics. The content of this course is an essential part of the training of a teacher of gen science. No prerequisites. Students may begin the study of college physics with this u Meets Mondays and Tuesdays for one and one-half hours lecture and classroom work in morning and for three hours laboratory work in the afternoon.
Begins Monday, July 1; 8:00 A. M.   -   45 hours   -   Credit: 2 S. H.   Room

Physics S304   Photography for High School Teachers   Dr. K. O. Sm
This is a beginning course in photography, consisting of laboratory and field work supplemer with lectures and demonstrations. Some of the topics studied are: the construction and op tion of cameras, film characteristics, use of exposure meters, development and printing of n tives and positives, taking pictures under very different lighting conditions, lantern s making, projection printing, production of colored transparencies with color film. A stu needs at least one camera for use in the course. No prerequisites. Meets Mondays, Tuesc Thursdays, and Fridays for one and one-half hours.
Begins Monday, July 1; 11:00 A. M.   -   30 hours   -   Credit: 2 S. H.   Room 8, (

28

Physics S511   Electronics and Electron Tubes   Dr. K. O. Smith

It is the aim of this course to give an understanding of the basic principles of electronics and then to proceed to the study of such familiar appliances as radio tubes, gas or vapor-filled electron tubes, cathode-ray tubes, photo-electric tubes, x-ray tubes, and Greuz-ray tubes. Applications in medicine are considered. To study the manufacture of such electron devices, trips may be arranged to some of the leading factories, as several are located in this section of New Jersey. Meets Mondays, Tuesdays, Thursdays, and Fridays for one and one-half hours.
Begins Monday, July 1; 8:00 A. M. - 30 hours - Credit: 2 S. H.   Room 8, CHS

Physics S518A   Industrial Physics, Part I   Dr. K. O. Smith

This course deals with the practical uses of the principles of physics in business, industrial, and recreational enterprises. The work consists of field trips, discussions, and library reference readings. Trips will be taken to: the World's Fair in New York; selected manufacturing plants in the metropolitan community; the Museum of Science and Industry; and the Franklin Institute in Philadelphia to study important uses of the laws of mechanics, heat, electricity, sound, and light, in the modern world. Meets Mondays and Tuesdays in the morning for one and one-half hours of lecture and classroom work and in the afternoons for the field trips mentioned.
Begins Monday, July 1; 9:30 A. M. - 45 hours - Credit: 2 S. H.   Room 8, CHS

Science S100A   Survey of Science—The Physical Sciences   Dr. McLachlan

This course is an introduction to the physical sciences. Attention is focused on some of the concepts in astronomy, chemistry, geology and physics, which have made possible the modern scientific age. Many simple demonstration experiments are used to promote understanding of the scientific method and the inescapable consequences of scientific development. Teachers, supervisors, and administrators find in this course an opportunity to explore the field of physical science and to discover some of the possibilities which it offers for vitalizing the teaching of all subjects. No previous work in science is required. Meets Mondays, Tuesdays, Thursdays, and Fridays, for one and one-half hours.
Begins Monday, July 1; 11:00 A. M. - 30 hours · Credit: 2 S. H.   Room 25

Science S406A   Astronomy for Teachers, Part I   Prof. Glenn

A first course for teachers of science and mathematics. There are no prerequisites for students in other fields. Such topics as the following are considered: motions of the earth; time; the moon; laws of gravitation; the planets, comets, and meteors; the sun; the constellations; distances and motions of the stars; the world's great telescopes; nebulae; and spectrum analysis. This course includes one visit to the Planetarium in New York and one trip to the Franklin Institute in Philadelphia. Meets Mondays, Tuesdays, Thursdays, and Fridays for one and one-half hours.
Begins Monday, July 1; 1:00 P. M. - 30 hours - Credit: 2 S. H.   Room 22

Science S410B   Junior High School Science Demonstrations, Part II
**   Prof. Glenn**

A course for teachers in service who wish to develop or extend experimental teaching in junior high school science. While about three hundred experiments are available for study, special attention is given to work with inexpensive equipment. Meets Mondays, Tuesdays, Thursdays, and Fridays for one and one-half hours.
Begins Monday, July 1; 9:30 A. M. - 30 hours - Credit: 2 S. H.   Room 22

Science S411A   Science in Transportation: Aviation, Part I   Dr. McLachlan

This course is designed to provide teachers and supervisors with knowledge and training which will help them to meet the rapidly growing demand for information about aviation as developed in the newer general science and high school physics books and in certain social studies courses. Some previous training in physics is desirable. Some of the topics covered are: history of aviation; theory of flight; principles and materials of construction; building model airplanes; parachutes; air navigation; uses of radio in air transportation; and the school aviation club. 411B, a continuation of this course, will be offered in the future. It deals with engines, instruments, studying and reporting weather conditions, and other aspects of the science of air transportation. The part now being offered meets Tuesdays, Thursdays, and Fridays in the morning for one and one-half hours lecture and demonstration work, and Thursday afternoons for three hours laboratory work and trips.
Begins Monday, July 1; 9:30 A. M. - 36 hours - Credit: 2 S. H.   Room 25

Science S505   Survey of Curricula and Science Courses in State and (
Prof. Glenn and Science S

This course is primarily for teachers of experience who wish to know about important
programs of science education being developed in the United States. The course satisfies
New Jersey State requirement in Curriculum Organization and Courses of Study in the ;
of science for the Limited Secondary Certificate. A survey is made of recent junior and se
high school science courses in state and city systems. Comparisons are made to determine
merits and deficiencies of these programs of instruction. The recent work of the Col
Entrance Examination Board, the Progressive Education Association, the Science Divisior
the National Education Association, and other national and local associations, is reviev
Meets daily for one and one-half hours.
Begins Monday, July 1; 8:00 A. M. - 45 hours - Credit: 3 S. H.   Roon

Science S601   Workshop: Current Problems in the Teaching of Science
Prof. Glenn and Science S

A course, conducted by personal conferences, for experienced teachers and school offic
The work of the entire session concerns a special problem of current interest and importa
to the student from the fields of junior or senior high school science education. Further de
on the scope of the work may be obtained from Professor Glenn.*
Begins Monday, July 1; 11:00 A. M. - 60 hours - Credit: 4 S. H.   Room :

DEPARTMENT OF SOCIAL STUDIES

Social Studies S200A   Contemporary Economic Life   Mr. Rellal

This course aims to acquaint the student with the basic nature of economic life, to point
the opposing economic doctrines in force in various parts of the world, and particularl;
investigate the functionings of economic life both here and abroad. Case studies from the
rent newspapers and periodicals are made the basis of this course. These suggest such to
as: working conditions; standards of living; economic security; governmental economic a(
ities; employer-employee relationships; etc. The sources of economic ideas and the evolu
of economic institutions are traced, when these appear necessary to an understanding of (
temporary affairs. Meets Mondays, Tuesdays, Thursdays, and Fridays for one and one-
hours.
Begins Monday, July 1; 1:00 P. M. - 30 hours - Credit: 2 S. H.   Room

Social Studies S200B   Contemporary Political Life   Mr. Gei

This course is designed to orient the student in the contemporary political situation—l(
national, and international. It provides an opportunity to think and talk about what
national state is; how the machinery of the state may be controlled through public opin
the suffrage, and political parties; how modern states are governed; how national states
with each other in war and peace; and what the outlook for the immediate future appears t(
Meets Mondays, Tuesdays, Thursdays, and Fridays for one and one-half hours.
Begins Monday, July 1; 8:00 A. M. - 30 hours - Credit: 2 S. H.   Roor

Social Studies S202B   United States History from 1900 to 1940   Prof. John

This course is devoted to the study of the United States as a world power, the developmer
"big business," the United States in the World War, and our present problems of the post
period. Meets Mondays, Tuesdays, Thursdays, and Fridays for one and one-half hours.
Begins Monday, July 1; 11:00 A. M. - 30 hours - Credit: 2 S. H.   Roor

Social Studies S301A   Economics I   Mr. Rella

The object of this course is to permit the teacher of the social studies to obtain a profess
understanding of the fundamental nature and functioning of our present economic sy
Emphasis is given to a study of the background of present-day economic institutions, an
manner in which the present system functions with respect to the economic and bu;
organization of production, the nature and laws of consumption, the principles involved i
determination of value and price under competition or monopoly, and the problem of dis
tion as related to an explanation of rent, interest, wages, and profits. Meets Mondays, Tue;
Thursdays, and Fridays for one and one-half hours.
Begins Monday, July 1; 8:00 A. M. - 30 hours - Credit: 2 S. H.   Roo

*For complete information as to the conduct of the Workshops, see page 12.

Social Studies S301B   Economics II   Mr. Rellahan

The aim of this course, which is a continuation of Economics I, is to acquaint the student with the basic economic principles and problems relating to risk and insurance, money, credit and banking, general price changes and their control; foreign trade and exchange; tariffs, international debts and imperialism; business combinations; and governmental regulation of business enterprise. Meets Mondays, Tuesdays, Thursdays, and Fridays for one and one-half hours.
Begins Monday, July 1; 9:30 A. M. - 30 hours - Credit: 2 S. H.   Room 21

Social Studies S401   The Teaching of Social Studies in the Secondary School
                                        Professors Hatch and Johnson

This course satisfies the state requirement in Curriculum Organization and Courses of Study in the social studies field. It meets in connection with a class in the College High School, so that students may have the opportunity to observe the demonstration of the methods presented. The course presents recent tendencies in the teaching of the social studies. Among the matters considered are: the social studies curriculum with special attention to the fusion organization; the objectives in the social studies; class procedures, including the problem-project method, unit mastery method, oral procedures, drill and review procedures, procedures in particular subjects, the teaching of current events; devices and aids, including visual, auditory, and motor aids; technique of field trips; use of text-books and supplementary reading; and testing and grading. Bibliographies and other teaching aids are supplied to students. Meets daily for one and one-half hours.
Begins Monday, July 1; 9:30 A. M. - 45 hours - Credit: 3 S. H.   Room 12, CHS

Social Studies S402A   American Government   Mr. Bye

The basic facts and principles necessary for the teaching of courses in civics, problems of American democracy, and United States history are studied in this course, through current problems in government and politics. Problems involving the relationship of the individual citizen to the government and to the political party, of the state to the United States, and of political machinery to its functions, are included. Meets Mondays, Tuesdays, Thursdays, and Fridays for one and one-half hours.
Begins Monday, July 1; 9:30 A. M. - 30 hours - Credit: 2 S. H.   Room E

Social Studies S407   New Jersey State and Local Government   Mr. Bye

A study is made of the State Constitution; New Jersey's place in the federal system; the rights and duties of citizens; suffrage, political parties; the legislative, the executive, and administrative systems; the courts, the law enforcement and correctional systems; revenues and expenditures; public health, educational, highway, and other services; county and municipal government; and other local political units. Meets Mondays, Tuesdays, Thursdays, and Fridays for one and one-half hours.
Begins Monday, July 1; 8:00 A. M. - 30 hours - Credit: 2 S. H.   Room E

Social Studies S413   Economic History of the United States   Mr. Geigle

This study of our national history from an economic point of view is particularly valuable in the period of economic reconstruction in which we are living. The great trends and movements in agriculture, finance, commerce, manufacturing, transportation, and industrial relations are traced from their beginnings in the colonial period to their contemporary expressions in the present crisis. This course supplements, but it does not duplicate, courses in the political history of the United States or courses in economic principles and problems. Meets Mondays, Tuesdays, Thursdays, and Fridays for one and one-half hours.
Begins Monday, July 1; 11:00 A. M. - 30 hours - Credit: 2 S. H.   Room D

Social Studies S415   Latin American Relations of the United States is not being offered this summer, due to the absence of Dr. Snyder, who is traveling this summer through South America, but will be offered at a later date.

Social Studies S417   American Archaeology   Dr. Freeman

This course aims to show the influence of Ancient America on Twentieth Century America. The New World of the early discoverers was in reality far from new. "Columbus came late." The course discusses the prehistoric pueblo dwellers and early mound builders. The truly remarkable civilizations of the Mayas and the Incas are examined and compared with that of

31

the Aztecs. North American tribes of Indians are also studied in order to evaluate their sig
cant cultures. Meets Mondays, Tuesdays, Thursdays, and Fridays for one and one-half h
Begins Monday, July 1; 1:00 P. M. - 30 hours - Credit: 2 S. H.   Roo

Social Studies S420A   The European Outlook, Part I   Dr. Witt
The complete course is aimed to give a better and broader understanding of European post
problems. Through a short survey of pre-war developments, the main causes, and, in s
aspects, the significance of the World War, are explained. Lectures on political, econo
social, and cultural topics help to interpret treaties and alliances concluded by European po
since 1918. Versailles and Locarno; disarmament and rearmament; the League of Nati
fascism, communism, and democracy; the corporative system; trends of thought inspire
Nietzsche, Spengler, Sorel, and Marx; the Danube and the Balkan problem; the situatlo
the Baltic states and Finland; are discussed. Special emphasis is given to the problem
Soviet Russia and Nazi Germany. Prerequisite: a course in modern European history. M
Mondays, Tuesdays, Thursdays, and Fridays for one and one-half hours.
Begins Monday, July 1; 9:30 A. M. - 30 hours - Credit: 2 S. H.   Roon

Social Studies S420B   The European Outlook, Part II   Dr. Witt
This is a continuation of the above course, which is not, however, necessarily prerequisite t
Special emphasis is given to the problem of Anglo-French cooperation, the Civil War in S
rivalries in the Mediterranean, and trends of Italian fascism. In connection with a stud
the economic, political, and strategic conditions of Great Britain, a survey of the world poli
situation is given. Africa, the Near East, India, and the nations of the Pacific are studie
factors influencing the political alignment of Europe. The latter half of the course is dev
to the interpretation of political news. Prerequisite: a course in modern European his
Meets Mondays, Tuesdays, Thursdays, and Fridays for one and one-half hours.
Begins Monday, July 1; 11:00 A. M. 30 hours - Credit: 2 S. H.   Room 12,

Social Studies S421   Oriental Civilization   Dr. Freer
This course aims to present the important contributions to civilization and social progress n
in antiquity in the three centers of the Near East—Egypt, Mesopotamia, and Crete. Discus
of the Oriental culture pattern is amplified by visual aids. Emphasis is laid on the resul
modern archaeological research in completing the picture of early life in the Near East.
dents of the social studies, English, and foreign languages should include this course a
important addition to the cultural background which they should carry to their high sc
teaching. Meets Mondays, Tuesdays, Thursdays, and Fridays for one and one-half hour
Begins Monday, July 1; 11:00 A. M. - 30 hours - Credit: 2 S. H.   Ro

Social Studies S428   Sociology I: Racial Contributions to American Lif
Mr. Cre
This course deals with the basic problems of quantity, quality, and distribution of popul
and emphasizes the adjustments and maladjustments which result from the inter-relatio.
Negroes, Asiatics, and various types of Europeans in the United States. Meets Mor
Tuesdays, Thursdays, and Fridays for one and one-half hours.
Begins Monday, July 1; 9:30 A. M. - 30 hours - Credit: 2 S. H.   Ro

Social Studies S432   Advanced Economics   Mr. Rell
Building upon the foundations laid in the introductory courses in economics, the purp
this study is to provide the student with an opportunity to use economic theory as a me
analyzing more intensively certain major problems and evaluating current economic po
Chief emphasis is given to the problems and programs concerned with business fluctua
the distribution of wealth and income; agriculture; labor and social legislation; transpoi
and public utility regulation; public revenues and expenditures; economic planning, anc
peting types of economic systems. In order to bring together the contributions of all pr
economic study and points of view, a brief summary of the history of economic thou
made. Meets Mondays, Tuesdays, Thursdays, and Fridays for one and one-half hours.
Begins Monday, July 1; 11:00 A. M. - 30 hours - Credit: 2 S. H.   Ro

Social Studies S434   Contemporary World Affairs   Dr. Wittmer

This course is designed to acquaint the student with the fundamentals of dynamic world strategy. It points out the significance of air and naval bases; highways and canals; production and exchange of raw materials; international monopolies; racial and religious divisions; and density of population. The Far East, Australia, India, Arabia, Africa, and Latin America, are shown in their relation to our foreign policy and the present world conflict. Meets Mondays, Tuesdays, Thursdays, and Fridays for one and one-half hours.

Begins Monday, July 1; 1:00 P. M. - 30 hours - Credit: 2 S. H.   Room 12, CHS

Social Studies S435A   The Americas: An Economic and Cultural Survey,
Part I   Mr. Labastille

This course deals with the functions and purposes of the Inter-American movement. It includes discussion, analysis, investigation, and evaluation of the Inter-American policy and its possibilities in the economic, cultural, and diplomatic fields. It presents historical background bearing upon present-day developments of governmental policies, discusses social evolution in Latin-America, and the nationalistic movements of today. Meets Mondays, Tuesdays, Thursdays, and Fridays for one and one-half hours.

Begins Monday, July 1; 9:30 A. M. - 30 hours - Credit: 2 S. H.   Room 7, CHS

Social Studies S436   Modern Men of Ancient Times   Dr. Freeman

This course is designed to present biographical sketches of some of the great leaders of past ages. The subjects for discussion are selected from all lines of human endeavor, and special attention is given to their influence on the thought of their own times and their contribution to the culture of the present day. The course is specially recommended to students who wish to know these leaders as real persons and not as lay figures in ancient history. Meets Mondays, Tuesdays, Thursdays, and Fridays for one and one-half hours.

Begins Monday, July 1; 9:30 A. M. - 30 hours - Credit: 2 S. H.   Room 7

Social Studies S437   The Political Party System in the United States Mr. Bye

In this course a realistic study is made of the dynamics of practical politics. Among the topics discussed are: party organization; the political boss; the political machine; party finances; the process of voting; election laws; primaries; conventions; platforms; presidential elections; majority rule; the development of the party system; sectional politics; the farm vote; the labor vote; and the future of party government in the United States. In the summer of 1940, particular attention will be given to the presidential campaign. Meets Mondays, Tuesdays, Thursdays, and Fridays for one and one-half hours.

Begins Monday, July 1; 11:00 A. M. - 30 hours - Credit: 2 S. H.   Room E

Social Studies S438   The Literature of American History   Prof. Johnson

A brief description of the materials available for the study of American history and how to find them is followed by class practice in finding and using the primary sources of some of the facts commonly taught in schools. Attention is then turned to representative American historians, their training for historical study, the sources they used, the degree of accuracy with which they used their sources, their point of view, their plan of organization, and their present importance. The contributions of the class consist of individual reports on selected passages. At each step, possible applications at various school levels are pointed out. Meets Mondays, Tuesdays, Thursdays, and Fridays for one and one-half hours.

Begins Monday, July 1; 8:00 A. M. - 30 hours - Credit: 2 S. H.   Room 20

Social Studies S504   International Economic Relations   Mr. Labastille

The purpose of this course is to show the importance of bringing full knowledge of the facts to the solution of international economic problems. Since the war and post-war years, the interdependence of all nations in the exchange of goods and services has been distinctly evident. The course deals with phases of economic nationalism and internationalism, the future of world trade, the United States as a creditor nation, and our commercial policy of reciprocal trade agreements. The course is valuable especially to teachers of modern history, current events, and problems of American democracy. Meets Mondays, Tuesdays, Thursdays, and Fridays for one and one-half hours.

Begins Monday, July 1; 8:00 A. M. - 30 hours - Credit: 2 S. H.   Room 12, CHS

Social Studies S509   Classical Archaeology   Dr. Freema

This course is designed to present a knowledge of source material in the fine arts of Gree and Rome that will enable the individual to reconstruct for himself various phases of Gre and Roman culture. This work is of particular importance to all prospective teachers of tl social studies, Latin, and English. The course is conducted by lectures liberally illustrated l an abundance of colorful material. Much of this material is verified by trips to the Metropolit Museum of Art and other local museums. Meets Mondays, Tuesdays, Thursdays, and Frida for one and one-half hours.
Begins Monday, July 1; 8:00 A. M. - 30 hours - Credit: 2 S. H.   Room

Social Studies S512   Field Studies in American Life—Central Eastern Regic
**   Mr. B}**

For the third time, this observational field study course, covering eastern Virginia, Marylan Pennsylvania, and West Virginia, is offered during the ten-day period following the summ session, August 12 to 21 inclusive. Among the historic places visited are: Valley Forge, o Philadelphia, Baltimore, Annapolis, Washington, Arlington, Alexandria, Mount Vernon, Fre ericksburg, Wakefield, Stratford, Richmond, Jamestown, Williamsburg, Yorktown, Charlotte ville, Natural Bridge, Skyline Drive, Luray Caverns, Winchester, Harpers Ferry, Frederic Gettysburg, Lancaster, Ephrata, Reading, Delaware Water Gap. The geography and history these regions, which were the setting for varied colonial settlements and for the Americ Revolution and the Civil War, may be studied at first hand under careful guidance. Send f special descriptive bulletin. Early registration in this course is necessary to assure reservation The class membership is limited in number. The course is open to all regular and part-tin students, but the director reserves the right to reject applications. Three graduate or unde graduate semester-hours credit may be earned upon presentation of satisfactory field not September 15 following the trip. The course may be taken for "no credit," but tuition fe must be paid by all and the usual college regulations apply to all alike. The cost, includir registration, tuition, transportation, rooms with bath, all fees, admissions, and hotel tips wi be $76.00. (Non-residents of New Jersey must add $6.00 for additional cost of tuition.) Mea are purchased and paid for individually. The cost of meals and personal purchases vari according to choice. Single rooms may be reserved at an additional charge of $5.00 for tl trip. Checks for registration and tuition ($19.00 for residents of New Jersey, $25.00 for no residents) must accompany registration. Write for registration blanks. The balance must I paid on or before July 15. Checks for registration and tuition should be drawn to the order Montclair State Teachers College; all other checks should be drawn to the order of the Fiel Studies Fund. It should be noted that the registration fee is paid only once for the summ session; if paid in connection with this course, it need not be paid again in connection wi the courses meeting from July 1 to August 10; and vice versa.

Social Studies S601   Workshop: Current Problems in the Teaching of Soci
Studies   Prof. Hatch and Social Studies St

This course is designed to give the secondary school teacher of the social studies an opp tunity to work under expert direction on a professional problem. The workshop method used. Such problems as the selection and organization of social studies materials, the use visual aids, the teaching of current events, character emphasis in education, the inter-relati of school and community, the validity of integrated or fused courses, and the organizati of worthwhile social studies courses in both the junior and the senior high school are studie Begins Monday, July 1; 11:00 A. M. - 60 hours - Credit: 4 S. H.   Room

Graduate S500A   Seminar and Thesis   Dr. Finl

Students writing a thesis for credit toward the Master's degree in any department of the coll are required to register for this course. The work is conducted under seminar or individ guidance. Students report to the Dean of Instruction, who calls a conference with the Head Department and the Sponsor. At this meeting, all matters pertaining to the topic, plan research, writing of manuscript, etc., are arranged.   Credit: 4 S. H.

*For complete information as to the conduct of the Workshops, see page 12.

34

Advance Announcement

OUR UNITED STATES

will be the subject of

Montclair's Second

TRANSCONTINENTAL FIELD TRIP

JULY & AUGUST, 1941
62 DAYS   12,000 MILES

10 CREDITS $500 TOTAL COST

MAKE TENTATIVE RESERVATIONS WELL IN ADVANCE.
GROUP WILL BE RESTRICTED TO FROM 25 TO 30
STUDENTS. CONSULT OR WRITE DIRECTOR.

HIGH POINTS

Mammoth Cave, Lincoln Country, Lake of the Ozarks, Great Plain,
Santa Fe Trail, Pikes Peak, Cripple Creek, Denver,
Rocky Mountain Park, Taos,
Cliff Dwellings, Pueblos, Petrified Forest,
Grand Canyon, Brice, Zion, Boulder Dam, Mojave Desert,
Los Angeles, Hollywood, California Missions, Sequoias Park,
Mexican Towns, Santa Barbara, Yosemite,
Monterey, San Francisco,
Lake Tahoe, Reno, Donner Pass, Gold Diggings,
Redwoods, Columbia River, Portland, Seattle, Mt. Rainier,
Grand Coulee Dam, Butte, Yellowstone,
Salt Lake City, Wyoming, Black Hills, Bad Lands, Chicago,
Detroit, Toronto, Niagara Falls.

SUMMER SESSION

Bulletin of

MONTCLAIR
STATE TEACHERS COLLEGE

1 9 4 1

July 7 to August 13

UPPER MONTCLAIR, NEW JERSEY

Officers of Administration

STATE BOARD OF EDUCATION

D. Stewart Craven, *President*..........................,......Salen

Oscar W. Jeffery, *Vice-President* ....Englewoo(

Mrs. Edward L. Katzenbach ....,.....Trento)

Gustave A. Hunziker.............................Little Fall

D. Howard Moreau...............................Flemingto)

Joseph W. Mott................................Atlantic Cit'

Miss May M. Carty..............................Jersey Cit'

Mrs. William F. Little..........................Rahwa'

Carl R. Woodward.·........................New Brunswic]

Miss Mary Merchant..............................Dove

COMMISSIONER OF EDUCATION

Charles H. Elliot..................Trenton Trust Bldg., Trento)

DIRECTOR OF TEACHER EDUCATION

Robert H. Morrison.................Trenton Trust Bldg., Trento)

OFFICERS OF ADMINISTRATION·
NEW JERSEY STATE TEACHERS COLLEGE
AT MONTCLAIR

Harry A. Sprague......................Director of Summer Sessio

Charles W. Finley...........................Dean of Instructio

Elizabeth S. Favor....................Secretary of Summer Sessio

Charlotte G. Marshall...............................Registr;

Maude L. Carter............................Dean of Wome

Zaidee Brown ....Libraria

Donald A. DeWitt ....Business Manag(

FACULTY

Harry A. Sprague, Ph.D. . . . . Director of the Summer Session
Wilford M. Aikin, LL.D. . . . . .Administration
Sylvia Block, A.B. . . . . .Applied Arts
Harold C. Bohn, A.M. . . . . .English
Edgar C. Bye, A.M. . . . . .Social Studies
• Eloise B. Cason, Ph.D. . . . . .Psychology
Harry G. Cayley, Ed.D. . . . . .English
Paul C. Clifford, A.M. . . . . .Mathematics
Lawrence H. Conrad, A.M. . . . . .English
E. Winifred Crawford, A. M. . . . . .Multi-Sensory Aids
Paul G. Cressey, A.M. . . . . .Sociology
David R. Davis, Ph.D. . . . . .Mathematics
Teresa De Escoriaza, A. M. . . . . .Spanish
Howard Franklin Fehr. Ph.D. .Mathematics
Avaline Folsom, Ph.D. . . . . .Social Studies
Walter H. Freeman, Ph.D. . . . . Acting Head, Dept. of Foreign Languages
Francis R. Geigle, A.M. . . . . .Business Education
Earl Rouse Glenn, A. M. . . . . .Head of the Department of Science
Charles E. Hadley, Ph.D. . . . . .Biology
William Paul Hamilton, A.M. . . . . .English
Roy Winthrop Hatch, A.M. . .Head of the Department of Social Studies
Claude E. Jackson, A.M. . . . . .Research
Emil L. Kahn, A.M. . . . . .Music
Ethel F. Littlefield, A.M. . . . . .Languages
Virgil S. Mallory, Ph.D. . . . . . .Head of the Department of Mathematics
Robert W. McLachlan, Ph.D. . . . . .Science
Harley P. Milstead, Ph.D. . . . . .Geography
Paul S. Nickerson, A.M. . . . . .English
Ernest DeAlton Partridge, Ph.D. . . . . .Integration
Chester M. Pittser, A.M. .Physical Education
Thomas Clark Pollock, Ph.D. . . . . . .Head of the Department of English
Rufus D. Reed, Ph.D. . . . . .Science
John J. Rellahan, A.M. . . . . .Social Studies
Heber Hinds Ryan, Ph.D. . . . . . .Head of the Department of Integration
Arthur M. Seybold, A.M. . . . . . . .Director, College H. S.; Integration
Kenneth O. Smith, Ph.D. . . . . .Science
W. Scott Smith, Ph.D. . . . . .Integration
W. Harry Snyder, Ph.D. . . . . .Social Studies
D. Henryetta Sperle, Ph.D. . . . . .Integration
Harry. L. Stearns, Ph.D. . . . . .Administration
Richard Voliva, A.M. . . . . .Physical Education
Harry A. Wann, Ph.D. . . . . .Administration
Felix Wittmer, Ph.D. . . . . .Social Studies
Roy R. Zimmerman, A.M. . . . . .Administration

SUMMER SESSION 1941

The Visiting Faculty Members

Wilford M. Aikin, LL.D.: Professor of Education, Ohio State University; Director of Commission on Relation of School and College (Thirty School Experiment) of the Progressive Education Association. Formerly, Principal of the John Burroughs School and of the Scarborough School.

Sylvia Block, A.B.: Director of the Puppet Center of New York, which is under the sponsorship and supervision of the Board of Education of that city.

Eloise B. Cason, Ph.D.: Psychologist of Montgomery County, Maryland. Formerly, psychologist, Rochester, New York, public schools, and instructor of psychology at Syracuse University.

E. Winifred Crawford, A.M.: Director of Visual Education, Public Schools of Montclair, New Jersey; Member of Executive Committee of the Dept. of Visual Education of the National Education Association.

Paul Cressey, A.M.: Special authority in the field of sociology; lecturer at New York University.

Harry L. Stearns, Ph.D.: Superintendent of Schools, Woodbury, New Jersey.

Harry A. Wann, Ph.D.: County Superintendent of Schools, Morris County, New Jersey.

Roy R. Zimmerman, A.M.: County Superintendent of Schools, Bergen County, New Jersey.

4

SUMMER SESSION OF THE
NEW JERSEY STATE TEACHERS COLLEGE AT MONTCLAIR

LOCATION AND GROUNDS

Located about three and one-half miles from the center of Montclair, on the first range of the Watchung mountains, with a campus of about seventy acres, of which thirty are undeveloped and wooded or rocky and precipitous and forty are beautifully developed with roadways, walks, shrubbery, trees, and lawns, with an amphitheatre, tennis courts, athletic fields, and college buildings, the State Teachers College at Montclair offers an admirable opportunity to pursue intellectual work and to enjoy recreational activities while doing so.

Because of the elevation and abundant shade, the campus has been considered generally comfortable and attractive throughout the summer session.

Eighteen miles away on the horizon rise the towers of the buildings and bridges of the city of New York. Still nearer, the city of Newark, New Jersey, can be seen.

Within a few miles of the college are the wooded reservations that afford delightful walks, horseback rides, and picnics. Lakes Mohawk, Hopatcong, Greenwood, and many smaller lakes are easily reached by car over beautiful roads through the mountains of northern New Jersey. To the south, the shore resorts of Asbury Park, Ocean Grove, Atlantic City, and other beaches invite one to the sea.

RESIDENCE HALLS FOR MEN AND WOMEN

Edward Russ Hall and Chapin Hall are Montclair's two well-appointed residences. In summer, Chapin is reserved as living quarters for all students. The main dining room is in Edward Russ Hall. The charge for living on campus is reasonable—$10.00 per week, including room, breakfast, and dinner. A la carte luncheons are served in the college cafeteria. For one student in a double room, an extra charge of $10.00 is made. The college provides all furnishings, with the exception of towels, blankets, and desk lamps. The fee must be paid on or before the first day of the summer session. No rebate is made for occasional absence or voluntary withdrawal during the session. Students who are absent on account of illness for two weeks or more will receive a rebate of $5.00 per week during the illness.

The elevation of the residence halls on the campus hill assures a cool breeze day and night, and also a magnificent view of the gardens and small farms in the valley and the jagged New York skyline just beyond.

The summer recreational activities include baseball, tennis, archery, swimming, riding, and hiking. These activities and others are easily planned and also easily accessible. The Dean of Women, athletic directors, and hostesses of the residence halls make a special effort to provide social and recreational activities for the men and women living on the campus.

For reservations in the college residence hall, address Mrs. Maude L. Carter; State Teachers College, Upper Montclair, New Jersey.

5

PURPOSE OF THE SUMMER SESSION AT MONTCLAIR

All courses have been organized and selected primarily for men an women engaged in or preparing for professional service in junior an senior high schools. This includes:

1. Candidates for a bachelor's degree in the field of secondar education;

2. Teachers holding a bachelor's degree who are candidates fc graduate credit or master's degree;

3. Junior and senior high school principals and supervisors seekin special courses or higher certificates and degrees;

4. Graduates of non-professional colleges who wish to take certif cate courses or a master's degree in special teaching fields:

5. Graduates of high schools, junior colleges, and four-year colleg who wish to take subject-matter courses for general culture.

FOR NON-MATRICULATED STUDENTS

The College feels a special responsibility to those who are interested i promoting the profession of teaching. It also serves laymen and wome who desire to take courses for cultural, vocational, or avocational purpose in which case the work may be taken with or without credit. High schoc graduates, or students who have not pursued college courses for credit, ma take for credit courses numbered 100 to 299 inclusive. Students who hav credit for at least two years of work on college level may take for cred courses numbered 300 to 499 inclusive. Courses numbered 500 and abov may be taken for credit only by those who have had three or more years c college work

AUDITORS

Those who desire merely to audit courses should indicate on the registrations that they are taking the work for no credit and have a clez understanding with their instructors at the beginning of the summer sessio to that effect. Failure to do this may result in the student's receiving a fai ing mark for the course.

MATRICULATION

Those who wish to become candidates for the A.B. or the A.M. d gree at Montclair must matriculate. Registration for courses does not cor stitute matriculation. Students should make application for matriculatio on the form provided for that purpose. This may be obtained from tl office of the Dean of Instruction. The request for it should make cle; which degree the student is interested in obtaining. When submitting tl application, properly filled in, the student must send his official transcrip of all previous work of college grade. The letter should be addressed t the Registrar. When an applicant has been accepted as a candidate for a d gree, a definite statement will be furnished him, showing the requiremen to be fulfilled in order to obtain the degree desired.

6

COURSES LEADING TO THE A.B. DEGREE

Candidates for the A.B. degree at Montclair should consult the complete catalogue of the college for the general requirements and for the details of the requirements in their particular major and minor fields. Also, they should confer with the Dean of Instruction regarding the general program of their work and with the Head of the Department in which they are majoring regarding the selection of their courses. Matriculated students should not take courses without this guidance.

COURSES LEADING TO THE A.M. DEGREE

Candidates for the A.M. degree at Montclair should consult the graduate bulletin of the college for the general requirements for that degree and for the details of the requirements in their major field. Also, they should confer with the Dean of Instruction regarding the general program of their work and with the Head of the Department in which they are majoring regarding the selection of their courses. Matriculated students should not take courses without this guidance.

A graduate student may not take a course on the 100 or 200 level for credit.

A student matriculated for the A.M. degree at Montclair may not take a course on the 300 level for credit unless the Head of the Department in which the student is majoring so requests in writing to the Dean of Instruction. Only one such course may be offered for credit toward the A.M. degree.

Courses numbered 400 and above may be taken for graduate credit.

Courses numbered 500 and above are designed for students holding baccalaureate degrees.

STUDENTS MATRICULATED AT OTHER COLLEGES

Graduate and undergraduate students matriculated at colleges other than Montclair who desire to take courses here this summer for credit to be presented at such other colleges should obtain in advance the approval of their own Deans of their selection of courses.

TEACHING CERTIFICATES

Anyone desiring information regarding the requirements for New Jersey teaching certificates should write to the State Board of Education at Trenton for the booklet entitled: "Rules Concerning Teachers Certificates."

Students definitely seeking New Jersey teaching certificates should submit official transcripts of all previous work on college level to Dr. John B. Dougall, State Department of Public Instruction, Trenton, N. J. No one working for a teaching certificate should select his courses until he has received a statement showing the evaluation of his previous work and the further courses needed to qualify him for the certificate he desires. As this requires time, the student who decides at the last minute to work for a teaching certificate will need to take his transcripts to Trenton, rather than to wait to mail them and receive a reply by mail.

LIST OF COURSE OFFERINGS FOR THE NEW JERSEY LIMITED
SECONDARY CERTIFICATE

This is not an official statement. It does not emanate from the State Department which issues the certificate. It is furnished the student merely for his convenience in selecting his courses. It shows where the courses of this college fit into the plan outlined by the State Department.

I Health Education—3 semester-hours required
    Biology 409 Human Physiology—3 s.h.
    Physical Education 301B—Health and Health Teaching, Part I—2 s.h.
    Physical Education 302B—Health and Health Teaching, Part II—2 s.h.

II Educational Psychology—3 semester-hours required
    Integration 200A Introduction to Educational Psychology and Mental Testing—2 s.h.
    Integration 200B Adolescent Psychology and Mental Hygiene—2 s.h.
    Integration 500B Advanced Educational Psychology—3 s.h.

III Aims and Organization (Principles) of Secondary Education—3 s.h. required
    Integration 300A Aims and Organization of Secondary Education—2 s.h.
    Integration 400A Principles and Philosophy of Secondary Education—2 s.h.
    Integration 405 Principles of Junior High School Teaching—2 s.h.
    Integration 500A History and Principles of Secondary Education—3 s.h.
    Integration 502A Organization and Administration of the Modern High School, Part I—2 s.h.
    Integration 502B Organization and Administration of the Modern High School, Part II—2 s.h.

IV Principles and Techniques of Teaching in the High School—3 s.h. required
    Integration 300B Principles and Techniques of Teaching in the Secondary School—2 s.h.
    Integration 500C Teaching Procedures in Secondary Education—3 s.h.

V Curriculum Organization and Courses of Study (Methods) in One Endorsed Teaching Field—3 semester-hours required
    Business Education 401 The Teaching of Business Education in the Secondary School—3 s.h.
    English 401 The Teaching of English in the Secondary School—3 s.h.
    Language 401 The Teaching of Foreign Languages in the Secondary School 3 s.h.
    Mathematics 401 The Teaching of Mathematics in the Secondary School 3 s.h.
    Music 401 The Teaching of High School Music—3 s.h.
    Science 401 The Teaching of Science in the Secondary School—3 s.h.
    Science 505 Survey of Curricula and Science Courses in State and City System—3 s.h.
    Biology 501 The Teaching of Biology—3 s.h.
    Chemistry 501 The Teaching of Chemistry—3 s.h.
    Physics 501 The Teaching of Physics—3 s.h.
    Social Studies 401 The Teaching of the Social Studies in the Secondary School—3 s.h.

VI Elective—3 semester-hours required
    Courses in the Department of Integration that are definitely in the field of Secondary Education and that have not been taken to satisfy one of the above requirements.

The student will note that either an undergraduate or a graduate course may be applied toward the certificate. Not all the above courses are offered during any one semester or summer session.

CONFERENCES

Students are urged not to wait until the opening of the summer session to consult their advisers. Between the date of publication of the bulletin and the close of the spring semester, students may arrange to confer with both the Dean of Instruction and the Department Heads relative to matriculation, courses, credit, etc., by writing directly to the particular official concerned for an appointment. For those who have found it impossible to make an earlier appointment, the Director of the Summer Session and the Heads of Departments will hold office hours on July 5. A representative of the Department of Public Instruction also will be at the college on July 5, between the hours of 10 A.M. and 3 P.M., to see students who desire a last word of advice. He cannot, however, undertake at this time to evaluate all the previous work of a student, as the interviews are but five minutes long. (See instructions on page 7, under "Teaching Certificates.") The Secretary of the Summer Session will receive requests for appointments with this State Official and will notify the student of the exact time of the appointment.

REGISTRATION

There is no advance registration, except for the Transcontinental Field Study course.* In all other courses, registration takes place on July 7, in the individual classes. Unless there are 10 students present, the course is discontinued. Students from such discontinued courses register in other classes on July 8. Registration is completed by calling at the Business Office, in the basement of the college, in the late afternoon or on the day following registration in class, to obtain the Class Admission Card. This must be delivered to the instructor not later than July 10. The mail clerk in the college bookstore will, if requested, place the Class Admission Card in the postbox of the instructor for the student.

Training Teachers, taking a course without charge, follow these same procedures. The Class Admission Card will be audited without payment of fees, upon presentation to the Business Manager of evidence that the teacher is entitled to this credit.

FEES

There is a registration fee of $1.00 for the summer session.

Legal residents of New Jersey are required to pay a tuition fee of $6.00 per point or semester-hour credit. Non-residents of New Jersey are required to pay $8.00 per point. Courses taken for no credit cost the same as those for credit.

Laboratory Fee: A fee of $1.50 will be charged in connection with each of the laboratory courses and for the crafts course.

Deferred payment fee: Students taking two or more courses may arrange in the Business Office for payment on a deferred basis; for this privilege, there is an extra charge of $1.00 per course. No deferred payment is permitted for a single course.

*Because of the necessity for knowing in advance how many students will take this course, students may register for it at any time, provided the fees accompany the registration. If interested, write for registration blanks.

WITHDRAWAL FROM COURSES

A student who finds it necessary to withdraw from any course after having completed his registration for it must so notify the Secretary of the Summer Session in writing immediately; otherwise the registration stands as a charge against the student and the fees for it are not refunded. No refunds of tuition fees are made except in cases of illness.

CREDITS AND TRANSCRIPTS

The total amount of credit which may be earned in one summer is 8 semester-hours.

Each course is in session at least thirty hours and receives credits as designated. Report cards, for the student's own use, and an official transcript for him to present at the State Department or at another college, are mailed directly to the student within a week or ten days of the close of the summer session. This first transcript is furnished to the student without charge. The cost of a second transcript depends upon the amount of work which the student has completed at this college, ranging from 25c for one semester or summer session to $1.00 for four or more. The college cannot provide a second transcript that covers less than all the work completed by the student. Stamps cannot be accepted as payment for transcripts; check or post-office money order should be used when remitting fees by mail.

The mark of "D" when earned in summer, part-time, or extension courses, is not accepted for credit at Montclair, but will be given when earned, for possible use elsewhere.

Courses that carry a credit of 4 semester-hours in the regular curriculum of the college are usually given in the summer session in two parts, each half course carrying a credit of 2 semester-hours. Occasionally, the nature of the course is such that the two parts must be taken in a designated sequence, in which case attention is drawn to that fact in the course description.

INCOMPLETE WORK

A student who has made an earnest endeavor to meet all requirements, but has failed in one particular, on account of illness, may see the instructor in charge of the course, and, if he thinks it advisable, the student may be granted two months' time in which to complete the work. If the work has not been finished by the end of this time, the mark for the course shall be "F." The responsibility regarding incomplete work rests with the student.

THE COLLEGE HIGH SCHOOL

The College High School will be continued this summer. Opportunities will thus be afforded students to observe demonstration lessons. College students who desire to place their own children in the demonstration school should make inquiries as early as possible. Families who desire to live in the residence hall, attend college, and place their children in the high school will be given special consideration.

10

SUPERVISED STUDENT TEACHING

The opportunity to do supervised student teaching is not offered during the summer session. Students desiring to do this work during the fall semester should write to Dr. Robert H. Morrison, Director of Teacher Education, State Department of Public Instruction, Trenton, New Jersey.

ROOM NUMBERS

Room numbers followed by the letters CHS indicate rooms in the College High School Building. All other room numbers refer to rooms in College Hall, the main building on the campus. Meetings and conferences that take place in the living rooms of the residence halls are indicated by ERH for Edward Russ Hall and CH for Chapin Hall.

SCHEDULE

Classes are so scheduled that all courses that meet daily are held in the morning, and that no afternoon class meets on either Wednesday or Saturday, thus leaving Wednesday and Saturday afternoons free each week for all students. Furthermore, no classes are held on Saturday, July 19, or on Saturday, August 2. This may be kept in mind in planning for afternoons and week-ends in New York or at shore or mountain resorts.

THE SCHOOLMEN'S CONFERENCE
July 17 and 18
"PROBLEMS OF OUR AMERICAN DEMOCRACY AND OUR RELATIONS WITH LATIN-AMERICA"

The aim of this conference is to bring together administrators and teachers for a discussion of:

1. The new State course of study in "Problems of American Democracy"
2. Courses in "Latin-American Relations"

CALENDAR

Saturday, July 5
　　10:00 A.M. - 3 P.M.—Registration Conferences
Monday, July 7
　　8:00 A.M.—Summer Session opens
Thursday, July 17
　　10:00 A.M.—Schoolmen's Conference begins
Friday, July 18
　　4:00 P.M.—Schoolmen's Conference ends
Saturday, July 19
　　No classes
Saturday, August 2
　　No classes
Tuesday, August 12
　　8:00 A.M. - 12:25 P.M. and 1:00 - 2:25 P.M.—Examinations in classes receiving 2 semester-hours credit
Wednesday, August 13
　　8:00 A.M. - 12:25 P.M. and 1:00 - 2:25 P.M.—Examinations in classes receiving 3 semester-hours credit
　　3:00 P.M.—Summer Session ends

11

DESCRIPTION OF COURSES

LEISURE TIME ACTIVITY COURSES

Applied Arts S411   Creative Crafts—Craft Work for Leisure Time

Dr. Partridge and Miss Block

This course is intended for teachers who want to develop a personal hobby or who have responsibility in conducting activities in school. The student has an opportunity to explore various craft hobbies, such as leather work, plaster casting, puppetry construction and manipulation, metal tooling, and similar crafts. Special emphasis is placed upon crafts involving little cost and using waste materials. Meets Mondays, Tuesdays, Thursdays, and Fridays for one and one-half hours.

Begins Monday, July 7; 9:30 A.M. - 30 hours - Credit: 2 S. H.   Room: Shop

Note: Students may earn credits in the above course toward a college degree or they may work solely for their own enjoyment and for the purpose of developing a hobby. In addition to this course, students will find in other departments one or more courses which may be taken with a view to their possibilities for the enrichment of leisure time. The following list is suggestive:

English S435—Play Production
Spanish—S1—Beginning Spanish, Part I
Physical Education S406—Games and Game Skills
Physics S304—Photography for High School Teachers
Social Studies S516—Field Studies: Continental United States

DEPARTMENT OF BUSINESS EDUCATION

Business Education S409   Consumer Education   **Mr. Geigle**

This course is a study of economic activities from the viewpoint of the consumer. It deals with such problems as the relation of the consumer to production, wasteful consumer practices, consumer propaganda, effective methods of consumer cooperation, and government aids to consumers. The main purpose is to present principles and methods of wise consumption as a guide to action in the purchase of the main varieties of goods and services. Meets Mondays, Tuesdays, Thursdays, and Fridays for one and one-half hours.

Begins Monday, July 7; 11:00 A.M. - 30 hours - Credit: 2 S. H.   Room D

Business Education S411A   Cost Accounting   **Mr. Geigle**

A thorough knowledge of bookkeeping is a prerequisite to a profitable study of this course. The course deals with the basic principles of modern cost finding and cost keeping, and endeavors to give a practical application of these principles to present-day conditions. The practical application consists of a laboratory budget containing business papers, vouchers, etc., together with full instructions for writing up a practice set of cost books. Meets Mondays, Tuesdays, Thursdays, and Fridays for one and one-half hours.

Begins Monday, July 7; 1:00 P.M. - 30 hours - Credit: 2 S. H.   Room D

DEPARTMENT OF ENGLISH

English S100B   World Literature, Part II   **Dr. Cayley**

Outstanding works of the Renaissance writers, the Elizabethans, the Romantics, and the Victorians are studied with the view of showing what each has contributed to the origin of forms and the development of the literature of the world, and how each in its turn has had its influence upon its own and succeeding times. Such writers as the following are considered: Dante, Boccaccio, Petrarch, Chaucer, Shakespeare, Milton, Calderon, Moliere, Racine, Pope, Boswell, Goethe, Wordsworth, and Tennyson. The first half of the course is not necessarily prerequisite to this half. Meets Mondays, Tuesdays, Thursdays, and Fridays for one and one-half hours.

Begins Monday, July 7; 9:30 A.M. - 30 hours - Credit: 2 S. H.   Room 2

English S401   The Teaching of English in the Secondary School   Mr. Nickerson

This course deals with the methods of teaching composition and literature in the high school. It aims to unify and organize the professional training and practical experience of all students in the course, and to provide new points of view for their active English teaching by setting up objectives and indicating concrete methods of obtaining those objectives. The required work in composition and literature, as outlined in city and state courses of study, receives attention. Demonstrations of composition, grammar, and literature teaching are given in the College High School classes for observation and criticism. (This course satisfies the requirement of Curriculum Organization and Courses of Study in the field of English for the Limited Secondary Certificate.) Meets daily for one and one-half hours. Begins Monday, July 7; 11:00 A.M. - 45 hours - Credit: 3 S. H. Room 13, CHS

English S402B   Survey of English Literature, Part II   Mr. Hamilton

The survey of English literature draws together into a systematic narrative the history of the development of literature in the English language. The course enables students to secure a sound background in English literature as a historical development, to become acquainted with a great number of masterpieces, and to fill in gaps in their reading. Part Two carries the study from 1660 to 1800. Meets Mondays, Tuesdays, Thursdays, and Fridays for one and one-half hours. Begins Monday, July 7; 8:00 A.M. - 30 hours - Credit: 2 S. H. Room 1

English S406   The Modern Novel   Mr. Conrad

Particular emphasis is given to British and American novels since 1870, and all important tendencies of present-day prose fiction are explored. Students are taught how to read a novel with profit, and how to guide and direct the reading of others. Meets Mondays, Tuesdays, Thursdays, and Fridays for one and one-half hours. Begins Monday, July 7; 8:00 A.M. - 30 hours - Credit: 2 S. H. Room C

English S413   Modern Poetry   Mr. Nickerson

This course deals with the work of contemporary poets, both British and American. A great deal of the best modern poetry is studied for interpretation and appreciation. The distinctive poetry "movements" that have occurred during the present century are examined as expressions of changing social ideals. Each student is assisted in developing a technique that will enable him to bring out in his own life and in the lives of others the best values that poetry can communicate. Meets Mondays, Tuesdays, Thursdays, and Fridays, for one and one-half hours. Begins Monday, July 7; 9:30 A.M. - 30 hours - Credit: 2 S. H. Room 13, CHS

English S419   Grammar for Teachers   Mr. Hamilton

This course is designed to give an understanding of the history and development of English grammar which will be useful to teachers of English. Out of this general study should come a broad, liberal attitude toward grammar and its function in speech and writing. The student should emerge from the course with an understanding of the structure of our language which will allow him to meet intelligently teaching problems involving grammatical relationships. Meets Mondays, Tuesdays, Thursdays, and Fridays for one and one-half hours. Begins Monday, July 7; 1:00 P.M. - 30 hours - Credit: 2 S. H. Room 1

English S431A   Shakespeare and the English Drama, Part I   Mr. Hamilton

The main emphasis of this course is upon eight Shakespearean tragedies and chronicle plays: Hamlet, Othello, King Lear, Macbeth, Richard II, Henry IV (part one), Henry V, and Richard III. The topics studied include Shakespeare's conception of tragedy; his dramatic art; his poetry; the sources of his plays; staging in Shakespeare's theatre and in our own; typical textual problems; and aids for the teaching of Shakespeare in the secondary school. Meets Mondays, Tuesdays, Thursdays, and Fridays for one and one-half hours. Begins Monday, July 7; 9:30 A.M. - 30 hours - Credit: 2 S. H. Room 1

English S435   Play Production   **Mr. Boh**

This course deals with the theory and art of play production. It is concerned with the
process of staging, lighting, costuming, and putting on of plays, and gives practical experience in the planning and making of properties, scenery, and costumes. Instruction is also
given concerning sources of supplies for stagecraft, materials suitable for various types of
costumes, methods of achieving artistic effects simply and the effects of lighting on color
and fabrics. Meets Mondays, Tuesdays, Thursdays, and Fridays for one and one-half
hours.
Begins Monday, July 7; 1:00 P.M. - 30 hours - Credit: 2 S. H.   Room A

English S442A   American Literature, Part I   **Mr. Conrad**

This course surveys the development of American Literature from its beginnings to the
height of the Romantic period. After studying the literature of colonial America and of
the Revolutionary and early national periods, the course emphasizes the flowering of American literature in the work of Irving, Hawthorne, Bryant, Poe, Emerson, Thoreau. Longfellow, Whittier, Holmes, Lowell, and Melville. Meets Mondays, Tuesdays, Thursdays, and
Fridays for one and one-half hours.
Begins Monday, July 7; 9:30 A.M. - 30 hours - Credit: 2 S. H.   Room C

English S447   Introduction to Philosophy   **Dr. Cayley**

This course is an introduction to the major problems of philosophic thought and to the
various ways in which thinkers throughout the ages have faced these problems. Meet
Mondays, Tuesdays, Thursdays, and Fridays for one and one-half hours.
Begins Monday, July 7; 11:00 A.M. - 30 hours - Credit: 2 S. H.   Room 2

English S515   Robert Browning   **Mr. Nickerson**

Browning's characteristic shorter poems are recalled or studied in order to define his fundamental ideas as a writer. This is followed by a study of his longer poems and dramas
the "soul-studies," Pauline, Paracelsus, and Sordello; the dramas, Strafford, Pippa Passes
A Blot in the 'Scutcheon, Colombe's Birthday, and In a Balcony; the translations, The
Agamemnon of Aeschylus, and Balaustrion's Adventure; and Browning's masterpiece, The
Ring and the Book. These works are studied for their literary and philosophical values
as showing the development of Browning as man, poet, and philosopher, and as a reflection
of certain phases of nineteenth-century life and thought. Meets Mondays, Tuesdays
Thursdays, and Fridays for one and one-half hours.
Begins Monday, July 7; 1:00 P.M. - 30 hours - Credit: 2 S. H.   Room 13, CH

English S516   Language Problems in the English Curriculum   **Mr. Conrad**

This course reviews the several theories of language and studies the problem of meaning i
order to arrive at a suitable technique for the interpretation of prose and verse. Thi
technique is then applied to the problems of reading, of composition, of speech, and c
appreciation of literature. The course has two aims: to increase the student's own skill i
dealing with language and to increase his effectiveness in teaching. Meets Mondays, Tues
days, Thursdays, and Fridays for one and one-half hours.
Begins Monday, July 7; 11:00 A.M. - 30 hours - Credit: 2 S. H.   Room

English S518   The Major Romantic Poets   **Dr. Cayle**

This course studies the work of Coleridge, Wordsworth, Scott, Byron, Shelley, and Keat
It devotes especial attention to those poems which are best adapted for the reading of hig
school students. Meets Mondays, Tuesdays, Thursdays and Fridays for one and one-ha
hours.
Begins Monday, July 7; 8:00 A.M. - 30 hours - Credit: 2 S. H.   Room

DEPARTMENT OF FOREIGN LANGUAGES

Language S300   Foundations of Language   Miss Littlefield

This course is required of all candidates for the A.B. degree regardless of their major subjects. A comprehensive survey is made of the background, growth, and structure of the English language, traced from its remote Indo-European ancestry down through the changes wrought by foreign additions and influences. By a systematic and comparative study of the main elements of Greek, Latin, French, Anglo-Saxon, and English, and of the phonetic phenomena recurring in language development, the course presents and augments the important diction values derived from foreign language study. It aims especially to train teachers of general language or of exploratory courses in foreign languages. Meets Mondays, Tuesdays, Thursdays, and Fridays for one and one-half hours.

Begins Monday, July 7; 11:00 A.M.   -   30 hours   -   Credit: 2 S. H.   Room 10

Language S401   The Teaching of Foreign Languages in Secondary Schools
                                                                        Miss Littlefield

This course is open to seniors and graduates majoring or minoring in foreign languages and satisfies the requirement in Curriculum Organization and Courses of Study in the foreign language field for the Limited Secondary Certificate. The work is focused on such topics as the following; ultimate and immediate aims in foreign language teaching; new fields opening up for the foreign language teacher; survey of outstanding methods, with emphasis on oral work; new methods of reading and of developing grammar; new realia; reports on new textbooks; review, tests, and supervised study. A unit on Comparative Phonetics is included. Special attention is given to the city and state courses of study in New Jersey. General language teachers find this course helpful to them also. Meets daily for one and one-half hours.

Begins Monday, July 7; 9:30 A.M.   -   45 hours   -   Credit: 3 S. H.   Room 10

Spanish S1   Beginning Spanish, Part I   Miss Escoriaza or substitute

This course is designed to prepare students to converse in and to read the Spanish language, to the extent that they may travel in Spanish-speaking countries, use Spanish in commercial relationships, and become more sensitive to the culture of our neighbors to the south. Meets Mondays, Tuesdays, Thursdays, and Fridays for one and one-half hours.

Begins Monday, July 7; 9:30 A.M.   -   30 hours   -   Credit: 2 S. H.   Room 9

Spanish S—C   Conversations in Spanish   Miss Escoriaza or substitute

This course is of a practical nature. It is intended for persons having a previous knowledge of the language. Work in the class stresses the spoken language. Correct pronunciation and rapid reading in Spanish are emphasized. Meets Mondays, Tuesdays, Thursdays, and Fridays for one and one-half hours.

Begins Monday, July 7; 11:00 A.M.   -   30 hours   -   Credit: 2 S. H.   Room 9

DEPARTMENT OF GEOGRAPHY

Geography S411   Geographic Influences in American History   Dr. Milstead

A study is made of the geographic factors influencing the development of social, economic, and political life in America. It is recommended especially to students of history and related subjects. Meets Mondays, Tuesdays, Thursdays, and Fridays for one and one-half hours.

Begins Monday, July 7; 11:00 A.M.   -   30 hours   -   Credit: 2 S. H.   Room 26

Geography S413   Economic Geography of South America   Dr. Milstead

This course constitutes a study of the influence of the natural environment upon production and utilization of resources in the economic, social, and political development of the various nations of South America. Meets Mondays, Tuesdays, Thursdays, and Fridays for one and one-half hours.

Begins Monday, July 7; 1:00 P.M. - 30 hours - Credit: 2 S. H.   Room 26

Geography S416   Conservation of Natural Resources   Dr. Milstead

This constitutes a study of the natural resources of the United States—soils, inland waters, forests, wild life, and minerals—their past and present exploitations; their influence on the development of the nation; their conservation and future use. Meets Mondays, Tuesdays, Thursdays, and Fridays for one and one-half hours.

Begins Monday, July 7; 9:30 A.M. - 30 hours - Credit: 2 S. H.   Room 26

Geography S504   Economic Geography of Europe   Dr. Milstead

This is a study of the economic and commercial development of the countries of Europe in relation to their environment. Meets Mondays, Tuesdays, Thursdays, and Fridays for one and one-half hours.

Begins Monday, July 7; 8:00 A.M. - 30 hours - Credit: 2 S. H.   Room 26

DEPARTMENT OF INTEGRATION

Integration S200A   Introduction to Educational Psychology and Mental Testing
Dr. Sperle

This course covers the psychology of classroom procedure. Growth and development of child and adolescent personality are studied from the physical, intellectual, social, and emotional aspects of individual pupils and their adjustment to the group. The relation of testing to the problems of understanding children as learners and to the problem of treating individual differences is studied through testing projects. Meets Mondays, Tuesdays, Thursdays, and Fridays for one and one-half hours.

Begins Monday, July 7; 8:00 A. M. - 30 hours - Credit: 2 S. H.   Room 6

Integration S300A   Aims and Organization of Secondary Education   Dr. W. Scott Smith

The content of this course may be summarized by the topics included, which are as follows: (1) nature and function of the American secondary school; (2) historical development of secondary education in the United States; (3) organization of the administrative units; (4) secondary education in other lands; (5) the students; (6) the program of studies and activities; (7) the staff; (8) buildings, grounds, and equipment; (9) cost and support of education; and (10) the secondary-school as a social and economic instrument. Meets Mondays, Tuesdays, Thursdays, and Fridays for one and one-half hours.

Begins Monday, July 7; 1:00 P.M. - 30 hours - Credit: 2 S. H.   Room 6

Integration S300B   Principles and Techniques of Teaching in the Secondary School
Dr. Sperle

After having established the fundamental principles underlying the teaching process, the following techniques and procedures are presented and evaluated: the question, the lesson plan, the assignment, testing and marking systems, classroom management and routine; and special procedures, such as supervised study. In addition to the above topics, based on subject-matter organization and administration, various types of classroom procedure are considered. The course seeks to develop a critical attitude with sound principles as bases. Meets Mondays, Tuesdays, Thursdays, and Fridays for one and one-half hours.

Begins Monday, July 7; 9:30 A.M. - 30 hours - Credit: 2 S.H.   Room 8

Integration S400A   Principles and Philosophy of Secondary Education   Dr. Ryan

This course evaluates educational objectives, techniques, procedures, and organizations in relation to the needs and demands made upon the school by society and by the developing personality. It involves a discussion of the meaning of philosophy and an interpretation of human values. Fundamental principles of education are evolved from previous work in the various fields of thought contributing to educational philosophy. Meets Mondays, Tuesdays, Thursdays, and Fridays for one and one-half hours.

Begins Monday, July 7; 8:00 A.M. - 30 hours - Credit: 2 S. H. Room 8

Integration S406   Educational Sociology   Mr. Cressey

This course deals with the application of sociological principles to educational problems. The school is treated as a part of the community, and the various social forces that affect the school and its administration are considered. The following topics are included: family backgrounds; community organization; social breakdown; socialized classroom methods; the social approach to individual behavior difficulties. Meets Mondays, Tuesdays, Thursdays, and Fridays for one and one-half hours.

Begins Monday, July 7; 1:00 P.M. - 30 hours - Credit: 2 S. H. Room C

Integration S408   Multi-Sensory Aids   Miss Crawford

Sources, principles of selection, standards of evaluation, and methods of use of the various multi-sensory aids are studied in relation to all phases of school work; the utilization of field trips, specimens, models, exhibits, and experiments; prints, stereopticon slides, film slides, silent and sound motion pictures; photoplay appreciation; maps, graphs, charts, diagrams, cartoons; and puppets and marionettes. Instruction is given in making many of the above aids and in the operation and care of the various projectors. Meets Mondays, Tuesdays, Thursdays, and Fridays for one and one-half hours.

Begins Monday, July 7; 8:00 A.M. - 30 hours - Credit: 2 S. H. Room 4

Integration S500A   History and Principles of Secondary Education   Dr. Stearns

This course traces the development of secondary education. Consideration is given to the meaning of liberal education as it was conceived by earlier civilizations. Special attention is given to organizations, curricula and methods of instruction, and to the social conditions affecting the development of secondary schools in England, Germany, France, and the United States. Meets daily for one and one-half hours.

Begins Monday, July 7; 8:00 A.M. - 45 hours - Credit: 3 S. H. Room 4, CHS

Integration S500B   Advanced Educational Psychology   Dr. Cason

Prerequisite: Integration 200A or its equivalent. In this course, a comparative study is made of contemporary schools of psychology with emphasis on their direct application to education. Practical applications are made to classroom problems and the work of guidance departments. Meets daily for one and one-half hours.

Begins Monday, July 7; 9:30 A.M. - 45 hours - Credit: 3 S. H. Room 30

Integration S500C   Teaching Procedures in Secondary Education   Mr. Seybold

This course emphasizes the fundamental principles underlying the technique of teaching on the secondary school level. Some of the topics considered are: organization of knowledge; the logical and psychological aspects of method; developing appreciations; social-moral education; teaching motor control; fixing motor responses; books and verbalism; meeting individual differences; guidance in study; tests and examinations; marks and marking. Meets daily for one and one-half hours.

Begins Monday, July 7; 11:00 A.M. - 45 hours - Credit: 3 S. H. Room 3, CHS

Integration S501   Tests and Measurements in Secondary Education   Mr. Jackson

The purpose of this course is to develop an appreciation of the meaning and importance of measurement in education and to give a working knowledge of instruments of measurement. The topics covered are: historical sketch of the development of educational tests and measurements; limitations of traditional types of examinations; newer types of examinations; standardized tests for teachers of English, mathematics, social studies, science, and the languages; criteria for the choice of tests; and applications of statistics in interpreting tests and measurements. Meets Mondays, Tuesdays, Thursdays, and Fridays for one and one-half hours.

Begins Monday, July 7; 11:00 A.M. - 30 hours - Credit: 2 S. H. Room 27

Integration S502A   Organization and Administration of the Modern High School, Part I   Dr. Wann

The problems considered are: the student personnel; building and revising the high school curriculum; providing for individual differences; making the school schedule; records, the guidance program; pupil participation in government; the extra-curricular program; the health program; the safety program; discipline; library and study hall; cafeteria; the principal's office; and evaluating results. Meets Mondays, Tuesdays, Thursdays, and Fridays for one and one-half hours.

Begins Monday, July 7; 9:30 A.M.   -   30 hours   -   Credit: 2 S. H.   Room 29

Integration S503   Methods and Instruments of Research   Mr. Jackson

This course is required of all candidates for the Master's degree without regard to their fields of major interest. Its purpose is to introduce students of education to research and its practical application to immediate problems. The course treats: the nature and types of educational research; methods and techniques of educational research; and the tools used in interpreting statistical data. During the course, the student sets up a problem and plans and carries out its solution. Meets Mondays, Tuesdays, Thursdays, and Fridays for one and one-half hours.

Begins Monday, July 7; 1:00 P.M.   -   30 hours   -   Credit: 2 S.H.   Room 9

Integration S504A   Curriculum Construction in the Secondary School   Mr. Seybold

This course purposes to introduce the student to constructive criticism of American culture, to consider the extent to which the secondary school curriculum meets the needs of a changing civilization, and to consider effective means of curriculum construction. Meets Mondays, Tuesdays, Thursdays, and Fridays for one and one-half hours.

Begins Monday, July 7; 9:30 A.M.   -   30 hours   -   Credit 2 S. H.   Room 3, CHS

Integration S504C   Current Curriculum Experimentation   Mr. Aikin

This course includes: a survey of recent systematic modifications of the secondary school offerings; an evaluation of results; promising departures; and probable future trends. No prerequisite courses. Meets Mondays, Tuesdays, Thursdays, and Fridays for one and one-half hours.

Begins Monday, July 7; 8:00 A.M.   -   30 hours   -   Credit: 2 S. H.   Room 9

Integration S505   Organization and Administration of Extra-Curricular Activities   Dr. W. Scott Smith

The first part of this course considers such general problems of extra-curricular activities as: their growing importance; their relation to the curriculum; the principles underlying their organization, administration, and supervision; and methods of financing. In the second part, an intensive study is made of the home room, the assembly, the student council, clubs, athletics, school publications, and other activities in which the class is especially interested. Meets Mondays, Tuesdays, Thursdays, and Fridays for one and one-half hours.

Begins Monday, July 7; 11:00 A.M.   -   30 hours   -   Credit: 2 S. H.   Room 29

Integration S507   Organization and Administration of Guidance Programs   Dr. Wann

The purpose of this course is to acquaint the student with the various agencies and methods for the guidance of students in school work, with certain implications in the choice of and the preparation for a vocation. Among the topics are: the abilities of students as related to guidance; the exploration of special interests; the organization of the guidance program; and the integration of the entire high school program for purposes of guidance. Meets Mondays, Tuesdays, Thursdays, and Fridays for one and one-half hours.

Begins Monday, July 7; 8:00 A.M.   -   30 hours   -   Credit: 2 S. H.   Room 29

Integration S508A   Supervision and Criticism of Teaching, Part I   Dr. Stearns

This course emphasizes the more practical phases of supervision which are met most frequently by those engaged in it. Among the topics are: the set-up for adequate supervision; supervision as encouraging and guiding the growth of teachers and the improvement

18

of educational procedures; the supervisory functions of teachers' meetings; discussion groups; general and professional reading; the writing of articles; cooperative curriculum modification; utilization of community resources; and teacher inter-visitation. Meets Mondays, Tuesdays, Thursdays, and Fridays for one and one-half hours.

Begins Monday, July 7; 11:00 A.M. - 30 hours - Credit: 2 S. H. Room 4, CHS

Integration S515 Guidance and Personnel Problems of Classroom Teachers
Mr. Seybold

This course considers all types of personnel problems with which the classroom teacher deals. It is concerned with the growth of pupils and seeks to point out the ways by which proper growth may be obtained. Classroom, health, social, and personal activities are analyzed in terms of the needs of present-day social life. The course seeks to show how the teacher may effectively direct pupils into worthwhile channels. The teacher's own personal problem of adjustment, as it affects dynamic guidance, is considered. Meets Mondays, Tuesdays, Thursdays, and Fridays for one and one-half hours.

Begins Monday, July 7; 1:00 P.M. - 30 hours - Credit: 2 S. H. Room 3, CHS

Integration S516 School Finance Dr. Stearns

This course is of special interest to school administrators, since it acquaints them with the field of finance in relation to a well-ordered school program. The topics considered are: basic problems of school support; systems of taxation; allocation of costs; computing school costs; sources of information; techniques; comparative costs; purchasing; and standards. Meets Mondays, Tuesdays, Thursdays, and Fridays for one and one-half hours.

Begins Monday, July 7; 9:30 A.M. - 30 hours - Credit: 2 S.H. Room 4, CHS

Integration S517 Administration of the Elementary School* Mr. Zimmerman

This course analyzes and evaluates the administrative duties and relationships of the elementary school principal. Particular consideration is given to: building management; effective use of the school plant; sanitation; health service; the library; personnel management; the administration of the curriculum; community relationships; publicity. Meets Mondays, Tuesdays, Thursdays, and Fridays for one and one-half hours.

Begins Monday, July 7; 9:30 A.M. - 30 hours - Credit: 2 S. H. Room 27

Integration S518 Supervision of Instruction in the Elementary School*
Mr. Zimmerman

This course is planned for those engaged in the supervision of the elementary school and those who are preparing for such responsibilities. Principles of classroom supervision are developed and applied to learning situations. Among the more important topics are: the nature and function of supervision; the organization necessary for effective supervision; the nature and significance of the teacher's purposes; the methods and techniques of group and individual supervision; the technique of observation; and the supervisory conference. Meets Mondays, Tuesdays, Thursdays, and Fridays for one and one-half hours.

Begins Monday, July 7; 8:00 A.M. - 30 hours - Credit: 2 S. H. Room 27

Integration S520 Principles of Mental Hygiene and Guidance Dr. Cason

This course is designed to be a general survey of the principles and practices of mental health with special reference to the mental health of teacher and pupil. It involves a thorough grounding in fundamental principles of mental hygiene with much practical consideration of the mental-health values of instructional programs and procedures. Discussion centers in practical efforts to develop wholesome personalities in our schools. Meets Mondays, Tuesdays, Thursdays, and Fridays for one and one-half hours.

Begins Monday, July 7; 11:00 A.M. - 30 hours - Credit: 2 S. H. Room 30

*The two courses offered in the field of the supervision and administration of Elementary Education are given as a part of the graduate major in Administration and Supervision.

19

Integration S524   The Study of the Failing Pupil   **Dr. Ryan**

The first part of the course is devoted to the "disparity technique," a method of evaluating the pupil's achievement in relation to his ability. The second part treats of procedures to be used in finding the causes of failure, and in planning treatment. Meets Mondays, Tuesdays, Thursdays, and Fridays for one and one-half hours.

Begins Monday, July 7; 11:00 A.M.   -   30 hours   -   Credit: 2 S. H.   Room 8

Integration S530A   In-Service Field Studies: Corrective and Remedial Reading in Secondary Schools   **Dr. Sperle**

This course offers an investigation and interpretation of the reading problems which are found in secondary school classes. A study is made of the causes of reading difficulties, methods of diagnosis, and techniques of remedial and corrective teaching. Particular attention is given to the selection and adaptation of suitable curriculum materials. Guidance is given to teachers with individual case problems of retarded, normal, and superior pupils. Illustrative material is taken from case studies developed by classroom teachers. Meets Mondays, Tuesdays, Thursdays, and Fridays, for one and one-half hours.

Begins Monday, July 7; 11:00 A.M.   -   30 hours   -   Credit: 2 S. H.   Room 1

Integration S601A   Workshop, Section I: Current Problems in Managing the School
Dr. Ryan and Staff

Problems in administration, guidance programs, curriculum construction, extra-curricular activities, finance, educational philosophy.

Begins Monday, July 7; 9:30 A.M.   -   60 hours   -   Credit: 4 S. H.   Room 4

Integration S601B   Workshop, Section II: Current Problems in Directing Instruction
Dr. Ryan and Staff

Problems in supervision, teaching techniques, curriculum experimentation, evaluation, corrective reading, multi-sensory aids.

Begins Monday, July 7; 9:30 A.M.   -   60 hours   -   Credit: 4 S. H.   Room 4

Integration S601C   Workshop, Section III: Current Problems and Understanding Youth   **Dr. Ryan and Staff**

Problems in adolescent psychology, "human relations," mental hygiene, the teacher in guidance, educational sociology, community relations, the visiting teacher.

Begins Monday, July 7; 9:30 A.M.   -   60 hours   -   Credit: 4 S. H.   Room 4

Each of these three Workshops is conducted as follows:

1. Under the supervision of the Director, general conference periods are held each week as arranged.

2. Conferences between the individual student and a special consultant are held by appointment.

3. Free unassigned time for individual study is allowed.

The work includes the definition, study, evaluation, and report on each individual problem.

DEPARTMENT OF MATHEMATICS

Mathematics S101A   Mathematical Analysis, Part I: College Algebra   Mr. Clifford

This course contains the usual topics found in a beginning course in college algebra, such as: study of functional relationships; graphing of functions; solution of equations; rational and irrational functions; permutations; combinations; probability; and the use of increments in finding rate of change. Meets Mondays, Tuesdays, Thursdays, and Fridays for one and one-half hours.

Begins Monday, July 7; 9:30 A.M.   -   30 hours   -   Credit: 2 S. H.   Room 3

Mathematics S101B   Mathematical Analysis, Part II: Trigonometry   Mr. Clifford

This course treats the following topics: functions and their graphical representation; functions of an acute angle; relationship of trigonometric functions; functions of any angle; reduction of functions; solution of triangles; complex numbers; trigonometric analysis; logarithms; slide rule; practical solution of triangles. When time permits, a study is made of Demoivre's theorem and its extension, the construction of trigonometric tables. Meets Mondays, Tuesdays, Thursdays, and Fridays for one and one-half hours.

Begins Monday, July 7; 11:00 A.M.   -   30 hours   -   Credit: 2 S. H.   Room 3

Mathematics S102A   Mathematical Analysis, Part III: Analytical Geometry   Dr. Davis

This course is recommended particularly to those students seeking a minor in mathematics or those in need of a review course in analytic geometry. The topics include: rectangular and polar coordinate systems; loci and their equations; the straight line; the conics—circle, parabola, ellipse, and hyperbola; parametric equations; transformation of coordinates; and the general equation of the second degree. Meets Mondays, Tuesdays, Thursdays, and Fridays for one and one-half hours.

Begins Monday, July 7; 8:00 A.M.   -   30 hours   -   Credit: 2 S. H.   Room 5

Mathematics S300   Social and Commercial Uses of Mathematics   Mr. Clifford

This course is required of all candidates for the A.B. degree, regardless of their major subjects. A consideration of the economic problems met by the intelligent citizen, independent of his vocation, forms the basis for selection of material for it. The mathematics is mostly arithmetic, and includes the problems met in home and civic life. Some of the topics are: budgeting and wise expenditure of income; providing for future independence through wise investments and insurance; taxation; cost of installment purchases; the operation of personal finance companies; cost of living versus the buying power of income, etc. Meets Mondays, Tuesdays, Thursdays, and Fridays for one and one-half hours.

Begins Monday, July 7; 8:00 A.M.   -   30 hours   -   Credit: 2 S. H.   Room 3

Mathematics S400   Educational Statistics   Dr. Fehr

The aim of this course is to provide a sufficient background to enable the student to comprehend and criticize articles of statistical nature in current educational literature, to apply statistical methods in testing and rating pupils, and to carry on the simpler types of educational research. Among the topics treated are: graphical and tabular representation; measures of central tendencies; measures of variability; linear correlation; the normal distribution; sampling; and reliability of measures. The application of the subject provides natural integration with psychology, tests and measurements, and procedures in secondary education. The methods are equally applicable to physical and social data. Meets Mondays, Tuesdays, Thursdays, and Fridays for one and one-half hours.

Begins Monday, July 7; 9:30 A.M.   -   30 hours   -   Credit: 2 S. H.   Room 14, CHS

Mathematics S401   The Teaching of Mathematics in the Secondary School
                                                                    Dr. Mallory and Dr. Fehr

This course is required of all candidates for the A.B. degree with a major in mathematics and meets the requirement for a course in Curriculum Organization and Courses of Study in the field of mathematics for the limited secondary certificate. In this course, special consideration is given to specific problems which arise in the teaching of junior and senior high school mathematics. These include the following: adaptation of material to students of varying abilities; selection and treatment of subject matter; use of texts and supplementary material; importance of the fundamental concepts; use of special methods and devices; how to treat the more difficult phases of the subject matter; and the preparation of students for college entrance examinations. Daily demonstrations in the College High School illustrate units in enriched teaching. Meets daily for one and one-half hours.

Begins Monday, July 7; 8:00 A.M.   -   45 hours   -   Credit: 3 S. H.   Room 14, CHS

Mathematics S410   Introduction to the Mathematics of Finance and Insurance

Instructor to be Assigned

A course introducing the student to the elementary theory of simple and compound interest and leading to the solution of practical problems in annuities, sinking funds, amortization, depreciation, stocks and bonds, installment buying, and building and loan associations; and to the mathematics of life insurance covering the subjects; the theory of probability as related to life insurance, the theory and calculation of mortality tables, various types of life annuities and insurance policies, and reserves. This course is designed to give a helpful background to the mathematics teacher as well as to be an aid to the student of economics and insurance. Meets Mondays, Tuesdays, Thursdays, and Fridays for one and one-half hours.

Begins Monday, July 7; 1:00 P.M.   -   30 hours   -   Credit: 2 S. H.   Room 3

Mathematics S507   General or Integrated Mathematics in the Junior High School

Dr. Mallory and Dr. Fehr

The seventh, eighth, and ninth grades afford an excellent opportunity to develop an integrated program in mathematics. The fundamental arithmetical processes require repeated and frequent drill. At the same time, the junior high school student may be made conscious of the importance of mathematics in everyday life and in its relation to the various fields of knowledge. This course considers some of the problems arising in the development of such a program and includes demonstrations in the College High School on methods of presenting some of the material discussed. Meets daily for one and one-half hours.

Begins Monday, July 7; 8:00 A.M.   -   45 hours   -   Credit: 3 S. H.   Room 7, CHS

Mathematics S509A   A Critical Interpretation of Mathematics in the Senior High School, Part I

Dr. Davis

The fundamental concepts of the algebra and geometry of the secondary school are analyzed and interpreted. The meaning and applications of secondary mathematics are stressed, together with the correlation of algebra and geometry. Among the topics discussed are: modes of thinking in algebra and geometry; fundamental laws of algebra and arithmetic; the function concept and its uses; recent trends in change of subject matter; etc. Meets Mondays, Tuesdays, Thursdays, and Fridays for one and one-half hours.

Begins Monday, July 7; 11:00 A.M.   -   30 hours   -   Credit: 2 S. H.   Room 5

Mathematics S515   Differential Equations

Dr. Davis

Various applications of differential equations and their standard methods of solution are fully treated in this course. Among the topics included are: linear differential equations of the first degree and of the first and higher orders; linear equations of the nth order with constant coefficients; linear equations of the second order; exact and total differential equations; simultaneous equations; numerical approximation; and partial differential equations. It is a continuation of the calculus considered from a new viewpoint. Meets Mondays, Tuesdays, Thursdays, and Fridays for one and one-half hours.

Begins Monday, July 7; 9:30 A.M.   -   30 hours   -   Credit: 2 S. H.   Room 5

Mathematics S524B   Statistical Inference and Sampling Theory

Dr. Fehr

This course deals with the planning and execution of a statistical study. Among the topics considered are: the interpretation of statistical functions, the general theory of sampling, students' distribution, chi-square distribution, analysis of variance and co-variance, statistical control, and the design for experiment. Special statistical devices for the solution of special problems are considered. The development of statistical reasoning is an important aim of the course. Applications are given to business, economics, agriculture, scientific, and social data. A course in elementary statistics is prerequisite to this course. Meets Mondays, Tuesdays, Thursdays, and Fridays for one and one-half hours.

Begins Monday, July 7; 11:00 A.M.   -   30 hours   -   Credit: 2 S. H. Room 14, CHS

DEPARTMENT OF MUSIC

Music S202B   Harmony, Part II   Mr. Kahn

This course is a continuation of Music 202A, given in the summer session of 1940, and includes four-part writing of primary and secondary triads in first and second inversions, seventh chords, modulation and harmonic analysis. The above theory is presented first as musical experiences, analyzed, defined, and used as a basis for sight singing, ear training, and melody writing. Special attention is given to the functional aspects of harmony as applied to the piano keyboard in the classroom. Prerequisites; knowledge of the rudiments of music, and the ability to play major and minor scales, intervals, fundamental chords, and dominant seventh chord. Meets Mondays, Tuesdays, Thursdays, and Fridays for one and one-half hours.

Begins Monday, July 7; 9:30 A.M. - 30 hours - Credit: 2 S. H.   Room 6

Music S402   Conducting and Score Reading   Mr. Kahn

The purpose of this course is to develop skills in conducting and score reading. It includes the particular type of ear training needed in conducting; technique of the baton, score reading and interpretation. A special feature of this course is the presentation of a large number of musical examples taken from standard orchestra repertoire which contain practically all technical and psychological problems which face a prospective conductor. Practical experience in conducting is given with the use of recorded music, piano, and orchestra. Prerequisites: knowledge of harmony and instrumentation acceptable to the instructor. Meets Mondays, Tuesdays, Thursdays, and Fridays for one and one-half hours.

Begins Monday, July 7; 11:00 A.M. - 30 hours - Credit: 2 S. H.   Room 6

DEPARTMENT OF PHYSICAL EDUCATION

Physical Education S201B   Organization of Physical Education   Mr. Voliva

In this course the student is made aware of the breadth of the field of physical education. The field is broken up into its integral parts, showing how each part is a unit in itself and how these units when combined form the physical education unit which in turn is a unit of the general education program. The following subjects are discussed: required physical examination; required program; restricted program; games and activities; elective program; intramural program; and interscholastic athletics program. Meets Mondays, Tuesdays, Thursdays, and Fridays for one and one-half hours.

Begins Monday, July 7; 1:00 P.M. - 30 hours - Credit: 2 S. H.   Room 5, CHS

Physical Education S202B   Management of Athletic Activities   Mr. Pittser

In this course information is provided which will enable the young teacher or director of physical education to avoid many of the common errors of management. Emphasis is placed upon: making schedules; care of equipment; care of playground; care of locker rooms; purchasing equipment; handling finances; budgeting; conduct of students while on trips; etc. Meets Mondays, Tuesdays, Thursdays, and Fridays for one and one-half hours.

Begins Monday, July 7; 11:00 A.M. - 30 hours - Credit: 2 S. H.   Room 6, CHS

Physical Education S302A   Methods and Practice in Physical Education   Mr. Voliva

Various methods used in assembling and handling classes on the field or gymnasium floor are discussed. The student is required to take charge of physical education activities of the fellow members of his class under the supervision of the instructor. Reports of systems used in nearby high schools are required. Meets Mondays, Tuesdays, Thursdays, and Fridays for one and one-half hours.

Begins Monday, July 7; 8:00 A.M. - 30 hours - Credit: 2 S. H.   Room 5, CHS

Physical Education S302B   Health and Health Teaching, Part II   Mr. Pittser

This course is a continuation of S301B—Health and Health Teaching, Part I, which was given in the summer of 1939. but which is not, however, necessarily prerequisite to this part. Some fields of subject-matter are considered intensively, the choice being governed by the needs of the group. Criteria for judging materials and procedures are developed. Meets Mondays, Tuesdays, Thursdays, and Fridays for one and one-half hours.

Begins Monday, July 7; 8:00 A.M. - 30 hours - Credit: 2 S. H.   Room 6, CHS

Physical Education S406   Games and Game Skills   Mr. Voliva

In recent years, much impetus has been given the physical education program in our high schools by the substitution of interesting games and contests for the calisthenics of yesterday. This course gives consideration to the rules of the games, methods of supervision, and to the acquiring of techniques by much practice and by individual and class competitions. Among the games and sports studied are archery, badminton, paddle tennis, shuffle board, horseshoes. indoor baseball, golf, and volley ball. Meets Mondays, Tuesdays, Thursdays, and Fridays for one and one-half hours.

Begins Monday, July 7; 11:00 A.M. - 30 hours - Credit: 2 S. H. Room 5, CHS

Physical Education S407   Safety Education   Mr. Pittser

In this course, a study is made of a number of safety controls which will have an influence upon the health and happiness of the individual throughout his entire life span. The subject matter is derived from the following sources: the study of anatomy, physiology, biology, growth of the child; hygiene; and from psychology, sociology, physical education, and athletics. The safety controls are discussed in chronological order, showing how it is possible for the teacher in the field of physical education to contribute to the welfare of each individual. Safety first and first aid on the playground and in the gymnasium are stressed. Meets Mondays, Tuesdays, Thursdays, and Fridays for one and one-half hours.

Begins Monday, July 7; 1:00 P.M. - 30 hours - Credit: 2 S. H.   Room 6, CHS

Physical Education S410   Principles and Philosophy of Physical Education Mr. Pittser

This course is designed for administrators in service and in training. The basic principles upon which the entire program of physical education is constructed and many of the vital problems which annoy administrators are studied. A practical application of physical education to the seven cardinal principles of education is made. It is shown how required physical education, varsity athletics and intramural sports are welded into a single unit of education. There is discussion of how health service and safety education are closely related to physical education. Finally, a philosophy of physical education is developed which is practical and usable. Meets Mondays, Tuesdays, Thursdays, and Fridays for one and one-half hours.

Begins Monday, July 7; 9:30 A.M. - 30 hours - Credit: 2 S. H.   Room 6, CHS

DEPARTMENT OF SCIENCE

Biology S406   Animal Histology   Dr. Hadley

This course includes a careful study of histological technique as illustrated by preparations made from various animal tissues. Tissues of different animals, both vertebrate and invertebrate, are studied in fresh preparations and in fixed, preserved condition. Students are trained in the making of microscopic slides which involve either whole mounts of small entire animals or serial sections of animals or parts of animals. Prerequisites: Biology 201 and 202, Zoology. Meets Mondays, Wednesdays, and Fridays at 11:00 A.M. and Wednesdays at 9:30 A. M. for lectures and classroom work; and Mondays, Wednesdays, and Fridays from 1:00 to 3:55 P.M. for laboratory work.

Begins Monday, July 7; 11:00 A.M. - 90 hours - Credit: 4 S. H.   Room 28

24

Biology S409   Human Physiology   Dr. Hadley

A careful study of human anatomy is used as a basis for discussion of both normal and abnormal physiology. In addition to an analysis of the part played by organs and tissues in carrying out the essential functions of the body, special attention is given to problems of hygiene and sanitation. Applications of the above problems are made in reference to children of school age and the physical condition of individual pupils is correlated with their behavior in the classroom. Meets daily for one and one-half hours.

Begins Monday, July 7; 8:00 A.M.   -   45 hours   -   Credit: 3 S. H.   Room 28

Chemistry S101 or S102   General College Chemistry   Dr. Reed

This is a course in beginning chemistry with laboratory work. The aims of the course are: to furnish an opportunity for mastering facts and principles of chemistry that serve as a basis for the subject-matter training of high school science teachers; to give training in scientific methods; to give experience in the use of carefully taken laboratory notes in solving problems; to give students an opportunity to become familiar with standard reference books in general chemistry. This course is planned in units and is conducted by conference and individual work so that the student may devote attention to those phases of elementary chemistry which are most essential to his particular needs. Those with no previous work in college chemistry should enroll in Chemistry S101, while those with previous work in college chemistry should enroll in Chemistry S102. Meets Monday, Wednesday, Friday, and Saturday mornings for one and one-half hours classroom and lecture work and on Monday, Wednesday, and Friday afternoons for three hours laboratory work.

Begins Monday, July 7; 11:00 A.M.   -   90 hours   -   Credit: 4 S. H.   Room 23

Chemistry S506A   Industrial Chemistry, Part I   Dr. Reed

The purpose of this course is to enable prospective science teachers to understand the kind of chemical industries in the State of New Jersey, the nature of their problems, and the effect of these industries on the lives of the people of the State. A survey is made by lectures, reports, and trips to several chemical plants of various types. Detailed study is made of some of the more important industries to ascertain some of the problems of chemistry, engineering, plant location, personnel, and marketing of product. Attention is given to the effect of the introduction of new chemical products upon competing materials and upon the industry in general. A study is made of the role of chemistry in national defense. Prerequisite: College Chemistry. Meets Tuesday and Thursday mornings for one and one-half hours lecture and class discussion and on those same afternoons for trips to industrial plants.

Begins Tuesday, July 8; 11:00 A.M.   -   45 hours   -   Credit: 2 S. H.   Room 23

Physics S102B   General College Physics, Part IV: Electricity   Dr. McLachlan

This part of the first course in college physics deals with the following topics: magnetism, static electricity, potential, resistance, capacitance, chemical and heating effects of electric currents, cells and batteries, electric power, electric lighting, electromagnetic induction, generators, motors, instruments, alternating currents, electric discharges in gases, electromagnetic waves, and modern methods of communication. Students may begin the study of physics with this unit. Meets Tuesdays and Thursdays for one and one-half hours lecture and classroom work in the morning and for three hours laboratory work in the afternoon.

Begins Tuesday, July 8; 8:00 A.M.   -   45 hours   -   Credit: 2 S. H.   Room 25

Physics S304   Photography for High School Teachers   Dr. K. O. Smith

This is a beginning course in photography, consisting of laboratory and field work supplemented with lectures and demonstrations. Some of the topics studied are: the construction and operation of cameras, film characteristics, use of exposure meters, development and printing of negatives and positives, taking pictures under very different lighting conditions, lantern slide making, projection printing, production of colored transparencies with color film. A student needs at least one camera for use in the course. No prerequisites. Meets Mondays, Tuesdays, Thursdays, and Fridays for one and one-half hours.

Begins Monday, July 7; 9:30 A.M.   -   30 hours   -   Credit: 2 S. H.   Room 8, CHS

25

Science S410A · Junior High School Science Demonstrations, Part I   Dr. K. O. Smith

A course primarily for teachers in service who wish to develop or extend experimental work in junior high school classes. Over three hundred experiments are available, from which students may make selections for special study. These experiments deal with a wide variety of subjects; such as: air, ventilation, fuels, fire prevention, winds and weather observation, foods, diet and digestion, soil and seed germination, machines, electric motors and generators, transformers, bell circuits, light and color, cameras. Some time is spent in planning lessons centered on demonstration experiments. Meets Mondays, Tuesdays, Thursdays, and Fridays for one and one-half hours.

Begins Monday, July 7; 8:00 A.M. - 30 hours - Credit: 2 S. H.   Room 8, CHS

Science S411A   Science in Transportation: Aviation   Dr. McLachlan

This course was organized to help teachers and supervisors to meet the growing and insistent demand of pupils for information about aviation. Some previous training in physics is desirable. Some of the topics covered are: history of aviation, theory of flight, principles and materials of construction, building and flying model airplanes, parachutes, air navigation, uses of radio in air transportation, and the school aviation club. One or more trips will be arranged if conditions permit. 411B, a continuation of this course, will be offered in the future. It deals with engines, instruments, studying and reporting weather conditions, and other aspects of air transportation. Meets Mondays, Tuesdays, Thursdays, and Fridays for one and one-half hours.

Begins Monday, July 7; 9:30 A.M. - 30 hours - Credit: 2 S. H.   Room 25

DEPARTMENT OF SOCIAL STUDIES

Social Studies S101A   European History from 1492 to 1713   Dr. Folsom

The course deals with the Lutheran, Calvinist, and Anglican aspects of the Reformation and the ensuing Counter-Reformation with their political and national significance in the 16th Century. The disintegration of Germany during the Thirty Years' War, the English constitutional conflict under the Stuarts, and the Age of Louis XIV are the main subjects for the 17th Century. Meets Mondays, Tuesdays, Thursdays, and Fridays for one and one-half hours.

Begins Monday, July 7; 9:30 A.M. - 30 hours - Credit: 2 S. H.   Room 21

Social Studies S200A   Contemporary Economic Life   Mr. Geigle

This course aims to acquaint the student with the basic nature of economic life, to point out the opposing economic doctrines in force in various parts of the world, and particularly to investigate the functionings of economic life both here and abroad. Case studies from the current newspapers and periodicals are made the basis of this course. These suggest such topics as: working conditions; standards of living; economic security; governmental economic activities; employer-employee relationships; etc. The sources of economic ideas and the evolution of economic institutions are traced, when these appear necessary to an understanding of contemporary affairs. Meets Mondays, Tuesdays, Thursdays, and Fridays for one and one-half hours.

Begins Monday, July 7; 8:00 A.M. - 30 hours - Credit: 2 S. H.   Room D

Social Studies S200B   Contemporary Political Life   Mr. Geigle

This course is designed to orient the student in the contemporary political situation— local, national, and international. It provides an opportunity to think and talk about what the national state is; how the machinery of the state may be controlled through public opinion, the suffrage, and political parties; how modern states are governed; how national states deal with each other in war and peace; and what the outlook for the immediate future appears to be. Meets Mondays, Tuesdays, Thursdays, and Fridays, for one and one-half hours.

Begins Monday, July 7; 9:30 A.M. - 30 hours - Credit: 2 S. H.   Room D

Social Studies S202A   United States History from 1860 to 1902   Dr. Snyder

This course covers the great struggle over slavery, the period of Reconstruction, the economic growth of the United States, and the political and social problems that developed during the latter part of the past century. Meets Mondays, Tuesdays, Thursdays, and Fridays for one and one-half hours.

Begins Monday, July 7; 8:00 A.M.   -   30 hours   -   Credit: 2 S. H.   Room 12, CHS

Social Studies S301A   Economics I   Mr. Rellahan

The object of this course is to permit the teacher of the social studies to obtain a professional understanding of the fundamental nature and functioning of our present economic system. Emphasis is given to a study of the background of present-day economic institutions, and the manner in which the present system functions with respect to the economic and business organization of production, the nature and laws of consumption, the principles involved in the determination of value and price under competition or monopoly, and the problem of distribution as related to an explanation of rent, interest, wages, and profits. Meets Mondays, Tuesdays, Thursdays, and Fridays for one and one-half hours.

Begins Monday, July 7; 9:30 A.M.   -   30 hours   -   Credit: 2 S. H.   Room 22

Social Studies S301B   Economics II   Mr. Rellahan

This course is a continuation of Economics I, which is not, however, prerequisite. The aim of this course is to acquaint the student with the basic economic principles and problems relating to risk and insurance; money, credit and banking; general price changes and their control; foreign trade and exchange; tariffs, international debts and imperialism; business combinations; and governmental regulation of business enterprise. Meets Mondays, Tuesdays, Thursdays, and Fridays for one and one-half hours.

Begins Monday, July 7; 11:00 A.M.   -   30 hours   -   Credit: 2 S. H.   Room 22

Social Studies S401   The Teaching of Social Studies in the Secondary School
Professor Hatch and Dr. Snyder

This course satisfies the state requirement in Curriculum Organization and Courses of Study in the social studies field. It meets in connection with a class in the College High School, so that students may have the opportunity to observe the demonstration of the methods presented. The course presents recent tendencies in the teaching of the social studies. Among the matters considered are: the social studies curriculum, with special attention to the fusion organization; the objectives in the social studies; class procedures, including the problem-project method, unit mastery method, oral procedures, drill and review procedures, procedures in particular subjects, the teaching of current events; devices and aids, including visual, auditory, and motor aids, technique of field trips; use of textbooks and supplementary reading; and testing and grading. Bibliographies and other teaching aids are supplied to students. Meets daily for one and one-half hours.

Begins Monday, July 7; 9:30 A.M.   -   45 hours   -   Credit: 3 S. H.   Room 12, CHS

Social Studies S402A   American Government   Mr. Bye

The basic facts and principles necessary for the teaching of courses in civics, problems of American democracy, and United States history are studied in this course, through current problems in government and politics. Problems involving the relationship of the individual citizen to the government and to the political party, of the state to the United States, and of political machinery to its functions, are included. Meets Mondays, Tuesdays, Thursdays, and Fridays for one and one-half hours.

Begins Monday, July 7; 8:00 A.M.   -   30 hours   -   Credit: 2 S. H.   Room E

Social Studies S402B   Comparative Government   Mr. Bye

Will democracy or dictatorship survive? This major world problem of today is approached in this course through a study of the nature and functions of states and governments, public opinion, civil rights, suffrage, political parties, and the machinery of government in England, France, the United States, Italy, Germany, and Russia. Since the course confines its attention to problems of internal political organization and the processes of politics and government, it may be taken along with courses in recent European history and the European outlook without undue duplication. Meets Mondays, Tuesdays, Thursdays, and Fridays for one and one-half hours.

Begins Monday, July 7; 9:30 A.M. - 30 hours - . Credit: 2 S. H.   Room E

Social Studies S420A   The European Outlook: Part I   Dr. Wittmer

The complete course is aimed to give a better and broader understanding of European post-war problems. Through a short survey of pre-war developments, the main causes, and in some aspects, the significance of the World War, are explained. Lectures on political, economic, social, and cultural topics help to interpret treaties and alliances concluded by European powers since 1918. Versailles and Locarno; disarmament and rearmament; the League of Nations; fascism, communism, and democracy; the corporative system; trends of thought inspired by Nietzsche, Spengler, Sorel, and Marx: the Danube and the Balkan states are discussed. Special emphasis is given to the problems of Soviet Russia and Nazi Germany. Prerequisite: a course in modern European history. Meets Mondays, Tuesdays, Thursdays, and Fridays for one and one-half hours.

Begins Monday, July 7; 8:00 A.M. - 30 hours - Credit: 2 S. H.   Room 20

Social Studies S420B   The European Outlook: Part II   Dr. Wittmer

Though this is a continuation of The European Outlook, Part I, the latter is not pre-requisite to it. Special emphasis is given to the causes of the fall of France, the low Countries, and Norway; Fascist activities in Portugal; Spain's role in the spread of Fascism to South America; Italy's strategic difficulties in the Mediterranean; and England's problems of Empire and insular defense. A survey of economic and strategic world conditions in their relation to the European conflict, as well as to America's future, is given. Part of the course is devoted to the interpretation of political news. Prerequisite: a course in modern European history. Meets Mondays, Tuesdays, Thursdays, and Fridays for one and one-half hours.

Begins Monday, July 7; 9:30 A.M. - 30 hours - Credit: 2 S. H.   Room 20

Social Studies S424   Mediaeval Civilization   Dr. Freeman

This course aims to trace the history and civilization of the different races which wandered about and finally settled in Europe during the Mediaeval period. The course presents a careful account of the importance of the Catholic Church in mediaeval civilization; th beginnings of modern nations; the effects of Arabic learning and scholarship; and socia awakening due to the Crusades and the capture of Constantinople by the Turks. Meet Mondays, Tuesdays, Thursdays, and Fridays for one and one-half hours.

Begins Monday, July 7; 8:00 A.M. - 30 hours - Credit: 2 S. H.   Room

Social Studies S428   Sociology I: Racial Contributions to American Life   Mr. By

This course deals with the basic problems of quantity, quality, and distribution of popula tion and emphasizes the adjustments and maladjustments which result from the inter-rela tion of Negroes, Asiatics, and various types of Europeans in the United States. Mee Mondays, Tuesdays, Thursdays, and Fridays for one and one-half hours.

Begins Monday, July 7; 11:00 A.M. - 30 hours - Credit: 2 S. H.   Room

Social Studies S432   Advanced Economics   Mr. Rellahan

Building upon the foundations laid in the introductory courses in economics, the purpose of this study is to provide the student with an opportunity to use economic theory as a means of analyzing more intensively certain major problems and evaluating current economic policies. Chief emphasis is given to the problems and programs concerned with business fluctuations; the distribution of wealth and income; agriculture; labor and social legislation; transportation and public utility regulation; public revenues and expenditures; economic planning; and competing types of economic systems. In order to bring together the contributions of all previous economic study and points of view, a brief summary of the history of economic thought is made. Meets Mondays, Tuesdays, Thursdays, and Fridays for one and one-half hours.
Begins Monday, July 7; 8:00 A.M.   -   30 hours   -   Credit: 2 S. H.   Room 22

Social Studies S433   American Political Thought   Mr. Bye

This is a survey of political thinking in America. It deals with contemporary trends and theories as they have emerged from social and economic conditions and as they are founded upon the bases laid down by such men as Hamilton, Madison, Washington, Jefferson, Marshall, Calhoun, Webster, Lincoln, Wilson, and others. A knowledge of American ideals as expressed in our political philosophy is especially important for teachers of American history, civics, and problems of democracy in this changing period through which we are passing. Meets Mondays, Tuesdays, Thursdays, and Fridays for one and one-half hours.
Begins Monday, July 7; 1:00 P.M.   -   30 hours   -   Credit: 2 S. H.   Room E

Social Studies S434   Contemporary World Affairs   Dr. Wittmer

This course is designed to acquaint the student with the fundamentals of dynamic world strategy. It points out the significance of air and naval bases; highways and canals; production and exchange of raw materials; international monopolies; racial and religious divisions; and density of population. The Far East, Australia, India, Arabia, Africa, and Latin-America, are shown in their relation to our foreign policy and the present world conflict. Meets Mondays, Tuesdays, Thursdays, and Fridays for one and one-half hours.
Begins Monday, July 7; 11.00 A.M.   -   30 hours   -   Credit: 2 S. H.   Room 20

Social Studies S436   Modern Men of Ancient Times   Dr. Freeman

This course is designed to present biographical sketches of some of the great leaders of past ages. The subjects for discussion are selected from all lines of human endeavor, and special attention is given to their influence on the thought of their own times and their contribution to the culture of the present day. The course is specially recommended to students who wish to know these leaders as real persons and not as lay figures in ancient history. Meets Mondays, Tuesdays, Thursdays, and Fridays for one and one-half hours.
Begins Monday, July 7; 9:30 A.M.   -   30 hours   -   Credit: 2 S. H.   Room 7

Social Studies S440A   The Development of South and Central America: Part I
                                                                                      Dr. Snyder
This course surveys the period of exploration and settlement in the colonies of South and Central America. It traces the revolutionary movements that led to their independence and national development as Latin-American countries. Meets Mondays, Tuesdays, Thursdays, and Fridays for one and one-half hours.
Begins Monday, July 7; 11:00 A.M.   -   30 hours   -   Credit: 2 S. H. Room 12, CHS

Social Studies S506   The British Empire from 1783   Dr. Folsom

This course tries to show the reasons why the members of the British Empire remain so loyal in time of crisis; the subtleties of the relationship existing between the members of the British Commonwealth of Nations. Many popular fallacies are exploded, from that which says England learned a lesson from the American Revolution to the one that declared that India, South Africa, French Canada would seize a chance to break away from exploitation. Meets Mondays, Tuesdays, Thursdays, and Fridays for one and one-half hours.
Begins Monday, July 7; 11:00 A.M.   -   30 hours   -   Credit: 2 S. H.   Room 21

29

Social Studies S509   Classical Archaeology   Dr. Freeman

This course is designed to present a knowledge of source material in the fine arts of Greece and Rome that will enable the individual to reconstruct for himself various phases of Greek and Roman culture. This work is of particular importance to all prospective teachers of the social studies, Latin, and English. The course is conducted by lectures liberally illustrated by an abundance of colorful material. Much of this material is verified by trips to the Metropolitan Museum of Art and other local museums. Meets Mondays, Tuesdays, Thursdays, and Fridays for one and one-half hours.
Begins Monday, July 7; 11:00 A.M. - 30 hours - Credit: 2 S. H.   Room 7

Social Studies S516   Field Studies in American Life: Continental United States
                                                                        Mr. Bye

This course consists of sixty-two days of directed travel, covers 12,000 miles, enters 26 states, visits most of the National Parks and the major points of geographic and historical interest in the West, including Mammoth Cave, Boulder and Grand Coulee Dams, Los Angeles, Tia Juana, Yosemite, Redwood Empire, Mt. Ranier, Yellowstone, Black Hills, and Toronto. The all-expense cost of the course is $500.00. This covers every expenditure necessary for a comfortable trip, including transportation, hotel expenses and tips, meals, fees, admissions, and tuition. Tuition must be paid whether credit is desired or not. Standard hotel accommodations include room for two with double bed and bath. (Single rooms or rooms with twin beds can be reserved for $30.00 extra. State regulations require non-residents of New Jersey to pay $20.00 additional for tuition.) Down payment of $50.00 must be made upon registration. The balance of $450.00 must be paid before June 1, 1941. Make out checks to Field Studies Fund. In case of illness, or withdrawal for cause, a refund in full will be made.
Begins Monday, June 30; 8:00 A.M. - 62 days - Credit: 10 S. H. DeLuxe Bus

GRADUATE DEPARTMENT

Graduate S500A   Seminar and Thesis   Dr. Finley

Students writing a thesis for credit toward the Master's degree in any department of the college are required to register for this course. The work is conducted under seminar or individual guidance. Students report to the Dean of Instruction, who calls a conference with the Head of Department and the Sponsor. At this meeting, all matters pertaining to the topic, plan of research, writing of manuscript, etc., are arranged.   Credit: 4 S. H.

PROPOSED COURSES FOR 1941--1942
BY DEPARTMENTS

Summer Session 1941	*Fall Semester* 1941	*Spring Semester* 1942

DEPARTMENT: *Applied Art*

Creative Crafts for Leisure
   Time

DEPARTMENT: *Business Education*

Consumer Education
Cost Accounting

DEPARTMENT: *English*

World Literature — Part II	The Short Story	Teaching of Speech
Teaching of English in Secondary Schools	Mediaeval Epic, Saga, and Romance	17th Century Literature
Survey of English Literature, Part II	Modern Drama	Shakespeare and the English Drama, Part I
The Modern Novel	18th Century Literature	John Milton
Modern Poetry	Public Speaking	Origin and Development of the Arthurian Legend
Grammar for Teachers		
Shakespeare and the English Drama, Part I		
Play Production		
American Literature, Part I		
Introduction to Philosophy		
Robert Browning		
Language Problems in the English Curriculum		
Major Romantic Poets		

DEPARTMENT: *Foreign Languages*

Foundations of Language	Foundations of Language	Foundations of Language.
Teaching of Foreign Languages in Secondary Schools	Beginning Spanish, Part I	Beginning Spanish—Part II
Beginning Spanish, Part I	Second Year Spanish, Part I	Second Year Spanish, Part II
Conversations in Spanish	Spanish 201B	Spanish 202A

DEPARTMENT: *Geography*

Geographic Influences in American History	Advanced Economic Geography, Part I	Advanced Economic Geography, Part II
Economic Geography of South America		
Conservation of Natural Resources		
Economic Geography of Europe		

DEPARTMENT: *Integration*

Introduction to Educational Psych. & Mental Testing

Aims and Organization of Secondary Education

Principles and Techniques of Teaching in Secondary Schools

Principles and Philosophy of Secondary Education

Educational Sociology

Multi-Sensory Aids

History and Principles of Secondary Education

Advanced Educational Psych.

Teaching Procedures in Secondary Education

Tests and Measurements In Secondary Education

Organization and Administration of the Modern High School, Part I

Methods and Instruments of Research

Curriculum Construction in the Secondary School

Current Curriculum Experimentation

Organization and Administration of Extra-Curricular Activities

Organization and Administration of Guidance Programs

Supervision and Criticism of Teaching, Part I

Guidance and Personnel Problems of Classroom Teachers

School Finance

Administration of the Elementary School

Supervision of Instruction in the Elementary School

Principles of Mental Hygiene and Guidance

Corrective and Remedial Reading in Secondary Schools

The Study of the Failing Pupil

Workshops, Sections I, II. and III

Educational Sociology

Radio and Sound Equipment in the Classroom

History and Principles of Secondary Education

Advanced Educational Psychology

Teaching Procedures in Secondary Education

Methods and Instruments of Research

Curriculum Construction in the Secondary School

Seminar in Curriculum Organization

Organization and Administration of Extra-Curricular Activities

Seminar in Educational Administration and Supervision

Field Work in Guidance

Organization and Administration of the Modern High School, Part I

Organization and Administration of the Modern High School, Part II

Methods and Instruments of Research

Seminar in Curriculum Organization

Supervision and Criticism of Teaching, Part I

Supervision and Criticism of Teaching, Part II

Principles of Mental Hygiene and Guidance

Field Work in Guidance

Teaching and Supervision of Reading in Elementary Schools

Vocational Guidance

Recreational and Activity Leadership

DEPARTMENT: *Mathematics*

College Algebra	Theory of Algebra	Educational Statistics
Trigonometry	Current Research in the	Mathematics in Relation to
Analytic Geometry	Teaching of Jr. & Sr. H.	Social Science
Social & Commercial Uses	S. Mathematics	Theory of Numbers
of Mathematics	Math. in Relation to Geo-	Statistical Analysis & Cor-
Educational Statistics	graphy & Astronomy	relation Theory
Teaching of Mathematics	Theory of Probability	Curriculum Construction in
in Secondary Schools	Statistical I n f e r e n c e and	Mathematics
Introduction to the Math.	Sampling Theory	
of Finance & Insurance		
General or Integrated		
Math. in the Junior H.		
S.		
A Critical Interpretation		
of Math. in the Sr.		
H. S.		
Differential Equations		
Statistical Inference and		
Sampling Theory		

DEPARTMENT: *Music*

Harmony, Part II	Seminar in Musicology	Wagner Music Drama
Conducting and S c o r e		
Reading		

DEPARTMENT: *Physical Education*

Organization of Physical	Health and Health Teaching,	Safety Education
Education	Part I	Games and Game Skills
Management of Athletics		
Methods in Physical Edu-		
cation		
Health and Health Teach-		
ing, Part II		
Games and Game Skills		
Safety Education		
Principles & Philosophy		
of Physical Education		

DEPARTMENT: *Science*

Animal Histology	Social Applications of	The Teaching of Biology
Human Physiology	Biology	Physical Chemistry
General College Chemis-	Advanced Organic Chemis-	Problems in Advanced
try, Parts I and II	try; Bio-Chemistry	Photography, Part II
Industrial Chemistry,	Problems in Advanced	Field Studies in Science;
Part I	Photography, Part I	Spring
General College Physics,	Physical Sciences in Modern	
Part IV: Electricity	Life	
Photography for H. S.	Field Studies in Science,	
Teachers	Autumn	
Junior H. S. Science		
Demonstrations, Part I		
Science in Transportation:		
Aviation		

DEPARTMENT: *Social Studies*

Summer Session 1941	Fall Semester 1941	Spring Semester 1942
European History, 1492-1713	European History, 1713-1815	European History, 1815-1870
Contemporary Economic Life	Contemporary Political Life	Contemporary Economic Life
Contemporary Political Life	United States History, 1900-1940	United States History, 1492-1789
American History, 1860-1902	Economics I	Economics II
Economics I	New Jersey State and Local Government	Economic History of the U. S.
Economics II	European Outlook, Part I	Latin-American Relations of the United States
Teaching the Social Studies in Secondary Schools	Oriental Civilization	European Outlook, Part II
American Government	Sociology II: Present-Day Social Problems	Greek Civilization
Comparative Government	Development of South and Central America, Part II	Sociology I: Racial Contributions to American Life
European Outlook, Part I	Economic History of Europe	The Political Party System in the United States
European Outlook, Part II	Origin and Development of the American Constitution	Recent Trends in American History
Mediaeval Civilization	Field Studies in the Metropolitan Community	
Sociology I: Racial Contributions to American Life		
Advanced Economics		
American Political Thought		
Contemporary World Affairs		
Modern Men of Ancient Times		
Development of South & Central America, Part I		
The British Empire		
Classical Archaeology		

SUMMER SESSION

Bulletin of

MONTCLAIR
STATE TEACHERS COLLEGE

1942
July 6 to August 14

UPPER MONTCLAIR, NEW JERSEY

THE VISITING FACULTY MEMBERS

Lawrence S. Chase, A.M.: Superintendent of Schools of Essex County, New Jersey.

E. Winifred Crawford, Ed.D. Director of Visual Education, Public Schools of Montclair; President, Zone II, Dept. of Visual Education of the National Education Association.

Robert W. Crawford, A.M.: Head of the Department of Recreation, Town of Montclair.

Alexander S. Hughes, Jr., A.B.: Head of the Department of Spanish, High School, Atlantic City.

Lemuel Roy Johnston, Ph.D.: Principal, Clifford J. Scott High School, East Orange.

Arthur S. Otis, Ph.D.: Author and Editor for World Book Co.; Private pilot; author, with Captain Francis Pope, TWA, of "Elements of Aeronautics."

George R. Placek, M.A.: Private pilot and designer of gliders; teacher of science, High School, Bogota.

FACULTY

Harry A. Sprague, Ph.D. ....Director of the Summer Session
Harold C. Bohn, A.M. ....English
Ethel M. Booth, R.N. ....First Aid
Edgar C. Bye, A.M. ....Social Studies
Harry G. Cayley, Ed.D. ....English
Lawrence S. Chase, A.M. ....Administration
Paul C. Clifford, A.M. ....Mathematics
Lawrence H. Conrad, A.M. ....English
E. Winifred Crawford, Ed.D. ....Multi-Sensory Aids
Robert W. Crawford, A.M. ....Recreation
Germaine P. Cressey, A.M. ....French
David R. Davis, Ph.D. ....Mathematics
Teresa de Escoriaza, A.M. ....Spanish
Howard Franklin Fehr, Ph.D. ....Mathematics
Avaline Folsom, Ph.D. ....Social Studies
Walter H. Freeman, Ph.D. Head of the Department of Foreign Languages
Francis R. Geigle, A.M. ..Head of the Department of Business Education
Earl Rouse Glenn, A.M. ....Head of the Department of Science
Charles E. Hadley, Ph.D. ....Biology
W. Paul Hamilton, A.M. ....English
Emanuel H. C. Hildebrandt, Ph.D. ....Mathematics
Alexander S. Hughes, Jr., A.B. ....Spanish
Otis C. Ingebritsen, Ph.D. ....Psychology
Claude E. Jackson, A.M. ....Research
Lemuel Roy Johnston, Ph.D. ....Administration
Florence M. Knowlton, A.M. ....Nutrition
Russell Krauss, Ph.D. ....English
Ethel F. Littlefield, A.M. ....Languages
Edna E. McEachern, Ph.D. ...... Director of the Department of Music
Harley P. Milstead, Ph.D. ....Geography
Paul S. Nickerson, A.M. ....English
Helen L. Ogg, Ph.D. ....Speech
Arthur S. Otis, Ph.D. ....Aeronautics
James P. Pettegrove, A.M. ....English
Chester M. Pittser, A.M. ....Physical Education
George R. Placek, A.M. ....Aeronautics
John J. Rellahan, A.M. ....Social Studies
Heber H. Ryan, Ph.D. ....Head of the Department of Integration
Arthur M. Seybold, A.M. ....Integration
Horace J. Sheppard, A.M. ....Business Education
Kenneth O. Smith, Ph.D. ....Science
W. Scott Smith, Ph.D. ....Integration
W. Harry Snyder, Ph.D. ....Social Studies
D. Henryetta Sperle, Ph.D. ....Integration
Felix Wittmer, Ph.D. ....Social Studies

Types of Courses

All courses are selected and organized for men and women engaged in or preparing for professional service in junior and senior high schools. Students may matriculate for the degree of Bachelor of Arts or for the degree of Master of Arts. In either case, those who do not already have the New Jersey Secondary Teaching Certificate must earn that while working for the degree.

This summer, in addition to the usual offerings, the college is making it possible for teachers and prospective teachers to take courses that enable them to assist in civilian defense; to prepare students to enter war service or war industries with more confidence and advance more rapidly; to interpret for themselves and to their classes the news of the war from the many parts of the world in which it is being fought; to build up the morale of their classes and their communities; to uphold democracy under the attacks of the enemy within and without the country; and thus to help in the winning of the war. For list of these, see page 24.

Matriculation

Those who wish to become candidates for the A.B. or the A.M. degree must request the Registrar of the college for the application form and return it properly filled in and accompanied by an official transcript of previous work. When the applicant has been accepted as a candidate for the degree, a definite statement will be furnished him, showing the requirements to be fulfilled by him individually. Candidates for the A.B. degree should thereafter consult the college catalogue for details of these requirements and for the general requirements for the degree. Candidates for the A.M. degree should consult the graduate bulletin in a similar manner. In both cases, the student should confer with the Dean of Instruction and with the Head of the Department in which he is majoring. Matriculated students should not take courses without this guidance.

Courses numbered 100-499, inclusive, may be taken for credit toward the degree of Bachelor of Arts.

Courses numbered 400-499, inclusive, may be taken for credit toward either the Bachelor of Arts or the Master of Arts degree.

Those numbered 500 and above are definitely graduate courses and may be taken only by those holding a Bachelor's degree.

Non-Matriculated Students

High school graduates, or students who have not pursued college courses for credit, may take for credit courses numbered 100 to 299, inclusive. Students who have credit for at least two years of work on college level may take for credit courses numbered 300 to 499, inclusive. Those holding Bachelor's degrees may take courses numbered 500 and above.

4

Auditors

The College feels a special responsibility to those who are interested in promoting the profession of teaching. Laymen and women who desire to take courses for cultural, vocational, or avocational purposes without college credit may register as auditors. This should be clearly indicated on the registration form.

Students Matriculated at Other Colleges

Such students should obtain in advance the approval of their own Deans of the courses they desire to take here this summer in order that the credits earned may be accepted in their own colleges without question.

Teaching Certificates

Students who do not matriculate at MONTCLAIR for a degree should write to the Sec'y to the State Board of Examiners at Trenton for the booklet entitled: "Rules Concerning Teachers Certificates." They should submit to Mr. John B. Dougall, State Department of Public Instruction, Trenton, official transcripts of all previous work on college level with an explanation of the kind of certificate for which they desire such transcripts evaluated. Do not select your summer courses until you have received a statement showing the work you lack for your teaching certificate. If you decide at the last minute to seek this advice, you may find it advisable to go to Trenton personally in order to enter your classes on time.

Registration

There is no advance registration. In all courses, registration takes place on July 6, in the individual classes, provided ten are present; if not, you wait until the second meeting. If there are not yet ten, the class is dismissed and the course discontinued. When you have thus registered for all your classes, call at the Business Office to pay your fees and obtain the Audited Class Admission Card. This must be handed to your instructor at the third meeting of your class; sooner if possible. Training Teachers, Staff Members, and Scholarship Students follow the above procedures also; the Class Admission Card will be audited without payment of fees upon presentation to the Business Manager of evidence that you are entitled to this credit. The Business Office is open until 3:30 P. M. in the summer.

Fees

Checks or money orders should be made payable to NEW JERSEY STATE TEACHERS COLLEGE. Registration service charge: $1.00 for the Summer Session. Tuition fees: to legal residents of New Jersey, $6.00 per semester-hour credit; to non-residents, $8.00 per credit. Courses taken for no credit cost the same. A Laboratory Service Charge of $1.50 is charged in connection with each of the following courses: Physics S304—Photography for High School Teachers, Physics S305A—First Course in Aeronautics and Physics S306A—Introduction to Radio Communication. This service charge is collected in class by your instructor. Do not include it in your check for tuition.

Withdrawal from Courses

The Registrar of the Summer Session should be notified at once if you withdraw from a course.

Credits and Transcripts

The total amount of credit which may be earned in the six weeks of the Summer Session is 8 semester-hours.

Each course is in session at least thirty hours and receives credits as designated. Report cards, for your own use, and an Official Transcript for you to present at the State Department or at another college, are mailed directly to you within a week or ten days of the close of the Summer Session. This first transcript is furnished free. The cost of a second transcript depends upon the amount of work you have completed at this college, ranging from 25c for one semester or summer session to $1.00 for four or more. The College cannot provide a second transcript that covers less than all the work completed by you. Stamps cannot be accepted for transcripts; check or money order should be used when remitting fees by mail.

The mark of "D" when earned in summer, part-time, or extension courses is not accepted for credit at MONTCLAIR, but will be given when earned for possible use elsewhere.

Courses that carry a credit of 4 s. h. in the regular curriculum are usually given in the summer session in two parts, each half course carrying a credit of 2 s. h. When the nature of the course is such that the two parts must be taken in a designated sequence, attention is drawn to that fact in the course description.

If prerequisites are indicated, make certain you have had them before registering in the course.

Incomplete Work

The responsibility regarding incomplete work rests with you. You should confer with your instructor and if he thinks it advisable, you may be granted as much as two months time in which to complete the work. If you do not finish at the end of two months, the mark for the course shall be "F".

Supervised Student Teaching

The opportunity to do supervised student teaching is not offered during the summer session. Matriculated students confer with Dr. Ryan. Non-matriculated students should write to Dr. Robert H. Morrison, Director of Teacher Education, State Department of Public Instruction, Trenton, New Jersey.

Residence Halls for Men and Women

Edward Russ Hall and Chapin Hall are MONTCLAIR's two well-appointed residences. In summer, Chapin Hall is reserved as living quarters for all students. The main dining room is in Edward Russ Hall. The charge for living on campus is reasonable—$10.00 per week, including room, breakfast, and dinner. A la carte luncheons are served in the college cafeteria. For one student in a double room, an extra charge of $2.00 is made. The college provides all furnishings, with the exception of towels, blankets, and desk lamps. The fee must be paid on or before the first day of the Summer Session. No rebate is made for occasional absence or voluntary withdrawal during the session. Students who are absent on account of illness for two weeks or more receive a rebate of $5.00 per week during the illness.

For reservations in the college residence hall, address Mrs. Maude L. Carter, State Teachers College, Upper Montclair, New Jersey.

Room Numbers

Room numbers followed by the letters CHS indicate rooms in the College High School Building. All other room numbers refer to rooms in College Hall, the main building on the campus.

S c h e d u l e

All courses will meet daily Monday through Friday for one hour, except where definitely indicated otherwise. The first period will begin at 8:30 A. M. The noon recess for luncheon will be one half-hour only, and the afternoon session will begin at 1:00 P. M., accordingly.

Due to the presence on the campus this summer of the undergraduate students who are speeding up their work to be graduated in three years time, it has been necessary to place Summer Session classes at hours and in rooms not used in previous summers. It is hoped that, should this result in personal inconvenience, you will realize it is due to the war and will cooperate cheerfully in consequence.

C o n f e r e n c e s

Students are urged not to wait until the opening of the summer session to consult their advisers. If, however, it has been impossible for you to make an earlier appointment, you may see the Head of your Department on Monday, July 6. A representative of the State Board of Examiners also will be at the college that day, between the hours of 10 A.M. and 3 P.M. to see students who desire a last word of advice. He cannot, however, undertake at this time to evaluate all the previous work of a student, as the interviews are but ten minutes long. (See instructions on page 5 under "Teaching Certificates.") The Registrar of the Summer Session will receive requests for appointments with this State Official.

COURSES THAT MAY BE TAKEN TOWARD
THE NEW JERSEY SECONDARY CERTIFICATE

This is not an official statement. It does not emanate from the State Department that issues the certificate. It is furnished merely for your convenience in selecting courses. You should check your selections with the State Department sending an official transcript of work already completed. Please note that either an undergraduate or a graduate course may apply on the certificate.

I Health Education—3 semester-hours required

*Biology 409A Human Physiology—2 s. h.
Physical Education 301B—Health and Health Teaching, Part I —2 s. h
*Physical Education 302B—Health and Health Teaching, Part II—2 s. h.

II Educational Psychology—3 semester-hours required

*Integration 200A--Introduction to Educational Psychology and Mental Testing—2 s. h.
Integration 200B—Adolescent Psychology and Mental Hygiene—2 s. h.
*Integration 500BW—Advanced Educational Psychology—2 s. h.

III Aims and Organization (Principles) of Secondary Education—3 s.h. required

*Integration 300A—Aims and Organization of Secondary Education—2 s. h.
*Integration 400A—Principles and Philosophy of Secondary Education—2 s. h.
Integration 405--Principles of Junior High School Teaching—2 s. h.
*Integration 500AW— History and Principles of Secondary Education—2 s. h.
*Integration 502A—Organization and Administration of the Modern High School, Part 1—2 s. h.
Integration 502B—Organization and Administration of the Modern High School, Part II—2 s. h.

IV—Principles and Techniques of Teaching in the High School—3 s.h. required

*Integration 300B—Principles and Techniques of Teaching in the Secondary School—2 s. h.
*Integration 500CW—Teaching Procedures in Secondary Education—2 s. h.

V Curriculum Organization and Courses of Study (Methods) in One Endorsed Teaching Field—3 semester-hours required

*Business Education 401W—The Teaching of Business Education in the Secondary School—2 s. h.
*English 401W—The Teaching of English in the Secondary School—2 s. h.
*Language 401W—The Teaching of Foreign Languages in the Secondary School—2 s. h.
*Integration 504A—Curriculum Construction in the Secondary School—2 s. h.
*Mathematics 401W—The Teaching of Mathematics in the Secondary School —2 s. h.
*Mathematics 532—Teaching Mathematics in a War Program—2 s. h.
*Music 401W—The Teaching of High School Music—2 s. h.
Science 401W—The Teaching of Science in the Secondary School—2 s. h.
Science 505W—Survey of Curricula and Science Courses in State and City Systems—2 s. h.
Biology 501W—The Teaching of Biology—2 s. h.
Chemistry 501W—The Teaching of Chemistry—2 s. h.
Physics 501W—The Teaching of Physics—2 s. h.
*Social Studies 401W--The Teaching of the Social Studies in the Secondary School—2 s. h.

VI Elective—3 semester-hours required

Courses in the Department of Integration that are definitely in the field of Secondary Education and that have not been taken to satisfy one of the above requirements.

---

*Not all the above courses are offered during any one semester or summer session. Those that are starred (*) are being offered this summer.

DESCRIPTION OF COURSES

Department of Business Education

Business Education S301A **Business Law, Part III** **Mr. Sheppard**

This is a treatment of business law from a practical, educational, and social point of view. The main points for consideration are: personal property, including the nature of personal property, sales, conditional sales, bailments, and chattel mortgages; real property, including landlord and tenant and mechanics' liens; and business organization, including partnerships and corporations.

IV: 11:30 A.M.-12:25 P.M. 30 hours Credit: 2 semester-hours Room 10

Business Education S302B **Salesmanship** - **Mr. Geigle**

The principal activities of the course are: practical application of the selling process through sales talks, discussions, and retail techniques, a knowledge of which is of value both to the seller and the buyer.

II: 9:30-10:25 A.M. 30 hours Credit: 2 semester-hours Room D

Business Education S401W **The Teaching of Business Education in Secondary Schools** **Mr. Geigle**

The history and development of business education, aims or objectives, laws of learning, lesson plans, teaching procedures, tests and measurements, and special helps for the teacher of business education are studied in this course. Consideration is given to the current trend in teaching in these fields, with emphasis on the viewpoint of the consumer as well as the social and vocational objectives.

I: 8:30-9:25 A.M. 30 hours Credit 2 semester-hours Room D

Business Education S409 **Consumer Education** **Mr. Sheppard**

This course deals with such problems as the relation of the consumer to production, wasteful consumer practices, consumer propaganda, effective methods of consumer cooperation, and government aids to consumers. The main purpose is to present principles and methods of wise consumption as a guide to action in the purchase of the main varieties of goods and services.

III: 10:30-11:25 A. M. 30 hours Credit: 2 semester-hours Room D

Department of English

English S204 **Extemporaneous Speaking** **Dr. Ogg**

This course provides maximum platform practice. Students speak on subjects of current interest, paying attention to content, organization of material, and essentials of effective oral presentation.

II: 9:30-10:25 A.M. 30 hours Credit: 2 semester-hours Room 29

English S208 **Fundamentals of Speech, II** **Dr. Ogg**

A study of the bases of speech and the relationship of speech to thought, emotion, and personality are the special concerns of this advanced course of fundamental principles.

I: 8:30-9:25 A.M. 30 hours Credit: 2 semester-hours Room 29

English S301A **Literature for Adolescents: Developing Faith for Living Through Literature** **Mr. Hamilton**

This course is a study of the best available literary material (fiction, drama, biography, essay), suitable to the interests and maturity of junior and senior high school adolescents, and of the use that can be made of it in enabling them to gain the knowledge and confidence necessary for courageous living in this world.

III: 10:30-11:25 A.M. 30 hours Credit: 2 semester-hours Room 1

English S401W **The Teaching of English in the Secondary School** **Mr. Hamilton**

This course deals with the methods of teaching composition and literature in the high school. It aims to unify and organize the professional training and practical experience of all students in the course, and to provide new points of view for their active English teaching by setting up objectives and indicating concrete methods of obtaining those objectives.

II: 9:30-10:25 A.M. 30 hours Credit: 2 semester-hours Room 1

9

English S402A and S402B   Survey of English Literature, I and II   Dr. Krauss

The survey of English literature draws together into a systematic narrative the history of the development of literature in the English language. The course enables students to secure a sound background in English literature as a historical development, to become acquainted with a great number of masterpieces, and to fill in gaps in their reading.
Part I: To 1660 V: 1:00-1:55 P.M.   30 hours   Credit: 2 semester-hours   Room 27
Part II: 1660-1800 IV: 11:30 A.M.-12:25 P.M.   30 hours   Credit: 2 semester-hours
Room 27

English S414   Public Relations and School Publicity   Mr. Pettegrove

This course is designed to prepare the teacher for inaugurating and directing a publicity program. How to develop a student staff for such a program, how to prepare copy for professional newspapers, how to get school news published, how to play fair with both the newspaper editor and the school, and how to make such a program constructively valuable to a school and community are typical problems which the course is planned to solve.
II: 9:30-10:25 A.M.   30 hours   Credit: 2 semester-hours   Room 2

English S421   The Short Story   Mr. Conrad

This course traces the history of this evolving literary form, emphasizing the productions of the nineteenth and twentieth centuries. Many stories are analyzed for both human and literary values. Professional use of the short story is the guiding purpose in the conduct of the course.
II: 9:30-10:25 A.M.   30 hours   Credit: 2 semester-hours   Room 27

English S431A   Shakespeare and the English Drama, Part I   Mr. Bohn

The main emphasis of this course is upon eight Shakespearean tragedies and chronicle plays: Hamlet, Othello, King Lear, Macbeth, Richard II, Henry IV (part one), Henry V, and Richard III. The topics studied include Shakespeare's conception of tragedy; his dramatic art; his poetry; the sources of his plays; staging in Shakespeare's theatre and in our own; typical textual problems; and aids for the teaching of Shakespeare in the secondary school.
III: 10:30-11:25 A.M.   30 hours   Credit: 2 semester-hours   Room A

**English S437   Humanities for Teachers of Literature and the Other Arts
Dr. Cayley**

This course enables teachers of literature, the fine arts, and music to interpret the movements, such as classicism, romanticism, realism, and abstractionism, which are similar in all the arts. Through the analysis of these movements and of the contrasting philosophies and psychologies of composition underlying them, the teacher is helped to understand better the art with which he is directly concerned and to evaluate current discussions as to the best methods of teaching aesthetic appreciation and creation.
III: 10:30-11:25 A.M.   30 hours   Credit: 2 semester-hours   Aud-CHS

**English S442A   American Literature: A Pageant of American Democracy.
Part I   Mr. Conrad**

This course surveys the development of American Literature from its beginnings to the height of the Romantic period. After studying the literature of colonial America and of the Revolutionary and early national periods, the course emphasizes the flowering of American literature in the work of Irving, Hawthorne, Bryant, Poe, Emerson, Thoreau, Longfellow, Whittier, Holmes, Lowell, and Melville.
IV: 11:30 A.M.-12:25 P.M.   30 hours   Credit: 2 semester-hours   Room 1

**English S442B   American Literature: A Pageant of American Democracy
Mr. Conrad**

This course surveys the development of American literature from the Civil War to the contemporary period. The writers studied include: Walt Whitman, Sidney Lanier, Emily Dickinson, William Dean Howells, Mark Twain, Henry James, Henry Adams, Hamlin Garland, Stephen Crane, Frank Norris, O. Henry, Vachel Lindsay, E. A. Robinson, Carl Sandburg, and Robert Frost.
I: 8:30-9:25 A.M.   30 hours   Credit: 2 semester-hours   Room 27

English S448   Choral Speaking   Dr. Ogg

The class is conducted as a regular speaking choir. Members of the group acquire skill in interpreting the various forms of literature suitable for group treatment and gain much as individuals in flexibility and beauty of speech.
V: 1:00-1:55 P.M.   30 hours   Credit: 2 semester-hours   Room 29

English S450   Contribution of American Drama to American Democracy

Mr. Bohn

American drama is now world-famous, having been produced in theatres throughout the world. Has it played any part in the evolution of American democracy? Has it reflected adequately American Democracy? These questions are answered by examining American drama from the beginning up to contemporary times. This examination, which includes not only plays and authors but theatre activity in general, reveals that this art with the most direct popular influence has played an important role in the development of democracy.

IV: 11:30 A.M.-12:25 P.M.   30 hours   Credit: 2 semester-hours   Room A

English S451   English Literature and the Rise of Modern Democracy

Mr. Pettegrove

The object of this course is to assist the high school teacher in evaluating English litera-ture as one of the most potent forces in the formation and crystallization of democratic attitudes and ideals. Our liberal heritage is derived largely from the fight for religious and political freedom of the last three centuries. This course studies the evolution of our way of life in such writers as Milton, Locke, Burke, Wordsworth, Byron, J. S. Mill, and Harold Laski.

IV: 11:30 A.M.-12:25 P.M.   30 hours   Credit: 2 semester-hours   Room 2

English S452   Conflicting Cultures in Contemporary Life   Dr. Cayley

This course contrasts the contemporary philosophic, social, religious, literary, and artistic institutions of today's civilizations. Following an examination of the philosophies of democracy and of representative works such as Mein Kampf, The Communist Manifesto, the biography of Gandhi, and other basic backgrounds, the course attempts to see what are the typical unresolved stresses and typical achievements of different societies, es-pecially as these are dramatized in the works of selected artists, playwrights, poets, novelists, and in the biographies of typical men and women. The nature of morale in individual, family, and state is considered.

V: 1:00-1:55 P.M.   30 hours   Credit: 2 semester-hours   Aud-CHS

English S503   Geoffrey Chaucer and His Times   Dr. Krauss

Some of the works of Chaucer are read rapidly, others studied intensively, so that the student may acquire a broad general understanding of Chaucer's place in the history of English literature, as well as facility in reading and interpreting the mediaeval text of his stories.

III: 10:30-11:25 A.M.   30 hours   Credit: 2 semester-hours   Room 27

English S506   John Milton   Mr. Hamilton

This course has for its primary aim the understanding and evaluation of Milton's poetry. Contributory to this end are the following topics: the Puritan struggle for civil and religious liberty; the growth of science in the seventeenth century; the life, personality, and prose writings of Milton; his literary heritage and influence; comparison of Milton with the Cavalier and Metaphysical poets.

I: 8:30-9:25 A.M.   30 hours   Credit: 2 semester-hours   Room C

Department of Foreign Languages

All courses in French and in Spanish are conducted entirely in those languages. The direct method of instruction is used to insure mastery of idiom and fluency of expression. There are prerequisite requirements. Students who think they have had equivalent courses or an equivalent knowledge of the language should consult the instructor of the course they wish to enter and should not register for such course unless they receive her permission to do so.

French S201B   Seventeenth Century Literature, Part II   Mrs. Cressey

In the sophomore year, the prospective teacher of French is expected to gain a literary understanding and cultural appreciation of the most important age of French literature. This course interprets the period from 1660 to 1715 through the study of such represent-ative authors as Bossuet, Fenelon, LaFontaine, LaRochefoucauld, LaBruyere, Mme. de Lafayette, Mme. de Sevigne, and Mme. de Maintenon.

IV: 11:30 A.M.-12:25 P.M.   30 hours   Credit: 2 semester-hours   Room 9

French S301B   Eighteenth Century Literature, Part II   Mrs. Cressey
This course deals with the novel and the theatre in the Eighteenth Century in France.
I: 8:30-9:25 A.M.   30 hours   Credit: 2 semester-hours   Room 9

French S402B   Advanced Grammar and Composition, Part II   Mrs. Cressey
This course deals with advanced composition work in French. It is open to teachers and is designed to give advanced students practice in French style and composition.
II: 9:30-10:25 A.M.   30 hours   Credit: 2 semester-hours   Room 9

Language S300   Foundations of Language   Miss Littlefield
A comprehensive survey is made of the background, growth, and structure of the English language, traced from its remote Indo-European ancestry down through the changes wrought by foreign additions and influence. By a systematic and comparative study of the main elements of Greek, Latin, French, Anglo-Saxon, and English, and of the phonetic phenomena recurring in language development, the course presents and augments the important diction values derived from foreign language study. It aims especially to train teachers of general language or of exploratory courses in foreign languages.
I: 8:30-9:25 A.M.   30 hours   Credit: 2 semester-hours   Room 24

**Language S401W   The Teaching of Foreign Languages in Secondary Schools
Dr. Freeman**
This course is designed to present the different phases of methodology in the foreign language field. It is required for the New Jersey Secondary Teaching Certificate.
1: 8:30-9:25 A.M.   30 hours   Credit: 2 semester-hours   Room 10

**Latin S101B   The Golden Age: Masterpieces of Prose Literature
Miss Littlefield**
Livy and Cicero are the two authors studied intensively in this course. Selected readings of Livy supply interesting material for the discussion of Roman history, and Cicero's De Senectute introduces the student to a study of ancient philosophy.
V: 1:00-1:55 P.M.   30 hours   Credit: 2 semester-hours   Room 7

**Latin S201B   The Silver Age: Masterpieces of Prose Literature
Miss Littlefield**
This course is designed to present the works of Pliny and Tacitus. Selected excerpts from both authors are studied with the aim of bringing out the inherent differences between the Golden and Silver Ages of Latin writing.
IV: 11:30 A.M.-12:25 P.M.   30 hours   2 semester-hours   Room 7

Latin S301B   Roman Comedy: Terence   Dr. Freeman
The life and works of Terence are studied in this course, with special reference to the history of the development of drama as a whole and the Roman contribution in particular.
III: 10:30-11:25 A.M.   30 hours   Credit: 2 semester-hours   Room 7

**Latin S402B   Advanced Latin Grammar and Composition, Part II
Dr. Freeman**
This is a very important course for prospective teachers in the field of Latin instruction. It presents the basic material of the High School Latin field against the background of intensive work in grammar and composition.
II: 9:30-10:25 A.M.   30 hours   Credit: 2 semester-hours   Room 7

Spanish S—1   Beginning Spanish, Part 1   Mr. Hughes
This course is designed to prepare students to converse in and to read the Spanish language, to the extent that they may travel in Spanish-speaking countries, use Spanish in commercial relationships, and become more sensitive to the culture of our neighbors to the south.
II: 9:30-10:25 A.M.   30 hours   Credit: 2 semester-hours   Room C

Spanish S—C   Conversations in Spanish   Mr. Hughes
This course is of a practical nature. It is intended for persons having a previous knowledge of the language. Work in the class stresses the spoken language. Correct pronunciation and rapid reading in Spanish are emphasized.
III: 10:30-11:25 A.M.   30 hours   Credit: 2 semester-hours   Room C

12

Spanish S101B   Spanish Civilization, Part II   Miss Escoriaza

This course is designed to introduce the student to the important eras in Spanish civilization with a view to building up the background out of which the Spanish civilization of the New World developed. Prerequisite: three years of high school Spanish; two years in special cases.

V: 1:00-1:55 P.M.   30 hours   Credit: 2 semester-hours   Room E

Spanish S201B   Hispanic-American Civilization, Part II   Miss Escoriaza

This course is designed to present the outstanding features in the civilization and history of two important South American States: Columbia and Venezuela.

IV: 11:30 A.M.-12:25 P.M.   30 hours   Credit: 2 semester-hours   Room E

Spanish S301B   Spanish Classics, Part II   Miss Escoriaza

The aim of this course is to present to advanced students the life and works of Miguel de Cervantes.

I: 8:30-9:25 A.M.   30 hours   Credit: 2 semester-hours   Room E

Spanish S402B   Advanced Grammar and Composition, Part II   Miss Escoriaza

This course is designed to give advanced students special practice in Spanish style and composition. This course is open to teachers of Spanish.

II: 9:30-10:25 A.M.   30 hours   Credit: 2 semester-hours   Room E

Spanish S407   The New World Before the Coming of the Spaniards
                                                            Dr. Freeman

This course aims to present to students of Spanish, of Spanish-American relations, and of the social studies, the brilliant civilization which had been built up in the New World before the times of Cortez and Pizarro. It employes the latest researches in American archaeology to fill out the picture of the culture which confronted the Spanish conquerors upon their arrival in America and shows that the New World was in reality a very old world. A visit to the New York Museum of the American Indian is regarded as an integral part of the course. Although this course is a part of the major in Spanish, it is offered in the English language to permit non-Spanish-speaking students to enroll in it also.

V: 1:00-1:55 P.M.   30 hours   Credit: 2 semester-hours   Room 10

Department of Geography

Geography S201B   Meteorology   Dr. Milstead

This course constitutes a study of the atmosphere, the sources of atmospheric heat, the temperature variations and their relation to the weather phenomena. Emphasis is placed on the nature of the large scale wind systems, air masses and fronts, and upon rainfall distribution. Special phenomena, such as thunderstorms, fog, and ice accretion, which affect the operation of aircraft, are treated, and the uses of meteorological instruments are explained.

I: 8:30-9:25 A.M.   30 hours   Credit: 2 semester-hours   Room 26

Geography S412   Geography of Africa, Australia, and New Zealand
                                                            Dr. Milstead

A study is made of the activities of the people of Africa, Australia, and New Zealand in relation to their natural environment. Emphasis is placed upon the location, relief, and climate of the continents. Attention is given to the influence of geographic factors upon the post-war adjustments and the possible future relations of these countries with the United States.

III: 10:30-11:25 A.M.   30 hours   Credit: 2 semester-hours   Room 26

Geography S413   Economic Geography of South America   Dr. Milstead

This constitutes a study of the influence of the natural environment upon production and utilization of resources in the economic, social, and political development of the various nations of South America.

II: 9:30-10:25 A.M.   30 hours   Credit: 2 semester-hours   Room 26

Geography S509   Economic Geography of Asia and the East Indies

Dr. Milstead

This course is a study of the relationship of the economic, social, and political development of the peoples of Asia in relation to their natural environment. Particular attention is given to the environmental background and resources of southeastern Asia, the Netherlands East Indies, China, and Japan, that have made their part of Asia one of the great battlegrounds of the world.

V: 1:00-1:55 P.M.   30 hours   Credit: 2 semester-hours   Room 26

Department of Integration

Integration S200A   Introduction to Educational Psychology and Mental Testing   Dr. Ingebritsen

This course covers the psychology of classroom procedure. Growth and development of child and adolescent personality are studied from the physical, intellectual, social, and emotional aspects of individual pupils and their adjustment to the group. The relation of testing to the problems of understanding children as learners and to the problem of treating individual differences is studied through testing projects.

II: 9:30-10:25 A.M.   30 hours   Credit: 2 semester-hours   Room 30

Integration S300A   Aims and Organization of Secondary Education

Dr. W. Scott Smith

This course includes the following topics: nature and function of the American secondary school; organization of administrative units; secondary education in America and other lands; the students; program of studies and activities; the staff; buildings, grounds, and equipment and the cost and support of education.

II: 9:30-10:25 A.M.   30 hours   Credit: 2 semester-hours   Room 24

Integration S300B   Principles and Techniques of Teaching in Secondary Schools   Dr. Sperle

The following techniques and procedures are presented and evaluated; the question, the lesson plan, the assignment, testing and marking systems, classroom management and routine; and special procedures such as supervised study. In addition to the above topics, based on subject-matter organization and administration, various types of classroom procedure are considered.

I: 8:30-9:25 A.M.   30 hours   Credit: 2 semester-hours   Room 7

Integration S400A   Principles and Philosophy of Secondary Education

Dr. Sperle

This course evaluates educational objectives, techniques, procedures, and organizations in relation to the needs and demands made upon the school by society and by the developing personality. It involves a discussion of the meaning of philosophy and an interpretation of human values. Fundamental principles of education are evolved from previous work in the various fields of thought contributing to educational philosophy.

III: 10:30-11:25 A.M.   30 hours   Credit: 2 semester-hours   Room 8

Integration S408   Multi-Sensory Aids   Dr. Crawford

Sources, principles of selection, standards of evaluation, and methods of use of the various multi-sensory aids are studied in relation to all phases of school work; the utilization of field trips, specimens, models, exhibits, and experiments; prints, stereopticon slides, film slides, silent and sound motion pictures; photoplay appreciation; maps, graphs, charts, diagrams, cartoons; and puppets and marionettes. Instruction is given in making many of the above aids and in the operation and care of the various projectors.

III: 10:30-11:25 A.M.   30 hours   Credit: 2 semester-hours   Room CHS-7

Integration S409   Radio and Sound Equipment in the Classroom

Mr. Nickerson

This course studies the ways in which radio programs and sound equipment may be used to achieve the recognized objectives of high school teaching. The class is given practice in the handling of radios, amplifying systems, and recording equipment as teaching aids. Problems of script writing, microphone and recording techniques, and simple production are considered. Students who have taken English 444 for credit may not receive credit for this course.

II: 9:30-10:25 A.M.   30 hours   Credit: 2 semester-hours   Room CHS-13

14

Integration S500AW   **History and Principles of Secondary Education**
Dr. Ryan

This course traces the development of secondary education. Consideration is given to the meaning of liberal education as it was conceived by earlier civilizations. Special attention is given to organizations, curricula and methods of instruction, and to the social conditions affecting the development of secondary schools in England, Germany, France, and the United States.

I: 8:30-9:25 A.M.   30 hours   Credit: 2 semester-hours   Room 8

Integration S500BW   **Advanced Educational Psychology**   **Dr. Ingebritsen**

In this course, a comparative study is made of contemporary schools of psychology with emphasis on their direct application to education. Practical applications are made to classroom problems and the work of guidance departments. Prerequisite: Integration 200A or its equivalent.

IV: 11:30 A.M.-12:25 P.M.   30 hours   Credit: 2 semester-hours   Room 30

Integration S500CW   **Teaching Procedures in Secondary Education**
Mr. Seybold

This course emphasizes the fundamental principles underlying the technique of teaching on the secondary school level. Some of the topics considered are: organization of knowledge; the logical and psychological aspects of method; developing appreciations; social-moral education; teaching motor control; fixing motor responses; books and verbalism; meeting individual differences; guidance in study; tests and examinations; marks and marking.

II: 9:30-10:25 A.M.   30 hours   Credit: 2 semester-hours   Room CHS-3

Integration S502A   **Organization and Administration of the Modern High School, Part I**   **Dr. Johnston**

The problems considered are: the student personnel; building and revising the high school curriculum; providing for individual differences; making the school schedule; records; the guidance program; pupil participation in government; the extra-curricular program; the health program; the safety program; discipline; library and study hall; cafeteria; the principal's office; and evaluating results.

II: 9:30-10:25 A.M.   30 hours   Credit: 2 semester-hours   Room CHS-14

Integration S503   **Methods and Instruments of Research**   **Mr. Jackson**

This course is required of all candidates for the Master's degree without regard to their fields of major interest. Its purpose is to introduce students of education to research and its practical application to immediate problems. The course treats: the nature and types of educational research; methods and techniques of educational research; and the tools used in interpreting statistical data. During the course, the student sets up a problem and plans and carries out its solution.

V: 1:00-1:55 P.M.   30 hours   Credit: 2 semester-hours   Room C

Integration S504A   **Curriculum Construction in the Secondary School**
Mr. Seybold

This course purposes to introduce the student to constructive criticism of American culture, to consider the extent to which the secondary school curriculum meets the needs of a changing civilization, and to consider effective means of curriculum construction

IV: 11:30 A.M.-12:25 P.M.   30 hours   Credit: 2 semester-hours   Room CHS-3

Integration S505   **Organization and Administration of Extra-Curricular Activities**   **Dr. W. Scott Smith**

The first part of this course considers such general problems of extra-curricular activities as: their growing importance; their relation to the curriculum; the principles underlying their organization, administration, and supervision; and methods of financing. In the second part, an intensive study is made of the home room, the assembly, the student council, clubs, athletics, school publications, and other activities in which the class is especially interested.

III: 10:30-11:25 A.M.   30 hours   Credit: 2 semester-hours   Room 9

Integration S507   Organization and Administration of Guidance Programs
Dr. Johnston

The purpose of this course is to acquaint the student with the various agencies and methods for the guidance of students in school work, with certain implications in the choice of and the preparation for a vocation. Among the topics are: the abilities of students as related to guidance; the exploration of special interests; the organization of the guidance program; and the integration of the entire high school program for purposes of guidance.

I: 8:30-9:25 A.M.   30 hours   Credit: 2 semester-hours   Room CHS-14

Integration S508A   Supervision and Criticism of Teaching, Part I
Dr. Johnston

Among the topics are: the set-up for adequate supervision; supervision as encouraging and guiding the growth of teachers and the improvement of educational procedures; the supervisory functions of teachers' meetings; discussion groups; general and professional reading; the writing of articles; cooperative curriculum modification; utilization of community resources; and teacher inter-visitation.

IV: 11:30 A.M.-12:25 P.M.   30 hours   Credit: 2 semester-hours   Room CHS-14

Integration S516   School Finance   Mr. Chase

This course is of special interest to school administrators, since it acquaints them with the field of finance in relation to a well-ordered school program. The topics considered are: Basic problems of school support; systems of taxation; allocation of costs; computing school costs; sources of information; techniques; comparative costs; purchasing; and standards.

III: 10:30-11:25 A.M.   30 hours   Credit: 2 semester-hours   Room CHS-4

Integration S517   Administration of the Elementary School*   Mr. Chase

This course analyzes and evaluates the administration duties and relationships of the elementary school principal. Particular consideration is given to: building management; effective use of the school plant; sanitation; health service; the library; personnel management; the administration of the curriculum; community relationships; and publicity.

II: 9:30-10:25 A.M.   30 hours   Credit: 2 semester-hours   Room CHS-4

Integration S518   Supervision of Instruction in the Elementary School*
Mr. Chase

This course is planned for those engaged in the supervision of the elementary school and those who are preparing for such responsibilities. Principles of classroom supervision are developed and applied to learning situations. Among the more important topics are: the nature and function of supervision; the organization necessary for effective supervision; the nature and significance of the teacher's purposes; the methods and techniques of group and individual supervision; the technique of observation; and the supervisory conference.

I: 8:30-9:25 A.M.   30 hours   Credit: 2 semester-hours   Room CHS-4

Integration S521   Psychological Tests in Guidance Programs Dr. Ingebritsen

This course is designed to familiarize the student with various psychological tests and scales that may be used in guidance programs in the secondary school. The student is given practice in administering many types of group tests. This includes scoring the tests and evaluating the results, with a discussion of ways in which these results may be used. Much time is spent in actual laboratory demonstration of tests, giving students an opportunity to serve as subjects and as examiners. Class discussion is based upon first-hand information gained through use of the tests, on readings, and on class reports.

III: 10:30-11:25 A.M.   30 hours   Credit: 2 semester-hours   Room 30

Integration S524   The Study of the Failing Pupil   Dr. Ryan

The first part of the course is devoted to the "disparity technique", a method of evaluating the pupil's achievement in relation to his ability. The second part treats of procedures to be used in finding the causes of failure, and in planning treatment.

III: 10:30-11:25 A.M.   30 hours   Credit: 2 semester-hours   Room 10

*The two courses offered in the field of the supervision and administration of Elementary Education are given as a part of the graduate major in Administration and Supervision.

Integration S532   **The Supervision and Teaching of Reading in Elementary Schools***   **Dr. Sperle**

The place of reading in the entire elementary school program is analyzed. Attention is given to necessary remedial work for junior high school students. Materials and their use in instructional programs are studied with a view toward increasing power. All growth levels are considered. Good first teaching is of primary concern; however, the analysis and correction of certain reading difficulties constitute an important portion of the course.

IV: 11:30 A.M.-12:25 P.M.   30 hours   Credit: 2 semester-hours   Room 8

Integration S601A   **Workshop, Section I: Current Problems in Managing the School**   **Dr. Ryan and Staff**

Problems in administration, guidance programs, curriculum construction, extra-curricular activities, finance, educational philosophy.

V: 1:00-1:55 P.M.   60 hours   Credit: 4 semester-hours   Room 8

Integration S601B   **Workshop, Section II: Current Problems in Directing Instruction**   **Dr. Ryan and Staff**

Problems in supervision, teaching techniques; curriculum experimentation, evaluation, corrective reading, multi-sensory aids.

V: 1:00-1:55 P.M.   60 hours   Credit: 4 semester-hours   Room 8

Integration S601C   **Workshop, Section III: Current Problems in Understanding Youth**   **Dr. Ryan and Staff**

Problems in adolescent psychology, "human relation," mental hygiene, the teacher in guidance, educational sociology, community relations, the visiting teacher.

V: 1:00-1:55 P.M.   60 hours   Credit: 4 semester-hours   Room 8

Each of these three Workshops is conducted as follows:

1. Under the supervision of the Director, general conference periods are held each week as arranged.
2. Conferences between the individual student and a special consultant are held by appointment.
3. Free unassigned time for individual study is allowed.

The work includes the definition, study, evaluation, and report on each individual problem.

*This course, like 517 and 518, is given as a part of the graduate major in Administration and Supervision.

Department of Mathematics

Mathematics S102D   **Spherical Trigonometry and Applications**   **Mr. Clifford**

A knowledge of plane trigonometry is a prerequisite. The course treats relations in spherical triangles, solutions of the right and oblique spherical triangle, special solutions, applications to map constructions, parallel sailing, middle latitude sailing, great circle sailing, rhumb lines, the celestial sphere, celestial navigation, and stereographic projection. Scale drawing and geometrical methods of solution are stressed along with the analytic derivations.

III: 10:30-11:25 A.M.   30 hours   Credit: 2 semester-hours   Room 2

Mathematics S300   **The Social and Commercial Uses of Mathematics**   **Dr. Hildebrandt**

The mathematics is mostly arithmetic, and includes the problems met in home and civic life. Some of the topics are: budgeting and wise investment of income; providing for future independence through wise investments and insurance; taxation; cost of installment purchases; the operation of personal finance companies; cost of living versus the buying power of income, etc.

II: 9:30-10:25 A.M.   30 hours   Credit: 2 semester-hours   Room 8

Mathematics S301B   Modern College Geometry, Part II

Dr. Davis and Dr. Hildebrandt

Special topics from the field of college geometry extend the student's background. These include the theorems of Euler, Stewart, Ptolemy, Menelaus, and Ceva, the Simson line, harmonic section, and harmonic properties of circles.

Section I: for Math. Juniors, I: 8:30-9:25 A.M.   Room 3

Section II: for Math. Sophomores, III: 10:30-11:25 A.M.   Room 5

30 hours   Credit: 2 semester-hours

Mathematics S400   Educational Statistics   Mr. Clifford and Dr. Hildebrandt

The aim of this course is to provide a sufficient background to enable the student to comprehend and criticize articles of statistical nature in current educational literature, to apply statistical methods in testing and rating pupils, and to carry on the simpler types of educational research. Among the topics treated are: graphical and tabular representation; measures of central tendencies; measures of variability; linear correlation; the normal distribution; sampling; and reliability of measures. The application of the subject provides natural integration with psychology, tests and measurements, and procedures in secondary education.

Section I: for general students only, IV: 11:30 A.M.-12:25 P.M.   Room 24
Section II: for Math. majors only, IV: 11:30 A.M.-12:25 P.M.   Room 5
30 hours   Credit 2 semester-hours

Mathematics S401A   The Teaching of Secondary Mathematics—The Junior High School   Dr. Fehr

The subject matter and methods of teaching the arithmetic, algebra, and geometry of Grades 7-9 are discussed in this course. Emphasis is placed on activities, general mathematics in the ninth grade, and differentiated work for bright and slow pupils.

II: 9:30-10:25 A.M., MTWTh 24 hours   Credit: 1½ semester-hours   Room 3

Mathematics S402B   Advanced Calculus   Dr. Davis

A study of certain selected topics from advanced calculus such as ordinary differential equations, partial differentiation and the applications of partial derivatives, and multiple integrals.

V: 1:00-1:55 P.M.   30 hours   Credit: 2 semester-hours   Room 5

Mathematics S430   Practical Avigation and Navigation   Dr. Fehr

Beginning with a graphical solution of important navigation problems, this course introduces such topics as map projections, use of instruments, piloting, dead reckoning, radio navigation and celestial navigation. Graduate and undergraduate credit.

III: 10:30-11:25 A.M.   30 hours   Credit: 2 semester-hours   · Room 3

Mathematics S431   Defense Mathematics of the Shop and Industry   Mr. Clifford

This course surveys the applications of mathematics in industry. Some of the topics covered are: the slide rule and computing machines; elements of engineering; drawing and blue print reading; use of measuring instruments and presentation of data; mathematics of standard engines and machines. Graduate or undergraduate credit.

V: 1:00-1:55 P.M.   30 hours   Credit: 2 semester-hours   Room 1

Mathematics S432   Artillery Mathematics   Dr. Davis

Elementary mathematical information required to solve certain problems arising in this field is clearly presented. The topics include a few fundamental geometric theorems, tables, triangle solutions, location, parallax, trajectory in vacuo and in a resisting medium, variable factors, and elementary problems in ballistics, probability, etc. Graduate and undergraduate credit allowed.

IV: 11:30 A.M.-12:25 P.M.   30 hours   Credit: 2 semester-hours   Room 3

Mathematics S532   Teaching Mathematics in a War Program   Dr. Fehr

A discussion of the special emphasis to be placed on problem material, on curriculum adjustments, modifications of subject matter in both general and college preparatory mathematics, and effective methods of teaching for the present emergency are taken up in this course. Graduate credit.

I: 8:30-9:25 A.M.   30 hours   Credit: 2 semester-hours   Room 5

Department of Music

Music S201B   **Sight Reading and Ear Training, Part II**   **Dr. McEachern**

This course aims to develop skill in the sight reading of music suitable for use in the junior and senior high school. It includes a study of rudiments of music, major and minor scales, intervals, music terminology, ear and eye recognition of commonly used tonal and rhythmic groups, and written dictation of a standard repertory of thematic material. The above subject-matter is taught through actual songs suitable for classroom use, thus assuring direct application of skill gained, and at the same time providing an extended song repertory for the student. Prerequistite: 201A or equivalent.

I: 8:30-9:25 A.M.   30 hours   Credit: 2 semester-hours   Room 6

Music S301A   **Music Literature**   **Dr. McEachern**

This course includes a study of folk song, art song, opera, oratorio, idealized dance forms, instrumental suite, symphony, and the symphonic poem. Abundant use of musical illustration, through directed listening and music making, acquaints the student with great masterpieces of musical art. In this connection, students are required to make a book of thematic materials of music frequently heard on the radio or in concert.

II: 9:30-10:25 A.M.   30 hours   Credit: 2 semester-hours   Room 6

Music S401W   **The Teaching of High School Music**   **Dr. McEachern**

This course deals with the aims, content, and procedure in the teaching of music in the junior and senior high school. It includes a study of the adolescent voice; music for boys; assembly music; material for special programs; song dramatizations; integration of music with other subjects in the school curriculum; music appreciation; and extra-curricular music activities. Opportunity is given students to work out special problems confronting them in the teaching of music in their respective high schools.

III: 10:30-11:25 A.M.   30 hours   Credit: 2 semester-hours   Room 6

Department of Physical Education

Physical Education S302B   **Health and Health Teaching, Part II**   **Mr. Pittser**

An analysis of the Health Service Program of a school system is made and the duties and responsibilities of the school physician, the school nurse and the classroom teacher are discussed so as to show how the school health program is coordinated. The responsibility of the classroom teacher is stressed. The Red Cross Standard First Aid Course is taught and practiced.

I: 8:30-9:25 A.M.   30 hours   Credit: 2 semester-hours   Room CHS 5

Physical Education S407   **Safety Education**   **Mr. Pittser**

Safety is the latest subject to be placed in the curriculum of elementary and secondary schools. There is a need for teachers who can teach safety and organize safety programs. A study is made of the causes which have made this an important subject and of its place in our present day method of living. What to teach and how to teach it constitutes much of the time spent on the course. Sources of reliable material for use by the teacher are made available.

III: 10:30-11:25 A.M.   30 hours   Credit: 2 semester-hours   Room CHS-5

Physical Education S410   Principles and Philosophy of Physical Education
Mr. Pittser

This course is designed for administrators in service and in training. The basic principles upon which the entire program of physical education is constructed and many of the vital problems which annoy administrators are studied. A practical application of physical education to the seven cardinal principles of education is made. It is shown how required physical education, varsity athletics, and intramural sports are welded into a single unit of education. There is discussion of how health service and safety education are closely related to physical education.

II: 9:30-10:25 A.M   30 hours   Credit: 2 semester-hours   Room CHS 5

Physical Education S412   Advanced First Aid and Home Nursing Miss Booth

Advanced First Aid requires ten hours, upon satisfactory completion of which, American Red Cross certificates will be granted. Prerequisites: Standard Red Cross First Aid Certificate. Home Nursing teaches practical procedures in the care of the sick in order that simple illnesses and home emergencies may be met with safety and efficiency. Demonstrations are made and student participation is required.

VI: 2:00-2:55 P.M.   30 hours   Credit: 2 semester-hours   Room CHS-13

Recreation S445   Community Recreation and the School   Mr. Crawford

This course covers the background for cooperation between schools and recreation programs of the community, the administration of school playgrounds, safety practices and requirements, training of recreation leaders, use of school facilities for various activities and programming for the playground around the calendar. Field trips are made to actual playgrounds.

I: 8:30-9:25 A.M.   30 hours   Credit: 2 semester-hours   Room 30

Department of Science

Biology S409A   Human Physiology, Part 1   Dr. Hadley

A careful study of human anatomy is used as a basis for discussion of both normal and abnormal physiology. In addition to an analysis of the part played by organs and tissues in carrying out the essential functions of the body, special attention is given to problems of hygiene and sanitation. Applications of the above problems are made in reference to children of school age and the physical condition of individual pupils is correlated with their behavior in the classroom.

IV: 11:30 A.M.-12:25 P.M.   30 hours   Credit: 2 semester-hours   Room 28

Physics S304   Photography for High School Teachers
Dr. K. O. Smith and Mr. Placek

This is a beginning course in photography, consisting of lectures, demonstrations, laboratory work. and field work. The topics covered are similar to those outlined in BASIC PHOTOGRAPHY, published by the United States Air Corps. Some of the topics are: construction and operation of cameras; the nature of chemical changes encountered in photographic work; developing and printing negatives and positives; taking pictures both indoors and outdoors; taking pictures at night; making lantern slides; and projection printing. A student needs at least one camera for the course.

I: 8:30-9:25A.M.   30 hours   Credit: 2 semester-hours   Room CHS-8

Physics S305A   First Course in Aeronautics
Dr. Otis, Mr. Placek, and Prof. Glenn

This introduction to aviation deals with the first two important aspects of aeronautics; first, learning to fly as related to ground school instruction; and, second, the fundamentals of aerodynamics. In the first part of the course, the following topics are considered: how an airplane flies, airplane instruments, starting and landing. Later, attention is given to engines and propellers, forces acting on a plane, speed and power, and airplane performance. While no flight training is given all of the work is based on studies of airplanes made available to students. This course is arranged for teachers and students who wish to acquire competence in aviation for school, industrial, or war services. No prerequisites.

IV: 11:30 A.M.-12:25 P.M.   30 hours   Credit: 2 semester-hours   Room 22

Physics S306A   Introduction to Radio Communication
Prof. Glenn and Mr. Placek

This first course in radio is designed for teachers and students who wish to acquire a knowledge of this field for aviation, school, or war services. The topics considered are: radio waves, principles of vacuum tubes, receiving sets, loud speakers, power supply, alternating current tubes, short-wave sets, aerials, and ultra-short-wave receivers. This is an experimental course and college physics is not a prerequisite for the work.

III: 10:30-11:25 A.M.   30 hours   Credit: 2 semester-hours   Room 22

20

Science S406A   Astronomy for Navigation   **Prof. Glenn**

This course consists of a study of the fundamental principles of the science of astronomy. Such topics as the following are considered: Motions of the earth; time; the moon; law of gravitation; the planets, comets, and meteors; the sun; evolution of the solar system; the constellations; distances and motions of the stars; spectrum analysis; and telescopic observations. Special attention is given to the astronomy used in marine and aerial navigation.

II: 9:30-10:25 A.M., TuThF*   30 hours   Credit: 2 semester-hours   Room 22

Science S413   Food and Nutrition in Defense   **Mrs. Knowlton**

This course is conducted by lectures, assigned readings, laboratory experiences, and inspection trips. Moving pictures are shown and feeding experiments carried out. The essentials of an adequate diet, the food needs of persons of different ages, daily sample meals, and the nutritive values of common food materials are studied, with special regard to the relation of such knowledge to food budgeting and health. The subject matter of this course is based on the findings of the 1941 National Nutrition Conference.

IV: 11:30 A.M.-12:25 P.M.   30 hours   Credit: 2 semester-hours   Room CHS-10

Sci. S406A will have other appointments in the evening.

Department of Social Studies

Social Studies S101B   European History, 1713 to 1815   Dr. Folsom

The rise of Russia and the rise of Prussia are treated. Primary consideration is given, however, to the political, economic, social, and intellectual conditions in France preceding the French Revolution, the French Revolution itself, and the Napoleonic period.

V: 1:00-1:55 P.M.   30 hours   Credit: 2 semester-hours   Room 21

Social Studies S102B   European History, 1870 to 1942   Dr. Folsom

This course aims to give a survey of historical trends before and after 1914. A study of the international diplomacy based upon conflicting economic imperialism leads to a brief consideration of the first World War. The treaty of Versailles is discussed as a basis for understanding post-war developments in the various European countries.

III: 10:30-11:25 A.M.   30 hours   Credit: 2 semester-hours   Room 29

Social Studies S301A   Economics I   Mr. Rellahan

Emphasis is given to a study of the background of present-day economic institutions, and the manner in which the present system functions with respect to the economic and business organization of production, the nature and laws of consumption, the principles involved in the determination of value and price under competition or monopoly; and the problem of distribution as related to an explanation of rent, interest, wages, and profits.

III: 10:30-11:25 A.M.   30 hours   Credit: 2 semester-hours   Room 21

Social Studies S301B   Economics II   Mr. Rellahan

This course is a continuation of Economics I, which is not, however, prerequisite. The aim of this course is to acquaint the student with the basic economic principles and problems relating to risk and insurance; money, credit, and banking; general price changes and their control; foreign trade and exchange; tariffs, international debts, and imperialism; business combinations; and governmental regulation of business enterprise.

II: 9:30-10:25 A. M.   30 hours   Credit: 2 semester-hours   Room 21

Social Studies S401W   The Teaching of Social Studies in Secondary Schools
Dr. Snyder

The course presents recent tendencies in the teaching of the social studies. Among the matters considered are: the social studies curriculum, with special attention to the fusion organization; the objectives in the social studies; class procedures, including the problem-project method, oral procedures, drill and review procedures; procedures in particular subjects, the teaching of current events; devices and aids, including visual, auditory, and motor aids; technique of field trips; use of textbooks and supplementary reading; and testing and grading. Bibliographies and other teaching aids are supplied to students.

II: 9:30-10:25 A.M.   30 hours   Credit: 2 semester-hours   Room CHS-12

Social Studies S402B   Comparative Government   Mr. Bye

Will democracy or dictatorship survive? This major world problem of today is approached in this course through a study of the nature and functions of states and governments; public opinion; civil rights, suffrage, political parties; and the machinery of government in England, France, the United States, Italy, Germany, and Russia. Since the course confines its attention to problems of internal political organization and the processes of politics and government, it may be taken along with courses in recent European history and the European outlook without undue duplication.

II: 9:30-10:25 A.M.   30 hours   Credit: 2 semester-hours   Room 20

Social Studies S407   New Jersey State and Local Government   Mr. Bye

A study is made of the State Constitution; New Jersey's place in the federal system; the rights and duties of citizens; suffrage, political parties; the legislative, the executive, and administrative systems; the courts, the law enforcement, and correctional systems; revenues and expenditures; public health, educational, highway, and other services; county and municipal government; and other local political units.

V: 1:00-1:55 P.M.   30 hours   Credit: 2 semester-hours   Room 20

Social Studies S420B   The European Outlook, Part II   Dr. Wittmer

This course is devoted to a study of contemporary Belgium, the Netherlands, France, Spain, Italy, and England. It is shown how the culture patterns of these nations can be preserved without impeding the growth of an all-embracing western democratic civilization. It shows how the Atlantic Charter may be applied to the particular conditions of the countries in question. The role of England as part of Europe on the one hand, and as a link between Europe and the world on the other, is discussed in detail. Prerequisite: a course in Modern European History.

IV: 11:30 A.M.-12:25 P.M.   30 hours   Credit: 2 semester-hours   Room 20

Social Studies S428   Sociology I: Racial Contributions to American Life   Mr. Bye

This course deals with the basic problems of quantity, quality, and distribution of population and emphasizes the adjustments and maladjustments which result from the inter-relation of Negroes, Asiatics, and various types of Europeans in the United States.

III: 10:30-11:25 A.M.   30 hours   Credit: 2 semester-hours   Room 20

Social Studies S434   Contemporary World Affairs   Dr. Wittmer

This course is designed to acquaint the student with the fundamentals of dynamic world strategy. It points out the significance of air and naval bases; highways and canals; production and exchange of raw materials; international monopolies; racial and religious divisions; and density of population. The Far East, Australia, India, Arabia, Africa, and Latin-America are shown in their relation to our foreign policy and the present world conflict.

III: 10:30-11:25 A.M.   30 hours   Credit: 2 semester-hours   Room CHS-12

Social Studies S436   Modern Men of Ancient Times   Dr. Freeman

This course is designed to present biographical sketches of some of the great leaders of past ages. The subjects for discussion are selected from all lines of human endeavor, and special attention is given to their influence on the thought of their own times and their contribution to the culture of the present day. The course is specially recommended to students who wish to know these leaders as real persons and not as lay figures in ancient history.

VI: 2:00-2:55 P.M.   30 hours   Credit: 2 semester-hours   Room 10

Social Studies S440B   The Development of South and Central America, Part II   Dr. Snyder

This course studies the experiences of the various Latin-American nations under different forms of government, ranging from absolute dictatorships to "popular front" administrations. It explains the economic and social standards of living accepted by the South and Central American people, and recognizes the contributions they have made to the growth of Pan-Americanism during the last century.

IV: 11:30 A.M.-12:25 P.M.   30 hours   Credit: 2 semester-hours   Room 21

Social Studies S446   Current and Post-War Problems in Economics and
                                        Government   **Mr. Rellahan**

This course is designed to analyze the relationship of economics to government in the United States. The causes, legislative treatment, administrative methods, and results of government activity are discussed in the light of their economic significance and their bearing upon public welfare. The studies of the National Resources Planning Board and Temporary National Economic Committee are reviewed and appropriate consideration is given to the problems of war and post-war adjustment.

I: 8:30 A.M.-9:25 A.M.   30 hours   Credit: 2 semester-hours   Room 21

Social Studies S447   Diplomatic History of the United States   **Dr. Wittmer**

This course is designed as a general survey of our diplomatic history. Its purpose is to show how we became gradually conscious of our world interests and responsibilities, and how we have come to play an important role in international politics. The growing concept of world democracy, as opposed to commercial and military imperialism, is stressed. Particular emphasis is given to the pressure of public opinion on the activities of our State Department.

V: 1:00-1:55 P.M.   30 hours   Credit: 2 semester-hours   Room 24

Social Studies S506   The British Empire from 1783   **Dr. Folsom**

This course deals with the evolution of the British Empire from the period of the old Colonial system to the present British Commonwealth of Nations. The rise of Dominion Government, the forces of anti-imperialism, and the various solutions suggested for the improvement of imperial relations are stressed. The histories of Canada, Australia, New Zealand, South Africa, and India, are included.

II: 9:30-10:25 A.M.   30 hours   Credit: 2 semester-hours   Room A

Social Studies S510   Field Studies: New England and French Canada
                                                                              Mr. Bye

Owing to the emergency restrictions on the use of gasoline and tires, the Field Studies Course to New England and French Canada will not be offered, as planned, in August. All field studies courses will be resumed when the transportation situation returns to normal. Plan ahead for Montclair's third transcontinental tour in 1944 if conditions permit.

Graduate Department

Graduate S500A   Seminar and Thesis   **Dr. Finley**

Students writing a thesis for credit toward the Master's degree in any department of the college are required to register for this course. The work is conducted under seminar or individual guidance. Students report to the Dean of Instruction, who calls a conference with the Head of Department and the Sponsor. At this meeting, all matters pertaining to the topic, plan of research, writing of manuscript, etc., are arranged.

Credit: 4 semester-hours

COURSES OF SPECIAL INTEREST AND VALUE IN WAR-TIME

Reference has been made to the following courses on page two of this bulletin. They are referred to as "special courses." They may be taken by teachers, industrial workers, and prospective service men.

Candidates for a teachers certificate may not elect more than three "special courses" to be credited toward certification in a major teaching field, nor more than two for credit toward certification in a minor teaching field. Candidates for state certification or for a degree at Montclair should consult Dean Finley relative to the selection of "special courses."

Mathematics S102D—Spherical Trigonometry and Applications
Mathematics S300—Social and Commercial Uses of Mathematics
Mathematics S430—Practical Avigation and Navigation
Mathematics S431—Defense Mathematics of the Shop and Industry
Mathematics S432—Artillery Mathematics
Mathematics S532—Teaching Mathematics in a War Program

Physics S304—Photography for Teachers
Physics S305A—First Course in Aeronautics
Physics S306A—Introduction to Radio Communication

Science S406A—Astronomy for Navigation
Science S413—Food and Nutrition in Defense

Business Education S409—Consumer Education

Physical Education S302B—Health and Health Teaching, Part II
Physical Education S407—Safety Education
Physical Education S412—Advanced First Aid and Home Nursing

Recreation S445—Community Recreation and the School

Spanish S—C—Conversations in Spanish
Spanish S201B—Hispanic-American Civilization, Part II

Geography S201B—Meteorology
Geography S412—Geography of Africa, Australia, and New Zealand
Geography S413—Economic Geography of South America
Geography S509—Economic Geography of Asia and the East Indies

Social Studies S102B—European History from 1870 to 1942
Social Studies S420B—The European Outlook, Part II
Social Studies S434—Contemporary World Affairs
Social Studies S440B—The Development of South and Central America, Part II
Social Studies S446—Current and Post-War Problems in Economics and Government
Social Studies S447—Diplomatic History of the United States
Social Studies S506—The British Empire from 1783

English S204—Extemporaneous Speaking
English S301A—Literature for Adolescents: Developing Faith for Living through Literature
English S442B—American Literature: A Pageant of American Democracy
English S450—Contribution of American Drama to American Democracy
English S451—English Literature and the Rise of Modern Democracy
English S452—Conflicting Cultures in Contemporary Life

24

IN WAR-TIME

two of this bul-
may be taken by teach-

than three "special
field, nor more
field. Candidates
Dean Finley

cations
mathematics

Industry

Part II

Nursing

Zealand

East Indies

America, Part II
Economics and Gov-

Living through

American Democracy
American Democracy
Democracy

SUMMER SESSION

Bulletin of

MONTCLAIR

STATE TEACHERS COLLEGE

July 6 to August 13
1943

UPPER MONTCLAIR, NEW JERSEY

SUMMER SESSION

Bulletin of

MONTCLAIR
STATE TEACHERS COLLEGE

1943

July 6 to August 13

UPPER MONTCLAIR

NEW JERSEY

SUMMER SESSION 1943

Visiting Faculty Member

Roy R. Zimmerman, A.M.
County Superintendent of Schools
Bergen County, New Jersey

FACULTY

HARRY A. SPRAGUE, Ph.D._____Director of the Summer Session

EDGAR C. BYE, A.M._____Social Studies

PAUL C. CLIFFORD, A.M._____Mathematics

LAWRENCE H. CONRAD, A.M._____English

GERMAINE P. CRESSEY, A.M._____French

DAVID R. DAVIS, Ph.D._____Mathematics

DOROTHY DUKE, A.M. _____ Physical Education

TERESA DE ESCORIAZA, A.M._____Spanish

HOWARD FRANKLIN FEHR, Ph.D._____Mathematics

AVALINE FOLSOM, Ph.D._____Social Studies

WALTER H. FREEMAN, Ph.D.___Head of Department of Foreign Languages

EDWIN S. FULCOMER, Ed.D._____Head of the Department of English

FRANCIS R. GEIGLE, Ed.D. _____ Accounting and Social Business

EARL ROUSE GLENN, A.M._____Head of the Department of Science

CHARLES E. HADLEY, Ph.D._____Biology

EMANUEL H. C. HILDEBRANDT, Ph.D._____Mathematics

OTIS C. INGEBRITSEN, Ph.D._____Psychology

CLAUDE E. JACKSON, A.M._____Research

RUSSELL KRAUSS, Ph.D._____English

ETHEL F. LITTLEFIELD, A.M._____Languages

EDNA E. McEACHERN, Ph.D._____Director of the Department of Music

HARLEY P. MILSTEAD, Ph.D._____Geography

JAMES P. PETTEGROVE, A.M._____English

CHESTER M. PITTSER, A.M._____Physical Education

RUFUS D. REED, Ph.D._____Chemistry

JOHN J. RELLAHAN, A.M._____Social Studies

HEBER H. RYAN, Ph.D._____Head of Department of Integration

ARTHUR M. SEYBOLD, A.M._____Integration

HORACE J. SHEPPARD, A.M. _____ Accounting and Social Business

MARGARET A. SHERWIN, A.M._____Physical Education

KENNETH O. SMITH, Ph.D._____Science

W. SCOTT SMITH, Ph.D._____Integration

W. HARRY SNYDER, Ph.D._____Social Studies

D. HENRYETTA SPERLE, Ph.D. _____ Integration

FELIX WITTMER, Ph.D._____Social Studies

ROY R. ZIMMERMAN, A.M. _____ Administration

SUMMER SESSION OF THE
NEW JERSEY STATE TEACHERS COLLEGE AT MONTCLAIR

How to Reach the Campus

Trains of the Greenwood Lake Division, Erie R. R., stop at College Station. Trains of the Lackawanna R. R. connect at Montclair with the following bus lines: No. 64, running between Brick Church and the college; No. 60, running between Newark and the college, and No. 76, which runs between Orange and Paterson, passing the college en route.

Schedule of Summer Session Classes

The Summer Session begins on Tuesday, July 6, and continues through Friday, August 13, on which day the Commencement exercises will be held at 4 P.M. All courses meet daily Monday through Friday for one hour, except where definitely indicated otherwise. The first period will begin at 8:30 A.M. The noon recess for luncheon will be one-half hour only, and the afternoon session will begin at 1:00 P.M.

Registration

There is no advance registration. In all courses, registration takes place on July 6, in the individual classes, provided ten are present; if not, you wait until the second meeting. If there are not yet ten, the class is dismissed and the course is discontinued. On your way to class the day after you register, call at the Business Office to pay your fees and obtain the Audited Class Admission Card. This must be handed to your instructor at the third meeting of your class; sooner if possible. Training Teachers, Staff Members and Scholarship Students follow the above procedures also; the Class Admission Card will be audited without payment of fees upon presentation to the Business Manager of evidence that you are entitled to this credit. The Business Office is open until 3:30 P.M. in the summer, if you prefer to call there the afternoon before the third meeting of your classes.

Fees

Checks or money orders should be made payable to NEW JERSEY STATE TEACHERS COLLEGE. Registration service charge: $1.00 for the Summer Session. Tuition fees: to legal residents of New Jersey, $6.00 per semester-hour credit; to non-residents, $8.00 per credit. Courses taken for no credit cost the same. A laboratory service charge of $1.50 is made in connection with each of the laboratory courses. This service charge is collected in class by your instructor. Do not include it in your check for tuition.

Residence Halls for Men and Women

Edward Russ Hall and Chapin Hall are Montclair's two well-appointed residences. The charge for living on campus is reasonable —$12.00 per week, including room, breakfast, and dinner. A la carte luncheons are served in the college cafeteria. For one student in a double room, an extra charge of $2.00 is made. The college provides all furnishings, with the exception of towels, blankets, and desk lamps. The fee must be paid on or before the first day of the Summer Session. No rebate is made for occasional absence or voluntary withdrawal during the session. Students who are absent on account of illness for two weeks or more receive a rebate of $6.00 per week during the illness.

For reservations in the college residence hall, address: Director of Personnel, State Teachers College, Upper Montclair, N. J.

General Objective

The New Jersey State Teachers College at Montclair is a professional school which prepares teachers for the Junior and Senior High Schools of the State. Students may matriculate for the degree of Bachelor of Arts or for the degree of Master of Arts. In either case, those who do not already have the New Jersey Secondary Teaching Certificate must earn that while working for the degree.

Students Matriculated at Other Colleges

Work taken for credit to be transferred to other colleges should be approved in advance by the Dean of the College to which the credit is sent. The numbering of courses at Montclair follows this order: 100-499, inclusive, are undergraduate courses; 500 and above, are graduate courses. Courses numbered 400-499, inclusive, may also be taken for graduate credit.

Students Matriculated at Montclair

Work taken for credit at Montclair must be with the advice and approval of the Head of the Department in which you are majoring and of the Dean of Instruction.

Teacher Re-Training Program

Many men have been called into service with our armed forces from teaching positions in the high schools in the fields of mathematics, science, and physical education. At the same time, the high schools have been asked to prepare other young men for similar service by giving them a year's work in mathematics, a like amount in physics, and vigorous work in physical education. This has created an emergency in our high schools. Teachers have had to take over courses for which they had only a minimum of preparation and for which they were not certified.

The State Department has cooperated by granting provisional certificates. The college at Montclair, through its Part-Time Division, provides an opportunity for teacher re-training in these three important fields. It is realized, however, that the transportation situation has made it very difficult for teachers to come to the campus more than once each week during the academic year. The Summer Session offers the opportuntiy to live on campus and to pursue a full program of work, so that the teacher-in-service may obtain six, or even eight semester-hours credit in any one of these fields.

Workshops

Workshop courses, numbered Mathematics S499, Physical Education S499, and Science S499, have been set up and will be found described in this Bulletin under their respective department headings.

Summer Term of Twelve Weeks

Included in this Bulletin of the Summer Session is a list of the courses of the twelve-weeks summer term of the undergraduate college. These classes are being opened this summer to students who have special need for a maximum amount of credit. Registration and payment for these courses must be made on May 24. Anyone desiring to enroll must report that day to the Summer Session Office. Classes begin on May 25 and continue for twelve weeks.

Auditors

Men and women who desire to take courses for cultural, vocational, or avocational purposes without college credit may register as auditors. This should be clearly indicated on the registration form.

Matriculation

Those who wish to become candidates for the A.B. or the A.M. degree must request the Registrar of the college for the application form and return it, properly filled in and accompanied by an official transcript of all previous college work. When an applicant has been accepted as a candidate for the degree, a definite statement will be furnished him, showing the requirements to be fulfilled by him individually.

Teaching Certificates

Students who do not matriculate at Montclair but who desire to teach in this State should write to the Secretary of the State Board of Examiners, Mr. John B. Dougall, for information concerning teachers' certificates. Mr. Dougall's address is: Department of Public Instruction, Trenton, N. J. With the inquiry, there must be submitted an official transcript of all previous work on college level, with an explanation of the kind of certificate for which it is to be evaluated. Some students who have decided at the last minute to seek this information and advice have found it helpful to go to Trenton personally in order to save time.

Supervised Student Teaching

The opportunity to do supervised student teaching cannot be offered during the summer session. Matriculated students confer with Dr. Ryan. Non-matriculated students should write to Dr. Robert H. Morrison, Director of Teacher Education, State Department of Public Instruction, Trenton, N. J., enclosing an official transcript of all work on college level.

6

Conferences

Students are urged not to wait until the opening of the summer session to consult their advisers. If, however, it has been impossible for you to make an earlier appointment, you may see the Head of your Department and the Dean of Instruction on Tuesday, July 6. A representative of the State Board of Examiners also will be at the college that day, between the hours of 10 A.M. and 3 P.M. to see students who desire a last word of advice. He cannot, however, undertake at this time to evaluate all the previous work of a student, as the interviews in each case are necessarily brief. (See instructions under "Teaching Certificates.") The Registrar of the Summer Session will receive requests for appointments with this State Official.

Credits and Transcripts

The total amount of credit which may be earned in the six weeks of the Summer Session is 8 semester-hours.

Each course is in session at least thirty hours and receives credit as designated. Report cards, for the student's own use, and an official transcript for him to present at the State Department or at another college, are mailed directly to him within a week or ten days of the close of the summer session. All transcripts are mailed on the same day in fairness to all students. This first transcript is furnished free. The cost of a second transcript depends upon the amount of work the student has completed at this college, ranging from 25 cents for one semester or summer session to $1.00 for four or more. The college cannot provide a second transcript that covers less than all the work completed. Stamps cannot be accepted for transcripts; check or money order should be used when remitting fees by mail. Men and women entering the armed forces are given this second transcript without the service charge.

The mark "D" when earned in summer, part-time, or extension courses is not accepted for degree credit at Montclair, but will be given, when earned, for possible use elsewhere.

Courses that carry a credit of 4 s.h. in the regular curriculum are usually given in the summer session in two parts, each half course carrying a credit of 2 s.h. When the nature of the course is such that the two parts must be taken in a designated sequence, attention is drawn to that fact in the course description.

If prerequisites are indicated, the student should make certain he has had them or the equivalent before enrolling in the course.

The responsibility regarding incomplete work rests with the student. He should confer with his instructor, who, if he considers it advisable, may grant as much as two months time in which the work can be completed. If, however, the work is not finished at the end of two months, the mark for the course shall be "F."

7

COURSES THAT MAY BE TAKEN TOWARD THE
NEW JERSEY SECONDARY CERTIFICATE

This is not an official statement. It does not emanate from the State Department that issues the certificate. It is furnished merely for your convenience in selecting courses. You should check your selections with the State Department, sending an official transcript of work already completed. Please note that either an undergraduate or a graduate course may apply on the certificate.

I   Health Education—3 semester-hours required
Biology 409A—Human Physiology—2 s. h.
. Physical Education 301B—Health and Health Teaching, Part I—2 s. h.
*Physical Education 302B—Health and Health Teaching, Part II—2 s. h.
II—Educational Psychology—3 semester-hours required
Integration 200A—Introduction to Educational Psychology and Mental Testing—2 s. h.
Integration 200B—Adolescent Psychology and Mental Hygiene—2 s. h.
*Integration 500BW—Advanced Educational Psychology—2 s. h.
III   Aims and Organization (Principles) of Secondary Education—3 s. h. required
*Integration 300A—Aims and Organization of Secondary Education—2 s.h.
*Integration 400A—Principles and Philosophy of Secondary Education —2 s. h.
Integration 405—Principles of Junior High School Teaching—2 s. h.
*Integration 500AW—History and Principles of Secondary Education— 2 s. h.
Integration 502A—Organization and Administration of the Modern High School, Part I—2 s. h.
Integration 502B—Organization and Administration of the Modern High School, Part II—2 s. h.
IV—Principles and Techniques of Teaching in the High School—3 s. h. required
*Integration 300B—Principles and Techniques of Teaching in the Secondary School—2 s. h.
*Integration 500CW—Teaching Procedure in Secondary Education—2 s.h.
V—Curriculum Organization and Courses of Study (Methods) in One Endorsed Teaching Field—3 semester-hours required
Business Education 401W—The Teaching of Business Education in the Secondary School—2 s. h.
*English 401W—The Teaching of English in the Secondary School— 2 s. h.
Language 401W—The teaching of Foreign Languages in the Secondary School—2 s. h.
*Integration 504A—Curriculum Construction in the Secondary School— 2 s. h.
Mathematics 401W—The Teaching of Mathematics in the Secondary School—2 s. h.
Mathematics 532—Teaching Mathematics in a War Program—2 s. h.
Music 401W—The Teaching of High School Music—2 s. h.
Science 401W—The Teaching of Science in the Secondary School— 2 s. h.
Science 505W—Survey of Curricula and Science Courses in State and City Systems—2 s. h.
Biology 501W—The Teaching of Biology—2 s. h.
Chemistry 501W—The Teaching of Chemistry—2 s. h.
Physics 501W—The Teaching of Physics—2 s. h.
*Social Studies 401W—The Teaching of the Social Studies in the Secondary School—2 s. h.
VI   Elective—3 semester-hours required
Courses in the Department of Integration that are definitely in the field of Secondary Education and that have not been taken to satisfy one of the above requirements.
*Not all the above courses are offered during any one semester or summer session. Those that are starred (*) are being offered this summer.

DESCRIPTION OF COURSES

Business Education

Business Education S301A—Business Law, Part III   **Mr. Sheppard**
This is a treatment of business law from a practical, educational, and social point of view. The main points for consideration are: personal property, including the nature of personal property; sales, conditional sales, bailments, and chattel mortgages; real property, including landlord and tenant and mechanics' liens; and business organization, including partnerships and corporations.
10:30-11:25 A.M.   30 hours   Credit: 2 semester-hours   Room C

Business Education S405B—Bookkeeping and Accounting   **Dr. Geigle**
This is a fundamental treatment of the subject and so planned that it will give the student an elementary understanding of the subject from a personal-use standpoint as well as a practical application. It deals with the fundamental theory of debit and credit; journalizing; posting; trial balance; adjustments; and preparation of financial statements. This course will be preceded by S405A, which will meet on Tuesday afternoons, May 25 to June 29, from 4:15-6:30 and the same evenings, from 7:15-9:30 P.M.: 30 hours, for 2 semester-hours credit. 405A is not, however, prerequisite.
9:30-10:25 A.M.   30 hours   Credit: 2 semester-hours   Room 30

Business Education S409—Consumer Education   **Mr. Sheppard**
This course deals with such problems as the relation of the consumer to production, wasteful consumer practices, consumer propaganda, effective methods of consumer cooperation, and government aids to consumers. The main purpose is to present principles and methods of wise consumption as a guide to action in the purchase of the main varieties of goods and services.
1:00-1:55 P.M.   30 hours   Credit: 2 semester-hours   Room D

Business Education S411A—Cost Accounting   **Dr. Geigle**
A thorough knowledge of bookkeeping is prerequisite to a profitable study of this course. The course deals with the basic principles of modern cost finding and cost keeping, and endeavors to give a practical application of these principles to present-day conditions. The practical application consists of a laboratory budget containing business papers, vouchers, etc., together with full instructions for writing up a practice set of cost books.
8:30-9:25 A.M.   30 hours   Credit: 2 semester-hours   Room D

English

English S100B—World Literature, Part II   **Dr. Krauss**
Outstanding works of the Renaissance writers, the Elizabethans, the Romantics, and the Victorians are studied with the view of showing what each has contributed to the origin of forms and to the development of the literature of the world, and how each in its turn has had its influence upon its own and succeeding times. Such writers as the following are considered: Dante, Boccaccio, Petrarch, Chaucer, Shakespeare, Milton, Calderon, Moliere, Racine, Pope, Boswell, Goethe, Wordworth, and Tennyson. The first half of the course is not prerequisite.
10:30-11:25 A.M.   30 hours   Credit: 2 semester-hours   Room 27

English S201B—British and American Poetry from Chaucer to Frost,
                 Part II   **Mr. Pettegrove**
This course surveys the development of English poetry from its beginnings to the present time. It includes study in the types of poetic statement, the historical development of the styles and forms of English poetry, the life and work of the major British and American poets, and the critical appreciation of poetry as an art and as an expression of life. Part II begins with the rise of the Romantic movement in poetry.
9:30-10:25 A.M.   30 hours   Credit: 2 semester-hours   Room C

English S301A—Literature for Adolescents: Developing Faith for
Living through Literature **Dr. Fulcomer**

This course is a study of the best available literary material (fiction, drama, biography, essay), suitable to the interests and maturity of junior and senior high school adolescents, and of the use that can be made of it in enabling them to gain the knowledge and confidence necessary for courageous living in this world.

930-10:25 A.M.   30 hours   Credit 2 semester-hours   Room 1

English S302B—American Literature: A Pageant of American
Democracy **Mr. Conrad**

This course surveys the development of American literature from the Civil War to the contemporary period. The writers studied include: Walt Whitman, Sidney Lanier, Emily Dickinson, William Dean Howells, Mark Twain, Henry James, Henry Adams, Hamlin Garland, Stephen Crane, Frank Norris, O. Henry, Vachel Lindsay, E. A. Robinson, Carl Sandburg, and Robert Frost.

10:'30-11:25 A.M.   30 hours   Credit: 2 semester-hours   CHS Aud.

English S401W—The Teaching of English in the Secondary
School **Dr. Fulcomer**

This course deals with the methods of teaching composition and literature in the high school. It aims to unify and organize the professional training and practical experience of all students in the course, and to provide new points of view for their active English teaching by setting up objectives and indicating concrete methods of obtaining those objectives.

8:30-9:25 A.M.   30 hours   Credit: 2 semester-hours   Room 1

English S404—Survey of British Literature from 1798 **Dr. Krauss**

This course draws together into a systematic narrative the story of the development of British literature from the Romantic triumph in 1798 and continues it to the present time. While this course is a continuation of English 402, the first course is not prerequisite.

9:30-10:25 A.M.   30 hours   Credit: 2 semester-hours   Room 27

English S406—The Modern Novel **Mr. Conrad**

Particular emphasis is given to British and American novels since 1870, and the important tendencies of present-day prose fiction are explored. Students are taught how to read a novel with profit, and how to guide and direct the reading of others.

8:30-9:25 A.M.   30 hours   Credit: 2 semester-hours   CHS Aud.

English S430—Reading in Secondary Schools **Dr. Sperle**

The study of reading interests and activities at various age levels in a school-wide program is undertaken. Methods of bridging the gap between undeveloped reading skills and the necessity for using these skills in content subjects are discussed and analyzed. Problems of vocabulary building, selected reading materials, and improving comprehension complete the course.

11:30 A.M.-12:25 P.M.   30 hours   Credit: 2 semester-hours   Room 8

English S431B—Shakespeare and the English Drama, Part II **Mr. Pettegrove**

The major emphasis of this course is upon the following Shakespearean comedies and tragi-comedies: A Comedy of Errors, A Midsummer Night's Dream, The Merchant of Venice, Much Ado About Nothing, As You Like It, Twelfth Night, Cymbeline, A Winter's Tale, and The Tempest. The topics studied include Shakespeare's conception of comedy; his dramatic art; his poetry; the sources of his plays; staging in Shakespeare's theatre and in our own; typical textual problems; and aids for the teaching of Shakespeare in the secondary school.

11:30 A.M.-12:25 P.M.   30 hours   Credit: 2 semester-hours   Room C

10

English S441—Mediaeval Epic, Saga, and Romance   Dr. Krauss

This course deals with the chief mediaeval epics, sagas, and romances from the literatures of England, France, Germany, Ireland, Iceland, Wales, and Italy in modern English translation. Attention is given both to those narratives which reflect the life of a particular country and to those which are international and express more generally the spirit of mediaeval Europe.

11:30 A.M.-12:25 P.M.   30 hours   Credit: 2 semester-hours   Room 27

English S443—Modern Drama   Dr. Fulcomer

This course is intended to stimulate interest in one of the most powerful expressions of contemporary life—the theatre. An historical survey of trends, dramatists, plays, and accomplishments from Ibsen to the latest prize plays on Broadway provides background. An examination of the structure and content of plays to determine what constitutes a good play stimulates appreciation. Students are encouraged to read widely and to see many of the current productions on Broadway.

10:30-11:25 A.M.   30 hours   Credit: 2 semester-hours   Room 1

English S445—Eighteenth Century Literature   Mr. Pettegrove

Major essayists, poets, dramatists, novelists, and letter writers are read and evaluated in terms of the thought, life, and literary movements of their own time and of their significance for the present generation. Authors studied include: Addison, Steele, Defoe, Swift, Goldsmith, Sheridan, Gray, Johnson, Boswell, Cowper, Richardson, Fielding, Sterne, Smollett, and Burke. High School classics receive special attention.

8:30-9:25 A.M.   30 hours   Credit: 2 semester-hours   Room C

English S516—Language Problems in the English Curriculum   Mr. Conrad

This course reviews the several theories of language and studies the problem of meaning in order to arrive at a suitable technique for the interpretation of prose and verse. This technique is then applied to the problems of reading, of composition, of speech, and of appreciation of literature. The course has two aims: to increase the student's own skill in dealing with language, and to increase his effectiveness in teaching.

11:30 A.M.-12:25 P.M.   30 hours   Credit: 2 semester-hours   CHS Aud.

Foreign Languages

French S101B—French Civilization: Early Periods, Part II   Mrs. Cressey

This Freshman course presents the background for all subsequent linguistic and literary studies in French. Special attention is devoted to bringing all the students up to a uniform level of development in speaking, reading, and writing French. The material used is French history and mediaeval literature. The course is conducted in French.

9:30-10:25 A.M.   30 hours   Credit: 2 semester-hours   Room 9

French S201B—Seventeenth Century Literature, Part II   Mrs. Cressey

In the Sophomore year, the prospective teacher of French is expected to gain a literary understanding and cultural appreciation of the most important age of French literature. This course interprets the period from 1660 to 1715 through the study of such representative authors as Bossuet, Fenelon, LaFontaine, LaRochefoucauld, LaBruyere, Mme, de Lafayette, Mme. de Sevigne, and Mme. de Maintenon. The course is conducted in French.

11:30 A.M.-12:25 P.M.   30 hours   Credit: 2 semester-hours   Room 9

11

French S302B—Eighteenth Century French Philosophers,
Part II   **Mrs. Cressey**

The first part of this course was devoted to a brief review of the history of the period studied and to the reading of the works of Montesquieu. In part II, the students read and evaluate some of the best known essays of Voltaire and Rousseau. The course is conducted in French. Part I is not prerequisite.

10:30-11:25 A.M.   30 hours   Credit: 2 semester-hours   Room 9

French S416B—French History from 1789 to 1939   **Mrs. Cressey**

This course aims to provide the prospective teacher of French with the historical background necessary to understand present-day conditions. The course is conducted in French.

1:00-1:55 P.M.   30 hours   Credit: 2 semester-hours   Room 9

Language S300—Foundations of Language   **Miss Littlefield**

A comprehensive survey is made of the background, growth, and structure of the English language, traced from its remote Indo-European ancestry down through the changes wrought by foreign additions and influence. By a systematic and comparative study of the main elements of Greek, Latin, French, Anglo-Saxon, and English, and of the phonetic phenomena recurring in language development, the course presents and augments the important diction values derived from foreign language study. It aims especially to train teachers of general language or of exploratory courses in foreign languages.

8:30-9:25 A.M.   30 hours   Credit: 2 semester-hours   Room 29

Language S415—War Languages   **Miss Littlefield**

This course presents a practical introduction to the learning of any foreign language. Through the use of International Phonetic Symbols and Linguaphone Records, students acquire skill in the recognition and identification of foreign speech sounds. Ear, lip, and tongue training are combined to ensure adequate ability in the pronunciation of foreign sounds with scientific accuracy. The course is designed for all students in the language field, but especially for all men and women in the college who intend to enter the Armed Forces, the Intelligence Division, Signal Corps, or any department of the war effort requiring acquaintance with foregn speech. Now that our troops are being brought into contact with every type of linguistic expression throughout the world, the practical value of this course in war languages is easily apparent.

9:30-10:25 A.M.   30 hours   Credit: 2 semester-hours   Room 29

Latin S201B—The Silver Age: Masterpieces of Prose
Literature   **Miss Littlefield**

This course is designed to present the works of Pliny and Tacitus. Selected excerpts from both authors are studied with the aim of bringing out the inherent differences between the Golden and Silver Ages of Latin writing.

11:30 A.M.-12:25 P.M.   30 hours   Credit: 2 semester-hours   Room 29

Latin S302B—Roman Philosophy: Lucretius   **Dr. Freeman**

The reading of Lucretius' "De Rerum Natura" serves to introduce the student to the evolution of abstract thought as developed in Greek and Roman philosophy.

10:30-11:25 A.M.   30 hours   Credit: 2 semester-hours   Room 10

Spanish S201B—Hispanic-American Civilization: Upper South American Area, Part II   Miss Escoriaza

This course is designed to present the outstanding features in the civilization and history of two important South American States: Columbia and Venezuela. The course is conducted in Spanish.

11:30 A.M.-12:25 P.M.   30 hours   Credit: 2 semester-hours   Room E

Spanish S202B—Hispanic-American Civilization: Lower South American Area, Part II   Miss Escoriaza

This course is designed to present outstanding features in the civilization and history of the following South American Republics: Chile, Argentina, Uruguay, and Paraguay. The course is conducted in Spanish.

1:00-1:55 P.M.   30 hours   Credit: 2 semester-hours   Room E

Spanish S302B—Spanish Classics, Part II   Miss Escoriaza

The aim of this course is to present to advanced students of Spanish the life and dramatic works of Calderon de la Barca and of Tirso de Molina.

9:30-10:25 A.M.   30 hours   Credit: 2 semester-hours   Room E

Geography

Geography S202B—Geography of the Western Hemisphere, Part II: South America   Dr. Milstead

A detailed regional study is made of the activities of the people of South America in relation to their natural environment. The commercial relations and possibilities for future development are emphasized.

8:30-9:25 A.M.   30 hours   Credit: 2 semester-hours   Room 26

Geography S302B—Economic Geography, Part II   Dr. Milstead

A study is made of the influence of the natural environment upon the production, trade, and utilization of the more important agricultural, mineral, forest, factory, and sea commodities; of the development of continental and ocean trade routes and trade regions of the world. The course affords preparation for the teaching of world geography and economic geography in secondary schools.

9:30-10:25 A.M.   30 hours   Credit: 2 semester-hours   Room 26

Science S417—Meteorology with Applications to Aviation   Dr. Milstead

For description of this course, see the Department of Science.

Integration

Integration S300A—Aims and Organization of Secondary Education   Dr. W. Scott Smith

This course includes the following topics: nature and function of the American secondary school; organization of administrative units; secondary education in America and other lands; the students; program of studies and activities; the staff; buildings, grounds, and equipment; and the cost and support of education.

9:30-10:25 A.M.   30 hours   Credit: 2 semester-hours   Room 5

Integration S300B—Principles and Techniques of Teaching in Secondary Schools   **Dr. Sperle**

The following techniques and procedures are presented and evaluated: the question, the lesson plan, the assignment, testing and marking systems, classroom management and routine; and special procedures such as supervised study. In addition to the above topics, based on subject-matter organization and administration, various types of classroom procedure are considered.

10:30-11:25 A.M.   30 hours   Credit: 2 semester-hours   Room 8

Integration S400A—Principles and Philosophy of Secondary Education   **Dr. Sperle**

This course evaluates educational objectives, techniques, procedures, and organizations in relation to the needs and demands made upon the school by society and by the developing personality. It involves a discussion of the meaning of philosophy and an interpretation of human values. Fundamental principles of education are evolved from previous work in the various fields of thought contributing to educational philosophy.

8:30-9:25 A.M.   30 hours   Credit: 2 semester-hours   Room 8

Integration S500AW—History and Principles of Secondary Education   **Dr. Ryan**

This course traces the development of secondary education. Consideration is given to the meaning of liberal education as it was conceived by earlier civilizations. Special attention is given to organizations, curricula and methods of instruction, and to the social conditions affecting the development of secondary schools in England, Germany, France, and the United States.

9:30-10:25 A.M.   30 hours   Credit: 2 semester-hours   Room 8

Integration S500BW—Advanced Educational Psychology   **Dr. Ingebritsen**

In this course, a comparative study is made of contemporary schools of psychology with emphasis on their direct application to education. Practical applications are made to classroom problems and the work of guidance departments. Prerequisite: Integration 200A or its equivalent.

11:30 A.M.-12:25 P.M.   30 hours   Credit: 2 semester-hours   Room 30

Integration S500CW—Teaching Procedures in Secondary Education   **Mr. Seybold**

This course emphasizes the fundamental principles underlying the technique of teaching on the secondary school level. Some of the topics considered are: organization of knowledge; the logical and psychological aspects of method; developing appreciations; social-moral education; teaching motor control; fixing motor responses; books and verbalism; meeting individual differences; guidance in study; tests and examinations; marks and marking.

9:30-10:25 A.M.   30 hours   Credit: 2 semester-hours   CHS-3

Integration S501—Tests and Measurements in Secondary Education   **Mr. Jackson**

The purpose of this course is to develop an appreciation of the meaning and importance of measurement in education, and to give a working knowledge of instruments of measurement.

9:30-10:25 A.M.   30 hours   Credit: 2 semester-hours   Room A

Integration S503—Methods and Instruments of Research   **Mr. Jackson**

This course is required of all candidates for the Master's degree without regard to their fields of major interest. Its purpose is to introduce students of education to research and its practical application to immediate problems. The course treats: the nature and types of educational research; methods and techniques of educational research; and the tools used in interpreting statistical data. During the course, the student sets up a problem and plans and carries out its solution.

11:30 A.M.-12:25 P.M.   30 hours   Credit: 2 semester-hours   Room A

Integration S504A—Curriculum Construction in the Secondary
School   **Mr. Seybold**

This course purposes to introduce the student to constructive criticism of American culture, to consider the extent to which the secondary school curriculum meets the needs of a changing civilization, and to consider effective means of curriculum construction.

11:30 A.M.-12:25 P.M.   30 hours   Credit: 2 semester-hours   CHS-3

Integration S505—Organization and Administration of Extra-Curricular
Activities   **Dr. W. Scott Smith**

The first part of this course considers such general problems of extra-curricular activities as: their growing importance; their relation to the curriculum; the principles underlying their organization, administration, and supervision; and methods of financing. In the second part, an intensive study is made of the home room, the assembly, the student council, clubs, athletics, school publications, and other activities in which the class is especially interested.

10:30-11:25 A.M.   30 hours   Credit: 2 semester-hours   Room 29

Integration S508A—Supervision and Criticism of Teaching,
Part I   **Mr. Seybold**

Among the topics are: the set-up for adequate supervision; supervision as encouraging and guiding the growth of teachers and the improvement of educational procedures; the supervisory functions of teachers' meetings; discussion groups; general and professional reading; the writing of articles; cooperative curriculum modification; utilization of community resources; and teacher inter-visitation.

10:30-11:25 A.M.   30 hours   Credit: 2 semester-hours   CHS-3

Integration S515—Guidance and Personnel Problems of Classroom
Teachers   **Mr. Seybold**

This course considers all types of personnel problems with which the classroom teacher deals. It is concerned with the growth of pupils and seeks to point out the ways by which proper growth may be attained. Classroom, health, social, and personal activities are analyzed in terms of the needs of present-day social life.

1:00-1:55 P.M.   30 hours   Credit: 2 semester-hours   CHS-3

Integration S517—Administration of the Elementary School*
Mr. Zimmerman

This course analyzes and evaluates the administration duties and relationships of the elementary school principal. Particular consideration is given to: building management; effective use of the school plant; sanitation; health service; the library; personnel management; the administration of the curriculum; community relationships; and publicity.

8:30-9:25 A.M.   30 hours   Credit: 2 semester-hours   Room 10

The courses offered in the field of the supervision and administration of Elementary Education are given as a part of the graduate major in Administration and Supervision.

15

Integration S520—Principles of Mental Hygiene and Guidance
Dr. Ingebritsen

This course is designed to be a general survey of the principles and practices of mental health with special reference to the mental health of teacher and pupil. It involves a thorough grounding in fundamental principles of mental hygiene with much practical consideration of the mental-health values of instructional programs and procedures. Discussion centers in practical efforts to develop wholesome personalities in our schools.

10:30-11:25 A.M.   30 hours   Credit 2 semester-hours   Room 30

Integration S524—The Study of the Failing Pupil   **Dr. Ryan**

The first part of the course is devoted to the "disparity technique"—a method of evaluating the pupil's achievement in relation to his ability. The second part treats of procedures to be used in finding the causes of failure, and in planning treatment.

8:30-9:25 A.M.   30 hours   Credit: 2 semester-hours   Room 9

Integration S536—Guiding High School Students into War Services
Dr. Ingebritsen

This course is designed to meet the immediate needs of counselors and guidance officers in high schools, in their job of helping students to orient themselves and to prepare to meet the requirements and demands of military services and work opportunities during the period of this emergency. It covers: all aspects of preparation for, induction into, and opportunities in military services; preparation for and guidance into critical and essential jobs in industry and for the business world; special opportunities for girls and women; orientation to the most available sources of current information on these topics.

8:30-9:25 A.M.   30 hours   Credit: 2 semester-hours   Room 30

Workshops

Integration S601A—Workshop, Section I: Current Problems in Managing the School   **Dr. Ryan and Staff**

Problems in administration; guidance programs; curriculum construction; extra-curricular activities; finance; educational philosophy.

1:00-1:55 P.M.   60 hours   Credit: 4 semester-hours   Room 8

Integration S601B—Workshop, Section II: Current Problems in Directing Instruction   **Dr. Ryan and Staff**

Problems in supervision; teaching techniques; curriculum experimentation; evaluation; corrective reading; multi-sensory aids.

1:00-1:55 P.M.   60 hours   Credit: 4 semester-hours   Room 8

Integration S601C—Workshop, Section III: Current Problems in Understanding Youth   **Dr. Ryan and Staff**

Problems in adolescent psychology; "human relations;" mental hygiene; the teacher in guidance; educational sociology; community relations; the visiting teacher.

1:00-1:55 P.M.   60 hours   Credit: 4 semester-hours   Room 8

Each of these three Workshops is conducted as follows:

1. Under the supervision of the Director, general conference periods are held each week as arranged.
2. Conferences between the individual student and a special consultant are held by appointment.
3. Free unassigned time for individual study is allowed.

The work includes the definition, study, evaluaton, and report on each individual problem.

16

Mathematics

Mathematics S102A—Trigonometry   Dr. Fehr

This course treats the following topics: functions and their graphical representation; functions of an acute angle; relationship of trigonometric functions; functions of any angle; reduction of functions; solution of triangles; complex numbers; trigonometric analysis; logarithms; slide rule; practical solution of triangles. When time permits, a study is made of Demoivre's theorem and its extension, the construction of trigonometric tables.

10:30-11:25 A.M.   30 hours   Credit: 2 semester-hours   CHS-14

Mathematics S102B—Analytical Geometry   Mr. Clifford

This course is recommended particularly to those students seeking a minor in mathematics or those in need of a review course in analytic geometry. The topics include: rectangular and polar coordinate systems; loci and their equations; the straight line; the conics—circle, parabola, ellipse, and hyperbola; parametric equations; transformation of coordinates; and the general equation of the second degree.

9:30-10:25 A.M.   30 hours   Credit: 2 semester-hours   Room 2

Mathematics S300—The Social and Commercial Uses of Mathematics   Mr. Clifford

This course is required of all candidates for the A.B. degree, regardless of their major subjects. A consideration of the economic problems met by the intelligent citizen, independent of his vocation, forms the basis for selection of material for it. The mathematics is mostly arithmetic, and includes the problems met in home and civic life. Some of the topics are: budgeting and wise expenditure of income; providing for future independence through wise investments and insurance; taxation; cost of installment purchases; the operation of personal finance companies; cost of living versus the buying power of income.

8:30-9:25 A.M.   30 hours   Credit: 2 semester-hours   Room 2

Mathematics S301B—Modern College Geometry, Part II   Dr. Hildebrandt

Special topics from the field of college geometry extend the student's background. These include the theorems of Euler, Stewart, Ptolemy, Menelaus, and Ceva; the Simson line, harmonic section, and harmonic properties of circles.

11:30 A.M.12:25 P.M.   30 hours   Credit: 2 semester-hours   Room 3

Mathematics S302B—Higher Algebra, Part II: Determinants and The Theory of Equations   Dr. Davis

A brief resume' is given of the various methods of solving algebraic equations with illustrative examples. The properties of determinants and matrices are fully treated which include short methods of evaluating determinants and their applications to the solution of linear simultaneous equations.

11:30 A.M.-12:25 P.M.   30 hours   Credit: 2 semester-hours   Room 5

Mathematics S400—Educational Statistics   Dr. Hildebrandt

The aim of this course is to provide a sufficient background to enable the student to comprehend and criticize articles of statistical nature in current educational literature, to apply statistical methods in testing and rating pupils, and to carry on the simpler types of educational research. Among the topics treated are: graphical and tabular representation; measures of central tendencies; measures of variability; linear correlation; the normal distribution; sampling; and reliability of measures. The application of the subject provides natural integration with psychology, tests and measurements, and procedures in secondary education.

10:30-11:25 A.M.   30 hours   Credit: 2 semester-hours   Room 3

17

Mathematics S402B—Advanced Calculus   **Dr. Davis**

A study of certain selected topics from advanced calculus such as ordinary differential equations, partial differentiation and the application of partial derivatives, and multiple integrals.

8:30-9:25 A.M.   30 hours   Credit: 2 semester-hours   Room 5

Mathematics S406B—Applications of Mathematics   **Mr. Clifford**

The course applies the use of surveying instruments in motivating the teaching of mathematics in the junior and senior high school. The material studied is of special value to teachers of slow-moving ninth grade pupils. Topics considered are: the use of transit and level to determine elevations, inaccessible distances, areas, volumes, etc.; mapping with the plane table; use of planimeter, pantograph, hand level hyposometer, cross staff, angle mirror, and sextant; the various types of slide rules, the accuracy obtained, and the fundamental ideas of approximate computation; and graphic representation of data. The method for constructing inexpensive instruments is shown.

10:30-11:25 A.M., M., Tu., Th., Fri. and one afternoon in the field.

        30 hours   Credit: 2 semester-hours   Room 2

Mathematics S429—Elements of Practical Navigation for Junior and
                Senior High School Classes   **Dr. Hildebrandt**

This course deals with those topics which introduce the high school student to the mathematics of air and sea navigation. It reviews the fundamentals of solid geometry, mathematical geography, and astronomy required in aviation. Unit headings include: the earth and its motions; latitude and longitude; celestial coordinate systems; time and the calendar; theory of map projections; the great circle course; pilotage and dead reckoning; radio navigation; scale drawing solutions of navigation problems; the triangle of velocities; radius of action; nautical astronomy. Films, filmstrips, instruments, maps, charts, simple models, and teaching aids are used and emphasized throughout the course. See the Department of Science for other courses in Aviation.

9:30-10:25 A.M.   30 hours   Credit: 2 semester-hours   Room 3

Mathematics S515—Differential Equations with War Applications—Dr. Davis

The treatment of many problems of modern warfare leads to the solution of various types of differential equations, such as: linear differential equations of first and higher order; simultaneous differential equations; and partial differential equations. The course is a continuation of the calculus considered from a new viewpoint. Prerequisite: Elements of Calculus.

10:30-11:25 A.M.   30 hours   Credit: 2 semester-hours   Room 5

Mathematcs S533—Astronomy and Celestial Navigation   **Dr. Fehr**

This course treats the following topics: the celestial sphere; celestial coordinates; motion of the sun, planets, and stars; lines of position from celestial observations; the sextant and its use; computation of altitude and azimuth by trigonometry and H.O. 211; time and its determination; the American Nautical Almanac; star charts; observations for latitude and longitude; applications to marine navigation. The course is designed primarily to acquaint teachers of secondary school mathematics with modern methods of astronomical calculations.

1:00-1:55 P.M.   30 hours   Credit: 2 semester-hours   CHS-14

Workshop

Mathematics S499—Mathematics for High School Teachers
Dr. Fehr and Mr. Clifford

Due to the war-time shortage of teachers, many mathematics classes in high schools are now being taught by teachers of English, history, and other academic fields. This course is planned to be of aid to such teachers.

Assignments will be made on the basis of a careful analysis of the training and experience of each student registering for the course. Students may be assigned for part of their work to regularly scheduled courses in mathematics. Some of the work may be individual tutoring by the instructor. Lectures will deal in general with high school algebra and geometry. Pupil difficulties and methods of teaching will be discussed. Guidance to work in the subject-matter of the junior high school and to work in trigonometry will be given. Individual difficulties and problems of the teacher will be given careful consideration. To those qualified, opportunity will be given to do advanced work in mathematics or special work in navigation.

Credit: 6 or 8 semester-hours   CHS-14

Music

Music S201B—Sight Reading and Ear Training, Part II   Dr. McEachern

This course aims to provide those knowledges and skills necessary for the effective teaching of music in the classroom. It includes sight-reading and ear-training; tonal and rhythmic dictation; keyboard harmony and the making of accompaniments to a given melody; transposition and modulation; elementary form and analysis. Prerequisite: Music 201A or its equivalent.

8:30-9:25 A.M.   30 hours   Credit: 2 semester-hours   Room 6

Music S417—Our American Music   Dr. McEachern

This course provides a survey of American folk and art music as related to various social-economic, political, and cultural epochs in the history of our country. It includes a study of our national songs and their use in the war effort. A feature of the course is the making and producing of programs of American music suitable for use in school and community.

11:30 A.M.-12:25 P.M.   30 hours   Credit: 2 semester-hours   Room 6

Workshop

Music S499—Workshop in High School Music   Dr. McEachern

This course deals with special phases of high school music which, for lack of time, are seldom covered in music education courses. It includes music for boys; the school choir; assembly music; song dramatization; integration of music with other subjects; music appreciation; extra-curricular music activities and materials for special programs. Opportunity is given to students to work out musical projects for use in their respective schools.

9:30-10:25 A.M.   30 hours   Credit: 2 semester-hours   Room 6

Physical Education

Physical Education S302A—Organization of and Methods for Teaching Physical Education   Mr. Pittser

In this course, for both men and women, the entire organization procedure for setting up a program of Physical Education is outlined and discussed. Beginning with the annual health examination of every student and taking up, step by step, the daily, weekly, and seasonal programs, the course covers that of the entire year. Daily lesson plans, methods of instruction, taking roll, class organization, group leadership, equality of competition, safety of the gymnasium and recreation fields, and the care of locker and shower rooms are among the topics discussed.

10:30-11:25 A.M.   30 hours   Credit: 2 semester-hours   CHS-4

19

Physical Education S302B—Health and Health Teaching, Part II

Mr. Pittser

This course is open to men and women. In it, the health aspects of physical education are established, analyzed, and discussed. Physiology of exercise, which is the foundation of successful physical fitness, is emphasized. First aid, as it applies to all aspects of physical education, as well as the safety factors, are stressed.

11:30 A.M.-12:25 P.M.   30 hours   Credit: 2 semester-hours   CHS-4

Physical Education S406—Games and Game Skills   .   Mr. Pittser

This course is open to men and women. It includes a close study and practice of all physical activities which conform to the requirements of the Army and Navy for the training and conditioning of boys for Military Service. The Victory Corps Manual is used as a guide. For women in this course, the physical skills and stunts will be directed by a woman instructor. Calisthenics, individual skills, stunts, combative stunts, sports, and games, rough and tumble team games, and indoor and outdoor obstacle courses are stressed.

8:30-9:25 A.M.   30 hours   Credit: 2 semester-hours   CHS-4

Physical Education S410—Principles and Philosophy of Physical
Education   Mr. Pittser

This course is open to men and women. It is designed to orient the student to the breadth and scope of the field of physical education and to develop a workable philosophy which will meet today's needs. The contents of the course include the following items: a brief history of physical education; development of physical education in the United States; basic principles upon which a program of physical education is developed; different philosophies of physical education; administrative problems; legal matters in the field of physical education.

9:30-10:25 A.M.   30 hours   Credit: 2 semester-hours   CHS-4

Workshop

Physical Education S499—Physical Education for High School Teachers

Mr. Pittser and Miss Duke

Many high schools in the State are having difficulty in securing men and women teachers prepared, even in a small way, to teach physical education. Aside from the draft, the insistence of Federal and State officials that more time be given to this work, and that all high school boys and girls take it, is the main cause of teacher shortage in this field. This workshop course is primarily designed to prepare teachers, already certified in other academic fields, to qualify for part-time or full-time work in physical education. The work embraces four main fields of preparation:

Games and Game Skills

This work involves study and practice in the physical activities which conform to the Army and Navy Program as outlined in the Victory Corps Manual.

Principles, Problems, and Curricula in Physical Education

Attention is here given to principles underlying high school work in physical education. Administrative problems of the work and legal responsibilities of the teacher and school are considered.

20

Organization and Procedure

Topics considered are: Annual health examinations; instructional materials, instructional procedures, inter-school and intra-mural athletics; competitive games; safety in the gymnasium, care of recreation fields, lockers, and shower rooms.

Health and Health Teaching

Attention is given to the physiology of exercise; exercise and health; first aid; and safety education in the school, the home, and on the street.

The instructors of this course will endeavor, insofar as possible, to adapt the program to the individual's needs in his teaching program. It is planned that the student shall be enabled, through this workshop, to do a good job of "pinch hitting" for the duration.

6 or 8 semester-hours   CHS-4

Science

Biology S102B—Morphology and Physiology of the Fungi, the Mosses, and the Ferns   Dr. Hadley

This course deals primarily with the economic importance of the fungi and with the evolution of the flowering plants from their ancestors among the Bryophytes and Pteridophytes. Class work involves a series of lectures accompanied by laboratory and field study of the organisms concerned. Prerequisite: Four semester-hours of General Botany or its equivalent.

8:30 A.M. Fri., 9:30 A.M. Tues. and Thurs., Lab. Mon. 1-5 P.M.

45 hours   Credit: 2 semester-hours   Room 28

Biology S201B—Entomology   Dr. Hadley

The study of insects is pursued from the standpoint of morphology, physiology, ecology, classification, and economic importance. Class procedures involve lectures, laboratory study, and field work for collecting and study of habitat. Prerequisites: Four semester-hours of General Zoology or its equivalent.

9:30 M. W. F., Lab: Tues. 1-5 P.M.   45 hours   Credit: 2 s.h.   Room 28

Biology S411B—Biological Technique (Medical), Part II   Dr. Hadley

This is a training course designed to prepare candidates for work as medical technicians. The course is divided into two parts: Part I, Blood Analysis, to be given from May 25th to July 2nd, and Part II, Urinalysis, to be given from July 6th to August 13th, but Part I is not prerequisite to Part II. Part II gives training in analysis of both normal and abnormal urine in respect to physical and chemical characteristics, the latter inclusive of qualitative and quantitative tests for such significant components as albumin, sugars, indican, acetone, diacetic acid, bile, urea, occult blood, and organic sediment including casts. Class procedure involves a minimum of lecturing and emphasis is placed on individual laboratory practice designed to develop certified technicians. Prerequisite: A minimum of four semester-hours of experience in biology or its equivalent.

10:30 Mon. and Tues., 11:30 Thurs., Lab: Wed. 1-5 P.M.

45 hours   Credit: 2 semester-hours   Room 28

Chemistry S101B—General College Chemistry, Part II   Dr. Reed

The aims of the course are: to provide opportunity for mastering the fundamentals of chemistry, of gases and solutions; to develop laboratory technique, and to use standard reference books. Chemistry 101A is given from May 25 to July 2, but is not prerequisite to this course.

10:30 Mon. and Tues., 11:30 Thurs., Lab: Wed. 1-5 P.M.

45 hours   Credit: 2 semester-hours   Room 23

Chemistry S201B—Analytical Chemistry, Part II   **Dr. Reed**

The purposes of this course are: to develop and apply the fundamental principles of chemistry of solutions; to perfect the techniques of chemistry as applied to preparation and utilization of solutions; and to understand and use methods of separating and identifying anions. Chemistry 201A, concerned with cations, is given from May 25 to July 2, but is not prerequisite to this course.

9:30 A.M. Mon., Wed., Fri. Lab: Thurs. 1:00-5:00 P.M.

         45 hours   Credit: 2 semester-hours   Room 23

Chemistry S510B—The Bio-Chemistry of Food and Nutrition,

         Part II   **Dr. Reed**

This course is planned to give students a knowledge of the composition and quality of foods now available, as ascertained by chemical analysis, microscopic study and comparative judgment; a knowledge of the chemistry of digestion and metabolism of foods; experience in calculation of diets, using standard references; and a knowledge of preserving and storing of common foods. The course 510A meets from May 25 to July 2, but is not prerequisite to this course. General College Chemistry is, however, prerequisite.

10:30 Wed., Thurs., Fri., Lab: Tues. 1-5 P.M.

         45 hours   Credit: 2 semester-hours   Room 23

Physics S101B and S102B—General College Physics,

         Parts II and IV   **Dr. K. O. Smith**

The major objective of physical science is to discover, describe, correlate, and explain the facts and phenomena of the inanimate world. For convenience, the subject-matter of physics is classified as mechanics; heat; magnetism and electricity; sound, and light. Physics 101A, Mechanics, meets from May 25 to July 2, followed by 101B, Heat, beginning on July 6 and ending on August 13. Physics 102A, Light and Sound, meets from May 25 to July 2, followed on July 6 by 102B, Magnetism and Electricity. Each of these four sections consists of lectures, demonstrations, discussions, problem-solving exercises, library assignments, and laboratory experiments. Each of the four sections meets for 45 hours and receives 2 semester-hours credit.

S101B: 8:30 M. W. F., Lab: Th. 1-5   45 hours   Credit: 2 s.h.   Room 25

S102B: 8:30 Tu., Th., 10:30 Wed., Lab: Fri. 1-5—45 hrs.   Credit: 2 s.h.   Room 25

Physics S304—Photography for High School Teachers   **Professor Glenn**

This is a beginning course in photography, consisting of lectures, demonstrations, laboratory work, and field work. The topics covered are similar to those outlined in BASIC PHOTOGRAPHY, published by the United States Air Corps. Some of the topics are: construction and operation of cameras; the nature of chemical changes encountered in photographic work; developing and printing negatives and positives; taking pictures both indoors and outdoors; taking pictures at night; making lantern slides; and projection printing. A student needs at least one camera for the course.

1:00-1:55 P.M.   30 hours   Credit: 2 semester-hours   Room 22

Physics S402B—Advanced Electricity and Radio   **Dr. K. O. Smith**

The course consists of lectures, demonstrations, reference readings, laboratory experiments, and construction of simple radio sets. Course 402A is given from May 25 to July 2, followed by 402B, beginning on July 6.

9:30 A.M. Tues., Thurs., Fri., Lab: Mon. 1-5 P.M.

         45 hours   Credit: 2 semester-hours   Room 25

Physics S407A—Aviation for Teachers   **Professor Glenn**

This introduction to aviation deals with the first two important aspects of aeronautics: first, learning to fly as related to ground school instruction; and, second, the fundamentals of aerodynamics. In the first part of the course, the following topics are considered: how an airplane flies, airplane instruments, starting, and landing. Later, attention is given to engines and propellers, forces acting on a plane, speed and power, and airplane performance. While no flight training is given, all of the work is based on studies of airplanes made available to students. Students interested in this course should note also: Science S417, Meteorology with Applications to Aviation; and Mathematics S429, Navigation for Junior and Senior High School Classes.

8:30-9:25 A.M.   30 hours   Credit: 2 semester-hours   Room 22

Science S417—Meteorology with Applications to Aviation   **Dr. Milstead**

This course constitutes a study of the atmosphere, the sources of atmospheric heat, the temperature variations and their relation to the weather phenomena. Emphasis is placed on the nature of the large scale wind systems, air masses and fronts, and upon rainfall distribution. Special phenomena, such as thunderstorms, fog, and ice accretion, which affect the operation of aircraft, are treated, and the uses of meteorological instruments are explained. See also: Physics S407A, Aviation for Teachers; and Mathematics S429, Navigation for Junior and Senior High School Classes.

10:30-11:25 A.M.   30 hours   Credit: 2 semester-hours   Room 26

Workshop

Science S499—Science for High School Teachers   **Prof. Glenn and Staff**

This course is designed to prepare teachers now in service (in subjects other than science) to begin the teaching of high school science in September, 1943. Three parallel lines of activity are planned which will use the entire summer session.

There will be a series of lectures covering the topics of current importance in war-time science, with intensive treatment of the texts, manuals, tests, demonstration equipment, and laboratory apparatus used in teaching high school science.

Personal conferences are planned for individual teachers, either daily or several times each week, on problems under intensive study in one subject-matter field, and the pre-induction courses now developing in the high schools of New Jersey.

In addition to the two types of work outlined above, the teacher will be asked to attend the laboratory and demonstration classes of certain courses in college physics, chemistry, or biology. Selection of these courses will be on the basis of individual needs for retraining in the science field. It is expected that the teacher will devote the entire summer session to this one course.

     6 or 8 semester-hours   Room 22

Social Studies

Social Studies S101A—European History from 1492 to 1713   **Dr. Folsom**

The course deals with the Lutheran, Calvinist, and Anglican aspects of the Reformation and the ensuing Counter-Reformation with their political and national significance in the 16th Century. The disintegration of Germany during the Thirty Years' War, the English constitutional conflict under the Stuarts, and the Age of Louis XIV are the main subjects for the 17th Century.

11:30 A.M.-12:25 P.M.   30 hours   Credit: 2 semester-hours   Room 21

Social Studies S101B—European History from 1713 to 1815   **Dr. Wittmer**

The Rise of Russia and the Rise of Prussia are treated. Primary consideration is given, however, to the political, economic, social, and intellectual conditions in France preceding the French Revolution; the French Revolution itself; and the Napoleonic period; with the inauguration of the spirit of nationalism.

9:30-10:25 A.M.   30 hours   Credit: 2 semester-hours   CHS-12

Social Studies S102B—European History from 1870 to the Present Day
    Dr. Folsom

The course discusses domestic problems in Germany, France, and Russia from 1870 to the World War in the light of the present world situation. The economic imperialism and international diplomacy of European states as they affected the Balkans, Africa, and the Far East form a major part of the course. Contemporary world affairs throughout serve as a basis for interpreting the European developments in modern times.

9:30-10:25 A.M.   30 hours   Credit: 2 semester-hours   Room 21

Social Studies S202B—American History from 1900 to the Present Day
    Dr. Snyder

This course is devoted to the study of the United States as a world power, the development of "big business," the United States in the first World War, and our problems of the depression and present war periods.

10:30-11:25 A.M.   30 hours   Credit: 2 semester-hours   Room 20

Social Studies S301B—Economics II   **Mr. Rellahan**

This course is a continuation of Economics I, which is not, however, prerequisite. The aim of this course is to acquaint the student with the basic economic principles and problems relating to risk and insurance; money, credit, and banking; general price changes and their control; foreign trade and exchange; tariffs, international debts, and imperialism; business combinations; and governmental regulation of business enterprise.

11:30 A.M.-12:25 P.M.   30 hours   Credit: 2 semester-hours   Room 24

Social Studies S401W—The Teaching of Social Studies in Secondary
    Schools   **Dr. Snyder**

The course presents recent tendencies in the teaching of the social studies. Among the matters considered are: the social studies curriculum, with special attention to the fusion organization; the objectives in the social studies; class procedures, including the problem-project method, oral procedures, drill and review procedures; procedures in particular subjects; the teaching of current events; devices and aids, including visual, auditory, and motor aids; technique of field trips; use of textbooks and supplementary reading; and testing and grading. Bibliographies and other teaching aids are supplied to students.

8:30-9:25 A.M.   30 hours   Credit: 2 semester-hours   Room 20

Social Studies S407—New Jersey State and Local Government   **Mr. Bye**

A study is made of the State Constitution; New Jersey's place in the federal system; the rights and duties of citizens; suffrage; political parties; the legislative, the executive, and administrative systems; the courts, the law enforcement and correctional systems; revenues and expenditures; public health, educational, highway, and other services; county and municipal government; and other local political units.

10:30-11:25 A.M.   30 hours   Credit: 2 semester-hours   Room 24

Social Studies S420B—The European Outlook, Part II   **Dr. Wittmer**

This course is devoted to a study of contemporary Belgium, the Netherlands, France, Spain, Italy, and England. It is shown how the culture patterns of these nations can be preserved without impeding the growth of an all-embracing western democratic civilization. It shows how the Atlantic Charter may be applied to the particular conditions of the countries being considered. The role of England as part of Europe on the one hand, and as a link between Europe and the world on the other, is discussed in detail. Prerequisite: a course in Modern European History.

10:30-11:25 A.M.   30 hours   Credit: 2 semester-hours   CHS-12

**Social Studies S428—Sociology I: Racial Contributions to
American Life**   **Mr. Bye**

This course deals with the basic problems of quantity, quality, and distribution of population and emphasizes the adjustments and maladjustments which result from the inter-relation of Negroes, Asiastics, and various types of Europeans in the United States.

9:30-10:25 A.M.   30 hours   Credit: 2 semester-hours   Room 20

Social Studies S433—American Political Thought   **Mr. Bye**

This is a survey of political thinking in America. It deals with contemporary trends and theories as they have emerged from social and economic conditions and as they are founded upon the bases laid down by such men as Hamilton, Madison, Washington, Jefferson, Marshall, Calhoun, Webster, Lincoln, Wilson, and others. A knowledge of American ideals as expressed in our political philosophy is especially important for teachers of American history, civics, and problems of democracy in this changing period through which we are passing.

11:30 A.M.-12:25 P.M.   30 hours   Credit: 2 semester-hours   Room 20

Social Studies S436—Modern Men of Ancient Times   **Dr. Freeman**

This course is designed to present biographical sketches of some of the great leaders of past ages. The subjects for discussion are selected from all lines of human endeavor, and special attention is given to their influence on the thought of their own times and their contribution to the culture of the present day. The course is specially recommended to students who wish to know these leaders as real persons and not as lay figures in ancient history.

11:30 A.M.-12:25 P.M.   30 hours   Credit: 2 semester-hours   Room 10

Social Studies S442—The Far East   **Dr. Wittmer**

A study is made of the economic, social, and cultural situation of the Far East, with particular emphasis on the historical background of China and Japan, and on our relations with the Philippines. Oriental folkways, religion, education, population shifts and strategic questions are discussed. This course provides an approach to the problems the United States is facing in the Far East.

11:30 A.M.-12:25 P.M.   30 hours   Credit: 2 semester-hours   CHS-12

**Social Studies S446—Current and Post-War Problems in Economics
and Government**   **Mr. Rellahan**

This course is designed to analyze the relationship of economics to government in the United States. The causes, legislative treatment, administrative methods, and results of government activity are discussed in the light of their economic significance and their bearing upon public welfare. The studies of the National Resources Planning Board and Temporary National Economic Committee are reviewed and appropriate consideration is given to the problems of war and post-war adjustment.

9:30-10:25 A.M.   30 hours   Credit: 2 semester-hours   Room 24

Social Studies S448—The British Empire in the Present Crisis   **Dr. Folsom**

The course deals with the coming to nationhood of England's daughter states: Canada, Australia, New Zealand, and South Africa; and the role that they are playing in present world affairs. Special emphasis is given to Canadian history and its dual position as an American state and a part of the Empire. The course also includes a study of India and her political ambitions.

10:30-11:25 A.M.   30 hours   Credit: 2 semester-hours   Room 21

Social Studies S450—Applied Economics, Part II   **Mr. Rellahan**

This course is devoted to an analysis of the application of economic principles in the operation and guidance of economic life with special attention given to an understanding of our economic problems and public policy relating to them. The scope of Part II (for which Part I is not necessarily required) covers such topics as agriculture, international trade and exchange, economic statistical analysis, public finance, the economics of war and post-war planning, comparative economic systems, and economic trends.

8:30-9:25 A.M.   30 hours   Credit: 2 semester-hours   Room 24

Graduate Department

Graduate S500A—Seminar and Thesis

Students writing a thesis for credit toward the Master's degree in any department of the college are required to register for this course. The work is conducted under seminar or individual guidance. Students report to the Dean of Instruction, who calls a conference with the Head of Department and the Sponsor. At this meeting, all matters pertaining to the topic, plan of research, writing of manuscript, etc., are arranged.

                                       Credit: 4 semester-hours

TWELVE WEEKS SUMMER TERM, 1943

The following courses will be given beginning May 25, 1943. Those marked with the numeral "I" are two-point courses and will end Friday, July 2. All other courses in this list will continue until August 13 and will give four semester-hours of credit.

Department	Cat. No.	Title of Course	Instructor
Business Ed.	I. 301B	Business Organization and Administration	Mr. Sheppard
	302	Salesmanship	Dr. Geigle
	303	Business Mathematics	Mr. Sheppard
	I. 304	Marketing	Mr. Sheppard
	407	Principles of Accounting	Dr. Geigle
English	201A, B	British Poetry from Chaucer to Frost I. A	Mr. Nickerson
		II. B	Mr. Pettegrove
	I. 208	Fundamentals of Speech	Dr. Ogg
	I. 301B	Shakespeare's Major Plays	Mr. Bohn
	302	Survey of American Literature I. A—Dr. Cayley	
			II. B—Mr. Conrad
	I. 322	Oral Interpretation of Literature	Dr. Ogg
	I. 405	Browning and Later Victorian Poets	Mr. Nickerson
	I. 413	Modern Poetry	Mr. Nickerson
	I. 435	Play Production	Mr. Bohn
	I. 447A	Introduction to Philosophy	Dr. Cayley
	I. 448	Choral Speaking	Dr. Ogg
Geography	I. 100C	The Earth Sciences	Dr. Milstead
	202	Geography of the Western Hemisphere	Dr. Milstead
	302	Economic Geography	Dr. Milstead
French	101	French Civilization	Mrs. Cressey
	201	XVII. Century French Literature	Mrs. Cressey
	302	XVIII. Century French Literature	Mrs. Cressey
	416	French History	Mrs. Cressey
Latin	201	Masterpieces of Latin Prose	Miss Littlefield
	302	Lucretius	Dr. Freeman
Spanish	201	Hispanic-American Civilization, Part One	Miss Escoriaza
	202	Hispanic-American Civilization, Part Two	Miss Escoriaza
	302	Spanish Classics	Miss Escoriaza
	I. 407	The New World before the Coming of Columbus	Dr. Freeman
Language	I. 300	Foundations of Language	Miss Littlefield
	I. 415	The War Languages	Miss Littlefield
Integration	I. 100B	Social Interpretations of Education (Fr. Course)	Dr. Ryan
	I. 200A	Educational Psychology: Tests and Measurements	Dr. Ingebritsen
	I. 300A	Aims and Organization of Junior and Senior H. S.	Dr. W. S. Smith, Mr. Seybold
	I.		
	I. 400A	Principles and Philosophy of Sec. Education	Dr. Ryan, Mr. Seybold

Department	Cat. No.	Title of Course	Instructor
Music	201	Sight Reading and Ear Training	Dr. McEachern
	I. 302A	Epochs in Musical Development	Dr. McEachern
Mathematics	102	Trigonometry and Analytic Geometry	Mr. Clifford
	301	Modern Geometry	Dr. Hildebrandt
	302	Higher Algebra	Dr. Davis
	402	Solid Analytic Geometry and Analysis	Dr. Davis
	406	Applications of Mathematics	Mr. Clifford
	I. 304B	Spherical Trigonometry	Dr. Fehr
	I. 405	History of Mathematics	Dr. Fehr
Biology	102	Botany, Part Two	Dr. Hadley
	201	Zoology, Part One	Dr. Hadley
	411	Biological Techniques (Medical)	Dr. Hadley
Chemistry	101	General College Chemistry	Dr. Reed
	201	Analytic Chemistry	Dr. Reed
	510	Food Inspection and Analysis	Dr. Reed
Physics	101	General College Physics, Part 1	Dr. K. O. Smith
	102	General College Physics, Part 2	Dr. K. O. Smith
	402	Advanced Electricity and Radio Com.	Dr. K. O. Smith
Social Studies	101	European History, 1492-1815	Dr. Wittmer
	202	American History, 1860-Present	Dr. Snyder
	301	Economics, Part One and Two	Mr. Rellahan
	I. 402B	Comparative Government	Mr. Bye
	I. 407	New Jersey State and Local Government	Mr. Bye
	420	European Outlook	Dr. Wittmer
	I. 429	Present Day Social Problems	Mr. Bye
	I. 440A	The Development of Central and South America	Dr. Snyder
	I. 446	Current and Post-war Problems in Economics and Government	Mr. Rellahan
	450	Applied Economics	Mr. Rellehan
	I. 451	The Middle East	Dr. Wittmer
Physical Education	W302A	Games and Game Skills	Miss Sherwin

(A practical class which meets on the laboratory basis, double periods, for two semester-hours of credit)

SUMMER SESSION

Bulletin of

MONTCLAIR
STATE TEACHERS COLLEGE

JULY 5 to AUGUST 15

1944

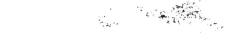

UPPER MONTCLAIR, NEW JERSEY

SUMMER SESSION

Bulletin of

MONTCLAIR
STATE TEACHERS COLLEGE

1944

July 5 to August 15

Upper Montclair, New Jersey

SUMMER SESSION 1944
FACULTY

HARRY A. SPRAGUE, Ph.D. _____Director of the Summer Session
HAROLD C. BOHN, A.M. _____English
EDGAR C. BYE, A.M. _____Social Studies
LAWRENCE S. CHASE, A.M. _____Administration
PAUL C. CLIFFORD, A.M. _____Mathematics
LAWRENCE H. CONRAD, A.M. _____English
GERMAINE P. CRESSEY, A.M. _____French
DAVID R. DAVIS, Ph.D. _____Mathematics
TERESA DeESCORIAZA, A.M. _____Spanish
HOWARD FRANKLIN FEHR, Ph.D. _____Mathematics
AVALINE FOLSOM, Ph.D. _____Social Studies
WALTER H. FREEMAN, Ph.D. _____Head of Department of
Foreign Languages
EDWIN S. FULCOMER, Ed. D. _____Head of the Department of English
FRANCIS R. GEIGLE, Ed. D. _____Head of Department of Social
Business and Accounting
CHARLES E. HADLEY, Ph.D. _____Biology
CLAUDE E. JACKSON, A.M. _____Research
RUSSELL KRAUSS, Ph.D. _____English
ETHEL F. LITTLEFIELD, A.M. _____Languages
HARLEY P. MILSTEAD, Ph.D. _____Geography
CHESTER M. PITTSER, A.M. _____Physical Education
JAMES S. PLANT, M. D. _____Integration
RUFUS D. REED, Ph.D. _____Chemistry
·JOHN J. RELLAHAN, A.M. _____Social Studies
HEBER H. RYAN, Ph.D. _____ Administration
ARTHUR M. SEYBOLD, A.M. _____ Integration
HORACE J. SHEPPARD, A.M. _____Social Business and Accounting
MARGARET A. SHERWIN, A.M. _____Dean of Women
KENNETH O. SMITH, Ph.D. _____Physics
W. SCOTT SMITH, Ph.D. _____Integration
W. HARRY SNYDER, Ph.D. ____Head of the Department of Social Studies
D. HENRYETTA SPERLE, Ph.D. _____Integration
MARGARET E. TIRRELL, A.M. _____Integration
FELIX WITTMER, Ph.D. _____Social Studies

The Visiting Faculty Members

Lawrence S. Chase, A.M.: Superintendent of Schools of Essex County, New Jersey

James S. Plant, M.D.: Director, Essex County Juvenile Clinic, Newark, N. J.

Heber H. Ryan, Ph.D.: Assistant Commissioner of Education, State of New Jersey; Supervisor of Secondary Education.

Margaret E. Tirrell, A.M.: Assistant to the Director, Essex County Juvenile Clinic, Newark, New Jersey.

3

SUMMER SESSION OF THE
NEW JERSEY STATE TEACHERS COLLEGE AT MONTCLAIR

How to Reach the Campus

Trains of the Greenwood Lake Division, Erie R. R., stop at College Station. Trains of the Lackawanna R. R. connect at Montclair with the following bus lines: No. 64, running between Brick Church and the college; No. 60, running between Newark and the college, and No. 76, which runs between Orange and Paterson, passing the college en route.

Schedule of Summer Session Classes

The Summer Session begins on Wednesday, July 5, and continues through Tuesday, August 15, on which day the Commencement exercises will be held. All courses meet daily, Monday through Friday, for one hour, except where definitely indicated otherwise.

Registration

There is no advance registration for courses. Students register in each class at the first meeting if a sufficient number is present. At the second meeting, classes too small to be enrolled at the first meeting are either registered or discontinued depending upon the number present.

Audited Class Admission Cards

Audited Class Admission Cards are due at the third meeting of each class. They are obtained in the Business Office on presentation of fees or credit slips. It is desirable that this be done in person, but if necessary students may send checks, money-orders, or credit slips by mail to the Business Managr, with the request that the Audited Class Admission Cards be placed in the postboxes of the respective teachers. The Business Office is open daily, Monday through Friday, at the following hours: 8:30 to 11:30 A.M., and 12:30 to 3:30 P.M.

Fees

Checks or money orders should be made payable to NEW JERSEY STATE TEACHERS COLLEGE. Registration service charge: $1.00 for the Summer Session. Tuition fees: to legal residents of New Jersey, $6.00 per semester-hour credit; to non-residents, $8.00 per credit. Courses taken for no credit cost the same. A laboratory service charge of $1.50 is made in connection with each of the laboratory courses. This service charge is collected in class by your instructor. Do not include it in your check for tuition.

Residence Halls for Men and Women

Edward Russ Hall and Chapin Hall are Montclair's two well-appointed residences. The charge for living on campus is reasonable—$12.00 per week, including room, breakfast, and dinner. A la carte luncheons are served in the college cafeteria. For one student in a double room, an extra charge of $2.00 is made. The college provides all furnishings, with the exceptions of towels, blankets, and desk lamps. The fee must be paid on or before the first day of the Summer Session. No rebate is made for occasional absence or voluntary withdrawal during the session. Students who are absent on account of illness for two weeks or more receive a rebate of $6.00 per week during the illness.

For reservations in the college residence hall, address: Director of Personnel, State Teachers College, Upper Montclair, N. J.

General Objective

The New Jersey State Teachers College at Montclair is a professional school which prepares teachers for the Junior and Senior High Schools of the State. Students may matriculate for the degree of Bachelor of Arts or for the degree of Master of Arts. In either case, those who do not already have the New Jersey Secondary Teaching Certificate must earn that while working for the degree.

Students Matriculated at Other Colleges

Work taken for credit to be transferred to other colleges should be approved in advance by the Dean of the College to which the credit is sent. The numbering of courses at Montclair follows this order: 100 - 399, inclusive, are undergraduate courses; 400 - 499 are senior-college and graduate courses; 500 and above are graduate courses.

Students Matriculated at Montclair

Work taken for credit at Montclair must be with the advice and approval of the Head of the Department in which you are majoring and of the Dean of Instruction.

Teacher Re-Training Program

Many men have been called into service with our armed forces from teaching positions in the high schools in the fields of mathematics, science, and physical education. At the same time, the high schools have been asked to prepare other young men for similar service by giving them a year's work in mathematics, a like amount in physics, and vigorous work in physical education. This has created an emergency in our high schools. Teachers have had to take over courses for which they had only a minimum of preparation and for which they were not certified.

The State Department has cooperated by granting provisional certificates. The college at Montclair, through its Part-Time Division, provides an opportunity for teacher re-training in these three important fields. It is realized, however, that the transportation situation has made it very difficult for teachers to come to the campus more than once each week during the academic year. The Summer Session offers the opportunity to live on campus and to pursue a full program of work, so that the teacher-in-service may obtain six, or even eight semester-hours credit in any one of these fields.

Summer Term of Twelve Weeks

Included in this Bulletin of the Summer Session is a list of the courses of the twelve-weeks summer term which is held for the benefit of the accelerated candidates for the A.B. degree at MONTCLAIR. Other

5

students who have special need for a maximum amount of credit may also enter these courses. Registration and payment of fees for them must be made on May 22nd. Anyone desiring to enroll should report that day to the Summer Session Office. These classes continue until August 15, with a recess July 1 to July 4, inclusive.

Auditors

Men and women who desire to take courses for cultural, vocational, or avocational purposes without college credit may register as auditors. This should be clearly indicated on the registration form.

Matriculation

Those who wish to become candidates for the A.B. or the A.M. degree must request the Registrar of the college for the application form and return it, properly filled in and accompanied by an official transcript of all previous college work. When an applicant has been accepted as a candidate for the degree, a definite statement will be furnished him, showing the requirements to be fulfilld by him individually.

Teaching Certificates

Students who do not matriculate at Montclair but who desire to teach in this State should write to the Secretary of the State Board of Examiners, Mr. John B. Dougall, for information concerning teachers' certificates. Mr. Dougall's address is: Department of Public Instruction, Trenton, N. J. With the inquiry, there must be submitted an official transcript of all previous work on college level, with an explanation of the kind of certificate for which it is to be evaluated. Some students who have decided at the last minute to seek this information and advice have found it helpful to go to Trenton personally in order to save time.

Supervised Student Teaching

The opportunity to do supervised student teaching cannot be offered during the summer session. Matriculated students confer with Dr. W. Scott Smith. Non-matriculated students should write to Dr. Robert H. Morrison, Director of Teacher Education, State Department of Public Instruction, Trenton, N. J., enclosing an official transcript of all work on college level.

Conferences

Students are urged not to wait until the opening of the summer session to consult their advisers. If, however, it has been impossible for you to make an earlier appointment, you may see the Head of your Department and the Dean of Instruction on Wednesday, July 5. A representative of the State Board of Examiners also will be at the college that day, between the hours of 10 A.M. and 3 P.M. to see students who desire a last word of advice. He cannot, however, undertake at this time to evaluate all the previous work of a student, as the interviews in each case are necessarily brief. (See instructions under "Teaching Certificates.") The Registrar of the Summer Session will receive requests for appointments with this State Official.

Credits and Transcripts

The maximum amount of credit which may be earned in the six weeks of Summer Session is 8 semester-hours.

Each course is in session at least thirty hours and receives credit as designated. Report cards, for the student's own use, and an official transcript for him to present at the State Department of Educaion or at another college, are mailed directly to him within a week or ten days of the close of the summer session. All transcripts are mailed on the same day in fairness to all students. This first transcript is furnished free. The cost of a second transcript depends upon the amount of work the student has completed at this college, ranging from 25 cents for one semester or summer session to $1.00 for four or more. The college cannot provide a second transcript that covers less than all the work completed. Stamps cannot be accepted for transcripts; check or money order should be used when remitting fees by mail. Men and women entering the armed forces are given this second transcript without the service charge.

The mark "D" when earned in summer, part-time, or extension courses is not accepted for degree credit at Montclair, but will be given, when earned, for possible use elsewhere.

Courses that carry a credit of 4 s.h. in the regular curriculum are frequently given in the summer session in two parts, each half course carrying a credit of 2 s.h. When the nature of the course is such that the two parts must be taken in a designated sequence, attention is drawn to that fact in the course dscription.

If prerequisites are indicated, the student should make certain he has had them or the equivalent before enrolling in the course.

The responsibility regarding incomplete work rests with the student. He should confer with his instructor, who, if he considers it advisable, may grant as much as two months time in which the work can be completed. If, however, the work is not finished at the end of two months, the mark for the course shall be "F."

This is not an official statement. It does not emanate from the State Department that issues the certificate. It is furnished merely for your convenience in selecting courses You should check your selections with the State Department, sending an official transcript of work already completed. Please note that either an undergraduate or a graduate course may apply on the certificate.

I **Health Education—3 semster-hours required**
Biology 409A—Human Physiology—2 s. h.
Physical Education 301B—Health and Health Teaching, Part 1—2 s. h.
Physical Education 302B—Health and Health Teaching, Part II—2 s. h.

II—**Educational Psychology—3 semester-hours required**
*Integration 200A—Introduction to Educational Psychology and Mental Testing—2 s. h.
Integration 200B—Adolescent Psychology and Mental Hygiene—2 s. h.
Integration 500BW—Advanced Educational Psychology—2 s. h.

III **Aims and Organization (Principles) of Secondary Education—3 s. h. required.**
Integration 300A—Aims and Organization of Secondary Education—2 s. h.
*Integration 400A—Principles and Philosophy of Secondary Education —2 s. h.
Integration 405—Principles of Junior High School Teaching—2 s. h.
*Integration 500AW—History and Principles of Secondary Education— 2 s. h.
*Integration 502A—Organization and Administration of the Modern High School, Part I—2 s. h.
Integration 502B—Organization and Administration of the Modern High School, Part II—2 s. h.

IV—**Principles and Techniques (General Methods) of Teaching in the High School—3 s. h. required.**
*Integration 300B—Principles and Techniques of Teaching in the Secondary School—2 s. h.
*Integration 500CW—Teaching Procedures in Secondary Education—2 s. h.

V—**Curriculum Organization and Courses of Study (Methods) in One Endorsed Teaching Field—3 semester-hours required.**
Business Education 401W—The Teaching of Business Education in the Secondary School—2 s. h.
*English 401W—The Teaching of English in the Secondary School—2 s. h.
*Language 401W—The Teaching of Foreign Languages in the Secondary School—2 s. h.
*Integration 504A—Curriculum Construction in the Secondary School—2 s.h.
*Mathematics 401W—The Teaching of Mathematics in the Secondary School—2 s. h.
Mathematics 532—Teaching Mathematics in a War Program—2 s. h.
Music 401W—The Teaching of High School Music—2 s. h.
Science 401W—The Teaching of Science in the Secondary School—2 s. h.
Science 505W—Survey of Curricula and Science Courses in State and City Systems—2 s. h.
*Biology 501—The Teaching of Biology—3 s. h.
Chemistry 501W—The Teaching of Chemistry—2 s. h.
Physics 501W—The Teaching of Physics—2 s. h.
*Social Studies 401—The Teaching of the Social Studies in the Secondary School—3 s. h.

DESCRIPTION OF COURSES

Business Education

Business Education S301A—Business Law, Part III   **Mr. Sheppard**
This is a treatment of business law from a practical, educational, and social point of view. The main points for consideration are: personal property, including the nature of personal property; sales, conditional sales, bailments, and chattel mortgages; real property, including landlord and tenant and mechanics' liens; and business organization, including partnerships and corporations. This is a continuation of Business Education 202, which is not, however, necessarily prerequisite.
8:30-9:25-11 A.M.   30 hours   Credit' 2 semester-hours   Room B

Business Education S301B—Business Organization and
**   Management**   **Mr. Sheppard**
The immediate purpose of a course in business organization and management is to give the student an understanding of the functions performed by the operating business unit. It is a practical application of the science of business. The topics covered are: the forms of business organization and their functions of ·selling, purchasing, financial operations, personnel, and recording.
10:30-11:25 A.M.   30 hours   Credit: 2 semester-hours   Room D

Business Education S310—Money and Banking   **Dr. Geigle**
This course provides a short historical survey of money and the evolution of banking, outside and within the United States. The organization of banks, the nature of their transactions, operations, and relations with other banks are considered. The functioning of the Federal Reserve System and the nature of the money markets are also examined.
9:30-10:25 A.M.   30 hours   Credit: 2 semester-hours   Room D

English

English S100A—World Literature, Part I   **Dr. Krauss**
This course surveys the main contributions of Egyptian, Babylonian, Persian, Hebrew, Arabian, Greek, and Roman Literature to world thinking. The specific contributions of such renowned writers as Homer, Sappho, Aeschylus, Sophocles, Euripides, Plato, Aristotle. Cicero, Virgil, Horace, Livy, and Tacitus are considered in detail. The objective of the course is three-fold: to increase literary appreciation, to trace the influence of a body of literature or a single author upon later writers, and to examine the thought of the past in relation to that of the present.
1:00-1:55 P.M.   30 hours   Credit: 2 semester hours   Room B

English S100B—World Literature, Part II   **Mr. Bohn**
Outstanding works of the Renaissance writers, the Elizabethans, the Romantics, and the Victorians are studied with the view of showing what each has contributed to the origin of forms and to the development of the literature of the world, and how each in its turn has had its influence upon its own and succeeding times. Such writers as the following are considered: Dante, Boccaccio, Petrarch, Chaucer, Shakespeare, Milton, Calderon, Moliere, Raciné, Pope, Boswell, Goethe, Wordsworth, and Tennyson.
10:30-11:25 A.M.   30 hours   Credit: 2 semester hours   Room A

English S102B—British and American Drama, Part II   **Mr. Bohn**
This course begins with the nineteenth century as a background for the modern and contemporary drama of England and the United States. It emphasizes drama as a literary form and a social force.
9:30-10:25 A.M.   30 hours   Credit: 2 semester hours   Room A

English S201A—British and American Poetry, Part I   **Dr. Krauss**
This course is designed to acquaint the student with the best known poems from Chaucer to Pope, and with the historical development of English poetry from the fourteenth to the eighteenth century. Chaucer, Spencer, Donne, Herrick, Milton, and Pope receive special stress.
11:30\A.M.-12-25 P.M.   30 hours   Credit: 2 semester-hours   Room B

9

English S202B—British and American Fiction, Part II   **Mr. Conrad**
This is the second half of the required course for English majors. Part B begins
with Dickens and continues to the present day. The course includes cultural and
professional studies, discussions, and reports.
8:30-9:25 A.M.   30 hours   Credit: 2 semester-hours   CHS-Auditorium

English S301A—Literature for Adolescents: Developing Faith for
                  Living through Literature   **Dr. Fulcomer**
This course is a study of the best available literary material (fiction, drama,
biography, essay), suitable to the interests and maturity of junior and senior
high school adolescents, and of the use that can be made of it in enabling them
to gain the knowledge and confidence necessary for courageous living in this
world.
10:30-11:25 A.M.   30 hours   Credit: 2 semester-hours   Room 1

English S401W—The Teaching of English in Secondary Schools   **Dr. Fulcomer**
This course deals with the methods of teaching composition and literature in the
high school. It aims to unify and organize the professional training and
practical experience of all students in the course, and to provide new points of
view for their active English teaching by setting up objectives and indicating
concrete methods of obtaining those objectives.
8:30-9:25 A.M.   30 hours   Credit: 2-semester-hours   Room 1

English S402B—Survey of English Literature, Part II   **Dr. Krauss**
The survey of English literature draws together into a systematic narrative the
history of the development of literature in the English language. The course
enables students to secure a sound background in English literature as a historical development, to become acquainted with a great number of masterpieces,
and to fill in gaps in their reading. Part II carries the study from 1660 to
1800.
10:30-11:25 A.M.   30 hours   Credit: 2 semester-hours   Room B

English S407—British and American Biography   **Mr Conrad**
Both the old and new types of biography are read and studied in this course,
with emphasis upon the nineteenth and twentieth centuries. Biography is presented for its cultural and informational values, for its use in integrating the
work of the various departments in the high school, and for its direct help in
the vocational guidance program.
11:30 A.M.-12-25 P.M. 30 hours Credit: 2 semester-hours CHS—Auditorium

English S419—Grammar for Teachers   **Dr. Fulcomer**
This course is a study of the basic facts of grammatical relationships in English, and of the current problems of "rules" as opposed to "usage." The problems of how much grammar to teach and how to teach it are given practical
application by analysis of typical high school themes. The primary aim of the
course is to acquaint students with the true function of grammar in speech and
writing.
9:30-10:25 A.M.   30 hours   Credit: 2 semester-hours   Room 1

English S430—Reading in Secondary Schools   **Dr. Sperle**
The study of reading interests and activities at various age levels in a school-
wide program is undertaken. Methods of bridging the gap between undeveloped
reading skills and the necessity for using these skills in content subjects are
discussed and analyzed. Problems of vocabulary building, selected reading
materials, and improving comprehension complete the course.
11:30 A.M.-12-25 P.M.   30 hours   Credit: 2 semester-hours   Room 8

English S431A—Shakespeare and the English Drama, Part I   **Mr. Bohn**
The main emphasis of this course is upon eight Shakespearean tragedies and
chronicle plays: Hamlet, Othello, King Lear, Macbeth, Richard II, Henry IV (part
one). Henry V, and Richard III. The topics studied include Shakespeare's conception of tragedy; his dramatic art; his poetry; the sources of his plays;
staging in Shakespeare's theatre and in our own; typical textual problems; and
aids for the teaching of Shakespeare in the secondary school.
11:30 A.M.-12:25 P.M.   30 hours   Credit: 2 semester-hours   Room A

English S442B—American Literature: A Pageant of American
Democracy, Part II   **Mr. Conrad**
This course surveys the development of American literature from the Civil War to the contemporary period. The writers studied include: Walt Whitman, Sidney Lanier, Emily Dickinson, William Dean Howells, Mark Twain, Henry James, Henry Adams, Hamlin Garland, Stephen Crane, Frank Norris, O. Henry, Vachel Lindsay, E. A. Robinson, Carl Sandburg, and Robert Frost.
10:30-11:25 A.M.   30 hours   Credit: 2 semester-hours   CHS-Auditorium

Foreign Languages

French S101B—French Civilization: Early Periods, Part II   **Mrs. Cressey**
This Freshman course presents the background for all subsequent linguistic and literary studies in French. Special attention is devoted to bringing all the students up to a uniform level of development in speaking, reading, and writing French. The material used is French history and mediaeval literature. The course is conducted in French.
9:30-10:25 A.M.   30 hours   Credit: 2 semester-hours   Room 9

French S202B—Seventeenth Century Literature, Part IV   **Mrs. Cressey**
In this course a study is made of Moliere and Racine against the background of Seventeenth Century French Theatre. The course is conducted in French.
11:30 A.M.-12:25 P.M.   30 hours   Credit: 2 semester hours   Room 9

French S301B—Eighteenth Century Literature, Part II   **Mrs. Cressey**
This course deals with the novel and the theatre in the Eighteenth Century in France. The course is conducted in French.
10:30-11:25 A.M.   30 hours   Credit: 2 semester-hours   Room 9

Language S300—Foundations of Language   **Miss Littlefield**
A comprehensive survey is made of the background, growth, and structure of the English language, traced from its remote Indo-European ancestry down through the changes wrought by foreign additions and influence. By a systematic and comparative study of the main elements of Greek, Latin, French, Anglo-Saxon, and English, and of the phonetic phenomena recurring in language development, the course presents and augments the important diction values derived from foreign language study. It aims especially to train teachers of general language or of exploratory courses in foreign languages.
1:00-1:55 P.M.   30 hours   Credit: 2 semester-hours   Room 10

Language S401W—The Teaching of Foreign Languages in
Secondary Schools   **Dr. Freeman**
The work of this course is focused on such topics as the following: values of foreign language teaching; ultimate and immediate aims in foreign language teaching; survey of the out-standing methods; pronunciation, oral work, reading, grammar; reviews, realia, examinations, tests; supervised study, etc. The course consists of readings and discussions, lesson planning and demonstrations, and organization of materials for use in teaching.
8:30-9:25 A.M.   30 hours   Credit: 2 semester-hours   Room 10

Language S415—War Languages   **Miss Littlefield**
This course presents a practical introduction to the learning of any foreign language. Through the use of International Phonetic Symbols and Linguaphone Records, students acquire skill in the recognition and identification of foreign speech sounds. Ear, lip, and tongue training are combined to ensure adequate ability in the pronunciation of foreign sounds with scientific accuracy. The course is designed for all students in the language field, but especially for all men and women who intend to enter the Armed Forces, the Intelligence Division, Signal Corps, or any department of the war effort requiring acquaintance with foreign speech. Now that our troops are being brought into contact with every type of linguistic expression throughout the world, the practical value of this course in war languages is easily apparent.
9:30-10:25 A.M.   30 hours   Credit: 2 semester-hours   Room 10

Latin S101B—The Golden Age: Masterpieces of Prose
.Literature, Part II   **Miss Littlefield**
Livy and Cicero are the two authors studied intensively in this course. Selected readings of Livy supply interesting material for the discussion of Roman history, and Cicero's De Senectute introduces the student to a study of ancient philosophy.   •
8:30-9:25 A.M.   30 hours   · Credit: 2 semester-hours   Room 7

Latin S202B—The Silver Age: Anthology of Latin Poetry,
Part II   **Miss Littlefield**
This course is designed to present the works of Latin poets. Selected excerpts from the Anthology are studied with the aim of bringing out the inherent differences between the Golden and Silver Ages of Latin writing.
11:30 A.M.-12:25 P.M.   30 hours   Credit: 2 semester-hours   Room 7

Latin S302B—Roman Philosophy: Lucretius, Part II   **Dr. Freeman**
The Reading of Lucretius' "De Rerum Natura" serves to introduce the student to the evolution of abstract thought as developed in Greek and Roman philosophy.
10:30-11:25 A.M.   30 hours   Credit: 2 semester-hours   Room 10

Spanish S101B—Spanish Civilization, Part II   **Miss Escoriaza**
This course is designed to introduce the student to the important eras in Spanish civilization with a view to building up the background out of which the Spanish civilization of the New World developed. Prerequisite: three years of high school Spanish; two years in special cases. The course is conducted in Spanish.
9:30-10-25 A.M.   30 hours   Credit: 2 semester-hours   Room E

Spanish S202B—Hispanic-American Civilization: Lower South
American Area, Part II   **Miss Escoriaza**
This course is designed to present outstanding features in the civilization and history of the following South American Republics: Chile, Argentina, Uruguay, and Paraguay. The course is conducted in Spanish.
11:30 A.M.-12:25 P.M.   30 hours   Credit: 2 semester-hours   Room E

Spanish S302B—The Spanish Classics, Part II   **Miss Escoriaza**
The aim of this course is to present to advanced students of Spanish the life and dramatic works of Calderon de la Barca and of Tirso de Molina.
10:30-11:25 A.M.   30 hours   Credit: 2 semester-hours   Room E

Geography

Geography S409—Economic Geography of the British Isles   **Dr. Milstead**
A comprehensive treatment of the resources of the British Isles is given and the influence of the natural environment upon the utilization of those resources in the economic, social, and political development of the British Empire.
8:30-9:25 A.M.   30 hours   Credit: 2 semester-hours   Room 26

Geography S411—Geographic Influences in American History   **Dr. Milstead**
A study is made of the geographic factors influencing the development of social, economic, and political life in America. It is recommended especially to students of history and related subjects.
9:30-10:25 A.M.   30 hours   Credit: 2 semseter-hours   Room 26

Geography S503—Economic Geography of the United States   **Dr. Milstead**
A study is made of the agricultural, industrial, and commercial development of the United States and of the geographic factors that have contributed to that development.
11:30 A.M.-12:25 P.M.   30 hours   Credit: 2 semester-hours   Room 26

Integration

Integration S100A & B—Social Interpretation of Education **Mr. Jackson**
The purposes of this course are: the orientation of students to life at the College; an appreciation of the purposes, the pleasures and the responsibilities of teaching; an understanding of the contributions of education to the evolution of social patterns; and the beginnings of an analytical attitude toward teaching.
8:30-9:25 A.M. 30 hours Credit: 2 semester-hours Room 8

Integration S200A—Introduction to Educational Psychology and Mental
Testing **Dr. Plant and Mrs. Tirrell**
Growth and development of child and adolescent personality are studied from the physical, intellectual, social, and emotional aspects—through readings, class discussions, and individual child study projects. The relation of testing to the problems of understanding children as learners, and to the problem of treating individual differences is studied through testing projects.
8:30-9:25 A.M. 30 hours Credit: 2 semester-hours Room 30

Integration S300B—Principles and Techniques of Teaching in
Secondary Schools **Dr. Sperle**
After having established the fundamental principles underlying the teaching process, the following techniques and procedures are presented and evaluated: the question, the lesson plan, the assignment, testing and marking systems, classroom management and routine; and special procedures, such as supervised study. In addition to the above topics, based on subject-matter organization and administration, various types of classroom procedure are considered.
10:30-11:25 A.M. 30 hours Credit: 2 semester-hours Room 8

Integration S400A—Principles and Philosophy of Secondary
Education **Dr. W. Scott Smith**
This course evaluates educational objectives, techniques, procedures, and organizations in relation to the needs and demands made upon the school by society and by the developing personality. It involves a discussion of the meaning of philosophy and an interpretation of human values. Fundamental principles of education are evolved from previous work in the various fields of thought contributing to educational philosophy.
9:30-10:25 A.M. 30 hours Credit: 2 semester-hours Room 27

Integration S412—The Teaching of Social Competence **Miss Sherwin**
This course is planned to enable the classroom teacher to become acquainted with the personal and social interests, problems, and needs of her students and to increase her own personnel counseling ability. It is organized to help her increase the student's social effectiveness, ease of manner, graciousness, and correct conduct and bearing in school, college, and community life. Personality traits, good grooming, and acceptable habit patterns are discussed. Possible handicaps and limitations are considered and constructively studied. Through reading materials, lectures and discussions, social experiences and observations, and classroom dramatizations the class learns and practices the teaching of satisfying social techniques.
1:00-1:55 P.M. 30 hours Credit: 2 semester-hours Room 6

Integration S500AW—History and Principles of Secondary Education **Dr. Sperle**
This course traces the development of secondary education. Consideration is given to the meaning of liberal education as it was conceived by earlier civilizations. Special attention is given to organizations, curricula, and methods of instruction, and to the social conditions affecting the development of secondary schools in England, Germany, France, and the United States.
9:30-10:25 A.M. 30 hours Credit: 2 semester-hours Room 8

13

Integration S500CW—Teaching Procedures in Secondary Education Mr. Seybold

This course emphasizes the fundamental principles underlying the technique of teaching on the secondary school level. Some of the topics considered are: organization of knowledge; the logical and psychological aspects of method; developing appreciations; social-moral education; teaching motor control; fixing motor responses; books and verbalism; meeting individual differences, guidance in study; tests and examinations; marks and marking.

10:30-11:25 A.M.   30 hours   Credit: 2 semester-hours   Room 3-CHS

**Integration S502A—Organization and Administration of the Modern
High School, Part I   Dr. Ryan**

The problems considered are: the student personnel; building and revising the high school curriculum; providing for individual differences; making the school schedule; records; the guidance program; pupil participation in government; the extra-curricular program; the health program; the safety program; discipline; library and study hall; cafeteria; the principal's office; and evaluating results.

10:30-11:25 A.M.   30 hours   Credit: 2 semester-hours   Room 6

Integration S503—Methods and Instruments of Research   Mr. Jackson

This course is required of all candidates for the Master's degree without regard to their fields of major interest. Its purpose is to introduce students of education to research and its practical application to immediate problems. The course treats; the nature and types of educational research; methods and techniques of educational research; and the tools used in interpreting statistical data. During the course, the student sets up a problem and plans and carries out its solution.

1:00-1:55 P.M.   30 hours   Credit: 2 semester-hours   Room 8

**Integration S504A—Curriculum Construction in the Secondary
School   Dr. W. Scott Smith**

This course purposes to introduce the student to constructive criticism of American culture, to consider the extent to which the secondary school curriculum meets the needs of a changing civilization, and to consider effective means of curriculum construction.

11:30 A.M.-12-25 P.M.   30 hours   Credit: 2 semester-hours   Room 27

**Integration S505—Organization and Administration of Extra-
Curricular Activities   Dr. W. Scott Smith**

The first part of this course considers such general problems of extra-curricular activities as: their growing importance; their relation to the curriculum; the principles underlying their organization, administration, and supervision; and methods of financing. In the second part, an intensive study is made of the home room, the assembly, the student council, clubs, athletics, school publications, and other activities in which the class is especially interested.

10:30-11:25 A.M.   30 hours   Credit: 2 semester-hours   Room 27

Integration S508A—Supervision and Criticism of Teaching, Part I Mr. Seybold

Among the topics are: the set-up for adequate supervision; supervision as encouraging and guiding the growth of teachers and the improvement of educational procedures; the supervisory functions of teachers' meetings; discussion groups; general and professional reading; the writing of articles; cooperative curriculum modification; utilization of community resources; and teacher inter-visitation.

11:30 A.M.-12-25 P.M.   30 hours   Credit: 2 semester-hours   Room 3-CHS

14

Integration S515—Guidance and Personnel Problems of Classroom Teachers   **Mr. Seybold**

This course considers all types of personnel problems with which the classroom teacher deals. It is concerned with the growth of pupils and seeks to point out the ways by which proper growth may be attained. Classroom, health, social, and personal activities are analyzed in terms of the needs of present-day social life.

8:30-9:25 A.M.   30 hours   Credit: 2 semester-hours   Room 3-CHS

Integration S516—School Finance   **Mr. Chase**

This course is of special interest to school administrators, since it acquaints them with the field of finance in relation to a well-ordered school program. The topics considered are: basic problems of school support; systems of taxation; allocation of costs; computing school costs; sources of information; techniques; comparative costs; purchasing; and standards.

9:30-10:25 A.M.   30 hours   Credit: 2 semester-hours   Room 29

Integration S517—Administration of the Elementary School   **Mr. Chase**

This course analyzes and evaluates the administrative duties and relationships of the elementary school principal. Particular consideration is given to: building management; effective use of the school plant; sanitation, health service; the library; personnel management; the administration of the curriculum; community relationships; and publicity.

8:30-9:25 A.M.   30 hours   Credit: 2 semester-hours.   Room 29

Integration S521—Psychological Tests in Guidance Programs   **Dr. Plant and Mrs. Tirrell**

This course is designed to familiarize the student with the various psychological tests and scales that may be used in guidance programs in the secondary school. The student is given practice in administering many types of group tests. This includes scoring the tests and evaluating the results, with a discussion of ways in which these results may be used. Much time is spent in actual laboratory demonstrations of tests, giving students an opportunity to serve as subjects and as examiners. Class discussion is based upon first-hand information gained through the use of the tests, on readings, and on class reports.

10:30-11:25 A.M.   30 hours   Credit: 2 semester-hours   Room 30

Integration S524—The Study of the Failing Pupil   **Dr. Ryan**

The first part of the course is devoted to the "disparity technique"—a method of evaluating the pupil's achievement in relation to his ability. The second part treats of procedures to be used in finding the causes of failure, and in planning treatment.

9:30-10:25 A.M.   30 hours   Credit: 2 semester-hours   Room 6

Integration S535—Vocational Guidance   **Dr. Plant and Mrs. Tirrell**

This course is especially intended to enable high school teachers to guide their pupils in planning for constructive vocational life. It is based upon the idea that real guidance must be self-guidance on the part of the pupil; the goal is therefore a growing independence of judgment on the part of the person who is being guided. The course is designed to be helpful also to adults who are seeking better vocational adjustment. Following are the topics included: the purpose of work; main areas of work; inventory of personal interests and traits; analyzing interests and traits; samples of personal inventories with analyses and interviews; exploring one's area of work; making the most of school days; finding the first job; adjustments on the way; who can expect to hold the higher positions; advancement—what it is and how to attain it; intelligent use of money; balanced use of time; and, cultivating pride of work.

11:30 A.M.-12-25 P.M.   30 hours   Credit: 2 semester-hours   Room 30

Workshops

**Integration..S601A—Workshop, Section I: Current Problems in Managing
the School**   **Dr. Ryan and Staff**

Problems in administration; guidance programs; curriculum construction; extra-curricular activities; finance; educational philosophy.

8:30-9:25 A.M.   60 hours   Credit: 4 semester-hours   Room 6

**Integration S601B—Workshop, Section II: Current Problems in
Directing Instruction**   **Dr. Ryan and Staff**

Problems in supervision; teaching techniques; curriculum experimentation; evaluation; corrective reading, multi-sensory aids.

8:30-9:25 A.M.   60 hours   Credit: 4 semester-hours   Room 6

**Integration S601C—Workshop, Section III: Current Problems in
Understanding Youth**   **Dr. Ryan and Staff**

Problems in adolescent psychology; "human relations;" mental hygiene; the teacher in guidance; educational sociology; community relations; the visiting teacher.

8:30-9:25 A.M.   60 hours   Credit: 4 semester-hours   Room 6

Each of these three Workshops is conducted as follows:
1. Under the supervision of the Director, general conference periods are held each week as arranged.
2. Conferences between the individual student and a special consultant are held by appointment.
3. Free unassigned time for individual study is allowed.

The work includes the definition, study, evaluation, and report on each individual problem.

Mathematics

Mathematics S102B—Mathematical Analysis, Part IV—Analytical Geometry   **Mr. Clifford**

This course is recommended particularly to those students seeking a minor in mathematics or those in need of a review course in analytic geometry. The topics include; rectangular and polar coordinate systems: loci and their equations; the straight line; the conics—circle, parabola, ellipse, and hyperbola; parametric equations; transformation of coordinates; and the general equation of the second degree.

9:30-10-25 A.M.   30 hours   Credit: 2 semester-hours   Room 2

Mathematics S300—The Social and Commercial Uses of Mathematics   **Dr. Fehr**

The aims of this course are: first, a consideration of the mathematical problems which are met in everyday life or general reading; and second, the establishment of a background for the teaching of junior high school mathematics. Some of the topics treated are: fundamental operations, graphs, solution of problems, numerical geometry, percentage, budgeting, installment buying, investments, banking, taxation, and insurance.

8:30-9:25 A.M.   30 hours   Credit: 2 semester-hours   Room 5

Mathematics S304B—Spherical Trigonometry, Part II   **Dr. Fehr**

This course treats the geometry of sphere and the solution of right and oblique spherical triangles. Applications are made to navigation and astronomy through a study of the terrestrial and celestial spheres. A knowledge of plane trigonometry is prerequisite.

9:30-10:25 A.M.   30 hours   Credit: 2 semester-hours   Room 5

**Mathematics S401W—The Teaching of Mathematics in Secondary
Schools**   **Dr. Davis**

In this course, special consideration is given to specific problems which arise in the teaching of junior and senior high school mathematics. These include the following: adaptation of material to students of varying abilities; selection and treatment of subject matter; use of texts and supplementary material; importance of the fundamental concepts; use of special methods and devices; how to treat the more difficult phases of the subject matter; and the preparation of students for college entrance examinations.

8:30-9:25 A.M.   30 hours   Credit: 2 semester-hours   Room 3

Mathematics S406B—Applications of Mathematics, Part II Mr. Clifford

The course applies the use of surveying instruments in motivating the teaching of mathematics in the junior and senior high school. The material studied is of special value to teachers of slow-moving ninth grade pupils. Topics considered are: the use of transit and level to determine elevations, inaccessible distances, areas, volumes, etc., mapping with the plane table; use of planimeter, pantograph, hand level hypsometer. cross staff, angle mirror, and sextant; the various types of slide rules, the accuracy obtained, and the fundamental ideas of approximate computation; and graphic representation of data. The method for constructing inexpensive instruments is shown.

11:30 A.M.-12:25 P.M. 30 hours Credit: 2 semester-hours Room 2

Mathematics S410—Introduction to the Mathematics of Finance
                and Insurance Mr. Clifford

This course introduces the student to the elementary theory of simple and compound interest and leads to the solution of practical problems in annuities, sinking funds, amortization, depreciation, stocks and bonds, installment buying, and building and loan associations. It also discusses the mathematics of life insurance covering the following subjects: the theory of probability as related to life insurance; the theory and calculation of mortality tables; various types of life annuities and insurance policies; and reserves. This course is designed to give a helpful background to the mathematics teacher as well as to be an aid to the student of economics and insurance.

10:30-11:25 A.M. 30 hours Credit: 2 semester-hours Room 2

Mathematics S509A—A Critical Interpretation of Mathematics
                in the Senior High School Part I Dr. Fehr

This course offers an investigation and interpretation of the algebra and geometry of the secondary school. The meaning and logical foundations of secondary school mathematics are stressed as essential to further application. Among the topics discussed are: algebra as a thought process and its mechanical operations; types of thinking in algebra and geometry; fundamental laws of algebra; geometrical interpretations of algebra; the function concept; the changing scope and subject matter of geometry; limits and incommensurables; and applications of geometry and algebra to military and naval problems.

11:30 A. M.-12:25 P.M 30 hours Credit: 2 semester-hours Room 5

Mathematics S511—Foundations of Geometry Dr. Davis

A critical study is made of the axioms and postulates which form the foundation of Euclidean and non-Euclidean geometries. This includes Pasch's axiom, the principle of continuity, the postulates of Archimedes and of Dedekind. the parallel postulate. From these premises, the development of Euclidean, of Hyperbolic Non-Euclidean, and of Elliptic Non-Euclidean geometry is carefully traced. Also, a brief survey of the historical development of each subject is given. This course is designed for teachers and students of mathematics who desire a proper perspective of the field of synthetic geometry.

9:30-10:25 A.M. 30 hours Credit: 2 semester-hours Room 3

Physical Education

Physical Education S406—Games and Game Skills Mr. Pittser

This course includes a close study and practice of all physical activities which conform to the requirements of the Army and Navy for the training and conditioning of students for Military Service. The Victory Corps Manual is used as a guide. Calisthenics. individual skills, stunts, combative stunts, sports, and games, rough and tumble team games, and indoor and outdoor obstacle courses are stressed.

10:30-11:25 A.M. 30 hours Credit: 2 semester-hours Room 4, CHS

17

Physical Education S407—Safety Education   **Mr. Pittser**

Safety is the latest subject to be placed in the curriculum of elementary and secondary schools. There is a need for teachers who can teach safety and organize safety programs. A study is made of the causes which have made this an important subject and of its place in our present-day method of living. What to teach and how to teach it constitutes much of the course. Sources of reliable material for use by the teacher are made available.

9:30-10-25 A.M.   30 hours   Credit: 2 semester-hours   Room 4, CHS

Physical Education S410—Principles and Philosophy of Physical Education   **Mr. Pittser**

This course is designed to orient the student to the breadth and scope of the field of physical education and to develop a workable philosophy which will meet today's needs. The contents of the course include the following items: a brief history of physical education; development of physical education in the United States; basic principles upon which a program of physical education is developed; different philosophies of physical education; administrative problems; legal matters in the field of physical education.

8:30-9:25 A.M.   30 hours   Credit: 2 semester-hours   Room 4, CHS

Science

Biology S408—Biological Technique   **Dr. Hadley**

This course is designed to furnish the prospective teacher of biology with the technical details necessary to enable him, as a secondary school teacher, to handle successfully biological materials and experiments and demonstrations in which these materials are employed. Students are trained in methods of collecting and preserving plants and animals for use in the laboratory and classroom. Study is made of the proper methods of preparing illustrative materials, with special emphasis laid upon the purpose of these materials. Prerequisite: A minimum of four semester-hours of experience in Biology or its equivalent.

11:30 A.M.-12:25 P.M., Mon. and Fri. Lab: 1:00-5:00 P.M., Tu. and Thurs..
     60 hours   Credit: 3 semester-hours   Room 28

Biology S501—The Teaching of Biology   **Dr. Hadley**

This is a seminar and research course designed to give opportunity for study of the best methods and practices being used in the teaching of secondary school biology. Major topics of discussion are: aims of a secondary school biology course, course content, functions of text-books, testing, laboratory exercises and demonstrations, and the collection and use of suitable and available laboratory materials. A study is made of recent research studies in the field of biology teaching. Open to teachers and prospective teachers of biology who have completed a minimum of 18 semester-hours in biological fields.

8:00-9:25 A.M.   45 hours   Credit: 3 semester-hours   Room 28

Chemistry S102—General College Chemistry   **Dr. Reed**

This course covers the chemistry of acids, carbon compounds, and metals. It meets eight class periods and two afternoons in laboratory a week for six weeks. The laboratory work is mainly qualitative in nature and is supplemented by lecture demonstrations and reports.

9:30-10:25 A.M., daily; 10:30-11:25 A.M., Mon., Wed., Fri.; Lab.: Tu. and Thurs.,
1:00-5:00 P.M.   90 hours   Credit: 4 semester-hours   Room 23

Chemistry S407B—Analytical Chemistry: Applied Quantitative Analysis Dr. Reed

This course offers experience in practical analysis which will enable the student to understand the use of analytical chemistry in control work in industry and various fields of science. The work covers practical problems and is adapted to pupils' needs and experiences. 11:30 A.M.-12:25 P.M., Tu., Wed., Thurs. Lab.:
1:00-5:00 P.M., Mon.   45 hours   Credit: 2 semester-hours   Room 23

Physics S102—General College Physics   **Dr. K. O. Smith**

The major objective of physical science is to discover, describe, correlate, and explain the facts and phenomena of the inanimate world. For convenience, the subject-matter of physics is classified as: mechanics, heat, magnetism and electricity, sound, and light. The course consists of lectures, demonstrations, discussions, problem-solving exercises, library assignments, and laboratory experiments. The work of this course pertains to the nature and propagation of sound, musical instruments, wave motion, the nature of light, optical instruments, color, spectra, polarization of light, magnetism, static electricity, electricity in motion, and electro-magnetic induction.

9:30-10:25 A.M., daily; 10:30-11:25 A.M., Mon., Wed., Fri., Lab: Tu. and Thurs., 1:00-5:00 P.M.   90 hours   Credit: 4 semester-hours   Room 25

Physics S301—Photography for High School Teachers   **Dr. K. O. Smith**

This is a beginning course in photography, consisting of lectures, demonstrations, laboratory work, and field work. The topics covered are similar to those outlined in "Basic Photography," published by the United States Air Corps. Some of the topics are: construction and operation of cameras; the nature of chemical changes encountered in photographic work; developing and printing negatives and positives; taking pictures both indoors and outdoors; taking pictures at night; making lantern slides; and projection printing. A student needs at least one camera for the course.

10:30-11:25 A.M., Tu., 11:30-12-25 P.M., Mon. and Fri.; Lab: 1:00-5:00 P.M., Wed.   30 hours   Credit: 2 semester-hours   Room 8-CHS

Social Studies

Social Studies S101B—European History from 1713 to 1815   **Dr. Folsom**

The rise of Russia and the rise of Prussia are treated. Primary consideration is given, however, to the political, economic, social, and intellectual conditions in France preceding the French Revolution; the French Revolution itself; and the Napoleonic period; with the inauguration of the spirit of nationalism.

9:30-10:25 A.M   30 hours   Credit: 2 semester-hours   Room 21

Social Studies S102B—European History from 1870 to the Present Day   **Dr. Folsom**

The course discusses domestic problems in Germany, France, and Russia from 1870 to the World War in the light of the present world situation. The economic imperialism and international diplomacy of European states as they affected the Balkans, Africa, and the Far East form a major part of the course. Contemporary world affairs throughout serve as a basis for interpreting the European developments in modern times.

11:30 A.M.-12-25 P.M.   30 hours   Credit: 2 semester-hours   Room 21

Social Studies S201B—American History from 1789 to 1860   **Dr. Snyder.**

The central interest during this period is the founding of the nation. The expansion of the nation territorially, the progress of the idustrialization of the North, the rise of the new West and the new Democracy, and the great struggle over slavery are the chief landmarks.

10:30-11:25 A.M.   30 hours   Credit: 2 semester-hours   Room 20

Social Studies S301A—Economics I   **Mr. Rellahan**

Emphasis is given to a study of the background of present-day economic institutions, and the manner in which the present system functions with respect to the economic and business organization of production, the nature and laws of consumption, the principles involved in the determination of value and price under competition or monopoly; and the problem of distribution as related to an explanation of rent, interest, wages, and profits.

8:30-9:25 A.M.   30 hours   Credit: 2 semester-hours   Room 22

Social Studies S301B—Economics II   **Mr. Rellahan**

This course is a continuation of Economics I, which is not, however, prerequisite. The aim of this course is to acquaint the student with the basic economic principles and problems relating to risk and insurance; money, credit, and banking; general price changes and their control; foreign trade and exchange; tariffs, international debts, and imperialism; business combinations; and governmental regulation of business enterprise.

11:30 A.M.-12:30 P.M.   30 hours   Credit: 2 semeter-hours   Room 22

Social Studies S401—The Teaching of the Social Studies
in Secondary Schools   **Dr. Snyder**

The course aims to present recent tendencies in educational method in teaching the social studies. A program is presented containing the fusion organization of the social studies in socialized recitation, the teaching of current events, projects in citizenship, and the use of the project-problem as a method of teaching history and civics. A laboratory containing texts and workbooks in the social studies field and other illustrative and concrete material is available to the students of this course.

8:00-9:25 A.M.   45 hours   Credit: 3 semester-hours   Room 20

Social Studies S407—New Jersey State and Local Government   **Mr. Bye**

The old and new State Constitutions of New Jersey are compared, and a study is made of New Jersey's place in the federal system; the rights and duties of citizens; suffrage; political parties; the legislative, the executive, and administrative systems; the courts; the law enforcement and correctional systems; revenues and expenditures; public health, educational, highway and other services; county and municipal government; and other local political units.

8:30-9:25 A.M.   30 hours   Credit: 2 semester-hours   Room 24

Social Studies S420A—The European Outlook, Part I   **Dr. Wittmer**

This course is designed to explain the conditions and events which have led to the present war. The first part presents each of Europe's nations in the light of its traditional influences. The historical perspective of the forces contending for supremacy in Europe today is emphasized throughout.

1:00-1:55 P.M.   30 hours   Credit: 2 semester-hours   Room 12, CHS

Social Studies S426B—Medieval History, Part II   **Dr. Folsom**

The course deals with the later Middle Ages in its political, economic, and cultural aspects. The development of England and France toward strong monarchies is contrasted with the disintegrating influences in the Germanies and Italy and the declining power of the Church over all. Economic growth in towns, commerce and industry, and the cultural changes, from Scholasticism through the Renaissance, form an important part of the course.

10:30-11:25 A.M.   30 hours   Credit: 2 semester-hours   Room 21

Social Studies S433—American Political Thought   **Mr. Bye**

This is a survey of political thinking in America. It deals with contemporary trends and theories as they have emerged from social and economic conditions and as they are founded upon the bases laid down by such men as Hamilton, Madison, Washington, Jefferson, Marshall, Calhoun, Webster, Lincoln, Wilson, and others. A knowledge of American ideals as expressed in our political philosophy is especially important for teachers of American history, civics, and problems of democracy in this changing period through which we are passing.

9:30-10:25 A.M.   30 hours   Credit: 2 semester-hours   Room 24

Social Studies S436—Modern Men of Ancient Times   **Dr. Freeman**

This course is designed to present biographical sketches of some of the great leaders of past ages. The subjects for discussion are selected from all lines of human endeavor, and special attention is given to their influence on the thought of their own times and their contributions to the culture of the present day. The course is specially recommended to students who wish to know these leaders as real persons and not as lay figures in ancient history.

11:30 A.M.-12:25 P.M.   30 hours   Credit: 2 semester-hours   Room 10

Social Studies S437—The Political Party System in the United States   **Mr. Bye**

It is the custom of the college to offer this course during the summer preceding the election of a President of the United States, with special attention to the current pre-election activities. In this course an objective study is made of the dynamics of practical politics. Among the topics discussed are: party organization; the political boss; the political machine; party finances; the process of voting; election laws; primaries; conventions; platforms; presidential elections; majority rule; the development of the party systems; sectional politics; the farm vote; the labor vote; and the future of party government in the United States.

11:30 A.M.-12-25 P.M.   30 hours   Credit: 2 semester-hours   Room 24

Social Studies S451—The Middle East   **Dr. Wittmer**

This course is devoted to a survey of Indian and Moslem civilizations. It reviews the cultural traditions of the peoples of the Middle East and studies the alternations and adjustments that they must make in order to take part and be happy in the fast-moving mechanized civilization of the twentieth century. It considers the problems of post-war planning for the region from the Near East through Persia, India, Burma, Thailand, and Malaya to the Netherland East Indies.

9:30-10:25 A.M.   30 hours   Credit: 2 semester-hours   Room 12, CHS

Social Studies S454—Post-War Economic Recostruction   **Mr. Rellahan**

The purpose of this course is to provide the student with the essentials necessary to appreciate the impact of reconstruction following the war upon existing economic institutions. Emphasis is placed upon Congressional plans for reconversion, the post-war public debt and related fiscal policies; the political economy of regional economic regulations, cartels, and foreign investments; the post-war distributive system; international monetary policy; labor and social security; post-war agriculture; and American economic philosophy as a national policy.

10:30-11:25 A.M.   30 hours   Credit: 2 semester-hours   Room 22

Graduate Department

Graduate S500—Seminar: Master's Thesis

Students writing a thesis for credit toward the Master's degree in any department of the college are required to register for this course. The work is conducted under seminar or individual guidance. Students report to the Dean of Instruction, who calls a conference with the Head of Department and the Sponsor. At this meeting, all matters pertaining to the topic, plan of research, writing of manuscript, etc., are arranged.

Credit: 4 semester-hours

21

TWELVE WEEKS SUMMER TERM, 1944

The following courses will be given beginning May 22, 1944. Those marked with the Roman numeral "I" will end Friday, June 30. All other courses in this list will continue until August 15. For descriptions and credit, see the regular undergraduate catalogue of the college.

Department	Cat. No.	Title of Course	Instructor
Art	I. 100	Art Appreciation	Dr. Cayley
Business Ed.	407	Principles of Accounting	Mr. Sheppard
	302	Salesmanship	Mr. Sheppard
	201	Junior Business Training	Mr. Sheppard
English	I. 451	Literature and Art in Western Culture	Dr. Cayley
	I. 446	The One Act Play	Mr. Bohn
	I. 445	18th Century Literature	Mr. Bohn
	I. 421	The Short Story	Mr. Conrad
	I. 406	The Modern Novel	Mr. Conrad
	I. 405	The Victorian Poets	Mr. Nickerson
	402	Survey of British Literature to 1798	Dr. Krauss
	I. 312	Acting, Directing, and Make-up	Mr. Bohn
	302	Survey of American Literature	Mr. Conrad
	I. 301B	Shakespeare's Major Plays	Dr. Krauss
	201	British and American Poetry	Mr. Nickerson
	102	British and American Drama	Dr. Krauss
	I. 100A	World Literature, Part I	Mr. Nickerson
	I. 100B	World Literature, Part II	Dr. Cayley
French	301	18th Century French Literature	Mrs. Cressey
	202	17th Century French Literature	Mrs. Cressey
	101	French Civilization: Early Periods ...	Mrs. Cressey
Language	I. 415	War Languages	Miss Littlefield
	I. 300	Foundations of Language	Miss Littlefield
Latin	302	Lucretius	Dr. Freeman
	202	Anthology of Latin Poetry	Miss Littlefield
	101	The Golden Age: Masterpieces of Prose Literature	Miss Littlefield
Spanish	I. 407	New World Before Columbus	Dr. Freeman
	302	Spanish Drama	Miss Escoriaza
	202	Hispanic-American Civilization	Miss Escoriaza
	101	Spanish Civilization	Miss Escoriaza
Geography	I. 410	Economic Geography of Caribbean America	Dr. Milstead
	I. 412	Geography of Africa, Australia, and New Zealand	Dr. Milstead
Integration	I. 400A	Principles and Philosophy of Secondary Education	Mr. Seybold and Dr. W. Scott Smith
	I. 300A	Aims and Organization of Secondary Education	Dr. W. Scott Smith
	I. 200A	Educational Psychology and Mental Testing	Dr. Ingebritsen

Department	Cat. No.	Title of Course	Instructor
Mathematics	406	Applications of Mathematics	Mr. Clifford
	I. 400	Educational Statistics	Dr. Fehr
	302	Higher Algebra	Dr. Davis
	301	Modern College Geometry	Dr. Davis
	I. 300	Social and Commercial Uses of Mathematics	Mr. Clifford
	102	Mathematical Analysis	Mr. Clifford
Music	I. 302B	Choral Technique	Dr. McEachern
	I. 301A	Music Literature	Dr. McEachern
	I. 100	Music Appreciation	Dr. McEachern
Chemistry	101, 102	General College Chemistry	Dr. Reed
	407	Analytical Chemistry	Dr. Reed
Physics	101, 102	General College Physics	Dr. K. O. Smith
Science	I. 417	Meteorology	Dr. Milstead
Social Studies	I. 450A	Applied Economics, Part I	Mr. Rellahan
	I. 442	The Far East	Dr. Wittmer
	I. 428	Racial Contributions to American Life	Mr. Bye
	426	Mediaeval History	Dr. Folsom
	420	The European Outlook	Dr. Wittmer
	I. 402A	American Government	Mr. Bye
	I. 402B	Comparative Government	Mr. Bye
	301	Economics	Mr. Rellahan
	I. 200A	Contemporary Economic Life	Mr. Rellahan
	102	European History, 1815 to the Present	Dr. Folsom
	101	European History, 1492 to 1815	Dr. Folsom

SUMMER SESSION

Bulletin of

MONTCLAIR
STATE TEACHERS COLLEGE

JULY 9 to AUGUST 17

1945

UPPER MONTCLAIR, NEW JERSEY

SUMMER SESSION

Bulletin of

Montclair
State Teachers College

1945

July 9 to August 17

Upper Montclair, New Jersey

STATE OFFICIALS
State Board of Education

Oscar W. Jeffery, *President* _____Englewood
Gustav A. Hunziker, *Vice President* _____Little Falls
D. Stewart Craven _____Salem
Mrs. Edward L. Katzenbach _____Princeton
D. Howard Moreau _____Flemington
Joseph W. Mott_____Atlantic City
Miss May M. Carty _____Jersey City
Miss Mary E. Merchant _____Dover
Clarence E. Partch_____Stelton
Mrs. Olive C. Sanford_____Nutley

Committee on Teacher Education

Mrs. Edward L. Katzenbach, *Chairman*

D. Stewart Craven   Clarence E. Partch
Gustav A. Hunziker   Miss Mary E. Merchant

Mrs. Olive C. Sanford

Commissioner of Education

John H. Bosshart

Director of Teacher Education

Robert H. Morrison

Officers of Administration

Harry A. Sprague_____President
John D. Messick_____Dean of Instruction
Charlotte G. Marshall_____Registrar
Elizabeth S. Favor _____Secretary of Extension and Summer Session
Robert Levy _____Business Manager
Claude E. Jackson_____Director of Personnel and Research
Margaret A. Sherwin _____Dean of Women
Francis R. Geigle_____Head of Business Education Department
Edwin S. Fulcomer_____Head of English Department
Harold Spears_____Head of Intergration Department
Walter H. Freeman_____Head of Language Department
Virgil S. Mallory _____Head of Mathematics Department
Edna E. McEachern _____Head of Music Department
Earl R. Glenn _____Head of Science Department
W. Harry Snyder_____Head of Social Studies Department
Arthur M. Seybold_____Director of College High School
Louis A. Fralick_____Superintendent of Buildings

2

SUMMER SESSION 1945

FACULTY

Harry A. Sprague, Ph.D.--President

John D. Messick, Ph.D.----------------------------------Dean of Instruction

Franklin G. Armstrong, A.M.----------------------------Health Education

Richard T. Beck, Ph.D.------------------------------------Administration

Edgar C. Bye, A.M.--Social Studies

Lawrence H. Conrad, A.M. --------------------------------------English

Margaret G Cook, AB., B.S.--------------------------------------Librarian

David R. Davis, Ph.D.--Mathematics

Vera Brooke Davis, A.M.--------------------------------------Mathematics

Teresa DeEscoriaza, A.M. --------------------------------------Spanish

Howard Franklin Fehr, Ph.D.----------------------------------Mathematics

L. Howard Fox A.M.--English

Walter H. Freeman, Ph.D.----------Head of Dept. of Foreign Languages

Francis R. Geigle, Ed.D. ------Head of Department of Business Education

Charles E. Hadley, Ph. D. --Biology

Otis C. Ingebritsen, Ph.D.----------------------------------Psychology

Claude E. Jackson, A.M.------------------------------------Research

Mark Karp, Ph.D.--English

Ethel F. Littlefield, A.M.----------------------------------Languages

Harley P. Milstead, Ph.D. --------------------------------Geography

Rufus D. Reed, Ph.D.--------------------------------------Chemistry

John J. Rellahan, A.M.------------------------------------Social Studies

Arthur M. Seybold, A.M. ----------------------------------Integration

Horace J. Sheppard, A.M.------------------------------Business Education

Margaret A. Sherwin, A.M.--------------------------------Dean of Women

Kenneth O. Smith, Ph.D --Physics

W. Scott Smith, Ph.D. --------------------------------------Integration

W. Harry Snyder, Ph.D------------Head of Department of Social Studies

Harold Spears, Ed. D. --------------Head of Department of Integration

D. Henryetta Sperle, Ph. D.--------------------------------Integration

Mollie C. Winchester, A.M.----------------Librarian, College High School

Felix Wittmer, Ph.D.--------------------------------------Social Studies

3

General Objective

The New Jersey State Teachers College at Montclair is a professional school which prepares teachers, supervisors, principals of high schools, and administrators of public school systems. The degrees offered by this college are those of Bachelor of Arts and Master of Arts. Certificate courses are offered for those who now hold degrees.

How to Reach the Campus

Trains of the Greenwood Lake Division, Erie R. R., stop at College Station. Trains of the Lackawanna R. R. connect at Montclair with the following bus lines: No. 64, running between Brick Church and the college; No. 60, running between Newark and the college, and No. 76, which runs between Orange and Paterson, passing the college en route. For those who come by car: the college is located about one mile north of the center of Upper Montclair.

Residence Halls for Men and Women

Edward Russ Hall and Chapin Hall are **Montclair's** two well-appointed residences. The charge for living on campus during the Summer Session is reasonable: $12.00 per week; which includes room, breakfast, and dinner. A la carte luncheons are served in the college cafeteria. For one student alone in a double room, an extra charge of $2.00 per week is made. The college provides all furnishings, with the exception of towels, blankets, and desk lamps. The boarding-hall fee must be paid on or before the first day of the Summer Session. No rebate is made for occasional absence or voluntary withdrawal during the session. Students who are absent on account of illness for two weeks or more receive a rebate of $6.00 per week during the illness.

For reservations in the college residence hall, address: Director of Personnel, State Teachrs College, Upper Montclair, New Jersey.

Schedule of the Summer Session

The Summer begins on Monday, July 9, and continues through Friday, August 17, on which day the summer Commencement will be held. All courses meet daily, Monday through Friday, for one hour, except where definitely indicated otherwise.

Summer Term of Twelve Weeks

Included in this Bulletin of the Summer Session is a list of the courses of the Twelve Weeks Summer Term which is held for the benefit of the accelerated candidates for the Bachelor of Arts degree at Montclair. Other students who have special need of a minimum amount of credit may also enter these courses. The list of these courses appears on the last two

4

pages of this Bulletin. The 1944-1946 Catalogue of the college contains descriptions of the courses. The mimeographed schedule of the Twelve Weeks Summer Term and the Catalogue will be sent upon request. Registration and payment of fees for this Term must be made on Wednesday, May 23. Anyone desiring to enroll should report that day to the office of the Summer Session. Classes begin the same day and continue through August 17.

Matriculation

Students planning to matriculate for the Master of Arts degree should note that not more than 8 semester-hours of credit earned prior to matriculation is accepted toward the degree.

Those who desire to become candidates for either the Bachelor of Arts or the Master of Arts degree at **Montclair** must request the Registrar for the application form and return it, properly filled in and accompanied by an official transcript of all previous work on college level. When such an applicant has been accepted by the college as a candidate for the degree, a definite statement will be furnished to him, showing the requirements which he must fulfill to earn it.

Auditors

Men and women who desire to take courses for cultural, vocational. or avocational purposes without college credit may register as auditors.

Students Matriculated at Montcalir

Work taken for credit at **Montclair** must be with the advice and approval of the Dean of Instruction and the Head of the Department in which the student is majoring. See paragraph under the heading: "**Conferences.**"

A student who expects to receive a degree should advise with the Registrar three months in advance of graduation.

Students Matriculated at Other Colleges

Work taken for credit to be transferred to other colleges should be approved in advance by the Dean of the college at which the student holds membership. Such students who are planning to attend **Montclair** this summer should take the Summer Session Bulletin to a conference with their Deans to arrange a program of work. For the Deans' information: the numbering of courses at **Montclair** follows this order: 100-399, inclusive, are undergraduate courses; 400-499, inclusive, are senior-college and graduate courses; 500 and above are graduate courses.

Certificates

The State Teachers College at **Montclair** offers work toward the following New Jersey Certificates: Limited Secondary Teaching Certificate; Permanent Secondary Teaching Certificate; Secondary School Principal's Certificate; Secondary School Subject Supervisor's Certificate; Supervising Principal's Certificate; and the Superintendent of Schools' Certificate.

Those who matriculate at **Montclair** for a degree will receive information from Dean Messick and the Head of the major department as to the requirements for each of these certificates.

Students who have not matriculated at **Montclair**, but who desire to obtain any of the above certificates, should write to Dr. E. C. Preston, Secretary of the State Board of Examiners, Department of Public Instruction, Trenton Trust Building, Trenton 8, New Jersey, for information as to the requirements and for an evaluation of work done previously. An official transcript of such previous work should accompany the inquiry, with a statement as to the particular certificate desired.

Students who must have this information immediately should go to Trenton to confer personally with Dr. Preston.

Supervised Student Teaching

The opportunity to do supervised student teaching cannot be offered during the Summer Session. Matriculated students confer with Dr. Spears. Non-matriculated students should write to Dr. Robert H. Morrison, Director of Teacher Education, State Department of Public Instruction, Trenton Trust Building, Trenton 8, New Jersey, enclosing an official transcript of all work done on college level.

Offerings to Veterans

Many Veterans have planned to continue their college work. Those who are discharged in the late spring or early summer may wish to use the Summer Session as a means of accelerating their program.

The College will make every effort to adjust its offerings and facilities to Veterans who are interested in teaching as a profession. It has printed a bulletin setting forth its policies and procedures in working with Veterans. This may be had upon request. It should be known that the College will recognize equivalency in courses taken and experiences gained by men and women in service. In general, credit may be allowed for:

(a) Armed Forces Institute courses or other courses at the college level,

(b) specialized training taken in service schools either on or off campus, and

(c) experiences of a more informal nature than can be judged from the standpoint of educational growth or development.

Veterans may receive government aid in financing Part-Time and Summer Session courses.

Conferences with Advisers

Students may make appointments by mail or telephone for a conference with Dean Messick or with the Head of a Department or the Director of Personnel. Do this at as early a date as possible. If, however, it has been impossible for you to make an earlier appointment, these officials or their representatives may be seen on July 9.

A representative of the State Board of Examiners will be at the College on July 9 to see students who desire advice on the selection of courses toward New Jersey Certificates. (See instructions under the heading "Certificates.")

The Registrar of the Summer Session will receive requests for appointments with this State Official.

Work Taken for Credit

The maximum amount of credit which may be earned in the six weeks of the Summer Session is 8 semester-hours. Students may not register for more. See paragraph under the heading "Summer Term of Twelve Weeks" for the opportunity to earn additional credit.

Each course is in session at least thirty hours and carries a designated amount of credit. It is not possible to earn three points credit in a two-point course.

If prerequisites are required, the student should make certain he has fulfilled them or their equivalent before enrolling in the course. If no previous work on college level has been taken, the student should advise with the Registrar before enrolling in any course.

Change of Status in a Course

If a student desires to change his status in a course from "credit" to "auditor," or from "auditor" to "credit," he must make formal application for such change not later than the middle of the course. Forms for this purpose may be procured from the Registrar of the Summer Session.

Registration

There is no advance registration for the Summer Session. Registration takes place in the first meeting of each class.

Withdrawal from a Course

The Registrar of the Summer Session must be notified in writing immediately if the student finds it necessary to withdraw from a course in which he has enrolled. Neglecting to do so may result in the student's receiving a failing mark for the course.

Audited Class Admission Cards

Audited Class Admission Cards are due at the third meeting of each class. They are obtained in the Business Office on presentation of fees or credit slips. It is desirable that this be done in person, but if necessary students may send checks, money-orders, or credit slips by mail to the Business Manager with the request that the Audited Class Admission Cards be placed in the postboxes of the respective teachers.

The Business Office is open daily, Monday through Friday, at the following hours: 8:30-11:30 A.M., and 12:30-3:30 P.M.

Fees

Checks or money-orders should be made payable to **New Jersey State Teachers College.** Registration service charge: $1.00 for the Summer Session. Tuition fees: to legal residents of New Jersey, $6.00 per semester-hour credit carried by the course; to non-residents,$8.00 per credit. Courses taken for "no credit" cost the same. A laboratory service charge of $2.00 is made in connection with each of the laboratory courses. This service charge is collected in class by the teacher and should not be included in the check for tuition fees and registration.

Final Marks

Following are the final marks which may be received for a course: A-Excellent; B-Good; C-Fair; D-Poor; F-Failure; Inc-Incomplete; Wd-Withdrew; N.C.: No Credit.

The mark of "D" when earned in the summer, part-time, or extension courses of this college is not accepted for degree credit at **Montclair.**

Very few marks of "Inc." are given. It may, however, be granted to a student whose work is incomplete in one particular at the end of the Summer Session and who is eager to finish the work for a higher grade than he could receive otherwise. All responsibility regarding incomplete work rests with the student. If the work of the course is not completed by the date indicated on the notification, the final grade will be recorded without further notice.

The mark of "N.C." is given only when the student has registered for "No Credit." See paragraph under "Auditors;" and also that under "Change of Status."

Report Cards and Transcripts

Report cards and an Official Transcript are mailed directly to the student himself as soon as possible after the close of the Summer Session. This is usually within one week or ten days at the most. This first transcript is furnished free of charge. The cost of a second one depends upon the amount of work the student has completed, ranging from 25 cents for one semester's work to $1.00 for four or more. Postage stamps are not accepted in payment for transcripts. Men and women entering or already in national service organizations are sent a second transcript without charge.

Catalogues and Bulletins

The following catalogues and bulletins may be obtained upon request: (1) Undergraduate Catalogue of Courses, 1944-1946; (2) Graduate Bulletin; (3) Veterans' Bulletin; (4) after July first, Announcement of the 1945-46 Part-Time and Extension Division.

8

COURSES THAT MAY BE TAKEN TOWARD THE
NEW JERSEY SECONDARY CERTIFICATE

This is not an official statement. It does not emanate from the State Department that issues the certificate. It is furnished merely for your convenience in selecting courses. You should check your selections with the State Department.

Please note that either an undergraduate or a graduate course may apply on the certificate and that the total requirements is 18 s.h. Often it is possible to take three courses of 2 s.h. credit each to satisfy a total of 6 s.h. in required work.

Courses of the Summer Session are preceded by the letter "S" and described in this Bulletin. Courses listed without this letter preceding the number are offered during the first six weeks of the Twelve Weeks Summer term.

I HEALTH EDUCATION—3 s.h. required.
   Biology S409—Human Physiology—Cr: 3 s.h.
II EDUCATIONAL PSYCHOLOGY—3 s.h. required.
   Integration 200A—Educational Psych. and Mental Testing—Cr: 2 s.h.
   Integration S500B—Advanced Educational Psychology—Cr: 2 s.h.
III AIMS AND ORGANIZATION (PRINCIPLES) OF SECONDARY
   EDUCATION—3 s.h. required.
   Integration 300A—Aims and Organization of Secondary Education—
                Cr: 2 s.h.
   Integration 400A—Principles and Philosphy of Secondary Education,
                Cr: 2 s.h.
   Integration S400A—Principles and Philosophy of Secondary Education,
                Cr: 2 s.h.
IV PRINCIPLES AND TECHNIQUES (GENERAL METHODS) OF
   TEACHING IN THE HIGH SCHOOL—3 s.h. required.
   Integration S300B—Principles and Techniques of Teaching in Second-
                ary Schools—Cr: 2 s.h.
   Integration S500C—Teaching Procedures in Secondary Education—
                Cr: 2 s.h.
V CURRICULUM ORGANIZATION AND COURSES OF STUDY
   (SPECIFIC METHODS) IN ONE ENDORSED TEACHING
   FIELD—3 s.h. required.
   Biology S501—The Teaching of Biology in Secondary Schools—Cr:
                3 s.h.
   Language S401—The Teaching of Foreign Languages in Secondary
                Schools, Cr: 3 s.h.
   Mathematics S401W—The Teaching of Mathematics in Secondary
                Schools, Cr: 2 s.h.
   Social Studies S401—The Teaching of Social Studies in Secondary
                Schools, Cr: 3 s.h.
VI ELECTIVE—3 s.h. required.
   Courses in the Department of Integration that are definitely in the
   field of Secondary Education and that have not been taken to satisfy
   one of the above requirements; for example:
   Integration S501—Tests and Measurements in Secondary
                Education: Cr. 2 s.h.

It is possible, also, to take a second course under one of the above headings to fulfill the elective; for example, a methods course in the minor field.

9

DESCRIPTION OF COURSES

Business Education

Business Education S301A—Business Law III Dr. Geigle

This is a continuation of course 202, but course 202 is not a prerequisite. Law topics treated are: sales, partnerships, property, deeds, mortgages, landlord and tenant, and torts.

9:30-10:25 A.M. 30 hours Credit: 2 semester-hours Room D

Business Education S301B—Business Organization and Management Mr. Sheppard

This course provides an opportunity to study the various types of business organization and some of the problems encountered in the establishment and operation of a business. These business problems deal with such matters as location, housing, equipment, arrangement and layout, internal organization, purchasing, shipping, personnel, and manufacturing.

10:30-11:25 A.M. 30 hours Credit: 2 semester-hours Room B

English

English S201B—British and American Poetry, Part II Dr. Karp

This course surveys the development of English poetry from its beginnings to the present time. It includes study in the types of poetic statement, the historical development of the styles and forms of English poetry, the life and work of the major British and American poets, and the critical appreciation of poetry as an art and as an expression of life. Part II begins with the rise of the Romantic movement in poetry.

11:30 A.M.-12:25 P.M. 30 hours Credit: 2 semester-hours Room 27

English S202A—British and American Fiction, Part I Mr. Conrad

This is the first half of the required course for English Majors. Part I studies the development of the novel in England and America from its beginnings to the time of Dickens.

8:30-9:25 A.M. 30 hours Credit: 2 semester-hours Auditorium, CHS*
*CHS means College High School building.

English S204—Extemporaneous Speaking Mr. Fox

This course provides maximum platform practice. Students speak on subjects of current interest, paying attention to content, organization of material, and essentials of effective oral presentation.

8:30-9:25 A.M. 30 hours Credit: 2 semester-hours Room 1

English S301A—Literature for Adolescents: Developing Miss Cook and
Faith for Living through Literature Mrs. Winchester

This course is a study of the best available literary material (fiction, drama, biography, essay), suitable to the interests and maturity of junior and senior high school adolescents, and of the use that can be made of it in enabling them to gain the knowledge and confidence necessary for courageous living in this world.

1:00-1:55 P.M. 30 hours Credit: 2 semester-hours Library, CHS

English S322—Oral Interpretation   **Mr. Fox**

This course is organized to increase the student's appreciation of poetic and dramatic literature from the standpoint of art in sound, and to develop his potentialities in oral reading.

11:30 A.M.-12:25 P.M.   30 hours   Credit: 2 semester-hours   Room 1

English S435—Play Production   **Mr. Fox**

This workshop course embraces both the theory and art of play production by providing training in staging, lighting, costuming, construction, and painting of scenery.

1:00-1:55 P.M.   30 hours   Credit: 2 semester-hours   Room 1

English S442A—American Literature: A Pageant of
American Democracy, Part I   **Mr. Conrad**

This is a survey, from the beginning through the Civil War, of those authors and works of literature that reflect the political, social, and economic turmoil out of which the national spirit emerged. Authors include the early historians, the political writers, and such full-scale literary figures as Irving, Cooper, Bryant, Emerson, Hawthorne, Lowell, Thoreau, and Holmes.

9:30-10:25 A.M.   30 hours   Credit: 2 semester-hours   Auditorium, CHS

English S515—Robert Browning   **Dr. Karp**

Selected works are studied for their literary and philosophical values, as showing the development of Browning as man, poet, and philosopher, and as a reflection of certain phases of nineteenth-century life and thought.

9:30-10:25 A.M.   30 hours   Credit: 2 semester-hours   Room 27

English S516—Language Problems in the English Curriculum   **Mr. Conrad**

This course reviews the several theories of language and studies the problem of meaning in order to arrive at a suitable technique for the interpretation of prose and verse. This technique is then applied to the problems of reading, of composition, of speech, and of appreciation of literature. The course has two aims: to increase the student's own skill in dealing with language, and to increase his effectiveness in teaching.

10:30-11:25 A.M.   30 hours   Credit: 2 semester-hours   Auditorium, CHS

Foreign Languages

Language S300—Foundations of Language   **Miss Littlefield**

A comprehensive survey is made of the background, growth, and structure of the English language, traced from its remote Indo-European ancestry down through the changes wrought by foreign additions and influence. By a systematic and comparative study of the main elements of Greek, Latin, French, Anglo-Saxon, and English, and of the phonetic phenomena recurring in language development, the course presents and augments the important diction values derived from foreign language study. It aims especially to train teachers of general language or of exploratory courses in foreign languages.

10:30-11:25 A.M.   30 hours   Credit: 2 semester-hours   Room 9

Language S401—The Teaching of Foreign Languages in
Secondary Schools   **Dr. Freeman**

The work of this course is focused on such topics as the following: values of

11

foreign language teaching; ultimate and immediate aims in foreign language teaching; survey of the out-standing methods; pronunciation, oral work, reading, grammar; reviews, realia, examinations, tests; supervised study, etc. The courses consists of readings and discussions, ·lesson planning and demonstrations, and organization of materials for use in teaching.

8:00-9:25 A.M.   45 hours   Credit: 3 semester-hours   Room 10

Language S415—War Languages ·   Miss Littlefield

This course presents a practical introduction to the learning of any foreign language. Through the use of International Phonetic Symbols and Linguaphone Records, students acquire skill in the recognition and identification of foreign speech sounds. Ear, lip, and tongue training are combined to ensure adequate ability in the pronunciation of foreign sounds with scientific accuracy. The course is designed for all students in the language field, but especially for all men and women in the college who intend to enter the Armed Forces, the Intelligence Division, Signal Corps, or any department of the war effort requiring acquaintance with foreign speech. Now that our troops are being brought into contact with every type of linguistic expression throughout the world, the practical value of this course in war languages is easily apparent.

9:30-10:25 A.M.   30 hours   Credit: 2 semester-hours   Room 9

Latin S101B—The Golden Age: Masterpieces of Prose   Miss Littlefield. Literature, Part II

Livy and Cicero are the two authors studied intensively in this course. Selected readings of Livy supply interesting material for the discussion of Roman history, and Cicero's De Senectute introduces the student to a study of ancient philosophy.

11:30 A.M.-12:25 P.M.   30 hours   Credit: 2 semester-hours   Room 9

Latin S202B—The Silver Age: Anthology of Latin Poetry, Part II   Miss Littlefield

This course is designed to present the works of Latin poets. Selected excerpts from the Anthology are studied with the aim of bringing out the inherent differences between the Golden and Silver Ages of Latin writing.

8:30-9:25 A.M.   30 hours   Credit: 2 semester-hours   Room 9

Latin S301B—Roman Comedy: Terence   Dr. Freeman

The life and works of Terence are studied in this course, with special reference to the history of the development of drama as a whole and the Roman contribution in particular.

9:30-10:25 A.M.   30 hours   Credit: 2 semester-hours   Room 10

Spanish S101B—Spanish Civilization, Part II   Miss Escoriaza

This course is designed to introduce the student to the important eras in Spanish civilization with a view to building up the background out of which the Spanish civilization of the New World developed. Prerequisite: three years of high school Spanish; two years in special cases. The course is conducted in Spanish.

8:30-9:25 A.M.   30 hours   Credit: 2 semester-hours   Room E

Spanish S202B—Hispanic-American Civilization: Lower South
American Area, Part II   **Miss Escoriaza**

This course is designed to present the outstanding features in the civilization and history of the following South American Republics: Chile, Argentina, Uruguay, and Paraguay. The course is conducted in Spanish.

9:30-10:25 A.M.   30 hours   Credit: 2 semester-hours   Room E

Spanish S302B—Spanish Classics, Part II   **Miss Escoriaza**

The aim of this course is to present to advanced students of Spanish the life and dramatic works of Calderon de la Barca of Tirso de Molina.

10:30-11:25 A.M.   30 hours   Credit: 2 semester-hours   Room E

Geography

Science S100C—Survey of Earth Sciences   **Dr. Milstead**

For the description of this course, see the Department of Science.

Geography S408B—Political Geography, Part II   **Dr. Milstead**

This course deals with the geographic conditions influencing the significant changes in the political divisions of the world. Emphasis is placed on geographic factors influencing racial, religious, commercial, and political adjustment between nations. It is especially recommended to students of history, economics and sociology. Part II deals with Russia, Northwestern Europe, Latin-America, and the United States.

9:30-10:25 A.M.   30 hours   Credit: 2 semester-hours   Room 26

Integration

Integration S300B—Principles and Techniques of Teaching
in Secondary Schools   **Mr. Seybold**

After having established the fundamental principles underlying the teaching process, the following techniques and procedures are presented and evaluated: the question, the lesson plan, the assignment, testing and marking systems, classroom management and routine; and special procedures, such as supervised study. In addition to the above topics, based on subject-matter organization and administration, various types of classroom procedure are considered.

10:30-11:25 A.M.   30 hours   Credit: 2 semester-hours   Room 3, CHS

Integration S400A—Principles and Philosophy of
Secondary Education   **Dr. W. Scott Smith**

This course evaluates educational objectives, techniques, procedures, and organizations in relation to the needs and demands made upon the school by society and by the student. It involves a discussion of the meaning of philosophy and an interpretation of human values. Fundamental principles of education are evolved from previous work in the various fields of thought contributing to educational philosophy.

11:30 A.M.-12:25 P.M.   30 hours   Credit: 2 semester-hours   Room 29

Integration S500B—Advanced Educational Psychology   **Dr. Ingebritsen**

In this course, a comparative study is made of contemporary schools of psychology with emphasis on their direct application to education. Practical applications are made to classroom problems and the work of guidance departments. Prerequisite: an introductory course in psychology.

10:30-11:25 A.M.   30 hours   Credit: 2 semester-hours   Room 30

Integration S500C—Teaching Procedures in Secondary Education   Mr. Seybold

This course emphasizes the fundamental principles underlying the techniques of teaching on the secondary school level. Some of the topics considered are: organization of knowledge, the logical and psychological aspects of method, developing appreciations, social-moral education, teaching motor control, fixing motor responses, books and verbalism, meeting individual differences, guidance in study, tests and examinations, marks and marking.

9:30-10:25 A.M.   30 hours   Credit: 2 semester-hours   Room 3, CHS

**Integration S501—Tests and Measurements in Secondary
                    Education   Dr. Ingebritsen**

The purpose of this course is to develop an appreciation of the meaning and importance of measurement in education, and to give a working knowledge of instruments of measurement.

11:30 A.M.-12:25 P.M.   30 hours   Credit: 2 semester-hours Room 30

**Integration S502B—Organization and Administration of
                    the Modern High School, Part II   Dr. Spears**

The topics treated reflect especially the wartime problems of the school as well as those presented by postwar proposals. Among the topics are these: administering the program for returning veterans and war workers, high school credit for military service, work experience in the school, scheduling the broader courses such as the core course, acceleration, selecting the staff, professional ethics, public relations, salary policies and principles involved, and cooperating parent organizations. A student may take Integration 502B before he takes 502A.

10:30-11:25 A.M.   30 hours -   Credit: 2 semester-hours   Room 24

Integration S503—Methods and Instruments of Research   Mr. Jackson

This course is required for all candidates for the Master's degree without regard to their field of major interest. Its purpose is to introduce students of education to research and its practical application to professional problems. The course treats; the nature and types of educational research; methods and techniques of educational research; and the tools used in interpreting statistical data. During the course, the student sets up a problem and plans and carries out its solution.

1:00-1:55 P.M.   30 hours   Credit: 2 semester-hours   Room A

**Integration S504C—Curriculum Trends in the Elementary
                    and Secondary Schools   Dr. Spears**

This course treats the emerging trends in the curriculum and the principles behind them, including the effects of the war upon the school program. Each student has an opportunity to do a constructive piece of work relating to curriculum needs in his or her particular school. Students who have already taken Integration 504A should not enroll for 504C without first consulting the instructor.

11:30 A.M.-12:25 P.M.   30 hours   Credit: 2 semester-hours   Room 24

**Integration S505—Organization and Administration of
                    Extra-Curricular Activities   Dr. W. Scott Smith**

The first part of this course considers such general problems of extra-curricular activities as: their growing importance; their relation to the curriculum;

14

the principles underlaying their organization, administration, and supervision; and methods of financing. In the second part, an intensive study is made of the home room, the assembly, the student council, clubs, athletics, school publications, and other activities in which the class is especially interested.

1:00-1:55 P.M. 30 hours Credit: 2 semester-hours Room 29

Integration S515—Guidance and Personnel Problems of Classroom Teachers Mr. Seybold

This course considers all types of personnel problems with which the classroom teacher deals. It is concerned with the growth of pupils and seeks to point out the ways by which proper growth may be attained. Classroom, health, social, and personal activities are analyzed in terms of the needs of present-day social life.

11:30 A.M.-12:25 P.M. 30 hours Credit: 2 semester-hours Room 3, CHS

Integration S517—Administration of the Elementary School Dr. Beck

This course analyzes and evaluates the administrative duties and relationships of the elementary school principal. Particular consideration is given to: building management, effective use of the school plant, sanitation, health service, the library, personnel management, the administration of the curriculum, community relationships, and publicity.

8:30-9:25 A.M. 30 hours Credit: 2 semester-hours Room 8

Integration S518—Supervision of Instruction in the Elementary School Dr. Beck

This course has been planned for those engaged in the supervision of the elementary school, and for those who are preparing for such responsibilities. Principles of classroom supervision are developed and applied to learning situations. Among the more important topics that receive attention are: the nature and function of supervision, the organization necessary for effective supervision, the nature and significance of the teacher's purposes, the methods and techniques of group and individual supervision, the technique of observation, and the supervisory conference.

9:30-10:25 A.M. 30 hours Credit: 2 semester-hours Room 8

Integration S520—Principles of Mental Hygiene Dr. Ingebritsen

This course is designed to be a general survey of the principles and practices of mental health with special reference to the mental health of teacher and pupil. It involves a thorough grounding in fundamental principles of mental hygiene with much practical consideration of the mental-health values of instructional programs and procedures. Discussion centers in practical efforts to develop wholesome personalities in our schools.

9:30-10:25 A.M. 30 hours Credit: 2 semester-hours Room 30

Integration S530B—Practicum in Remedial and Corrective Reading in Secondary Schools Dr. Sperle

This course represents a special workshop in remedial and corrective reading for graduate students interested in the reading problem. The student has an opportunity to explore the current method and materials used for improving reading ability and to work on a program for his or her own school. The course has been scheduled to meet from June 25 to July 6, intensively, so that teach-

15

e:s-in-service may take the course after their schools have closed and yet complete it before the opening of the Summer Session on July 9. Prerequisite: either Integration 530—Corrective and Remedial Reading in Secondary Schools, or Integration 532—The Supervision and Teaching of Reading in Elementary Schools. Students register in class on June 25.

9:30 A.M.-12:25 P.M.   30 hours   Credit: 2 semester-hours   Room 7

Integration S601—Workshop in Education   Dr. Spears and Staff

Section A—Organizing and Administering the School
Section B—Supervising Instruction
Section C—Dealing with and Understanding Youth

The workshop course enables the graduate student to devote his time to an educational topic or school problem of current interest to him and to secure the help of the staff, fellow students, and college facilities in pursuing this study. Workshoppers may meet together to discuss matters of common concern in respect to the current school situation. In addition, the student works independently on his own project and at times meets with a small group interested in the same area.

The four credits in the course can be handled together, or be broken down into two courses, to meet specific needs such as requirements for a particular teaching certificate or course needs to meet Master's degree requirements here; and individual work in the course is pointed accordingly. For instance, the student needing credit in a specific course in school supervision may well arrange to work off such requirement through the workshop.

In the past, students have worked on topics in such areas as these: problems in administration, guidance programs, extra-curricular activities; school philosophies, problems in supervision, curriculum planning, and community relations. The success of a workshop depends much upon the student knowing what he wants to accomplish in six weeks, and the procedure being flexible enough to support his purposes.

8:30-10:25 A.M.   60 hours   Credit: 4 semester-hours •   Room 7

Mathematics

Mathematics S102B—Mathematical Analysis, Part IV:
Analytical Geometry   Mrs. Davis

This course is recommended particularly to those students seeking a minor in mathematics or those in need of a review course in analytic geometry. The topics include: rectangular and polar coordinate systems; loci and their equations; the straight line; the conics—circle, parabola, ellipse, and hyperbola; parametric equations; transformation of coordinates; and the general equation of the second degree.

10:30-11:25 A.M.   30 hours   Credit: 2 semester-hours   Room 5

Mathematics S300—The Social and Commercial Uses of Mathematics   Mrs. Davis

The aims of this course are: first, a consideration of the mathematical problems which are met in everyday life or general reading; and second, the establishment of a background for the teaching of junior high school mathematics. Some of the topics treated are: fundamental operations, graphs, solution of problems, numerical geometry, percentage, budgeting, installment buying, investments, banking, taxation, and insurance.

9:30-10:25 A.M.   30 hours   Credit: 2 semester-hours   Room 5

16

Mathematics S400—Educational Statistics   Dr. Davis

The aim of this course is to prepare the student first, to comprehend and criticize articles of statistical nature in current educational literature; second, to apply statistical methods in testing and rating pupils; and, third, to carry on the simpler types of educational research. By analysis of real data from the secondary field, the student becomes familiar with the measures of central tendency and variability, short methods of computation, graphic representation of material, the properties of the normal curve, and linear correlation. Inasmuch as statistical methods in education are almost identical with those employed in the natural, physical, and social sciences, there is natural integration with these fields.

9:30-10:25 A.M.   30 hours   Credit: 2 semester-hours   Room 3

Mathematics S401W—The Teaching of Mathematics in Secondary Schools   Mrs. Davis

In this course, special consideration is given to specific problems which arise in the teaching of junior and senior high school mathematics. These include the following: adaptation of material to students of varying abilities; selection and treatment of subject matter; use of texts and supplementary material; importance of the fundamental concepts; use of special methods and devices; how to treat the more difficult phases of the subject matter; and the preparation of students for college entrance examinations.

8:30-9:25 A.M.   30 hours   Credit: 2 semester-hours   Room 5

Mathematics S406B—Applications of Mathematics, Part II   Dr. Fehr

The course applies the use of surveying instruments in motivating the teaching of mathematics in the junior and senior high school. The material studied is of special value to teachers of slow-moving ninth grade pupils. Topics considered are: the use of transit and level to determine elevations, inaccessible distances, areas, volumes, etc., mapping with the plane table; use of planimeter, pantograph, hand level hypsometer, cross staff, angle mirror and sextant; the various types of slide rules, the accuracy obtained, and the fundamental ideas of approximate computation; and graphic representation of data. The method of constructing inexpensive instruments is shown.

11:30 A.M.-12:25 P.M.   30 hours   Credit: 2 semester-hours   Room 2

Mathematics S510C—Mathematics in its Relation and Application to Other Fields of Knowledge, Part III: Geography and Astronomy   Dr. Fehr

Part III offers an opportunity for mathematics teachers to become acquainted with the mathematics of mapping, astronomy, and navigation closely related to the algebra, solid geometry, and trigonometry taught in high school. A study of spherical geometry and trigonometry leads to topics in mathematical astronomy and geography, and to navigation. The discussion includes such topics as: latitude and longitude; time and the calendar; map projections; the making of star maps; sizes and distances of the sun, moon, planets, and stars; weighing the earth and moon; and relativity.

9:30-10:25 A.M.   30 hours   Credit: 2 semester-hours   Room 2

Mathematics S515—Differential Equations   **Dr. Davis**

This course is a continuation of the calculus considered from a new viewpoint. Various applications of differential equations and their standard methods of solution are fully treated in this course. Among the topics included are: linear differential equations of the first degree and of the first and higher orders, linear equations of the nth order with constant coefficients, linear equations of numerical approximation and partial differential equations.

10:30-11:25 A.M.   30 hours   Credit: 2 semester-hours   Room 3

Physical Education

Physical Education SW302A—Theory and Practice of Self-Testing, Athletic Games and Archery   **Dean Sherwin**

In this course students participate in self-testing activities, athletic games, and archery. At least one hour a week is spent in discussing the adaptation of these activities to age levels, physical abilities, and particular situations.

1:00-1:55 P.M.   30 hours   Credit: 2 semester-hours   Room 9

Physical Education S302B—Health and Health Teaching, Part II

         Mr. Armstrong

First Aid forms the major part of this course with certification by the American Red Cross. In addition, the organs of special sense, eye and ear, are studied with the object of fostering good eyesight and good hearing. An opportunity is afforded for testing groups with modern diagnostic methods.

11:30 A.M.-12:25 P.M.   30 hours   Credit: 2 semester-hours   Room 4, CHS

Science

Biology S409—Human Physiology   **Dr. Hadley**

A careful study of human anatomy is used as a basis for discussion of both normal and abnormal physiology. In addition to an analysis of the part played by organs and tissues in carrying out the essential functions of the body, special attention is given to problems of hygiene and sanitation. Applications of the above problems are made in reference to children of school age and the physical condition of individual pupils is correlated with their behavior in the classroom.

1:00-2:25 P.M.   45 hours   Credit: 3 semester-hours   Room 28

Biology S501—The Teaching of Biology in Secondary Schools   **Dr. Hadley**

This is a seminar and research course designed to give opportunity for study of the best methods and practices being used in the teaching of secondary school biology. Major topics of discussion are: aims of a secondary school biology course, course content, functions of text-books, testing, laboratory exercises and demonstrations, and the collection and use of suitable and available laboratory materials. A study is made of recent research studies in the field of biology teaching. Open to teachers and prospective teachers of biology who have completed a minimum of 18 semester-hours in biological fields.

8:00-9:25 A.M.   45 hours   Credit: 3 semester-hours   Room 28

Chemistry S406—Organic Chemistry, Part II   **Dr. Reed**

The work of this semester covers the chemistry of multiple functional chain compounds, the ring compounds, proteins, vitamins, hormones, and the application of these compounds in industry, in foods and in medicine.

10:30-11:25 A.M., daily; plus Tu. & Th. at 11:30 A.M-12:25 P.M., and Laboratory 1:00-5:00 P.M., W. & F. 90 hours   Credit: 4 semester hours   Room 23

Chemistry S509A—Advandced Inorganic Chemistry, Part I   **Dr. Reed**

This course offers opportunity for intensive and systematic study of the elements in the light of the periodic classification. Selected theories and principles of inorganic chemistry and some of their applications are studied in detail. Directed use of chemical literature is an important part of∙this course. Individual experimental work in the laboratory consists chiefly of preparation and purification of inorganic compounds. In this half of the course, the chemistry of metals is stressed.

9:30-10:25. MWF; Lab. Tu., 1-5 P.M.

45 hours   Credit: 2 semester- hours   Room 23

Physics S101—General College Physics, Part I:
Mechanics and Heat   **Dr. K. O. Smith**

The major objective of physical science is to discover, describe, correlate, and explain the facts and phenomena of the inanimate world. For convenience, the subject-matter of physics is classified as: mechanics, heat, magnetism and electricity, sound, and light. The work of this course consists of a study of mechanics of fluids and solids, properties of matter, and heat energy and phenomena. The course includes lectures, demonstrations, discussions, problem-solving exercises, library assignments, and laboratory experiments.

9:30-10:25 A.M. daily, plus M. & W. at 10:30-11:25 A.M., and Laboratory 1:00-5:00 P.M., Tu. & Th.   90 hours   Credit: 4 semester-hours   Room 25

Physics S304B—Photography for High School
Teachers, Part II   **Dr. K. O. Smith**

This is an elementary course in photography, consisting of lectures, demonstrations, laboratory work, and field work. Some of the topics covered in this course are: projection printing and controls used in projection printing, making of lantern slides, corrections of negatives and positives, taking of pictures with black and white and colored film. Physics 304A or a knowledge of film development and contact printing is a prerequisite .

11:30 A.M.-12:25 P.M. MWF; Lab. W-1-5 P.M.

45 hours   Credit: 2 semester-hours   Room 25

Science S100C—Survey of Earth Sciences   **Dr. Milstead**

In this course, emphasis is laid on the effect of soil, climate, and physical features on the welfare of plants, animals, and mankind. The keynote of the course is to show the influence of a constantly changing physical environment on the life activities and welfare of mankind.

10:30-11:25 A.M.   ·30 hours   Credit: 2 semester-hours   Room 26

Social Studies

Social Studies S101B—European History from 1713 to 1815   **Dr. Wittmer**

The rise of Russia and the rise of Prussia are treated. Primary consideration is given, however, to the political, economic, social, and intellectual conditions in France, preceding the French Revolution; the French Revolution itself; and the Napoleonic period; with the inauguration of the spirit of nationalism.

9:30-10:25 A.M.   30 hours   Credit: 2 semester-hours   Room 12, CHS

Social Studies S202B—United States History since 1900   **Dr. Snyder**

This course is devoted to the study of the United States as a world power; the development of "big business," the United States in the first World War, and our problems of the depression and present war periods.

9:30-10:25 A.M.   30 hours   Credit: 2 semester-hours   Room 20

Social Studies S301B—Economics Part II   **Mr. Rellahan**

This course is a continuation of Economics I, which is not however, prerequisite. The aim of this course is to acquaint the student with the basic economic principles and problems relating to risk and insurance; money, credit, and banking; general price changes and their control; foreign trade and exchange; tariffs, international debts, and imperialism; business combinations; and governmental regulation of business enterprise.

9:30-10:25 A.M.   30 hours   Credit: 2 semester-hours   Room 22

Social Studies S401—The Teaching of Social Studies in Secondary Schools   **Dr. Snyder**

The course aims to present recent tendencies in educational method in teaching the social studies. A program is presented containing the fusion organizatio in socialized recitation, the teaching of current events, projects in citizenship, and the use of the project-problem as a method of teaching history and civics. A laboratory containing texts and workbooks in the social studies field is available to the students of this course.

8:00-9:25 A.M.   45 hours   Credit: 3 semester-hours   Room 20

Social Studies S420B—The European Outlook, Part II   **Dr. Wittmer**

This course is devoted to a study of contemporary Belgium, the Netherlands, France, Spain, Italy, and England. It is shown how the culture patterns of these nations can be preserved without impeding the growth of an all-embracing western democratic civilization. It shows how the Atlantic Charter may be applied to the particular conditions of the countries being considered. The role of England as part of Europe on the one hand, and as a link between Europe and the world, on the other, is discussed in detail.

8:30-9:25 A.M.   30 hours   Credit: 2 semester-hours   Room 12, CHS

Social Studies S433—American Political Thought   **Mr. Bye**

This is a survey of political thinking in America. It deals with the contemporary trends and theories as they have emerged from social and economic conditions and as they are founded upon the bases laid down by such men as Hamilton, Madison, Washington, Jefferson, Marshall, Calhoun, Webster, Lincoln, Wilson, and others.

9:30-10:25 A.M.   30 hours   Credit: 2 semester-hours   Room 21

Social Studies S442—The Far East   **Dr. Wittmer**

A study is made of the economic, social, and cultural situation of the Far East, with particular emphasis on the historical background of China and Japan, and our relations with the Philippines. Oriental folkways, religion, education, population shifts and strategic questions are discussed. This course provides an approach to the problems the United States must face in the Far East.

10:30-11:25 A.M.   30 hours   Credit: 2 semester-hours   Room 12,CHS

Social Studies S447—Diplomatic History of the United States   **Mr. Bye**

The purpose of this course is to show how we have become gradually conscious of our world interests and responibilities, and the important role we have come to play in international politics. The growing concept of world democracy, as opposed to commercial and military imperialism, is stressed.

10:30-11:25 A.M.   30 hours   Credit: 2 semester-hours   Room 21

Social Studies S450A—Applied Economics: Problems and Policies, Part I   **Mr. Rellahan**

This, the first half of the course, is devoted to an analysis of economic principles in the operation and guidance of our everyday economic life.

10:30-11:25 A.M.   30 hours   Credit: 2 semester-hours   Room 22

Social Studies S455—Social Legislation   **Mr. Rellahan**

This course analyzes the social, economic, and political adjustments which have come about in our society due to technologcal progress. The content covers such subjects as public policy relative to immigration; the problems of national income and its distribution; labor legislation such as the regulation of wages and hours of work, industrial hazards and social insurance, women and children in industry, and the problem of unemployment; social legislation relating to the conflict between organized labor and capital; public policy to aid and protect the consumer; and an analysis of competing philosophies pertaining to industrial and social progress.

11:30 A.M.-12:25 P.M.   30 hours   Credit: 2 semester-hours   Room 22

Graduate Department

Graduate S500—Seminar: Master's Thesis   **Dean Messick**

Students writing a thesis for credit towards the Master's degree in any department of the College are required to register for this course. The work is conducted under seminar or individual guidance. Students report to the Dean of Instruction, who calls a conference with the Head of the Department and the Sponsor. At this meeting, all matters pertaining to the topic, plan of research, writing of manuscript, etc., are arranged.

Credit: 4 semester hours   Dean's Office

On page 4 of this Bulletin, there is a paragraph concerning the Twelve Weeks Summer Term. The list of courses below is the one referred to in that paragraph.

The Roman Numeral "I" precedes the catalogue number of the courses that will end Friday, July 6. All other courses in this list will continue through Friday, August 17.

Courses that carry a credit of 4 s.h. in the regular college curriculum are frequently given in the Summer Session in two parts, each half course carrying a credit of 2 s.h. Usually, the second half of such a course may be taken without the student's having already taken the first half. If, however, the description of the second half is omitted from the Summer Session Bulletin, it is an indication that the first half is prerequisite. Students able to enroll for the Twelve Weeks Summer Term, therefore, have the opportunity to take both halves of such a course.

Department	Cat. No.	Title of Course	Teacher
Business Ed.	201	Introduction to Business	Mr. Sheppard
Business Ed.	302	Salesmanship	Mr. Sheppard
Business Ed.	405	Bookkeeping and Accounting	Mr. Sheppard
English	I. 100B	World Literature, Part II	Mr. Bohn
English	201	British and American Poetry	Dr. Krauss
English	I. 202B	British and American Fiction, Part II	Mr. Conrad
English	I. 301B	Shakespeare's Major Plays	Mr. Bohn
English	I. 312	Fundamentals of Acting and Directing	Mr. Fox
English	I. 404	Survey of British Literature	Dr. Krauss
English	I. 421	The Short Story	Mr. Conrad
English	I. 430	Reading in Secondary Schools	Dr. Sperle
English	I. 441	Medieval Epic, Saga, and Romance	Dr. Krauss
English	I. 443	Modern Drama	Mr. Bohn
English	I. 446	The One-Act Play	Mr. Fox
Language	I. 300	Foundations of Language	Miss Littlefield
Language	I. 415	War Languages	Miss Littlefield
Latin	101	The Masters of Prose Literature	Miss Littlefield
Latin	202	The Anthology of Latin Poetry	Miss Littlefield
Latin	301	Roman Drama	Dr. Freeman
Spanish	101	The Civilization of Spain	Miss Escoriaza
Spanish	202	Hispanic-American Civilization	Miss Escoriaza
Spanish	302	The Spanish Classics:	Miss Escoriaza
Spanish	I. 407	New World Before the Spaniards	Dr. Freeman
Geography	408	Political Geography	Dr. Milstead
Geography	I. 410	Economic Geography of Caribbean America	Dr. Milstead
Geography	I. 413	Economic Geography of South America	Dr. Milstead

22

Integration	I. 200A	Educational Psychology and Mental Testing_____Dr. Sperle
Integration	I. 300A	Aims and Organization of Secondary Education _____Dr. Spears
Integration	I. 400A	Principles and Philosophy of Secondary Education_____Dr. Smith
Integration	I. *530B	Practicum in Remedial and Corrective Reading in Seconary Schools Dr. Sperle

*Courses numbered 500 and above are graduate courses. Their descriptions will be found in the Graduate Bulletin. Integration 530B will be given intensively, beginning June 25. For further information concerning it, see page 15 of this Summer Session Bulletin.

Mathematics	I. 102A	Mathematical Analysis: Trigonometry_____Mr. Clifford
Mathematics	I. 300	Social and Commercial Uses of Math._____Mr. Clifford
Mathematics	301	Modern College Geometry_____Dr. Fehr
Mathematics	302	Higher Algebra_____Dr. Davis
Mathematics	I. 400	Educational Statistics_____Mr. Clifford
Mathematics	406	Applications of Mathematics_____Dr. Fehr

Music	I. 100	Music Appreciation_____Dr. McEachern
Music	I. 201A	Harmony, Part I_____Dr. McEachern
Music	I. 301	Choral Technique_____Dr. McEachern

| Chemistry | I. 405 | Organic Chemistry, Part I_____Dr. Reed |

| Physics | I. 102 | General College Physics_____Dr. K. O. Smith |

Social Stud.		100B	Civilization and Citizenship_____ Dr. Freeman
Social Stud.		101	European History: 1492-1815_____Dr. Wittmer
Social Stud.	I.	200A	Contemporary Economic Life_____Mr. Rellahan
Social Stud.	I.	200B	Contemporary Political Life_____Mr. Bye
Social Stud.	I.	200C	Contemporary Social Life _____Dr. Link
Social Stud.	I.	202A	United States History: 1860-1900____Dr. Link
Social Stud.		301	Economics_____Mr. Rellahan
Social Stud.	I.	402B	Comparative Government	Mr. Bye
Social Stud.	I.	407	New Jersey State and Local Government Mr. Bye
Social Stud.	I.	420	The European Outlook _____Dr. Wittmer
Social Stud.	I.	444	The Social Bases of Human Relations__Dr. Link
Social Stud.	I.	451	The Middle East_____Dr. Wittmer

SUMMER SESSION

Bulletin of

MONTCLAIR
STATE TEACHERS COLLEGE

JULY 8 to AUGUST 16

1946

UPPER MONTCLAIR, NEW JERSEY

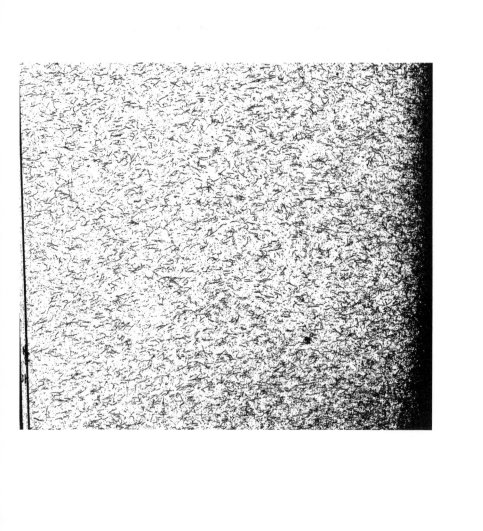

Summer Session

Bulletin of

Montclair
State Teachers College

1946

July 8 to August 16

Upper Montclair, New Jersey

STATE OFFICIALS

STATE BOARD OF EDUCATION

Gustav A. Hunziker, *President*	Little Falls
George O. Smalley, *Vice-President*	Bound Brook
Joseph Clayton	Point Pleasant Beach
John S. Gray	Newton
Mrs. Edward L. Katzenbach	Princeton
William Kirk	Penns Grove
A. Harry Moore	Jersey City
Paul V. Murphy	Metuchen
Amos J. Peaslee	Clarksboro
Mrs. Herbert Reim	Maywood
Mrs. Olive C. Sanford	Nutley
Richard E. Swift	Ventnor City

COMMISSIONER OF EDUCATION
John H. Bosshart

ASSISTANT COMMISSIONER FOR HIGHER EDUCATION
Robert H. Morrison

OFFICERS OF ADMINISTRATION
NEW JERSEY STATE TEACHERS COLLEGE AT MONTCLAIR

Harry A. Sprague	President
John D. Messick	Dean of Instruction
Frances Van Etten	Registrar
Elizabeth S. Favor	Secretary of Extension and Summer Session
Robert Levy	Business Manager
Claude E. Jackson	Director of Personnel and Research
Margaret A. Sherwin	Dean of Women
Richard Voliva	Dean of Men
Horace J. Sheppard	Acting Head of Business Education Department
Edwin S. Fulcomer	Head of English Department
Arthur E. Morr,	Director, Health, Physical Education and Recreation Department
Harold Spears	Head of Integration Department
Walter H. Freeman	Head of Language Department
Virgil S. Mallory	Head of Mathematics Department
Edna McEachern	Head of Music Department
Earl R. Glenn	Head of Science Department
W. Harry Snyder	Head of Social Studies Department
Arthur M. Seybold	Director of College High School
Otto Cordes	Engineer in Charge, Maintenance

SUMMER SESSION 1946

FACULTY

Harry A. Sprague, Ph.D............President
John D. Messick, Ph.D............Dean of Instruction
Franklin G. Armstrong, A.M............Health Education
Harold C. Bohn, A.M............English
Thomas A. Budne, A.M............Mathematics
J. Herbert Burgy, Ph.D............Geography
Paul C. Clifford, A.M............Mathematics
Lawrence H. Conrad, A.M............English
Margaret G. Cook, A.B., B.S............Librarian
David R. Davis, Ph.D............Mathematics
Jerome DeRosa, A.M............Physical Education
Emma Fantone, A.M............Multi-Sensory Aids
L. Howard Fox, A.M............English
Walter H. Freeman, Ph.D............Head of Department of Foreign Languages
Paul E. Froelich, A.M............Business Education
Edwin S. Fulcomer, Ed.D............Head of Department of English
Lili Heimers, Ph.D............Director, Auditory and Visual Aids Service
Leo W. Jenkins, Ed.D............Social Studies
Claude E. Jackson, A.M............Research
Russell Krauss, Ph.D............English
Ethel F. Littlefield, A.M............Languages
John A. Milligan, Ed.D............Administration
Arthur E. Morr, A.M.-Director, Dept. of Health, Physical Ed., and Recreation
E. DeAlton Partridge, Ph.D............Multi-Sensory Aids
George R. Placek, A.M............Aeronautics
Rufus D. Reed, Ph.D............Chemistry
John J. Rellahan, A.M............Social Studies
Arthur M. Seybold, A.M............Integration
Horace J. Sheppard, A.M....Acting Head, Department of Business Education
Kenneth O. Smith, Ph.D............Physics
V. Scott Smith, Ph.D............Integration
O. Henryetta Sperle, Ph.D............Integration
Richard Voliva, A.M............Physical Education
Felix Wittmer, Ph.D............Social Studies

3

SUMMER SESSION OF THE
NEW JERSEY STATE TEACHERS COLLEGE AT MONTCLAIR

General Objective

The New Jersey State Teachers College at Montclair is a professional school which prepares teachers, supervisors, principals of high schools, and administrators of public school systems. The degrees offered by this college are those of Bachelor of Arts and Master of Arts. Certificate courses are offered for those who now hold degrees.

How to Reach the Campus

Trains of the Greenwood Lake Division, Erie R. R., stop at College Station. Trains of the Lackawanna R. R. connect at Montclair with the following bus lines: No. 64, running between Brick Church and the college; No. 60, running between Newark and the college; and No. 76, which runs between Orange and Paterson, passing the college en route. For those who come by car: the college is located about one mile north of the center of Upper Montclair.

Residence Halls for Men and Women

Edward Russ Hall and Chapin Hall are **Montclair's** two well-appointed residences. The charge for living on campus during the Summer Session is reasonable: $12:00 per week; which includes room, breakfast, and dinner. A la carte luncheons are served in the college cafeteria. For one student alone in a double room, an extra charge of $2.00 per week is made. The college provides all furnishings, with the exception of towels, blankets, and desk lamps. The boarding-hall fee must be paid on or before the first day of the Summer Session. No rebate is made for occasional absence or voluntary withdrawal during the session. Students who are absent on account of illness for two weeks or more receive a rebate of $6.00 per week during the illness.

For reservations in the college residence hall, address: Dean of Women, State Teachers College, Upper Montclair, New Jersey.

Schedule of the Summer Session

The Summer begins on Monday, July 8, and continues through Friday, August 16, on which day the summer Commencement will be held All courses meet daily, Monday through Friday, for one hour, except where definitely indicated otherwise.

Summer Term of Twelve Weeks

Included in this Bulletin of the Summer Session is a list of the courses of the Twelve Weeks Summer Term which is held for the benefi of the accelerated candidates for the Bachelor of Arts degree at Montclair Other students who have special need of a maximum amount of credit may also enter these courses. The list of these courses appears on the las page of this Bulletin. The 1944-1946 Catalogue of the College contain:

4

descriptions of the courses. The mimeographed schedule of the Twelve Weeks Summer Term and the Catalogue will be sent upon request. Registration and payment of fees for this Term must be made on Wednesday, May 22. Anyone desiring to enroll should report that day to the office of the Summer Session. Classes begin the same day and continue through August 16.

Matriculation

Students planning to matriculate for the Master of Arts degree should note that not more than 8 semester-hours of credit earned prior to matriculation is accepted toward the degree.

Those who desire to become candidates for either the Bachelor of Arts or the Master of Arts degree at **Montclair** must request the Registrar for the application form and return it, properly filled in and accompanied by an official transcript of all previous work on college level. When such an applicant has been accepted by the college as a candidate for the degree, a definite statement will be furnished to him, showing the requirements which he must fulfill to earn it.

Auditors

Men and women who desire to take courses for cultural, vocational, or avocational purposes without college credit may register as auditors.

Students Matriculated at Montclair

Work taken for credit at **Montclair** must be with the advice and approval of the Dean of Instruction and the Head of the Department in which the student is majoring. See paragraph under the heading **"Conferences."**

A student who expects to receive a degree should consult the Registrar three months in advance of graduation.

Students Matriculated at Other Colleges

Work taken for credit to be transferred to other colleges should be approved in advance by the Dean of the college at which the student holds membership. Such students who are planning to attend **Montclair** this summer should take the Summer Session Bulletin to a conference with their Deans to arrange a program of work. For the Dean's information: the numbering of courses at **Montclair** follows this order: 100-399, inclusive, are undergraduate courses; 400-499, inclusive, are senior-college and graduate courses; 500 and above are graduate courses.

Certificates

The State Teachers College at **Montclair** offers work toward the following New Jersey Certificates: Limited Secondary Teaching Certificate; Permanent Secondary Teaching Certificate; Secondary School Principal's Certificate; Secondary School Subject Supervisor's Certificate; Supervising Principal's Certificate; and the Superintendent of Schools' Certificate.

Those who matriculate at **Montclair** for a degree will receive information from Dean Messick and the Head of the major department as to the requirements for each of these certificates.

5

Students who have not matriculated at **Montclair**, but who desire to obtain any of the above certificates, should write to Dr. E. C. Preston, Secretary of the State Board of Examiners, Department of Public Instruction, Trenton Trust Building, Trenton 8, New Jersey, for information as to the requirements and for an evaluation of work done previously. An official transcript of such previous work should accompany the inquiry with a statement as to the particular certificate desired.

Students who must have this information immediately should go to Trenton to confer personally with Dr. Preston.

Supervised Student Teaching

The opportunity to do supervised student teaching cannot be offered during the Summer Session. Matriculated students confer with Dr. W. Scott Smith. Non-matriculated students should write to Dr. Robert H. Morrison, Ass't Commissioner for Higher Education, State Department of Public Instruction, Trenton Trust Building, Trenton 8, New Jersey, enclosing an official transcript of all work done on college level.

Offerings to Veterans

Many Veterans have planned to continue their college work. Those who are discharged in the late spring or early summer may wish to use the Summer Session as a means of accelerating their program.

The College will make every effort to adjust its offerings and facilities to Veterans who are interested in teaching as a profession. It has printed a bulletin setting forth its policies and procedures in working with Veterans. This may be had upon request. It should be known that the College will recognize equivalency in courses taken and experiences gained by men and women in service. In general, credit may be allowed for:

(a) Armed Forces Institute courses or other courses at the college level,

(b) specialized training taken in service schools either on or off campus, and

(c) experiences of a more informal nature that can be judged from the standpoint of educational growth or development.

Veterans may receive government aid in financing Part-Time and Summer Session courses.

Conferences with Advisers

Students may make appointments by mail or telephone for a conference with Dean Messick or with the Head of a Department or the Director of Personnel. Do this at as early a date as possible. If, however, it has been impossible for you to make an earlier appointment, these officials or their representatives may be seen on July 8.

A representative of the State Board of Examiners will be at the College on July 8 to see students who desire advice on the selection of courses toward New Jersey Certificates. (See instructions under the heading "Certificates.")

The Registrar of the Summer Session will receive requests for appointments with this State Official.

6

Work Taken for Credit

The maximum amount of credit which may be earned in the six weeks of the Summer Session is 8 semester-hours. Students may not register for more. See paragraph under the heading "Summer Term of Twelve Weeks" for the opportunity to earn additional credit.

Each course is in session at least thirty hours and carries a designated amount of credit. It is not possible to earn three points credit in a two-point course.

If prerequisites are required, the student should make certain he has fulfilled them or their equivalent before enrolling in the course. If no previous work on college level has been taken, the student should consult with the Registrar before enrolling in any course.

Change of Status in a Course

If a student desires to change his status in a course from "credit" to "auditor," or from "auditor" to "credit," he must make formal application for such change not later than the middle of the course. Forms for this purpose may be procured from the Registrar of the Summer Session.

Registration

There is no advance registration for the Summer Session. Registration takes place in the first meeting of each class.

Withdrawal from Course

The Registrar of the Summer Session must be notified in writing immediately if the student finds it necessary to withdraw from a course in which he has enrolled. Neglecting to do so may result in the student's receiving a failing mark for the course.

Audited Class Admission Cards

Audited Class Admission Cards are due at the third meeting of each class. They are obtained in the Business Office on presentation of fees or credit slips. It is desirable that this be done in person, but if necessary students may send checks, money-orders, or credit slips by mail to the Business Manager with the request that the Audited Class Admission Cards be placed in the postboxes of the respective teachers.

The Business Office is open daily, Monday through Friday, at the following hours: 8:30-11:30 A.M., and 12:30-3:30 P.M.

Fees

Checks or money-orders should be made payable to **New Jersey State Teachers College.** Registration service charge: $1.00 for the Summer Session. Tuition fees: to legal residents of New Jersey, $6.00 per semester-hour credit carried by the course; to non-residents, $8.00 per credit. Courses taken for "no credit" cost the same. A laboratory service charge of $2.00 is made in connection with each of the laboratory courses. This service charge is collected in class by the teacher and should not be included in the check for tuition fees and registration.

Final Marks

Following are the final marks which may be received for a course: A-Excellent; B-Good; C-Fair; D-Poor; F-Failure; Inc-Incomplete; Wd-Withdrew; N.C.—No Credit.

The mark of "D" when earned in the summer, part-time, or extension courses of this college is not accepted for degree credit at **Montclair.**

Very few marks of "Inc." are given. It may, however, be granted to a student whose work is incomplete in one particular at the end of the Summer Session and who is eager to finish the work for a higher grade than he could receive otherwise. All responsibility regarding incomplete work rests with the student. If the work of the course is not completed by the date indicated on the notification, the final grade will be recorded without further notice.

The mark of "N.C." is given only when the student has registered for "No Credit." See paragraph under "Auditors", and also that under "Change of Status."

Report Cards and Transcripts

Report cards and an Official Transcript are mailed directly to the student himself as soon as possible after the close of the Summer Session. This is usually within one week or ten days at the most. The first transcript is furnished free of charge. The cost of a second one depends upon the amount of work the student has completed, ranging from 25 cents for one semester's work to $1.00 for four or more. Postage stamps are not accepted in payment for transcripts. Men and women entering or already in national service organizations are sent a second transcript without charge as are veterans of such service.

Catalogues and Bulletins

The following catalogues and bulletins may be obtained upon request: (1) Undergraduate Catalogue of Courses, 1944-1946; (2) Graduate Bulletin; (3) Veterans' Bulletin; (4) after July first, Announcement of the 1946-47 Part-Time and Extension Division.

COURSES THAT MAY BE TAKEN TOWARD THE NEW JERSEY SECONDARY CERTIFICATE

This is not an official statement. It does not emanate from the State Department that issues the certificate. It is furnished merely for your convenience in selecting courses. You should check your selections with the Secretary of the State Board of Examiners.

Please note that either an undergraduate or a graduate course may apply on the certificate and that the total requirement is 18 semester-hours Often it is possible to take three courses of 2 s.h. credit each to satisfy a total of 6 s.h. in required work.

Courses of the Summer Session are preceded by the letter "S" and described in this Bulletin. Courses listed without this letter preceding the number are offered during the first six weeks of the Twelve Weeks Summer Term.

8

I HEALTH EDUCATION—3 s.h. required

Physical Education S301B—Health and Health Teaching, Part I—Cr: 2 s.h.

Biology S409—Human Physiology—Cr: 4 s.h.

Physical Education 101—Applied Physiology—Cr: 4 s.h.

II EDUCATIONAL PSYCHOLOGY—3 s.h. required

Integration 200A—Educational Psychology and Mental Testing—Cr: 2 s.h.

Integration S200B—Adolescent Psychology and Mental Hygiene—Cr: 2 s.h.

Integration S500B—Advanced Educational Psychology—Cr: 2 s.h.

III AIMS AND ORGANIZATION (PRINCIPLES) OF SECONDARY EDUCA-TION—3 s.h. required

Integration 300A—Aims and Organization of Secondary Education—Cr: 2 s.h.

Integration 400A—Principles and Philosophy of Secondary Educa-tion—Cr: 2 s.h.

Integration S400A—Principles and Philosophy of Secondary Educa-tion—Cr: 2 s.h.

IV PRINCIPLES AND TECHNIQUES (GENERAL METHODS) OF TEACH-ING IN THE HIGH SCHOOLS—3 s.h. required

Integration S300B—Principles and Techniques of Teaching in the Secondary School—Cr: 2 s.h.

Integration S500C—Teaching Procedures in Secondary Education—Cr: 2 s.h.

V CURRICULUM ORGANIZATION AND COURSES OF STUDY (SPECIFIC METHODS) IN ONE ENDORSED TEACHING FIELD—3 s.h. required

English S401—The Teaching of English in Secondary Schools—Cr: 3 s.h.

Language S401—The Teaching of Foreign Languages in Secondary Schools—Cr: 3 s.h.

Mathematics S401—The Teaching of Mathematics in Secondary Schools—Cr: 3 s.h.

Physical Education SM302A—Organization and Methods in Physical Education—Cr: 2 s.h.

Biology S408—Biological Technique—Cr: 3 s.h.

Chemistry S501—The Teaching of Chemistry in Secondary Schools—Cr: 3 s.h.

Science S401D—The Teaching of Aviation in Secondary Schools—Cr: 2 s.h.

Social Studies S401—The Teaching of the Social Studies in Secondary Schools—Cr: 3 s.h.

VI ELECTIVE—3 s.h. required

Courses in the Department of Integration that are definitely in the field of Secondary Education and that have not been taken to satisfy one of the above requirements; for example:

Integration S530B—Practicum in Remedial and Corrective Reading in Secondary Schools—Cr: 2 s.h.

It is possible, also, to take a second course under one of the above headings to fulfill the elective; for example, a methods course in the minor field.

COURSES THAT MAY BE TAKEN TOWARD SUPERVISOR'S, PRINCIPAL'S, AND ADMINISTRATOR'S CERTIFICATES DURING THE SUMMER SESSION 1946

(Check your selections with Dr. Preston.)

Courses in the Field of Administration

Integration S502B—Organization and Administration of the Modern High School, Part II—Cr: 2 s.h.

Integration S510—Seminar in Educational Administration and Supervision* Cr: 2 s.h.

Integration S517—Administration of the Elementary School—Cr: 2 s.h.

Integration S548—The Elementary School Curriculum—Cr: 2 s.h.

Integration S503—Methods and Instruments of Research—Cr: 2 s.h.

Courses in the Field of Supervision

Integration S508B—Supervision of Teaching, Part II—Cr: 2 s.h.

Integration S510—Seminar in Educational Administration and Supervision* Cr: 2 s.h.

Integration S518—Supervision of Instruction in the Elementary School, Cr: 2 s.h.

Courses of Interest to High School Principals

Integration S500C—Teaching Procedures in Secondary Education—Cr: 2 s.h.

Integration S530B—Practicum in Remedial and Corrective Reading in Secondary Schools—Cr: 2 s.h.

Integration S502B—Org. and Adminis. of the Modern H.S.-II—Cr: 2 s.h.

Courses of Interest to Elementary School Principals

Integration S517—Administration of the Elementary School—Cr: 2 s.h.

Integration S518—Supervision of Instruction in the Elementary School, Cr: 2 s.h.

Integration S548—The Elementary School Curriculum—Cr: 2 s.h.

Courses in the Field of Personnel and Guidance

Integration S500B—Advanced Educational Psychology—Cr: 2 s.h.

Integration S515—Guidance and Personnel Problems of Classroom Teachers, Cr: 2 s.h.

Integration S521—Psychological Tests in Guidance Programs—Cr: 2 s.h.

Courses of Interest to Subject Supervisors

English S401—The Teaching of English in Secondary Schools—Cr 3 s.h.

Language S401—The Teaching of Foreign Languages in Secondary Schools—Cr: 3 s.h.

Mathematics S401—The Teaching of Mathematics in Secondary Schools—Cr: 3 s.h.

Physical Education SM302A—Organization and Methods in Physical Education (Men), Cr: 2 s.h.

Biology S408—Biological Technique—Cr: 3 s.h.

Chemistry S501—The Teaching of Chemistry in Secondary Schools—Cr: 3 s.h.

Science S401D—The Teaching of Aviation in Secondary Schools—Cr: 2 s.h.

Social Studies S401—The Teaching of the Social Studies in Secondary Schools, Cr: 3 s.h.

Integration S508B—Supervision of Teaching, Part II—Cr: 2 s.h.

Integration S510—Seminar in Educational Administration and Supervision* Cr: 2 s.h.

Integration S518—Supervision of Instruction in the Elementary School—Cr: 2 s.h.

See also offerings in the Subject Matter fields.

*This course may be credited toward either Administration or Supervision depending upon the nature of the problem study undertaken by the student.

DESCRIPTION OF COURSES

Business Education

**Business Education S301B—Business Organization and
Management**   Mr. Froelich

This course provides an opportunity to study the various types of business organization and some of the problems encountered in the establishment and operation of a business. These business problems deal with such matters as location, housing, equipment, arrangement and layout, internal organization, purchasing, shipping, personnel, and manufacturing.

9:30-10:25 A.M.   30 hours   Credit: 2 semester-hours   Room D

Business Education S308—Advertising   Mr. Sheppard

This course aims to acquaint the student with the social and economic aspects of advertising so that a fair evaluation may be made of its worth as well as its undesirable aspects. Copy appeals, the writing of copy, advertising layouts, and the selection of appropriate types of media for various advertisements are considered.

11:30 A.M.-12:25 P.M.   30 hours   Credit: 2 semester-hours   Room B

Business Education S406—Business Economics   Mr. Froelich

This is a course in applied economics, specifically planned for the business student or teacher. It stresses the practicable, tangible side as a means of interpreting the actual business world. It deals with the structure of our economic system, the place of the individual in our social organization, human wants, and the factors of production.

10:30-11:25 A.M.   30 hours   Credit: 2 semester-hours   Room D

English

**English S100A—World Literature: Its Forms and Its Masters,
Part I**   Mr. Bohn

The various culture-epochs represented in world literature are considered in a time-sequence parallel to that of the courses *Civilization and Citizenship* and *Art-Music Appreciation*. These three first-year courses provide an historical survey of the evolution of the humanities. The work of the first half year comprises the Bible, Aeschylus, Sophocles, Euripides, Aristophanes, Plato, Aristotle and Thucydides.

8:00-9:25 A.M.   45 hours   Credit: 3 semester-hours   Room A

**English S100B—World Literature: Its Forms and Its Masters,
Part II**   Dr. Krauss

The second half-year is given to Plutarch, Virgil, medieval legend, Dante, Boccaccio, Chaucer, Cellini, Cervantes, Machiavelli, and Shakespeare. As a whole, the study attempts to attain the ends both of professional usefulness and of general cultural education.

1:00-2:25 P.M.   45 hours   Credit: 3 semester-hours   Room 27

English S200A—Composition   Mr. Conrad

This course is designed to help the student improve his ability in writing so that he may understand and fulfill the requirements of the College in the organization and presentation of written materials. Exposition is stressed in order to provide practice in the fundamentals of effective organization.

11

Outlining, handling of research and source materials, and general organization of term papers are introduced. The Style Book of the College serves as a basis for the mechanics of the course.

8:00-9:25 A.M.   45 hours   Credit: 3 semester-hours   Aud. CHS

English S200B—Fundamentals of Speech, Part I   Mr. Fox

This basic course is designed to help the student improve his ability in speaking. The instruction includes practice in the fundamentals of effective voice production and the development of clear and pleasing diction. The work of the course is adapted to the individual needs of the students as revealed by phonograph recordings and diagnostic tests.

1:00-2:25 P.M.   45 hours   Credit: 3 semester-hours   Room E

English S301A—Literature for Adolescents   Dr. Fulcomer

A study of the reading interests of different age levels introduces problems involved in the selection of literature for high school students. Extensive reading and analysis of literature designed for adolescents, including those in the junior high school, are required.

11:30 A.M.-12:25 P.M.   30 hours   Credit: 2 semester-hours   Room 1

English S322—Oral Interpretation   Mr. Fox

This course is organized to increase the student's appreciation of poetic and dramatic literature from the standpoint of art in sound, and to develop his potentialities in oral reading.

9:30-10:25 A.M.   30 hours   Credit: 2 semester-hours   Room E

English S401—The Teaching of English in Secondary Schools   Dr. Fulcomer

Here theory gives way to practice. Students are required to develop and use materials of the classroom. Lesson plans and units of work are prepared and presented for criticism. Textbooks are analyzed for training in their use. Bulletin board exhibits and visual education materials are prepared by students for the class.

8:00-9:25 A.M.   45 hours   Credit: 3 semester-hours   Room 1

English S405—The Victorian Poets   Dr. Krauss

This course covers the work of the Brownings, Tennyson, Arnold, Clough, Morris, the Rossettis, and Swinburne. The authors are presented in relation to the moral, religious, social and political life of nineteenth-century England.

9:30-10:25 A.M.   30 hours   Credit 2 semester-hours   Room 27

English S407—British and American Biography   Mr. Conrad

Both the old and new types of biography are read and studied in this course, with emphasis upon the nineteenth and twentieth centuries. Biography is presented for its cultural and informational values, for its use in integrating the work of the various departments in the high school, and for its direct help in the vocational guidance program.

10:30-11:25 A.M.   30 hours   Credit: 2 semester-hours   Aud. CHS

English S419—Grammar for Teachers   Dr. Fulcomer

This course is a study of the basic facts of grammatical relationships in English, and of the current problems of "rules" as opposed to "usage." The primary aim of the course is to acquaint students with the true function of grammar in speech and writing.

10:30-11:25 A.M.   30 hours   Credit: 2 semester-hours   Room 1

English S431B—Shakespeare, Part II   **Mr. Bohn**

This course deals with Shakespeare's plays in relation to his life, his times, his contemporaries, and Elizabethan drama generally. Extensive reading is required from Shakespeare, his predecessors, contemporaries, and successors. The problems of stage production in both Elizabethan and modern theatres, of Shakespearean criticism are analyzed. Part II deals with the Shakespearean comedies and tragi-comedies

9:30-10:25 A.M.   30 hours   Credit: 2 semester-hours   Room A

English S435—Play Production   **Mr. Fox**

This workshop course embraces both the theory and art of play production by providing training in staging, lighting, costuming, construction, and painting of scenery. A minimum of twelve clock hours of craft work upon a production of the College is required for credit in this course.

10:30-11:25 A.M.   30 hours   Credit: 2 semester-hours   Room A

English S442B—American Literature: A Pageant of American Democracy, Part II   **Mr. Conrad**

This course surveys the development of American literature from the Civil War to the contemporary period. The writers studied include: Walt Whitman, Sidney Lanier, Emily Dickinson, William Dean Howells, Mark Twain, Henry James, Henry Adams, Hamlin Garland, Stephen Crane, Frank Norris, O. Henry, Vachel Lindsay, E. A. Robinson, Carl Sandburg, and Robert Frost.

11:30 A.M.-12:25 P.M.   30 hours   Credit: 2 semester-hours   Aud. CHS

English S446—The One-Act Play   **Mr. Bohn**

This course studies the one-act play as an art form, devoting special attention to plays which are suitable for high school production.

11:30 A.M.-12:25 P.M.   30 hours   Credit: 2 semester-hours   Room A

English S510—Edmund Spenser   **Dr. Krauss**

This course studies the "Poet's Poet" of Elizabethan England, devoting special attention to his exquisite melodious art, his "roots" in the literary Renaissance of Italy, France, and England, and the aesthetic Spenserian tradition in later English verse, notably in the Romantic and Victorian eras. In comprehending the great Elizabethan, the student enriches his knowledge of over five centuries of a vital poetic tradition.

11:30 A.M.-12:25 P.M.   30 hours   Credit: 2 semester-hours   Room 27

Foreign Languages

Language S300—Foundations of Language   **Miss Littlefield**

This course is required of all candidates for the A.B. degree at Montclair. Its purpose is to give every one of them as prospective high school teachers (1) a survey of the background, growth, and structure of the English language from its Indo-European orgin to modern times, (2) an introduction to the science of linguistics, (3) an appreciation of several foreign language patterns, and (4) a rich fund of information in the field of general language. The course consists of lectures, student reports, maps and charts, class disussions and frequent objective tests.

8:30-9:25 A.M.   30 hours   Credit: 2 semester-hours   Room 9

Language S401—The Teaching of Foreign Languages in
                          Secondary Schools   .Dr. Freeman

The work of this course is focused on such topics as the following: values of foreign language teaching; ultimate and immediate aims in foreign language teaching; survey of the outstanding methods; pronunciation, oral work, reading, grammar, reviews, realia, examinations, tests, supervised study, etc. The course consists of readings and discussions, lesson planning and demonstrations, and organization of materials for use in student-teaching.

8:00-9:25 A.M.   45 hours   Credit 3 semester-hours   Room 10

Language S402—Comparative Phonetics   **Miss Littlefield**

This course consists of an analysis of speech production from both a physiological and an acoustic standpoint. Upon this phonetic basis is built up a scientific comparison of French, Spanish, German, and English speech-sounds. The prospective teacher of foreign languages is trained in recognizing, producing, and writing these sounds both with and without the accepted symbols of the International Phonetic Association. Practice is given in detecting, analyzing, and correcting errors in pronunciation in each of the above-named foreign languages. Modern textbooks in foreign languages are examined for their treatment of pronunciation. Emphasis is laid upon scientific laboratory methods.

10:30-11:25 A.M. '   30 hours   Credit: 2 semester-hours   Room 9

Spanish S407—The New World Before the Coming
                          of the Spaniards   **Dr. Freeman**

The purpose of this course is to present our present knowledge of the remarkable civilizations of the New World (Mayan, Aztec, Incan) as they had developed before the coming of Europeans placed them under Old World direction. Today it is important that teachers, particularly those of Spanish and Social Studies, should acquire much wider horizons in matters respecting our Hispanic American neighbors. This course is given in English.

11:30 A.M.-12:25 P.M.   30 hours   Credit 2 semester-hours   Room 10

Geography

Geography S503—Economic Geography of the United States   **Dr. Burgy**

A study is made of the agricultural, industrial, and commercial development of the United States and of the geographic factors that have contributed to that development.

8:30-9:25 A.M.   30 hours   Credit: 2 semester-hours   Room 26

Geography S504—Economic Geography of Europe   **Dr. Burgy**

This course constitutes a study of the economic development of the nations of Europe in relation to the environmental background and resources that have made Europe one of the world's leading continents.

10:30-11:25 A.M.   30 hours   Credit 2 semester-hours   Room 26

Integration

Integration S200B—Adolescent Psychology and
                          Mental Hygiene   (teacher to be assigned

The work of this semester deals with problems of adjustment and mal-adjustment, particularly those to be found at the high school level and those

14

peculiar to the adolescent. Students read and discuss case reports written by student-teachers while in service, study current works on adolescent and adjustment problems of this period, and make a rather complete study of social and psychological factors in the life of a normal adolescent. The mental hygiene aims of the work are two-fold: to build up in the mind of the student a picture of the normal, wholesome adolescent personality and its needs, and to help the student through observation, reading, and discussion, to grow toward a well-adjusted adult, teacher personality.

9:30-10:25 A.M.　　30 hours　　Credit: 2 semester-hours　　Room 30

Integration S300B—Principles and Techniques of Teaching
in the Secondary School　　　　　　Dr. W. Scott Smith

The course is divided into four major parts as follows: (1) a general view, with the emphasis upon the nature and function of teaching, inherited nature, attention, interest and motivation, and how learning takes place; (2) teaching techniques such as the assignment, the question, oral presentation, using illustrative material, and testing; (3) specialized procedures including supervised study, socialized recitations, projects, and individual instruction; (4) integration through lesson planning, social control, and extra-curricular activities.

10:30-11:25 A.M.　　30 hours　　Credit: 2 semester-hours　　Room 8

Integration S400A—Principles and Philosophy
of Secondary Education　　　　　Dr. W. Scott Smith

This course evaluates educational objectives, techniques, procedures, and organizations in relation to the needs and demands made upon the school by society and by the student. It involves a discussion of the meaning of philosophy and an interpretation of human values. Fundamental principles of education are evolved from previous work in the various fields of thought contributing to educational philosophy.

9:30-10:25 A.M.　　30 hours　　Credit: 2 semester-hours　　Room 8

Integration S408—Multi-Sensory Aids　　　Dr. Partridge, Dr. Helmers,
and Miss Fantone

Sources, principles of selection, standards of evaluation and methods of use of the various multi-sensory aids are studied in relation to all phases of school work. Other phases of the work concern field trips, specimens, models, exhibits, experiments, radio and phonograph, prints, stereopticon slides, film slides, motion pictures, maps, graphs, charts, diagrams, cartoons, and marionettes. Instruction is given in making many of the above aids and in the operation and care of the various projectors.

8:30 A.M.-9:25 A.M.　　30 hours　　Credit 2 semester-hours　　Room 4

Integration S500B—Advanced Educational Psychology (teacher to be assigned)

In this course a comparative study is made of contemporary schools of psychology with emphasis on their direct application to education. Prerequisite: An introductory course in psychology.

11:30 A.M.-12:25 P.M.　　30 hours　　Credit: 2 semester-hours　　Room 30

Integration S500C—Teaching Procedures in
Secondary Education　　　　　　　Mr. Seybold

This course emphasizes the fundamental principles underlying the technique of teaching on the secondary school level. Some of the topics considered are:

15

organization of knowledge, the logical and psychological aspects of method, developing appreciation, social-moral education, teaching motor control, fixing motor responses, books and verbalism, meeting individual differences, guidance in study, tests and examinations, marks and marking.

10:30-11:25 A.M.　30 hours　Credit: 2 semester-hours　Room 3, CHS

**Integration S502B—Organization and Administration of
the Modern High School, Part II** Mr. Seybold

This course takes up the broader and more intricate problems of high school administration. Some of the topics studied are: the meaning of American education; current developments in educational philosophy; types of secondary school organization; articulation programs; standardizing agencies; public relations; cooperation with other educational agencies, such as vocational and industrial schools; legal aspects; the plant and equipment; selecting and assigning the staff, making the high school budget; relation of principal to special supervisors. Prerequisite: Integration 502A.

11:30 A.M.-12:25 P.M.　30 hours　Credit 2 semester-hours　Room 3, CHS

Integration S503—Methods and Instruments of Research Mr. Jackson

This course is required of all candidates for the Master's degree without regard to their field of major interest. Its purpose is to introduce students of education to research and its practical application to professional problems. The course treats: the nature and types of educational research, methods and techniques of educational research; and the tools used in interpreting statistical data. During the course, the student sets up a problem and plans and carries out its solution.

1:00-1:55 P.M.　30 hours　Credit: 2 semester-hours　Room 6

Integration S508B—Supervision of Teaching, Part II Dr. Messick

This course is offered to students who have completed Integration 508A, which is prerequisite to this part of the course, and who desire advanced work in supervision. It deals with the supervisory platform, the supervisor as a philosopher and social engineer, the selection of teachers, helping beginner teachers, the relation of administration to supervision, and supervision through class observation.

10:30-11:25 A.M.　30 hours　Credit: 2 semester-hours　Room 6

**Integration S510—Seminar in Educational Administration
and Supervision** Dr. Messick

In this course the class makes an intensive study of administrative and supervisory problems suggested by the educational events and trends of the year, by the interests and responsibilities of the members of the class, and by educational movements in New Jersey. Each student does an individual piece of research which he reports to the class. Prerequisites: Integration 502A or 517, and 508A or 518.

1:00-1:55 P.M.　30 hours　Credit: 2 semester-hours　Room 7

**Integration S515—Guidance and Personnel Problems
of Classroom Teachers** Mr. Seybold

This course considers all types of personnel problems with which the classroom teacher deals. It is concerned with the growth of pupils and seeks to point out the ways by which proper growth may be attained. Classroom,

16

health, social, and personal activities are analyzed in terms of the needs of present-day social life.

9:30-10:25 A.M.   30 hours   Credit: 2 semester-hours   Room 3, CHS

* Integration S517—Administration of the Elementary School   Dr. Milligan

This course analyzes and evaluates the administrative duties and relationships of the elementary school principal. Particular consideration is given to: building management, effective use of the school plant, sanitation, health service, the library, personnel management, the administration of the curriculum, community relationships, and publicity.

8:30-9:25 A.M.   30 hours   Credit: 2 semester-hours   Room 24

* Integration S518—Supervision of Instruction in
                    the Elementary School   Dr. Milligan

This course has been planned for those engaged in the supervision of the elementary school, and for those who are preparing for such responsibilities. Principles of classroom supervision are developed and applied to learning situations. Among the more important topics that receive attention are: the nature and function of supervision, the organization necessary for effective supervision, the nature and significance of the teacher's purposes, the methods and techniques of group and individual supervision, the technique of observation, and the supervisory conference.

11:30 A.M.-12:25 P.M.   30 hours   Credit: 2 semester-hours   Room 3, CHS

Integration S521—Psychological Tests in Guidance·
                  Programs   (Teacher to be assigned)

This course is designed to familiarize the student with various psychological tests and scales that may be used in guidance programs in the secondary school. The student is given practice in administering many types of group tests. This includes scoring the tests and evaluating the results, with a discussion of ways in which these results may be used. Much time is spent in actual laboratory demonstrations of tests, giving students an opportunity to serve as subjects and as examiners. Class discussion is based upon first-hand information gained through use of the tests, on readings, and on class reports.

10:30-11:25 A.M.   30 hours   Credit: 2 semester-hours   Room 30

Integration S530B—Practicum in Remedial and Corrective
                   Reading in Secondary Schools   Dr. Sperle

This course represents a special workshop in remedial and corrective reading for graduate students interested in the reading problem. The student has an opportunity to explore the current method and materials used for improving reading ability and to work on a program for his or her own school. The course has been scheduled to meet from June 24 to July 6, intensively, so that teachers-in-service may take the course after their schools have closed and yet complete it before the opening of the Summer Session on July 8. Prerequisite: either Integration 530A—Corrective and Remedial Reading in Secondary Schools, or Integration 532—The Supervision and Teaching of Reading in Elementary Schools, or the equivalent. Students register in class on June 24.

10:30 A.M.-1:30 P.M.   30 hours   Credit: 2 semester-hours   Room 7

---

* The courses offered in the field of the supervision and administration of Elementary Education are given as a part of the graduate major in Administration and Supervision.

17

* Integration S548—The Elementary School Curriculum Dr. Milligan

This course offers an opportunity to review State and city elementary curricula; to discuss the principles of curriculum construction; to collect new teaching materials for the various subjects; and to evaluate, organize, and grade these materials. Teaching procedures in the use of materials are discussed and evaluated in terms of pupil needs, the objectives set up, and the results obtained. The course offers an opportunity to make a special study of the materials and procedures to be used in the teaching of the language arts.

11:30 A.M.-12:25 P.M.   30 hours   Credit: 2 semester-hours   Room 24

Mathematics

Mathematics S102B—Mathematical Analysis, Part IV:
Analytical Geometry Mr. Budne

This course is recommended particularly to those students seeking a minor in mathematics or those in need of a review course in analytic geometry. The topics include: rectangular and polar coordinate systems; loci and their equations; the straight line; the conics—circle, parabola, ellipse, and hyperbola; parametric equations; transformation of coordinates; and the general equation of the second degree.

8:30-9:25 A.M.   30 hours   Credit: 2 semester-hours   Room 5

Mathematics S400—Educational Statistics Mr. Budne

The aim of this course is to prepare the student (1) to comprehend and criticize articles of statistical nature in current educational literature; (2) to apply statistical methods in testing and rating pupils; (3) to carry on the simpler types of educational research. By analysis of real data from the secondary field, the student becomes familiar with the measures of central tendency and variability, short methods of computation, graphic representation of material, the properties of the normal curve, and linear correlation. Inasmuch as statistical methods in education are almost identical with those employed in the natural, physical, and social sciences, there is natural integration with these fields.

11:30 A.M.-12:25 P.M.   30 hours   Credit: 2 semester-hours   Room 5

Mathematics S401—The Teaching of Mathematics
in Secondary Schools Dr. Davis

In this course, special consideration is given to specific problems which arise in the teaching of junior and senior high school mathematics. These include the following: adaptation of material to students of varying abilities; selection and treatment of subject matter; use of texts and supplementary material; importance of the fundamental concepts; use of special methods and devices; how to treat the more difficult phases of the subject matter; and the preparation of students for college entrance examinations.

8:00-9:25 A.M.   45 hours   Credit: 3 semester-hours   Room 3

Mathematics S402—Applications of Mathematics Mr. Clifford

The student is taught how to use and adjust those modern instruments of precision which can be used to motivate the teaching of mathematics in the

---

* The courses offered in the field of the supervision and administration of Elementary Education are given as a part of the graduate major in Administration and Supervision.

junior and senior high school. Included among these are the slide rule, transit, sextant, planimeter, plane table, solar telescope, and astronomical telescope with equatorial mountings. Such early instruments as the astrolabe, hypsometer, baculum, and optical square are also considered. The student must also make some of the simpler instruments and devise and solve problems which can be used in the classroom instruction.

9:30-11:25 A.M.   60 hours   Credit: 4 semester-hours   Room 2

Mathematics S407—Consumer Mathematics. A Background for
Teaching in the Junior High School   Mr. Budne

This course aims to survey the field of consumer problems, to display the placement and methods of teaching this material in the intermediate grades and in the junior high school. Some of the topics included are: the cost of raising children; the money value of a man; the cost of owning or renting a home; insurance; pensions and social security; stocks, bonds, and the financial page; the quality and cost of consumer goods; business cycles and indices of business activity. This course may be taken in lieu of Math. 300.

10:30-11:25 A.M.   30 hours   Credit: 2 semester-hours   Room 5

Mathematics S410—Introduction to the Mathematics of
Finance and Insurance   Dr. Davis

This course introduces the student to the elementary theory of simple and compound interest and leads to the solution of practical problems in annuities, sinking funds, amortization, depreciation, stocks and bonds, installment buying, and building and loan associations. It also discusses the mathematics of life insurance covering the following subjects: the theory of probability as related to life insurance; the theory and calculation of mortality tables; various types of annuities and insurance policies and reserves. This course is designed to give a helpful background to the mathematics teacher as well as to be an aid to the student of economics and insurance.

11:30 A.M.-12:25 P.M.   30 hours   Credit: 2 semester-hours   Room 3

Mathematics S510B—Mathematics in its Relation and Appli-
cation to Other Fields of Knowledge,
Part II: Science, Art and Music   Mr. Clifford

Part II of this course introduces such topics as mechanics and vector analysis, wave motion, geometrical optics, weather forecasting, mathematics in biology, chemistry, medicine, and geology, phyllotaxis (leaf arrangement in plants), spirals, laws of growth; static and dynamic symmetry, perspective, designs; and mathematics in music. Many of these topics should serve to enrich the background of secondary school teachers and encourage further study in special fields.

11:30 A.M.-12:25 P.M.   30 hours   Credit: 2 semester-hours   Room 3

Mathematics S514—Foundations of Algebra   Dr. Davis

Careful consideration is given to the fundamental concepts, assumptions, and postulates which form the foundational structure of algebra. Upon this basis, the development of our number system is demonstrated by application of algebraic operations. Algebraic Analysis is applied in establishing the criteria for possibility of geometrical constructions. This course gives a large fund of useful and essential information to teachers of high school mathematics.

9:30-10:25 A.M.   30 hours   Credit: 2 semester-hours   Room 3

19

Physical Education

Physical Education S100—Hygiene and Health   Mr. Voliva

The basis for work in this course is the physical examination which is given to each student on entering the College. The examination is followed, when necessary, by a conference in which the student is encouraged to take any remedial measures that are necessary. The class work is a study of the principles of hygienic living, and is based on a study of physiology, anatomy, and psychology. Special effort is made to help each student realize the importance of observing the rules of hygiene in his daily life.

8:30-9:25 A.M.   30 hours   Credit: 2 semester-hours   Room 4, CHS

Recreation S202A—Elements of Recreational Leadership   Mr. De Rosa

This course is an introduction to the field of recreational leadership. A brief survey is made of the various areas of recreation and their relation to the schools. Primary skills and techniques are taught in game and activity leadership, party planning, simple folk dancing and group singing. The student is introduced to the extensive source material in this field.

8:30-9:25 A.M.   30 hours   Credit: 2 semester-hours   Room 14, CHS

Physical Education SM202B—Management of Athletic Activities   Mr. Voliva

In this course information is provided which will enable the young teacher or director of physical education to avoid many of the common errors of management. Emphasis is placed upon: making schedules, care of equipment, care of playgrounds, care of locker rooms, purchasing equipment, handling finances, budgeting, conduct of students while on trips, etc.

10:30-11:25 A.M.   30 hours   Credit: 2 semester-hours   Room 14, CHS

**Physical Education S301A—Principles and Problems
of Physical Education**   Mr. Morr

This course acquaints the student with the scope of the field of physical education. The philosophy, aims, and objectives are outlined. Many of the problems are outlined, and suggestions are made which should prepare the young teacher to meet them successfully. A brief study of the history of physical education is made.

9:30-10:25 A.M.   30 hours   Credit: 2 semester-hours   Room 4, CHS

Physical Education S301B—Health and Health Teaching, Part I   Mr. Voliva

Community health. Principles of healthy community living as applied to family, school, and society are considered. This course includes field trips to nearby health and sanitation centers.

9:30-10:25 A.M.   30 hours   Credit: 2 semester-hours   Room 13, CHS

**Physical Education S302A—Organization and Methods in
Physical Education**   Mr. Morr

The details of organizing the units of the physical education program into its component parts are studied. Physical education classes, intramural programs, tournaments, and other units are discussed. Classification of students as to their physical ability or the quality of their health is emphasized. The construction and use of lesson plans are studied.

10:30-11:25 A.M.   30 hours   Credit: 2 semester-hours   Room 4, CHS

Physical Education S407—Safety Education   Mr. Morr

Safety is the latest subject to be placed in the curriculum of elementary and secondary schools. There is a need for teachers who can teach safety and organize safety programs. A study is made of the causes which have made this an important subject and of its place in our present-day method of living as well as of materials and methods of safety education.

11:30 A.M.-12:25 P.M.   30 hours   Credit: 2 semester-hours   Room 4, CHS

Physical Education S411—School Health Service Program   Mr. Armstrong

Due to the present emphasis upon health and the close relationship between Physical Education and Health, it is advisable that the student minoring in Physical Education should be well informed as to the details of the School Health Service Program. The organization and administration of this work is studied. The duties of the school nurse and the part which the classroom teacher plays in this important field of education are emphasized

9:30-10:25 A.M.   30 hours   Credit: 2 semester-hours   Room 14, CHS

Science

Biology S408—Biological Technique

This course is designed to furnish the prospective teacher of biology with the technical details necessary to enable him to handle successfully biological materials, experiments, and demonstrations. Prerequisites: Biology 101, 102, 201, and 202, Botany and Zoology.

9:30-10:25 A.M.,   TuTh&F;   Laboratory Tu&Th. Aft.   60 hours
Cr: 3 s.h.   Room 28

Biology S409—Human Physiology

A careful stduy of human anatomy is used as a basis for discussion of both normal and abnormal physiology. Prerequisites: Biology 201 and 202, Zoology.

8:30-9:25 A.M., daily; 9:30-10:25 M&W; Lab. M&W Aft.
90 hours   Cr: 4 s.h.   Room 28

Chemistry S501—The Teaching of Chemistry in Secondary Schools   Dr. Reed

This course satisfies the requirements in the field of teaching of chemistry for the limited secondary certificate. A study is made of the objectives, recent trends, methods of presentation, courses of study, instructional aids, and subject-matter of high school chemistry. Prerequisite: Eighteen semester-hours in chemistry.

8:00-9:25 A.M.   45 hours   Credit: 3 semester-hours   Room 23

Chemistry S506A—Industrial Chemistry, Part I   Dr. Reed

The purpose of this course is to enable science teachers to understand the chemical industries in the metropolitan region. The course involves field trips, reading assignments, and class discussions. In addition, a survey is made of the economic foundations of chemical industry, the relation of chemistry to industry in general, and the effects of synthetics upon social, economic, and political life. Prerequisite: General college chemistry.

9:30-10:25 A.M., M&W;   Field Trips M&W Aft.
45 hours   Cr: 2 s.h.   Room 23

Chemistry S509B—Advanced Inorganic Chemistry, Part II　　　　　**Dr. Reed**

This course offers opportunity for intensive and systematic study of the elements in the light of the periodic classification. Selected theories and principles of inorganic chemistry and some of their applications are studied in detail. Directed use of chemical literature is an important part of this course. Individual experimental work in the laboratory consists chiefly of preparation and purification of inorganic compounds. Prerequisite: General inorganic chemistry and analytical chemistry.

10:30-11:25 A.M.,　　TuThF;　　Laboratory Th, Aft.

　　　　　　　　　　　　　45 hours　　Cr: 2 semester-hours　Room 23

Physics S102—General College Physics, Part II　　　　　**Dr. K. O. Smith**

The major objective of physical science is to discover, describe, correlate, and explain the facts and phenomena of the inanimate world. For convenience, the subject-matter of physics is classified as: mechanics, heat, magnetism and electricity, sound, and light. The course consists of lectures, demonstrations, discussions, problem-solving exercises, library assignments, and laboratory experiments. The work of this part of the course pertains to the nature and propagation of sound, musical instruments, wave motion, the nature of light, optical instruments, color, spectra, polarization of light, magnetism, static electricity, electricity in motion, and electromagnetic induction. Part I is not prerequisite.

8:30-9:25 A.M., daily;　　9:30-10:25 M&W;　　Lab. M&W Aft.

　　　　　　　　　　　　　90 hours　　Cr: 4 s.h.　　Room 25

Physics S407—Aviation　　　　　**Mr. Placek**

This course treats types of airplanes, structures, motion of a plane, stability, lift, drag, principles of flying, engines, speed, power, physics of flight, and airplane performance. At least eight hours of flight instruction should precede or parallel this course. Prerequisites: General college physics and adequate college training in mathematics.

10:30 A.M.-12:25 P.M.　　60 hours　　Credit: 4 semester-hours　　Room 22

Physics S409A—Principles of Radio Communication, Part I　　**Dr. K. O. Smith**

Types of tubes are studied in circuits for which they have been designed. A study is made of audio and high-frequency amplifiers, rectifiers and power apparatus, oscillators, transmitters, antennas, and television transmission. Prerequisites: General college physics and a course in electrical measurements.

10:30-11:25 A.M., TuThF;　　Laboratory Tu. Aft.

　　　　　　　　　　　　　45 hours　　Credit: 2 semester-hours　　Room 25

Science S100C—Survey of Earth Sciences　　　　　**Dr. Burgy**

In this course, emphasis is laid on the effect of soil, climate, and physical features on the welfare of plants, animals, and mankind. The keynote of the course is to show the influence of a constantly changing physical environment on the life activities and welfare of mankind.

9:30-10:25 A.M.　　30 hours　　Credit: 2 semester-hours　　Room 26

Science S401D—The Teaching of Aviation in Secondary Schools　　**Mr. Placek**

This course deals with texts, bulletins, demonstration equipment, tests, working models, visual aids, and reference works needed to teach aerodynamics,

22

aircraft engines, meteorology, navigation and aircraft communication in high schools.

9:30-10:25 A.M.   30 hours   Credit: 2 semester-hours   Room 22

Social Studies

Social Studies S100B—Civilization and Citizenship, Part II   Dr. Wittmer
This course carries to completion the problems set up by the preceding course, but with the modern world the main theme. First, a study is made of the transformation of culture through the medium of great epochs: the Renaissance, the Protestant Reformation, the Commercial Revolution, and, finally, the Industrial Revolution and the industrial society of our world today. Then an effort is made to evaluate and organize the various remedies which have been proposed as desirable answers to the problems with which the course started. The focus of attention, however, is upon questions of a political, economic, and sociological nature.

10:30-11:55 A.M.   45 hours   Credit: 3 semester-hours   Room 12, CHS

Social Studies S200A—Contemporary Economic Life   Mr. Rellahan
This course aims to acquaint the student with the basic nature of economic life, to point out the opposing economic doctrines in force in various parts of the world, and particularly to investigate the functionings of economic life both here and abroad. Case studies from the current newspapers and periodicals are made the basis of this course.

10:30-11:25 A.M.   30 hours   Credit: 2 semester-hours   Room 20

Social Studies S200C—Contemporary Social Life   Dr. Jenkins
This course is designed to create in prospective teachers an awareness of the tensions in the community and their effects upon pupils and the school. The student is given guidance in dealing with social issues and in discovering the constructive community forces which may be used by the teachers.

11:30 A.M.-12:25 P.M.   30 hours   Credit: 2 semester-hours   Room 21

Social Studies S401—The Teaching of the Social Studies
in Secondary Schools   Dr. Jenkins
The course aims to present recent tendencies in educational method in teaching the social studies. A program is presented containing the fusion organization in socialized recitation, the teaching of current events, projects in citizenship, and the use of the project-problem as a method of teaching history and civics. A laboratory containing texts and workbooks in the social studies field is available to all students of this course.

8:00-9:25 A.M.   45 hours   Credit: 3 semester-hours   Room 21

Social Studies S402A—American Government   Dr. Jenkins
The basic facts and principles necessary for the teaching of civics, history, and the political aspects of Problems of American Democracy are studied. This, the first part, is devoted to American national government, including the obligations and rights of citizens, the suffrage, political parties, the changing nature of the federal system, and the executive, administrative, legislative, and judicial systems.

10:30-11:25 A.M.   30 hours   Credit: 2 semester-hours   Room 21

Social Studies S436—Modern Men of Ancient Times   Dr. Freeman

This course is designed to present biographical sketches of some of the great leaders of past ages. The subjects for discussion are selected from all lines of human endeavor, and special attention is given to their influence on the thought of their own times and the contribution to the culture of the present day. The course is specially recommended to students who wish to know these leaders as real persons and not as lay figures in ancient history.

9:30-10:25 A.M.   30 hours   Credit: 2 semester-hours   Room 10

Social Studies S442—The Far East   Dr. Wittmer

A study is made of the economic, social, and cultural situation of the Far East, with particular emphasis on the historical background of China and Japan, and on our relations with the Philippines. Oriental folkways, religion, education, population shifts, and strategic questions are discussed. This course provides an approach to the problems the United States must face in the Far East.

8:30-9:25 A.M.   30 hours   Credit: 2 semester-hours   Room 12, CHS

Social Studies S450B—Applied Economics: Problems and Policies, Part II   Mr. Rellahan

Special attention is given to an understanding of our broader economic problems and the public policy relating to them.

9:30-10:25 A.M.   30 hours   Credit: 2 semester-hours   Room 20

Social Studies S454—Post-War Economic Reconstruction   Mr. Rellahan

The purpose of this course is to provide the student with the essentials necessary to appreciate the impact of reconstruction following the war upon existing economic institutions. Emphasis is placed upon Congressional plans for reconversion, the post-war public debt and related fiscal policies; the political economy of regional economic regulations, cartels, and foreign investments; the post-war distributive system; international monetary policy; labor and social security; post-war agriculture; and American economic philosophy as a national policy.

11:30 A.M.-12:25 P.M.   30 hours   Credit: 2 semester-hours   Room 20

Social Studies S457—Development of Russia   Dr. Wittmer

Factors which have shaped the evolution of the Russian people, such as the Byzantinism and the Greek Orthodox faith, the Synod, Tartar state organization, the Mir, Westernization from Peter to Lenin, Slavophilism and dialectic materialism, are emphasized. An account is presented of Soviet internal organization, sovkhoz, kolkhoz, and the Five-Year Plans. In addition to the historical background, Russia's great writers are discussed in the light of social and political developments.

9:30-10:25 A.M.   30 hours   Credit: 2 semester-hours   Room 12, CHS

TWELVE WEEKS SUMMER TERM, 1946

On page 4 of this Bulletin, there is a paragraph concerning the Twelve Weeks Summer Term. The list of courses below is the list referred to in that paragraph.

The Roman numeral "I" precedes the catalogue number of the courses that will end Wednesday, July 3. All other courses in this list will

24

continue through Friday, August 16. Courses that carry a credit of 4 s.h. in the regular college curriculum are frequently given in the Summer Session in two parts, each half course carrying a credit of 2 s.h. If the description of the second half is omitted from the Summer Session Bulletin, it is an indication that the first half is prerequisite and that only those students able to enroll for the entire Twelve Weeks may enter the course.

Courses in progress from May 22 through July 3, 1946

Department	Cat. No.		Sem. Hr. Cr.
Business Ed.	201	Introduction to Business (May 22-August 16)	4
Business Ed.	I 301A	Business Law, III	2
Business Ed.	302	Salesmanship (May 22-August 16)	4
English	I 100A	World Literature: Its Forms and Its Masters	3
English	I 200A	Composition	3
English	I 431A	Shakespeare, Part I	2
English	I 442A	American Literature, Part I	2
Integration	I 200A	Educational Psychology and Mental Testing	2
Integration	I 300A	Aims and Organization of Secondary Education	2
Integration	I 400A	Principles and Philosophy of Secondary Education	2
Integration	*I 530B	Practicum in Remedial and Corrective Reading	2
Mathematics	I 102A	Mathematical Analysis: Trigonometry	2
Mathematics	I 300	Social and Commercial Uses of Mathematics	2
Mathematics	I 400	Educational Statistics	2
Physical Ed.	I 101	Applied Physiology	4
Physics	I 101	General College Physics	4
Science	I 100A	Survey of Physical Science	4
Science	I 100B	Survey of Biology	4
Social Stud.	I 100A	Civilization and Citizenship Part I	3 / 3
Social Stud.	I 100B	Civilization and Citizenship Part II	3
Social Stud.	I 101A	European History from 1492 to 1713	2
Social Stud.	I 101B	European History from 1713 to 1815	2
Social Stud.	I 451	The Middle East	2
Social Stud.	I 455	Social Legislation	2
Social Stud.	*I 518	Recent Trends in American History	2

* Courses numbered 500 and above are graduate courses and their descriptions are to be found in the Graduate Bulletin. Integration 530B will be given intensively, beginning June 24. For further information concerning this course, see page 17 of this Summer Session Bulletin.

SUMMER SESSION

Bulletin of

MONTCLAIR
STATE TEACHERS COLLEGE

JULY 1 to AUGUST 15

1947

UPPER MONTCLAIR, NEW JERSEY

Summer Session

Bulletin of

Montclair
State Teachers College

1947

July 1 to August 15

Upper Montclair, New Jersey

STATE OFFICIALS

State Board of Education

GUSTAV A. HUNZIKER, *President* ....Little Fall

GEORGE O. SMALLEY, *Vice-President* ....,.......Bound Broo

JOSEPH CLAYTON ....Point Pleasant Beac

JOHN S. GRAY ....Newto

MRS. EDWARD L. KATZENBACH ....Princeto

WILLIAM KIRK ....Penns Grov

A. HARRY MOORE ....Jersey Cit

PAUL V. MURPHY ....Metuche

AMOS J. PEASLEE ....Clarksbor

MRS. HERBERT REIM ....Maywoo

MRS. OLIVE C. SANFORD ....Nutle

RICHARD E. SWIFT ....Ventnor Cit

Commissioner of Education
John H. Bosshart

Assistant Commissioner for Higher Education
Robert H. Morrison

Officers of Administration
New Jersey State Teachers College at Montclair

HARRY A. SPRAGUE, Ph.D. ....Presider

JOHN D. MESSICK, Ph.D. ....Dean of Instructio

FRANCES VAN ETTEN, Ed.B. ....Registra

ELIZABETH S. FAVOR, A.M., Administrative Assistant in Part-time and Summer Wor

CARL E. SNEDEKER, B.Acc. ....Business Manage

CLAUDE E. JACKSON, A.M. ....Director of Personnel and Researc

MARGARET A. SHERWIN, A.M. ....Dean of Wome

HORACE J. SHEPPARD, A.M. ....Acting Head of Business Education Departmei

EDWIN S. FULCOMER, Ed.D. ....Head of English Departmei

ARTHUR E. MORR, Ed.M.
Director, Health, Physical Education and Recreation Departmei

HAROLD SPEARS, Ed.D. ....Head of Integration Departmei

WALTER H. FREEMAN, Ph.D. ....Head of Language Departmei

VIRGIL S. MALLORY, Ph.D. ....Head of Mathematics Departmei

EDNA McEACHERN, Ph.D. ....Head of Music Departmei

EARL R. GLENN, A.M. ....Head of Science Departmei

ELWYN C. GAGE, Ph.D. ....Head of Social Studies Departmei

ARTHUR M. SEYBOLD, A. M. ....Director of College High Scho

OTTO CORDES ....Engineer in Charge, Maintenani

SUMMER SESSION 1947

FACULTY

HARRY A. SPRAGUE, Ph.D. ....President
JOHN D. MESSICK, Ph.D. ....Dean of Instruction
FRANKLIN G. ARMSTRONG, A.M. ....Health Education
HAROLD C. BOHN, A.M. ....English
EDGAR C. BYE, A.M. ...,..Field Studies
ALDEN C. CODER, Ed.M. ....Physical Education
LAWRENCE H. CONRAD, A.M. ....English
MARGARET G. COOK, A.M. ....Librarian
VERA BROOKE DAVIS, A.M. ....Mathematics
DAVID R. DAVIS, Ph.D. ....Mathematics
JEROME DEROSA, A.M. ....Physical Education
L. HOWARD FOX, A.M. ....English
WALTER H. FREEMAN, Ph.D. ......(.....Head of Department of Foreign Languages
PAUL E. FROEHLICH, A.M. ....:.....Business Education
EDWIN S. FULCOMER, Ed.D. ....Head of Department of English
PAUL GLASS, B.S. ....Music
EARL R. GLENN, A.M. ....Head of Department of Science
HERBERT B. GOODEN, Ed. D. ....Social Studies
CHARLES E. HADLEY, Ph.D. ....Biology
WILLIAM PAUL HAMILTON, A.M. ....English
LILI HEIMERS, Ph.D. ....Director, Auditory and Visual Aids Service
OTIS C. INGEBRITSEN, Ph.D. ....Psychology
CLAUDE E. JACKSON, A.M. ....Research
RUSSELL KRAUSS, Ph.D. ....English
ETHEL F. LITTLEFIELD, A.M. ....Languages
EDNA E. McEACHERN, Ph. D. ....Head of Department of Music
RALPH MILLER, A.M. ....Mathematics
JOHN P. MILLIGAN, Ed.D. ....Administration
HARLEY P. MILSTEAD, Ph.D. ....Geography
MAURICE P. MOFFATT, Ph.D. ....Social Studies
ARTHUR E. MORR, A.M....Department of Health, Physical Education and Recreation
RUFUS D. REED, Ph.D. ....Chemistry
JOHN J. RELLAHAN, A.M. ....Social Studies
PAUL J. RITTER, Ph.D. ....Integration
ARTHUR M. SEYBOLD, A.M. ....Integration
HORACE J. SHEPPARD, A.M.........:..Acting Head, Department of Business Education
W. SCOTT SMITH, Ph.D. ....Integration
HAROLD SPEARS, Ed.D. ....Head of Department of Integration
D. HENRYETTA SPERLE, Ph.D. ....Integration
EVAN H. THOMAS, A.M. ....Guidance
FELIX WITTMER, Ph.D. ....Social Studies
CHIH MENG, Ph.D. ....China Workshop

SUMMER SESSION OF THE
NEW JERSEY STATE TEACHERS COLLEGE AT MONTCLAIR

Professional and Academic Status

The New Jersey State Teachers College at Montclair is a fully accredited member of the American Association of Teachers Colleges; the Middle States Association of Colleges and Secondary Schools, and the Association of American Universities.

The College is a professional school which prepares teachers, supervisors, and principals of high schools, and administrators of public school systems. The degrees offered by this College are those of Bachelor of Arts and Master of Arts. Certificate courses are offered for those who now hold degrees.

How to Reach the Campus

Trains of the Greenwood Lake Division, Erie R. R., stop at College Station. Trains of the Lackawanna R. R. connect at Montclair with the following bus lines: No. 64, running between Brick Church and the College; No. 60, running between Newark and the College; and No. 76, which runs between Orange and Paterson, passing the College en route. For those who come by car: the College is located about one mile north of the center of Upper Montclair.

Residence Halls for Men and Women

Edward Russ Hall and Chapin Hall are Montclair College's two well-appointed Residences. The charge for living on campus during the Summer Session is reasonable: $12.00 per week; which includes room, breakfast, and dinner. A la carte luncheons are served in the College cafeteria. For one student alone in a double room, an extra charge of $2.00 per week is made. The College provides and launders sheets, pillowcase, and bedpad. Towels, table lamps, blankets, clocks, and similar items must be provided and cared for by the student. The boarding-hall fee must be paid on or before the first day of the Summer Session. No rebate is made for occasional absence or voluntary withdrawal during the session. Students who are absent on account of illness for two weeks or more receive a rebate of $6.00 per week during the illness.

For reservations in a College Residence Hall, both men and women address: Dean of Women, State Teachers College, Upper Montclair, N. J.

Schedule of the Summer Session

The Summer Session begins on Tuesday, July 1, and continues through Friday, August 15, on which day the summer Commencement will be held. All courses meet daily, Monday through Friday, for one hour, except where definitely indicated otherwise.

4

Summer Session of Nine Weeks

On page 26 of this Bulletin is a list of the courses of the Nine-Weeks Summer Session which is held for the benefit of the accelerated candidates for the Bachelor of Arts degree at Montclair. Other students who have special need for a maximum amount of credit may enroll in this session. Descriptions of the courses will be found in the Undergraduate Catalogue of the College. The mimeographed schedule will be sent upon request. All students other than the regular undergraduates of this College must register and pay the fees on Monday, June 16. Report to Room 8 in College Hall. Classes begin the next day and continue to August 15.

Matriculation

Those who desire to become candidates for either the Bachelor of Arts or the Master of Arts degree at Montclair must request the Registrar for the application form and return it, properly filled in and accompanied by an official transcript of all previous work on college level. When such an applicant has been accepted by the College as a candidate for the degree, a definite statement will be furnished to him, showing the requirements which he must fulfill to earn the degree.

Auditors

Men and women who desire to take courses for cultural, vocational, or avocational purposes without college credit may register as auditors.

A student who desires to enroll in a course for which he already holds credit must register as an auditor in that course.

Change of Status in a Course

If a student desires to change his status in a course from "credit" to "auditor," or from "auditor" to "credit," he must make formal application for such change not later than the middle of the course. Forms for this purpose may be procured from the Secretary of the Summer Session.

Students Matriculated at Montclair

Work taken for credit at Montclair must be with the advice and approval of the Dean of Instruction and the Head of the Department in which the student is majoring. See paragraph under the heading "Conferences."

A student who expects to receive a degree should consult the Registrar, Miss Van Etten, three months in advance of graduation.

Students Matriculated at Other Colleges

Work taken for credit to be transferred to other colleges should be approved in advance by the Dean of the college at which such student holds membership. A student who is planning to attend Montclair this summer should take the Summer Session Bulletin to a conference with his Dean to arrange a program of work. For the Dean's information: the numbering of courses at Montclair follows this order: 100-399, inclusive, are undergraduate courses; 400-499, inclusive, are senior-college and graduate courses; 500 and above are graduate courses.

Certificates

The State Teachers College at Montclair offers work toward the following New Jersey Certificates: Limited Secondary Teaching Certificate;

Permanent Secondary Teaching Certificate; Secondary School Principal's Certificate; Secondary School Subject Supervisor's Certificate; Supervising Principal's Certificate; and the Superintendent of Schools' Certificate.

Those who matriculate at Montclair for a degree will receive information from Dean Messick and the Head of the major department as to the requirements for each of these certificates. Students who have not matriculated at Montclair, who desire to obtain any of the above certificates, should write to Dr. E. C. Preston, Secretary of the State Board of Examiners, Department of Public Instruction, Trenton Trust Building, Trenton 8, New Jersey, for information as to the requirements and for an evaluation of work already completed. An official transcript of such previous work should accompany the inquiry, with a statement as to the particular certificate desired.

Students who must have this information immediately should go to Trenton to confer personally with Dr. Preston or his assistant, Miss Smith.

Supervised Student Teaching

The opportunity to do supervised student teaching cannot be offered during the Summer Session. For fall teaching, matriculated students confer with Dr. Harold Spears. Non-matriculated students should write to Dr. Robert H. Morrison, Assistant Commissioner for Higher Education, State Department of Public Instruction, Trenton Trust Building, Trenton 8, New Jersey, enclosing an official transcript of all work done on college level.

Offerings to Veterans

Many Veterans have planned to continue their college work. Those who are discharged in the late spring or early summer may wish to use the Summer Session as a means of accelerating their program.

The College makes every effort to adjust its offerings and facilities to Veterans who are interested in teaching as a profession. It has printed a bulletin setting forth its policies and procedures in working with Veterans. This bulletin may be had upon request to Mr. Lawrence T. Clark, Veterans' Counselor. It should be known that the College will recognize equivalency in courses taken and experiences gained by men and women in service. In general, credit may be allowed for:

(a) Courses at undergraduate and graduate level taken while in service,

(b) specialized training taken in service schools either on or off campus, and

(c) experiences of a more informal nature that can be judged from the standpoint of educational growth or development.

Veterans may receive government aid in financing Part-Time and Summer Session courses. They should be sure to obtain the Certificate of Eligibility from the Veterans' Administration before the start of the Summer Session.

Conferences with Advisers

Appointments with the Dean of Instruction, a Department Head, or the Veterans' Counselor may be made by mail or by telephone to their offices. This should be done at as early a date as possible. Student

6

unable to do so earlier may, however, see these officials or their representatives on July 1.

A representative of the State Board of Examiners will be at the College on July 1 to see students who desire advice on the selection of courses toward New Jersey Certificates. (See paragraph under heading "Certificates.") The Secretary of the Summer Session will receive requests for appointments with this State Official.

Work Taken for Credit

The maximum amount of credit which may be earned in the Summer Session is 8 semester-hours. There is no provision for a student to audit additional courses; consequently, the total of all courses may not exceed that amount and students should not register for more. If additional credit is necessary, the student should plan to attend the Nine-Weeks Summer Session, mentioned previously.

Each course is in session at least thirty hours and carries a designated amount of credit. It is not possible to earn three points credit in a two-point course.

If prerequisites are required, the student should make certain he has fulfilled them or their equivalent before enrolling in the course. If no previous work on college level has been taken, the student should consult the Dean of Instruction before enrolling in any course.

A student may not register for credit in any course for which he already holds credit.

Registration

There is no advance registration for the Summer Session. Registration takes place in the first meeting of each class on July 1. All registrations received subsequent to July 1 are subject to a late registration service charge of $2.00.

Withdrawal from a Course

The Secretary of the Summer Session must be notified in writing immediately if the student finds it necessary to withdraw from a course in which he has enrolled. Teachers are required to give the student a failing mark unless the notice of withdrawal is received by them from the Secretary of the Summer Session.

Audited Class Admission Cards

Audited Class Admission cards are due at the third meeting of each class. They are obtained in the Business Office on presentation of fees, credit slips, or Veteran's cards, following registration.

The Business Office is open daily, Monday through Friday, at the following hours: 8:30-11:30 A. M., and 12:30-3:30 P. M.

The late registration service charge is collected from students who fail to obtain their Audited Cards by the third meeting.

Fees and Service Charges

Check or money-order should be made payable to New Jersey State Teachers College.

Registration service charge: $1.00 for the Summer Session.

Late registration service charge: $2.00. This is collected from all students who enroll after July 1 or who fail to obtain their Audited cards by the third meeting.

Tuition fees: to legal residents of New Jersey, $8.00 per semester-hour credit carried by the course; to non-residents, $10.00 per credit. Courses taken by auditors for no credit cost the same.

Laboratory service charge: $2.00 for each laboratory course. This is collected in class by the teacher and should not be included in the check for tuition and registration.

Final Marks

Following are the final marks which may be received for a course: A-Excellent; B-Good; C-Fair; D-Poor; F-Failure; Inc.-Incomplete; Wd-Withdrew; N. C.-No Credit.

The mark of "D" when earned in summer, part-time, or extension courses of this College is not accepted for degree credit at Montclair.

The mark of "F" is given when earned and when the student has failed to notify the Secretary of the Summer Session promptly of his withdrawal from a course.

The mark of "N. C." is given only to auditors.

The mark of "Wd" is given only when prompt notice of withdrawal has been given to the Secretary and when the student's work to that time has been satisfactory to the teacher of the course.

The mark of "Inc." is seldom given. It may, however, be granted to a student whose work is incomplete in one particular at the end of the Session and who is eager to finish the work for a higher grade than he could receive otherwise. All responsibility regarding incomplete work rests with the student. He will be notified of a date after which, if the work remains incomplete, the final grade will be recorded without further notice.

Report Cards and Transcripts

A report card for each course and an Official Transcript are mailed directly to the student himself as soon as possible after the close of the Summer Session. This is usually within one week or ten days at the most. This first transcript is furnished free of charge. The student is urged to present it without delay to the State, college, or school official who is awaiting it, together with a statement as to the purpose for which the transcript is being filed. A student whose college requires that the transcript be mailed directly to the Dean or Registrar should so notify the Secretary of the Summer Session not later than the middle of the Session.

The cost of a second transcript depends upon the amount of work the student has completed at Montclair, ranging from 25 cents for one summer's or semester's work to $1.00 for four or more. All transcripts subsequent to the first one must include all work taken at this College..

Postage stamps cannot be accepted in payment. Check or money-order should be used. Men and women entering or already in national service are sent a second transcript without charge, as are Veterans of such service, upon request.

8

Catalogues and Bulletins

The following catalogues and bulletins may be obtained upon request: (1) Undergraduate Catalogue; (2) Graduate Bulletin; (3) Veterans' Bulletin; (4) Announcement of the 1947-1948 Part-Time and Extension Division.

This last will be printed about June 15, 1947.

Text-Book Exhibit

In the College Gymnasium, from July 7 to August 1, inclusive, there will be an exhibit of high school text-books. While primarily for the benefit of the principals and teachers attending the Summer Session, the exhibit will be open to undergraduate students and to members of the general public who may be interested in seeing the latest text-books for high school students.

COURSES THAT MAY BE TAKEN TOWARD THE NEW JERSEY SECONDARY CERTIFICATE

This is not an official statement. It does not emanate from the State Department that issues the certificate. It is furnished merely for your convenience in selecting courses. You should check your selections with the Secretary of the State Board of Examiners, Department of Education, Trenton Trust Building, Trenton, New Jersey.

Please note that either an undergraduate or a graduate course may apply on the certificate and that the total requirement is 18 semester-hours. Often it is possible to take three courses of 2 s. h. credit each to satisfy a total of 6 s. h. in required work.

Courses of the Summer Session are preceded by the letter "S" and described in this Bulletin. Courses listed without this letter preceding the number are offered during the Nine Weeks Session, beginning June 16.

I HEALTH EDUCATION—3 s.h required

The combination of *Physical Education 100—Hygiene and Health,* and *Physical Education 411—School Health Services,* each of which carries 2 semester-hours credit, provides the prospective teacher with an understanding of health education such as the classroom teacher needs. Neither of these courses, however, is being offered this summer. Graduate students may take both courses next year during the regular daytime hours of the College, and both courses will be offered during the Summer Session of 1948.

II EDUCATIONAL PSYCHOLOGY—3 s.h. required

Integration 200A—Introduction to Educational Psychology and Mental Testing—Cr: 2 s.h.

Integration 200B—Adolescent Psychology and Mental Hygiene—Cr: 2 s.h.

Integration S500B—Advanced Educational Psychology—Cr: 2 s.h.

9

III AIMS AND ORGANIZATION (PRINCIPLES) OF SECONDARY EDUCA-TION—3 s.h. required

Integration 300A—Aims and Organization of Secondary Education—Cr: 2 s.h.

Integration 400A—Principles and Philosophy of Secondary Education—Cr: 2 s.h.

Integration S500A—History and Principles of Secondary Education—Cr: 2 s.h.

IV PRINCIPLES AND TECHNIQUES (GENERAL METHODS) OF TEACHING IN THE HIGH SCHOOLS—3 s.h required

Integration S300B—Principles and Techniques of Teaching in the Secondary School—Cr: 2 s.h.

Integration S500C—Teaching Procedures in Secondary Education—Cr: 2 s.h.

V CURRICULUM ORGANIZATION AND COURSES OF STUDY (SPECIFIC METHODS) IN ONE ENDORSED TEACHING FIELD—3 s.h. required

English S519—English in the Modern High School—Cr: 2 s.h.

Language S401—The Teaching of Foreign Languages in Secondary Schools—Cr: 3 s.h.

Health Education S401—Methods and Materials in Health Education—Cr: 2 s.h.

Mathematics S401—The Teaching of Mathematics in Secondary Schools—Cr: 3 s.h.

Science S401—The Teaching of Science in Secondary Schools—Cr: 3 s.h.

Social Studies S401—The Teaching of the Social Studies in Secondary Schools—Cr: 3 s.h.

VI ELECTIVE—3 s.h required

Courses in the Department of Integration that are definitely in the field of Secondary Education and that have not been taken to satisfy one of the above requirements; for example:

Integration S505—Organization and Administration of Extra-Curricular Activities—Cr: 2 s.h.

It is possible, also, to take a second course under one of the above headings to fulfill the elective; for example, a methods course in the minor field.

COURSES THAT MAY BE TAKEN TOWARD SUPERVISOR'S, PRINCIPAL'S, AND ADMINISTRATOR'S CERTIFICATES

As in the case of the Secondary Certificate, this list is not an official one and selections from it should be checked with Dr. Preston or Miss Smith. See paragraph under heading *"Certificates."*

Courses in the Field of Administration

Integration S503—Methods and Instruments of Research—Cr: 2 s.h.

Integration S505—Organization and Administration of Extra-Curricular Activities—Cr: 2 s.h.

Integration S517—Administration of the Elementary School—Cr: 2 s.h.

Integration S548—The Elementary School Curriculum—Cr: 2 s.h.

Integration S601A—Workshop in Organizing and Administering the School—Cr.: 2 s.h.

Courses in the Field of Supervision

Integration S518—Supervision of Instruction in the Elementary School—Cr: 2 s.h.

Integration S601B—Workshop in Supervising Instruction—Cr: 2 s.h.

Courses of Interest to High School Principals

Integration S501—Tests and Measurement in Secondary Education—Cr: 2 s.h.

Integration S500C—Teaching Procedures in Secondary Education—Cr: 2 s.h.

Integration S530B—Workshop in Corrective and Remedial Reading in Secondary Schools—Cr: 2 s.h.

Courses of Interest to Elementary School Principals

Integration S517—Administration of the Elementary School—Cr: 2 s.h.

Integration S518—Supervision of Instruction in the Elementary School—Cr: 2 s.h.

Integration S548—The Elementary School Curriculum—Cr: 2 s.h.

Courses in the Field of Personnel and Guidance

Integration S500B—Advanced Educational Psychology—Cr: 2 s.h.

Integration S515—Guidance and Personnel Problems of Classroom Teachers—Cr: 2 s.h.

Integration S520—Principles of Mental Hygiene—Cr: 2 s.h.

Integration S535—Vocational Guidance—Cr: 2 s.h.

Integration S601C—Workshop in Dealing With and Understanding Youth—Cr: 2 s.h.

Integration S500C—Teaching Procedures in Secondary Education —Cr: 2 s.h.

Integration S518—Supervision of Instruction in the Elementary School—Cr: 2 s.h.

Integration S601B—Workshop in Supervising Instruction—Cr: 2 s.h.

See also offerings in the Subject Matter fields.

DESCRIPTION OF COURSES

Business Education

Business Education S405—Marketing   **Mr. Sheppard**

Marketing is the process of transferring goods from the producer to the consumer. The functions involved in this process, the various channels of distribution, marketing institutions, and the costs of marketing are considered in this course. Such topics as auctions, produce exchanges, wholesalers, retailing, department and mail-order stores, chain stores, co-operatives, profits, and prices are included.

9:30-10:25 A.M.   Credit: 2 semester-hours   Room B

Business Education S409—Money and Banking   **Mr. Froelich**

This course provides a short historical survey of money and the evolution of banking, outside and within the United States. The organization of banks, the nature of their transactions, operations, and relations with other banks are considered. The functioning of the Federal Reserve System and the nature of the money markets are also examined.

10:30-11:25 A.M.   Credit: 2 semester-hours   Room D

English

English S406——The Modern Novel   **Mr. Conrad**

Particular emphasis is given to British and American novels since 1870, and the important tendencies of present-day prose fiction are explored. Students are taught how to read a novel with profit, and how to guide and direct the reading of others.

9:30-10:25 A.M.   Credit: 2 semester-hours   Room CHS-7

English S431A—Shakespeare, Part I   **Mr. Bohn**

This course deals with Shakespeare's plays in relation to his life, his times, his contemporaries, and Elizabethan drama generally. Extensive reading is required from Shakespeare, his predecessors, contemporaries, and successors. The problems of stage production in both Elizabethan and modern theatres, of Shakespearean criticism are analyzed. Part I deals with Shakespearean tragedies.

9:30-10:25 A.M.   Credit: 2 semester-hours   Room A

English S439—Contemporary American Literature   Dr. Fulcomer

This course studies the major authors and literary movements in America during the contemporary period. Beginning where the course in *Masters of American Literature* normally ends, it is designed to complete a unit in this subject.

10:30-11:25 A.M.   .   Credit: 2 semester-hours   Room 1

English S442A—American Literature, Part I   Mr. Conrad

This chronological survey examines American Literature to observe its reflection of the political, social, and ethical principles of the American people. Part A begins with the Revolutionary period of the eighteenth century and ends with the Civil War.

10:30-11:25 A.M.   Credit: 2 semester-hours   Room CHS-7

English S442B—American Literature, Part II   Mr. Conrad

Part B embraces Reconstruction and the New South, Immigration and the Development of the West, Urban America, and the present reaffirmation of the American tradition of Democracy.
(These two courses are not open for credit to students who have credit for English 302, *Survey of American Literature*.)

11:30 A.M.-12:25 P.M.   Credit: 2 semester-hours   Room CHS-7

English S456—Play Direction   Mr. Fox

This course covers the choosing and casting, as well as directing, of plays. Scenes will be directed for class criticism, and a detailed prompt book of one play will be prepared. This course will complement English 435, which covers the technical aspects of play production.

11:30 A.M.-12:25 P.M.   Credit: 2 semester-hours.   Room A

English S503—Geoffrey Chaucer and His Time   Dr. Krauss

Some of the works of Chaucer are read rapidly, others studied intensively, so that the students may acquire a broad general understanding of Chaucer's place in the history of English literature as well as facility in reading and interpreting the medieval text of his stories.

9:30-10:25 A.M.   Credit: 2 semester-hours   Room CHS-14

English S518—The Major Romantic Poets   Mr. Hamilton

This course studies the work of Coleridge, Wordsworth, Scott, Byron, Shelley, and Keats. It devotes especial attention to the poems which are best adapted for the reading of high school students.   .

11:30 A.M.-12:25 P.M.   Credit: 2 semester-hours   Room 1

English S519—English in the Modern High School   Dr. Fulcomer

This is a seminar in which the methods and materials requisite to the development of a program in the language arts (listening, speaking, reading, and writing) are considered.

8:30-9:25 A.M.   Credit: 2 semester-hours   Room 1

Foreign Languages

Language S401—The Teaching of Foreign Languages in
Secondary Schools   **Dr. Freeman**

The work of this course is focused on such topics as the following: values
of foreign language teaching; ultimate and immediate aims in foreign
language teaching; survey of the outstanding methods, pronunciation, oral
work, reading, grammar, reviews, realia, examinations, tests, supervised
study, etc. The course consists of readings and discussions, lesson planning
and demonstrations, and organization of materials for use in student-teaching.

8:00-9:25 A.M.   Credit: 3 semester-hours   Room 9

Language S415—World Languages   **Miss Littlefield**

This course presents a practical introduction to the learning of any foreign
language. Through the use of International Phonetic Symbols and Linguaphone Records, students acquire skill in the recognition and identification
of foreign speech sounds. Ear, lip, and tongue training are combined to
ensure adequate ability in the pronunciation of foreign sounds with scientific
accuracy. The course is designed for all students in the language field.

9:30-10:25 A.M.   Credit: 2 semester-hours   Room 10

Geography

Geography S411—Geographic Influences in American History   **Dr. Milstead**

A study is made of the geographic factors influencing the development of
social, economic, and political life in America.

10:30-11:25 A.M.   Credit: 2 semester-hours   Room 26

Geography S509—Economic Geography of Asia   **Dr. Milstead**

This course constitutes a treatment of the economic and commercial development of the countries of Asia in relation to their natural environment.

8:30-9:25 A.M.   Credit: 2 semester-hours   Room 26

Health, Physical Education, and Recreation

Physical Education S202—History and Principles of
Physical Education   **Mr. Morr**

The student is acquainted with the scope of physical education. The course
deals with the history, philosophies, and objectives underlying the present
program of physical education. Emphasis is given to organic development
and physical education leadership.

10:30-11:25 A.M.   Credit: 2 semester-hours   Room CHS-4

Recreation S203—Introduction to Recreation   **Mr. DeRosa**

This course is an introduction to the field of recreational leadership. The
social influence and the historical movements which have created the philosophy of American recreation are stressed. A study is made of the various
areas of recreation and their relation to the secondary school pupil.

8:30-9:25 A.M.   Credit: 2 semester-hours   Room CHS-3

Health Education S304—Driver Education   Mr. Morr

In this course the student is instructed in the causes of highway accidents and in the methods of safe driving. Prospective teachers will be given an opportunity to qualify as teachers of Driver Education in the high schools of New Jersey.

11:30 A.M.-12:25 P.M.   Credit: 2 semester-hours   Room CHS-4

Recreation S307—Arts and Crafts   Mr. DeRosa

Techniques in arts and crafts used in the various recreational programs are presented so that teachers will be familiar with materials and tools. Wood craft, paper craft, leather craft, metal craft, music, dramatics, and special features of programs are included.

9:30-10:25 A.M.   Credit: 2 semester-hours   Studio Workshop

Physical Education SM307–308—Methods of Coaching and Officiating   Mr. Coder

The offensive and defensive strategy of the various varsity sports are discussed. A knowledge of the rules and techniques of officiating the various sports, together with actual experience in coaching and officiating are required.

10:30 A.M.-12:25 P.M. and 1:00-1:55 P.M.   Cr: 6 s.h.   Room E

Health Education S401—Methods and Materials in Health Education   Mr. Armstrong

This course prepares the teacher to assume the responsibility of formulating a course of study in health and safety instruction. The group method and individual counseling techniques of dealing with health problems will be discussed. The integration of health topics with other subjects in the secondary school curriculum will be considered. Special emphasis is given to the use of visual aids and basal and supplemental textbooks.

8:30-9:25 A.M.   Credit: 2 semester-hours   Room CHS-4

Physical Education S409—Organization and Administration of Physical Education   Mr. Morr

The details of organizing the units of the physical education program are discussed. Various topics, such as legislation, financing, curriculum construction, grading, excuses, plant facilities, supplies and equipment, and office management are considered.

9:30-10:25 A.M.   Credit: 2 semester-hours   Room CHS-4

Integration

Integration S300B—Principles and Techniques of Teaching in the Secondary School   Mr. Seybold

The purpose of this course is to help each student: (1) to acquire a knowledge of general and specific techniques and the basic principles involved in their utilization; (2) to acquire skill in selecting and preparing materials and in manipulating tools and instruments which will be utilized in vitalizing instruction; (3) to study the problems and techniques of effective instructional planning. Activities: reading and discussion of

15

case studies and other professional literature dealing with current problem
and practices, exploring courses of study, learning to operate projectors
and preparing both a unit and a daily lesson plan.

9:30-10:25 A.M.   Credit: 2 semester-hours   Room CHS-

Integration S410—Teaching Aids Workshop   **Dr. Ritte**

This is a practical course designed for both in-service and student teachers
with emphasis upon the development and use of teaching aids. A specia
study is made in the use of photographs, film strips, glass slides, charts
motion pictures, radio programs, television, etc. In the course, the studen
has the opportunity to handle and to perfect his use of these materials an
equipment. Presumably he has secured a more general knowledge of sucl
teaching aids through Integration 408, 409, or similar experiences. H
will have the benefit of class round-table discussion of his work, and wil
have the opportunity to demonstrate materials or the use of them befor
the group.

8:30-9:25 A.M.   Credit: 2 semester-hours   Room 4

Integration S500A—History and Principles of Secondary
Education   **Dr. Spear**

In this course we are concerned with the larger movements in America
secondary education. While a portion of the work is devoted to th
beginnings of secondary schools in this country, much of the emphasis i
upon current trends in thought and practice, such as the relationship o
general education and specialized, the growing concern for citizenshi
training, etc. In the course are treated the latest national reports an
studies dealing with this field.

10:30-11:25 A.M.   Credit: 2 semester-hours   Room 2

Integration S500B—Advanced Educational Psychology   **Dr. Ingebritse**

In this course a comparative study is made of contemporary schools o
psychology with emphasis on their direct application to education. Pre
requisite: An introductory course in psychology.

9:30-10:25 A.M.   Credit: 2 semester-hours   Room 3

Integration S500C—Teaching Procedures in Secondary Education   **Mr. Seybol**

This course emphasizes the fundamental principles underlying the techniqu
of teaching on the secondary school level. Some of the topics considere
are: the organization of knowledge, the logical and psychological aspec
of method, developing appreciations, social-moral education, teaching motc
control, fixing motor responses, books and verbalism, meeting individu
differences, guidance in study, tests and examinations, marks and marking

11:30 A.M.-12:25 P.M.   Credit: 2 semester-hours   Room CHS

Integration S501—Tests and Measurements in Secondary
Education   **Dr. Ingebritse**

The purpose of this course is to develop an appreciation of the meanii
and importance of measurement in education, and to give a working knov
edge of instruments of measurement.

10:30-11:25 A.M.   Credit: 2 semester-hours   Room

16

Integration S503—Methods and Instruments of Research   Mr. Jackson

This course is required of all candidates for the Master's degree without regard to their field of major interest. Its purpose is to introduce students of education to research and its practical application to professional promlems. The course treats: the nature and types of educational research; methods and techniques of educational research; and the tools used in interpreting statistical data. During the course, the student sets up a problem and plans and carries out its solution.

1:00-1:55 P.M.   Credit: 2 semester-hours   Room 9

Integration S505—Organization and Administration of Extra-Curricular Activities   Dr. Smith

The first part of this course considers such general problems of extra-curricular activities as: their growing importance; their relation to the curriculum; the principles underlying their organization, administration, and supervision; and methods of financing. In the second part, an intensive study is made of the home room, the assembly, the student council, clubs, athletics, school publications, and other activities in which the class is especially interested.

10:30-11:25 A.M.   Credit: 2 semester-hours   Room 8

Integration S515—Guidance and Personnel Problems of Classroom Teachers   Mr. Seybold

This course considers all types of personnel problems with which the classroom teacher deals. It is concerned with the growth of pupils and seeks to point out the ways by which proper growth may be attained. Classroom, health, social, and personal activities are analyzed in terms of the needs of present-day social life.

10:30-11:25 A.M.   Credit: 2 semester-hours   Room CHS-3

*Integration S517—Administration of the Elementary School   Dr. Milligan

This course analyzes and evaluates the administrative duties and relationships of the elementary school principal. Particular consideration is given to: building management, effective use of the school plant, sanitation, health service, the library, personnel management, the administration of the curriculum, community relationships, and publicity.

8:30-9:25 A.M.   Credit: 2 semester-hours   Room 29

*Integration S518—Supervision of Instruction in the Elementary School   Dr. Milligan

This course has been planned for those engaged in the supervision of the elementary school, and for those who are preparing for such responsibilities. Principles of classroom supervision are developed and applied to learning situations. Among the more important topics that receive attention are: the nature and function of supervision, the organization necessary for effective supervision, the nature and significance of the teacher's purposes, the methods and techniques of group and individual supervision, the technique of observation, and the supervisory conference.

11:30 A.M.-12:25 P.M.   Credit: 2 semester-hours   Room 29

---

* The courses offered in the field of the supervision and administration of Elementary Education are given as a part of the graduate major in Administration and Supervision.

Integration S520—Principles of Mental Hygiene   **Dr. Ingebritsen**

This course is designed to be a general survey of the principles and prac_tices of mental health with special reference to the mental health of teacher and pupil. It involves a thorough grounding in fundamental principles of mental hygiene with much practical consideration of the mental-health values of instruction programs and procedures. Discussion centers in practical efforts to develop wholesome personalities in our schools.

11:30 A.M.-12:25 P.M.   Credit: 2 semester-hours   Room 30

Integration S530 B—Workshop in Corrective and Remedial
    Reading in Secondary Schools   **Dr. Sperle**

This course is designed for students who are directing or instituting pro_grams of remedial and corrective reading and for those who are teaching individuals and classes in such programs. For the most part each student works intensively on his own teaching problem, receiving suggestions and recommendations as the work progresses. Some topics of common interest are: diagnosis, remediation, evaluation, organization and administration of reading programs; use and cost of materials and equipment; relation to the rest of the educational program of the school.
Prerequisite: *Integration 530A—Corrective and Remedial Reading in Secondary Schools,* or the equivalent, or considerable experience in remedial work.

9:30-10:25 A.M.   Credit: 2 semester-hours   Room 7

Integration S535—Vocational Guidance   **Mr. Thomas**

This course is especially intended to enable high school teachers to guide their pupils in planning for constructive vocational life. The course is designed to be helpful also to adults who are seeking better vocational adjustment. Following are the topics included: the purpose of work, main areas of work, inventory of personal interests and traits, analyzing interests and traits, samples of personal inventories with analyses and interviews, exploring one's area of work, making the most of school days, finding the first job, adjustments on the way, advancement—what it is and how to attain it, intelligent use of money, balanced use of time, and cultivating pride of work. To make the course practical, special features include lectures by outstanding management and labor specialists and a series of field trips to industries in this area. Among outstanding men who will participate are Glen Gardner, management consultant; Walter Kidde, industrialist; William Orchard, industrial relations specialist; and Leo Carlin, well-known in New Jersey labor circles.

8:30-9:25 A.M.   Credit: 2 semester-hours   Room 30

*Integration S548—The Elementary School Curriculum   **Dr. Milligan**

This course offers an opportunity to review State and city elementary cur_ricula; to discuss the principles of curriculum construction; to collect new teaching materials for the various subjects; and to evaluate, organize, and grade these materials. Teaching procedures in the use of materials are

---

* The courses offered in the field of the supervision and administration of Elementary Education are given as a part of the graduate major in Administration and Supervision.

discussed and evaluated in terms of pupil needs, the objectives set up, and the results obtained. This course offers an opportunity to make a special study of the materials and procedures to be used in the teaching of the language arts.

9:30-10:25 A.M. Credit: 2 semester-hours Room 29

Integration S601—Workshop in Education Dr. Spears
Section A—Organizing and Administering the School
Section B—Supervising Instruction
Section C—Dealing With and Understanding Youth

The workshop course enables the graduate student to devote his time to an educational topic or school problem of current interest to him and to secure the help of the staff, fellow students, and college facilities in pursuing this study. Workshoppers may meet together to discuss matters of common concern in respect to the current school situation. In addition, the student works independently on his own project and at times meets with a small group interested in the same area.

In the past, students have worked on topics in such areas as these: problems in administration, guidance programs, extra-curricular activities, school philosophies; problems in supervision, curriculum planning, and community relations. The success of the workshop depends much upon the student knowing what he wants to accomplish in six weeks, the procedure being flexible enough to support his purposes. He must have his proposed problems for study approved by the Director of the Workshop before he enrolls for the course.

The workshop is offered only in the summer session. It is divided into three sections, as noted above. The student may enroll for four semester-hours credit or for two, the four calling for two periods of scheduled time in the course daily, the two calling for one period of scheduled time in the course. The student taking the course for two credits enrolls for one of the three fields: A-Administration, B-Supervision, or C-Guidance. The student taking it for four credits may do all the work in one of these three fields, or he may enroll for two hours credit in one and two in another.

8:30-9:25 A.M. and 9:30-10:25 A.M. Credit: 2 or 4 s.h. Room 24

Mathematics

Mathematics S308—Teaching of Junior High School Mathematics Mrs. Davis

In this course a critical examination is made of the curriculum content of junior high school mathematics with suggested grade placement of topics in arithmetic, intuitive geometry, and introductory algebra. Methods of teaching and the use of multi-sensory devices are considered. Special emphasis is given to the material and teaching of general mathematics in the ninth grade.

9:30-10:25 A.M. Credit: 2 semester-hours Room 3

Mathematics S401—The Teaching of Mathematics in
Secondary Schools Mr. Miller

The student in this course studies the methods of teaching the different units of work in the junior and senior high school. A study of recent

19

trends in the teaching of mathematics, of noteworthy research, and of modern texts and tests is included.

8:00-9:25 A.M.   Credit: 3 semester-hours   Room 22

Mathematics S508—Tests and Measurements in Mathematics   Mrs. Davis

A careful study is made of representative tests in secondary school mathematics. The technique of administering and scoring tests, the tabulation and manipulation of data, the interpretation of results and certain types of remedial measures are considered in detail. The student has access to up-to-date material and to the publications of standard authorities in this field.

11:30 A.M.-12:25 P.M.   Credit: 2 semester-hours   Room 3

**Mathematics S509A—A Critical Interpretation of Mathematics
in the Senior High School, Part I   Dr. Davis**

An opportunity is here offered for an investigation and interpretation of the algebra and geometry of the secondary school. The meaning and use of secondary mathematics are stressed, rather than the methods of teaching. Among the topics discussed are: algebra as a thought process and not a mechanical operation, types of thinking in algebra and geometry, fundamental laws of arithmetic, algebra as generalized arithmetic, geometrical interpretation of algebra, the function concept in algebra and geometry, the changing scope and subject-matter of Euclidean geometry, limits and incommensurables, and integration (i.e. correlation and fusion) of all secondary mathematics.

9:30-10:25 A.M.   Credit: 2 semester-hours   Room 5

Mathematics S515—Differential Equations   Dr. Davis

This course is a continuation of the calculus considered from a new viewpoint. Various applications of differential equations and their standard methods of solution are fully treated in this course. Among the topics included are: linear differential equations of the first degree and of the first and higher orders, linear equations of the nth order with constant coefficients, linear equations of the second order, exact and total differential equations, simultaneous equations, numerical approximation, and partial differential equations.

10:30-11:25 A.M.   Credit: 2 semester-hours   Room

Music

Music S417—Our American Music   Mr. Glas

This course provides a survey of American folk and art music as relate to various social, economic, political, and cultural epochs in the histor of our country. It deals with the European backgrounds and native source of American music, the growth of the American idiom in music, and i use in our contemporary musical life. A special feature of the course the making and producing of programs of American music suitable for u in school and community.

9:30-10:25 A.M.   Credit: 2 semester-hours   Room CHS

20

Music S499—Workshop in High School Music   Dr. McEachern

This course deals with special phases of high school music. It is organized on the unit plan and includes music for boys, folk song dramatizations, integration of music with other subjects, music appreciation, visual aids, small vocal and instrumental ensembles, operettas, pageants and festivals. Students are given opportunity to work out units in fields of special interest. Prerequisite: Music 401, or the equivalent.

11:30 A.M.-12:25 P.M.   Credit: 2 semester-hours   Room 6

Science

Biology S402—Mammalian Anatomy and Histology   Dr. Hadley

A study is made of the gross structure of a typical mammal and of the structural peculiarities of its various tissues. This course prepares the student for the study of human physiology. Prerequisites: Biology 201 and 202.

9:30-10:25 A.M.; Lab. Tu. and Th. Afternoons   Cr: 4 s.h.   Room 28

Biology S508—Social Applications of Biology   Dr. Hadley

This field-study course offers to teachers of science an opportunity to gain first hand knowledge of the uses made of biological principles in industry, and in modern laboratories. Field trips are designed to cover such varied interests as public health and hospital routine laboratories, medical botanical research laboratories, and the inspection of model industries developing biological products.

11:30 A.M.-12:25 P.M., M&W; Field Trips M&W Afternoons
                                        Cr: 2 s.h.   Room 28

Chemistry S101—General College Chemistry, Part I   Dr. Reed

The course provides opportunity for mastering the fundamentals of chemistry, for understanding the numerous and far-reaching effects of contributions of chemistry to modern living, for training in scientific method, for developing facility in taking and utilizing laboratory notes, and for learning to use standard reference books. The laboratory contains many experiments of value for demonstration in high school chemistry. Accompanying such laboratory assignments are supplementary questions requiring reading of library reference books in chemistry.

9:30-10:25 A.M.; Lab. M&W Afternoons   Cr: 4 s.h.   Room 23

Chemistry S506B—Industrial Chemistry, Part II   Dr. Reed

The purpose of this course is to enable science teachers to understand the chemical industries in the metropolitan region. The course involves field trips, reading assignments, and class discussions. In addition, a survey is made of the economic foundations of chemical industry, the relation of chemistry to industry in general, and the effects of synthetics upon social, economic, and political life. Prerequisite: General College Chemistry.

11:30 A.M.-12:25 P.M., Tu. and Th.; Field Trips Tu. and Th. Aft.
                                        Cr: 2 s.h.   Room 23

21

Science S100C—Survey of Earth Sciences Dr. Milstead

In this course emphasis is laid on the effect of soil, climate, and physica features on the welfare of plants, animals, and mankind. The keynote o the course is to show the influence of a constantly changing physical envi ronment on the life activities and welfare of mankind.

9:30-10:25 A.M.   Credit: 2 semester-hours   Room 2(

Science S401—The Teaching of Science in Secondary Schools Prof. Glen

The chief purposes of this course are: to review the educational objective of science in public schools; to consider a program of instruction planned for all grades of the public school system; to study the chief aids to instruc tion such as texts, manuals, workbooks, tests, and materials for the enrich ment of teaching; to make a critical review of standards of classroom and laboratory instruction; and to participate in classroom activities in biology chemistry, and physics prior to student-teaching. This course is required of all science majors.

8:00-9:25 A.M.   Credit: 3 semester-hours   Room CHS-

Social Studies

Social Studies S200A—Contemporary Economic Life Mr. Rellahar

This course acquaints the student with the basic nature of economic life points out the opposing economic doctrines in force in various parts of the world, and investigates the functionings of economic life both here and abroad. Case studies from current newspapers and periodicals are made the basis of this course.

9:30-10:25 A.M.   Credit: 2 semester-hours   Room 2

Social Studies S200C—Contemporary Social Life Dr. Moffa

This course is designed to create in prospective teachers an awareness o the tensions in the community and their effects upon pupils and the school The student is given guidance in dealing with social issues and in discover ing the constructive community forces which may be used by teachers.

11:30 A.M.-12:25 P.M.   Credit: 2 semester-hours   Room 2

Social Studies S401—The Teaching of the Social Studies in the Secondary Schools Dr. Moffat

The course aims to present recent tendencies in educational method i teaching the social studies. A program is presented containing the fusio organization in socialized recitation, the teaching of current events, project in citizenship, and the use of the project-problem as a method of teachin history and civics. A laboratory containing texts and workbooks in th social studies field is available to the students of this course.

8:00-9:25 A.M.   Credit: 3 semester-hours   Room CHS-1

Social Studies S402B—Comparative Government Dr. Good

The basic facts and principles necessary for the teaching of civics, histor and the political phenomena in England, France, Germany, Italy, ar Russia, are studied.

8:30-9:25 A.M.   Credit: 2 semester-hours   Room 4

22

Social Studies S412—International Government **Mr. Bye**

The attempts of the international community of States to express itself in a formal world organization are the subject of this course. The agencies which have been established to deal with international legislative, executive, administrative, and judicial problems are studied. Specifically, among the topics discussed are the national State system, sovereignty, equality, intervention, international law, diplomatic services and procedures, international conferences and unions, sanctions, treaties, arbitration, international courts of justice, armaments and war, League of Nations, International Labor Organization, regional agreements, and the United Nations. The United Nations Organization and related problems in world politics will be stressed. Field trips to United Nations headquarters and to meetings of the Council and Assembly will be an essential part of the course and representative speakers will be secured. Films and other visual materials will be used.

11:30 A.M.-12:25 P.M.　　　Credit: 3 semester-hours　　　Room 20

**Social Studies S415—Latin-American Relations of the
United States** **Dr. Gooden**

This course aims to provide the information necessary to a clear understanding and accurate appreciation of the political, economic, and social relations that have developed between us and our Latin-American neighbors. To achieve this end, it considers the geographical conditions, the historical events, and the civic circumstances that have motivated and directed the growth of these relations and that will determine our Latin-American policy in the future.

10:30-11:25 A.M.　　　Credit: 2 semester-hours　　　Room 4B

Social Studies S417—American Archæology **Dr. Freeman**

This course shows that the New World of the early discoverers was in reality far from new. The course discusses the prehistoric pueblo dwellers and early mound builders. The truly remarkable civilizations of the Mayas and the Incas are examined and compared with that of the Aztecs. North American tribes of Indians are also studied in order to evaluate their significant cultures.

9:30-10:25 A. M.　　　Credit: 2 semester-hours　　　Room 9

Social Studies S419—American Political Biography **Dr.Moffatt**

This is the study of the life and influence of the leading figures in American political and social history. It is the aim here to show the relation of each of these characters to the times in which he lived and to point out how he influenced the trend of American life. The study includes such leaders as Washington, Jefferson, Hamilton, Webster, Lincoln, Cleveland, Roosevelt, and Wilson.

10:30-11:25 A.M.　　　Credit: 2 semester-hours　　　Room 9

Social Studies S451—The Middle East **Dr. Wittmer**

This course is a survey of Indian and Moslem civilizations. It shows that economic and political changes alone do not suffice to adjust the peoples of the Middle East to twentieth century civilization, and that many cultural traditions must vanish while some forgotten features of the past are to be

23

revived. Post-war planning for the region from the Near East through Persia, India, Burma, Thailand, and Malaya to the Netherlands East Indies is discussed.

10:30-11:25 A.M.   Credit: 2 semester-hours   Room 20

Social Studies S457—Development of Russia   Dr. Wittmer

Factors which have shaped the evolution of the Russian people, such as Byzantinism and the Greek Orthodox faith, the Synod, Tartar state organization, the Mir, Westernization from Peter to Lenin, Slavophilism, and dialectic materialism, are emphasized. An account is presented of Soviet internal organization, sovkhoz, kolkhoz, and the Five-Year plans. In addition to the historical background, Russia's great writers are discussed in the light of social and political developments.

9:30-10:25 A. M.   Credit: 2 semester-hours   Room 20

*Social Studies S461—New England and French Canada   Mr. Bye

This field study course gives an opportunity to study by direct observation the historical and geographical features of New England and the Province of Quebec. The trip, occupying the twelve days immediately following the summer session, is made in a modern chartered motor coach with overnight stops at first-class hotels. The route covers the lower Connecticut valley, including Hartford, Springfield, Northampton, and Deerfield; the Rhode Island cities of Providence and Newport; historical Massachusetts towns, such as Plymouth, Boston, Lexington, Concord, Salem, and Marblehead; the coast of New Hampshire and southern Maine; the White Mountains in the Mt. Washington and Franconia Notch area; the Canadian Province of Quebec, including the ancient French city of Quebec, Montmorency Falls, Ste. Anne de Beaupre, Montreal; the western shores of Lake Champlain, Lake George, and the Hudson River. It is an indispensable background for an understanding of Colonial and Revolutionary life and history in this region.

Credit: 3 semester-hours

Social Studies S470—History and Principles of Philosophy   Dr. Freeman

This course presents a study of the history of philosophy and of the important principles contributed by outstanding philosophers from Thales to Gentile. Much of the discussion is centered on three types of philosophic thought: naturalism, idealism, and pragmatism. Among the philosophers considered are: Plato, Aristotle, Bacon, Spencer, Rousseau, Hegel, James, Dewey, and Gentile.

11:30 A.M.-12:25 P.M.   Credit: 2 semester-hours   Room 9

Social Studies S499—China Workshop   Dr. Chih Meng

This course is given in twelve days. Twenty-four hours of lectures and class discussions are devoted to the study of Chinese History and Contemporary Chinese Life under the direction of Chinese scholars. Twenty-four hours of directed study in the library are devoted to the preparation of teaching units and background materials on China for use in our schools.

---

* This course was fully enrolled, with a waiting list, by January 15, 1947.

This year, the course begins June 30 and continues through July 12. Note the enclosed leaflet for further details, including daily schedule. If interested, write for registration materials.

9:30 A.M.-4:00 P. M.   Credit: 3 semester-hours   CHS-Auditorium

Social Studies S497—China Workshop, Advanced Course   Dr. Chih Meng

This course is given in twelve days. Twenty-four hours of lectures and class discussion are devoted to the study of Chinese philosophy under the direction of Professor Fung Yu-lan, Professor of Philosophy at National Tsing Hua University, China; visiting professor at the University of Pennsylvania. Professor Fung did his graduate work in this country at Columbia University (Ph.D., 1923), and is the author of a number of standard works on Chinese philosophy, one of which has been translated into English (*A History of Chinese Philosophy*) and is widely used in the United States.

Prerequisite: Social Studies 499, or equivalent in general philosophy or history of philosophy.

9:30 A.M.-4:00 P.M.   Credit: 3 semester-hours   Room CHS-12

Courses in Session from June 16 through August 15, 1947

(See paragraph at the top of page 5)

The detailed Schedule of these Courses available upon request.

Department	Cat. No.	Title of Course	Sem. Hrs. Cr.
Business Ed.	101	Introduction to Business	4
Business Ed.	201A	Business Law III	2
Business Ed.	201B	Business Org. and Management	2
Business Ed.	301	Bookkeeping and Accounting	4
English	100A	World Literature, Part I	3
English	100B	World Literature, Part II	3
English	200A	Composition	3
English	200B	Fundamentals of Speech, Part I	3
Language	300	Foundations of Language	2
Integration	200A	Introduction to Educational Psychology and Mental Testing	2
Integration	200B	Adolescent Psychology and Mental Hygiene	2
Integration	300A	Aims and Organization of Secondary Education	2
Integration	400A	Principles and Philosophy of Secondary Education	2
Mathematics	300	Social and Commercial Uses of Mathematics	2
Mathematics	301	Modern College Geometry	4
Mathematics	302	Higher Algebra	4
Mathematics	400	Educational Statistics	2
Music	100	Music Appreciation	1
Music	201	Harmony	4
Music	202	Advanced Harmony	4
Music	207	Epochs in Musical Development, Part I	2
Music	301	Choral Technique	2
Physics	101	General College Physics, Part I	4
Physics	407	Aviation	4
Science	100A	Survey of Physical Science	4
Social Stud.	100A	Civilization and Citizenship, Part I	3
Social Stud.	102	European History: 1815 to the Present	4
Social Stud.	200A	Contemporary Economic Life	2
Social Stud.	200B	Contemporary Political Life	2
Social Stud.	200C	Contemporary Social Life	2
Social Stud.	201	American History to 1860	4
Social Stud.	301	Economics	4

Descriptions of the above courses are to be found in the Undergraduate Catalogue o
the College.

IMPORTANT NOTICE!

NEW REGISTRATION PROCEDURES

Please note that registration no longer takes place in class, but in advance of the opening of the Summer Session. Read carefully the section on page 7 that gives dates and hours for registration.

Summer Session

Bulletin of
Montclair
State Teachers College

1948

June 29 to August 13

Upper Montclair, New Jersey

STATE OFFICIALS

STATE BOARD OF EDUCATION

GUSTAV A. HUNZIKER, *President* ....Little Falls
GEORGE O. SMALLEY, *Vice-President* ....Bound Brook
JOSEPH CLAYTON ....Point Pleasant Beach
JOHN S. GRAY ....Newton
MRS. EDWARD L. KATZENBACH ....Princeton
A. HARRY MOORE ....Jersey City
AMOS J. PEASLEE ....Clarksboro
MRS. HERBERT REIM ....Maywood
MRS. OLIVE C. SANFORD ....Nutley
RICHARD E. SWIFT ....Ventnor City
HUGH C. THUERK ....Morristown

COMMISSIONER OF EDUCATION
JOHN H. BOSSHART

ASSISTANT COMMISSIONER FOR HIGHER EDUCATION
ROBERT H. MORRISON

OFFICERS OF ADMINISTRATION

NEW JERSEY STATE TEACHERS COLLEGE AT MONTCLAIR

HARRY A. SPRAGUE, Ph.D. ....President
E. DEALTON PARTRIDGE, Ph.D. ....Dean of Instruction
FRANCES VAN ETTEN, A.M. ....Registrar
ELIZABETH S. FAVOR, A.M., Administrative Assistant in Part-Time and Summer Work
CARL E. SNEDEKER, B.Acc. ....Business Manager
CLAUDE E. JACKSON, A.M. ....Director of Personnel and Research
MARGARET A. SHERWIN, A.M. ....Dean of Women
PAUL J. RITTER, Ph.D. ....Dean of Men
HORACE J. SHEPPARD, A.M. ....Acting Head of Business Education Department
EDWIN S. FULCOMER, Ed.D. ....Head of English Department
CHARLES G. DESHAW, Ed.D.,
        Director, Health, Physical Education and Recreation Department
MOWAT G. FRASER, Ph.D. ....Head of Integration Department
WALTER H. FREEMAN, Ph.D. ....Head of Language Department
VIRGIL S. MALLORY, Ph.D. ....Head of Mathematics Department
EDNA MCEACHERN, Ph.D. ....Head of Music Department
EARL R. GLENN, A.M. ....Head of Science Department
ELWYN C. GAGE, Ph.D. ....Head of Social Studies Department
MORRIS SEIBERT, A.B. ....Veterans' Counselor
ARTHUR M. SEYBOLD, A.M. ....Director of College High School
OTTO CORDES, P.E. ....Engineer in Charge, Maintenance

2

SUMMER SESSION 1948

FACULTY

HARRY A. SPRAGUE, Ph.D. ....President
E. DEALTON PARTRIDGE, Ph.D. ....Dean of Instruction
WILLIAM A. BALLARE, A.M. ....Speech
HAROLD C. BOHN, A.M. ....English
EDGAR C. BYE, A.M. ....Social Studies
FRANK L. CLAYTON, Ph.D. ....Social Studies
PAUL C. CLIFFORD, A.M. ....Mathematics
LAWRENCE H. CONRAD, A.M. ....English
~~MARGARET G. COOK, A.M.~~ *Cridlelaugh*............................~~Librarian~~
DAVID R. DAVIS, Ph.D. ....Acting Head, Department of Mathematics
VERA BROOKE DAVIS, A.M. ....Mathematics
CHARLES G. DESHAW, Ed.D.,
        Director of Department of Health and Physical Education
L. HOWARD FOX, A.M. ....Speech
MOWAT G. FRASER, Ph.D. ....Head of Department of Integration
WALTER H. FREEMAN, Ph.D. ....Head of Department of Foreign Languages
PAUL E. FROELICH, A.M. ....Business Education
EDWIN S. FULCOMER, Ed.D. ....Head of Department of English
HERBERT B. GOODEN, Ed.D. ....Social Studies
CHARLES E. HADLEY, Ph.D. ......Biology and Acting Head, Department of Science
W. PAUL HAMILTON, A.M. ....English
OTIS C. INGEBRITSEN, Ph.D. ....Psychology
CLAUDE E. JACKSON, A.M. ....Personnel and Research
RUSSELL KRUASS, Ph.D. ....English
CHIH MENG, Ph.D. ....Director of China Institute
JOHN P. MILLIGAN, Ed.D. ....Administration
HARLEY P. MILSTEAD, Ph.D. ....Geography
MAURICE P. MOFFATT, Ph.D. ....Social Studies
ALLAN MOREHEAD, A.M. ....Integration
RUFUS D. REED, Ph.D. ....Chemistry
JOHN J. RELLAHAN, A.M.,
        Acting Head, Department of Social Studies for Graduate Students
PAUL J. RITTER, Ph.D. ....Integration
ARTHUR M. SEYBOLD, A.M. ....Integration
KENNETH O. SMITH, Ph.D. ....Physics
W. SCOTT SMITH, Ph.D. ....Integration
RICHARD W. WILLING, A.M. ....Business Education
FELIX WITTMER, Ph.D.,
        Acting Head, Department of Social Studies for Undergraduate Students

3

SUMMER SESSION OF THE
NEW JERSEY STATE TEACHERS COLLEGE AT MONTCLAIR

Professional and Academic Status

The New Jersey State Teachers College at Montclair is a fully accredited member of the American Association of Teachers Colleges; the Middle States Association of Colleges and Secondary Schools, and the Association of American Universities.

The College is a professional school which prepares teachers, supervisors, and principals of high schools, and administrators of public school systems. The degrees offered by this College are those of Bachelor of Arts and Master of Arts. Certificate courses are offered for those who now hold degrees.

How to Reach the Campus

Trains of the Greenwood Lake Division, Erie R. R., stop at College Station. Trains of the Lackawanna R. R. connect at Montclair with the following bus lines: No. 64, running between Brick Church and the College; No. 60, running between Newark and the College; and No. 76, which runs between Orange and Paterson, passing the College en route. For those who come by car: the College is located about one mile north of the center of Upper Montclair.

Residence Halls for Men and Women

Edward Russ Hall and Chapin Hall are Montclair College's two well-appointed Residences. The charge for living on campus during the Summer Session is: $12.00 per week; which includes room, breakfast, and dinner. A la carte luncheons are served in the College cafeteria. For one student alone in a double room, an extra charge of $2.00 per week is made. The College provides and launders sheets, pillowcase, and bedpad. Towels, table lamps, blankets, clocks, and similar items must be provided and cared for by the student. The boarding-hall fee must be paid on or before the first day of the Summer Session. No rebate is made for occasional absence or voluntary withdrawal during the session. Students who are absent on account of illness for two weeks or more receive a rebate of $6.00 per week during the illness. These prices are subject to change.

For reservations in a College Residence Hall, women address: Dean of Women, State Teachers College, Upper Montclair, N. J. Men address the Dean of Men.

Schedule of the Summer Session

Registration will take place on Saturday morning, June 26, and Tuesday, June 29. Classes for the Summer Session will begin June 30 and continue through Friday, August 13. All classes meet daily Monday to Friday, inclusive. Classes will also meet on Saturday, July 3. Monday, July 5, is a legal holiday. No classes will be held on that date.

4

Summer Session of Nine Weeks

On pages 23 and 24 of this Bulletin is a list of the courses of the Nine-Weeks Session which is held for the benefit of the accelerated candidates for the Bachelor of Arts degree at Montclair. Other students who have special need for a maximum amount of credit may enroll in this session. Descriptions of the courses will be found in the Undergraduate Catalogue of the College. The mimeographed schedule will be sent upon request. All students other than the regular undergraduates of this College must register and pay the fees on Monday, June 14. Report to Room 8 in College Hall. Classes begin June 15 and continue to August 13.

Matriculation

Those who desire to become candidates for either the Bachelor of Arts or the Master of Arts degree at Montclair must request the Registrar for the application form and return it, properly filled in and accompanied by an official transcript of all previous work on college level. When such an applicant has been accepted by the College as a candidate for the degree, a definite statement will be furnished to him, showing the requirements which he must fulfill to earn the degree.

Auditors

Men and women who desire to take courses for cultural, vocational, or avocational purposes without college credits may register as auditors.

A student who desires to enroll in a course for which he already holds credit must register as an auditor in that course.

Change of Status in a Course

If a student desires to change his status in a course from "credit" to "auditor," or from "auditor" to "credit," he must make formal application for such change not later than the middle of the course. Forms for this purpose may be procured from the Secretary of the Summer Session.

Students Matriculated at Montclair

Work taken for credit at Montclair must be with the advice and approval of the Dean of Instruction and the Head of the Department in which the student is majoring. See paragraph under the heading "Conferences."

A student who expects to receive a degree should consult the Registrar, Miss Van Etten, three months in advance of graduation.

Students Matriculated at Other Colleges

Work taken for credit to be transferred to other colleges should be approved in advance by the Dean of the college at which such student holds membership. A student who is planning to attend Montclair this summer should take the Summer Session Bulletin to a conference with his Dean to arrange a program of work. For the Dean's information: the numbering of courses at Montclair follows this order: 100-399, inclusive, are undergraduate courses; 400-499, inclusive, are senior-college and graduate courses; 500 and above are graduate courses.

Certificates

The State Teachers College at Montclair offers work toward the fol
lowing New Jersey Certificates: Limited Secondary Teaching Certificate
Permanent Secondary Teaching Certificate; Secondary School Principal'
Certificate; Secondary School Subject Supervisor's Certificate; Supervisin
Principal's Certificate; and the Superintendent of Schools' Certificate.

Those who matriculate at Montclair for a degree will receive informa
tion from Dean Partridge and the Head of the Major Department as t
the requirements for each of these certificates. Students who have no
matriculated at Montclair who desire to obtain any of the above certificate
should write to Dr. E. C. Preston, Secretary of the State Board o
Examiners, Department of Education, 175 West State Street, Trenton E
N. J., for information as to the requirements and for an evaluation of worl
already completed. An official transcript of such previous work shoul
accompany the inquiry, with a statement as to the particular certificat
desired.

Students who must have this information immediately should go t
Trenton to confer personally with Dr. Preston or his assistant, Miss Smith

Supervised Student Teaching

The opportunity to do supervised student teaching cannot be offere
during the Summer Session. For fall teaching, students confer with Dr
Fraser at the College.

Offerings to Veterans

The College makes every effort to adjust its offerings and facilities t
Veterans who are interested in teaching as a profession. It has printed
bulletin setting forth its policies and procedures in working with Veteran
This bulletin may be had upon request to Mr. Morris Seibert, Veteran
Counselor. It should be known that the College will recognize equivalenc
in courses taken and experiences gained by men and women in servic
In general, credit may be allowed for:

   (a) Courses at undergraduate and graduate level taken while
       service,

   (b) specialized training taken in service schools either on or o
       campus, and

   (c) experiences of a more informal nature that can be judged fro
       the standpoint of educational growth or development.

Veterans may receive government aid in financing Part-Time ar
Summer Session courses. They should be sure, however, to obtain tl
Certificate of Eligibility from the Veterans' Administration before the sta
of the Summer Session. Failure to do this will mean that the usual fe
must be paid by the student for all courses taken; these fees to be refund
when the Letter of Eligibility is presented to the College.

6

Conferences with Advisers

Appointments with the Dean of Instruction, the chairman of the Graduate Committee, a Department Head, or the Veterans' Counselor may be made by mail or telephone to their respective offices. This should be done at as early a date as possible. Students unable to do so earlier may, however, see these officials or their representatives on June 26 and June 29.

A representative of the State Board of Examiners will be at the College on June 29 to see students who desire advice on the selection of courses toward a New Jersey Certificate. (See paragraph under heading "Certificates.") The Secretary of the Summer Session will receive requests for appointments with this State Official.

Work Taken for Credit

The maximum amount of credit which may be earned in the Regular Summer Session is 8 semester-hours. There is no provision for a student to audit additional courses; consequently, the total of all courses may not exceed that amount and students should not register for more. If additional credit is necessary, the student should plan to attend the Nine-Weeks Session mentioned previously.

Each course is in session at least thirty hours and carries a designated amount of credit. It is *not* possible to earn three points credit in a two-point course.

If prerequisites are required, the student should make certain that he has fulfilled them or their equivalent before enrolling in the course. If no previous work on college level has been taken, the student should consult the Dean of Instruction before enrolling in any course.

A student may *not* register for credit in any course for which he already holds credit except with permission of the Dean of Instruction.

Registration

Beginning this summer, registration for courses will take place before the opening of the session, not in class as formerly.

Registration for the Summer Session will be on Saturday, June 26, between 9 A. M. and 12 Noon; and on Tuesday, June 29, between 9 A. M. and 12 Noon and between 1 and 4 P. M. Students must have their programs approved by their advisers, pay for their courses, and receive their class admission cards to admit them to classes on June 30. Students who enroll subsequent to June 29 will be charged the late registration service charge of $2.00, and no students will be admitted for credit after July 3.

The College reserves the right to close on June 30 any course for which the enrollment is insufficient. Notice of the closing will be sent to the Business Office and students will call there for adjustments of tuition fees.

Withdrawal from a Course

The Secretary of the Summer Session must be notified in writing immediately if the student finds it necessary to withdraw from a course. (The student is urged not to enroll in a course until it has been approved by his advisers.) Refunds of fees are computed from the date on which the student's notification is received by the Secretary. Teachers are notified by the Secretary that the student has withdrawn. Students who neglect to follow these instructions receive a failing mark for the courses from which they withdraw.

Tuition Fees and Service Charges

Check or money-order should be made payable to New Jersey State Teachers College, except for the China Workshop.

Registration service charge: $1.00 for the Summer Session.

Late registration service charge: $2.00. This is collected from all students who fail to enroll on June 26 or June 29.

Tuition fees: to legal residents of New Jersey, $8.00 per semester-hour credit carried by the course; to non-residents, $10.00 per credit. Courses taken by auditors for no credit cost the same.

Laboratory service charge: $2.50 for each laboratory course. This is collected by the business office. It should not be included in the check for tuition and registration.

Final Marks

Following are the final marks which may be received for a course: A-Excellent; B-Good; C-Fair; D-Poor; F-Failure; Inc.-Incomplete; Wd-Withdrew; N. C.-No Credit.

The mark of "D" when earned in summer, part-time, or extension courses of this College is not accepted for degree credit at Montclair.

The mark of "F" is given when earned and when the student has failed to notify the Secretary of the Summer Session promptly of this withdrawal from a course.

The mark of "N. C." is given only to auditors.

The mark of "Wd" is given only when prompt notice of withdrawal has been given to the Secretary and when the student's work to that time has been satisfactory to the teacher of the course.

The mark of "Inc." is seldom given. It may, however, be granted to a student whose work is incomplete in one particular at the end of the Session and who is eager to finish the work for a higher grade than he could receive otherwise. All responsibility regarding incomplete work rests with the student. He will be notified of a date after which, if the work remains incomplete, the final grade will be recorded without further notice.

Report Cards and Transcripts

A report card for each course and an Official Transcript are mailed directly to the student himself as soon as possible after the close of the Summer Session. This is usually within one week or ten days at the most. This first transcript is furnished free of charge. The student is urged to present it without delay to the State, college, or school official who is awaiting it, together with a statement as to the purpose for which the transcript is being filed. A student whose college requires that the transcript be mailed directly to the Dean or Registrar should so notify the Secretary of the Summer Session not later than the middle of the Session.

All transcripts are photostated copies of the complete record of the student. The cost of a second one is $1.00. Check or money-order should be used; postage stamps cannot be accepted. Men and women entering or already in national service are sent a second transcript without charge, as are Veterans of such service, upon request.

Room Numbers

Room numbers used in this Bulletin, if unaccompanied by other designation, refer to rooms in College Hall, the main building of the College.

Other designations are as follows:

CHS: College High School Building; to the northeast of the main building;

Annex No. 1: Federal Works Administration Building No. 1; at the northwest corner of the main building;

Annex No. 2: Federal Works Administration Building No. 2; next to No. 1;

Annex No. 3: Federal Works Administration Building No. 3; directly east of the main building.

DESCRIPTION OF COURSES

Business Education

Business Education S404—Business Economics   Mr. Froehlich

This course deals with the business aspects of the economics of war and peace; immediate and long range post-war problems; operation and government control of public utilities; taxation; government finance; and labor and management problems.

10:30-11:20 A.M.   Credit: 2 semester-hours   Room 1, Annex No. 2

Business Education S407B—Consumer Education II   Mr. Willing

This course is a continuation of 407A, but course 407A is not a prerequisite. Topics considered include the wise buying of textiles, furs, shoes, clothing, food, and home furnishings and supplies

11:30 A.M.-12:20 P.M. Credit: 2 semester-hours Room 2, Annex No. 2

English

English S401—The Teaching of English in Secondary Schools   Dr. Fulcomer

Here theory gives way to practice. Students are required to develop and use materials of the classroom. Lesson plans and units of work are prepared and presented for criticism. Textbooks are analyzed for training in their use. Bulletin board exhibits and visual education materials are prepared by students for the class.

8:00-9:20 A.M.   Credit: 3 semester-hours   Room 1

9

English S404—Survey of British Literature   **Dr. Krauss**

This course is a continuation of English 402. It takes up the story with the romantic triumph in 1798 and continues it to the present time.

11:30 A.M.-12:20 P.M.   Credit: 2 semester-hours   Room 14,CHS

English S431B—Shakespeare II   **Mr. Bohn**

This course deals with Shakespeare's plays in relation to his life, his times, his contemporaries, and Elizabethan drama generally. Extensive reading is required from Shakespeare, his predecessors, contemporaries, and successors. The problems of stage production in both Elizabethan and modern theatres, of Shakespearean criticism are analyzed. Part II deals with the Shakespearean comedies and tragi-comedies.

11:30 A.M.-12:20 P.M.   Credit: 2 semester-hours   Room 3

English S435—Play Production   **Mr. Fox**

This workshop course deals with both the theory and art of play production by providing training in staging, lighting, costuming, construction, and painting of scenery. A minimum of twelve clock hours of craft work upon a production of the College is required for credit in this course.

1:00-1:50 P.M.   Credit: 2 semester-hours   Aud-CHS

English S442A—American Literature I   **Mr. Conrad**

This chronological survey examines American Literature to observe its reflection of the political, social, and ethical principles of the American people. Part A begins with the Revolutionary period of the eighteenth century and ends with the Civil War. Not open to students who have credit for English 302A.

10:30-11:20 A.M.   Credit: 2 semester-hours   Room 4-CHS

English S442B—American Literature II   **Mr. Conrad**

Part B embraces Reconstruction and the New South, Immigration and the Development of the West, Urban America, and the present reaffirmation of the American tradition of Democracy. Not open to students who have credit for English 302B.

11:30 A.M.-12:20 P.M.   Credit: 2 semester-hours   Room 4-CHS

English S446—The One-Act Play   **Mr. Ballard**

This course studies the one-act play as an art form, devoting special attention to plays which are suitable for high school production

9:30-10:20 A.M.   Credit: 2 semester-hours   Room

English S449—Public Speaking   **Mr. Ballard**

This is an advanced course in the theory and practice of public speaking It provides opportunity for training in the more complex speech skills especially in the techniques of leadership in speech situations and the techniques for making creative speech responses in cooperative situation

10:30-11:20 A.M.   Credit: 2 semester-hours   Room

English S455—Reading Interests of High School Students   Dr. Fulcomer

Through wide reading, study and preparation of bibliographies, and establishing criteria for judging current books, the student is prepared to guide the recreational reading of junior and senior high school students. Students holding credit for Eng. 301A may not have credit for this course.

10:30-11:20 A. M.   Credit: 2 semester-hours   Room 1

English S457—Workshop in Speech Activities   Mr. Ballare

It is the purpose of this course to prepare students to organize and conduct assembly programs, PTA demonstrations, and similar activities. Class lectures and discussions cover all phases of the director's responsibilities. Groups conduct research on suitable program materials and share their findings with classmates. Each student prepares a list of programs of various types he could present during a school year.

11:30 A.M.-12:20 P.M.   Credit: 2 semester-hours   Room 2

English S506—John Milton   Mr. Hamilton

This course has for its primary aim the understanding and evaluation of Milton's poetry. Contributory to this end are the following topics: the Puritan struggle for civil and religious liberty; the growth of science in the seventeenth century; the life, personality, and prose writings of Milton; his literary heritage and influence; comparison of Milton with the Cavalier Metaphysical poets.

10:30-11:20 A.M.   Credit: 2 semester-hours   Room 5-CHS

English S511—The History of Literary Criticism   Dr. Krauss

The purpose of this course is to familiarize the student with the chief doctrines of the great critics from Aristotle to Arnold and to correlate these critical doctrines with the outstanding writings of each age. By such a study it is possible for the student to evaluate the historical interrelations of expert criticism and literary production. A basic text is used, but much of the information is gleaned from source materials.

9:30-10:20 A.M.   Credit: 2 semester-hours   Room 14-CHS

English S516—Language Problems in the English Curriculum   Mr. Conrad

This course reviews the several theories of language and studies the problem of meaning in order to arrive at a suitable technique for the interpretation of prose and verse. This technique is then applied to the problems of reading, of composition, of speech, and of appreciation of literature. The course has two aims; to increase the student's own skill in dealing with language, and to increase his effectiveness in teaching.

9:30-10:20 A.M.   Credit: 2 semester-hours   Room 4-CHS

Geography

Geography S410—Economic Geography of Caribbean America   Dr. Milstea

This is a study and interpretation of the major and important minc
economic areas of Caribbean America in relation to the natural enviror
ment. Attention is also given to the historical factors which have playe
a part in the economic and social life of the people.

10:30-11:20 A.M.   Credit: 2 semester-hours   Room 2

Geography S418—Regional Geography of North America   Dr. Milstea

This course constitutes a detailed regional treatment of the continent c
North America. Emphasis is placed upon the human activities of th
various regions in relation to their natural environment and the relatior
of the regions to each other. Attention is given to the techniques c
presenting the material and the use of geographic tools in the treatmer
of the subject-matter.

9:30-10:20 A. M.   Credit: 2 semester-hours   Room 2

Science S100C—The Earth Sciences   Dr. Milstea

See description and other data under the heading of "Science."

Health and Physical Education

Health Education S304—Driver Education   Mr. DeSha

In this course the student is instructed in the causes of highway acciden
and in the methods of safe driving. Prospective teachers are given a
opportunity to qualify as teachers of Driver Education in the high schoo
of New Jersey.

10:30-11:20 A.M.   Credit: 2 semester-hours   Room

Health Education S411—School Health Services   Mr. DeSha

The student is familiarized with the health services available in t
secondary schools. The part which the teacher plays in coordinating l
activities with the school medical staff is emphasized.

11:30 A.M.-12:20 P. M.   Credit: 2 semester-hours   Room

Physical Education—SM405—Management of Athletic Activities   Mr. DeSh

The student is provided with information essential to the good manageme
of an intramural and interscholastic athletic program. Some of the maj
problems to be considered are: educational values, health and safety
participants, insurance, transportation, scheduling, management of financ
budgeting, maintenance of play areas, care of supplies and equipment, st
and local athletic associations and the organization of leagues and meets

8:30-9:20 A.M.   Credit: 2 semester-hours   Room

12

Physical Education S409—Organization and Administration of
Physical Education   Mr. DeShaw

The details of organizing the units of the physical education program are discussed. Various topics, such as legislation, financing, curriculum construction, grading, excuses, plant facilities, supplies and equipment, and office management are considered. ·

9:30-10:20 A.M.   Credit: 2 semester-hours   Room D

Integration

Integration S410—Teaching Aids Workshop   Dr. Ritter

This is a practical course designed for both in-service and student teachers, with emphasis upon the development and use of teaching aids. A special study is made in the use of photographs, film strips, glass slides, charts, motion pictures, radio programs, television, etc. In the course the student has the opportunity to handle and to perfect his use of these materials and equipment. Presumably he has secured a more general knowledge of such teaching aids through Integration 408, 409, or similar experiences. He will have the benefit of class round-table discussion of his work, and will have the opportunity to demonstrate materials or the use of them before the group.

10:30-11:20 A.M.   Credit: 2 semester-hours   Room 5

Integration S500A—History and Principles of Secondary
Education   Dr. Fraser

In this course we are concerned with the larger movements in American secondary education. While a portion of the work is devoted to the beginnings of secondary schools in this country, much of the emphasis is upon current trends in thought and practice, such as the relationship of general education and specialized, the growing concern for citizenship training, etc. In the course are treated the latest national reports and studies dealing with this field.

10:30-11:20 A.M.   Credit: 2 semester-hours   Room 4, Annex No. 2

Integration S500B—Advanced Educational Psychology   Dr. Ingebritsen

The course covers the various aspects of growth. Individual differences, their measurement and their bearing on educational practices and principles furnish topics of study and discussion. Principles and laws of learning are reviewed. Some time is given to problems of personality as encountered in school work. The several points of view which have been prominent in the psychology of the past fifty to seventy-five years are examined for their contributions to our thinking about human nature.

Prerequisite: An introductory course in psychology.

9:30-10:20 A. M.   Credit: 2 semester-hours   Room 30

13

Integration S500C—Teaching Procedures in Secondary Education
Mr. Seybold

This course emphasizes the fundamental principles underlying the technique of teaching on the secondary school level. Some of the topics considered are: organization of knowledge, the logical and psychological aspects of method, developing appreciations, social-moral education, teaching motor control, fixing motor responses, books and verbalism, meeting individual differences, guidance in study, tests and examinations, marks and marking.

Credit: 2 semester-hours

Two sections of this course are being offered this summer, as follows:

9:30-10:20 A.M.   Room 3-CHS

11:30 A.M.-12:20 P.M.   Room 3-CHS

Integration S502B—Organization and Administration of the Modern High School II
Mr. Morehead

This course takes up the broader and more intricate problems of high school administration. Some of the topics studied are: types of secondary school organization; articulation programs; standardizing agencies; public relations; cooperation with other educational agencies; legal aspects; work-experience in the school; scheduling the broader core courses; professional ethics; salary policies and principles involved; the plant and equipment; selecting and assigning the staff; making the high school budget; relation of principal to special supervisors. (Integration 502A is not a prerequisite.)

9:30-10:20 A.M.   Credit: 2 semester-hours   Room B

Integration S503—Methods and Instruments of Research
Mr. Jackson

This course is required of all candidates for the Master's degree without regard to their field of major interest. Its purpose is to introduce students of education to research and its practical application to professional problems. The course treats: the nature and types of educational research; methods and techniques of educational research; and the tools used in interpreting statistical data. During the course, the student sets up a problem and plans and carries out its solution.

1:00-1:50 P.M.   Credit: 2 semester-hours   Room 9

Integration S504A—Curriculum Construction in the Secondary School
Dr. Smith

The purpose of this course is to introduce the student to constructive criticism of American culture, to consider the extent to which the secondary school curriculum meets the needs of a changing civilization, and to consider effective means of curriculum construction. (A student may not receive credit for both Integration 504A and Integration 504C.)

9:30-10:20 A.M.   Credit: 2 semester-hours   Room 8

14

Integration S505—Organization and Administration of
Extra-Curricular Activities   Mr. Morehead

The first part of this course considers such general problems of extra-curricular activities as: their growing importance; their relation to the curriculum; the principles underlying their organization, administration, and supervision; and methods of financing. In the second part, an intensive study is made of the home room, the assembly, the student council, clubs, athletics, school publications, and other activities in which the class is especially interested.

11:30 A.M.-12:20 P. M.   Credit: 2 semester-hours   Room B

Integration S508A—Supervision of Teaching I   Dr. Fraser

This course emphasizes the more practical phases of supervision which are met most frequently by those engaged in it. Among the topics are: the set-up for adequate supervision, supervision as encouraging and guiding the growth of teachers and the improvement of educational procedures, the supervisory functions of teachers' meetings, discussion groups, general and professional reading, the writing of articles, cooperative curriculum modification, utilization of community resources, and teacher intervisitation.

8:30-9:20 A.M.   Credit: 2 semester-hours   Room 4, Annex No. 2

Integration S515—Guidance and Personnel Problems of
Classroom Teachers   Mr. Seybold

This course considers all types of personnel problems with which the classroom teacher deals. It is concerned with the growth of pupils and seeks to point out the ways by which proper growth may be attained. Classroom, health, social, and personal activities are analyzed in terms of the needs of present-day social life.

10:30-11:20 A.M.   Credit: 2 semester-hours   Room 3-CHS

Integration S517—Administration of the Elementary School   Dr. Milligan

This course analyzes and evaluates the administrative duties and relationships of the elementary school principal. Particular consideration is given to: building management, effective use of the school plant, sanitation, health service, the library, personnel management, the administration of the curriculum, community relationships, and publicity.

8:30-9:20 A.M.   Credit: 2 semester-hours   Room 29

Integration S518—Supervision of Instruction in the
Elementary School   Dr. Milligan

This course has been planned for those engaged in the supervision of the elementary school, and for those who are preparing for such responsibilities. Principles of classroom supervision are developed and applied to learning situations. Among the more important topics that receive attention are: the nature and function of supervision, the organization necessary for effective supervision, the nature and significance of the teacher's purposes, the methods and techniques of group and individual supervision, the technique of observation, and the supervisory conference.

11:30 A.M.-12:20 P.M.   Credit: 2 semester-hours   Room 29

Integration S520—Principles of Mental Hygiene   Dr. Ingebritsen

This course is designed to be a general survey of the principles and practices of mental health with special reference to the mental health of teacher and pupil. It involves a thorough grounding in fundamental principles of mental hygiene with much practical consideration of the mental-health values of instructional programs and procedures. Discussion centers in practical efforts to develop wholesome personalities in our schools.

8:30-9:20 A.M.   Credit: 2 semester-hours   Room 30

Integration S521—Psychological Tests in Guidance Programs   Dr. Ingebritsen

This course is designed to familiarize the student with various psychological tests and scales that may be used in guidance programs in the secondary school. The student is given practice in administering many types of group tests. This includes scoring the tests and evaluating the results, with a discussion of ways in which these results may be used. Much time is spent in actual laboratory demonstrations of tests, giving students an opportunity to serve as subjects and as examiners. Class discussion is based upon first-hand information gained through use of the tests, on readings, and on class reports.

11:30 A.M.-12:20 P. M.   Credit: 2 semester-hours   Room 30

**Integration S548—Administration of the Elementary School
         Curriculum**   Dr. Milligan

This course offers an opportunity to review State and city elementary curricula; to discuss the principles of curriculum construction; to collect new teaching materials for the various subjects; and to evaluate, organize, and grade these materials. Teaching procedures in the use of materials are discussed and evaluated in terms of pupil needs, the objectives set up, and the results obtained. This course offers an opportunity to make a special study of the materials and procedures to be used in the teaching of the language arts.

9:30-10:20 A. M.   Credit: 2 semester-hours   Room 29

Mathematics

**Mathematics S300—The Social and Commercial Uses of
         Mathematics**   Mr. Clifford

Some of the toics treated are: review of fundamental operations, approximate computation, use of slide rule and computing devices, graphs and scale drawing, percentage, simple and compound interest, consumer credit and installment buying, savings and investment, mortgages, taxation, insurance, cost of housing and budgeting. Commercial, industrial, and consumer applications are stressed.

9:30-10:20 A.M.   Credit: 2 semester-hours   Room 3, Annex No. 1

16

Mathematics S308—The Social and Commercial Uses of Mathematics
    for Mathematics Majors   **Mrs. Davis**

This course covers in general the same content as Mathematics S300, but it presupposes a broader background in mathematics and an ability to cover the work more thoroughly.

9:30-10:20 A.M.   Credit: 2 semester-hours   Room 2, Annex No. 1

Mathematics S401—The Teaching of Mathematics in
    Secondary Schools   **Mrs. Davis**

The student in this course studies the methods of teaching the different units of work in the junior and senior high school. A study of recent trends in the teaching of mathematics, of noteworthy research, of courses in general mathematics, and of modern texts and tests is included.

8:00-9:20 A.M.   Credit: 3 semester-hours   Room 2, Annex No. 1

Mathematics S410—Mathematics of Finance   **Mr. Clifford**

This course introduces the student to the elementary theory of simple and compound interest and leads to the solution of practical problems in annuities, sinking funds, amortization, depreciation, stocks and bonds, installment buying, and building and loan associations. It also discusses the mathematics of life insurance covering the following subjects: the theory of probability as related to life insurance; the theory and calculation of mortality tables; various types of life annuities and insurance policies and reserves. This course is designed to give a helpful background to the mathematics teacher as well as to be an aid to the student of economics and insurance.

10:30-11:20 A.M.   Credit: 2 semester hours   Room 3, Annex No. 1

Mathematics S501A—Administration and Supervision of
    Mathematics—I   **Dr. Davis**

This course is concerned with the problems met in organizing and supervising the teaching of mathematics. There are considered the functions and qualifications of the supervisor of mathematics, in-service training of teachers, demonstration lessons, professional attitude and preparation of teachers, departmental meetings, selection of texts, current problems, research, and the basis for determining objectives. Attention is paid to efficient methods of securing mastery of skills, the development of power in problem solving, and the organization of testing programs.

9:30-10:20 A.M.   Credit: 2 semester-hours   Room 1, Annex No. 1

Mathematics S509C—A Critical Interpretation of Mathematics
    in the Junior High School   **Mr. Clifford**

The aim of this course is to give teachers a deeper insight into the subject-matter usually taught in the seventh, eighth, and ninth grades. Among the topics considered are: the nature of graphs, intuition and experimentalism in geometry, the arithmetic and algebra for social use and interpretation, approximate measures and mensuration, enrichment material for class and clubs, use of models, and integration with other subject fields. The course is open to all junior and senior high school teachers and those elementary school teachers who have had two years of high school mathematics.

8:30-9:20 A.M.   Credit: 2 semester-hours   Room 3, Annex No. 1

Science

Biology S501—The Teaching of Biology in Secondary Schools   Dr. Hadley

This is a seminar and research course designed to give opportunity for study of the best methods and practices being used in the teaching of secondary school biology. Major topics of discussion are: aims of secondary school biology, course content, functions of text-books, testing, laboratory exercises and demonstrations, and the collection and use of suitable and available laboratory materials. A study is made of recent research studies in the field of biology teaching.

Prerequisite: 18 semester-hours of work in biology.

8:00-9:20 A.M.   Credit: 3 semester-hours   Room 4, Annex No. 3

Biology S508—Social Applications of Biology   Dr. Hadley

This field-study course offers to teachers of science an opportunity to gain first-hand knowledge of the uses made of biological principles in industry and in modern laboratories. Field trips are designed to cover such varied interests as public health and hospital routine laboratories, medical botanical research laboratories, and the inspection of model industries developing biological products.

Credit: 2 semester-hours

11:30 A.M.-12:20 P.M., Mon. and Wed.   Room 4, Annex No. 3
Field Trips: Monday and Wednesday afternoons

Chemistry S406—Organic Chemistry—II   Dr. Reed

The work of this semester covers the chemistry of multiple functional chain compounds, the ring compounds, proteins, vitamins, hormones, and the application of these compounds in industry, in foods, and in medicine.

9:30-10:20 A.M.   Credit: 4 semester-hours   Room 23

Laboratories: Tuesday and Thursday afternoons

Chemistry S506A—Industrial Chemistry—I   Dr. Reed

The purpose of this course is to enable science teachers to understand the chemical industries in the metropolitan region. The course involves field trips, reading assignments, and class discussions. In addition, a survey is made of the economic foundations of chemical industry, the relation of chemistry to industry in general, and the effects of synthetics upon social, economic, and political life.

Prerequisite: General College Chemistry.

Credit: 2 semester-hours

11:30 A.M.-12:20 P.M., Mon. and Wed.   Room 23
Field Trips: Monday and Wednesday afternoons

18

Physics S304B—Introduction to Photography—II　　　　**Dr. Smith**

This is a beginning course in photography consisting of laboratory work and field work supplemented by lectures and demonstrations. Some of the topics covered are: the construction and operation of cameras, common films and papers, fundamental chemistry of photography, development and printing. A student needs at least one camera. Part II emphasizes projection printing.

9:30-10:20 A. M.　　　　Credit: 2 semester-hours　　　　Room 25

Physics S512—Modern Physics　　　　**Dr. Smith**

This course is a survey of recent experimental research in physics and of the newer theories concerning nuclear physics and electricity. Such topics as atomic spectra, radioactivity, artificial transmutation of the elements, and cosmic rays are discussed.

Prerequisites: General College Physics and a course in electrical measurements.

8:00-9:20 A. M.　　　　Credit: 4 semester-hours　　　　Room 25
Field Trips: By arrangement

Science S100C—The Earth Sciences　　　　**Dr. Milstead**

In this course, emphasis is placed on the effect of soil, climate, and physical features on the welfare of plants, animals, and mankind. The keynote of the course is to show the influence of a constantly changing physical environment on the life activities and welfare of mankind.

11:30 A.M.-12:20 P.M.　　　　Credit: 2 semester-hours　　　　Room 26

Social Studies

**Social Studies S401—The Teaching of the Social Studies
in Secondary Schools**　　　　**Dr. Moffatt**

The course aims to present recent tendencies in educational method in teaching the social studies. A program is presented containing the fusion organization in socialized recitation, the teaching of current events, projects in citizenship, and the use of the project-problem as a method of teaching history and civics. A laboratory containing texts and workbooks in the social studies field is available to the students of this course.

8:00-9:20 A.M.　　　　Credit: 3 semester-hours　　　　Room 21

Social Studies S407—New Jersey State and Local Government　　　　**Dr. Moffatt**

A study is made of the State Constitution; New Jersey's place in the Federal system; the rights and duties of citizens; suffrage; political parties; the legislative, the executive, and administrative systems; the courts, the law enforcement and correctional systems; revenues and expenditures; public health, educational, highway, and other services; county and municipal government; and other local political units.

9:30-10:20 A.M.　　　　Credit: 2 semester-hours　　　　Room 21

19

Social Studies S428—Racial Contributions to American Life   Dr. Clayton

This course deals with the basic problems of quantity, quality, and distribution of population and emphasizes the adjustments and maladjustments which result from the interrelations of Negroes, Asiatics, and various types of Europeans in the United States.

11:30 A.M.-12:20 P.M.   Credit: 2 semester-hours   Room 27

Social Studies S433—American Political Thought   Dr. Clayton

This course deals with contemporary trends and theories as they have emerged from social and economic conditions and as they are founded upon the bases laid down by such men as Hamilton, Madison, Washington, Jefferson, Marshall, Calhoun, Webster, Lincoln, and Wilson.

10:30-11:20 A. M.   Credit: 2 semester-hours   Room 27

**Social Studies S437—The Political Party System in the
   United States   Mr. Bye**

Among the topics discussed are: party organization, the political boss, the political machine, party finances, the process of voting, election laws, primaries, conventions, platforms, presidential elections, majority rule, the development of the party system, sectional politics, the farm vote, the labor vote, and the future of party government in the United States.

11:30 A.M.-12:20 P.M.   Credit: 2 semester-hours   Room 20

Social Studies S442—The Far East   Dr. Wittmer

A study is made of the economic, social, and cultural situation of the Far East, with particular emphasis on the historical background of China and Japan, and on our relations with the Philippines. Oriental folkways, religion, education, population shifts, and strategic questions are discussed. This course provides an approach to the problems the United States must face in the Far East.

9:30-10:20 A.M.   Credit: 2 semester-hours   Room 13-CHS

Social Studies S447—Diplomatic History of the United States   Dr. Gooden

The purpose of this course is to show how we have become gradually conscious of our world interests and responsibilities, and the important role we have come to play in international politics. The growing concept of world democracy, as opposed to commercial and military imperialism, is stressed.

10:30-11:20 A.M.   Credit: 2 semester-hours   Room 5, Annex No. 2

Social Studies S470—History and Principles of Philosophy   Dr. Freeman

This course presents a study of the history of philosophy and of the important principles contributed by outstanding philosophers from Thales to Gentile. Much of the discussion is centered on three types of philosophic thought: naturalism, idealism, and pragmatism. Among the philosophers considered are: Plato, Aristotle, Bacon, Spencer, Rousseau, Hegel, James, Dewey, and Gentile.

10:30-11:20 A.M.   Credit: 2 semester-hours   Room 9

CHINA INSTITUTE OF NEW JERSEY

The China Institute of New Jersey is a permanent year-round organization composed of former students of the China Workshop. The policies and program of the Institute are determined by an elected executive committee, an advisory board of laymen and representatives from the faculty of Montclair Teachers College, in consultation with the Chinese Director. Dr. Chih Meng, Director of the China Institute in America, whose purpose is to promote cultural and educational relations between China and the United States, is Chinese Director of the China Institute of New Jersey. The College provides the facilities necessary for the courses sponsored by the Institute and grants credit for the satisfactory completion of such courses.

Social Studies S499—China Workshop   **Dr. Chih Meng**

This course is given in twelve days. Twenty-four hours of lectures and class discussions are devoted to the study of Chinese history and contemporary Chinese life under the direction of Chinese scholars. Twenty-four hours of directed study in the library are devoted to the preparation of teaching units and background materials on China for use in our schools. If interested, write for registration materials.

Credit: 3 semester-hours

9:30 A. M.-4 P. M., June 28-July 10   Auditorium-CHS

In addition to the above China Workshop, the China Institute of New Jersey places on our campus each summer a more advanced course, open only to students who have received credit for the Workshop. This second course is selected late in the spring, the selection being dependent upon the special field of work of a particular Chinese scholar resident in the United States at this time and able to arrange his affairs so as to give to Montclair his entire time for twelve days. Last year, the course was "Chinese Philosophy" taught by Dr. Fung Yu-lan, Professor of Philosophy at National Tsing Hua University, China. The course for 1948 will be The Chinese Society.

The presence on our campus and in our residence halls of the Chinese scholars who are in charge of these two courses is most welcome. It permits the students of these courses to become personally acquainted with their professors and for the College to offer to all the students and to the general public an opportunity to hear a Chinese lecturer at one of the College assemblies.

While the primary and definite purpose of the institute is to assist the teachers of New Jersey, men and women who desire to take these courses for cultural, vocational, or avocational purposes are welcome also. They may enroll for college credit or simply as auditors for no credit. The cost is the same in all cases. If it be desired to attend a single lecture, the Institute Treasurer collects the fee of $2.00 at the door of the Auditorium. Students who enroll for the entire course must register in advance of the opening day.

21

POST-SUMMER SESSION COURSES

This fifteen-day tour of Pennsylvania, Maryland, Virginia, West Virginia, North Carolina, and Tennessee covers the major points of historic interest associated with the Colonial Period, the American Revolution, and the Civil War, and the geographic features of the coastal plain, the Piedmont, the Great Valley, and the Appalachian Mountains in these States. Travel is by modern chartered motor coach, and overnight stops are made at first-class hotels. Among the places visited are: Valley Forge, Philadelphia, Baltimore, Annapolis, Washington, Arlington, Alexandria, Mt. Vernon, Fredericksburg, Richmond, Washington's birthplace at Wakefield, Lee's plantation at Stratford, Yorktown, Williamsburg, Jamestown, Raleigh, Durham, Winston-Salem, Asheville, Great Smoky Mountains, Norris Dam, Jefferson's Monticello at Charlottesville, Natural Bridge, Skyline Drive in the Shenandoah National Park, Luray Caverns, Winchester, Harper's Ferry, Frederick, Gettysburg, and the Pennsylvania Dutch area around Lancaster and Ephrata.

Credit: 3 semester-hours

Immediate registration for this course is necessary, since there is a quota of 33 persons and no more can be taken after the quota is filled. The all-expense price, including tuition: $150.00. Address the Bureau of Field Studies. Starts Tuesday, August 17, 1948; ends August 31.

Course for Veterans

Veterans who have been in attendance at this College from June 14 to August 13 and who desire to remain on subsistence, will have the opportunity to take an additional 2 semester-hours credit following the close of the Regular Summer Session. The work will be given intensively, so as to end before the beginning of the fall semester. Registration in this course must be made on June 14.

Health Education S207—Safety Education   **Mr. DeShaw**

This course is designed to prepare teachers for a relatively new field in education. Opportunities are presented for acquiring knowledge and skills related to safety in the school building, on the school grounds, and going to and from school.

Credit: 2 semester-hours   Room 24

Courses in Session from June 14 through August 13, 1948

Descriptions of these courses are to be found in the Undergraduate Catalogue. The detailed Schedule and the Catalogue are available upon request. See also paragraph at the top of page 5 of this Bulletin.

Department	Cat. No.	Title of Course	Sem. Hrs. Cr.
Bus. Ed.	101	Introduction to Business	4
Bus. Ed.	201A	Business Law—III	2
Bus. Ed.	201B	Business Organization and Management	2
Bus. Ed.	301	Bookkeeping and Accounting	4
Bus. Ed.	302	Principles of Accounting	4
Bus. Ed.	401	The Teaching of Business Education	3
Bus. Ed.	402	Salesmanship	4
English	100A	World Literature—I	3
English	100B	World Literature—II	3
English	200A	Composition	3
English	200B	Fundamentals of Speech	3
English	202	British and American Fiction	4
English	401	The Teaching of English in Secondary Schools	3
Language	300	Foundations of Language	2
Mathematics	102	Mathematical Analysis—II	4
Mathematics	301	Modern College Geometry	4
Mathematics	302	Higher Algebra	4
Mathematics	400	Educational Statistics	2
Mathematics	402	Applications of Mathematics	4
Music	100	Music Appreciation	1
Music	102	Advanced Sight Reading and Ear Training	2
Music	201	Harmony	4
Physical Ed.	M307	Methods of Coaching and Officiating—I	3
Physical Ed.	M308	Methods of Coaching and Officiating—II	3

Department	Cat. No.	Title of Course	Sem. Hrs. Cr.
Chemistry	201	Analytical Chemistry: Qualitative Analysis	4
Physics	407	Aviation	4
Science	100A	Survey of Science: The Physical Sciences	4
Social Stud.	100A	Civilization and Citizenship—I	3
Social Stud.	100B	Civilization and Citizenship—II	3
Social Stud.	102	European History from 1815 to the Present	4
Social Stud.	200A	Contemporary Economic Life	2
Social Stud.	200B	Contemporary Political Life	2
Social Stud.	200C	Contemporary Social Life	2
Social Stud.	301	Economics	4
Integration	100	Introduction to Teaching	2
Integration	200A	Introduction to Educational Psychology and Mental Testing	2
Integration	200B	Adolescent Psychology and Mental Hygiene	2
Integration	300A	Aims and Organization of Secondary Education	2
Integration	400A	Principles and Philosophy of Secondary Education	2

SUMMER SESSION

Bulletin of

MONTCLAIR
STATE TEACHERS COLLEGE

JULY 5 TO AUGUST 18

1949

UPPER MONTCLAIR, NEW JERSEY

NEW JERSEY STATE SCHOOL OF CONSERVATION

July 5-23

Stokes State Forest, N. J.

Graduate students who wish to spend an enjoyable and profitable summer will be interested in the School of Conservation to be held at Lake Wapalanne, Stokes State Forest, N. J. The graduate session from July 5 to 23 will carry four points of graduate credit applicable toward the Master's degree and will include two different courses—Field Studies in Science and Materials and Methods of Conservation Education. The camp on Lake Wapalanne has excellent physical facilities and is one thousand feet above sea level. All inquiries should be addressed to Dr. E. D. Partridge, Dean of Instruction, State Teachers College, Upper Montclair, N. J.

TEACHERS NEEDED IN ELEMENTARY GRADES

Graduates of colleges other than teachers colleges who wish to secure teaching positions in the elementary schools of New Jersey can meet the minimum requirements for emergency certification in one summer session by attending the New Jersey State Teachers Colleges at Paterson, Newark, Trenton, or Glassboro. Those interested should address inquiries to the registrar of one of the colleges listed above.

Summer Session

Bulletin of
Montclair
State Teachers College

1949
July 5 to August 18

Upper Montclair, New Jersey

OFFICERS OF ADMINISTRATION

2

SUMMER SESSION 1949

FACULTY

HARRY A. SPRAGUE, Ph.D. .... President
E. DeALTON PARTRIDGE, Ph.D. .... Dean of Instruction
HAROLD C. BOHN, A.M. .... English
EDGAR C. BYE, A.M. .... Field Studies
FRANK L. CLAYTON, Ph.D. .... Social Studies
PAUL C. CLIFFORD, A.M. .... Mathematics
LAWRENCE H. CONRAD, A.M. .... English
ANNE BANKS CRIDLEBAUGH, B.S. .... Acting Librarian
DAVID R. DAVIS, Ph.D. .... Acting Head, Department of Mathematics
CHARLES G. DeSHAW, Ed.D.,
            Director, Department of Health & Physical Education
EMMA FANTONE, A.M. .... Audio-Visual Aids
MOWAT G. FRASER, Ph.D. .... Head of Department of Integration
WALTER H. FREEMAN, Ph.D. .... Head of Department of Foreign Languages
PAUL E. FROEHLICH, A.M. .... Business Education
EDWIN S. FULCOMER, Ed.D. .... Head of Department of English
HERBERT B. GOODEN, Ed.D. .... Social Studies
W. PAUL HAMILTON, A.M. .... English
T. ROLAND HUMPHREYS, A.M. .... Mathematics
OTIS C. INGEBRITSEN, Ph.D. .... Psychology
CLAUDE E. JACKSON, A.M. .... Personnel and Research
BENJAMIN KARP, A.M. .... Art
GEORGE W. KAYS, A.M. .... Mathematics
RUSSELL KRAUSS, Ph.D. .... English
EDNA E. McEACHERN, Ph.D. .... Head of Department of Music
ROBERT W. McLACHLAN, Ph.D. .... Chemistry
CHIH MENG, Ph.D. .... Director of China Institute
HARLEY P. MILSTEAD, Ph.D. .... Geography
MAURICE P. MOFFATT, Ph.D. .... Social Studies
ALLAN MOREHEAD, A.M. .... Integration
ULRICH J. NEUNER, A.M. .... Business Education
WILLIAM R. PHIPPS, Ed.D. .... Integration
GEORGE F. PLACEK, A.M. .... Aeronautics
JOHN J. RELLAHAN, Ph.D. .... Acting Head, Department of Social Studies
PAUL J. RITTER, Ph.D. .... Integration
EDNA D. SALT, A.M. .... Elementary Education
ARTHUR M. SEYBOLD, A.M. .... Integration
HORACE J. SHEPPARD, A.M.....Acting Head, Department of Business Education
KENNETH O. SMITH, Ph.D. .... Physics
W. SCOTT SMITH, Ph.D. .... Integration
D. HENRYETTA SPERLE, Ph.D. .... Integration
EVAN H. THOMAS, A.M. .... Guidance
ELIZABETH T. VANDERVEER, A.M. .... Business Education
RICHARD W. WILLING, A.M. .... Business Education
FELIX WITTMER, Ph.D. .... Social Studies
ANNETTA L. WOOD, A.M. .... Speech

GRADUATE COMMITTEE
OTIS C. INGEBRITSEN, *Chairman*

E. DeALTON PARTRIDGE	DAVID R. DAVIS	HORACE J. SHEPPARD
D. HENRYETTA SPERLE		ELIZABETH S. FAVOR, *Secretary*
W. PAUL HAMILTON	RUFUS D. REED	JOHN J. RELLAHAN

3

SUMMER SESSION OF THE

NEW JERSEY STATE TEACHERS COLLEGE AT MONTCLAIR

Professional and Academic Status

The New Jersey State Teachers College at Montclair is a fully accredited member of the American Association of Teachers Colleges; the Middle States Association of Colleges and Secondary Schools, and the Association of American Universities.

The College is a professional school which prepares teachers, supervisors, and principals of high schools, and administrators of public school systems. The degrees offered by this College are those of Bachelor of Arts and Master of Arts. Certificate courses are offered for those who now hold degrees.

How to Reach the Campus

Trains of the Greenwood Lake Division, Erie R. R., stop at College Station. Trains of the Lackawanna R. R. connect at Montclair with the following bus lines: No. 64, running between Brick Church and the College; No. 60, running between Newark and the College; and No. 76, which runs between Orange and Paterson, passing the College en route. For those who come by car: the College is located about one mile north of the center of Upper Montclair.

Residence Halls for Men and Women

Edward Russ Hall and Chapin Hall are Montclair College's two well-appointed Residences. The charge for living on campus during the Summer Session is: $13.00 per week; which includes room, breakfast, and dinner. A la carte luncheons are served in the College cafeteria. For one student alone in a double room, an extra charge of $2.00 per week is made. The College provides and launders sheets, pillowcase, and bedpad. Towels, table lamps, blankets, clocks, and similar items must be provided and cared for by the student. The boarding-hall fee must be paid on or before the first day of the Summer Session. No rebate is made for occasional absence or voluntary withdrawal during the session. Students who are absent on account of illness for two weeks or more receive a rebate of $6.00 per week during the illness. These prices are subject to change.

For reservations in a College Residence Hall, women address: Dean of Women, State Teachers College, Upper Montclair, N. J. Men address the Dean of Men.

Schedule of the Summer Session

Registration will take place on Saturday, June 25, between the hours of 9 to 12 and 1 to 3; and on Friday, July 1, at those same hours. Classes for the Summer Session will begin Tuesday, July 5, and continue through Thursday, August 18. All classes meet daily, Monday to Friday, inclusive, except when definitely otherwise indicated.

4

Summer Session of Nine Weeks

On page 26 of this Bulletin is a statement concerning the courses of the Nine Weeks Session, which begins earlier than does the regular Summer Session and runs concurrently with it during the last seven weeks. Students who desire more credit than can be earned during the regular Summer Session should consult this statement.

Matriculation

Those who desire to become candidates for either the Bachelor of Arts or the Master of Arts degree at Montclair must request the Registrar for the application form and return it, properly filled in and accompanied by an official transcript of all previous work on college level. When such an applicant has been accepted by the College as a candidate for the degree, a definite statement will be furnished to him, showing the requirements which he must fulfill to earn the degree.

Auditors

Men and women who desire to take courses for cultural, vocational, or avocational purposes without college credits may register as auditors.

A student who desires to enroll in a course for which he already holds credit must register as an auditor in that course.

Change of Status in a Course

If a student desires to change his status in a course from "credit" to "auditor," or from "auditor" to "credit," he must make formal application for such change not later than the middle of the course. Forms for this purpose may be procured from the Secretary of the Summer Session.

Students Matriculated at Montclair

Work taken for credit at Montclair must be with the advice and approval of the Dean of Instruction or the Chairman of the Graduate Committee and the Head of the Department in which the student is majoring. See paragraph under the heading "Conferences."

A student who expects to receive a degree should consult the Registrar, Miss Van Etten, three months in advance of graduation.

Students Matriculated at Other Colleges

Work taken for credit to be transferred to other colleges should be approved in advance by the Dean of the college at which such student holds membership. A student who is planning to attend Montclair this summer should take the Summer Session Bulletin to a conference with his Dean to arrange a program of work. For the Dean's information: the numbering of courses at Montclair follows this order: 100-399, inclusive, are undergraduate courses; 400-499, inclusive, are senior-college and graduate courses: 500 and above are graduate courses.

5

Certificates

The State Teachers College at Montclair offers work toward the following New Jersey Certificates: *Limited Secondary Teaching Certificate; Permanent Secondary Teaching Certificate; Secondary School Principal's Certificate; Secondary School Subject Supervisor's Certificate; Junior College Teacher's Certificate; Supervising Principal's Certificate; and the Superintendent of Schools' Certificate.

Those who matriculate at Montclair for a degree will receive information from Dr. Fraser, Head of the Integration Department as to the requirements for each of these certificates. Students who have not matriculated at Montclair who desire to obtain any of the above certificates should write to Dr. E. C. Preston, Secretary of the State Board of Examiners, Department of Education, 175 West State Street, Trenton 8, N. J., for information as to the requirements and for an evaluation of work already completed. An official transcript of such previous work should accompany the inquiry, with a statement as to the particular certificate desired.

Students who must have this information immediately should go to Trenton to confer personally with Dr. Preston or his assistant, Miss Smith.

Supervised Student Teaching

The opportunity to do supervised student teaching cannot be offered during the Summer Session. For fall teaching, students confer with Dr. Fraser at the College.

Offerings to Veterans

The College makes every effort to adjust its offerings and facilities to Veterans who are interested in teaching as a profession. It has printed a bulletin setting forth its policies and procedures in working with Veterans. This bulletin may be had upon request to Mr. Morris Seibert, Veterans' Counselor. It should be known that the College will recognize equivalency in courses taken and experiences gained by men and women in service. In general, credit may be allowed for:

(a) Courses at undergraduate and graduate level taken while in service,

(b) specialized training taken in service schools either on or off campus, and

(c) experiences of a more informal nature that can be judged from the standpoint of educational growth or development.

Veterans may receive government aid in financing Part-Time and Summer Session courses. They should be sure, however, to obtain the Certificate of Eligibility from the Veterans' Administration before the start of the Summer Session. Failure to do this will mean that the usual fees must be paid by the student for all courses taken; these fees to be refunded when the Letter of Eligibility is presented to the College.

* See page 10.

Conferences with Advisers

Appointments with the Dean of Instruction, the Chairman of the Graduate Committee, a Department Head, or the Veterans' Counselor may be made by mail or telephone to their respective offices. This should be done at as early a date as possible. Students unable to do so earlier may, however, see these officials or their representatives on June 25 and July 1.

A representative of the State Board of Examiners will be at the College on July 1 to see students who desire advice on the selection of courses toward a New Jersey Certificate. (See paragraph under heading "Certificates.") The Secretary of the Summer Session will receive requests for appointments with this State Official.

Work Taken for Credit

The maximum amount of credit which may be earned in the Regular Summer Session is 8 semester-hours, but only 6 s. h. is recommended. There is no provision for a student to audit additional courses; consequently, the total of all courses may not exceed that amount and students should not register for more. If additional credit is necessary, the student should plan to attend the Nine-Weeks Session mentioned previously, or the Post Summer Session Course.

Each course is in session at least thirty hours and carries a designated amount of credit. It is *not* possible to earn three points credit in a two-point course.

If prerequisites are required, the student should make certain that he has fulfilled them or their equivalent before enrolling in the course. If no previous work on college level has been taken, the student should consult the Registrar before enrolling in any course.

A student may *not* register for credit in any course for which he already holds credit except with permission of the Dean of Instruction.

Registration

Registration for courses now takes place before the opening of the session, not in class as formerly.

Registration for the Summer Session will be on Saturday, June 25, between 9 A. M. and 12 Noon and between 1 and 3 P. M.; and on Friday, July 1, between 9 A. M. and 12 Noon and between 1 and 3 P. M. Students must have their programs approved by their advisers, pay for their courses, and receive their class admission cards to admit them to classes on July 5. Students who enroll subsequent to July 1 will be charged the late registration service charge of $2.00, and no student will be admitted for credit after July 8.

The College reserves the right to close any course for which the enrollment is insufficient. Notice of the closing will be sent to the Business Office and students will call there for adjustments of tuition fees.

Withdrawal from a Course

The Secretary of the Summer Session must be notified in writing immediately if the student finds it necessary to withdraw from a course. (The student is urged not to enroll in a course until it has been approved by his advisers.) Refunds of fees are computed from the date on which the student's notification is received by the Secretary. Teachers are notified by the Secretary that the student has withdrawn. Students who neglect to follow these instructions receive a failing mark for the courses from which they withdraw.

Tuition Fees and Service Charges

Check or money-order should be made payable to New Jersey State Teachers College, except for the China Institute courses.

Registration service charge: $1.00 for the Summer Session.

Late registration service charge: $2.00. This is collected from all students who fail to enroll on June 25 or July 1.

Tuition fees: to legal residents of New Jersey, $8.00 per semester-hour credit carried by the course; to non-residents, $10.00 per credit. Courses taken by auditors for no credit cost the same.

Laboratory service charge: $2.50 for each laboratory course. This is collected by the business office. It should not be included in the check for tuition and registration.

Final Marks

Following are the final marks which may be received for a course: A-Excellent; B-Good; C-Fair; D-Poor; F-Failure; Inc.-Incomplete; Wd-Withdrew; N. C.-No Credit.

The mark of "D" when earned in summer, part-time, or extension courses of this College is not accepted for degree credit at Montclair.

The mark of "F" is given when earned and when the student has failed to notify the Secretary of the Summer Session promptly of his withdrawal from a course.

The mark of "N. C." is given only to auditors.

The mark of "Wd" is given only when prompt notice of withdrawal has been given to the Secretary and when the student's work to that time has been satisfactory to the teacher of the course.

The mark of "Inc." is seldom given. It may, however, be granted to a student whose work is incomplete in one particular at the end of the Session and who is eager to finish the work for a higher grade than he could receive otherwise. All responsibility regarding incomplete work rests with the student. He will be notified of a date after which, if the work remains incomplete, the final grade will be recorded without further notice.

Report Cards and Transcripts

A report card for each course and an Official Transcript are mailed directly to the student himself as soon as possible after the close of the Summer Session. This is usually within one week or ten days at the most. This first transcript is furnished free of charge. The student is urged to present it without delay to the State, college, or school official who is awaiting it, together with a statement as to the purpose for which the transcript is being filed. A student whose college requires that the transcript be mailed directly to the Dean or Registrar should so notify

8

the Secretary of the Summer Session not later than the middle of the Session.

All transcripts are photostated copies of the complete record of the student. The cost of a second one is $1.00. Check or money-order should be used; postage stamps cannot be accepted. Men and women entering or already in national service are sent a second transcript without charge, as are Veterans of such service, upon request.

Room Numbers

Room numbers used in this Bulletin, if unaccompanied by other designation, refer to rooms in College Hall, the main building of the College.

Other designations are as follows:

CHS: College High School Building; to the northeast of the main building;

Campus Studio Workshop: near the eastern end of the parking area;

Annex No. 1: Federal Works Administration Building No. 1; at the northwest corner of the main building;

Annex No. 2: Federal Works Administration Building No. 2; next to No. 1;

Annex No. 3: Federal Works Administration Building No. 3; directly east of the main building;

Music Building: at the Northeast corner of the College High School Building.

Recreation Building: at extreme north end of campus.

Elementary Education Courses

Although the New Jersey State Teachers College at Montclair is engaged primarily in preparing secondary school teachers, during the present shortage of teachers in the elementary schools it was deemed expedient to offer courses in the field of elementary education leading toward certification to teach in these subjects. Those offered this summer are:

Integration S470—Child Growth and Development

Integration S472—The Elementary School Curriculum

Integration S473—Teaching the Elementary School Language Arts

Integration S474—Elementary School Art

Integration S475A—Fundamentals of Elementary School Music

The following courses are offered as a part of the curriculum for the graduate major in Educational Administration and Supervision:

Integration S517—Administration of the Elementary School

Integration S518—Supervision of Instruction in the Elementary School

Integration S532—The Supervision and Teaching of Reading in Elementary Schools

Integration S548—Curriculum Construction in the Elementary School

9

EXCERPTS FROM THE SEVENTEENTH EDITION STATE OF NEW JERSEY RULES CONCERNING TEACHERS' CERTIFICATES

SECONDARY

AUTHORIZATION—To teach the endorsed subject fields in grades seven through twelve.

REQUIREMENTS—

1. A bachelor's degree based upon an accredited curriculum in a four-year college.

2. A minimum of thirty semester-hour credits in general background courses distributed in at least three of the following fields: English, social studies, science, fine arts, mathematics, and foreign languages. Six semester-hour credits in English and six in social studies will be required.

3. A minimum of eighteen semester-hour credits in courses distributed over four or more of the following groups including at least one course in a, b, and c below:

   a. Methods of teaching. This group includes such courses as: (1) methods of teaching in secondary schools, (2) visual aids in education, and (3) individualizing instruction.

   b. Educational psychology. This group includes such courses as: (1) psychology of learning, (2) human growth and development, (3) adolescent psychology, (4) educational measurements, and (5) mental hygiene.

   c. Health education. This group includes such courses as: (1) personal health problems, (2) school health problems, (3) nutrition, (4) health administration, and (5) biology.

   d. Curriculum. This group includes such courses as: (1) principles of curriculum construction, (2) the high school curriculum, (3) a study of the curriculum in one specific field, and (4) extra-curricular activities.

   e. Foundations of education. This group includes such courses as: (1) history of education, (2) principles of education, (3) philosophy of education, (4) comparative education, and (5) educational sociology.

   f. Guidance. This group includes such courses as: (1) principles of guidance, (2) counseling, (3) vocational guidance, (4) educational guidance, (5) research in guidance, and (6) student personnel problems.

4. Two teaching fields are required, one of which must contain thirty semester-hour credits and the other eighteen.

5. One hundred and fifty clock hours of approved student teaching. At least ninety clock hours must be devoted to responsible classroom teaching; sixty clock hours may be employed in observation and participation.

DESCRIPTION OF COURSES

Please note that the numbering of courses at this College follows this order: 100-399, inclusive, are undergraduate courses; 400-499, inclusive, are senior-college and graduate courses; 500 and above are graduate courses.

Art

Art S406—Studio Workshop for Secondary Teachers   Mr. Karp

This course offers practice in the use of the commoner media for students who wish to employ the creative visual arts in the teaching of other subjects. Students are encouraged to work out projects definitely related to the various subject-matter fields; and to the exploration of the various media as a means of personal expression and of increased sensitiveness to art.

10:30-11:20 A. M.   Credit: 2 semester-hours   Campus Studio Workshop

Art S408—Creative Painting   Mr. Karp

This course gives the student an opportunity to use the materials of the painter for personal creative experience. Oils, water colors, and pastels are used. The student is encouraged to work in landscape, figure, and free imaginative composition. No previous experience is necessary.

11:30 A. M.-12:20 P.M.   Credit: 2 semester-hours   Campus Studio Workship

Integration S474—Elementary School Art   Mr. Karp

See description and other data under the heading of "Integration."

Business Education

Business Education S401—
The Teaching of Business Education   Mr. Froehlich

In this course a study is made of the history and development of business education, aims or objectives, human learning processes, lesson plans, teaching procedures, tests and measurements, and special helps for the teachers of business education. Consideration is given to the current trend in teaching in these fields with emphasis on the viewpoint of the consumer as well as the social and vocational objectives.

11:30 A. M.-12:45 P. M.   Credit: 3 semester-hours   Room 2, Annex No. 2

Business Education S404—Business Economics   Mr. Froehlich

This course deals with the business aspects of the economics of war and peace; immediate and long range post-war problems; operation and government control of public utilities; taxation; government finance; and labor and management problems.

10:30-11.20 A. M.   Credit: 2 semester-hours   Room 2, Annex No. 2

11

Business Education S410—Cost Accounting I & II   **Mr. Neuner**

A thorough knowledge of bookkeeping is a prerequisite to a profitable study of this course. The course deals with the basic principles of modern cost finding and cost keeping, and endeavors to give a practical application of these principles to present-day conditions. The practical application consists of a laboratory budget containing business papers, vouchers, payrolls, etc., together with full instructions for writing up a practice set of cost books.

8:30-10:10 A. M.   Credit: 4 semester-hours   Room 3, Annex No. 2

Business Education S412—Transportation and Communication   Mr. Willing

The student in this course becomes acquainted with the various kinds of services rendered by transportation and communication agencies. He also receives some insight as to how to use these services most efficiently; the practices of the agencies; how and why they are controlled by the government.

9:30-10:20 A. M.   Credit: 2 semester-hours   Room 1, Annex No. 2

Business Education S504—
Improvement of Instruction in Business Education   Mrs. VanDerveer

This course seeks to bring together business education teachers regardless of subject matter fields to consider common problems involving general subject matter and methods of instruction including visual and auditory aids. It also offers opportunity for an individual to investigate and evaluate materials and methods in specific subject matter areas.

8:30-9:20 A. M.   Credit: 2 semester-hours   Room 4, Annex No. 2

Business Education S602—Seminar in Economics   Mr. Sheppard

This seminar is designed to meet the individual needs of the graduate student in business education or social studies by allowing him to pursue areas of work along economic lines in which he is not well-versed. The direction of his study will be determined by the co-ordinator of the seminar and himself, after the results of his student diagnostic test are analyzed. The program of participation will consist of oral and written reports, developed through independent reading and individually directed field studies. The field studies are planned so as to give the student a first-hand knowledge of business organization methods and practices. It is expected that the reports arising from these experiences will be in such form that they will be capable of being published or delivered as speeches before groups of people. An opportunity will also be given to view, evaluate, and work with a variety of related visual and auditory aids. The plan of this seminar assists the students in preparing for the final comprehensive examination for the Master of Arts degree, and at the same time offers certain personal and professional advantages.

9:30 A. M.-12:20 P. M.   Credit: 6 semester-hours   Room 5, Annex No. 2

English

English S324—Minor Speech Disorders   Miss Wood

An introduction to the problems inherent in such abnormalities as lisping, cluttering, vocal monotony, and general articulatory inaccuracies is undertaken in order that the nature of the problems and their diagnosis may be understood. *Prerequisite: English 208—Fundamentals of Speech-Part II.*

9:30-10:20 A. M.   Credit: 2 semester-hours   Room 2

English S401—The Teaching of English in Secondary Schools   Dr. Fulcomer

Here theory gives way to practice. Students are required to develop and use materials of the classroom. Lesson plans and units of work are prepared and presented for criticism. Textbooks are analyzed for training in their use. Bulletin board exhibits and visual education materials are prepared by students for the class.

8:00-9:20 A. M.   Credit: 3 semester-hours   Room 1

English S407—British and American Biography   Mr. Conrad

Both the old and new types of biography are read and studied in this course, with emphasis upon the nineteenth and twentieth centuries. Biography is presented for its cultural and informational values, for its use in integrating the work of the various departments in the high school, and for its direct help in the vocational guidance program.

9:30-10:20 A. M.   Credit: 2 semester-hours   Room 4-CHS

English S409—The Teaching and Appreciation of Poetry   Dr. Fulcomer

This course is both personal and professional. It develops the student's appreciation of poetry as an expression of life and as a form of art, and it considers in detail the aims and methods of teaching poetry.

11:30 A. M.-12:20 P. M.   Credit: 2 semester-hours   Room 1

English S417—Methods in the Teaching of Speech   Miss Wood

This course studies the objectives of speech education, modern trends in instruction, speech textbooks and teaching materials, and the integration of speech with other academic departments of study.

8:30-9:20 A. M.   Credit: 2 semester-hours   Room 2

English S431A—Shakespeare—Part I   Mr. Bohn

This course deals with Shakespeare's plays in relation to his life, his times, his contemporaries, and Elizabethan drama generally. Extensive reading is required from Shakespeare, his predecessors, contemporaries, and successors. The problems of stage production in both Elizabethan and modern theatres, and of Shakespearean criticism are analyzed. Part I deals with Shakespearean tragedies.

11:30 A. M.-12:20 P. M.   Credit: 2 semester-hours   Room 3

English S432—The Development of the Drama   Mr. Bohn

The development of the drama is studied in all periods from ancient Greece and Rome through the Middle Ages and the Renaissance to the beginning of modern drama with Ibsen. The emphasis of the course is placed on trends, developments, and major characteristics of the drama and its necessary complement, the theatre. Representative plays are read and discussed.

9:30-10:20 A. M.   Credit: 2 semester-hours   Room 3

English S442A—American Literature—Part I   Mr. Conrad

This chronological survey examines American Literature to observe its reflection of the political, social, and ethical principles of the American people. Part A begins with the Revolutionary period of the eighteenth century and ends with the Civil War. (*Not open to students who have credit for English* 302A.)

10:30-11:20 A. M.   Credit: 2 semester-hours   Room 4-CHS

13

English S442B—American Literature—Part II **Mr. Conrad**
Part B embraces Reconstruction and the New South, Immigration and the
Development of the West, Urban America, and the present reaffirmation of
the American tradition of Democracy. (*Not open to students who have
credit for English 302B.*)
11:30 A. M.-12:20 P. M. Credit: 2 semester-hours Room 4-CHS

English S445—Eighteenth Century Literature **Mr. Bohn**
Major essayists, poets, dramatists, novelists, and letter writers are read
and evaluated in terms of the thought, life, and literary movements of their
own time and of their significance for the present generation. Authors
studied include Addison, Steele, Defoe, Swift, Goldsmith, Sheridan, Gray,
Johnson, Boswell, Cowper, Richardson, Fielding, Sterne, Smollett, and
Burke. High School classics receive special attention.
8:30-9:20 A. M. Credit: 2 semester-hours Room 3

English S502—Victorian Poetry **Mr. Hamilton**
The most important English poets who wrote during the transition from the
Victorian to the modern period are read and discussed. An important feature
of the course is the analysis and appreciative reading of the lyric poetry
of Rossetti, Swinburne, Hardy, Bridges, G. M. Hopkins, Francis Thompson,
A. E. Housman, Kipling, and W. B. Yeats.
10:30-11:20 A. M. Credit: 2 semester-hours Room 1

English S503—Goeffry Chaucer and His Times **Dr. Krauss**
Some of the works of Chaucer are read rapidly, others studied intensively,
so that the students may acquire a broad general understanding of Chaucer's
place in the history of English literature as well as facility in reading and
interpreting the medieval text of his stories.
9:30-10:20 A. M. • Credit: 2 semester-hours Room 5-CHS

English S514—
  Origin and Development of the Arthurian Legend **Dr. Krauss**
This course deals with the vague and tentative beginnings of the Arthur
story in early chronicle and legend; with Geoffrey of Monmouth's pseudo-
historical and Chretian de Troye's romantic treatments; with the great
medieval recapitulations of Gottfried von Strassburg, Wolfram von Eschenbach, and Sir Thomas Malory; with the Victorian retellings of Tennyson,
Arnold, and Morris; with the musical adaptations of Wagner; and with
the modern versions of E. A. Robinson. It includes a detailed history of the
development of the legend in its divers forms.
10:30-11:20 A. M. Credit: 2 semester-hours Room 5-CHS

Geography

Geography S411—Geographic Influences in American History **Dr. Milstead**
A study is made of the geographic factors influencing the development of
social, economic, and political life in America.
11:30 A. M.-12:20 P. M. Credit: 2 semester-hours Room 26

Geography S413—Economic Geography of South America **Dr. Milstead**
This course constitutes a study of the influence of the natural environment
upon production and utilization of resources in the economic, social, and
political development of the various nations of South America.
10:30-11:20 A. M. Credit: 2 semester-hours Room 26

14

Science S100C—The Earth Sciences   Dr. Milstead
See description and other data under the heading of "Science."

Health and Physical Education

Health Education S411—School Health Services   Dr. DeShaw
The student is familiarized with the health services available in the secondary
schools. The part which the teacher plays in co-ordinating his activities
with the school medical staff is emphasized.
11:30 A. M.-12:20 P. M.   Credit: 2 semester-hours   Room D

Physical Education SM405—Management of Athletic Activities Dr. DeShaw
The student is provided with information essential to the good management
of an intramural and interscholastic athletic program. Some of the major
problems to be considered are: educational values, health and safety of
participants, insurance, transportation, scheduling, management of finances,
budgeting, maintenance of play areas, care of supplies and equipment, state
and local athletic associations and the organization of leagues and meets.
8:30-9:20 A. M.   Credit: 2 semester-hours   Room D

Physical Education S409—Organization and Administration of
Physical Education   Dr. DeShaw
The details of organizing the units of the physical education program are
discussed. Various topics, such as legislation, financing, curriculum construction, grading, excuses, plant facilities, supplies and equipment, and
office management are considered.
9:30-10:20 A. M.   Credit: 2 semester-hours   Room D

Integration

Integration S410—Teaching Aids Workshop   '   Miss Fantone and Others
This is a practical course designed for both in-service and student teachers,
with emphasis upon the development and use of teaching aids. A special study
is made in the use of photographs, film strips, glass slides, charts, motion
pictures, radio programs, television, etc. In the course, the student has the
opportunity to handle and to perfect his use of these materials and equipment. The course is given co-operatively by various members of the College
staff, supplemented by experts from educational and trade circles.
10:30-11:20 A. M.   Credit: 2 semester-hours   Room 5

Integration S470—Child Growth and Development   Mrs. Salt
This course is planned to help teachers understand how children grow and
develop. Such understanding will help teachers in guiding the total personality development of the child. The course will help college students apply
their learnings of biology, psychology, and sociology to the teaching of
children.
11:30 A. M.-12:20 P. M.   Credit: 2 semester-hours   Room 28

Integration S472—The Elementary School Curriculum   Mrs. Salt
This course will acquaint the College student with the subject matter of
the elementary school curriculum for grades 3-6 inclusive. In addition,
the following will be studied: (1) correlation among subjects, (2) the appraisal and use of textbooks, (3) the use of visual aids, (4) the methods
adapted to each subject, and (5) use of course of study materials.
8:00-9:20 A. M.   Credit: 3 semester-hours   Room 28

Integration S473—Teaching the Elementary School Language Arts
Mrs. Salt

This course gives an overview of modern practices' that are used in teaching reading, creative writing, speaking, spelling, and handwriting in the elementary grades. Students are helped to recognize and to make provision for readiness for learning in these areas, to learn or devise various techniques that will meet the needs of different children and situations, and to evaluate, select, and create suitable materials to be used at various maturity levels. Special emphasis is placed on the functional use of the language arts in the total curriculum and life of the elementary school child.

10:30-11:20 A. M.   Credit: 2 semester-hours   Room 28

Integration S474—Elementary School Art
Mr. Karp

This course provides a wide range of creative manipulative experience with the materials, tools, and techniques of art work in the elementary school and an insight into significant art work of children of various age levels. Work is done in crayon, paint, chalk, clay, wood, papier-maché, finger paints, and other easily accessible materials. The work of the course includes simple weaving, block prints, murals, and the making of puppets. Attention throughout is directed toward an insight into the significance of art work and of manipulative experience as a medium of expression and a means of growth for the child.

9:30-10:20 A. M.   Credit: 2 semester-hours   Room 11-CHS

Integration S475A—Fundamentals of Elementary School Music
Dr. McEachern

The elements of music, including notation, the formation of scales and various modes, key and clef signatures, Italian musical terms, abbreviations, rhythm, and intervals are included in this course. The student should acquire the ability to write a simple melody from dictation and to read at sight any part in a simple three-part selection in a musician-like manner. Ability to carry a tune is necessary for success in this course.

11:30 A. M.-12:20 P. M.   Credit: 2 semester-hours   Room 13-Music Bldg.

Integration S500A—Basic Educational Trends
Dr. Fraser

This course deals with the historical background which administrators and supervisors, as well as teachers, need in order to evaluate problems and policies in due perspective. It emphasizes the current trends in American society and their bearing upon education. It also considers philosophies concerning the causes of rises and declines in outstanding civilizations and the part education could play among them.

10.30-11:20 A. M.   Credit: 2 semester-hours   Room 27

Integration S500B—Advanced Educational Psychology
Dr. Sperle

The course cover the various aspects of growth. Individual differences, their measurement, and their bearing on educational practices and principles furnish topics of study and discussion. Principles and laws of learning are reviewed. Some time is given to problems of personality as encountered in school work. The several points of view which have been prominent in the psychology of the past fifty to seventy-five years are examined for their contributions to thinking about human nature. *Prerequisite: an introductory course in psychology.*

9:30-10:20 A. M.   Credit: 2 semester-hours   Room 29

Integration S500C—Recent Trends in Secondary School
Methods   **Dr. Sperle**

This course emphasizes the fundamental principles underlying the technique of teaching on the secondary school level. Some of the topics considered are: organization of knowledge, the logical and psychological aspects of method, developing appreciations, social-moral education, teaching motor control, fixing motor responses, books and verbalism, meeting individual differences, guidance in study, tests and examinations, marks and marking.

11:30 A. M.-12:20 P. M.   Credit: 2 semester-hours   Room 29

Integration S500D—School Administration I; Functions
and Organization   **Mr. Morehead**

This introductory course in educational administration is concerned with general functions and personnel, as well as with the general organization of public education on local, state, and national levels. It deals also with federal-state relations, the state and sectarian education, the expanding scope of modern school systems, types and bases of school organization, and professional ethics.

10:30-11:20 A. M.   Credit: 2 semester-hours   Room B

Integration S501—Tests and Measurements in Education   **Dr. Ritter**

The purpose of this course is to develop an appreciation of the meaning and importance of measurement in education, and to give a working knowledge of instruments of measurement.

9:30-10:20 A. M.   Credit: 2 semester-hours   Room 5

Integration S502A—Organization and Administration of the
Modern High School—Part I   **Dr. W. S. Smith**

The following problems are considered: the student personnel, building and revising the high school curriculum, providing for individual differences, making the school schedule, records, the guidance program, pupil participation in government, the extra-curricular program, the health program, the safety program, discipline, library and study hall, cafeteria, the principal's office, and evaluating results.

9:30-10:20 A. M.   Credit: 2 semester-hours   Room 9

Integration S503—Methods and Instruments of Research   **Mr. Jackson**

This course is required of all candidates for the Master's degree without regard to their field of major interest. Its purpose is to introduce students of education to research and its practical application to professional problems. The course treats: the nature and types of educational research; methods and techniques of educational research; and the tools used in interpreting statistical data. During the course, the student sets up a problem and plans and carries out its solution.

1:00-1:50 P. M.   Credit: 2 semester-hours   Room 9

Integration S504A—Curriculum Construction in the
Secondary School   **Mr. Seybold**

The purpose of this course is to introduce the student to constructive criticism of American culture, to consider the extent to which the secondary school curriculum meets the needs of a changing civilization, and to consider effective means of curriculum construction. (A student may not receive credit for both Integration 504A and Integration 504C.)

9:30-10:20 A. M.   Credit: 2 semester-hours   Room 3-CHS

17

**Integration S505—Organization and Administration of
Extra-Curricular Activities**   **Mr. Morehead**

The first part of this course considers such general problems of extra-curricular activities as: their growing importance; their relation to the curriculum; the principles underlying their organization, administration, and supervision; and methods of financing. In the second part, an intensive study is made of the home room, the assembly, the student council, clubs, athletics, school publications, and other activities in which the class is especially interested.

8:30-9:20 A. M.   Credit: 2 semester-hours   Room B

**Integration S507—Organization and Administration of
Guidance Programs**   **Mr. Seybold**

The purpose of this course is to acquaint the student with the various agencies and methods for the guidance of students in school work, with certain implications in the choice of and the preparation for a vocation. Among the topics are: the abilities of students as related to guidance, the exploration of special interests, the organization of the guidance program, and the integration of the entire high school program for purposes of guidance.

11:30 A. M.-12:20 P. M.   Credit: 2 semester-hours   Room 3-CHS

**Integration S508A—Supervision of Instruction in
Secondary Schools**   **Dr. Fraser**

This course emphasizes the more practical phases of supervision which are met most frequently by those engaged in it. Among the topics are: the set-up for adequate supervision, supervision as encouraging and guiding the growth of teachers and the improvement of educational procedures, the supervisory functions of teachers' meetings, discussion groups, general and professional reading, the writing of articles, co-operative curriculum modification, utilization of community resources, and teacher inter-visitation.

8:30-9:20 A. M.   Credit: 2 semester-hours   Room 27

**Integration S510—Seminar in Secondary Administration
and Supervision**   **Mr. Morehead**

In this course the class makes an intensive study of administrative and supervisory problems suggested by the educational events and trends of the year, by the interests and responsibilities of the members of the class, and by educational movements in New Jersey and the country. Each student does an individual piece of research which he reports to the class. This represents advanced work which depends upon previous study or experience in educational administration or supervision. *Prerequisites: Integration* 502A, 502B, or 601A, and 508A, 508B, 508C, or 601B.

1:00-1:50 P. M.   Credit: 2 semester-hours   Room B

**Integration S515—Guidance and Personnel Problems of
Classroom Teachers**   **Mr. Seybold**

This course considers all types of personnel problems with which the classroom teacher deals. It is concerned with the growth of pupils and seeks to point out the ways by which proper growth may be attained. Classroom, health, social, and personal activities are analyzed in terms of the needs of present-day social life.

10:30-11:20 A. M.   Credit: 2 semester-hours   Room 3-CHS

18

Integration S517—Administration of the Elementary School   Dr. Phipps

This course analyzes and evaluates the administrative duties and relationships of the elementary school principal. Particular consideration is given to: building management, effective use of the school plant, sanitation, health service, the library, personnel management, the administration of the curriculum, community relationships, and publicity.

9:30-10:20 A. M.   Credit: 2 semester-hours   Room 2, Annex No. 2

Integration S518—Supervision of Instruction in the Elementary School   Dr. Phipps

This course has been planned for those engaged in the supervision of the elementary school, and for those who are preparing for such responsibilities. Principles of classroom supervision are developed and applied to learning situations. Among the more important topics that receive attention are: the nature and function of supervision, the organization necessary for effective supervision, the nature and significance of the teacher's purposes, the methods and techniques of group and individual supervision, the technique of observation, and the supervisory conference.

10:30-11:20 A. M. *   Credit: 2 semester-hours   Room 4, Annex No. 2

Integration S520—Principles of Mental Hygiene   Dr. Ingebritsen

This course is designed to be a general survey of the principles and practices of mental health with special reference to the mental health of teacher and pupil. It involves a thorough grounding in fundamental principles of mental hygiene with much practical consideration of the mental-health values of instructional programs and procedures. Discussion centers in practical efforts to develop wholesome personalities in our schools.

11:30 A. M.-12:20 P. M.   Credit: 2 semester-hours   Room 30

Integration S532—The Supervision and Teaching of Reading in Elementary Schools   Dr. Sperle

The place of reading in the entire elementary school program is analyzed. Attention is given to necessary remedial work for junior high school students. Materials and their use in instructional programs are studied with a view toward increasing power. All growth levels are considered. Good first teaching is of primary concern; however, the analysis and correction of certain reading difficulties constitute an important portion of the course.

8:30-9:20 A. M.   Credit: 2 semester-hours   Room 29

Integration S535A—Vocational Guidance   Mr. Thomas

This course is especially intended to enable high school teachers to guide their pupils in planning for constructive vocational life. The course is designed to be helpful also to adults who are seeking better vocational adjustment. Following are the topics included: the purpose of work, main areas of work, inventory of personal interests and traits, analyzing interests and traits, samples of personal inventories with analyses and interviews, exploring one's area of work, making the most of school days, finding the first job, adjustments on the way, advancement—what it is and how to attain it, intelligent use of money, balanced use of time, and cultivating pride of work.

9:30-10:20 A. M.   Credit: 2 semester-hours   Room 30

**Integration S548—Curriculum Construction in the
Elementary School**   **Dr. Phipps**

This course offers an opportunity to review State and city elementary curricula; to discuss the principles of curriculum construction; to collect new teaching materials for the various subjects; and to evaluate, organize, and grade these materials. Teaching procedures in the use of materials are discussed and evaluated in terms of pupil needs, the objectives set-up, and the results obtained. This course offers an opportunity to make a special study of the materials and procedures to be used in the teaching of the language arts.

11:30 A. M.-12:20 P. M.   Credit: 2 semester-hours   Room 4, Annex No. 2

Integration S550—Child and Adolescent Development   **Mr. Thomas**

This course reviews the general characteristics of child and adolescent development; motor and physiological, social, emotional, language, intellectual, and interests and ideals. The influence of home, school, community, and institutional life on child and adolescent development are considered as well as problems of guidance presented by children in the normal course of development and also those presented by deviations from the normal course.

8:30-9:20 A. M.   Credit: 2 semester-hours   Room 30

Mathematics

Mathematics S400—Educational Statistics   **Mr. Clifford**

The aim of this course is to prepare the student (1) to comprehend and criticize articles of statistical nature in current educational literature; (2) to apply statistical methods in testing and rating pupils; (3) to carry on the simpler types of educational research. By analysis of real data from the secondary field, the student becomes familiar with the measures of central tendency and variability, short methods of computation, graphic representation of material, the properties of the normal curve, and linear correlation. Inasmuch as statistical methods in education are almost identical with those employed in the natural, physical, and social sciences, there is natural integration with these fields.

9:30-10:20 A. M.   Credit: 2 semester-hours   Room 4, Annex No. 1

**Mathematics S401—The Teaching of Mathematics in
Secondary Schools**   **Mr. Humphreys**

The student in this course studies the methods of teaching the different units of work in the junior and senior high school. A study of recent trends in the teaching of mathematics, of noteworthy research, of courses in general mathematics, and of modern texts and tests is included.

8:00-9:20 A. M.   Credit: 3 semester-hours   Room 2, Annex No. 1

**Mathematics S505—Consumer Mathematics. A Background for
Teaching in the Junior High School**   **Mr. Clifford**

This course aims to survey the field of consumer problems, to display mathematics as a powerful tool in analyzing these problems, and to consider the placement and methods of teaching this material in the intermediate grades and in the junior high school. Some of the topics included are: the cost of raising children; the money value of a man; the cost of owning or renting a home; insurance; pensions and social security; stocks, bonds, and the financial page; the quality and cost of consumer goods; business cycles and indices of business activity.

8:30-9:20 A. M.   Credit: 2 semester-hours   Room 4, Annex No. 1

**Mathematics S509A—A Critical Interpretation of Mathematics
in the Senior High School—I** Dr. Davis

An opportunity is here offered for an investigation and interpretation of
the algebra and geometry of the secondary school. The meaning and use of
secondary mathematics are stressed, rather than the methods of teaching.
Among the topics discussed are: algebra as a thought process and not a
mechanical operation, types of thinking in algebra and geometry, fundamental
laws of arithmetic, algebra as generalized arithmetic, geometrical interpretation of algebra, the function concept in algebra and geometry, the changing
scope and subject matter of Euclidean geometry, limits and incommensurables,
and integration* (i.e. correlation and fusion) of all secondary mathematics.

10:30-11:20 A. M. Credit: 2 semester-hours Room 1, Annex No. 1

Mathematics S511B—Non-Euclidean Geometry Mr. Kays

The development of Hyperbolic-Non-Euclidean and of Elliptic Non-Euclidean
geometry is carefully traced. A brief survey of the historical development
of each is given. This course is designed for teachers and students of
mathematics who desire a better perspective of the field of geometry.

9:30-10:20 A. M. Credit: 2 semester-hours Room 3, Annex No. 1

Mathematics S521—Analytical Mechanics Mr. Humphreys

The fundamental basic principles of this course are Newton's laws of motion,
whose applications and consequences are carefully considered in the study of
such topics as: the composition and resolution of forces, the statics of a
particle and of a rigid body, forces acting upon a body, friction, straight
line motion, curvi-linear motion, work and energy, moment of inertia, etc.
The need and usefulness of mathematics for the explanation of physical
phenomena are clearly shown. *Prerequisite: Elementary calculus.*

11:30 A. M.-12:20 P. M. Credit: 2 semester-hours . Room 2, Annex No. 1

Music

**Integration S475A—Fundamentals of Elementary School
Music** Dr. McEachern

See description and other data under the heading of "Integration."

Science

Chemistry S407A—Advanced Quantitative Analysis—I Dr. McLachlan

This course is adapted to the needs and preparation of students. The work
is mainly instrument analysis applied to control work in industry, agriculture,
and biochemistry.

10:30-11:20 A. M.-MWF-Lab. Tu. 1-5 P. M. Credit: 2 s.h. Room 22

Chemistry S412—Physical Chemistry—II Dr. McLachlan

This course deals with electrical conductance, electrolytic equilibrium, electromotive force, electrolysis, polarization, chemical kinetics, photo-chemical reactions, atomic structure, molecular structure, and radioactivity. *Prerequisites:
General college chemistry, analytical chemistry, and general college physics.*

9:30-10:20 A. M.-Labs. M&W 1-5 P. M. Credit: 4 s.h. Room 22

Physics S304A—Introduction to Photography—I   **Dr. K. O. Smith**

This is a beginning course in photography consisting of laboratory work and field work supplemented by lectures and demonstrations. Some of the topics covered are: the construction and operation of cameras, common films and papers, fundamental chemistry of photography, development and printing. A student needs at least one camera. Part I emphasizes film development and contact printing.

10:30-11:20 A. M.-MWF-Lab. Th. 1-5 P. M.   Credit: 2 s.h.   Room 25

Physics S407—Aviation   ·   **Mr. Placek**

This course treats types of airplanes, structures, motions of a plane, stability, lift, drag, principles of flying, engine, speed, power, physics of flight, and airplane performance. *Prerequisites: General college physics and adequate college training in mathematics.*

9:30-11:20 A. M.   Credit: 4 semester-hours   Room 8-CHS

Physics S512—Modern Physics   **Dr. K. O. Smith**

This course is a survey of recent experimental research in physics and of the newer theories concerning nuclear physics and electricity. Such topics as atomic spectra, radioactivity, artificial transmutation of the elements, and cosmic rays are discussed. *Prerequisites: General college physics and a course in electrical measurements.*

8:00-9:20 A. M. and   Credit: 4 semester-hours   Room 25
Field Trips by Arrangement

Science S100C—The Earth Sciences   **Dr. Milstead**

In this course emphasis is placed on the effect of soil, climate, and physical features on the welfare of plants, animals, and mankind. The keynote of the course is to show the influence of a constantly changing environment on the life activities and welfare of mankind.

9:30-10:20 A. M.   Credit: 2 semester-hours   Room 26

**Science S401D—The Teaching of Aviation in
Secondary Schools**   **Mr. Placek**

This course deals with texts, bulletins, demonstration equipment, tests, working models, visual aids, and reference works needed to teach aerodynamics, aircraft engines, meteorology, navigation, and aircraft communication in high schools.

11:30 A. M.-12:20 P. M.   Credit: 2 semester-hours   Room 8-CHS

Social Studies

**Social Studies S401—The Teaching of the Social Studies
in Secondary Schools**   **Dr. Moffatt**

The course aims to present recent tendencies in educational method in teaching the social studies. A program is presented containing the correlation of subject-matter organization in socialized recitation, the teaching of current events, projects in citizenship, and the use of the project-problem as a method of teaching history and civics. A laboratory containing texts and workbooks in the social studies field is available to the students of this course.

8:00-9:20 A. M.   Credit: 3 semester-hours   Room 21

Social Studies S402B—Comparative Government   **Dr. Gooden**

The basic facts and principles necessary for the teaching of civics, history, and the political phenomena in England, France, Germany, Italy, and Russia, are studied.

10:30-11:20 A. M.   Credit: 2 semester-hours   Room 21

Social Studies S404—The Philosophy of History   **Dr. Clayton**

It is the purpose of this course to investigate the relation of history to the other social studies and also the major attempts to find the meaning of history. A brief survey is made of the leading philosophies of history.

9:30-10:20 A. M.   Credit: 2 semester-hours   Room 14-CHS

Social Studies S407—New Jersey State and Local Government   **Dr. Moffatt**

A study is made of the State Constitution; New Jersey's place in the Federal system; the rights and duties of citizens; suffrage; political parties; the legislative, the executive, and administrative systems; the courts; the law enforcement and correctional systems; revenues and expenditures; public health, educational, highway, and other services; county and municipal government; and other local political units.

9:30-10:20 A. M.   ·   Credit: 2 semester-hours   Room 20

Social Studies—S435A—The Americas: A Contemporary
     Political, Economic, and Cultural Survey—Part 1   **Dr. Gooden**

This course deals specifically with the relations of the United States and the Caribbean countries. Attention is given to the dependencies of the United States in this region as well as to the independent republics. Twentieth century political, economic, and cultural developments of this region are stressed in light of the inter-American system.

9:30-10:20 A. M.   Credit: 2 semester-hours   Room 21

Social Studies S439—The Family and Its Problems   **Dr. Clayton**

This course gives a history of the family, our American family patterns, the effects of social change, marital patterns of interaction, social roles, sources of conflicts and frustration, divorce and desertion, special problems in family life, economics of children and the home, social legislation pertaining to family problems, marital adjustments, personality change after marriage, parent-child relationships, and personality reorientation.

8:30-9:20 A. M.   Credit: 2 semester-hours   Room 14-CHS

Social Studies S451—The Middle East   **Dr. Wittmer**

This course is a survey of Indian and Moslem civilizations. It shows that economic and political changes alone do not suffice to adjust the peoples of the Middle East to twentieth century civilization, and that many cultural traditions must vanish while some forgotten features of the past are to be revived. Post-war planning for the region from the Near East through Persia, India, Burma, Thailand, and Malaya to the Netherland East Indies is discussed.

9:30-10:20 A. M.   Credit: 2 semester-hours   Room 13-CHS

Social Studies S457—Development of Russia   **Dr. Wittmer**

Factors which have shaped the evolution of the Russian people, such as Byzantinism and the Greek Orthodox faith, the Synod, Tartar state organization, the Mir, Westernization from Peter to Lenin, Slavophilism, and dialectic materialism, are emphasized. An account is presented of Soviet internal organization, sovkhoz, kolkhoz, and the Five-Year plans. In addition to the historical background, Russia's great writers are discussed in the light of social and political developments.

10:30-11:20 A.M.   Credit: 2 semester-hours   Room 13-CHS

Social Studies S462—Continental United States   **Mr. Bye**

This field study course consists of sixty-two days of directed travel, including all of July and August, and provides an opportunity for gaining an integrated view of our country as a whole. The trip is made in a modern chartered motor coach with overnight stops at first-class hotels. The route covers about 12,500 miles and visits 26 states and 6 National Parks. Among the major points of interest are Gettysburg, Natural Bridge, Blue Ridge and blue grass region, Mammoth Cave, Lincoln shrines in Kentucky and Illinois, Ozark Mountains, Dodge City, Royal Gorge, Pikes Peak, Denver, Rocky Mountain National Park, Taos and other Indian Reservations, Santa Fe, Petrified Forest, Painted Desert, Grand Canyon, Bryce and Zion National Parks, Hoover Dam, Los Angeles, Hollywood, San Diego, San Capistrano and other Missions; Tia Juana, Santa Barbara, Sequoia and Yosemite National Parks, Monterey, San Francisco, Sacramento, Lake Tahoe, Reno, Donner Pass, mammoth redwood groves, Crater Lake, Columbia River Valley, Portland, Seattle, Mt. Rainier, Grand Coulee Dam, Spokane, Butte, Yellowstone National Park, Salt Lake City, pioneer trails of Wyoming, Black Hills, Chicago, Detroit, Toronto, and Niagara Falls. All important geographic and historical features are studied under the instruction of members of the college faculty and local specialists. Write for descriptive folder, addressing the Bureau of Field Studies.

Credit: 10 semester-hours

The quota for the above course has been filled. In case of withdrawals, vacancies will be filled from the waiting list in order of applications received, preference being given to those taking the course for credit. The all-expense price will be $750.00. This includes tuition, transportation, hotels, meals, tips, and a laboratory fee of $80.00 covering all other expenses. Starts Saturday, July 2; ends Wednesday, August 31, 1949.

Social Studies S470—History and Principles of Philosophy   **Dr. Freeman**

This course presents a study of the history of philosophy and of the important principles contributed by outstanding philosophers from Thales to Gentile. Much of the discussion is centered on three types of philosophic thought: Naturalism, idealism, and pragmatism. Among the philosophers considered are: Plato, Aristotle, Bacon, Spencer, Rousseau, Hegel, James, Dewey, and Gentile.

10:30-11:20 A.M.   Credit: 2 semester-hours   Room 10

Social Studies S474—America in Transition   **Dr. Gooden**

This course surveys rapidly the results of the Civil War and then emphasizes the major trends, economic and social, which have made modern America. It is intended as a more advanced study than that which is made in the undergraduate course. The period covered is from 1867 to around 1914.

11:30 A.M.-12:20 P.M.   Credit: 2 semester-hours   Room 21

24

CHINA INSTITUTE OF NEW JERSEY

The China Institute of New Jersey is a permanent year-round organization composed of former students of the China Workshop course. The policies and program of the Institute are determined by an elected executive committee, an advisory board of laymen and representatives from the faculty of Montclair Teachers College, in consultation with the Chinese Director. Dr. Chih Meng, Director of the China Institute of America, whose purpose is to promote cultural and educational relations between China and the United States, is Chinese Director of the China Institute of New Jersey. The College provides the facilities necessary for the courses sponsored by the Institute and grants credit for the satisfactory completion of such courses. The courses are given on the senior-graduate level, so that students may work toward either undergraduate or graduate credit.

While the primary and definite purpose of the Institute is to assist the teachers of New Jersey, men and women who desire to take these courses for cultural, vocational, or avocational purposes are welcome also. They may enroll for college credit or simply as Auditors for no credit. The cost is the same in both cases. If it be desired to attend a single lecture, the Institute Treasurer collects the fee of $2.00 at the door of the Auditorium. Students who enroll for the entire course follow the instructions below

The presence on our campus and in our residence halls of the Chinese scholars who are in charge of these two courses is most welcome. It permits the students of these courses to become personally acquainted with their professors and for the College to offer to all students of the Summer Session and to the general public an opportunity to hear a Chinese speaker at one of the College assemblies.

OFFERINGS FOR 1949: JUNE 27 - JULY 9

Social Studies S499—China Workshop   **Dr. Chih Meng**

This course is given in twelve days. Twenty-four hours of lectures and class discussions are devoted to the study of Chinese history and contemporary Chinese life under the direction of Chinese scholars. Twenty-four hours of directed study in the library are devoted to the preparation of teaching units and background materials on China for use in our schools.

9:30 A. M.-4 P. M.   Credit: 3 semester-hours   Auditorium-CHS

Social Studies S496B—China: The Evolution of a Nation   Dr ....

This course is an intensive study of the Chinese civilization, the forces underlying the development of the national character of the Chinese people, their contacts and conflicts with other peoples and cultures from historical times to the present. Chinese folklore, folkways, biographies and contributions to world civilization are considered. Because of its voluminous material, this course does not attempt to cover the whole span of Chinese history, but it is an integrated presentation of the maturing of the Chinese people as a nation. There are twenty-four hours of lectures in the morning, and round table discussion and library work in the afternoon. *Prerequisite: Social Studies 499—China Workship.*

9:30 A. M.-4 P. M.   Credit: 3 semester-hours   Room 12-CHS

Registration for either of the above courses must be made on forms provided by the College. Write to Miss Favor, the Secretary of the Summer Session, for these forms. Return them to her not later than June 17, with check made payable to the *China Institute of New Jersey* for $25.00. A late service charge of $2.00 will be made for all registrations not received by June 17.

Courses in Session from June 21 through August 18, 1949

Following is a list of the courses of the Nine Weeks Session, which is held for the benefit of the accelerated candidates for the Bachelor of Arts degree at Montclair.

Other students who have special need for these courses may enroll in them also. This includes undergraduate students from other colleges, graduate students who require these courses for certification or prerequisite purposes, and teachers-in-service who are seeking to complete the requirements for a bachelor's degree. Students matriculated at other colleges should note carefully the paragraph directed to them on page 5.

Descriptions of these courses are to be found in the Undergraduate Catalogue. The hours and room numbers will be shown on a mimeographed list provided at the time of registration.

All students (other than the regular undergraduate students of this College) who are taking any of the following courses must register and pay the fees on Monday, June 20. They should report to Room 9 in the Main Building, and come prepared to enroll at the same time in the courses they expect to take in the Regular Summer Session, in order that the total amount of credit to be taken will appear on the Registration Form. It should be remembered that not more than 9 s. h. credit may be taken during the Nine Weeks Session, but students may enroll in the Post-Summer Session course also, thus earning a total of 11 s. h. for the summer.

Department	Cat. No.	Title of Course	Sem. Hrs. Cr.
Bus. Ed.	201A	Business Law III	2
Bus. Ed.	201B	Business Organization and Management	2
Bus. Ed.	301	Bookkeeping and Accounting	4
Bus. Ed.	302	Principles of Accounting	4
English	200A	Composition	3
English	200B	Fundamentals of Speech—I	3
Language	300	Foundations of Language	2
Integration	200A	Introduction to Educational Psychology and Mental Testing	2
Integration	300A	Aims and Organization of Secondary Education	2
Integration	400A	Principles and Philosophy of Secondary Education	2
Mathematics	300	The Social and Commercial Uses of Mathematics	2
Mathematics	301	Modern College Geometry	4
Mathematics	302	Higher Algebra	4
Mathematics	400	Educational Statistics	2
Mathematics	402	Applications of Mathematics	4
Physical Ed.	M307	Methods of Coaching and Officiating	3
Physical Ed.	M308	Methods of Coaching and Officiating	3
Science	100A	Survey of Physical Science	4
Physics	406	Astronomy	4
Social Stud.	200A	Contemporary Economic Life	2
Social Stud.	200B	Contemporary Political Life	2
Social Stud.	200C	Contemporary Social Life	2
Social Stud.	301	Economics	4

Post-Summer Session Course

Students have the opportunity to take an additional 2 semester-hours credit following the close of the Regular Summer Session. The work will be given intensively, so as to end before the beginning of the fall semester. Registration for this course will be accepted up to and including the opening day of the course. However, students should register early as there is a limit to the number of registrations which may be accepted.

Health Education S408—Principles and Practices of Safety
Education for High School Teachers   Dr. N. O. Schneider and Staff
Dr. DeShaw, Coordinator

This course is intended for teachers-in-service and prospective teachers who may teach safety education in the high schools of New Jersey. Special emphasis is given to driver education with actual outdoor practice in the handling of a motor vehicle. The driver education phase of the course consists of two parts: (1) classroom instruction and (2) actual experience behind the wheel. A dual-control car is provided for this latter part of the course. The section of the course devoted to general safety education covers safety principles in industry, at home, on the street, and in recreational activities. A variety of teaching units and integrated teaching aids is furnished to the student.

Credit: 2 semester-hours   Room 24

Text-Book Exhibit

In the Gymnasium of the Main Building, from July 11 through July 22, there will be an exhibit of high school and elementary school textbooks. While primarily for the benefit of the principals and teachers attending the Summer Session, the exhibit will be open to undergraduate students and to members of the general public who may be interested in seeing the latest textbooks.

Mrs. Paul J. Ritter will be in charge of the exhibit again this year.

SUMMER SESSION

Bulletin of

MONTCLAIR
STATE TEACHERS COLLEGE

JULY 5 TO AUGUST 17

1950

UPPER MONTCLAIR, NEW JERSEY

SUMMER SESSION

Bulletin Of

MONTCLAIR
STATE TEACHERS COLLEGE

1 9 5 0
July 5th to August 17th

UPPER MONTCLAIR, NEW JERSEY

OFFICERS OF ADMINISTRATION

NEW JERSEY STATE TEACHERS COLLEGE AT MONTCLAIR

HARRY A. SPRAGUE, Ph.D. ....Presider

E. DEALTON PARTRIDGE, Ph.D. ....Dean of Instructic

OTIS C. INGEBRITSEN, Ph.D. ....Chairman of the Graduate Committe

CLAUDE E. JACKSON, A.M. ....Director of Admissions, Records and Researc

MORRIS SEIBERT, A.B. ....Acting Registrar and Veterans' Counsele

ELIZABETH S. FAVOR, A.M. ....Assistant in Graduate Personn

BERNARD SIEGEL, B.S. ....Business Manag

EARL C. DAVIS, M.S. ....Director of Personnel and Guidan

MARGARET A. SHERWIN, A.M. ....Dean of Wom

HENRY E. SCHMIDT, A.M.,

    Dean of Men and Director, Health, Physical Education and Recreatic

HORACE J. SHEPPARD, A.M. ....Acting Head of Business Education Departme

EDWIN S. FULCOMER, Ed.D. ....Head of English Departme

MOWAT G. FRASER, Ph.D. ....Head of Integration Departme

VIRGIL S. MALLORY, Ph.D. ....Head of Mathematics Departme

EDNA McEACHERN, Ph.D. ....Head of Music Departme

EARL R. GLENN, A.M. ....Head of Science Departme

ELWYN C. GAGE, Ph.D. ....Head of Social Studies Departme

ANNE BANKS CRIDLEBAUGH, B.S. ....Acting Librari

EDGAR C. BYE, A.M. ....Director, New Tools for Learning Bure

ARTHUR M. SEYBOLD, A.M. ....Director of College High Sch

OTTO CORDES, P.E. ....Engineer in Charge, Maintenai

2

SUMMER SESSION 1950

FACULTY

HARRY A. SPRAGUE, Ph.D. ....President
E. DEALTON PARTRIDGE, Ph.D. ....Dean of Instruction
EDGAR C. BYE, A.M. ....Field Studies
PAUL C. CLIFFORD, A.M. ....Mathematics
ALDEN C. CODER, Ed.M. ....Health and Physical Education
ANNE BANKS CRIDLEBAUGH, B.S. ....Acting Librarian
DAVID R. DAVIS, Ph.D. ....Acting Head, Department of Mathematics
EARL C. DAVIS, M.S. ....Personnel and Guidance
JEROME DE ROSA, A.M. ....Health and Physical Education
EMMA FANTONE, A.M. ....Audio-Visual Aids
L. HOWARD FOX, A.M. ....Speech
PAUL E. FROEHLICH, A.M. ....Business Education
EDWIN S. FULCOMER, Ed.D. ....Head of Department of English
HERBERT B. GOODEN, Ed.D. ....Social Studies
W. PAUL HAMILTON, A.M. ....English
OTIS C. INGEBRITSEN, Ph.D. ....Psychology
BENJAMIN KARP, A.M. ....Art
GEORGE W. KAYS, A.M. ....Mathematics
WALTER KOPS, A.M. ....Field Studies
RUSSELL KRAUSS, Ph.D. ....English
RICHARD H. LAMPKIN, Ph.D. ....Science
CHIH MENG, Ph.D. ....Director of China Institute
JOHN P. MILLIGAN, Ed.D. ....Administration
HARLEY P. MILSTEAD, Ph.D. ....Geography
MAURICE P. MOFFATT, Ph.D. ....Social Studies
ALLAN MOREHEAD, A.M. ....Integration
CLYDE M. NARRAMORE, Ed.D. ....Integration
JAMES P. PETTEGROVE, A.M. ....English
WILLIAM R. PHIPPS, Ed.D. ....Integration
GEORGE F. PLACEK, A.M. ....Science
RUFUS D. REED, Ph.D. ....Chemistry
JOHN J. RELLAHAN, Ph.D. ....Acting Head, Department of Social Studies
ARTHUR M. SEYBOLD, A.M. ....Integration
HORACE J. SHEPPARD, A.M. ....Acting Head, Department of Business Education
KENNETH O. SMITH, Ph.D. ....Physics
W. SCOTT SMITH, Ph.D. ....Integration
ELIZABETH T. VANDERVEER, A.M. ....Business Education
RICHARD W. WILLING, A.M. ....Business Education
FELIX WITTMER, Ph.D. ....Social Studies
ANNETTA L. WOOD, A.M. ....Speech
FREDERIC H. YOUNG, Ph.D. ....Integration

GRADUATE COMMITTEE

OTIS C. INGEBRITSEN, *Chairman*

E. DEALTON PARTRIDGE   RUFUS D. REED
D. HENRYETTA SPERLE   HORACE J. SHEPPARD
W. PAUL HAMILTON   ELIZABETH S. FAVOR, *Secretary*
DAVID R. DAVIS   JOHN J. RELLAHAN

Main Building—Montclair College Campus

SUMMER SESSION OF THE
NEW JERSEY STATE TEACHERS COLLEGE AT MONTCLAIR

Objectives and Academic Status

The College is a professional school which prepares teachers, supervisors, and principals of high schools, and administrators of public school systems. The degrees offered by this College are those of Bachelor of Arts and Master of Arts. Certificate courses are offered for those who now hold degrees from other colleges.

The New Jersey State Teachers College at Montclair is a fully accredited member of the American Association of Teachers Colleges, the Middle States Association of Colleges and Secondary Schools, the Association of American Universities, and the American Association of University Women.

How to Reach the Campus

Trains of the Greenwood Lake Division, Erie R. R., stop at College Station. Trains of the Lackawanna R. R. connect at Montclair with the following bus lines: No. 64, running between Brick Church and the College; No. 60, running between Newark and the College; and No. 76, which runs between Orange and Paterson, passing the College en route. For those who come by car: the College is located about one mile north of the center of Upper Montclair.

Residence Halls for Men and Women

Edward Russ Hall and Chapin Hall are Montclair College's two well-appointed Residences. The charge for living on campus during the Summer Session is: $13.50 per week; which includes room, breakfast, and dinner. A la carte luncheons are served in the College cafeteria. For one student alone in a double room, an extra charge of $2.00 per week is made. The College provides and launders sheets, pillowcase, and bedpad. Towels, table lamps, blankets, clocks, and similar items must be provided and cared for by the student. The boarding-hall fee must be paid on or before the first day of the Summer Session. No rebate is made for occasional absence or voluntary withdrawal during the session. Students who are absent on account of illness for two weeks or more receive a rebate of $6.00 per week during the illness. These prices are subject to change.

For reservations in a College Residence Hall, women address: Dean of Women, State Teachers College, Upper Montclair, N. J. Men address the Dean of Men.

Schedule of the Summer Session

Registration will take place on Wednesday, July 5: Hours, 1-4 and 7-9 P. M.; also, Thursday, July 6: Hours, 1-3 P. M. Classes will begin on Thursday morning, July 6, at 8 A. M. and will continue through Thursday, August 17. All classes meet daily, Monday to Friday, inclusive, at the hours indicated for each.

Matriculation

Those who desire to become candidates for either the Bachelor of Arts or the Master of Arts degree at Montclair must request the Registrar for the application form and return it, properly filled in and accompanied by an Official Transcript of all previous work on college level. When such an applicant has been accepted by the College as a candidate for the degree, a definite statement will be furnished to him, showing the requirements which he must fulfill to earn the degree. This sheet becomes the student's Work Program.

Auditors

Men and women who desire to take courses for cultural, vocational, or avocational purposes without college credits may register as auditors.

A student who desires to enroll in a course for which he already holds credit must register as an auditor in that course.

A student who desires to enroll in a course for which he has not completed the prerequisites must enroll as an auditor in that course.

Change of Status in a Course

If a student desires to change his status in a course from "credit" to "auditor" or from "auditor" to "credit," he must make formal application for such change not later than the middle of the course. Forms for this purpose may be procured from the Secretary of the Summer Session. Such changes cannot be made after the midpoint of the course is passed.

Students Matriculated at Montclair

Work taken for credit at Montclair must be with the advice and approval of the Dean of Instruction or the Chairman of the Graduate Committee and the Head of the Department in which the student is majoring. See paragraph under the heading "Conferences."

Candidates for a degree must file with the Registrar an application for conferment of the degree before November 30 of the college year in which the work is to be completed. Application blanks for this purpose may be secured in the Registrar's Office. The burden of responsibility for the request rests with the candidate. This is of special significance to the teacher-in-service who may have distributed the work for the degree over several years.

Students Matriculated at Other Colleges

In recent summers, the State Teachers College at Montclair has offered courses to its own accelerated candidates for the Bachelor's degree. It has therefore, been possible to accept students from other colleges in freshman sophomore, and junior year courses, as well as in courses of the senior year Beginning in the summer of 1950, however, the College returns to its pre-war custom of offering courses primarily to teachers-in-service in its Summer Session Since such teachers already hold the Bachelor's degree, with few exceptions, the College will offer for the most part only Graduate and Senior-Graduate courses

A student who is planning to attend Montclair this summer should take the Summer Session Bulletin to a conference with the Dean of his own college to arrange a program of work. For the Dean's information: the numbering of courses at Montclair follows this order: 100-399, inclusive, are undergraduate courses; 400-499, inclusive, are senior-college and graduate courses; 500 and above are graduate courses.

Certificates

The State Teachers College at Montclair offers work toward the following New Jersey Certificates: Secondary Teaching Certificate; Secondary School Principal's Certificate; Elementary School Principal's Certificate; Subject Supervisor's Certificate; General Supervisor's Certificate; Guidance; School Administrator's Certificate; Junior College Teacher's Certificate; and the Advanced Professional Certificate.

Those who matriculate at Montclair for a degree will receive information from Dr. Fraser, Head of the Integration Department, as to the requirements for each of these certificates. Students who have not matriculated at Montclair should write to Dr. E. C. Preston, Secretary of the State Board of Examiners, Department of Education, 175 West State Street, Trenton 8, N. J., for information as to the requirements. For an evaluation of work already completed, address Dr. Preston. An official transcript of such previous work should accompany the inquiry, with a statement as to the particular certificate desired. The student should bring Dr. Preston's reply with him when conferring with Dr. Fraser as to his program of work.

Students who must have this information immediately should go to Trenton to confer personally with Dr. Preston or his assistant, Miss Smith.

Supervised Student Teaching

The opportunity to do supervised student teaching cannot be offered during the Summer Session. For fall teaching, students confer with Dr. Fraser at the College.

Veterans

Veteran students taking work under the G. I. Bill for the first time at Montclair State Teachers College must see the Veterans' Counselor at least two weeks prior to the registration day. Veterans should be sure to obtain the Certificate of Eligibility from the Veterans' Administration before the start of the Summer Session. Failure to do so will mean that the usual fees must be paid by the student at the time of registration. Veterans transferring to this institution, who have previously been training under the G. I. Bill, will be required to present a Supplemental Certificate of Eligibility at the time of registration.

Conferences with Advisers

Appointments with the Dean of Instruction, the Chairman of the Graduate Committee, a Department Head, or the Veterans' Counselor may be made by mail or telephone to their respective offices. This should be done at as early a date as possible. Students unable to do so earlier may, however, see these officials or their representatives on July 5 and 6.

A representative of the State Board of Examiners will be at the College on July 5, 1-4 P. M., to see students who desire advice on the selection of courses toward a New Jersey Certificate. (See paragraph under the heading "Certificates.") The Secretary of the Summer Session will receive requests for appointments with this State Official.

Work Taken for Credit

The maximum amount of credit which may be earned in the Summer Session is 8 semester-hours, but only 6 s. h. are recommended. There is no provision for a student to audit additional courses; consequently, the total of all courses taken during the Summer Session may not exceed 8 s. h. and students should not register for more. Additional credits may be earned by attending one of the sessions at the State School of Conservation that precedes or follows the

Summer Session. Attention is called also to the post-Summer Session course i Safety Education and to the Feild Studies course in New England and Frenc Canada, as well as to the courses of the China Institute of New Jersey.

Each course is in session at least thirty hours and carries a designated amour of credit. It is not possible to earn three s. h. credit for a two s. h. course.

If prerequisites are required, the student should make certain that he ha fulfilled them or their equivalent before enrolling in the course. If no previou work on college level has been taken, the student should consult the Registra before enrolling in any course, unless as an Auditor.

A student may not register for credit in any course for which he alread holds credit except by permission of the Dean of Instruction.

Registration Information

Registration takes place in the College Library, on Wednesday, July 5, fror 1-4 and from 7-9 P. M.; also, on Thursday, July 6, from 1-3 P. M. Anyon unable to enroll during the hours shown must register on Friday, July 7 or o Monday, July 10, during the regular office hours. The late registration Servic Charge will be made on such registrations, and no course may be taken fc credit after Monday, July 10. Late students must report first to the Registrar' Office for the necessary forms.

Matriculated students should bring their "Worksheets' when they come t enroll.

The College reserves the right to close any course for which the enrollmer is insufficient. The class will meet at least once, however, before this decisio is made. Students may then enter another course in place of the one dis continued by going to the Registrar's Office to re-enroll and to receive the nev Class Admission Card in exchange for, the card of the discontinued course Students who decide not to enroll in an alternate course must return to th Registrar's Office to have the Class Admission Card of the discontinued cours stamped "Discontinued" before going to the Business Office for an adjustmer of tuition fees.

Withdrawal from a Course

Written notice to the Secretary of the Summer Session must be given a once by the student. Refunds are computed from the date of the receipt of th written notice. Teachers of the courses from which the student is withdrawin are notified by the Secretary. Students who neglect to follow this procedur receive a failing mark for the course or courses which they cease to attend.

Tuition Fees and Service Charges

Check or money-order should be made payable to New Jersey State Teache College, except for the China Institute courses.

Registration service charge: $1.00 for the Summer Session.

Late registration service charge: $2.00. This is collected from all studen who fail to enroll on July 5 or July 6.

Tuition fees: to students who have not taught regularly as a public scho teacher: $8.00 per semester-hour credit carried by the course; to students wl have taught regularly as a public school teacher: $11.00 per credit. Cours taken by auditors for no credit cost the same.

Laboratory service charge: $4.00 for each laboratory course. This is cc lected by the Business Office. It should not be included in the check for tuiti and registration.

Teachers who have supervised Montclair student-teachers and who have their possession old Montclair credit slips may take them to the office of t

8

Integration Department, where new ones will be issued. The Business Office cannot return any unused portion of a credit slip, so it is necessary that the new type credit slip be obtained before presenting it in payment of tuition fees. Training teachers may use the credit slips of any one of the six New Jersey State Teachers Colleges when taking courses at Montclair, but should bring only the new type slip in all cases.

Final Marks

Following are the final marks which may be received for a course: A-Excellent; B-Good; C-Fair; D-Poor; F-Failure; Inc.-Incomplete; Wd-Withdrew; N. C.-No Credit.

The mark of "D" when earned in summer, part-time, or extension courses of this College is not accepted for degree credit at Montclair.

The mark of "F" is given when earned and when the student has failed to notify the Secretary of the Summer Session promptly of his withdrawal from a course.

The mark of "N. C." is given only to auditors.

The mark of "Wd" is given only when prompt notice of withdrawal has been given to the Secretary and when the student's work to that time has been satisfactory to the teacher of the course.

The mark of "Inc." is seldom given. It may, however, be granted to a student whose work is incomplete at the end of the Session and who is eager to finish the work for a higher grade than he could receive otherwise. All responsibility regarding incomplete work rests with the student. He will be notified of a date after which, if the work remains incomplete, the final grade will be recorded without further notice.

Report Cards and Transcripts

An Official Transcript showing the credits earned is sent to the student personally ten days to two weeks following the close of the Session. A report card for each course taken is sent with the transcript. The transcript is sent without cost, but a service charge of $1.00 is made for a duplicate copy.

A student whose college requires that the transcript be mailed directly to the Dean or Registrar should call during the Summer Session at the Registrar's Office to address an envelope for this purpose.

Room Numbers

Room numbers used in this Bulletin, if unaccompanied by other designation, refer to rooms in College Hall, the main building of the College.

Other designations are as follows:

CHS: College High School Building; to the northeast of the main building;

Campus Studio Workshop: near the eastern end of the parking area;

Annex No. 1: Federal Works Administration Building No. 1; at the northwest corner of the main building;

Annex No. 2: Federal Works Administration Building No. 2; next to No. 1;

Annex No. 3: Federal Works Administration Building No. 3; directly east of the main building;

Music Building: at the northeast corner of the College High School Building;

Recreation Building: at the extreme north end of campus.

9

Elementary Education Courses

Although the New Jersey State Teachers College at Montclair is engaged primarily in preparing secondary school teachers, during the present shortage of teachers in the elementary schools it is deemed expedient to offer courses in the field of elementary education to those students who are eligible to enroll at this College in such courses.

Students eligible to enroll at Montclair in courses leading to certification in elementary education are:

(1) those who already hold a degree from Montclair with a certificate in secondary education; and

(2) those who are now matriculated at Montclair for such a degree.

Montclair cannot accept any other students in these courses.

The eligible students should consult Mr. Seibert, Acting Registrar of the College, for an evaluation of their previous work and a statement concerning the courses to be taken in order to receive the endorsement in elementary education on the secondary certificate already held or to be conferred.

Graduate students ineligible to enroll at Montclair who wish to secure teaching positions in the elementary schools of New Jersey can meet the minimum requirements for emergency certification in one Summer Session by attending the New Jersey State Teachers College at Paterson, Newark, Trenton, or Glassboro. Those interested should address inquiries to the Registrar of one of the aforementioned colleges.

Courses offered as a part of the curriculum for the graduate major in Educational Administration and Supervision should be carefully distinguished from those offered toward certification in elementary education. Courses that apply on the Elementary Principal's Certificate do not apply on the Teacher's Certificate.

Textbook Exhibit

In the Gymnasium of the Main Building, from July 10 through July 21, there will be an exhibit of high school and elementary school textbooks. While primarily for the benefit of the principals and teachers attending the Summer Session, the exhibit will be open to undergraduate students and to members of the general public who may be interested in seeing the latest textbooks.

Mrs. E. S. Fulcomer will be in charge of the exhibit this year.

NEW JERSEY STATE SCHOOL OF CONSERVATION

Stokes State Forest, Branchville, N. J.

1950 Summer Offerings

While the following courses are given as a part of the Summer Session offerings of the State Teachers College at Montclair, registration in them and payment for them is made at the School of Conservation. The credits earned are recorded on the permanent record card of the student at the College and thus appear on the photostated transcript thereafter.

Pre-Summer Session: June 19 to 29, Inclusive

This session is primarily for undergraduates. During the eleven-day period, the student may take one of the following courses:

Integration 440—Camping Education

This course is designed to prepare students for positions in summer camps. The areas covered include nature lore, craft, overnight trips, outdoor cooking, woodcraft, evening programs, and a general philosophy of camping education.

Credit: 2 semester-hours

Integration 441—Conservation Education

The social, economic, and scientific implications of conservation are considered together in this course. Discussion periods are interspersed with field trips to forest areas and demonstrations of conservation problems. Outside experts bring special contributions in their fields. Visual aids are used extensively.

Credit: 2 semester-hours

Physical Education 410—Water Safety and First Aid

This course includes intensive instruction in swimming, diving, water sports, boating, canoeing, water safety, and first aid. Students can qualify for Red Cross certification during this course. Credit: 2 semester-hours

Total fee, including tuition fees for the 2 s. h. credit: $40.00.

Summer Sessions

The following sessions offer opportunities for teachers-in-service, senior, and graduate students to pursue special courses during short periods of the summer. Credits earned in these courses may be applied as graduate or as undergraduate credit at the Montclair State Teachers College, Newark State Teachers College, and Trenton State Teachers College, subject to approval in advance by the institution concerned. Credit toward a bachelor's or an advanced degree may be transferred to other institutions where such transfer is permitted.

Courses Offered July 5 to 23, Inclusive

Integration 441—Conservation Education

See description above, under Pre-Summer Session.

Credit: 2 semester-hours

Science 405C—Field Studies in Science: Summer

Emphasis in this course is given to the ecology of plant life, a study of wild flowers, of brook and pond life, and of insects. Some attention is given to summer birds, trees in summer condition, and to minerals of the region.

Credit: 2 semester-hours

Total fee for this session, including tuition fees for 4 s. h. credit: $80.00.

Courses Offered July 26 to August 13, Inclusive

Integration 441—Conservation Education

See description above, under Pre-Summer Session.

Credit: 2 semester-hours

Integration 478—Elementary School Science

This course is based upon the assumption that science teaching in the elementary school should include scientific inquiry at the child's level as well as scientific information. Specific methods and materials are developed to meet these purposes. Emphasis is placed upon using the school community, learning through activity, and integrating science with other subject matter areas.

Credit: 2 semester-hours

Science 405C—Field Studies in Science: Summer

See description in previous session, above.

Credit: 2 semester-hours

Total fee for this session, including tuition fees for 4 s. h. credit: $80.00.

Courses Offered Post-Summer Session: August 18 to 28, Inclusive

In this session the student may complete either one of the following courses

Science 411—Problems in Field Studies in Science

In this course each student selects a phase of field science in which he does advanced study under the guidance of the instructor. Plant ecology, bird-life pond life, fungi, tree diseases, insect life are a few of the areas from which the student may choose. Prerequisites: Field Studies in Science or its equivalent plus at least 12 s. h. points of biology.

Credit: 2 semester-hour

Social Studies 477—Rural Sociology

During this course the student comes face to face with rural life in norther New Jersey. Social processes and problems are considered. Opportunities are provided for students to attend Grange meetings, county fairs, rural dances an parties, and to live for a day or two with a farm family.

Credit: 2 semester-hour

Total fee for this session, including tuition fees for 2 s. h. credit: $40.00.

August 30 to September 9, Inclusive

In this session the student may complete either one of the following courses

Integration 441—Conservation Education

See description above, under Pre-Summer Session.

Credit: 2 semester-hour

Science 405C—Field Studies in Science: Summer

See description above, under the session of July 5 to 23.

Credit: 2 semester-hour

Total fee for this session, including tuition fees for 2 s. h. credit: $40.00.

In all of the sessions listed above, there is a rich program of recreation activities, including picnics, cook-outs, water sports, folk-dancing, and music. Address inquiries to New Jersey State School of Conservation, State Teacher College, Montclair, New Jersey. Camp address: Branchville, N. J.

SPECIAL OPPORTUNITY TO TAKE ELEMENTARY EDUCATION COURSES ON CAMPUS AND AT LAKE WAPALANNE

Because of the demand for elementary education courses and the desire on the part of Montclair students to participate in the program of the New Jersey State School of Conservation in the Stokes State Forest, a special offering in elementary education will be presented this summer. Under this arrangement a student or a former student of Montclair State Teachers College may complete four semester-hours of elementary education during the three weeks from July 5th to July 25th at the New Jersey State Teachers College at Montclair and then be free to register for two courses at the New Jersey State School of Conservation beginning July 26th. During this latter period a special course in the Teaching of Elementary School Science together with the course in Conservation Education will be offered at Lake Wapalanne. Details of these offerings are listed below.

First Three Weeks Session on the Montclair Campus
—July 5th to 25th

A. Integration 474—Elementary School Arts and Crafts　　　**Mr. Karp**
10:30 A. M.-12:20 P. M.　　　　　　　　　　　Credit: 2 semester-hours

B. Geography 418—Regional Geography of North America　　　**Dr. Milstead**
8:30-10:20 A. M.　　　　　　　　　　　　　Credit: 2 semester-hours

Second Three Weeks Session at the New Jersey State School of Conservation, Lake Wapalanne, Stokes State Forest
July 26 to August 13

A. Integration 478—Elementary School Science
　　　　　　　　　　　　　　　　　Credit: 2 semester-hours

B. Integration 441—Conservation Education
　　　　　　　　　　　　　　　　　Credit: 2 semester-hours

Description of the course in Conservation Education will be found on page 10.

Description of the course in Regional Geography of North America will be found on page 21.

Descriptions of these and other courses in the field of Elementary Education will be found on pages 26 and 27.

Please note also the statement on page 10 concerning elementary education courses offered by this College.

CHINA INSTITUTE OF NEW JERSEY

The China Institute of New Jersey is a permanent year-round organization composed of former students of the China Workshop course. The policies and program of the Institute are determined by an elected executive committee, an advisory board of laymen, and representatives from the faculty of Montclair Teachers College, in consultation with the Chinese Director.

Dr. Chih Meng, Director of the China Institute of America, whose purpose is to promote cultural and educational relations between China and the United States, is Chinese Director of the China Institute of New Jersey. The College provides the facilities necessary for the courses sponsored by the Institute and grants credit for the satisfactory completion of such courses. These are given on the senior-graduate level, so that students may work toward either undergraduate or graduate credit.

While the primary and definite purpose of the Institute is to assist the teachers of New Jersey, men and women who desire to take these courses for cultural, vocational, or avocational purposes are welcome also. They may enroll for college credit or simply as Auditors for no credit. The cost is the same in both cases. If it be desired to attend a single lecture, the Institute Treasurer collects the fee of $2.00 at the door of the Auditorium in the College High School. Students who enroll for the entire course follow the instructions below.

Registration for one of the following courses must be made on forms provided by the College. Write to Miss Favor, the Secretary of the Summer Session, for these forms. Refer to the list below for the proper number and title of the course you expect to take. Note that the course **Social Studies S499 —China Workshop** is prerequisite to the course in Chinese Literature and do not enroll for credit in the Literature course unless you have completed the prerequisite course. Return the forms to Miss Favor not later than June 17, with check or money order **made payable to the China Institute of New Jersey** for $25.00. A **late service charge of $2.00** will be made for all registrations not received by June 17. Your class admission card will be mailed to you by the Treasurer of the Institute. It should be presented to your teacher on the opening day.

Offerings for 1950: June 26-July 8, Inclusive

Art S414—History of Chinese Art

In this course the developments and distinguishing characteristics of the major arts of China are traced by specialists and are surveyed from the point of view of their historical developments. There are twenty-four hours of lectures in the morning, and round-table discussion and library work in the afternoon. During this afternoon workshop period, the technique of Chinese painting is demonstrated and taught by the noted Chinese artist, Professor Ya Chin Wang, whose paintings have been exhibited in the Metropolitan Museum of New York and other art centers in this country. No Prerequisite.

9:30 A. M.-4 P. M.   Credit: 3 semester-hours   Room 11, CHS

English S459—A Survey of Great Chinese Literature

Some of the contributions which have gone into the making of this immortal literature, such as the work of Tao Teh Ching, the *Analects* of Confucius, the *Monkey*, and the poetry of Tang, are considered. Aside from a general insight into the great literature of China, special attention is given to English translations of masterpieces of Chinese literature. There are twenty-four hours of lectures in the morning, and round-table discussion and library work in the

afternoon. During this afternoon workshop period, individual students work on specific phases under the guidance of the instructor. **Prerequisite: Social Studies 499—China Workshop.**
9:30 A. M.-4 P. M.   Credit: 3 semester-hours   Room 12, CHS

Social Studies S499—China Workshop   **Dr. Chih Meng**
This course is given in twelve days. Twenty-four hours of lectures and class discussions are devoted to the study of Chinese history and contemporary Chinese life under the direction of Chinese scholars. Twenty-four hours of directed study in the library are devoted to the preparation of teaching units and background materials on China for use in our schools.
9:30 A. M.-4 P. M.   Credit: 3 semester-hours   Auditorium, CHS

BUREAU OF FIELD STUDIES

While the following courses are given as a part of the Summer Session offerings of the State Teachers College at Montclair, registration for them must be made in advance through the Bureau of Field Studies. Likewise, the cost of the courses includes both tuition fees and travel expenses and payment is made as requested by the Bureau. Interested students should address Mr. E. C. Bye, Director, Bureau of Field Studies, New Jersey State Teachers College, Upper Montclair, New Jersey. This should be done at once, as the number of students in each course must be limited to a definite quota.

Social Studies S461—New England and French Canada   **Mr. Kops**
This field study course gives an opportunity to study by direct observation the historical and geographical features of New England and the Province of Quebec. The trip, occupying the twelve days immediately following the Summer Session, is made in a modern chartered motor coach with overnight stops at first-class hotels. The route covers the lower Connecticut Valley, including Hartford, Springfield, Northampton, and Deerfield; the Rhode Island cities of Providence and Newport; historic Massachusetts towns, such as Plymouth, Boston, Lexington, Concord, Salem, and Marblehead; the coast of New Hampshire and southern Maine; the White Mountains in the Mt. Washington and Franconia Notch area; the Canadian Province of Quebec, including the ancient French city of Quebec, Montmorency Falls, Ste. Anne de Beaupre, Montreal; the western shores of Lake Champlain, Lake George, and the Hudson River. It is an indispensable background for an understanding of Colonial and Revolutionary life and history in this region.
Credit: 3 semester-hours

The all-expense price for this 1,800 miles' trip is $150.00. This includes tuition, transportation, hotels, meals, tips, and admissions—no extras. Starts Monday, August 21; ends Friday, September 1, 1950.

Social Studies S462—Continental United States   **Mr. Bye**
This field study course consists of sixty-two days of directed travel, including all of July and August, and provides an opportunity for gaining an integrated view of our country as a whole. The trip is made in a modern chartered motor coach with over-night stops at first-class hotels. The route covers about 12,500 miles and visits twenty-six States and six National Parks. Among the major points of interest are Gettysburg, Natural Bridge, Blue Ridge and blue grass region, Mammoth Cave, Lincoln shrines in Kentucky and Illinois, Ozark Mountains, Dodge City, Royal Gorge, Pikes Peak, Denver, Rocky Mountain National Park, Taos and other Indian Reservations, Santa Fe, Petrified Forest, Painted

Desert, Grand Canyon, Bryce and Zion National Parks, Hoover Dam, Los Angeles, Hollywood, San Diego, San Capistrano and other Missions; Tia Juana, Santa Barbara, Sequoia and Yosemite National Parks, Monterey, San Francisco, Sacramento, Lake Tahoe, Reno, Donner Pass, mammoth redwood groves, Crater Lake, Columbia River Valley, Portland, Seattle, Mt. Rainier, Grand Coulee Dam, Spokane, Butte, Yellowstone National Park, Salt Lake City, pioneer trails of Wyoming, Black Hills, Chicago, Detroit, Toronto, and Niagara Falls. All important geographic and historical features are studied under the instruction of members of the college faculty and local specialists.

Credit: 10 semester-hours

The all-expense price for this trip will be $750.00. Starts Saturday, July 1; ends Friday, September 1, 1950.

COURSES OF THE SUMMER SESSION LOCATED ON THE COLLEGE CAMPUS

July 6-August 17, Inclusive

Please note that the numbering of courses at this College follows this order: 100-399, inclusive, are undergraduate courses; 400-499, inclusive, are senior-college and graduate courses; 500 and above are graduate courses.

Art

Art S408—Creative Painting   **Mr. Karp**

This course gives the student an opportunity to use the materials of the painter for personal creative experience. Oils, water colors, and pastels are used. The student is encouraged to work in landscape, figure, and free imaginative composition. No previous experience is necessary.

9:30-10:20 A. M.   Credit: 2 semester-hours   Campus Studio Workshop

Art S414—The History of Chinese Art

For description and other data, see section under "China Institute of New Jersey."

Integration S474—Elementary School Arts and Crafts   **Mr. Karp**

See description and other data under the heading of "Integration."

Business Education

Business Education S401—

     The Teaching of Business Education   **Mr. Froehlich**

In this course a study is made of the history and development of business education, aims and objectives, human learning processes, lesson plans, teaching procedures, tests and measurements, and special helps for the teachers of business education. Consideration is given to the current trend in teaching in these fields with emphasis on the viewpoint of the consumer as well as the social and vocational objectives.

8:00-9:20 A. M.   Credit: 3 semester-hours   Room 2, Annex No. 2

Business Education S404—Business Economics   **Mr. Froehlich**

This course deals with the business aspects of the economics of war and peace; immediate and long range post-war problems; operation and government control of public utilities; taxation; government finance; and labor and management problems.

10:30-11:20 A. M.   Credit: 2 semester-hours   Room 2, Annex No. 2

Business Education S406—Advertising   **Mr. Willing**

This course aims to acquaint the student with the social and economic aspects of advertising so that a fair evaluation may be made of its worth as well as its undesirable aspects. Copy appeals, the writing of copy, advertising layouts, and the selection of appropriate types of media for various advertisements are considered.

9:30-10:20 A. M.   Credit: 2 semester-hours   Room 1, Annex No. 2

Administration Building—School of Conservation, Stokes State Forest
See Pages 10-12 for Complete Information

Business Education S504

Improvement of Instruction in Business Education   Mrs. VanDerveer

This course seeks to bring together business education teachers regardless of subject matter fields to consider common problems involving general subject matter and methods of instruction including visual and auditory aids. It also offers opportunity for an individual to investigate and evaluate materials and methods in specific subject matter areas.

8:30-9:20 A. M.   Credit: 2 semester-hours   Room 4, Annex No. 2

Business Education S513—Labor Problems   Mr. Willing

This course provides an opportunity to study Federal and State Labor Laws and regulations. It also includes consideration of such matters as arbitration, collective bargaining, labor organizations, the labor contract, personnel management, and case problems.

11:30 A. M.-12:20 P. M.   Credit: 2 semester-hours   Room 1, Annex No. 2

Business Education S602—
Seminar in Economics   Mr. Sheppard and Mrs. VanDerveer

This seminar is designed to meet the individual needs of the graduate student in business education or social studies by allowing him to pursue areas of work along economic lines in which he is not well-versed. The direction of his study is determined by the co-ordinator of the seminar and himself, after the results of his student diagnostic test are analyzed. The program of participation consists of oral and written reports, developed through independent reading and individually directed field studies. The field studies are planned so as to give the student a first-hand knowledge of business organization methods and practices. It is expected that the reports arising from these experiences will be in such form that they will be capable of being published or delivered as speeches before groups of people. An opportunity is also given to view, evaluate, and work with a variety of related visual and auditory aids. The plan of this seminar assists the students in preparing for the final comprehensive examination for the Master of Arts degree, and at the same time offers certain personal and professional advantages.

9:30 A. M.-12:20 P. M.   Credit: 6 semester-hours   Room 5, Annex No. 2

English

English S401—The Teaching of English in Secondary Schools   Dr. Fulcomer

Students are taught to develop and use materials of the classroom. Lesson plans and units of work are prepared and presented for criticism; textbooks are analyzed for training in their use; and bulletin board exhibits and visual education materials are prepared by students for the class.

8:00-9:20 A. M.   Credit: 3 semester-hours   Room 1

English S404—Survey of British Literature from 1798   Dr. Krauss

This course is a continuation of English 402. It takes up the story with the romantic triumph in 1798 and continues it to the present time.

11:30 A. M.-12:20 P. M.   Credit: 2 semester-hours   Room 27

English S410—Speech Pathology   Miss Wood

This course deals with diagnostic and corrective procedures, causes and treatment for stuttering, cleft palate, spastic speech, and aphasia. This course is required to teach speech, and speech defectives. Prerequisites: English 208 and 324.

3:30-9:20 A. M.   Credit: 2 semester-hours   Room 2

English S422—Seventeenth Century Literature   **Mr. Pettegrove**

This course covers the period from Donne through Dryden. It deals with Jacobean and Restoration drama; the Jonsonian, Metaphysical, and Restoration lyric; the prose of Browne, Walton, Donne, Taylor, Hobbes, Burton, and Bunyan; the prose and verse of Milton; the prose and verse of Dryden. .

9:30-10:20 A. M.   Credit: 2 semester-hours   Room 5, CHS

English S426—The Victorian Novel   **Mr. Pettegrove**

This is an intensive unit of work on the novel in Victorian England. A review of the development of the English novel before this period is followed by studies in the works of Dickens, Thackeray, Austen, Eliot, Trollope, Meredith, and Hardy. Novels studied in the high school are treated professionally in class.

1:00-1:50 P. M.   Credit: 2 semester-hours   Room 5, CHS

English S431B—Shakespeare II (Comedies)   **Mr. Hamilton**

This course deals with Shakespeare's plays in relation to his life, his times, his contemporaries, and Elizabethan drama generally. Extensive reading is required from Shakespeare, his predecessors, contemporaries, and successors. The problems of stage production in both Elizabethan and modern theatres, and of Shakespearean criticism are analyzed. Part II deals with Shakespearean comedies.

9:30-10:20 A. M.   Credit: 2 semester-hours   Room 3

English S438—Masters of American Literature   **Dr. Fulcomer**

Significant American writers, including Irving, Hawthorne, Poe, Emerson, Melville, Whitman, and Mark Twain are studied to discover their contributions to American life and to reveal important forces in our national background.

10:30-11:20 A. M.   Credit: 2 semester-hours   Room 1

English S454—Training the Speaking Voice   **Miss Wood**

This is a course in the study of the problems of speech, the development of a pleasing speaking voice with precision in diction, and the application of speech skills to practical speaking situations.

10:30-11:20 A. M.   Credit: 2 semester-hours   Room

English S456—Play Direction   **Mr. Fox**

This course covers the choosing and casting, as well as directing, of plays. Scenes are directed for class criticism, and a detailed prompt-book of one play is prepared. This course complements English 435.

11:30 A. M.-12:20 P. M.   Credit: 2 semester-hours   Room

English S459—A Survey of Great Chinese Literature

For description and other data, see section under "China Institute of New Jersey."

English S506—John Milton   **Mr. Hamilton**

This course has for its primary aim the understanding and evaluation of Milton's poetry. Contributory to this end are the following topics: the Puritan struggle for civil and religious liberty; the growth of science in the seventeenth century; the life, personality, and prose writings of Milton; his literary heritage and infl   comparison of Milton with the Cavalier Metaphysical poets.

11   M.-12:20 P. M.   Credit: 2 semester-hours   Room

20

English S511—History of Literary Criticism   Dr. Krauss

The purpose of this course is to familiarize the student with the chief doctrines of the great critics from Aristotle to Arnold and to correlate these critical doctrines with the outstanding writings of each age. By such a study it is possible for the student to evaluate the historical interrelations of expert criticism and literary production. A basic text is used, but much of the information is gleaned from source materials.

9:30-10:20 A. M.   Credit: 2 semester-hours   Room 27

English S518—The Major Romantic Poets   Mr. Pettegrove

This course studies the work of Coleridge, Wordsworth, Scott, Byron, Shelley, and Keats. It devotes especial attention to the poems which are best adapted for the reading of high school students.

10:30-11:20 A. M.   Credit: 2 semester-hours   Room 5, CHS

English S520—Great Books in Education   Dr. Krauss

Students examine the classics dealing with educational theory and practice which they so often read about, but rarely consult: Plato's *Republic*, Xenophen's *Cyropaedia*, Cicero's *De Oratore*, Castiglione's *Courtier*, Machiavelli's *Prince*, Rabelais's *Abbey of Thelome*, Ascham's *Schoolmaster*, Bacon's *Novum Organum*, Defoe's *Projects*, Milton's *To Samuel Hartlit on Education*, Rousseau's *Emile*, Byron's *Don Juan*, Hughes' *Tom Brown's Schooldays*, Newman's *Idea of a University*, the Arnold-Huxley debates, and the works of John Dewey and Jacques Barzmin. This course is recommended for graduate students in the Department of Integration.

8:30-9:20 A. M.   Credit: 2 semester-hours   Room 27

English S522—Advanced Phonetics   Miss Wood

This course provides ear-training to develop skill in recognizing and distinguishing typical English speech sounds, regional differences in pronouncing American English, and foreign sounds heard in English speech. This is followed by extensive practice in transcribing speech sounds into International Phonetic Alphabet symbols and in reading International Phonetic Alphabet transcriptions. A thorough study of the speech characteristics of some geographical region with which the student is personally familiar is required of each student.

11:30 A. M.-12:20 P. M.   Credit: 2 semester-hours   Room 2

Geography

Geography S411—Geographic Influences in American History   Dr. Milstead

A study is made of the geographic factors influencing the development of social, economic, and political life in America.

11:30 A. M.-12:20 P. M.   Credit: 2 semester-hours   Room 26

Geography S418—Regional Geography of North America   Dr. Milstead

This course constitutes a detailed regional treatment of the continent of North America. Emphasis is placed upon the human activities of the various regions in relation to their natural environment and the relations of the regions to each other. Attention is given to the techniques of presenting the material and the use of geographic tools in the treatment of the subject-matter.

8:30-9:20 A. M.   Credit: 2 semester-hours   Room 26
8:30-10:20 A. M. for those students completing the course in three weeks in order to proceed to the School of Conservation to continue work there

21

Geography S504—Economic Geography of Europe Dr. Milste

This course constitutes a study of the economic development of the nations
Europe in relation to the environmental background and resources that ha
made Europe one of the world's leading continents.

10:30-11:20 A. M. Credit: 2 semester-hours Room

Integration

Integration S400A—
Principles and Philosophy of Secondary Education Dr. You

This course evaluates educational objectives, techniques, procedures, and orga
zations in relation to the needs and demands made upon the school by socie
and by the student. It aims to help the student develop an adequate philosop
of life and of education.

11:30 A. M.-12:20 P. M. Credit: 2 semester-hours Room

Integration S409—Radio and Sound Equipment in the Classroom Mr. F

This course trains teachers and school executives in the use of radio progran
amplifying systems, recording equipment, and record players. Actual practice
given in the use of these educational aids. Problems of script-writing, micr
phone and recording techniques, and program directing are considered. T
class visits radio stations for equipment and program observation. Each stude
develops a teaching unit using radio or sound equipment to vary, vitalize, a
improve educational practices.

9:30-10:20 A. M. Credit: 2 semester-hours Room

Integration S410—Teaching Materials Workshop Miss Fanto

This course is for those persons who wish to study advanced problems in t
utilization and administration of audio-visual materials. Individual research
stressed, and there is an opportunity to work out individual projects. Su
problems as budget requirements, administrative set-up, establishment of fi
libraries, etc., are emphasized. It is assumed that the student will have tak
Integration 408 or will have had the equivalent in practical experiences.

10:30-11:20 A. M. Credit: 2 semester-hours Room

Integration S500C—
Recent Trends in Secondary School Methods Mr. Seyb

This course emphasizes the fundamental principles underlying the technique
teaching on the secondary school level. Some of the topics considered a
organization of knowledge, the logical and psychological aspects of meth
developing appreciations, social-moral education, teaching motor control, fix
motor responses, books and verbalism, meeting individual differences, guida
in study, tests and examinations, marks and marking.

10:30-11:20 A. M. Credit: 2 semester-hours Room 3, C

Integration S500D—
School Administration I: Functions and Organization Mr. Moreh

This introductory course in educational administration is concerned with gen
functions and personnel, as well as with the general organization of public edi
tion on local, state, and national levels. It deals also with federal-state relati
the state and sectarian education, the expanding scope of modern school syste
types and bases of school organization, and professional ethics.

10:30-11:20 A. M. Credit: 2 semester-hours Room

22

Integration S500E—
School Administration II: Law and Finance   Mr. Morehead

This course acquaints the student with the allied fields of school law and school finance, with special reference to New Jersey. Its topics include basic principles of public school support, taxation, federal aid, educational finance, legal provisions for school district borrowing, tenure provisions, and rights and duties of school boards and officials.

8:30-9:20 A. M.   Credit: 2 semester-hours   Room B

Integration S502A—Organization and Administration
of the Modern High School   Dr. W. S. Smith

The following problems are considered: the student personnel, building and revising the high school curriculum, providing for individual differences, making the school schedule, records, the guidance program, pupil participation in government, the extra-curricular program, the health program, the safety program, discipline, library and study hall, cafeteria, the principal's office, and evaluating results.

9:30-10:20 A. M.   Credit: 2 semester-hours   Room 9

Integration S503—Methods and Instruments of Research   Dr. Narramore

This course is required of all candidates for the Master's degree without regard to their field of major interest. Its purpose is to introduce students of education to research and its practical application to professional problems. The course treats: the nature and types of educational research; methods and techniques of educational research; and the tools used in interpreting statistical data. During the course, the student sets up a problem and plans and carries out its solution. Mathematics 400 or its equivalent is recommended before taking this course.

1:00-1:50 P. M.   Credit: 2 semester-hours   Room 9

Integration S504A—
Curriculum Construction in the Secondary School   Dr. W. S. Smith

The purpose of this course is to introduce the student to constructive criticism of American culture, to consider the extent to which the secondary school curriculum meets the needs of a changing civilization, and to consider effective means of curriculum construction. (A student may not receive credit for both Integration 504A and Integration 504C.)

8:30-9:20 A. M.   Credit: 2 semester-hours   Room 9

Integration S505—Organization and Administration
of Extra-Curricular Activities   Mr. Morehead

The first part of this course considers such general problems of extra-curricular activities as: their growing importance, their relation to the curriculum; the principles underlying their organization, administration, and supervision; and methods of financing. In the second part, an intensive study is made of the home room, the assembly, the student council, clubs, athletics, school publications, and other activities in which the class is especially interested.

11:30 A. M.-12:20 P. M.   Credit: 2 semester-hours   Room B

Integration S507—
Organization and Administration of Guidance Programs   Mr. Seybold

The purpose of this course is to acquaint the student with the various agencies and methods for the guidance of students in school work, with certain implications in the choice of and the preparation for a vocation. Among the topics are: the abilities of students as related to guidance, the exploration of special interests, the organization of the guidance program, and the integration of the entire high school program for purposes of guidance.

9:30-10:20 A. M.   Credit: 2 semester-hours   Room 3, CHS

Integration S508A—
     Supervision of Instruction in Secondary Schools   Mr. Seybol
This course emphasizes the more practical phases of supervision which are me
most frequently by those engaged in it. Among the topics are: the set-up fo
adequate supervision, supervision as encouraging and guiding the growth c
teachers and the improvement of educational procedures, the supervisory func
tions of teachers' meetings, discussion groups, general and professional reading
the writing of articles, co-operative curriculum modification, utilization of com
munity resources, and teacher intervisitation.
11:30 A. M.-12:20 P. M.   Credit: 2 semester-hours   Room 3, CH:

Integration S515—Guidance and Personnel Problems
     of Classroom Teachers   Dr. Narramor
This course considers all types of personnel problems with which the classroor
teacher deals. It is concerned with the growth of pupils and seeks to point ou
the ways by which proper growth may be attained. Classroom, health, socia
and personal activities are analyzed in terms of the needs of present-day socia
life.
9:30-10:20 A. M.   Credit: 2 semester-hours   Room 1

Integration S517—Administration of the Elementary School   Dr. Milliga
This course analyzes and evaluates the administrative duties and relationships o
the elementary school principal. Particular consideration is given to: buildin,
management, effective use of the school plant, sanitation, health service, th
library, personnel management, the administration of the curriculum, communit
relationships, and publicity.
8:30-9:20 A. M.   Credit: 2 semester-hours   Room 4, CH:

Integration S518—
     Supervision of Instruction in the Elementary School   Dr. Milliga
This course has been planned for those engaged in the supervision of th
elementary school, and for those who are preparing for such responsibilitie:
Principles of classroom supervision are developed and applied to learnin
situations. Among the more important topics that receive attention are: th
nature and function of supervision, the organization necessary for effectiv
supervision, the nature and significance of the teacher's purposes, the methoc
and techniques of group and individual supervision, the technique of observatio1
and the supervisory conference.
9:30-10:20 A. M.   Credit: 2 semester-hours   Room 4, CH

Integration S521—
     Psychological Tests in Guidance Programs   Dr. Ingebritse
This course is designed to familiarize the student with various psychologic:
tests and scales that may be used in guidance programs in the secondary schoc
The student is given practice in administering many types of group tests. Th
includes scoring the tests and evaluating the results, with a discussion of wa;
in which these results may be used. Much time is spent in actual laborato1
demonstrations of tests, giving students an opportunity to serve as subjects a1
as examiners. Class discussion is based upon first-hand information gain(
through use of the tests, on readings, and on class reports.
11:30 A. M.-12:20 P. M.   Credit: 2 semester-hours   Room

Integration S535A—Vocational Guidance   Mr. E. C. Da
This course is especially intended to enable high school teachers to guide th(
pupils in planning for constructive vocational life. The course is designed to
helpful also to adults who are seeking better vocational adjustment. The follo\
ing topics are included: the purpose of work, main areas of work, inventory
personal interests and traits, analyzing interests and traits, samples of persor

inventories with analyses and interviews, exploring one's area of work, making the most of school days, finding the first job, adjustments on the way, advancement—what it is and how to obtain it, intelligent use of money, balanced use of time, and cultivating pride of work.

8:30-9:20 A. M.   Credit: 2 semester-hours   Room 30

Integration S548—
Curriculum Construction in the Elementary School   Dr. Milligan

This course offers an opportunity to review State and city elementary curricula; to discuss the principles of curriculum construction; to collect new teaching materials for the various subjects; and to evaluate, organize, and grade these materials. Teaching procedures in the use of materials are discussed and evaluated in terms of pupil needs, the objectives set up, and the results obtained. This course offers an opportunity to make a special study of the materials and procedures to be used in the teaching of the language arts.

11:30 A. M.-12:20 P. M.   Credit: 2 semester-hours   Room 4, CHS

Integration S550—Child and Adolescent Development   Dr. Phipps

This course reviews the general characteristics of child and adolescent development: motor and physiological, social, emotional, language, intellectual, and interests and ideals. The influence of home, school, community, and institutional life on child and adolescent development are considered as well as problems of guidance presented by children in the normal course of development and also those presented by deviations from the normal course.

9:30-10:20 A. M.   Credit: 2 semester-hours   Room 29

Integration S551—
Principles and Techniques of Guidance   Dr. Narramore

Topics included in this course cover: philosophy of guidance, history of the guidance movement, the need for guidance presented by children and adolescents. The methods of gathering useful data are studied, and school records, exploratory activities, tests, inventories, the case study approach, occupational information, and occupational data are treated as well as general methods of guidance with special stress on interviewing and counseling of students.

10:30-11:20 A. M.   Credit: 2 semester-hours   Room 10

Integration S602—Seminar in Guidance   Mr. E. C. Davis

The general objective of this course is to acquaint the student with school guidance problems as they relate to industry. The objective is obtained through group discussions growing out of individual research and group field trips to personnel departments of large and small industries, offices of labor unions, a job placement agency, a large group industrial insurance firm, and state employment offices. Each student makes a job analysis in some one occupation. From these visits and discussions a guidance program is evolved. Prerequisites: Integration 507 and 551, or permission of the instructor.

10:30 A. M.-12:20 P. M.   Credit: 4 semester-hours   Room 5

25

ELEMENTARY EDUCATION

These courses in Elementary Education are open to the following only:

(1) Those who already hold a degree from Montclair with a certificate in Secondary Education, and

(2) Those who are now matriculated at Montclair for a degree and the certificate in Secondary Education.

Students ineligible to enroll at Montclair in the above courses should note the statement on page 10 concerning other colleges where the courses are offered.

Students interested both in Elementary Education courses and in the courses offered at the Stokes State Forest this summer should refer to page 13 for complete information concerning the special opportunity this summer to combine these programs of work.

Integration S472—The Elementary School Curriculum   Dr. Phipps

This course acquaints the College student with the subject matter of the elementary school curriculum for grades 3-6, inclusive. In addition, the following are studied: (1) correlation among subjects, (2) the appraisal and use of textbooks, (3) the use of visual aids, (4) the methods adapted to each subject, and (5) use of course of study materials.

1:00-1:50 P. M.   Credit: 2 semester-hours   Room 29

Integration S473—The Elementary School Language Arts   Dr. Phipps

This course gives an overview of modern practices that are used in teaching reading, creative writing, speaking, spelling, and handwriting in the elementary grades. Students are helped to recognize and to make provision for readiness for learning in these areas, to learn or devise various techniques that will meet the needs of different children and situations, and to evaluate, select, and create suitable materials to be used at various maturity levels. Special emphasis is placed on the functional use of the language arts in the total curriculum and life of the elementary school child.

10:30-11:20 A. M.   Credit: 2 semester-hours   Room 29

Integration S474—Elementary School Arts and Crafts   Mr. Karp

This course provides a wide range of creative manipulative experience with the materials, tools, and techniques of art work in the elementary school and an insight into significant art work of children of various age levels. Work is done in crayon, paint, chalk, clay, wood, papier-mache, finger paints, and other easily accessible materials. The work of the course includes simple weaving, block prints, murals, and the making of puppets. Attention throughout is directed toward an insight into the significance of art work and of manipulative experience as a medium of expression and a means of growth for the child.

8:30-9:20 A. M.   Credit: 2 semester-hours   Campus Studio Workshop

10:30 A. M.-12:20 P. M. for students completing the course in three weeks in order to proceed to the School of Conservation to continue work there.

Integration S476—
Elementary School Health and Physical Education   Mr. DeRosa

The purpose of this course is to induct the perspective elementary classroom teacher into the field of health and physical education. Such phases as state courses of study, selection and organization of materials, grading, class organization, and others will be discussed. To give the student a more functional approach, the programs of surrounding communities are studied.

9:30-10:20 A. M.   Credit: 2 semester-hours   Room D

Integration S477—Elementary School Mathematics   **Mr. Kays**

This course includes a study of the development of the number concept in young children, the problem of number readiness, and an analysis of the various number skills. Consideration is given to the development of methods of presenting the units of elementary mathematics to children. Emphasis is placed on the meaningful use of the fundamental operations with integers, fractions, decimals, and problem solving. Experience is given to students in effective methods of lesson planning, testing, and diagnostic and remedial work.

11:30 A. M.-12:20 P. M.   Credit: 2 semester-hours   Room 3, Annex No. 1

Integration S478—Elementary School Science   **Dr. Lampkin**

This course is based upon the assumption that science teaching in the elementary school should include scientific inquiry at the child's level as well as scientific information. Specific methods and materials are developed to meet these purposes. Emphasis is placed upon using the school community, learning through activity, and integrating science with other subject matter areas.

8:30-9:20 A. M.   Credit: 2 semester-hours   Room 5, Annex No. 3

Health and Physical Education

Health Education S407—
Prevention and Care of Athletic Injuries   **Mr. Coder**

This is a lecture and laboratory course designed to acquaint the student with ways to prevent and to care for the common injuries sustained in athletics. Attention is given to sprains, strains, bruises, burns, and fractures. The responsibility of the coach in caring for injuries is emphasized.

8:00-8:50 A. M.   Credit: 2 semester-hours   Room E

Health Education S408—Driver Education and Training   **Mr. Coder**

See page 33 under the heading "Post-Summer Session Course" for the description and other data concerning this course.

Health Education S411—School Health Services   **Mr. DeRosa**

The student is familiarized with the health services available in the school. The part which the teacher plays in co-ordinating his activities with the school medical staff is emphasized.

11:30 A. M.-12:20 P. M.   Credit: 2 semester-hours   Room D

Integration S476—
Elementary School Health and Physical Education   **Mr. DeRosa**

See description and other data under the heading "Elementary Education."

Physical Education SM405—Management of Athletic Activities   **Mr. DeRosa**

The student is provided with information essential to the good management of an intra-mural and interscholastic athletic program. Some of the major problems to be considered are: educational values, health and safety of participants, insurance, transportation, scheduling, management of finances, budgeting, maintenance of play area, care of supplies and equipment, State and local athletic associations, and the organization of leagues and meets.

10:30-11:20 A. M.   Credit: 2 semester-hours   Room D

27

Mathematics

Mathematics S300—Social and Commercial Uses of Mathematics   Mr. Kay

Some of the topics treated are: review of fundamental operations, approximat computation, use of slide rule and computing devices, graphs and scale drawing percentage, simple and compound interest, consumer credit and installmen buying, savings and investment, mortgages, taxation, insurance, cost of housing and budgeting. Commercial, industrial, and consumer applications are stressed
9:30-10:20 A. M.   Credit: 2 semester-hours   Room 3, Annex No.

Mathematics S400—Educational Statistics   Mr. Cliffor

The aim of this course is to prepare the student (1) to comprehend and criticiz articles of statistical nature in current educational literature; (2) to apply statis tical methods in testing and rating pupils; (3) to carry on the simpler types o educational research. By analysis of real data from the secondary field, th student becomes familiar with the measures of central tendency and variability short methods of computation, graphic representation of material, the propertie of the normal curve, and linear correlation. Inasmuch as statistical methods i education are almost identical with those employed in the natural, physical, an social sciences, there is natural integration with these fields.
10:30-11:20 A. M.   Credit: 2 semester-hours   Room 4, Annex No.

Mathematics S407—Advanced Calculus   Mr. Kay

A study of continuity, the theory of limits, the generalized theorem of the mean and its extension to series with a remainder term is made in this course. Also studied are partial differentiation with applications to tangent planes, normals envelopes, and approximations; multiple integration with applications to areas volumes, center of gravity, pressure, moment of inertia, and work; and th solution of ordinary differential equations of the first order with applications.
1:00-1:50 P. M.   Credit: 2 semester-hours   Room 3, Annex No.

Mathematics S410—Mathematics of Finance   Mr. Cliffor

This course introduces the student to the elementary theory of simple and com pound interest and leads to the solution of practical problems in annuitie sinking funds, amortization, depreciation, stocks and bonds, installment buyin and building and loan associations. It also discusses the mathematics of li insurance covering the following subjects: the theory of probability as relate to life insurance; the theory and calculation of mortality tables; various typ of life annuities and insurance policies and reserves. This course is designed give a helpful background to the mathematics teacher as well as to be an a to the student of economics and insurance.
11:30 A. M.-12:20 P. M.   Credit: 2 semester-hours   Room 4, Annex No.

Integration S477—Elementary School Mathematics   Mr. Ka

See description and other data under the heading "Elementary Education."

Mathematics S501C—
The Teaching of Advanced Secondary School Mathematics   Dr. Da

This course presents the best modern practices in teaching advanced algeb trigonometry, solid geometry, and analysis in the last two years of the seni

28

high school. Topics include: introducing trigonometry, teaching applications of trigonometry, variations in the sequence of topics, recent trends in the curriculum, the aims of teaching solid geometry, the elimination of certain subject matter and proofs, the use of algebra and trigonometry in solid geometry, making algebra thinking rather than manipulation, applications of advanced algebra, and the use of the function concept in unifying the mathematical knowledge of the student. A study is made of outstanding experiments in teaching these subjects and methods of adapting the material to the abilities and interests of the students.

8:30-9:20 A. M.   Credit: 2 semester-hours   Room 1, Annex No. 1

**Mathematics S509C—A Critical Interpretation of Mathematics
in the Junior High School**   **Mr. Clifford**

The aim of this course is to give teachers a deeper insight into the subject-matter usually taught in the seventh, eighth, and ninth grades. Among the topics considered are: the nature of graphs, intuition and experimentalism in geometry, the arithmetic and algebra for social use and interpretation, approximate measures and mensuration, enrichment material for class and clubs, use of models, and integration with other subject fields. The course is open to all junior and senior high school teachers and those elementary school teachers who have had two years of high school mathematics.

9:30-10:20 A. M.   Credit: 2 semester-hours   Room 4, Annex No. 1

Mathematics S517—The Theory of Numbers   **Dr. Davis**

This course offers a systematic treatment of certain fundamental properties of numbers. It includes such topics as: properties of integers; prime numbers; composite numbers; factorization; relatively prime numbers; properties of congruences and their solutions; fundamental theorems of Fermat, Euler, Wilson, Gauss, etc., primitive roots of a congruence; quadratic residues; and certain types of Diophantine equations. Prerequisite: Two years of college mathematics.

10:30-11:20 A. M.   Credit: 2 semester-hours   Room 1, Annex No. 1

Science

Chemistry S408B—Industrial Chemistry, Part II   **Dr. Reed**

This course is a study of the chemical industries of the metropolitan area, utilizing the method outlined in Chemistry 408A. Also, a study is made of the economics of chemical industry, chemistry and industry in general, and the effects of chemical discoveries upon living conditions. Prerequisite: General and Organic Chemistry, or special permission of the instructor. Class meets for two recitations and two afternoon trips to industrial plants.

11:30 A. M.-12:20 P. M.—Tues. and Thurs.

Field Trips: Tues. and Thurs. Afternoons   Credit: 2 semester-hours   Room 23

**Chemistry S501—
The Teaching of Chemistry in Secondary Schools**   **Dr. Reed**

This course satisfies the requirements in the teaching of chemistry for the limited secondary certificate. A study is made of the objectives, recent trends, methods of presentation, courses of study, instructional aids, and subject-matter of high school chemistry. Prerequisite: 18 semester-hours in chemistry.

9:30-10:20 A. M.   Credit: 3 semester-hours   Room 23

Research: Wed. Afternoon

29

Physics S304B—Introduction to Photography, Part II   **Dr. Smith**

This is a beginning course in photography consisting of laboratory work and field work supplemented by lectures and demonstrations. Some of the topics covered are: the construction and operation of cameras, common films and papers, fundamental chemistry of photography, development and printing. A student needs at least one camera. Part II emphasizes projection printing.

10:30-11:20 A. M., Mon., Wed., Fri.

Laboratory: Mon. Afternoon   Credit: 2 semester-hours   Room 25

Physics S406—Astronomy   **Dr. Lampkin**

The course consists of a study of the fundamental principles of the science of astronomy. Such topics as the following are considered: motions of the earth; time; the moon; law of gravitation; the planets, comets, and meteors; the sun; evolution of the solar system; the constellations; distances and motions of the stars; spectrum analysis; and telescopic observations.

10:30 A. M.-12:20 P. M.   Credit: 4 semester-hours   Room 5, Annex No. 3

Physics S407A—Aviation, Part I   **Mr. Placek**

This course deals with the historical development of aviation, air traffic rules, air-worthiness regulations, pilot certification, types of aircraft, aircraft structures, principles of aerodynamics, lift, drag, stability, motions of an airplane, piloting, motorless flight, and aircraft engines. Flight experience is made available as a part of this course.

11:30 A. M.-12:20 P. M.   Credit: 2 semester-hours   Room 8, CHS

Physics S512—Modern Physics   **Dr. Smith**

This course is a survey of recent experimental research in physics and of the newer theories concerning nuclear physics and electricity. Such topics as atomic spectra, radioactivity, artificial transmutation of the elements, and cosmic rays are discussed. Prerequisites: General college physics and a course in electrical measurements.

8:00-9:20 A. M.   Credit: 4 semester-hours   Room 25

Field Trips: By Arrangement

Science S410—Junior High School Science Demonstrations   **Mr. Placek**

This course covers the methods of experimental instruction in grades seven, eight, and nine. A detailed study is made of about three hundred demonstrations.

8:30-10:20 A. M.   Credit: 4 semester-hours   Room 8, CHS

Integration S478—Elementary School Science   **Dr. Lampkin**

See description and other data under the heading of "Elementary Education."

Social Studies

Social Studies S419—American Political Biography   **Dr. Moffat**

This is the study of the life and influence of the leading figures in American political and social history. It is the aim here to show the relation of each of these characters to the times in which he lived and to point out how he influenced the trend of American life. The study includes such leaders as Washington, Jefferson, Hamilton, Webster, Lincoln, Cleveland, Theodore Roosevelt, and Wilson.

11:30 A. M.-12:20 P. M.   Credit: 2 semester-hours   Room 2

Social Studies S435B—The Americas: A Contemporary
Political, Economic, and Cultural Survey, Part II   Dr. Gooden

This course deals specifically with the twentieth century political, economic, and cultural life of the South American nations. The role which the South American States play in world affairs is stressed. Attention is given to post-World War II developments and adjustments in South America.

11:30 A. M.-12:20 P. M.   Credit: 2 semester-hours   Room 21

Social Studies S446—
Current Problems in Economics and Government   Dr. Rellahan

This course is designed to analyze the relationship of economics to government. The causes and results of governmental activity are discussed in the light of their economic significance and their bearing on public welfare.

11:30 A. M.-12:20 P. M.   Credit: 2 semester-hours   Room 28

Social Studies S447—
Diplomatic History of the United States   Dr. Gooden

The purpose of this course is to show how we have become gradually conscious of our world interests and responsibilities, and the important role we have come to play in international politics. The growing concept of world democracy, as opposed to commercial and military imperialism, is stressed.

10:30-11:20 A. M.   Credit: 2 semester-hours   Room 21

Social Studies S453B—The Development of Canada   Dr. Gooden

This course is devoted to the study of the historical background, geographical environment, governmental organization, economic behavior, and social conditions of the northern neighbor of the United States. Its professional objective is to provide the understanding and appreciation necessary to the student and teacher who may follow and interpret the growth, internal and external, of the Dominion of Canada and of its relation to the United States as well as to the British Commonwealth of Nations.

8:30-9:20 A. M.   Credit: 2 semester-hours   Room 21

Social Studies S456—International Economic Relations   Dr. Rellahan

The purpose of this course is to study the significance of international trade and exchange to the economic life of our nation and the world economy. An analysis of the contrasting economic philosophies relating to international economic organization is made. Special emphasis is given to those policies which tend to promote freer trade, including the classical doctrine of comparative costs, the Reciprocal Trade Agreements Act, and the International Bank and Currency Stabilization Fund.

9:30-10:20 A. M.   Credit: 2 semester-hours   Room 28

Social Studies S458—Russia as a World Power   Dr. Wittmer

An analysis of Russia's relations with China, Iran, Turkey, the European continent, England, and the United States is presented. Marxist world policy, as interpreted by Kautsky, Plekhanov, Jaures, Bukharin, Trotsky, Lenin, and Stalin, is described. The changing views of the Second and Third Internationals, and the organization and methods of the Comintern are discussed. A chronological account of Soviet diplomacy, since Chicherin, is offered.

10:30-11:20 A. M.   Credit: 2 semester-hours   Room 13, CHS

Social Studies S461—New England and French Canada   Mr. Kops

See description and other data under the heading "Bureau of Field Studies."

Social Studies S462—Continental United States   **Mr. Bye**

See description and other data under the heading "Bureau of Field Studies."

Social Studies S472—
Modern Social Studies Instruction and Supervision   **Dr. Moffatt**

This course is designed primarily to assist teachers and supervisors to obtain a comprehensive view of recent curriculum trends, current subject-matter tendencies, and newer practices in secondary school social studies. Topics discussed include: materials, methods, and techniques; use of audio-visual aids; courses of study and experimental programs; professional literature; and problems of the critic teacher and the supervisor.

8:30-9:20 A. M.   Credit: 2 semester-hours   Room 20

Social Studies S478—
Theories of Social Justice from Antiquity to Our Time   **Dr. Wittmer**

This course is designed to show how specific ideas of social justice resulted from specific historical conditions and events. A comparison of social upheavals among the ancient Hebrews, Greeks, and Romans; the early Christians; the peasants in the Middle Ages; the religious rebels of the early Renaissance; and the revolutionaries of the modern age is to furnish background material for an understanding of present social thought. Lectures and discussions cover the social prophets of the Hebrews; Lycurgus; Cleomenes; Plato; Gracchus; Spartacus; the Essenes, the Waldensians, the Albigensians, and the Hussites; Wycliffe, John Hall; and on selected social thinkers of the last few centuries, such as Hobbes, Locke, Hume, Rousseau, the Utopians, the Socialists, and the Anarchists.

8:30-9:20 A. M.   Credit: 2 semester-hours   Room 13, CHS

Social Studies S499—China Workshop   **Dr. Chih Meng**

For description and other data, see section under "China Institute of New Jersey."

Social Studies S502—
Origin and Development of the American Constitution   **Dr. Moffat**

This course is an intensive study of the origin and framing of the Constitution of the United States. It aims to search out the roots and influences that determined our basic political institutions. The seminar method is employed and attention is given to the techniques of historical research and historical writing.

9:30-10:20 A. M.   Credit: 2 semester-hours   Room 2

POST-SUMMER SESSION COURSE

August 21 through September 1, 1950

To Meet an Urgent Need, the following course is being offered by the State Teachers College at Montclair, with the assistance of the **New Jersey State Safety Council,** the **New Jersey Automobile Club,** the **American Automobile Association,** the **New Jersey State Police,** and the **New Jersey Department of Motor Vehicles.** Last year, over 32,300 persons lost their lives in traffic accidents. One-fourth of these were persons of high school and college age (15-24). The development of qualified young drivers can no longer be left to chance. The responsibility of our high schools in such a program is of vital importance. Training youth in skillful driving and in their responsibility toward other highway users, assumed when a person gets behind the wheel, will go far toward developing a new generation of skillful accident-free drivers. The lack of teachers for such training courses is all that prevents their being offered in most of the high schools of the country.

This Course Offers the Necessary Opportunity for men and women to prepare themselves to teach driver education in high schools. Enrollees completing the work of the course are presented with a certificate indicating the work done. Those who took this course at Montclair last summer were given enthusiastic co-operation by principals and school boards eager to establish driver education courses in their high schools, so that classes were opened in September taught by those who had received the Certificate of Completion in late August.

College Credit Required in New Jersey. In order to teach Driver Education in New Jersey, this course must be taken for credit.

Veterans may take this course under the G.I. Bill, if they have so arranged with the Veterans' Counselor of the College.

Living Expenses and Traveling Expenses must be paid by the student. Those desiring hotel accommodations should write to Mr. F. K. Schultze, Mgr., New Jersey Auto Club AAA, 156 Clinton Avenue, Newark 5, New Jersey. The College Residence Halls are closed at this time.

Textbooks and Other Text Materials will be furnished to each enrollee without charge.

Registration for this course will be accepted up to and including the opening day of the course. However, students should register early if possible, preferably on the regular registration days for the Summer Session. There is a limit to the number of registrations which may be accepted.

Description of the Course

Health Education S408—Driver Education and Training   Mr. Coder

Part I

This part consists of a minimum of 20 hours of class recitations and discussions, for which home reading and study have been assigned. The following topics are included: (1) history and development of driver education and training programs; (2) objectives of driver education; (3) local, State, and national traffic safety programs; (4) driver qualifications; (5) psychophysical testing; (6) curriculum content of school courses in driver education and training; (7) construction, operation, and maintenance of automobiles; (8) traffic laws and driver licensing; (9) traffic engineering; (10) pedestrian education and protection; (11) equipment for teaching driver education; (12) liability, costs, and insurance; (13) planning driver education as a part of the daily program of the high school; (14) public relations; (15) records and reports; and (16) visual·aids in teaching driver education.

33

Part II

This part consists of a minimum of 20 hours devoted to the following: (
behind-the-wheel instruction; (2) demonstrations and student-teacher practice
the car; and (3) road tests in traffic. Home reading and study are required
preparation for these projects.
Full attendance at all sessions is required. Prerequisite: a license to drive
car in New Jersey.

9:00-12:00 and 1:00-4:00 daily   Credit: 2 semester-hours   Room

SUMMER SESSION

Bulletin of

MONTCLAIR

STATE TEACHERS COLLEGE

JUNE 25 TO AUGUST 8

1951

SUMMER SESSION

Bulletin Of

MONTCLAIR
STATE TEACHERS COLLEGE

1 9 5 1
June 25th to August 8th

UPPER MONTCLAIR, NEW JERSEY

OFFICERS OF ADMINISTRATION

STATE BOARD OF EDUCATION

GUSTAV A. HUNZIKER, *President* ....Little Falls
GEORGE O. SMALLEY, *Vice-President* ....Bound Brook
ARTHUR E. ARMITAGE ....Collingswood
JOHN S. GRAY ....Newton
MRS. EDWARD L. KATZENBACH ....Princeton
JOHN C. KINAHAN ....Carney's Point
A. HARRY MOORE ....Jersey City
AMOS J. PEASLEE ....Clarksboro
MRS. HERBERT REIM ....Maywood
MRS. FREDERIC H. SANFORD ....Nutley
RICHARD E. SWIFT ....Margate City
HUGH C. THUERK ....Morristown

COMMISSIONER OF EDUCATION
JOHN H. BOSSHART

ASSISTANT COMMISSIONERS FOR HIGHER EDUCATION
ROBERT H. MORRISON

NEW JERSEY STATE TEACHERS COLLEGE AT MONTCLAIR

HARRY A. SPRAGUE, Ph.D. ....President
E. DEALTON PARTRIDGE, Ph.D. ....Dean of Instruction
OTIS C. INGEBRITSEN, Ph.D. ....Chairman of the Graduate Committee
CLAUDE E. JACKSON, A.M. ....Director of Admissions, Records and Research
MARY M. HOUSE, B.C.S. ....Acting Registrar
CHARLES J. SENSALE, A.M. ....Veterans' Counselor
ELIZABETH S. FAVOR, A.M. ....Assistant in Graduate Personnel
BERNARD SIEGEL, B.S. ....Business Manager
EARL C. DAVIS, M.S. ....Director of Personnel and Guidance
MARGARET A. SHERWIN, A.M. ....Dean of Women
HENRY E. SCHMIDT, A.M.,
    Dean of Men and Director, Health, Physical Education and Recreation
HORACE J. SHEPPARD, A.M. ....Acting Head of Business Education Department
EDWIN S. FULCOMER, Ed.D. ....Head of English Department
MOWAT G. FRASER, Ph.D. ....Head of Integration Department
VIRGIL S. MALLORY, Ph.D. ....Head of Mathematics Department
EDNA McEACHERN, Ph.D. ....Head of Music Department
EARL R. GLENN, A.M. ....Head of Science Department
ELWYN C. GAGE, Ph.D. ....Head of Social Studies Department
ANNE BANKS CRIDLEBAUGH, B.S. ....Acting Librarian
EDGAR C. BYE, A.M. ....Director, New Tools for Learning Bureau
OTTO CORDES, P.E. ....Engineer in Charge, Maintenance

SUMMER SESSION 1951

HARRY A. SPRAGUE, Ph.D. ....President
E. DEALTON PARTRIDGE, Ph.D. ....Dean of Instruction
WILLIAM A. BALLARE, A.M. ....Speech
HAROLD C. BOHN, A.M. ....English
EDGAR C. BYE, A.M. ....Field Studies
FRANK L. CLAYTON, Ph.D. ....Social Studies
PAUL C. CLIFFORD, A.M. ....Mathematics
ALDEN C. CODER, Ed.M. ....Health and Physical Education
LAWRENCE H. CONRAD, A.M. ....English
JOHN W. CRAFT, A.M. ....Music
ROBERT J. DARLING, A.M. ....Personnel and Guidance
DAVID R. DAVIS, Ph.D. ....Acting Head, Department of Mathematics
EARL C. DAVIS, M.S. ....Personnel and Guidance
JEROME DEROSA, A.M. ....Health and Physical Education
EMMA FANTONE, A.M. ....Audio-Visual Aids
L. HOWARD FOX, A.M. ....Speech
MARION W. FOX, Ed.M. ....Elementary Education
ELVIRA K. FRADKIN, A.M. ....United Nations Institute
PAUL E. FROEHLICH, A.M. ....Business Education
EDWIN S. FULCOMER, Ed.D. ....Head of Department of English
EARL ROUSE GLENN, A.M. ....Head of Department of Science
CHARLES E. HADLEY, Ph.D. ....Biology
OTIS C. INGEBRITSEN, Ph.D. ....Psychology
GEORGE W. KAYS, A.M. ....Mathematics
WU-CHI LIU, Ph.D. ....Chinese Philosophy
ROBERT W. MCLACHLAN, Ph.D. ....Science
CHIH MENG, Ph.D. ....Director of China Institute
HARLEY P. MILSTEAD, Ph.D. ....Geography
MAURICE P. MOFFATT, Ph.D. ....Social Studies
ALLAN MOREHEAD, A.M. ....Integration
MILDRED M. OSGOOD, A.M. ....Art
WILLIAM R. PHIPPS, Ed.D. ....Integration
JOHN J. RELLAHAN, Ph.D. ....Acting Head, Department of Social Studies
HARRY M. RICE, A.M. ....Integration
CHARLES J. SENSALE, A.M. ....Research
HORACE J. SHEPPARD, A.M. ....Acting Head, Department of Business Education
MEYER P. SMITH, Ph.D. ....Business Education
W. SCOTT SMITH, Ph.D. ....Acting Head, Department of Integration
ELIZABETH T. VANDERVEER, Ed.D. ....Business Education
FELIX WITTMER, Ph.D. ....Social Studies
NA-SUN WU, A.M. ....Chinese Art

GRADUATE COMMITTEE

OTIS C. INGEBRITSEN, *Chairman*

E. DEALTON PARTRIDGE	RUFUS D. REED
D. HENRYETTA SPERLE	HORACE J. SHEPPARD
W. PAUL HAMILTON	ELIZABETH S. FAVOR, *Secretary*
DAVID R. DAVIS	JOHN J. RELLAHAN

3

MAIN BUILDING—MONTCLAIR COLLEGE CAMPUS

SUMMER SESSION OF THE
NEW JERSEY STATE TEACHERS COLLEGE AT MONTCLAIR
Objectives and Academic Status

The College is a professional school which prepares teachers, supervisors, and principals of high schools, and administrators of public school systems. The degrees offered by this College are those of Bachelor of Arts and Master of Arts. Certificate courses are offered for those who now hold degrees from other colleges.

The New Jersey State Teachers College at Montclair is a fully accredited member of the American Association of Colleges of Teacher Education, the Middle States Association of Colleges and Secondary Schools, the Association of American Universities, and the American Association of University Women.

How to Reach the Campus

Trains of the Greenwood Lake Division, Erie R. R., stop at Montclair Heights, the College Station. Trains of the Lackawanna R. R. connect at Montclair with the following bus lines: No. 64, running between Brick Church and the College; No. 60, running between Newark and the College; and No. 76, which runs between Orange and Paterson, passing the College en route. For those who come by car: the College is located about one mile north of the center of Upper Montclair.

Residence Halls for Men and Women

Edward Russ Hall and Chapin Hall are Montclair College's two well-appointed Residences. The charge for living on campus during the Summer Session is: $13.50 per week; which includes room, breakfast, and dinner. A la carte luncheons are served in the College cafeteria. For one student alone in a double room, an extra charge of $2.00 per week is made. The College provides and launders sheets, pillowcase, and bedpad. Towels, table lamps, blankets, clocks, and similar items must be provided and cared for by the student. The boarding-hall fee must be paid on or before the first day of the Summer Session. No rebate is made for occasional absence or voluntary withdrawal during the session. Students who are absent on account of illness for two weeks or more receive a rebate of $6.00 per week during the illness. These prices are subject to change.

For reservations in a College Residence Hall, women address: Dean of Women, State Teachers College, Upper Montclair, N. J. Men address the Dean of Men.

Schedule of the Summer Session

Registration will take place on Monday, June 25: Hours, 9-12 and 1-5. Classes will begin on Tuesday morning, June 26, at 8 A. M. and will continue through Wednesday, August 8. All classes meet daily, Monday to Friday, inclusive, at the hours indicated for each.

Matriculation for the Master of Arts Degree

Not more than 8 semester-hours of work taken prior to matriculation ar allowed to apply on the Master of Arts degree.

Those who desire to become candidates for the degree must request an ap plication form from the Chairman of the Graduate Committee and return i properly filled in and accompanied by an Official Transcript of all previou work on college level. When such an applicant has been accepted by the Colleg as a candidate for the degree, a definite statement is furnished to him, showing th requirements which he must fulfill to earn the degree. This sheet of requir ments becomes the student's Work Program and should be brought by th student each time he comes to enroll for courses.

Auditors

Men and women who desire to take courses for cultural, vocational, c avocational purposes without college credits may register as auditors.

A student who desires to enroll in a course for which he already holds cred must register as an auditor in that course.

A student who desires to enroll in a course for which he has not complete the prerequisites must enroll as an auditor in that course.

Change of Status in a Course

If a student desires to change his status in a course from "credit" to "audito or from "auditor" to "credit," he must make formal application for such chang not later than the middle of the course. Forms for this purpose may be procure from Miss Favor, in the Registrar's Office. Such changes cannot be made aft the midpoint of the course is passed.

Students Matriculated at Montclair for A.M. Degree

The selection of courses must be in accordance with the student's Wor Program, and his registration form will be signed by the Head of the Depar ment in which the student is majoring or by a representative of that departme present in the registration room.

Candidates for a degree must file with the Registrar an application for co ferment of the degree before November 30 of the college year in which the wo is to be completed. Application blanks for this purpose may be secured in t Registrar's Office. The burden of responsibility for the request rests with t candidate. This is of special significance to the teacher-in-service who may ha distributed the work for the degree over several years.

Students Matriculated at Other Colleges

In previous summers, when the State Teachers College at Montclair offer courses to its own accelerated candidates for the Bachelor's degree, it w possible to accept students from other colleges in freshman, sophomore, a junior year courses, as well as in courses of the senior year. Beginning in t summer of 1950, however, the College returned to its pre-war custom of offeri courses in its Summer Session primarily to teachers-in-service. Since su teachers already hold the Bachelor's degree, with few exceptions, the cour shown in this Bulletin are for the most part only Graduate and Senior-Gradu courses.

A student who is planning to attend Montclair this summer should take t Bulletin to a conference with the Dean of his own college to arrange a progr of work. For the Dean's information: the numbering of courses at Montc

Arts Degree

follows this order: 100-399, inclusive, are undergraduate courses: 400-499, inclusive, are senior-college and graduate courses; 500 and above are graduate courses.

At the time of registration, the student should go to the table of the Department in which the courses are listed that he plans to take. The registration form must be signed by the Representative of the Department at that table. The College reserves the right to decide whether the student has fulfilled necessary prerequisites. If the student is seeking certification to teach in New Jersey, he must confer with Dr. Fraser, Head of the Department of Integration. Please note paragraph under the Heading: "Certificates."

Certificates

The State Teachers College at Montclair offers work toward the following New Jersey Certificates: Secondary Teaching Certificate; Secondary School Principal's Certificate; Elementary School Principal's Certificate; Subject Supervisor's Certificate; General Supervisor's Certificate; Guidance Certificate; School Administrator's Certificate; Junior College Teacher's Certificate; and the Advanced Professional Certificate.

Those who matriculate at Montclair for a degree will receive information from Dr. Fraser, Head of the Integration Department, as to the requirements for each of these certificates. Students who have not matriculated at Montclair should write to Dr. E. C. Preston, Secretary of the State Board of Examiners, Department of Education, 175 West State Street, Trenton 8, N. J., for information as to the requirements. For an evaluation of work already completed, address Dr. Preston. An official transcript of such previous work should accompany the inquiry, with a statement as to the particular certificate desired.

The student should bring Dr. Preston's reply with him when conferring with Dr. Fraser as to his program of work.

Students who must have this information immediately should go to Trenton to confer personally with Dr. Preston or his assistant, Miss Smith.

Supervised Student Teaching

The opportunity to do supervised student teaching cannot be offered during the Summer Session. For fall teaching, students confer with Dr. Fraser at the College. Ask his secretary for an appointment.

Veterans

Since July 25, 1951, is the last date to commence training under the G. I. Bill, it is recommended that veterans attend the summer session of 1951 to insure their continued eligibility under this bill.

Veteran students taking work under the G. I. Bill for the first time at Montclair State Teachers College must see the Veterans' Counselor at least two weeks prior to the registration day. Veterans should be sure to obtain the Certificate of Eligibility from the Veterans' Administration before the start of the Summer Session. Failure to do so will mean that the usual fees must be paid by the student at the time of registration.

It will be necessary for Veterans who have completed the work for either the A.B. or the A.M. degree at Montclair to secure and present to the Veterans' Counselor the Supplemental Certificate of Eligibility before registering for further work at Montclair. Veterans transferring to Montclair who have previously been training under the G. I. Bill will be required to present a Supplemental Certificate of Eligibility at the time of registration.

Conferences with Advisers

Appointments with the Dean of Instruction, the Chairman of the Graduat Committee, a Department Head, or the Veterans' Counselor may be made b mail or telephone to their respective offices. This should be done at as early date as possible to avoid delay at the time of registration.

In order to assist students who have been unable to go to Trenton for th information, a representative of the State Board of Examiners will be at th College on June 25, from 10 A. M. to 3 P. M., to see students who need advic on the selection of courses toward a New Jersey Certificate. (See paragrap under the heading: "Certificates.") The Assistant in Graduate Personnel wi receive requests for appointments with this State Official.

Summer Session Credit Load

The maximum amount of credit which may be earned in the Summer Sessio is 8 semester-hours, but only 6 s. h. are recommended. There is no provisio for a student to audit additional courses; consequently, the total of all course taken during the Summer Session may not exceed 8 s. h. and students should nc register for more.

Additional credits may be earned by attending one of the sessions at th State School of Conservation that precedes or follows the Summer Sessior Attention is called also to the post-Summer Session course in Safety Educatio and to the Field Studies course in the Central Eastern Region.

Each Summer Session course is in session at least thirty hours and carries designated amount of credit. It is not possible to earn three s. h. credit in two s. h. course.

Registration Information

Registration takes place in the College Gymnasium, on Monday, June 2! from 9 A. M. to 12 noon, and from 1 to 5 P. M. Anyone unable to enroll dui ing the hours shown must register during the regular office hours of the Colleg in the Registrar's Office and pay the Late Registration Service Charge. N Summer Session course may be taken for credit after Thursday, June 28. Th summer office hours are from 8:30 A. M. to 3:30 P. M.

Matriculated students should bring their "Work Programs" when they com to enroll.

The College reserves the right to close any course for which the enrollmei is insufficient. The class will meet at least once, however, before this decisic is made. Students may then enter another course in place of the one discoi tinued, by going to the Registrar's Office to re-enroll and to receive the ne Class Admission Card in exchange for the card of the discontinued cours Students who decide not to enroll in an alternate course must return to tl Registrar's Office to have the Class Admission Card of the discontinued cour: stamped "Discontinued" before going to the Business Office for an adjustme: of tuition fees.

If prerequisites are required, the student should make certain that he h fulfilled them or their equivalent before enrolling in the course. If no previo: work on college level has been taken, the student should consult the Registr before enrolling in any course, unless as an Auditor.

A student may not register for credit in any course for which he already hol credit except by permission of the Dean of Instruction.

The Registration form of every student must be signed by an Adviser. R port to the table of that Adviser.

8

Withdrawal from a Course

Written notice to Miss Favor, Assistant in Graduate Personnel, must be given at once by the student. Students who neglect to follow this procedure receive a failing mark for the course or courses which they cease to attend. Miss Favor will notify the teachers of the courses from which the student is withdrawing, as well as the Business Office of the College. Refunds are computed from the date of the receipt of the letter of withdrawal. Inquiries regarding refunds should be addressed to the Business Manager.

Tuition Fees and Service Charges

Check or money-order should be made payable to New Jersey State Teachers College.

Registration service charge: $1.00 for the Summer Session.

Late registration service charge: $2.00. This is collected from all students who fail to enroll on June 25.

Tuition fees: to students who have not been professionally employed: $8.00 per semester-hour credit carried by the course; to students who are or have been professionally employed: $11.00 per credit. **Courses taken by auditors for no credit cost the same.**

Laboratory service charge: $4.00 for each laboratory course.

Teachers who have supervised Montclair student-teachers and who have in their possession old Montclair credit slips may take them to the office of the Integration Department, where new ones will be issued. The Business Office cannot return any unused portion of a credit slip, so it is necessary that the new type credit slip be obtained before presenting it in payment of tuition fees. Training Teachers may use the credit slips of any one of the six New Jersey State Teachers Colleges when taking courses at Montclair, but should bring only the new type slip in all cases.

Final Marks

Following are the final marks which may be received for a course: A-Excellent; B-Good; C-Fair; D-Poor; F-Failure; Inc.-Incomplete; Wd-Withdrew; N. C.-No Credit.

The mark of "D" when earned in summer, part-time, or extension courses of this College is not accepted for degree credit at Montclair.

The mark of "F" is given when earned and when the student has failed to notify the Assistant in Graduate Personnel promptly of his withdrawal from a course.

The mark of "N. C." is given only to auditors.

The mark of "Wd" is given only when prompt notice of withdrawal has been given and when the student's work to that time has been satisfactory to the teacher of the course.

The mark of "Inc." is seldom given. It may, however, be granted to a student whose work is incomplete at the end of the Session and who is eager to finish the work for a higher grade than he could receive otherwise. All responsibility regarding incomplete work rests with the student. He will be notified of a date after which, if the work remains incomplete, the final grade will be recorded without further notice

Report Cards and Transcripts

An Official Transcript showing the credits earned is sent to the student personally ten days to two weeks following the close of the Session. A report card for each course taken is sent with the transcript. The transcript is sent without cost, but a service charge of $1.00 is made for a duplicate copy.

A student whose college requires that the transcript be mailed directly to the Dean or Registrar should call during the Summer Session at the Registrar's Office to address an envelope for this purpose.

Elementary Education Courses

Courses offered as a part of the curriculum for the graduate major in Educational Administration and Supervision should be carefully distinguished from those offered toward the endorsement in elementary education on the teacher's certificate. The courses in the Administration and Supervision of Elementary Education apply on the Elementary Principal's certificate, but not on the Elementary Teacher's certificate.

Although the New Jersey State Teachers College at Montclair is engaged primarily in preparing secondary school teachers, during the present shortage of teachers in the elementary schools it is deemed expedient to offer courses in the field of elementary education to those students who are eligible to enroll at this College in such courses.

Students eligible to enroll at Montclair in courses leading to certification in elementary education are:

(1) those who already hold a degree from Montclair with a certificate in secondary education; and

(2) those who are now matriculated at Montclair for such a degree.

Montclair cannot accept any other students in these courses.

The eligible students should consult the Registrar's Office for an evaluation of their previous work and a statement concerning the courses to be taken in order to receive the endorsement in elementary education on the secondary certificate already held or to be conferred.

Textbook Exhibit

In the Gymnasium of the Main Building, from July 9 through July 20, there will be an exhibit of high school and elementary school textbooks. While primarily for the benefit of the principals and teachers attending the Summer Session, the exhibit will be open to undergraduate students and to members of the general public who may be interested in seeing the latest textbooks.

Mrs. E. S. Fulcomer will be in charge of the Exhibit.

Room Numbers

Room numbers used in this Bulletin, if unaccompanied by other designation refer to rooms in College Hall, the main building of the College.

Other designations are as follows:

CHS: College High School Building; to the northeast of the main building Campus Studio Workshop: near the eastern end of the parking area;
Annex No. 1: Federal Works Administration Building No. 1; at the north west corner of the main building;
Annex No. 2: Federal Works Administration Building No. 2; next to No. 1
Annex No. 3: Federal Works Administration Building No. 3; directly east of the main building;
Music Building: at the northeast corner of the College High School Building
Recreation Building: at the extreme north end of campus.

BUREAU OF FIELD STUDIES

Social Studies S460—Central Eastern Region   **Mr. Bye**

This fifteen-day tour of Pennsylvania, Maryland, Virginia, West Virginia, North Carolina, and Tennessee covers the major points of historic interest associated with the Colonial Period, the American Revolution, and the Civil War; and the geographic features of the coastal plain, the Piedmont, the Great Valley, and the Appalachian Mountains in these states. Travel is by modern chartered motor coach, and overnight stops are made at first-class hotels. Among the places visited are: Valley Forge, Philadelphia, Baltimore, Annapolis, Washington, Arlington, Alexandria, Mt. Vernon, Fredericksburg, Richmond, Washington's birthplace at Wakefield, Lee's plantation at Stratford, Yorktown, Williamsburg, Jamestown, Raleigh, Chattanooga, Asheville, Great Smoky Mountains, Norris Dam, Jefferson's Monticello at Charlottesville, Natural Bridge, Skyline Drive in the Shenandoah National Park, Luray Caverns, Winchester, Harper's Ferry, Frederick, Gettysburg, and the Pennsylvania Dutch area around Lancaster and Ephrata.

Credit: 3 semester-hours

While the above course is given as a part of the Summer Session offerings of the State Teachers College at Montclair, registration for it must be made in advance through the Bureau of Field Studies. Likewise, payment is made as requested by the Bureau. Interested students should address Mr. E. C. Bye, Bureau of Field Studies, New Jersey State Teachers College, Upper Montclair, New Jersey. This should be done at once, as the number of students in the course must be limited to a definite number. The all-expense price for this 2,500 mile trip is $175.00. This includes tuition, transportation, hotels, meals, tips, and admissions—no extras. Starts Tuesday, August 14; ends Monday, August 27, 1951.

A student matriculated in one New Jersey State Teachers College may enroll for a field studies course conducted by another New Jersey College provided he presents written approval from the college where he is matriculated. The New Jersey Council for Field Studies will determine the number of semester-points credit for each field studies course given under its jurisdiction. The allocation of this credit for specific purposes for each student concerned shall be determined by the officials of each college. Students who enroll for a field study course shall register and pay tuition in the Teachers College which sponsors the course. Students may register for graduate or undergraduate credit provided graduate courses are offered by the college sponsoring the course. A limited number of students may enroll for No Credit provided they pay the regular tuition fees and service charges.

Trenton State Teachers College

Post-Term Field Trip

Geography S505—The Piedmont and Southern Appalachians   **Dr. Botts**

The third annual post-term field trip sponsored by the New Jersey State Teachers College at Trenton will spend the last fifteen days of August, 1951, studying the geography of the southeastern part of Pennsylvania, the Shenandoah Valley, the Cumberland Plateau, the Great Smoky Mountains, the Piedmont, and the Coastal Plain. In addition to visits to cities, farms, factories, and mines, the group will spend much time in places of great historic and scenic interest.

Credit: 3 semester-hours

Fifteen days; 2,200 miles. Begins August 17, ends August 31, 1951. For additional information, write to: Dr. Adelbert K. Botts, Head, Department of Geography, State Teachers College, Trenton 5, New Jersey.

11

INSTITUTES AND WORKSHOPS

China Institute of New Jersey

The China Institute of New Jersey is a permanent year-round organization composed of former students of the China Workshop course. The policies and program of the Institute are determined by an elected executive committee, an advisory board of laymen, and representatives from the faculty of Montclair Teachers College, in consultation with the Chinese Director.

Dr. Chih Meng, Director of the China Institute of America, whose purpose is to promote cultural and educational relations between China and the United States, is Chinese Director of the China Institute of New Jersey. The College provides the facilities necessary for the courses sponsored by the Institute and grants credit for the satisfactory completion of such courses. These are given on the senior-graduate level, so that students may work toward either under-graduate or graduate credit.

While the primary and definite purpose of the Institute is to assist the teachers of New Jersey, men and women who desire to take these courses for cultural, vocational, or avocational purposes are welcome also. They may enroll for college credit or simply as Auditors for no credit. The cost is the same in both cases. If it be desired to attend a single lecture, the Institute Treasurer collects the fee of $2.00 at the door of the Auditorium in the College High School. Students who enroll for the entire course follow the instructions below.

Registration for one of the following courses must be made on forms provided by the College. Write to: **Mrs. Flora Dayton, China Institute of New Jersey, State Teachers College, Upper Montclair, N. J.**, for these forms, and for any additional information you require. Refer to the list below for the proper number and title of the course you expect to take. Note that the course **Social Studies S499—China Workshop** is prerequisite to the course in **Chinese Philosophy** and do not enroll for credit in the Philosophy course unless you have completed the prerequisite course. Return the forms to Mrs. Dayton not later than Saturday, June 16, with check or money order **made payable to the China Institute of New Jersey, for $34.00.** A late service charge of $2.00 will be made for all registrations not received by June 16. Your class admission card will be mailed to you by the Treasurer of the Institute. It should be presented to your teacher on the opening day of the course.

Offerings for 1951: June 25—July 7, Inclusive

Art S414—History of Chinese Art   **Mr. Na-Sun Wu**

In this course the developments and distinguishing characteristics of the major arts of China are traced by specialists and are surveyed from the point of view of their historical developments. There are twenty-four hours of lectures in the morning, and round-table discussion and library work in the afternoon. During this afternoon workshop period, the technique of Chinese painting is demonstrated and taught by the noted Chinese artist, Professor Ya Chin Wang, whose paintings have been exhibited in the Metropolitan Museum of New York and other art centers in this country. **No prerequisite.**

9:30 A. M.-4 P. M.   Credit: 3 semester-hours   Room 11, CHS

Social Studies S497—Chinese Philosophy   **Dr. Wu-Chi Li**

This course shows how the ancient philosophies, Confucianism, Taoism, Buddhism, Mohism, can be applied to the China of today and how they affect modern Chinese thought. There are twenty-four hours of lectures in the morn

ing, and round-table discussion and library work in the afternoon. **Prerequisite:** Social Studies S499, China Workshop, or an equivalent course in philosophy.
9:30 A. M.-4 P. M.   Credit: 3 semester-hours   Room 14, CHS

Social Studies S499—China Workshop   **Dr. Chih Meng**
A number of authorities introduce first-year students to the rise, growth, and maturing of Chinese civilization, as well as to the fundamental problems of China today, including the conflict of ideologies. The course is given in twelve days. Each day there are two hours of lectures in the morning; after lunch a period of forty-five minutes is devoted to informal talks including further discussion on Chinese music, philosophy, Chinese school days, festivals, and calligraphy. Some time is also given to the singing of Chinese songs and the showing of motion pictures. During the two-hour workshop period, the students prepare their projects, teaching units, and background material under the direction of faculty members.
9:30 A. M.-4 P. M.   Credit: 3 semester-hours   Auditorium, CHS

Montclair State Teachers College Workshops

Social Studies S490—United Nations Institute   **Mrs. Fradkin**

July 9—July 20, 1951

This course covers four and one-half hours per day for ten consecutive days excluding Saturday and Sunday. It consists of basic lectures on factual backgrounds by the instructor, supplementary lectures by visiting lecturers from the United Nations and other organizations, discussions, workshop and library projects, demonstrations of the use of audio-visual materials, and field trips to the United Nations. Included among the subjects studied are the national State system, war and peace, world organizations (past, present, and proposed), the national armaments problem, international law, the international police proposal, pacific methods of settling international disputes, and the outlook for international co-operation.
9:30 A. M.-3 P. M.   Credit: 2 semester-hours   Room 3, Annex No. 2

Social Studies S491—Workshop in Citizenship Education   **Dr. Clayton**

June 25—July 6, 1951

Americans are becoming increasingly aware of the severe test to which the democratic way of life is put by the developing world situation. The need to strengthen citizenship to meet this crisis is reflected in renewed efforts to find ways better to educate for membership in a democratic society. To help meet this need, Montclair State Teachers College plans a workshop in citizenship education from June 25 to July 6. It will be a short period of intensive study carrying two credit hours on the graduate level. In this workshop it is planned to study what has been done in some of the many projects in citizenship education throughout the country. Special emphasis will be placed on the plans and materials developed by the Citizenship Education Project now being conducted by Teachers College, Columbia University, and financed by the Carnegie Corporation. Montclair has been one of the eight teachers colleges co-operating in this project. Consultants will be called in to give a variety of points of view. Attention will be given to programs and practices already in use in the schools. New means for citizenship education will be sought. Methods of evaluation will be reviewed. There will be experience in the group processes essential to

13

democratic action. It is hoped especially to include in the workshop those who have been or who may be serving as training teachers for Montclair student teachers, especially those who teach social studies. Principals and administrators who want to join with others in learning how to make more effective the citizenship education in the schools with which they are connected are also invited to participate. The number in the workshop will, of necessity, have to be limited to insure individual guidance and participation.

Application for participation in this workshop should be addressed to Dr. Frank L. Clayton, State Teachers College, Upper Montclair, New Jersey. Actual registration and payment of fees will take place on June 25.

9:30 A. M.-3 P. M.   Credit: 2 semester-hours   Room 3, Annex No. 2

Workshops at the Trenton State Teachers College

Geography S452—Workshop for Teachers of Geography and
Social Studies   **Dr. Botts**

The purpose of this course is to provide an opportunity for a selected group of elementary teachers to consider together their classroom problems relating to the teaching of geography in the social studies. Opportunities will be provided for such activities as: forums on the philosophy of geography teaching; lectures by guests who are specialists in various phases of educational geography; research in the library; viewing and evaluating audio-visual aids; planning and conducting field trips; preparation of individual projects, consultation on problems common to all geography teachers.

2 points (undergraduate)   July 30-August 10, 1951

Science S502—Conservation Education Workshop   **Dr. Crowell**

The workshop will be held on the college campus and will consist of trips in the college bus, illustrated lectures, conferences and round-table discussions. Representatives of Federal and State Governments and of other organizations will cooperate in this program, and particular attention will be paid to the needs of the elementary and junior high school teachers. Teachers will be encouraged to develop individual programs in conservation education for their particular needs.

4 points (graduate or undergraduate)   July 9-27, 1951

14

NEW JERSEY STATE SCHOOL OF CONSERVATION

Stokes State Forest, Branchville, New Jersey

COURSES IN CONSERVATION, FIELD SCIENCES, CAMPING EDUCATION, AND WATER FRONT SAFETY

Spring and Summer, 1951

Application for admission to any of the courses at the School of Conservation should be made in advance. Write to School of Conservation, Montclair State Teachers College, Upper Montclair, N. J., for this preliminary application form. Final registration, with payment of fees, will be made at the School itself. At that time, the student should indicate to which of the New Jersey State Teachers Colleges his record should be mailed at the end of the summer.

The following sessions, June 17 to August 23, offer opportunities for teachers-in-service, senior students, and graduate students to pursue special courses during short periods of the summer. It is possible to earn 10 semester-credits for the five sessions, or a minimum of 2 semester-credits for a single session. Credits for these courses may be applied for graduate or undergraduate credit at the New Jersey State Teachers Colleges, subject to approval in advance by the institution. Credit may be transferred to other institutions where such transfer is permitted toward an undergraduate or an advanced degree.

June 17-26

Integration 440—Camping Education
The purpose of this course is to familiarize the students with camping and outdoor education as educational methods utilized by the schools of America. The aims and methods of camping are studied, and consideration is given to the communities that have active camping and outdoor education programs in operation.
Credit: 2 semester-hours

Integration 441—Conservation Education
The social, economic, and scientific implications of conservation are considered in this course. Discussion periods are interspersed with field trips to forest areas and demonstrations of conservation problems.
Credit: 2 semester-hours

Physical Education 410—Water Safety and First Aid
This course includes intensive instruction in swimming, diving, water sports, boating, canoeing, water safety, and first aid. Students can qualify for Red Cross certificates during this course.
Credit: 2 semester-hours

July 2-12

Science 412—Field Studies in Science: Biological
Emphasis in this course is given to the ecology, life-history, and identification of plant and animal communities (terrestrial and aquatic) with an introduction to their conservation.
Credit: 2 semester-hours

July 16-26

Science 414—Conservation of Plants and Animals
The social, economic, and ecological implications of plant and animal conservation are considered together in this course. Discussion periods are interspersed with field trips to forest and wildlife management areas. Co-operating experts from State and Federal agencies bring special contributions in their fields. Visual aids are used extensively.

Credit: 2 semester-hours

July 30—August 9

Science 413—Field Studies in Science: Physical
Emphasis in this course is given to local and New Jersey geology, minerals, soils, and waters, with emphasis on the chemical and physical aspects of soil and water. Field trips are taken through the Kittatinny Mountains and to the Delaware Water Gap.

Credit: 2 semester-hours

August 13-23

Social Studies 477—Rural Sociology
During this course the student comes face to face with rural life in northern New Jersey. Social processes and problems are considered. Opportunities are provided for students to attend Grange meetings, county fairs, rural dances and parties, and to live for a day or two with a farm family.

Credit: 2 semester-hours

Fees

The total fee for each **ten-day session** listed above will be $50.00. This includes tuition, board, and lodging.

SPECIAL SEMINARS

July 2—August 23

Science 411—Problems in Field Studies in Science
In this course each student selects a phase of field science in which he does advanced research under the guidance of the instructor. Plant ecology, bird-life, pond-life, fungi, tree diseases, and insect-life are a few of the areas from which the student may choose. Prerequisites: Science 405, Field and Laboratory Studies in Science, or its equivalent, plus at least 12 points in Biology.

Credit: To be determined by length of stay and nature of problem.

Science 416—Problems in Conservation
In this course, a student or a group of students selects a phase of conservation in which he or the group does original research, either at the School of Conservation or within New Jersey. The research may be done any time during the summer with the approval of the instructor. This course is intended primarily to encourage individuals or groups from institutions of higher learning in New Jersey to use the School of Conservation as a base for research in conservation. Enrollment is limited and subject to advanced approval. Fees are determined by the number of hours of credit allowed and the number of days or weeks spent in research.

Credit: to be determined by length of stay and nature of problem.

16

ADMINISTRATION BUILDING—SCHOOL OF CONSERVATION, STOKES STATE FOREST
SEE PAGES 15-16 FOR COMPLETE INFORMATION

DESCRIPTIONS OF THE COURSES OF THE SUMMER SESSION SHOWN BY DEPARTMENTS

Please note that the numbering of courses at this College follows this order: 100-399, inclusive, are undergraduate courses; 400-499, inclusive, are senior-college and graduate courses; 500 and above are graduate courses.

Art

Art S406—Creative Arts Workshop   **Miss Osgood**
This course offers experience in painting, drawing, sculpture, ceramics, and print-making for students who wish to employ the creative visual arts in the teaching of other subjects. No previous art training is required.
10:30-11:20 A. M.   Credit: 2 semester-hours   Campus Studio Workshop

Art S414—The History of Chinese Art
For description and other data, see section under "China Institute of New Jersey."

Integration S474—Elementary School Arts and Crafts   **Miss Osgood**
For description and other data, see section under "Elementary Education."

Business Education

Business Education S401—The Teaching of Business Education   **Mr. Froehlich**
In this course a study is made of the history and development of business education, aims and objectives, human learning processes, lesson plans, teaching procedures, tests and measurements, and special helps for the teachers of business education. Consideration is given to the current trend in teaching in these fields with emphasis on the viewpoint of the consumer as well as the social and vocational objectives.
8-9:20 A. M.   Credit: 3 semester-hours   Room 2, Annex No. 2

Business Education S408—Business Finance   **Dr. Meyer P. Smith**
This course deals with the processes involved in the financing of business organizations from the time of their inception and promotion, during operation and expansion, and during the period of reorganization. Included are problems of financing by means of stock, borrowed capital, bonds, mortgages, and notes.
10:30-11:20 A. M.   Credit: 2 semester-hours   Room 1, Annex No. 2

Business Education S414—Merchandising I   **Dr. VanDerveer**
This course analyzes the problems of how, what, where, and when to buy; the terms of purchasing; tested receiving and marketing procedures; the mathematics of merchandising—setting the retail price, planning mark-up and mark-down; and inventory controls. It is designed to assist the teacher of the prospective or actual small businessman.
9:30-10:20 A. M.   Credit: 2 semester-hours   Room 4, Annex No. 2

18

Business Education S504—
Improvement of Instruction in Business Education   Dr. VanDerveer
This course seeks to bring together business education teachers regardless of subject matter fields to consider common problems involving general subject matter and methods of instruction including visual and auditory aids. It also offers opportunity for an individual to investigate and evaluate materials and methods in specific subject matter areas.
8:30-9:20 A. M.   Credit: 2 semester-hours   Room 4, Annex No. 2

Business Education S519A—Advanced Accounting I   Dr. Meyer P. Smith
The content of this course emphasizes an intensive study of the items making up accounting statements and the principles of valuation and income determination. Problem solving is an integral part of the course. At least eight semester-hours of accounting are required as a prerequisite.
11:30 A. M.-12:20 P. M.   Credit: 2 semester-hours   Room 1, Annex No. 2

Business Education S602—
Seminar in Economics   Mr. Sheppard and Mr. Froehlich
This seminar is designed to meet the individual needs of the graduate student in business education or social studies by allowing him to pursue areas of work along economic lines in which he is not well-versed. The program of participation consists of oral and written reports, developed through independent reading and individually directed field studies. In addition, group field trips are planned so as to give the student a first-hand knowledge of methods and practices of such organizations as banks, organized exchanges, manufacturing and marketing businesses. It is expected that the reports arising from these experiences will be in such form that they will be capable of being published or delivered as speeches before groups of people. An opportunity is given to view, evaluate, and work with a variety of related visual and auditory aids.
9:30 A. M.-12:20 P. M.   Credit: 6 semester-hours   Room 5, Annex No. 2

English

English S401—The Teaching of English in Secondary Schools   Dr. Fulcomer
Students are taught to develop and use materials of the classroom: lesson plans and units of work are prepared and presented for criticism; textbooks are analyzed for training in their use; and bulletin board exhibits and visual education materials are prepared by students for the class.
8-9:20 A. M.   Credit: 3 semester-hours   Room 1

English S406—The Modern Novel   Mr. Conrad
Particular emphasis is given to British and American novels since 1870, and the important tendencies of present-day prose fiction are explored. Students are taught how to read a novel with profit, and how to guide and direct the reading of others.
11:30 A. M.-12:20 P. M.   Credit: 2 semester-hours   Room 4, CHS

English S431A—Shakespeare I (Tragedies)   Mr. Bohn
This course deals with Shakespeare's plays in relation to his life, his times, his contemporaries, and Elizabethan drama generally. Extensive reading is required from Shakespeare, his predecessors, contemporaries, and successors. The problems of stage production in both Elizabethan and modern theatres, and of Shakespearean criticism are analyzed. Part I deals with Shakespearean tragedies.
9:30-10:20 A. M.   Credit: 2 semester-hours   Room 1

19

English S435—Stagecraft   **Mr. Fox**
This workshop course provides training in construction and painting of scenery
and lighting the stage. A minimum of twelve clock hours of craft work upon a
production of the College or the College High School is required for credit in
this course.
8:30-9:20 A. M.   Credit: 2 semester-hours   Auditorium, CHS

English S442A-B—American Literature   **Mr. Conrad**
This chronological survey examines American Literature to observe its reflection
of the political, social, and ethical principles of the American people. Part A
begins with the Revolutionary period of the eighteenth century and ends with
the Civil War. Part B embraces Reconstruction and the New South, immigration and the development of the West, urban America, and the present reaffirmation of the American tradition of Democracy. (Not open for credit to students
who have credit for English 302, Survey of American Literature.)
8:30-10:20 A. M.   Credit: 4 semester-hours   Room 4, CHS

English S443—Modern Drama   **Mr. Bohn**
An historical survey of trends, dramatists, plays, and accomplishments from
Ibsen to the latest prize plays on Broadway provides background for this course.
An examination of the structure and content of plays to determine what constitutes a good play stimulates appreciation. Students are encouraged to read
widely and to see current productions on Broadway.
10:30-11:20 A. M.   Credit: 2 semester-hours   Room 1

English S455—Reading Interests of High School Students   **Dr. Fulcomer**
Through wide reading, study and preparation of bibliographies, and establishing
criteria for judging current books, the student is prepared to guide the recreational reading of junior and senior high school students. Credit cannot be given
for both English 301A, Literature for Adolescents, and this course.)
10:30-11:20 A. M.   Credit: 2 semester-hours   Library, CHS

English S457—Workshop in Speech Activities   **Mr. Ballare**
It is the purpose of this course to prepare students to organize and to conduct
assembly programs, PTA demonstrations, and similar activities. Class lectures
and discussions cover all phases of the director's responsibilities. Groups conduct research on suitable program materials and share their findings with classmates. Each student prepares a list of programs of various types which he
could present during a school year. This course is open, not only to students
majoring in Speech, but to teachers and principals interested in these activities.
11:30 A. M.-12:20 P. M.   Credit: 2 semester-hours   Room 3

English S458—Radio Directing   **Mr. Fox**
This course offers training in the organization and direction of radio programs,
and equips the student to select material for broadcasting and to cast and to
rehearse programs. Listening is directed toward an analysis of common radio
presentation techniques and the appreciation of successful programs.
10:30-11:20 A. M.   Credit: 2 semester-hours   Audio-Aids Laboratory

English S462—Group Discussion and Leadership   **Mr. Ballare**
Students are taught the principles of democratic discussion and methods for
guiding the committee meeting, panel symposium, lecture, and debate forums
Frequent opportunities to apply these principles and methods are given through
discussion of topics chosen by the class.
9:30-10:20 A. M.   Credit: 2 semester-hours   Room

Integration S473—The Elementary School Language Arts   **Mrs. Fox**
See description and other data under the heading "Elementary Education."

English S528—Perspectives in World Literature   **Mr. Bohn**
The point of view of our own democratic culture is surveyed and established in
an attempt to see how the literature of Western Europe, the Middle East, and the
Orient have influenced and are influencing modern thinking. Such perspectives
are designed to provide adequacy in teaching a world point of view through
literature.
11:30 A. M.-12:20 P. M.   Credit: 2 semester-hours   Room 1

Geography

Geography S410—Economic Geography of Caribbean America   **Dr. Milstead**
This is a study and interpretation of the major and important minor economic
areas of Caribbean America in relation to the natural environment. Attention
is also given to the historical factors which have played a part in the economic
and social life of the people.
8:30-9:20 A. M.   Credit: 2 semester-hours   Room 26

Geography S416—Conservation of Natural Resources   **Dr. Milstead**
This course includes a study of the natural resources of the United States, their
past and present exploitation, their influence on the development of the Nation,
their conservation and future use.
9:30-10:20 A. M.   Credit: 2 semester-hours   Room 26

Geography S418—Regional Geography of North America   **Dr. Milstead**
This course constitutes a detailed regional treatment of the continent of North
America. Emphasis is placed upon the human activities of the various regions
in relation to their natural environment and the relations of the regions to each
other. Attention is given to the techniques of presenting the material and the
use of geographic tools in the treatment of the subject-matter.
11:30 A. M.-12:20 P. M.   Credit: 2 semester-hours   Room 26

Health and Physical Education

Health Education S407—Prevention and Care of Athletic Injuries   **Mr. Coder**
This is a lecture and laboratory course designed to acquaint the student with
ways to prevent and care for the common injuries sustained in athletics. Attention is given to sprains, strains, bruises, burns, and fractures. The responsibility
of the coach in caring for injuries is emphasized.
8:30-9:20 A. M.   Credit: 2 semester-hours   Room D

Health Education S408—Driver Education and Training   **Mr. Coder**
See page 33 under the heading "Post-Summer Session Course" for the description and other data concerning this course.

Health Education S411—School Health Services   **Mr. DeRosa**
The student is familiarized with the health services available in the school. The
part which the teacher plays in co-ordinating his activities with the school
medical staff is emphasized.
9:30-10:20 A. M.   Credit: 2 semester-hours   Room 13, CHS

Recreation S405—Principles and Problems in Recreation　　　　**Mr. DeRosa**

Under supervision, the student collects recreational and activity materials suited to his own particular needs. Visits are made to playgrounds, recreational centers, and the student is given an opportunity for practical experience in the planning and direction of recreational activities on the campus.

11:30 A. M.-12:20 P. M.　　　　Credit: 2 semester-hours　　　　Room 13, CHS

Integration S476—
Elementary School Health and Physical Education　　　　**Mr. DeRosa**

See description and other data under the heading "Elementary Education."

Integration

Integration S400A—Principles and Philosophy
of Secondary Education　　　　**Dr. Clayton**

This course evaluates educational objectives, techniques, procedures, and organizations in relation to the needs and demands made upon the school by society and by the student. It aims to help the student develop an adequate philosophy of life and education.

11:30 A. M.-12:20 P. M.　　　　Credit: 2 semester-hours　　　　Room 27

* Integration S408—Selection and Utilization
of Audio-Visual Materials　　　　**Miss Fantone**

Sources, selection, and evaluation of audio-visual aids are studied in this course. Techniques in developing individual reference catalogs of audio-visual aids are stressed. The production of school-made aids is also an important aspect of the course. The use of the latest audio-visual equipment is demonstrated.

10:30-11:20 A. M.　　　　Credit: 2 semester-hours　　　　Room 4

* Integration S409—Radio and Sound Equipment in the Classroom　　　**Mr. Fox**

This course trains teachers and school executives in the use of radio programs, amplifying systems, recording equipment, and record players. Actual practice is given in the use of these educational aids. Problems of script-writing, microphone and recording techniques, and program directing are considered. The class visits radio stations for equipment and program observation. Each student develops a teaching unit using radio or sound equipment to vary, vitalize, and improve educational practices.

9:30-10:20 A. M.　　　　Credit: 2 semester-hours　　　　Audio-Aids Laboratory

Integration S500B—Advanced Educational Psychology　　　　**Mr. Darling**

This course covers the various aspects of growth. Individual differences, their measurement, and their bearing on education practices and principles furnish topics of study and discussion. Principles and laws of learning are reviewed. Some time is given to problems of personality as encountered in school work. The several points of view which have been prominent in the psychology of the past fifty to seventy-five years are examined for their contributions to thinking about human nature. Prerequisite: An introductory course in psychology.

10:30-11:20 A. M.　　　　Credit: 2 semester-hours　　　　Room 30

Integration S500D—School Administration I:
Functions and Organization　　　　**Mr. Morehead**

This introductory course in educational administration is concerned with general functions and personnel, as well as with the general organization, of public education on local, State, and national levels. It deals also with Federal-State relations, the State and sectarian education, the expanding scope of modern school systems, types and bases of school organization, and professional ethics.

9:30-10:20 A. M.　　　　Credit: 2 semester-hours　　　　Room B

---

* See page 25.

22

Integration S500E—School Administration II:
Law and Finance   **Mr. Morehead**
This course acquaints the student with the allied fields of school law and school finance, with special reference to New Jersey. Its topics include basic principles of public school support, taxation, Federal aid, educational finance, legal provisions for school district borrowing, tenure provisions, and rights and duties of school boards and officials.
11:30 A. M.-12:20 P. M.   Credit: 2 semester-hours   Room B

Integration S500F—School Administration III: Community Relations   Mr. Rice
The course concerns the relation of the school to other educational efforts of the community. It considers the scope and types of agencies and informal influences of an educational nature, and also the agencies and methods by which the best total co-operative effort can be attained. It deals also with methods and plans of publicity. Constant reference throughout is made to New Jersey localities.
10:30-11:20 A. M.   Credit: 2 semester-hours   Room 9

Integration S502—Organization and Administration
of the Modern High School   **Dr. W. Scott Smith**
The following topics are considered: the student personnel, building and revising the high school curriculum, providing for individual differences, making the school schedule, records, the guidance program, pupil participation in government, the extra-curricular program, the health program, the safety program, discipline, library and study hall, cafeteria, the principal's office, and evaluating results.
10:30-11:20 A. M.   Credit: 2 semester-hours   Room 27

Integration S503—Methods and Instruments of Research   Mr. Sensale
This course is required of all candidates for the Master's Degree without regard to their field of major interest. Its purpose is to introduce students of education to research and its practical application to professional problems. The course treats the nature and types of educational research; methods and techniques of educational research; and the tools used in interpreting statistical data. During the course the student sets up a problem and plans and carries out the solution. Mathematics 400 or its equivalent is recommended before taking this course.
1-1:50 P. M.   Credit: 2 semester-hours   Room 9

Integration S504A—Curriculum Construction
in the Secondary School   **Dr. W. Scott Smith**
The purpose of this course is to introduce the student to constructive criticism of American culture, to consider the extent to which the secondary school curriculum meets the needs of a changing civilization, and to consider effective means of curriculum construction. (A student may not receive credit for both Integration 504A and Integration 504C.)
8:30-9:20 A. M.   Credit: 2 semester-hours   Room 27

Integration S508—Supervision of Instruction
in Secondary Schools   **Mr. Morehead**
This course emphasizes the more practical phases of supervision which are met most frequently by those engaged in it. Among the topics are: the set-up for adequate supervision, supervision as encouraging and guiding the growth of teachers and the improvement of educational procedures, the supervisory functions of teachers' meetings, discussion groups, general and professional reading, the writing of articles, co-operative curriculum modification, utilization of community resources, and teacher intervisitation.
8:30-9:20 A. M.   Credit: 2 semester-hours   Room B

23

Integration S517—Administration of the Elementary School   Dr. Phipps
This course analyzes and evaluates the administrative duties and relationships of
the elementary school principal. Particular consideration is given to: building
management, effective use of the school plant, sanitation, health service, the
library, personnel management, the administration of the curriculum, community
relationships, and publicity.
8:30-9:20 A. M.   Credit: 2 semester-hours   Room 28

Integration S518—Supervision of Instruction
in the Elementary School   Dr. Phipps
This course has been planned for those engaged in the supervision of the elementary school and for those who are preparing for such responsibilities. Principles of classroom supervision are developed and applied to learning situations.
Among the more important topics that receive attention are: the nature and
function of supervision, the organization necessary for effective supervision, the
nature and significance of the teacher's purposes, the methods and techniques
of group and individual supervision, the techniques of observation, and the supervisory conference.
9:30-10:20 A. M.   Credit: 2 semester-hours   Room 28

Integration S520—Principles of Mental Hygiene   Dr. Ingebritsen
This course is designed to be a general survey of the principles and practices of
mental health with special reference to the mental health of teacher and pupil.
It involves a thorough grounding in fundamental principles of mental hygiene
with much practical consideration of the mental-health values of instructional
programs and procedures. Discussion centers in practical efforts to develop
wholesome personalities in our schools.
11:30 A. M.-12:20 P. M.   Credit: 2 semester-hours   Room 30

Integration S536—Educational Guidance   Mr. E. C. Davis
This course is concerned with the facilities available for education after high-
school graduation, the problem of further training for pupils leaving school
before completing high school, and the academic problems of students while in
school. A brief survey of colleges and college-admission procedures is made.
8:30-9:20 A. M.   Credit: 2 semester-hours   Room 5

Integration S538—Group Guidance and Counseling Activities   Mr. Darling
This course is concerned with the various techniques for helping individual pupils
and for using group activities including role-playing as a guidance technique.
The group activities considered include those of home rooms, activity periods,
occupation courses, student field trips, placement follow-ups, college nights, and
career days.
9:30-10:20 A. M.   Credit: 2 semester-hours   Room 30

Integration S548—Curriculum Construction
in the Elementary School   Dr. Phipps
This course offers an opportunity to review State and city elementary curricula;
to discuss the principles of curriculum construction; to collect new teaching
materials for various subjects; and to evaluate, organize, and grade these materials. Teaching procedures in the use of materials are discussed and evaluated
in terms of pupil needs, the objectives set up, and the results obtained. This
course offers an opportunity to make a special study of the materials and procedures to be used in the supervision of the language arts.
11:30 A. M.-12:20 P. M.   Credit: 2 semester-hours   Room 28

Integration S551—Principles and Techniques of Guidance   Mr. Darling
Topics included in this course cover: philosophy of guidance, history of the guidance movement, the need for guidance presented by children and adolescents. The methods of gathering useful data are studied, and school records, exploratory activities, tests, inventories, the case study approach, occupational information, and occupational data are treated as well as general methods of guidance with special stress on interviewing and counseling of students.
8:30-9:20 A. M.   Credit: 2 semester-hours   Room 30

Integration S553—Core-Curriculum and
**   Life Adjustment Programs in High Schools   Mr. Rice**
This course concerns two leading educational developments of the last decade after a discussion of their philosophy and historical antecedents. The most significant school programs already adopted to put these developments into practice are presented in detail.
9:30-10:20 A. M.   Credit: 2 semester-hours   Room 9

Integration S602—Seminar in Guidance   Mr. E. C. Davis
The general objective of this course is to acquaint the student with school guidance problems as they relate to industry. The objective is obtained through group discussions growing out of individual research and group field trips to personnel departments of large and small industries, offices of labor unions, a job placement agency, a large group industrial insurance firm, and State employment offices. Each student makes a job analysis in some one occupation. From these visits and discussions a guidance program is evolved. Prerequisite: Integration 551 or permission of the instructor.
10:30 A. M.-12:20 P. M.   Credit: 4 semester-hours   Room 5

Scholarships Available

Encyclopedia Brittanica Films, Inc. is offering a scholarship in each of two courses this summer: one in Integration S408 and one in Integration S409. These courses are described on page 22. Further information may be obtained from Miss Emma Fantone at the College.

ELEMENTARY EDUCATION

These courses in Elementary Education are open to the following only:
(1) Those who already hold a degree from Montclair with a Certificate in Secondary Education, and
(2) Those who are now matriculated at Montclair for a degree and the Certificate in Secondary Education.

The courses starred (*) do not carry graduate credit. Only 6 semester-hours credit in Elementary Education may apply on the Master of Arts Degree. These courses are offered to assist Montclair students to obtain the State of New Jersey Certificate for Elementary School Teachers, for which 24 semester-hours credit is necessary.

Integration S472—The Elementary School Curriculum   **Mrs. Fox**
This course acquaints the college student with the subject matter of the elementary school curriculum for grades 3-6, inclusive. In addition, the following are studied: (1) correlation among subjects, (2) the appraisal and use of textbooks, (3) the use of visual aids, (4) the methods adapted to each subject, and (5) use of course of study materials.
10:30-11:20 A. M.   Credit: 2 semester-hours   Room 29

Integration S473—The Elementary School Language Arts   **Mrs. Fox**
This course gives an overview of modern practices that are used in teaching reading, creative writing, speaking, spelling, and handwriting in the elementary grades. Students are helped to recognize and to make provision for readiness for learning in these areas, to learn or devise various techniques that will meet the needs of different children and situations, and to evaluate, select, and create suitable materials to be used at various maturity levels. Special emphasis is placed on the functional use of the language arts in the total curriculum and life of the elementary school child.
11:30 A. M.-12:20 P. M.   Credit: 2 semester-hours   Room 29

* Integration S474—Elementary School Arts and Crafts   **Miss Osgood**
This course provides a wide range of creative manipulative experience with the materials, tools, and techniques of art work in the elementary school and an insight into significant art work of children of various age levels. Work is done in crayon, paint, chalk, clay, wood, papier-mache, finger paints, and other easily accessible materials. The work of the course includes simple weaving, block prints, murals, and the making of puppets. Attention throughout is directed toward an insight into the significance of art work and of manipulative experience as a medium of expression and a means of growth for the child.
9:30-10:20 A. M.   Credit: 2 semester-hours   Campus Studio Workshop

* Integration S475A—Fundamentals of Elementary School Music   **Mr. Craf**
The elements of music, including notation, the formation of scales and various modes, key and clef signatures, Italian musical terms, abbreviations, rhythm and intervals are included in this course. The student should acquire the ability to write a simple melody from dictation and to read at sight any part in a simple three-part selection in a musician-like manner. Ability to carry a tune is necessary for success in this course.
8:30-9:20 A. M.   Credit: 2 semester-hours   Room 5, CHS

*** Integration S476—Elementary School Health
and Physical Education**   **Mr. DeRosa**

The purpose of this course is to induct the prospective elementary classroom teacher into the field of health and physical education. Such phases as state courses of study, selection and organization of materials, grading, class organization, and others are discussed. To give the student a more functional approach, the programs of surrounding communities are studied.

10:30-11:20 A. M.   Credit: 2 semester-hours   Room 13, CHS

Integration S477—Elementary School Mathematics   **Mr. Kays**

This course includes a study of the development of the number concept in young children, the problem of number readiness, and an analysis of the various number skills. Consideration is given to the development of methods of presenting the units of elementary mathematics to children. Emphasis is placed on the meaningful use of the fundamental operations with integers, fractions, decimals, and problem solving. Experience is given to students in effective methods of lesson planning, testing, and diagnostic and remedial work.

8:30-9:20 A. M.   Credit: 2 semester-hours   Room 3, Annex No. 1

Integration S478—Elementary School Science   **Professor Glenn**

This course is based upon the assumption that science teaching in the elementary school should include scientific inquiry at the child's level as well as scientific information. Specific methods and materials are developed to meet these purposes. Emphasis is placed upon using the school community, learning through activity, and integrating science with other subject-matter areas.

9:30-10:20 A. M.   Credit: 2 semester-hours   Room 9, Annex No. 3

Integration S479—Elementary School Social Studies   **Dr. Moffatt**

This course is designed to familiarize the student with the materials and methods for teaching man's relation to his environment and other human beings in the elementary grades. The integration of the various phases of social living with other subjects, grade placement of subject-matter, the source and use of visual aids, and student projects are all stressed.

9:30-10:20 A. M.   . Credit: 2 semester-hours   Room 21

In addition to the above courses, **Geography S418, Regional Geography of North America**, applies on the Limited Elementary Certificate. For description and other data regarding this course, see page 21 under the heading "Geography."

Mathematics

Mathematics S300—Social and Commercial Uses of Mathematics   **Mr. Kays**

Some of the topics treated are: review of fundamental operations, approximate computation, use of slide rule and computing devices, graphs and scale drawing, percentage, simple and compound interest, consumer credit and installment buying, savings and investment, mortgages, taxation, insurance, cost of housing, and budgeting. Commercial, industrial, and consumer applications are stressed.

10:30-11:20 A. M.   Credit: 2 semester-hours   Room 3, Annex No. 1

Mathematics S400—Educational Statistics   **Mr. Clifford**

The aim of this course is to prepare the student (1) to comprehend and criticize articles of statistical nature in current educational literature; (2) to apply statistical methods in testing and rating pupils; (3) to carry on the simpler types of educational research. By analysis of real data from the secondary field, the student becomes familiar with the measures of central tendency and variability, short methods of computation, graphic representation of material, the propertie: of the normal curve, and linear correlation. Inasmuch as statistical methods in education are almost identical with those employed in the natural, physical, and social sciences, there is natural integration with these fields.

9:30-10:20 A. M.   Credit: 2 semester-hours   Room 2, Annex No. :

Mathematics S405—The History of Mathematics   Dr. D. R. Davi
A cultural background in the field of elementary mathematics is furnished by thi: course. Emphasis is placed on the history of the development of the number systems of elementary mathematics, computational devices, mathematica symbolism, space concepts, and simple logical processes. Other topics treated are: methods of problem solving, historical references in teaching, mathematica recreations, and the biographies of outstanding mathematicians.

11:30 A. M.-12:20 P. M.   Credit: 2 semester-hours   Room 1, Annex No. .

Mathematics S410—Mathematics of Finance   Mr. Clifforc
This course introduces the student to the elementary theory of simple and com pound interest and leads to the solution of practical problems in annuities, sink ing funds, amortization, depreciation, stocks and bonds, installment buying, and building and loan associations. It also discusses the mathematics of life insur ance; the theory and calculation of mortality tables; various types of life an nuities and insurance policies and reserves. This course is designed to give a helpful background to the mathematics teacher as well as to be an aid to the student of economics and insurance.

11:30 A. M.-12:20 P. M.   Credit: 2 semester-hours   Room 2, Annex No. :

Integration S477—Elementary School Mathematics   Mr. Kay:
See description and other data under the heading "Elementary Education."

**Mathematics S505—Consumer Mathematics. A Background
for Teaching in the Junior High School   Mr. Clifforc**
This course aims to survey the field of consumer problems, to display mathe matics as a powerful tool in analyzing these problems, and to consider th placement and methods of teaching this material in the intermediate grades an in the junior high school. Some of the topics included are: the cost of raisin children; the money value of a man; the cost of owning or renting a home; in surance; pensions and social security; stocks, bonds, and the financial page the quality and cost of consumer goods; business cycles, and indices of busines activity.

10:30-11:20 A. M.   Credit: 2 semester-hours   Room 2, Annex No.

**Mathematics S510C—Mathematics in Its Relation to Other Fields
of Knowledge: Geography, Astronomy and Navigation   Mr. Kay**
An opportunity is here offered for mathematics teachers to become acquainte with the mathematics of mapping, astronomy, and navigation closely related the algebra, solid geometry, and trigonometry taught in high school. A study spherical geometry and trigonometry leads to topics in mathematical astronom and geography, and to navigation. The discussion includes such topics a latitude and longitude; time and the calendar; map projections; the making star maps; sizes and distances of the sun, moon, planets, and stars; weighing t earth and moon; and relativity.

9:30-10:20 A. M.   Credit: 2 semester-hours   Room 3, Annex No.

28

Mathematics S511A—Foundations of Geometry   **Dr. D. R. Davis**

A careful study is made of the fundamental postulates and basic principles underlying Euclidean synthetic and projective geometrics. Past and present trends in this field and the resulting modifications are considered in connection with the historical background of each. Finally, the development of the subject is briefly traced through certain fundamental groups of associated theorems and their generalizations.

8:30-9:20 A. M.   Credit: 2 semester-hours   Room 1, Annex No. 1

Science

Biology S402—Mammalian Anatomy and Histology   **Dr. Hadley**

A study is made of the gross structure of a typical mammal and of the structural peculiarities of its various tissues. This course prepares the student for the study of human physiology. Prerequisites: Biology 201 and 202, Zoology.

Lectures: 9:30-10:20 A. M.
Laboratories: Tues. and Thurs. P. M.

          Credit: 4 semester-hours   Room 1, Annex No. 3

Biology S501—The Teaching of Biology in Secondary Schools   **Dr. Hadley**

This is a seminar and research course designed to give opportunity for study of the best methods and practices being used in the teaching of secondary school biology. Major topics of discussion are: aims of secondary school biology, course content, functions of textbooks, testing, laboratory exercises and demonstrations, and the collection and use of suitable and available laboratory materials. A study is made of recent research studies in the field of biology teaching. Prerequisite: 18 semester-hours of work in biology.

8-9:20 A. M.   Credit: 3 semester-hours   Room 1, Annex No. 3

Chemistry S412—Physical Chemistry II   **Dr. McLachlan**

This course deals with electrical conductance, electrolytic equilibrium, electromotive force, electrolysis, polarization, chemical kinetics, photochemical reactions, atomic structure, molecular structure, and radioactivity. Prerequisites: General college chemistry, analytical chemistry, and general college physics.

Lectures: 10:30-11:20 A. M.
Laboratories: Mon. and Wed. P. M.   Credit: 4 semester-hours   Room 22

Chemistry S413—Atomic Structure and Atomic Energy   **Dr. McLachlan**

This is a lecture course designed to familiarize the student with a modern conception of the structure of matter and to acquaint him with some significant aspects of atomic energy. Some of the topics studied include the following: discoveries leading to knowledge of the structure of the atom; isotopes; nuclear fission; nuclear reactions; chemical versus atomic explosions; the chain-reacting pile; production of plutonium; detection and measurement of nuclear radiation and incendiary effects of atomic explosions; atomic energy for peace-time uses; radio-active isotopes in agricultural, biological, and chemical research; and availability of materials for atomic energy. Prerequisites: General college chemistry and general college physics, or special permission of the instructor.

9:30-10:20 A. M.   Credit: 2 semester-hours   Room 22

Integration S478—Elementary School Science   **Professor Glenn**

For description and other data, see listing under "Elementary Education."

Physics S406—Astronomy   **Professor Glenn**
The course consists of a study of the fundamental principles of the science of
astronomy. Such topics as the following are considered: motions of the earth;
time; the moon; law of gravitation; the planets; comets; meteors; the sun, evolution of the solar system; the constellations; distances and motions of the stars;
spectrum analysis; and telescopic observations. Prerequisites: General college
physics and college chemistry.
Lectures: 11:30 A. M.-12:20 P. M.

Trips to the Planetarium in Philadelphia and to the Planetarium in New York at
the mutual convenience of the class members and the instructor.

Credit: 4 semester-hours   Room 9, Annex No. 3

Social Studies

Social Studies S419—American Political Biography   **Dr. Moffatt**
This is the study of the life and influence of the leading figures in American
political and social history. It is the aim here to show the relation of each of
these charatcers to the times in which he lived and to point out how he influenced the trend of American life. The study includes such leaders as Washington, Jefferson, Hamilton, Webster, Lincoln, Cleveland, Theodore Roosevelt,
and Wilson.
11:30 A. M.-12:20 P. M.   Credit: 2 semester-hours   Room 21

Social Studies S429—Present-Day Social Problems   **Dr. Clayton**
Beginning with a survey of levels of living in the United States and their relation
to the distribution of wealth and income, this course proceeds with a study of
poverty and crime, their sources, treatment, and prevention. Among the topics
discussed are: housing, wages, unemployment, physical illness, accidents, old
age, physical and mental defectiveness, the nature and extent of crime, police and
prison systems, the criminal courts, and methods of punishment and reformation.
8:30-9:20 A. M.   Credit: 2 semester-hours   Room 3, Annex No. 2

Social Studies S442—The Far East   **Dr. Wittmer**
A study is made of the economic, social, and cultural situation of the Far East,
with particular emphasis on the historical background of China and Japan, and
on our relations with the Philippines. Oriental folkways, religion, education,
population shifts, and strategic questions are discussed. This course provides an
approach to the problems the United States must face in the Far East.
8:30-9:20 A. M.   Credit: 2 semester-hours   Room 12, CHS

Social Studies S450—Modern Economic Problems   **Dr. Rellahan**
After a brief recapitulation of the material contained in Social Studies 200A
Contemporary Economic Life, the class proceeds to make a detailed study of our
broader economic problems and of the public policy relating to them. (Students
who have had credit for Social Studies 450B should not enroll in this course.)
10:30-11:20 A. M.   Credit: 2 semester-hours   Room 20

30

Social Studies S451—The Middle East   Dr. Wittmer
This course is a survey of Indian and Moslem civilizations. It shows that economic and political changes alone do not suffice to adjust peoples of the Middle East to twentieth century civilization, and that many cultural traditions must vanish while some forgotten features of the past are to be revived. Post-war planning for the region from the Near East through Persia, India, Burma, Thailand, and Malaya to the Netherland East Indies is discussed.
9:30-10:20 A. M.   Credit: 2 semester-hours   Room 12, CHS

Social Studies S460—Central Eastern Region   Mr. Bye
See description and other data on page 11, under the heading "Bureau of Field Studies."

Integration S479—Elementary School Social Studies   Dr. Moffatt
See description and other data on page 27, under the heading "Elementary Education."

Social Studies S490—United Nations Institute   Mrs. Fradkin
See description and other data on page 13, under the heading "Montclair State Teachers College Workshops."

Social Studies S491—Workshop in Citizenship Education   Dr. Clayton
See description and other data on page 13, under the heading "Montclair State Teachers College Workshops."

Social Studies S497—Chinese Philosophy   Dr. Wu-Chi Liu
See description and other data on page 12, under the heading "China Institute of New Jersey."

Social Studies S499—China Workshop   Dr. Chih Meng
See description and other data on page 13, under the heading "China Institute of New Jersey."

Social Studies S518—Recent Trends in American History
    1918 to the Present   Dr. Moffatt
Without attempting to reach final conclusions, this course analyzes the major problems which have influenced American life since the First World War. The new position of the Nation in world affairs, the modifications of the old economic order, the progress of social and political change are all surveyed. While the treatment is historical, it is intended to present materials which are serviceable in teaching the Problems of American Democracy.
10:30-11:20 A. M.   Credit: 2 semester-hours   Room 21

Social Studies S523—Economics of the Business Cycle   Dr. Rellahan
The purpose of this course is to consider the nature of business cycles and their impact on the national economy, to survey business cycle theories, and to analyze the significant proposed methods of control for the purpose of developing a desirable public program conducive to economic stability.
11:30 A. M.-12:20 P. M.   Credit: 2 semester-hours   Room 20

Announcement of a new Social Studies course appears on the next page.

31

NEW BACKGROUND COURSES FOR EDUCATIONAL TRAVEL

For those who have traveled in the United States, for those who hope to travel and for those who cannot travel but wish they could, a new course is being offered in the Summer School, Social Studies S492A, Studies in American Life—Eastern United States. This course will be followed later, probably in the spring of 1952, by Social Studies S492B, Western United States. Together the two courses will provide an integrated understanding of the United States as a cultural, historic, geographic, economic, social, and political unit and, at the same time, an appreciation of the regional differences which characterize American unity in diversity, but either course may be taken without the other. In both courses, the geography, the history, the literature, the art, the music, the architecture, the people, the manners and customs, the flora and fauna, the economic, social, and political problems, and the significant personalities of the regions studied are discussed and illustrated with slides, films, and other audio-visual materials. These two courses will be closely correlated with the Field Study Courses given every summer by the College but may be taken independently. They will provide a rich background for teachers in elementary and high schools as well as a foundation for intelligent travel.

Social Studies S492A—Studies in American Life—Eastern
United States   **Mr. Bye**
This is a descriptive survey of the region east of the Mississippi River including New England, the Central Eastern States, the South and the Middle West. It is an integrated and comprehensive study which cuts across subject matter lines. See above for further description.

9:30-10:20 A. M.   Credit: 2 semester-hours   Room 5

POST-SUMMER SESSION COURSE

August 13 through August 24, 1951

To Meet an Urgent Need, the following course is being offered by the State Teachers College at Montclair, with the assistance of the **New Jersey State Safety Council,** the **New Jersey Automobile Club,** the **American Automobile Association,** the **New Jersey State Police,** and the **New Jersey Department of Motor Vehicles.** Last year, over 32,300 persons lost their lives in traffic accidents. One-fourth of these were persons of high school and college age (15-24). The development of qualified young drivers can no longer be left to chance. The responsibility of our high schools in such a program is of vital importance. Training youth in skillful driving and in their responsibility toward other highway users, assumed when a person gets behind the wheel, will go far toward developing a new generation of skillful accident-free drivers. The lack of teachers for such training courses is all that prevents their being offered in most of the high schools of the country.

This Course Offers the Necessary Opportunity for men and women to prepare themselves to teach driver education in high schools. Enrollees completing the work of the course are presented with a certificate indicating the work done. Those who took this course at Montclair last summer were given enthusiastic co-operation by principals and school boards eager to establish driver education courses in their high schools, so that classes were opened in September taught by those who had received the Certificate of Completion in late August.

College Credit Required in New Jersey. In order to teach Driver Education in New Jersey, this course must be taken for credit.

Veterans may take this course under the G.I. Bill, if they have so arranged with the Veterans' Counselor of the College.

Living Expenses and Traveling Expenses must be paid by the student. Those desiring hotel accommodations should write to Mr. F. K. Schultze, Mgr., New Jersey Auto Club AAA, 156 Clinton Avenue, Newark 5, New Jersey. The College Residence Halls are closed at this time.

Textbooks and Other Text Materials will be furnished to each enrollee without charge.

Registration for this course will be accepted up to and including the opening day of the course. However, students should register early if possible, preferably on the regular registration days for the Summer Session. There is a limit to the number of registrations which may be accepted.

Description of the Course

Health Education S408—Driver Education and Training   **Mr. Coder**

Part I

This part consists of a minimum of 20 hours of class recitations and discussions, for which home reading and study have been assigned. The following topics are included: (1) history and development of driver education and training programs; (2) objectives of driver education; (3) local, State, and national traffic safety programs; (4) driver qualifications; (5) psychophysical testing; (6) curriculum content of school courses in driver education and training; (7) construction, operation, and maintenance of automobiles; (8) traffic laws and driver

33

licensing; (9) traffic engineering; (10) pedestrian education and pro
equipment for teaching driver education; (12) liability, costs, an
(13) planning driver education as a part of the daily program of the
(14) public relations; (15) records and reports; and (16) visual aid:
driver education.

Part II

This part consists of a minimum of 20 hours devoted to the fo
behind-the-wheel instruction; (2) demonstrations and student-teache
the car; and (3) road tests in traffic. Home reading and study are
preparation for these projects.
Full attendance at all sessions is required. Prerequisite: a licens
car in New Jersey.
9-12 and 1-4 daily   Credit: 2 semester-hours

Driver Education Course at Trenton

The above course will be offered from June 18 through June 29
Jersey State Teachers College at Trenton. Inquiries regarding
should be addressed to that college.

SUMMER SESSION

Bulletin of

MONTCLAIR
STATE TEACHERS COLLEGE

JUNE 30 to AUGUST 13

1952

SUMMER SESSION

Bulletin of

MONTCLAIR
STATE TEACHERS COLLEGE

1952
June 30th to August 13th

UPPER MONTCLAIR, NEW JERSEY

OFFICERS OF ADMINISTRATION

State Board of Education

GEORGE O. SMALLEY, *President* ....Bound Brool
ARTHUR E. ARMITAGE ....Collingswoo
JOHN S. GRAY ....Newtoi
MRS. EDWARD L. KATZENBACH ....Princetoi
JOHN C. KINAHAN ....Carney's Poin
A. HARRY MOORE ....Jersey Cit
AMOS J. PEASLEE ....Clarksbor
MRS. HERBERT REIM ....Maywoo
MRS. FREDERICK H. SANFORD ....Nutle
HUGH C. THUERK ....Morristowi

Commissioner of Education
JOHN H. BOSSHART

Assistant Commissioner for Higher Education
ROBERT H. MORRISON

New Jersey State Teachers College at Montclair

E. DeALTON PARTRIDGE, Ph.D. ....Presiden
CLYDE M. HUBER, Ph.D. ....Dean of Instructio
OTIS C. INGEBRITSEN, Ph.D. ....Chairman of the Graduate Committe
ELIZABETH S. FAVOR, A.M. ....Assistant in Graduate Personne
CLAUDE E. JACKSON, A.M. ....Director of Admissions, Records and Researc
MARY M. HOUSE, B.C.S. ....Acting Registra
EARL C. DAVIS, M.S. ....Director of Personnel and Guidanc
MARGARET A. SHERWIN, A.M. ....Dean of Wome
ULRICH J. NEUNER, A.M. ....Veterans' Counselc
BERNARD SIEGEL, B.S. ....Business Manage
HORACE J. SHEPPARD, A.M. ....Head of Business Education Departmei
EDWIN S. FULCOMER, Ed.D. ....Head of English Departmei
MOWAT G. FRASER, Ph.D. ....Head of Integration Departmei
VIRGIL S. MALLORY, Ph.D. ....Head of Mathematics Departmei
EDNA McEACHERN, Ph.D. ....Head of Music Departmei
RUFUS D. REED, Ph.D. ....Chairman of Science Departmei
ELWYN C. GAGE, Ph.D. ....Head of Social Studies Departmei
EDGAR C. BYE, A.M. ....Director, New Tools for Learning Burea
ANNE BANKS CRIDLEBAUGH, A.M. ....Librari
OTTO CORDES, P.E. ....Engineer in charge, Maintenan

FACULTY

SUMMER SESSION 1952

E. DeAlton Partridge, Ph.D. ....President
Clyde M. Huber, Ph.D. ....Dean of Instruction
Hugh Allen, Jr., M.S. ....Science
Keith W. Atkinson, Ph.D. ....Integration
Ruth Bristol, A.M. ....Elementary Education
Edgar C. Bye, A.M. ....Director, New Tools for Learning Bureau
Paul Louis Cambreleng, A.M. ....Guidance
Frank L. Clayton, Ph.D. ....Social Studies
Alden C. Coder, Ed.M. ....Health and Physical Education
John W. Craft, A.M. ....Music
Anne Banks Cridlebaugh, A.M. ....Librarian
David R. Davis, Ph.D. ....Acting Head, Department of Mathematics
Earl C. Davis, M.S. ....Personnel and Guidance
Jerome G. DeRosa, A.M. ....Health and Physical Education
George Forbes, A.M. ....Audio-Visual Aids
L. Howard Fox, A.M. ....Speech
Elvira K. Fradkin, A.M. ....United Nations Institute
Mowat G. Fraser, Ph.D. ....Head of Department of Integration
Paul E. Froehlich, A.M. ....Business Education
Edwin S. Fulcomer, Ed.D. ....Head of Department of English
Charles E. Hadley, Ph.D. ....Biology
W. Paul Hamilton, A.M. ....English
T. Rowland Humphreys, A.M. ....Mathematics
Ellen Kauffman, A.M. ....Speech
Walter E. Kops, A.M. ....Social Studies
Russell Krauss, Ph.D. ....English
Chih Meng, Ph.D. ....Director, China Institute
Harley P. Milstead, Ph.D. ....Geography
Maurice P. Moffatt, Ph.D. ....Social Studies
Allan Morehead, A.M. ....Integration
Mildred M. Osgood, A.M. ....Art
James P. Pettegrove, A.M. ....English
Josephine M. Phillips, A.M. ....Mathematics
Edward C. Rasp, Jr., A.M. ....Director, Television and Education Project
Rufus D. Reed, Ph.D. ....Chairman, Department of Science
John J. Rellahan, Ph.D. ....Acting Head, Department of Social Studies
Horace J. Sheppard, A.M. ....Head of Department of Business Education
Kenneth O. Smith, Ph.D. ....Physics
W. Scott Smith, Ph.D. ....Integration
D. Henryetta Sperle, Ph.D. ....Integration
Elizabeth T. VanDerveer, Ed.D. ....Business Education

GRADUATE COMMITTEE

Otis C. Ingebritsen, *Chairman*

Clyde M. Huber	Rufus D. Reed,
D. Henryetta Sperle	Elizabeth T. VanDerveer
W. Paul Hamilton	Elizabeth S. Favor, *Secretary*
David R. Davis	John J. Rellahan

AMPHITHEATER

**DORMI
LOUN**

Outdoor and inside centers for a wide variety of cool and comfortable activities make Montclair's summer program enjoyable and beneficial.

SUMMER SESSION OF THE
NEW JERSEY STATE TEACHERS COLLEGE
AT MONTCLAIR

Objectives and Academic Status

The College is a professional school which prepares teachers, supervisors, and principals of high schools, and administrators of public school systems. The degrees offered by this College are those of Bachelor of Arts and Master of Arts. Certificate courses are offered for those who now hold degrees from other colleges.

The New Jersey State Teachers College at Montclair is a fully accredited member of the American Association of Colleges of Teacher Education, the Middle States Association of Colleges and Secondary Schools, the Association of American Universities, and the American Association of University Women.

How to Reach the Campus

Trains of the Greenwood Lake Division, Erie R. R., stop at Montclair Heights, the College Staion. Trains of the Lackawanna R. R. connect at Montclair with the following bus lines: No. 64, running between Brick Church and the College; No. 60, running between Newark and the College; and No. 76, which runs between Orange and Paterson, passing the College en route. For those who come by car; the College is located about one mile north of the center of Upper Montclair.

Residence Halls for Men and Women

Edward Russ Hall and Chapin Hall are Montclair College's two well-appointed Residences. The charge for living on campus during the Summer Session is: $14.50 per week; which includes room, breakfast, and dinner. A la carte luncheons are served in the College cafeteria. For one student alone n a double room, an extra charge of $2.00 per week is made. The College proides and launders sheets, pillowcase, and bedpad. Towels, table lamps, blankets, locks, and similar items must be provided and cared for by the student. The oarding-hall fee must be paid on or before the first day of the Summer Session. 'o rebate is made for occassional absence or voluntary withdrawal during the ession. These prices are subject to change.   t

For reservations in a College Resident Hall, women address: Dean of Women, tate Teachers College, Upper Montclair, N. J. Men address the Dean of Men.

Schedule of the Summer Session

Registration will take place on Monday, June 30: Hours, 9-12 and 1-5. Classes 'ill begin on Tuesday morning, July 1, at 8 A. M. and will continue through ednesday, August 13. All classes meet daily, Monday to Friday, inclusive, at he hours indicated for each.

Matriculation for the Master of Arts Degree

Not more than 8 semester-hours of work taken prior to matriculation are llowed to apply on the Master of Arts degree.

Those who desire to become candidates for the degree must request an application form from the Chairman of the Graduate Committee and return it, roperly filled on and accompanied by an Official Transcript of all previous 'ork on college level. When such an applicant has been accepted by the College s a candidate for the degree, a definite statement is furnished to him, showing the equirements which he must fulfill to earn the degree. This sheet of requirements becomes the student's Work Program and should be brought by the student each time he comes to enroll for courses.

Auditors

Men and women who desire to take courses for cultural, vocational, or avocational purposes without college credits may register as auditors.

A student who desires to enroll in a course for which he already holds credit must register as an auditor in that course.

A student who desires to enroll in a course for which he has not completed the prerequisites must enroll as an auditor in that course.

Change of Status in a Course

If a student desires to change his status in a course from "credit" to "auditor" or from "auditor" to "credit," he must make formal application for such change not later than the middle of the course. Forms for this purpose may be procured from Miss Favor, in the Registrar's Office. Such changes cannot be made after the midpoint of the course is passed.

Students Matriculated at Montclair for A.M. Degree

The selection of courses must be in accordance with the student's Work Program, and his registration form will be signed by the Head of the Department in which the student is majoring or by a representative of that department present in the registration room.

Candidates for a degree must file with the Registrar an application for conferment of the degree before November 30 of the college year in which the work is to be completed. Application blanks for this purpose may be secured in the Registrar's Office. The burden of responsibility for the request rests with the candidate. This is of special significance to the teacher-in-service who may have distributed the work for the degree over several years.

Students Matriculated at Other Colleges

In previous summers, when the State Teachers College at Montclair offere courses to its own accelerated candidates for the Bachelor's degree, it wa possible to accept students from other colleges in freshman, sophomore, an junior year courses, as well as in courses of the senior year. Beginning in th summer of 1950, however, the College returned to its pre-war custom of offerin courses in its Summer Session primarily to teachers-in-service. Since suc teachers already hold the Bachelor's degree, with few exceptions, the course shown in this Bulletin are for the most part only Graduate and Senior-Graduat courses.

A student who is planning to attend Montclair this summer should take thi Bulletin to a conference with the Dean of his own college to arrange a progra of work. For the Dean's information: the numbering of courses at Montcla follows this order: 100-399, inclusive, are undergraduate courses: 400-499; incl sive, are senior-college and graduate courses; 500 and above are graduate course

At the time of registration, the student should go to the table of the Depar ment in which the courses are listed that he plans to take. The registratio form must be signed by the Representative of the Department at that table. Th College reserves the right to decide whether the student has fulfilled necessar prerequisites. He should bring with him, however, a letter from his own colleg If the student is seeking certification to teach in New Jersey, he must confer wit Dr. Fraser, Head of the Department of Integration. Please note paragrap under the Heading: "Certificates."

6

Certificates

The State Teachers College at Montclair offers work toward the following New Jersey Certificates: Secondary Teaching Certificate; Secondary School Principal's Certificate; Elementary School Principal's Certificate; Subject Supervisor's Certificate; General Supervisor's Certificate; Guidance Certificate; School Administrator's Certificate; Junior College Teacher's Certificate; and the Advanced Professional Certificate.

Those who matriculate at Montclair for a degree will receive information from Dr. Fraser, Head of the Integration Department, as to the requirements for each of these certificates. Students who have not matriculated at Montclair should write to Dr. E. C. Preston, Secretary of the State Board of Examiners, Department of Education, 175 West State Street, Trenton 8, N. J., for information as to the requirements. **For an evaluation of work already completed, address Dr. Preston.** An official transcript of such previous work should accompany the inquiry, with a statement as to the particular certificate desired.

The student should bring Dr. Preston's reply with him when conferring with Dr. Fraser as to his program of work.

Students who must have this information immediately should go to Trenton to confer personally with Dr. Preston or his assistant, Miss Smith.

Supervised Student Teaching

The opportunity to do supervised student teaching cannot be offered during the Summer Session. For fall teaching, students confer with Dr. Fraser at the College. Ask his secretary for an appointment.

Veterans

Veteran students taking work under the G. I. Bill for the first time at Montclair State Teacher College must see the Veterans' Counselor **at least two weeks prior to the registration day.** Veterans should be sure to obtain the Certificate of Eligibility from the Veterans' Administration before the start of the Summer Session. Failure to do so will mean that **the usual fees must be paid by the student at the time of registration.**

It will be necessary for Veterans who have completed the work for either the A.B. or A.M. degree at Montclair to secure and present to the Veterans' Counselor the **Supplemental Certificate of Eligibility** before registering for further work at Montclair. Veterans transferring to Montclair who have previously been training under the G. I. Bill will be required to present a Supplemental Certificate of Eligibility at the time of registration.

Conferences with Advisers

Appointments with the Dean of Instruction, the Chairman of the Graduate Committee, a Department Head, or the Veterans' Counselor may be made by mail or telephone to their respective offices. This should be done at as early a date as possible to avoid delay at the time of registration.

In order to assist students who have been unable to go to Trenton for the information, a representative of the State Board of Examiners will be at the College on June 30, from 10 A. M. to 3 P. M., to see students who need advice on the selection of courses toward a New Jersey Certificate. (See paragraph under the heading: "Certificates.") The Assistant in Graduate Personnel will receive requests for appointments with this State Official.

Summer Session Credit Load

The maximum amount of credit which may be earned in the Summer Session is 8 semester-hours, but only 6 s. h. are recommended. There is no provision for a student to audit additional courses; consequently, the total of all courses taken during the Summer Session may not exceed 8 s. h. and students should not register for more.

Additional credits may be earned by attending one of the sessions at the State School of Conservation that precedes or follows the Summer Session. Attention is called also to the post-Summer Session course in Safety Education and to the Field Studies course in the Central Region.

Each Summer Session course is in session at least thirty hours and carries a designated amount of credit. **It is not possible to earn three s. h. credit in a two s. h. course.**

Registration Information

Registration takes place in the College Gymnasium, on Monday, June 30, from 9 A. M. to 12 noon, and from 1 to 5 P. M. Anyone unable to enroll during the hours shown must register during the regular office hours of the College in the Registrar's Office and pay the late Registration Service Charge. No Summer Session course may be taken for credit after Thursday, July 3. The summer office hours are from 8:30 A. M. to 3:30 P. M.

Matriculated students should bring their "Work Programs" when they come to enroll.

The College reserves the right to close any course for which the enrollment is insufficient. The class will meet at least once, however, before this decision is made. Students may then enter another course in place of the one discontinued, by going to the Registrar's Office to re-enroll and to receive the new Class Admission Card in exchange for the card of the discontinued course. Students who decide not to enroll in an alternate course must return to the Registrar's Office to have the Class Admission Card of the discontinued course stamped "Discontinued" before going to the Business Office for an adjustment of tuition fees.

If prerequisites are required, the student should make certain that he has fulfilled them or their equivalent before enrolling in the course. If no previous work on college level has been taken, the student should consult the Registrar before enrolling in any course, unless as an Auditor.

A student may not register for credit in any course for which he already holds credit except by permission of the Dean of Instruction.

The Registration form of every student must be signed by a Department Head or his Representative. The student should report to the table of the Department in which he is majoring; or, if not matriculated here for a degree at present, of the Department in which he is taking courses. Signs on the tables indicate the various Departments.

Withdrawal from a Course

Written notice to Miss Favor, Assistant in Graduate Personnel, must be given at once by the student. Students who neglect to follow this procedure receive a failing mark for the course or courses which they cease to attend. Miss Favor will notify the teachers of the courses from which the student is withdrawing, as well as the Business Office of the College. Refunds are computed from the date of the receipt of the letter of withdrawal. Inquiries regarding refunds should be addressed to the Business Manager.

Tuition Fees and Service Charges

Check or money-order should be made payable to New Jersey State Teachers College.

Registration service charge: $1.00 for the Summer Session.

Late registration service charge: $2.00. This is collected from all students who fail to enroll on June 30.

Tuition fees: to students who have not been professionally employed: $8.00 per semester-hour credit carried by the course; to students who are or have been professionally employed: $11.00 per credit. Non-Residents of New Jersey pay $13.00 per credit. **Courses taken by auditors for no credit cost the same.**

Laboratory service charge: $4.00 for each laboratory course.

Teachers who have supervised Montclair student-teachers and who have in their possession old Montclair credit slips may take them to the Office of the Integration Department, where new ones will be issued. The Business Office cannot return any unused portion of a credit slip, so it is necessary that the new type credit slip be obtained before presenting it in payment of tuition fees. Training Teachers may use the credit slips of any one of the six New Jersey State Teachers Colleges when taking courses at Montclair, but should bring only the new type slip in all cases.

Final Marks

Following are the final marks wrich may be received for a course: A-Excellent; B-Good; C-Fair; D-Poor; F-Failure; Inc.-Incomplete; Wd-Withdrew; N. C.-No Credit.

The mark of "D" when earned in summer, part-time, or extension courses of this College is not accepted for degree credit at Montclair.

The mark of "F" is given when earned and when the student has failed to notify the Assistant in Graduate Personnel promptly of his withdrawal from a course.

The mark of "N. C." is given only to auditors.

The mark of "Wd" is given only when prompt notice of withdrawal has been given and when the student's work to that time has been satisfactory to the teacher of the course.

The mark of "Inc." is seldom given. It may, however, be granted to a student whose work is incomplete at the end of the Session and who is eager to finish the work for a higher grade than he could receive otherwise. All responsibility regarding incomplete work rests with the student. He will be notified of a date after which, if the work remains incomplete, the final grade will be recorded without further notice.

Report Cards and Transcripts

An Official Transcript showing the credits earned is sent to the student personally ten days to two weeks following the close of the Session. A report card for each course taken is sent with the transcript. The transcript is sent without cost, but a service charge of $1.00 is made for a duplicate copy.

A student whose college requires that the transcript be mailed directly to the Dean or Registrar should call during the Summer Session at the Registrar's Office to address an envelope for this purpose.

Elementary Education Courses

Courses offered as a part of the curriculum for the graduate major in Educational Administration and Supervision should be carefully distinguished from those offered toward the endorsement in elementary education on the teacher's certificate. The courses in the Administration and Supervision of Elementary Education apply on the Elementary Principal's certificate, but not on the Elementary Teacher's certificate.

Although the New Jersey State Teachers College at Montclair is engaged primarily in preparing secondary school teachers, during the present shortage of teachers in the elementary schools it is deemed expedient to offer courses in the field of elementary education to those students who are eligible to enroll at this College in such courses.

Students eligible to enroll at Montclair in courses leading to certification in elementary education are:
  (1) those who already hold a degree from Montclair with a certificate in secondary education; and
  (2) those who are now matriculated at Montclair for such a degree.
Montclair cannot accept any other students in these courses.

The eligible students should consult the Registrar's Office for an evaluation of their previous work and a statement concerning the courses to be taken in order to receive the endorsement in elementary education on the secondary certificate already held or to be conferred.

Textbook Exhibit

In the Gymnasium of the Main Building, from July 7 through July 18, there will be an exhibit of high school and elementary school textbooks. While primarily for the benefit of the principals and teachers attending the Summer Session, the exhibit will be open to undergraduate students and to members of the general public who may be interested in seeing the latest textbooks.

Mrs. E. S. Fulcomer will be in charge of the Exhibit.

Location of Buildings on Campus

Main Building faces south; clock over doorway. If no other building is named, the room is in the Main Building.

College High School Building; to the northeast of Main

Annex No. 1: Federal Works Administration Building No. 1; at the northwest corner of Main.

Annex No. 2: Federal Works Administration Building No. 2; next to No. 1.

Annex No. 3: Federal Works Administration Building No. 3; directly east of Main.

Campus Studio Workshop; near the western end of the Parking Area.

Music Building: at the northeast corner of the College High School Building.

Recreation Building: at the extreme northern end of the campus.

BUREAU OF FIELD STUDIES

Social Studies S462—Continental United States   **Mr. By**

This Field Study course consists of sixty-two days of directed travel, including all of July and August, and provides an opportunity for gaining an integrated view of our country as a whole. The trip is made in a modern chartered motor coach with overnight stops at first-class hotels. The route covers about 12,500 miles and visits 26 states and 6 National Parks. Among the major points of interest are Gettysburg, Natural Bridge, Blue Ridge and blue grass region, Mammoth Cave, Lincoln shrines in Kentucky and Illinois, Dodge City, Pikes Peak, Denver, Rocky Mountain National Park, Taos and other Indian Reservations, Santa Fe, Petrified Forest, Painted Desert, Grand Canyon, Bryce and Zion National Parks, Hoover Dam, Los Angeles, Hollywood, San Diego, San Capistrano and other Missions; Tia Juana, Santa Barbara, Sequoia and Yosemite National Parks, Monterey, San Francisco, Sacramento, Lake Tahoe, Reno, Donner Pass, mammoth redwood groves, Crater Lake, Mt. Hood, Columbia River Valley, Portland, Seattle, Mt. Rainier, Grand Coulee Dam, Spokane, Butte, Yellowstone

10

National Park, Salt Lake City, pioneer trails of Wyoming, Black Hills, Chicago, Detroit, and Niagara Falls. All important geographic and historical features are studied under the instruction of members of the College faculty and local specialists. Write for descriptive folder, addressing the Bureau of Field Studies.

Credit. 10 semester-hours

While the above course is given as a part of the Summer Session offerings of the State Teachers College at Montclair, registration for it must be made in advance through the Bureau of Field Studies. Likewise, payment is made as requested by the Bureau. Interested students should address Mr. E. C. Bye, Bureau of Field Studies, New Jersey State Teachers College, Upper Montclair, New Jersey. This should be done at once, as the number of students in the course must be limited to a definite number. The price will be $595. This includes tuition, transportation, hotels, twenty meals, (other meals extra) tips, and admissions. Starts Saturday, June 28; ends Tuesday, August 26, 1952.

A student matriculated in one New Jersey State Teachers College may enroll for a field studies course conducted by another New Jersey College provided he presents written approval from the college where he is matriculated. The New Jersey Council for Field Studies will determine the number of semester-points credit for each field studies course given under its jurisdiction. The allocation of this credit for specific purposes for each student concerned shall be determined by the officials of each college. Students who enroll for a field study course shall register and pay tuition in the Teachers College which sponsors the course. Students may register for graduate or undergraduate credit provided graduate courses are offered by the college sponsoring the course. A limited number of students may enroll for No Credit provided they pay the regular tuition fees and service charges.

Trenton State Teachers College

College Field Studies, Geography S507—Geography of the Middlewest

This sixteen-day field trip by bus through the eastern states of the middle west includes visits to geographical and historical points in and near Pittsburgh, Cleveland, Cincinnati, Springfield, Milwaukee, Detroit, and Buffalo. Very few stops are made in route to and from this region so that most of the time can be spent studying the industries, agriculture, and culture of that very interesting section of our country. The trip from Milwaukee, Wisconsin, to Muskegon, Michigan, is made by boat across Lake Michigan. Two or three days are spent in several of the largest cities.

Credit: 4 semester-hours; graduate or undergraduate

June 20 through July 5, 1952. For additional information, write to the Director of the trip, Dr. Adelbert K. Botts, Professor of Geography, State Teachers College, Trenton, New Jersey.

Paterson State Teachers College

Geography 16.50—New England and French Canada   Dr. Shannon

August 7 through August 18, 1952

This field study course consists of 12 days of directed travel. The route covers approximately 1400 miles. It includes visits to key points of interest in the St. Lawrence Area of the Province of Quebec, and in the six New England States. Dr. Edith R. Shannon will conduct the trip. Cost: $160.00 includes tuition, transportation, hotels, certain admissions and twelve meals.

Credit: 3 semester-hours toward Geography or Social Science

For information and registration forms for this course write to Secretary of the Summer Session, State Teachers College, Paterson 22, New Jersey; P.O. Box 2259.

11

CHINA INSTITUTE

Workshops, Institutes and Field Studies provide real learning experiences.

TELEVISION WORKSHOP

MATHEMATICS LABORATORY

INSTITUTES AND WORKSHOPS

China Institute of New Jersey

Founded by a missionary who had spent twenty years in China and learned to know and love the Chinese people, China Institute of New Jersey was initiated in 1944. The purpose of the Institute then was to give the American people facts on which to build informed understanding of the Chinese. The presentation of those same facts is even more imperative today in order that Americans may understand the true character of the Chinese people and appreciate how fundamentally un-Chinese are the philosophy and behavior of the communist regime.

China Institute of New Jersey is a permanent year-round organization composed of former students of the China Workshop course. The policies and program of the Institute are determined by an elected executive committee, an advisory board of laymen, and representatives from the Faculty of Montclair Teachers College, in consultation with the Chinese Director.

Dr. Chih Meng, Director of the China Institute of America, whose purpose is to promote cultural and educational relations between China and the United States, is Chinese Director of China Institute of New Jersey. The College provides the facilities necessary for the courses sponsored by the Institute and grants credit for the satisfactory completion of such courses. These are given on the senior-graduate level, so that students may work either undergraduate or graduate credit.

While the primary and definite purpose of the Institute is to assist the teachers of New Jersey, men and women who desire to take these courses for cultural, vocational, or avocational purposes are welcome also. Students may enroll for college credit if eligible to do so, or simply as Auditors for no credit. The cost is the same in both cases. Those who enroll for credit are expected to complete such notebooks, papers, and projects as are assigned by the course instructors. The preliminary grading of these papers and projects is done by the Chinese teachers, while the final grading and coordinating is done by a representative of the regular Faculty of the College.

Those who wish to attend a single lecture will pay a fee of $2.00 at the door of the Auditorium in the College High School Building. Students who enroll for the entire course follow the instructions below.

Registration for one of the following courses must be made on forms provided by the College. Write to: Mrs. Willard Church, China Institute of New Jersey, State Teachers College, Upper Montclair, N. J., for these forms, and for any additional information you may require. Refer to the list below for the proper number and title of the course you expect to take. Note that the course Social Studies S499 is prerequisite to two of these courses and is recommended before taking any other course offered by the Institute. Please do not, therefore, enroll for credit in either English S459 or Social Studies S496B unless you already hold credit for Social Studies S499. Return the forms to Mrs. Church not later than Saturday, June 21, with check or money order made payable to New Jersey State Teachers College. A late service charge of $2.00 will be made for all registrations received after June 21. A receipt for fees and your Class Admission Card will be mailed to you following the arrival of your registration and check. The Class Admission Card should be presented to your class teacher on the opening day of the course.

Offerings for 1952: June 30—July 12, Inclusive

ART S414—History of Chinese Art   **Mr. Nelson Wu**

In this course, the developments and distinguishing characteristics of the major arts of China are traced by specialists and are surveyed from the point of view

13

of their historical developments. An historical survey of the development of Chinese art from the dawn of civilization to the present day is made which includes the role played by foreign influences, such as the spreading of Buddaism, and the Chinese influence on other parts of the world. There are twenty-four hours of lectures in the morning, and round-table discussion and library work in the afternoon. During the afternoon workshop period, the technique of Chinese painting is demonstrated. A student selecting a research paper or project in this course is required to write 5,000 words, as in all other courses in the Institute. If, however, the student prefers to paint a picture of his own creation in the Chinese manner, he is then required to write only 2,000 words. Although there is no prerequisite for this course, it is suggested that those who enroll for it should have some knowledge of art or have taken Social Studies S499—China Workshop.

9:30 A. M.-4 P. M.   Credit: 3 semester-hours   Room 12 CHS

English S459—A Survey of Great Chinese Literature   Dr. Wu-Chi-Liu

Some of the contributions which have gone into the making of Chinese literature, such as the **Book of Odes** of Confucius, the poems of Li Po and Tu Fu, the **Lute Song,** and the **Dream of the Red Chamber,** are considered in this course. Aside from a general survey of the great literature of China, special attention is given to English translations of the masterpieces of Chinese literature. There are twenty-four hours of lectures in the morning; after lunch each day, a period of forty-five minutes is devoted to informal talks, story-telling, singing of Chinese songs, and showing of motion pictures. During the two-hour workshop period that follows, individual students work on specific topics under the guidance of the instructor. **Prerequisite: Social Studies S499—China Workshop.**

9:30 A. M.-4 P. M.   Credit: 3 semester-hours   Room 3, CHS

Social Studies S496B—China: The Evolution of a Nation   Dr. William Hung

This course is an intensive study of the Chinese civilization, the forces underlying the development of the national character of the Chinese people, their contacts and conflicts with other peoples and cultures from historical times to the present. Because of its voluminous material, the course does not attempt to cover the whole span of Chinese history, but it is an integrated presentation of the maturing of the Chinese people as a nation. There are twenty-four hours of lectures in the morning, and round-table discussion and library work in the afternoon. **Prerequisite: Social Studies S499—China Workshop.**

9:30 A. M.-4 P. M.   Credit: 3 semester-hours   Room 4, CHS

Social Studies S499—China Workshop   Dr. Chih Meng

A number of authorities introduce first-year students to the rise, growth, and maturing of Chinese civilization, as well as to the fundamental problems of China today, including the conflict of ideologies. The course is given in twelve days. Each day; there are two hours of lectures in the morning; after lunch, a period of forty-five minutes is devoted to informal talks, including further discussion on Chinese music, philosophy, Chinese school days, festivals, and calligraphy. Some time is given also to the singing of Chinese songs and the showing of motion pictures. During the two-hour workshop period, the students prepare their projects, teaching units, and background material, under the direction of faculty members.

MONTCLAIR STATE TEACHERS COLLEGE WORKSHOPS
July 1—August 13, 1952

Integration S407—Television in Education Workshop:
Programming and Production   **Mr. Rasp**

This is a laboratory course designed to develop the techniques, methods, standards, procedures, and criteria pertaining to the special place of television in education. Through the utilization of studio equipment together with the resources of all the academic departments of the College, student potentialities, campus life, and the community, students receive experience in planning, developing, and producing television programs of educational value. Actual training is given in the use of standard television equipment on campus, and field trips are made to local television laboratories and studios. **Registration in this course is limited to fifteen students.**

8:00-9:50 A. M., M. W. F. and 8:00-8:50 Tu. & Th.

Credit: 2 semester-hours   Room A

Inasmuch as registration in Integration S407 will be limited to fifteen, students interested in that course are urged to write immediately to: Mr. Edward C. Rasp, Jr., care of this College, for an application for admission to the course.

Workshop in Citizenship Education

In the summer of 1951, the Montclair State Teachers College offered for the first time a workshop course in citizenship education. The success of this undertaking was such that a similar workshop was offered in the spring semester of 1952 through the Part-Time and Extension Division. For the summer of 1952, the Workshop in Citizenship Education will be given in two parts, so that it may include students who are participating for the first time and those who have been involved in either of the previous workshops.

Social Studies S491A—Workshop in Citizenship Education, Part I   Dr. Clayton

The purpose of this workshop is to present a study of what has been done in some of the many projects in citizenship education throughout the country. Special emphasis is placed on the plans and materials developed by the Citizenship Education Project now being conducted by Teachers College, Columbia University, and financed by the Carnegie Corporation. Montclair has been one of the eight teachers colleges cooperating in this project, and the College High School is now a co-operating school. Consultants are invited in as needed. Attention is given to programs and practices already in use in the schools, and advantage is taken of the state-wide project of this past year in collecting from the schools experience in education for character and citizenship. New means for citizenship education are sought, and methods of evaluation are reviewed. Experience in the group processes essential to democratic action is provided. It is hoped especially to include in the workshop those who have been or may be serving as training teachers for Montclair student teachers, especially in the fields of social studies and English. Principals and administrators who want to join with others in learning how to make more effective the citizenship education in the schools with which they are connected are invited to participate. Each participant in the workshop works on actual plans for carrying out such education in the school and the classroom.

10:30-11:20 A. M.   Credit: 2 semester-hours   Room 3, Annex No. 2

Social Studies S491B—Workshop in Citizenship Education, Part II   Dr. Clayton

Membership in this workshop course is limited to those who have completed Social Studies 491A, and participants in this advanced workshop meet and work

15

with the members of the Social Studies 491A workshop. On the basis of previous experience, each member of the Social Studies S491B group is expected to
work out several laboratory practices or similar projects for use in the classroom or the school.
10:30-11:20 A. M.   Credit: 2 semester-hours   Room 3, Annex No. ?

UNITED NATIONS INSTITUTE
July 14—July 25, 1952

Social Studies S490A—United Nations Institute   Mrs. Fradkin and Mr. Kop
This course covers four and one-half hours per day for ten consecutive day:
excluding Saturday and Sunday. It consists of basic lectures on factual back
grounds by the instructor, supplementary lectures by visiting lecturers from the
United Nations and other organizations, discussions, workshop and library
projects, demonstrations of the use of audio-visual materials, and field trips to
the United Nations. Included among the subjects studied are the national State
system, war and peace, world organizations (past, present, and proposed), the
national armaments problem, international law, the international police proposal
pacific methods of settling international disputes, and the outlook for inter
national co-operation.
9:30 A. M.-3:00 P. M.   Credit: 3 semester-hours   Auditorium, CHS

**Social Studies S490B—The United Nations and
American Foreign Policy   Mrs. Fradkin and Mr. Kop**
The purpose of this course is to help provide an understanding of the United
Nations in its operation as a basis for American foreign policy. In that the
Charter of the United Nations forms the backbone of American cultural, eco
nomic, and military cooperation with other nations, its interpretation and the
application of our aid to needy people open a wide area of disagreement within
the nation. Following the principle that American foreign policy should res
upon an intelligent understanding on the part of the electorate and working
within the framework of the policy of the State Board of Education with re
gard to controversial issues, the United Nations Institute deals with the strong
as well as the weak aspects of this newly created world organization. This
institute serves the needs of teachers of all grades, students of foreign policy
the public at large, as well as visitors from other lands who are here to stud
the ways of American democracy. It is available to students who have com
pleted the requirements for **Social Studies S490A, United Nations Institute,** o
the equivalent.
9:30 A. M.-3:00 P. M.   Credit: 3 semester-hours   Auditorium,.CH

As it is desired that all registrations for the United Nations Institute be mad
in advance in order to obviate the use of time on the opening day, intereste
students should write immediately to Mr. Walter E. Kops, care of the Colleg
for a set of the registration materials. The student should indicate careful
whether he is enrolling for the A or the B course and enclose a check to cov
the tuition fees and registration service charge.

WORKSHOPS AT THE TRENTON STATE TEACHERS COLLEG

**Science S502—Conservation Education Workshop   ·
Dr. Victor L. Crowell, Professor of Scien**
July 7—July 25, 1952
The session consists of field trips, illustrated lectures by cooperating specialis

motion pictures and discussion periods. $25.00 scholarships are available. A descriptive bulletin will be mailed upon request.

Credit: 4 semester-hours, graduate or undergraduate

Education S513—Workshop in Early Childhood Education
Dr. Irene S. Brauer, Associate Professor of Education

July 28—August 8, 1952

This course includes the study of the development of children between the ages of five and ten. On the basis of their characteristics and needs, a desirable program, including all areas of development, receives consideration. Problems of the students concerning the tool subjects as well as the arts are included in the course.

Credit: 3 semester-hours, graduate or undergraduate

Students interested in these courses should write directly to the college concerned for further information.

NEW JERSEY STATE SCHOOL OF CONSERVATION
Branchville, New Jersey

COURSES IN CONSERVATION, FIELD SCIENCES, CAMPING EDUCATION, AND WATER FRONT SAFETY

Spring and Summer, 1952

Application for admission to any of the courses at the N. J. State School of Conservation should be made in advance. Write to the N. J. State School of Conservation, State Teachers College, Upper Montclair, N. J., for this preliminary application form. Final registration, with payment of fees, will be made at the School itself. At that time, the student should indicate to which of the New Jersey State Teachers Colleges his record should be mailed at the end of the summer.

The following sessions, June 15 to September 2, offer opportunities for teachers-in-service, senior students, and graduate students to pursue special courses during short periods of the Summer. It is possible to earn 12 semester-credits for the five sessions, or a minimum of two semester-credits for a single session. Credits for these courses may be applied for graduate or undergradute credit at the New Jersey State Teachers Colleges, subject to approval in advance by the institution. Credit may be transferred to other institutions where such transfer is permitted toward an undergraduate or an advanced degree.

The State Board of Examiners has issued the following directive:

"Credit for the completion of one or more of the following courses when submitted on an official transcript of an accredited college will be accepted toward meeting requirements for certification to teach in the public schools of New Jersey in accord with the Eighteenth Edition of the Rules Concerning Teachers' Certificates. Each course is accepted as an elective in the field in which classified. In addition, the following substitutions for courses specifically required for certification are approved:
1. Art 415, **School Arts and Crafts with Native Materials**, may be substituted for the required course, elementary school art.
2. Integration 480, **Field Science for Elementary Teachers**, may be substituted for the required course, elementary school science." *

---

* Approved 12/12/51, Everett C. Preston, Secretary, State Board of Examiners for Teachers.

June 15-24

Integration 440—Camping Education

The purpose of this course is to familiarize the students with camping and outdoor education as educational methods utilized by the schools of America. The aims and methods of camping are studied, and consideration is given to the communities that have active camping and outdoor education programs in operation.

Credit: 2 semester-hours

Integration 441—Conservation Education

The social, economic, and scientific implications of conservation are considered in this course. Discussion periods are interspersed with field trips to forest areas and demonstrations of conservation problems.

Credit: 2 semester-hours

Physical Education 410—Water Safety and First Aid

This course includes intensive instruction in swimming, diving, water sports, boating, canoeing, water safety, and first aid. Students can qualify for Red Cross certificates during this course.

Credit: 2 semester-hours

June 29—July 19

Integration 443—Practicum in Camping Education and Administration

This course is designed to provide practical experience in the identification and solution of problems arising in camp administration. Among the phases considered are discussion of current practices at both private and institutional camps, interpretation of educational philosophies and objectives as they relate to camping, finances, personnel selection, waterfront organization, food purchasing, staff supervision, sanitation, health and safety, camp management, records and reports, insurance, kitchen management, maintenance, and other phases of camp administration. Practical application is provided through the techniques used in the children's demonstration camp.

Prerequisite: Integration 440, **Camping Education,** or the equivalent.

Credit: 3 semester-hours

Integration 444—Practicum in Conservation Education

This course is designed to provide teachers and supervisors with a background of experience and knowledge which will enable them to organize and to conduct conservation education programs in their own communities. Using an extensive library of conservation education material, students formulate teaching units, lists of teaching aids, and projects suitable for use in their own communities. Participation in conservation projects with the children in the demonstration camp furnishes a practical background for research and discussion.

Prerequisite: Integration 441. **Conservation Education,** or Science 412,Field **Studies in Science: Biological,** or Science 413, **Field Studies in Science: Physical** or the equivalent.

Credit: 3 semester-hours

July 20—August 9

Integration 443—Practicum in Camping Education and Administration

Credit: 3 semester-hours

(See description as listed above.)

18

Integration 444—Practicum in Conservation Education
Credit: 3 semester-hours

(See description as listed above.)

August 13-23

Art 415—School Arts and Crafts with Native Materials
In this course the student gains an appreciation and understanding of art expression growing out of the immediate environment as he learns to work creatively with native materials. Useful and decorative articles are made from wood, fruit pits, seeds, grasses, reeds, and native clay. The use of natural dyes for coloring is demonstrated. The construction of teaching aids using simple, native matérials is also shown. Flower and plant arrangements for room and table decoration in keeping with good conservation practices are presented.

Credit: 2 semester-hours

Integration 480—Field Science for Elementary Teachers

Working in a natural setting, rather than an artificial laboratory, this course stresses firsthand experience with natural phenomena and suggests what can be done to convey understanding of these things to the elementary-school student. In developing an understanding of natural resources consideration is given to such areas as rocks and minerals, plant and animal life, astronomy, weather, and all outdoor phenomena, both physical and biological. If desired, collections are made under supervision, and some latitude is provided for individual specialization in some phase of field science. The student needs no formal scientific background for this course. Methods of teaching on the elementary-school level as well as subject-matter content are included. Simple demonstrations, experiments, collections, acquisition of free and inexpensive materials, reference publications, and the most recent methods and trends in field-trip procedure are considered.

Credit: 2 semester-hours

Mathematics 411—Field Mathematics

In this course the student learns how to make a map using the alidade and plane table and how to find heights and inaccessible distances by scale drawings. Simple devices for estimating heights and distances are taught. The use of the surveying transit is explained as well as the use of simple devices, easily made, such as the hypsometer and geometric square. A knowledge of the elementary processes in arithmetic is sufficient background for this course.

Credit: 2 semester-hours

Science 413—Field Studies in Science: Physical

Emphasis in this course is given to local and New Jersey geology, minerals, soils, and waters, with emphasis on the chemical and physical aspects of soil and water. Field trips are taken through Kittatinny Mountains and to the Delaware Water Gap.

Credit: 2 semester-hours

Science 417—Science Problems in Conservation

This course is designed for students who already have a background in science and who wish to organize units of instruction dealing with conservation problems in their own immediate environment. By utilizing visiting experts, the rich environment of the camp, and the library resources, each student can prepare materials dealing with the relation between science and conservation, suitable for use with pupils in the schools of New Jersey.

Credit: 2 semester-hours

19

August 23—September 2

Geography 420—Field Geography and Conservation

This course constitutes a study of the relation between relief features of north
ern New Jersey, the location of natural resources, and the way in which lan
use and population distribution follow these patterns. Emphasis is given t
the reading and interpretation of topographical maps and aerial photograph
and to a study of the United States Geological and Soil Surveys of thi
region. By means of an actual land-use survey the student comes to appreci
ate the problems of conservation as they grow out of man's use of natural re
sources.

Credit: 2 semester-hours

Science 411—Problems in Field Studies in Science

In this course each student selects a phase of field science in which he doe
advanced research under the guidance of the instructor. Plant ecology, bird
life, pond-life, fungi, tree diseases, and insect-life are a few of the areas fron
which the student may choose.

Prerequisites: Science 405, **Field and Laboratory Studies in Science**, or it
equivalent, plus at least 12 points in biology.

Credit: 2 semester-hours

Science 412—Field Studies in Science: Biological

Emphasis in this course is given to the ecology, life-history, and identificatio
of plant and animal communities (terrestrial and aquatic) with an introduc
tion to their conservation.

Credit: 2 semester-hours

Science 414—Conservation of Plants and Animals

The social, economic, and ecological implications of plant and animal conser
vation are considered together in this course. Discussion periods are inter
spersed with field trips to forest and wildlife management areas. Cooperatin
experts from State and Federal agencies bring special contributions in thei
fields. Visual aids are used extensively.

Credit: 2 semester-hours

Social Studies 477—Rural Sociology

During this course the student comes face to face with rural life in norther
New Jersey. Social processes and problems are considered. Opportunities ar
provided for students to attend Grange meetings, county fairs, rural dance
and parties, and to live for a day or two with a farm family.

Credit: 2 semester-hours

Fees

The total fee for each ten-day session listed above will be $55.00. The tot
fee for each "practicum" course will be $105.00. These prices include tuitio
board, and lodging.

DESCRIPTIONS OF THE COURSES OF THE SUMMER SESSION SHOWN BY DEPARTMENTS

Please note that the numbering of courses at this College follows this order: 100-399, inclusive, are undergraduate courses; 400-499, inclusive, are senior-college and graduate courses; 500 and above are graduate courses.

Art

Art S406—Creative Arts Workshop   **Miss Osgood**
This course offers experience in painting, drawing, sculpture, ceramics, and print-making for students who wish to employ the creative visual arts in the teaching of other subjects. No previous art training is required.
10:30-11:20 A. M.   Credit: 2 semester-hours   Campus Studio Workshop

Art S414—The History of Chinese Art   **Mr. Nelson Wu**
For description and other data, see section on page 13 under "China Institute of New Jersey."

Integration S474—Elementary School Arts and Crafts   **Miss Osgood**
For description and other data, see section under "Elementary Education."

Business Education

Business Education S404—Business Economics   **Mr. Froehlich**
This course deals with the business aspects of economics as related to contemporary and long range problems; operation and government control of public utilities; taxation, government finance, and labor and management problems.
8:30-9:20 A. M.   Credit: 2 semester-hours   Room 2, Annex No. 2

Business Education S409—Money and Banking   **Mr. Froehlich**
This course provides a short historical survey of money and the evolution of banking, outside and within the United States. The organization of banks, the nature of their transactions, operations, and relations with other banks are considered. The functioning of the Federal Reserve System and the nature of the money markets are also examined.
9:30-10:20 A. M.   Credit: 2 semester-hours   Room 2, Annex No. 2

Business Education S411—Retail Store Management   **Dr. VanDerveer**
The work of the store manager in retail store operation is fully explored in this course. The problems of organization and management as they are encountered in various types of retail stores are discussed. Consideration is given to trends, principles, and practices in small and large stores in both the independent and chain store fields.
10:30-11:20 A. M.   Credit: 2 semester-hours   Room 4, Annex No. 2

Business Education S504—Improvement of Instruction in Business Education   **Dr. VanDerveer**
This course seeks to bring together business education teachers regardless of subject matter fields to consider common problems involving general subject matter and methods of instruction including visual and auditory aids. It also offers opportunity for an individual to investigate and evaluate materials and methods in specific subject matter areas.
8:30-9:20 A. M.   Credit: 2 semester-hours   Room 4, Annex No. 2

Business Education S602—Seminar in Economics
                                       Mr. Sheppard and Mr. Froehlich
This seminar is designed to meet the individual needs of the graduate student in business education or social studies by allowing him to pursue areas of work along economic lines in which he is not well versed. The program of participation consists of oral and written reports, developed through independent reading and individually directed field studies. In addition, group field trips are planned so as to give the student a first-hand knowledge of methods and practices of such organizations as banks, organized exchanges, manufacturing, and marketing businesses. It is expected that the reports arising from these experiences will be in such form that they will be capable of being published or delivered as speeches before groups of people. An opportunity is given to view, evaluate, and work with a variety of related visual and auditory aids.
9:30 A. M.-12:20 P. M.   Credit: 6 semester-hours   Room 5, Annex No. 2

English

English S431B—Shakespeare II (Comedies)   **Mr. Hamilton**
This course, in two parts, presents all of Shakespeare's plays as opposed to those taught only in high school, which is the chief concern of English 301B. Here the poet's full development can be seen, providing a complete critical experience. Critical analysis, contentual evaluation, and textual problems are the main areas of concern. Part A deals with the tragedies; Part B, the comedies. The chronicle plays are woven into the discussion.
9:30-10:20 A. M.   Credit: 2 semester-hours   Room 1

English S441—Medieval Epic, Saga, and Romance   **Dr. Krauss**
This course deals with the chief medieval epics, sagas, and romances from the literatures of England, France, Germany, Ireland, Iceland, Wales, and Italy in modern English translation. Attention is given both to those narratives which reflect the life of a particular country and to those which are international and express more generally the spirit of medieval Europe.
9:30-10:20 A. M.   Credit: 2 semester-hours   Room 2

English S459—A Survey of Great Chinese Literature   **Dr. Wu-Chi-Liu**
See description and other data on pages 13 and 14 of this Bulletin.

English S502—Victorian Poetry   **Mr. Pettegrove**
The most important English poets who wrote during the transition from the Victorian to the modern period are read and discussed. An important feature of the course is the analysis and appreciative reading of the lyric poetry of Rossetti, Swinburne, Hardy, Bridges, G. M. Hopkins, Francis Thompson, A. E. Houseman, Kipling, and W. B. Yeats.
8:30-9:20 A. M.   Credit: 2 semester-hours   Room 2

English S503—Geoffrey Chaucer and His Times   **Dr. Krauss**
Some of the works of Chaucer are read rapidly, others studied intensively, so that the students may acquire a broad general understanding of Chaucer's place in the history of English literature as well as facility in reading and interpreting the medieval text of his stories.
11:30 A. M.—12:20 P. M.   Credit: 2 semester-hours   Room 2

English S518—The Major Romantic Poets   **Mr. Hamilton**
This course studies the work of Coleridge, Wordsworth, Scott, Byron, Shelley, and Keats. It devotes especial attention to the poems which are best adapted for the reading of high school students.
11:30 A. M.-12:20 P. M.   Credit: 2 semester-hours   Room 1

English S519—English in the Modern High School   **Dr. Fulcomer**

This is a seminar in which the methods and materials requisite to the development of a program in the language arts (listening, speaking, reading, and writing) are considered. The course may be taken as equivalent for Specific Methods in English for certification in secondary education.

:30-9:20 A. M.   Credit: 2 semester-hours   Room 1

English S521—English Literature of Social Problems   **Mr. Pettegrove**

This course surveys English literature as English 460 deals with American literature. The period from 1800 to 1914 is covered, and the principal authors discussed include Shelley, Dickens, Kingsley, Tennyson, Carlyle, Butler, Meredith, Galsworthy, Bennett, Shaw, and Wells. English 460 is not prerequisite to this course.

0:30-11:20 A. M.   Credit: 2 semester-hours   Room 2

Speech

English S410—Speech Pathology   **Miss Kauffman**

This course deals with diagnostic and corrective procedures, cause and treatment of stuttering, cleft palate, spastic speech, and aphasia. This course is required to teach speech and speech defectives. Prerequisites: English 208 and 209.

1:30 A. M.-12:20 P. M.   Credit: 2 semester-hours   Room 3

English S417—Methods in the Teaching of Speech   **Mr. Fox**

In this course a study is made of the objectives of speech education, modern trends in instruction, speech textbooks and teaching materials, and the integration of speech with other academic departments of study. This course is required to teach speech.

00-9:20 A. M.   Credit: 3 semester-hours   Room 3

English S456—Play Direction   **Mr. Fox**

This course covers the choosing and casting, as well as directing, of plays. Scenes are directed for class criticism, and a detailed prompt-book of one play is prepared. This course complements English 435.

9:30-11:20 A. M.   Credit: 2 semester-hours   Room 3

English S466—Speech Development: Improvement and Reeducation   **Miss Kauffman**

This course is intended for superintendents, principals, and classroom teachers who have little or no background in speech education. Consideration is given to the following topics: (1) speech development; (2) speech difficulties or problems found on the kindergarten, elementary, and secondary school levels; (3) acquisition of good voice and speech characteristics; (4) use of techniques and materials in classrooms to motivate good speech patterns; and (5) ways of setting up and integrating speech education in school systems. Demonstrations with individuals and groups are made, and students are expected to prepare a practical project.

30-10:20 A. M.   Credit: 2 semester-hours   Room 3

Geography

Geography S411—Geographic Influences in American History   **Dr. Milstead**

A study is made of geographic factors influencing the development of social, economic, and political life in America.

9:30-11:20 A. M.   Credit: 2 semester-hours   Room 26

23

Geography S418—Regional Geography of North America   **Dr. Milst**

This course constitutes a detailed regional treatment of the continent of No America. Emphasis is placed upon the human activities of the various regi in relation to their natural environment and the relations of the regions to e other. Attention is given to the techniques of presenting the material and the of geographic tools in the treatment of the subject-matter.

11:30 A. M.-12:20 P. M.   Credit: 2 semester-hours ·   Room

Geography S509—Economic Geography of Asia   **Dr. Milst**

This course constitutes a treatment of the economic and commercial devel ment of the countries of Asia in relation to their natural environment.

8:30-9:20 A. M.   Credit: 2 semester-hours   Room

Health and Physical Education

Health Education S407—Prevention and Care of Athletic Injuries   **Mr. Co**

This is a lecture and laboratory course designed to acquaint the student v ways to prevent and care for the common injuries sustained in athletics. Att tion is given to sprains, strains, bruises, burns, and fractures. The responsibi of the coach in caring for injuries is emphasized.

8:00-8:50 A. M.   Credit: 2 semester-hours   Room

Health Education S408—Driver Education and Training   **Mr. Co**

See page 34 under the heading "Post-Summer-Session Course" for the desc tion and other data concerning this course.

Health Education S411—School Health Services   **Mr. DeR**

The student is familiarized with the health services available in the school. part which the teacher plays in co-ordinating his activities with the sch medical staff is emphasized.

11:30 A. M.-12:20 P. M.   Credit: 2 semester-hours   Room 7, C

**Integration S476—Elementary School Health and
Physical Education**   **Mr. DeR**

See description and other data under the heading "Elementary Education."

Integration

**Integration S400A—Principles and Philosophy
of Secondary Education**   **Dr. Fr**

This course evaluates educational objectives, techniques, procedures, and org zations in relation to the needs and demands made upon the school by soc and by the student. It aims to help the student develop an adequate philoso of life and education.

11:30 A. M.-12:20 P. M.   Credit: 2 semester-hours   Roon

**Integration S407—Television in Education Workshop:
Programming and Production**   **Mr. I**

For description and other data, see page 15 under "Montclair State Teac College Workshops."

**Integration S408—Selection and Utilization of
Audio-Visual Materials**   **Mr. Fo**

Sources, selection, and evaluation of audio-visual aids are studied in this co Techniques in developing individual reference catalogs of audio-visual aids

24

stressed. The production of school-made aids is also an important aspect of the course. The use of the latest audio-visual equipment is demonstrated.
9:30-10:20 A. M.   Credit: 2 semester-hours   Room 4

Integration S500A—Basic Educational Trends   Dr. Fraser
This course deals with the historical background which administrators and supervisors, as well as teachers, need in order to evaluate problems and policies in due perspective. It emphasizes the current trends in American society and their bearing upon education. It also considers philosophies concerning the causes of rises and declines in outstanding civilizations and the part education could play among them.
8:30-9:20 A. M.   Credit: 2 semester-hours   Room 28

Integration S500B—Advanced Educational Psychology   Mr. Cambreleng
This course covers the various aspects of growth. Individual differences, their measurement, and their bearing on education practices and principles furnish topics of study and discussion. Principles and laws of learning are reviewed. Some time is given to problems of personality as encountered in school work. The several points of view which have been prominent in the psychology of the past fifty to seventy-five years are examined for their contributions to thinking about human nature. Prerequisite: An introductory course in Psychology.
9:30-10:20 A. M.   Credit: 2 semester-hours   Room 30

Integregation S500C—Recent Trends in Secondary School Methods   Dr. Sperle
This course emphasizes the fundamental principles underlying the technique of teaching on the secondary school level. Some of the topics considered are: organization of knowledge, the logical and psychological aspects of method, developing appreciations, social-moral education, teaching motor control, fixing motor responses, books and verbalism, meeting individual differences, guidance in study, tests and examinations, marks and marking.
10:30-11:20 A. M.   Credit: 2 semester-hours   Room D

Integration S500D—School Administration I:
Functions and Organization   Mr. Morehead
This introductory course in educational administration is concerned with general functions and personnel, as well as with the general organization, of public education on local, State, and national levels. It deals also with Federal-State relations, the State and sectarian education, the expanding scope of modern school systems, types and bases of school organization, and professional ethics.
9:30-10:20 A. M.   Credit: 2 semester-hours   Room 29

Integration S500E—School Administration II: Law and Finance   Mr. Morehead
This course acquaints the student with the allied fields of school law and school finance, with special reference to New Jersey. Its topics include basic principles of public school support, taxation, Federal aid, educational finance, legal provisions for district borrowing, tenure provisions, and rights and duties of school boards and officials.
11:30 A. M.-12:20 P. M.   Credit: 2 semester-hours   Room 29

Integration S500F—School Administration III:
Community Relations   Dr. Atkinson
This course concerns the relation of the school to other educational efforts of the community. It considers the scope and types of agencies and informal influences of an educational nature, and also the agencies and methods by which the best total cooperative effort can be attained. It deals also with methods and plans of publicity. Constant reference throughout is made to New Jersey localities.
10:30-11:20 A. M.   Credit: 2 semester hours   Room 9

Integration S502—Organization and Administration of the
Modern High School   **Dr. Atkins**

The following topics are considered: the student personnel, building and revisi:
the high school curriculum, providing for individual differences, making t
school schedule, records, the guidance program, pupil participation in gover
ment, the extra-curricular program, the health program, the safety progra
discipline, library and study hall, cafeteria, the principal's office, and evaluati
results.

11:30 A. M.-12:20 P. M.   Credit: 2 semester-hours   Room

Integration S503—Methods and Instruments of Research   **Dr. Fras**

This course is required of all candidates for the Master's degree without rega
to their field of major interest. Its purposes is to introduce students of educati
to research and its practical application to professional problems. The cour
treats: the nature and types of educational research; methods and techniques
educational research; and the tools used in interpreting statistical data. Duri
the course, the student sets up a problem and plans and carries out its solutic
Prerequisite: Mathematics 400 or its equivalent.

9:30-10:20 A. M.   Cedit: 2 semester-hours   Room

Integration S504A—Curriculum Construction in the
Secondary School   **Dr. W. Scott Smi**

The purpose of this course is to introduce the student to constructive criticis
of American. culture, to consider the extent to which the secondary schc
curriculum meets the needs of a changing civilization, and to consider effecti
means of curriculum construction.

10:30-11:20 A. M.   Credit: 2 semester-hours   Room

Integration S505—Organization and Administration of
Extra-Curricular Activities   **Dr. W. Scott Smi**

The first part of this course considers such general problems of extra-curricu
activities as: their growing importance; their relation to the curriculum; t
principles underlying their organization, administration, and supervision; a
methods of financing. In the second part, an intensive study is made of t
home room, the assembly, the student council, clubs, athletics, school publi
tions, and other activities in which the class is especially interested.

11:30 A. M.-12:20 P. M.   Credit: 2 semester-hours   Room

Integration S508—Supervision of Instruction in
Secondary Schools   **Dr. Atkins**

This course emphasizes the more practical phases of supervision which are n
most frequently by those engaged in it. Among the topics are: the set-up :
adequate supervision, supervision as encouraging and guiding the growth
teachers and the improvement of educational procedures, the superviso
functions of teachers' meetings, discussion groups, general and professio
reading, the writing of articles, cooperative curriculum modification, utilizati
of community resources, and teacher intervisitation.

9:30-10:20 A. M.   Credit: 2 semester-hours   Room

Integration S518—Supervision of Instruction in the
Elementary School   **Miss Bris**

This course has been planned for those engaged in the supervision of
elementary school, and for those who are preparing for such responsibilit
Principles of classroom supervision are developed and applied to learn
situations. Among the more important topics that receive attention are:
nature and function of supervision, the organization necessary for effect

26

upervision, the nature and significance of the teacher's purposes, the methods
nd techniques of group and individual supervision, the techniques of observa-
on, and the supervisory conference.

:30-10:20 A. M.　　　　　　　　Credit: 2 semester-hours　　　　　Room 10

ntegration S520—Principles of Mental Hygiene　　　　　Mr. Cambreleng

'his course is designed to be a general survey of the principles and practices of
1ental health with special reference to the mental health of teacher and pupil.
t involves a thorough grounding in fundamental principles of mental hygiene
'ith much practical consideration of the mental-health values of instructional
rograms and procedures. Discussion centers in practical efforts to develop
·holesome personalities in our schools.

0:30-11:20 A. M.　　　　　　　Credit: 2 semester-hours.　　　　　Room 30

ntegration S521A—Educational and Psychological
Measurement　　　　　　　　　　　　　　　　Mr. Morehead

'his course deals with fundamentals of educational and psychological measure-
1ent: test theory, statistical concepts, test construction, evaluation, and inter-
retation. The place of tests in the instructional program is stressed.

:30-9:20 A. M.　　　　　　　　Credit: 2 semester-hours　　　　　Room 29

ntegration S532—The Supervision and Teaching of Reading in
Elementary Schools　　　　　　　　　　　　　Dr. Sperle

'he place of reading in the entire elementary school program is analyzed.
.ttention is given to necessary remedial work for junior high school students.
faterials and their use in instructional programs are studied with a view
)ward increasing power. All growth levels are considered. Good first teach-
1g is of primary concern; however, the analysis and correction of certain
:ading difficulties constitute an important portion of the course.

1:30 A. M.-12:20 P. M.　　　　　Credit: 2 semester-hours　　　　　Room D

ntegration S537—Social-Moral Guidance　　　　　Mr. E. C. Davis

'his course is concerned with the non-vocational and non-academic personal
nd social problems of pupils as well as with the development of techniques by
'hich counselors can integrate the pupil's personal life with the mores and
ustoms of society. It also includes a study of the possible services of
arious community agencies and a study of the counselor's relation to prob-
:ms of discipline and citizenship education.

:30-9:20 A. M.　　　　　　　　Credit: 2 semester-hours　　　　　Room 30

ntegration S548—Curriculum Construction in the
Elementary School　　　　　　　　　　　　　Miss Bristol

'his course offers an opportunity to review state and city elementary cur-
icula; to discuss the principles of curriculum construction; to collect new
:aching materials for the various subjects; and to evaluate, organize, and
rade these materials. Teaching procedures in the use of materials are
iscussed and evaluated in terms of pupil needs, the objectives set up, and the
esults obtained. This course offers an opportunity to make a special study
f the materials and procedures to be used in the supervision of the language
rts.

0:30-11:20 A. M.　　　　　　　Credit: 2 semester-hours　　　　　Room 10

ntegration S602—Seminar in Guidance　　　　　Mr. E. C. Davis

'his course is designed to provide a laboratory situation for the exploration
nd study of the present practices with respect to the three major phases of

the guidance program. Usually this seminar is given in conjunction wi either Vocational (Integration 535A), Educational (Integration 536), or Soci Moral (Integration 537) Guidance. The major portion of the time is spent field trips, in private investigation, and in research. Prerequisites: Integrati 551, and have taken or be taking in conjunction one of the courses of maj emphasis listed above.

10:30 A. M.-12:20 P. M.   Credit: 4 semester-hours   Room

ELEMENTARY EDUCATION

These courses in Elementary Education are open to the following only:

(1) Those who already hold a degree from Montclair with a Certificate Secondary Education, and

(2) Those who are now matriculated at Montclair for a degree and the Ce tificate in Secondary Education.

The courses starred (*) do not carry graduate credit. Only 6 semester-hou credit in Elementary Education may apply on the Master of Arts degree. The courses are offered to assist Montclair students to obtain the State of New Jers Certificate for Elementary School Teachers, for which 24 semester-hours credit necessary.

*Integration S474—Elementary School Arts and Crafts   Miss Osgo

This course provides a wide range of creative manipulative experience with t materials, tools, and techniques of art work in the elementary school and insight into significant art work of children of various age levels. Work is do in crayon, paint, chalk, clay, wood, papier-mache, finger paints, and other eas accessible materials. The work of the course includes simple weaving, blo prints, murals, and the making of puppets. Attention throughout is direct toward an insight into the significance of art work and of manipulative experien as a medium of expression and a means of growth for the child.

9:30-10:20 A. M.   Credit: 2 semester-hours   Campus Studio Worksh

*Integration S475A—Fundamentals of Elementary School Music   Mr. Cr

The elements of music, including notation, the formation of scales and varic modes, key and clef signatures, Italian musical terms, abbreviations, rhyth and intervals are included in this course. The student should acquire the abil to write a simple melody from dictation and to read at sight any part in a sim three-part selection in a musician-like manner. Ability to carry a tune is nec sary for success in this course.

8:30-9:20 A. M.   Credit: 2 semester hours   Room 5, Cl

*Integration S476—Elementary School Health and
**   Physical Education   Mr. DeR**

The purpose of this course is to induct the prospective elementary classro teacher into the field of health and physical education. Such phases as st courses of study, selection and organization of materials, grading, class org: zation, and others are discussed. To give the student a more functional appro: the programs of surrounding communities are studied. (There are two secti of this course being offered this summer. See hours below.)

Section one: 9:30-10:20 A. M.   Credit: 2 semester-hc
          Room 7, CHS, and Gym, CHS
Section two: 10:30-11:20 A. M.   Credit: 2 semester-hc
          Room 7, CHS, and Gym, CHS

28

Integration S477—Elementary School Mathematics   Mr. Humphreys

This course includes a study of the development of the number concept in young children, the problem of number readiness, and an analysis of the various number skills. Consideration is given to the development of methods of presenting the units of elementary mathematics to children. Emphasis is placed on the meaningful use of the fundamental operations with integers, fractions, decimals, and problem solving. Experience is given to students in effective methods of lesson planning, testing, and diagnostic and remedial work.

10:30-11:20 A. M.   Credit: 2 semester-hours   Room 2, Annex No. 1

Integration S478—Elementary School Science   Mr. Allen

This course is based upon the assumption that science teaching in the elementary school should include scientific inquiry at the child's level as well as scientific information. Specific methods and materials are developed to meet these purposes. Emphasis is placed upon using the school community, learning through activity, and integrating science with other subject-matter areas.

8:30-9:20 A. M.   Credit: 2 semester-hours   Room 5, Annex No. 3

Integration S479—Elementary School Social Studies   Dr. Moffatt

This course is designed to familiarize the student with the materials and methods for teaching man's relation to his environment and other human beings in the elementary grades. The integration of the various phases of social living with other subjects, grade placement of subject-matter, the source and use of visual aids, and student projects are all stressed.

11:30 A. M.-12:20 P. M.   Credit: 2 semester-hours   Room 21

In addition to the above courses, **Geography S418, Regional Geography of North America**, applies on the Limited Elementary Certificate. For description and other data regarding this course, see page 24 under the heading "Geography."

Mathematics

Mathematics S400—Educational Statistics   Mr. Humphreys

The aim of this course is to prepare the student (1) to comprehend and criticize articles of statistical nature in current educational literature; (2) to apply statistical methods in testing and rating pupils; (3) to carry on the simpler types of educational research. By analysis of real data from the secondary field, the student becomes familiar with the measures of central tendency and variability, short methods of computation, graphic representation of material, the properties of the normal curve, and linear correlation. Inasmuch as statistical methods in education are almost identical with those employed in the natural, physical, and social sciences, there is natural integration with these fields. (This course is required of all Montclair undergraduate students and it, or its equivalent, is now prerequisite to the required graduate course Integration 503—Methods and Instruments of Research.)

9:30-10:20 A. M.   Credit: 2 semester-hours   Room 2, Annex No. 1

Mathematics S406—Solid Analytic Geometry   Mrs. Phillips

A review and extension of the theory of determinants, a study of lines and planes in space, of space-coordinates, transformation of coordinates, loci in space, the sphere, and of quadric surfaces are considered in this course. The study of the general quadratic equation in three variables, invariance under motion, and the classification of numerical equations completes the course.

9:30-10:20 A. M.   Credit: 2 semester-hours   Room 3, Annex No. 1

Integration S477—Elementary School Mathematics   **Mr. Humphre**
See description and other data under the heading "Elementary Education."

Mathematics S501A—Administration and Supervision of
Mathematics, Part I   **Dr. D. R. Da·**
This course is concerned with the problems met in organizing and supervisi
the teaching of mathematics. There are considered the functions and qualific
tions of the supervisor of mathematics, in-service training of teachers, demonstr
tion lessons, professional attitude and preparation of teachers, department me·
ings, selection of texts, current problems, research, and the basis for determi
ing objectives. Attention is paid to efficient methods of securing mastery
skills, the development of power in problem solving, and the organization
testing programs.
9:30-10:20 A. M.   Credit: 2 semester hours   Room 1, Annex No.

Mathematics S509C—A Critical Interpretation of Mathematics
in the Junior High School   **Mrs. Philli**
The aim of this course is to give teachers a deeper insight into the subject-matt
usually taught in the seventh, eighth, and ninth grades. Among the top·
considered are: the nature of graphs, an intuitive and experimental approach
geometry, the arithmetic and algebra for social use and interpretation, appro:
mate measures and mensuration, and integration with other subject fields. T
course is open to all junior and senior high school teachers and those elementa
school teachers who have had two years of high school mathematics.
10:30-11:20 A. M.   Credit: 2 semester-hours   Room 3, Annex No.

Mathematics S510B—Mathematics in its Relation to Other Fields of
Knowledge: Science, Art, and Music   **Mrs. Philli**
In this course there are introduced such topics as mechanics and vector analys
wave motion, geometrical optics, weather forecasting, mathematics in biolo
chemistry, medicine, and geology; phyllotaxis (leaf arrangement in plant
spirals, laws of growth; static and dynamic symmetry, perspective, designs; a
mathematics in music. Many of these topics should serve to enrich the ba·
ground of secondary school teachers and encourage further study in special fiel
11:30 A. M.-12:20 P. M.   Credit: 2 semester-hours   Room 3, Annex No

Mathematics S515—Differential Equations   **Dr. D. R. Da·**
This course is a continuation of the calculus considered from a new viewpoi
Various applications of differential equations and their standard methods
solution are fully treated in this course. Among the topics included are: lin·
differential equations of the first degree and of the first and higher orders, lin·
equations of the nth order with constant coefficients, linear equations of
second order, exact and total differential equations, simultaneous equatio
numerical approximation, and partial differential equations.
8:30-9:20 A. M.   Credit: 2 semester-hours   Room 1, Annex Nc

New Tools for Learning

Integration S407—Television in Education Workshop: Programming
and Production   **Mr. R·**
For description and other data, see page 15 of this bulletin.

Integration S408—Selection and Utilization of Audio-Visual
Materials   **Mr. For·**
For description and other data, see page 24 of this bulletin.

Social Studies S462—Continental United States **Mr. Bye**

For description and other data, see page 10 of this bulletin.

Science

Biology S409—Human Physiology **Dr. Hadley**

A study is made of normal and abnormal physiology based on previous study of mammalian anatomy. In addition to an analysis of the part played by organs and tissues in carrying out the essential functions of the body, special attention is given to problems of hygiene and sanitation. **Prerequisite: A course in comparative anatomy or Biology 402.**

Lectures: 8:30-9:20 A. M.

Laboratories: Tues. and Thurs. P. M.

Credit: 4 semester-hours   Room 1, Annex No. 3

Chemistry S408A—Industrial Chemistry, Part I **Dr. Reed**

The purpose of this course is to enable science teachers to understand the type of chemical industries in the State of New Jersey and the nature of their problems. A survey is made by lectures, reports, and trips to plants of the chemical industries in the state. This section of the course stresses the importance and the characteristics of chemical industry, the various unit operations used by the industry to carry out chemical reactions, the controls used to insure quality, organization for research, and the type of workers employed. **Prerequisites: General and organic chemistry, or special permission of the instructor.**

Lectures: 11:30 A. M.-12:20 P. M., Tues. and Thurs.

Field Trips: Tues. and Thurs. P. M.

Credit: 2 semester-hours   Room 22

Chemistry S412—Physical Chemistry, Part II **Dr. Reed**

This course deals with electrical conductance, electrolytic equilibrium, electromotive force, electrolysis, polarization, chemical kinetics, photochemical reactions, atomic structure, molecular structure, and radioactivity. **Prerequisites: General college chemistry, analytical chemistry, and general college physics.**

Lectures: 9:30-10:20 A. M.

Laboratories: Mon. and Wed. P. M.

Credit: 4 semester-hours   Room 22

Physics S510A—Advanced Problems in Photography, Part I **Dr. K. O. Smith**

This course is intended to give teachers who supervise photography in high school a working knowledge of the different phases of the subject. It is also intended to enable those who follow photography as a hobby to do work of exhibition quality. The underlying principles of physics and chemistry in the various processes are emphasized. The topics covered are: projection and printing controls, toning processes, making of diapositives and paper negatives, intensification and reduction of negatives, reduction of positives, retouching and corrections on negatives and positives. **Prerequisite: Physics 304 or the permission of the instructor.**

Lectures: 10:30-11:20 A. M., Mon., Wed. and Friday.

Laboratory: Mon. P. M.   Credit: 2 semester-hours   Room 25

Physics S512—Modern Physics **Dr. K. O. Smith**

This course is a survey of recent experimental research in physics and of the newer theories concerning nuclear physics and electricity. Such topics as atomic spectra, radioactivity, artificial transmutation of the elements, and cosmic rays

are discussed. **Prerequisites: General college physics, general college chemistry, and a course in electrical measurements.**
Lectures: 8:00-9:20 A.M.
Field Trips by Arrangement   Credit: 4 semester-hours   Room 25

Integration S478—Elementary School Science   **Mr. Allen**
For description and other data, see listing under "Elementary Education."

SOCIAL STUDIES

Social Studies S404—The Philosophy of History   **Dr. Clayton**
It is the purpose of this course to investigate the relation of history to the other social studies and also the major attempts to find the meaning of history. A brief survey is made of the leading philosophies of history.
9:30-10:20 A. M.   Credit: 2 semester-hours   Room 3, Annex No. 2

Social Studies S419—American Political Biography   **Dr. Moffat**
This is the study of the life and influence of the leading figures in American political and social history. It is the aim here to show the relation of each of these characters to the times in which he lived and to point out how he influenced the trend of American life. The study includes such leaders as Washington Jefferson, Hamilton, Webster, Lincoln, Cleveland, Theodore Roosevelt, and Wilson.
9:30-10:20 A. M.   Credit: 2 semester-hours   Room 21

Social Studies S439—The Family and Its Problems   **Dr. Clayton**
This course gives a history of the family, our American family patterns, the effects of social change, marital patterns of interaction, social roles, sources of conflicts and frustration, divorce and desertion, special problems in family life economics of children and the home, social legislation pertaining to family problems, marital adjustments, personality change after marriage, parent-child relationships, and personality reorientation.
8:30-9:20 A. M.   Credit: 2 semester-hours   Room 3, Annex No.

Social Studies S455—Social Legislation   **Dr. Rellahan**
This course analyzes the social, economic, and political adjustments which have come about in our society, due to technological progress. The content covers such subjects as public policy relative to immigration; the problems of national income and its distribution; labor legislation; public policy to aid and protect the consumer; and an analysis of competing philosophies pertaining to industrial and social progress.
9:30-10:20 A. M.   Credit: 2 semester-hours   Room 2

Social Studies S462—Continental United States   **Mr. By**
For description and other data, see "Bureau of Field Studies" on page 10 of this bulletin.

Social Studies S474—America in Transition   **Dr. Moffa**
This course surveys rapidly the results of the Civil War and then emphasize the major trends, economic and social, which have made modern America. It intended as a more advanced study than that which is made in the undergraduate course. The period covered is from 1867 to around 1914.
10:30-11:20 A. M.   Credit: 2 semester-hours   Room

ntegration S479—Elementary School Social Studies   Dr. Moffatt

See description and other data on page 29, under the heading "Elementary Education."

ocial Studies S490A—United Nations Institute   Mrs. Fradkin and Mr. Kops

ocial Studies S490B—The United Nations and American
    Foreign Policy   Mrs. Fradkin and Mr. Kops

For descriptions and other data concerning these two courses, see page 16 of this ulletin.

ocial Studies S491A and Social Studies S491B—Workshop in
    Citizenship Education, Part I and Part II   Dr. Clayton

For descriptions and other data concerning these two courses, see page 15 of this ulletin.

ocial Studies S496B—China: The Evolution of a Nation   Dr. Hung

ocial Studies S499—China Workshop   Dr. Meng

For descriptions and other data concerning these two courses, see pages 13 and 4 of this bulletin.

ocial Studies S522—The Development of Economic
    Institutions and Ideas   Dr. Rellahan

This course deals with the changing principles, institutions, and ideas which letermine the character of economic society. The doctrines of the more important chools of economic thought, such as the Classical, Historical, and Institutional ;roups are emphasized, and the teachings of the Mercantilists, Physiocrats, Adam Smith, Malthus, Ricardo, Marx, Henry George, Veblen, Hobson, Commons, Keynes, and others are examined in relation to the important problems of money, redit, prices, business cycles, foreign and domestic commerce, property, wages, he nature of wealth and value, and economic planning.

:30-9:20 A. M.   Credit: 2 semester-hours   Room 20

POST-SUMMER SESSION COURSE
August 11 through August 22, 1952

To Meet an Urgent Need, the following course is being offered by the State Teachers College at Montclair, with the assistance of the **New Jersey State Safety Council,** the **New Jersey Automobile Club,** the **American Automobile Association,** the **New Jersey State Police,** and the **New Jersey Department of Motor Vehicles.** Last year, over 32,000 persons lost their lives in traffic accidents. One-fourth of these were persons of high school and college age (15-24). The development of qualified young drivers can no longer be left to chance. The responsibility of our high schools in such a program is of vital importance. Training youth in skillful driving and in their responsibility toward other highway users, assumed when a person gets behind the wheel, will go far toward developing a new generation of skillful accident-free drivers. The lack of teachers for such training courses is all that prevents their being offered in most of the high schools of the country.

This Course Offers the Necessary Opportunity for men and women to prepare themselves to teach driver education in high schools. Enrollees completing the work of the course are presented with a certificate indicating the work done. Those who took this course at Montclair last summer were given enthusiastic cooperation by principals and school boards eager to establish driver education courses in their high schools, so that classes were opened in September taught by those who had received the Certificate of Completion in late August.

College Credit Required in New Jersey. In order to teach Driver Education in New Jersey, this course must be taken for credit.

Veterans may take this course under the G. I. Bill, if they have so arranged with the Veterans' Counselor of the College.

Living Expenses and Traveling Expenses must be paid by the student. Those desiring hotel accommodations should write to Mr. F. K. Schultze, Mgr., New Jersey Auto Club AAA, 156 Clinton Avenue, Newark 5, New Jersey. The College Residence Halls are closed at this time.

Textbooks and Other Text Materials will be furnished to each enrollee without charge.

Registration for this course will be accepted up to and including the opening day of the course. However, students should register early if possible, preferably on the regular registration days for the Summer Session. There is a limit to the number of registrations which may be accepted.

Description of the Course

Health Education S408—Driver Education and Training   **Mr. Cod**

Part I

This part consists of a minimum of 20 hours of class recitations and discussion for which home reading and study have been assigned. The following topics are included: (1) history and development of driver education and training programs; (2) objectives of driver education; (3) local, State and national traffic safety programs; (4) driver qualifications; (5) psychophysical testing; (6) curriculum content of school courses in driver education and training; (7) construction, operation, and maintenance of automobiles; (8) traffic laws and driver licensing; (9) traffic engineering; (10) pedestrian education and pu

ction; (11) equipment for teaching driver education; (12) liability, costs, and
surance; (13) planning driver education as a part of the daily program of the
gh school; (14) public relations; (15) records and reports; and (16) visual
ds in teaching driver education.

Part II

his part consists of a minimum of 20 hours devoted to the following: (1)
:hind-the-wheel instruction; (2) demonstrations and student-teacher practice
the car; and (3) road tests in traffic. Home reading and study are required in
·eparation for these projects.

ull attendance at all sessions is required. Prerequisite: a license to drive a
r in New Jersey.

'-12 and 1-4 daily   Credit: 2 semester-hours   Room D

* Because Health Education S408 begins on August 11 and the courses of the
1mmer Session do not end until August 13, Health Education S408 will meet
1 August 11, 12, and 13 at the following hours: 1:00-9:00 P.M.

Driver Education Course at Trenton

The above course will be offered from June 16 through June 27 at the New
:rsey State Teachers College at Trenton. Inquiries regarding this course
1ould be addressed to that college.

Montclair State Teachers College

1953

T 11

NEW JERSEY

SUMMER SESSION

Bulletin of

MONTCLAIR

STATE TEACHERS COLLEGE

1953
June 29th to August 11th

UPPER MONTCLAIR, NEW JERSEY

OFFICERS OF ADMINISTRATION

State Board of Education

GEORGE O. SMALLEY, *President* .... Bound Brook
MRS. EDWARD L. KATZENBACH, *Vice-President* .... Princeton
ARTHUR E. ARMITAGE, SR. .... Collingswood
JOHN S. GRAY .... Newton
JOHN C. KINAHAN .... Carney's Point
*A. HARRY MOORE .... Jersey City
JAMES W. PARKER .... Red Bank
AMOS J. PEASLEE .... Clarksboro
MRS. HERBERT REIM .... Maywood
MRS. FREDERICK H. SANFORD .... Nutley
HENRY A. WILLIAMS .... Paterson
*Deceased

Commissioner of Education

FREDERICK RAUBINGER

Assistant Commissioner for Higher Education

ROBERT H. MORRISON

New Jersey State Teachers College at Montclair

E. DEALTON PARTRIDGE, Ph.D. .... President
CLYDE M. HUBER, Ph.D. .... Dean of Instruction
OTIS C. INGEBRITSEN, Ph.D. .... Chairman of the Graduate Committee
ELIZABETH S. FAVOR, A.M. .... Assistant in Graduate Personnel
MARY M. HOUSE, B.C.S. .... Acting Registrar
EARL C. DAVIS, M.S. .... Director of Personnel and Guidance
MARGARET A. SHERWIN, A.M. .... Dean of Women
ULRICH J. NEUNER, A.M. .... Veterans' Counselor
BERNARD SIEGEL, B.S. .... Business Manager
HORACE J. SHEPPARD, A.M. .... Head of Business Education Department
EDWIN S. FULCOMER, Ed.D .... Head of English Department
MOWAT G. FRASER, Ph.D. .... Head of Integration Department
VIRGIL S. MALLORY, Ph.D. .... Head of Mathematics Department
EDNA MCEACHERN, Ph.D. .... Head of Music Department
RUFUS D. REED, Ph.D. .... Chairman of Science Department
ELWYN C. GAGE, Ph.D. .... Head of Social Studies Department
EDGAR C. BYE, A.M. .... Director, New Tools for Learning Bureau
ANNE BANKS CRIDLEBAUGH, A.M. .... Librarian
OTTO CORDES, P.E. .... Engineer in charge, Maintenance

2

FACULTY
SUMMER SESSION 1953

E. DeALTON PARTRIDGE, Ph.D.	President
CLYDE M. HUBER, Ph.D.	Dean of Instruction
HUGH ALLEN, JR., M.S.	Science
KEITH W. ATKINSON, Ph.D.	Integration
WILLIAM A. BALLARE, A.M.	Speech
HAROLD C. BOHN, A.M.	English
RUTH BRISTOL, A.M.	Elementary Education
EDGAR C. BYE, A.M.	Director, New Tools for Learning Bureau
FRANK L. CLAYTON,. Ph.D.	Social Studies
PAUL C. CLIFFORD, A.M.	Mathematics
ALDEN C. CODER, Ed.M.	Health and Physical Education
LAWRENCE H. CONRAD, A.M.	English
ANNE BANKS CRIDLEBAUGH, A.M.	Librarian
DAVID R. DAVIS, Ph.D.	Acting Head, Department of Mathematics
EARL C. DAVIS, M.S.	Personnel and Guidance
JEROME G. DeROSA, A.M.	Health and Physical Education
GEORGE FORBES, A.M.	Audio-Visual Materials
MOWAT G. FRASER, Ph.D.	Head of Department of Integration
PAUL E. FROEHLICH, A.M.	Business Education
EDWIN S. FULCOMER, Ed.D.	Head of Department of English
T. ROLAND HUMPHREYS, A.M.	Mathematics
OTIS C. INGEBRITSEN, Ph.D.	Psychology
WALTER E. KOPS, A.M.	United Nations Institute
CHIH MENG, Ph.D.	Director, China Institute
HARLEY P. MILSTEAD, Ph.D.	Geography
MAURICE P. MOFFATT, Ph.D.	Social Studies
ALLAN MOREHEAD, A.M.	Integration
DOROTHY J. MORSE, A.M.	Music
GEORGE F. PLACEK, A.M.	Physics
ROBERT J. POLGLAZE, A.M.	Guidance
RUFUS D. REED, Ph.D.	Chairman, Department of Science
JOHN J. RELLAHAN, Ph.D.	Acting Head, Department of Social Studies
HORACE J. SHEPPARD, A.M.	Head of Department of Business Education
W. SCOTT SMITH, Ph.D.	Integration
HARRY L. STEARNS, Ph.D.	Integration
ELIZABETH T. VanDERVEER, Ed.D.	Business Education
RALPH A. VERNACCHIA, A.M.	Art

GRADUATE COMMITTEE

OTIS C. INGEBRITSEN, *Chairman*

CLYDE M. HUBER	RUFUS D. REED
D. HENRYETTA SPERLE	ELIZABETH T. VANDERVEER
W. PAUL HAMILTON	ELIZABETH S. FAVOR, *Secretary*
DAVID R. DAVIS	JOHN J. RELLAHAN

3

LIVING ROOM   STUDENT ROOM

Dormitory rooms for women students are pleasant and comfortable.

Plans are made by the Administrative Council

SUMMER SESSION OF THE
NEW JERSEY STATE TEACHERS COLLEGE
AT MONTCLAIR

Objectives and Academic Status

The College is a professional school which prepares teachers, supervisors, and principals of high schools, and administrators of public school systems. The degrees offered by this College are those of Bachelor of Arts and Master of Arts. Certificate courses are offered for those who now hold degrees from other colleges.

The New Jersey State Teachers College at Montclair is a fully accredited member of the American Association of Colleges of Teacher Education, the Middle States Association of Colleges and Secondary Schools, the Association of American Universities, and the American Association of University Women.

How to Reach the Campus

Trains of the Greenwood Lake Division, Erie R. R., stop at Montclair Heights, the College Station. Trains of the Lackawanna R. R. connect at Montclair with the following bus lines: No. 64, running between Brick Church and the College; No. 60, running between Newark and the College; and No. 76, which runs between Orange and Paterson, passing the College en route. For those who come by car; the College is located about one mile north of the center of Upper Montclair.

Residence Halls for Men and Women

Edward Russ Hall and Chapin Hall are Montclair College's two well-appointed Residences. The charge for living on campus during the Summer Session is: $14.50 per week; which includes room, breakfast, and dinner. A la carte luncheons are served in the College cafeteria. For one student alone in a double room, an extra charge of $2.00 per week is made. The College provides and launders sheets, pillowcase, and bedpad. Towels, table lamps, blankets, clocks, and similar items must be provided and cared for by the student. The boarding-hall fee must be paid on or before the first day of the Summer Session. No rebate is made for occasional absence or voluntary withdrawal during the session. These prices are subject to change.

For reservations in a College Resident Hall, women address: Dean of Women, State Teachers College, Upper Montclair, N. J. Men address: Dean of Men.

Schedule of the Summer Session

Registration will take place on Monday, June 29: Hours, 9-12 and 1-4. Classes will begin on Tuesday morning, June 30, at 8 A. M. and will continue through Tuesday, August 11. All classes meet daily, Monday to Friday, inclusive, at the hours indicated for each.

Matriculation for the Master of Arts Degree

Not more than 8 semester-hours of work taken prior to matriculation are allowed to apply on the Master of Arts degree.

Those who desire to become candidates for the degree must request an application form from the Chairman of the Graduate Committee and return it, properly filled and accompanied by an Official Transcript of all previous work on college level. When such an applicant has been accepted by the College as a candidate for the degree, a definite statement is furnished to him, showing the requirements which he must fulfill to earn the degree. This sheet of requirements becomes the student's Work Program and should be brought by the student each time he comes to enroll for courses.

Auditors

Men and women who desire to take courses for cultural, vocational, or avocational purposes without college credits may register as auditors.

A student who desires to enroll in a course for which he already holds credit must register as an auditor in that course.

A student who desires to enroll in a course for which he has not completed the prerequisites must enroll as an auditor in that course.

Change of Status in a Course

If a student desires to change his status in a course from "credit" to "auditor" or from "auditor" to "credit," he must make formal application for such change not later than the middle of the course. Forms for this purpose may be procured from Miss Favor, in the Registrar's Office. Such changes cannot be made after the midpoint of the course is passed.

Students Matriculated at Montclair for A.M. Degree

All students matriculating in the Graduate Division after September 1, 1952 will be required to complete at least one full-time summer session, or in lieu thereof at least one regular semester of full-time graduate attendance.

The selection of courses must be in accordance with the student's Work Program, and his registration form will be signed by the Head of the Department in which the student is majoring or by a representative of that department present in the registration room.

Candidates for a degree must file with the Registrar an application for conferment of the degree before November 30 of the college year in which the work is to be completed. Application blanks for this purpose may be secured in the Registrar's Office. The burden of responsibility for the request rests with the candidate. This is of special significance to the teacher-in-service who may have distributed the work for the degree over several years.

Students Matriculated at Other Colleges

In previous summers, when the State Teachers College at Montclair offered courses to its own accelerated candidates for the Bachelor's degree, it was possible to accept students from other colleges in freshmen, sophomore, and junior year courses, as well as in courses of the senior year. Beginning in the summer of 1950, however, the College returned to its pre-war custom of offering courses in its Summer Session primarily to teachers-in-service. Since such teachers already hold the Bachelor's degree, with few exceptions, the courses shown in this Bulletin are for the most part only Graduate and Senior-Graduate courses.

A student who is planning to attend Montclair this summer should take this Bulletin to a conference with the Dean of his own College to arrange a program of work. For the Dean's information: the numbering of courses at Montclai follows this order: 100-399, inclusive, are undergraduate courses: 400-499; inclu sive, are senior-college and graduate courses; 500 and above are graduat courses.

At the time of registration, the student should go to the table of the De partment in which the courses are listed that he plans to take. The registratio form must be signed by the Representative of the Department at that table. Th College reserves the right to decide whether the student has fulfilled necessar prerequisites. He should bring with him, however, a letter from his own college If the student is seeking certification to teach in New Jersey, he must confe with Dr. Fraser, Head of the Department of Integration. Please note paragrap under the Heading: "Certificates."

Certificates

The State Teachers College at Montclair offers work toward the followin New Jersey Certificates: Secondary Teaching Certificate; Secondary Schoo Principal's Certificate; Elementary School Principal's Certificate; Subjec Supervisor's Certificate; General Supervisor's Certificate; Guidance Certificate

School Administrator's Certificate; Junior College Teacher's Certificate; and the Advanced Professional Certificate.

Those who matriculate at Montclair for a degree will receive information from Dr. Fraser, Head of the Integration Department, as to the requirements for each of these certificates. Students who have not matriculated at Montclair should write to Dr. E. C. Preston, Secretary of the State Board of Examiners, Department of Education, 175 West State Street, Trenton 8, N. J., for information as to the requirements. **For an evaluation of work already completed, address Dr. Preston.** An official transcript of such previous work should accompany the inquiry, with a statement as to the particular certificate desired.

The student should bring Dr. Preston's reply with him when conferring with Dr. Fraser as to his program of work.

Students who must have this information immediately should go to Trenton to confer personally with Dr. Preston or his assistant, Miss Smith.

Supervised Student Teaching

The opportunity to do supervised student teaching cannot be offered during the Summer Session. For fall teaching, students confer with Dr. Fraser at the College. Ask his secretary for an appointment.

Veterans

Veteran students taking work under the G. I. Bill for the first time at Montclair State Teachers College must see the Veteran's Counselor **at least two weeks prior to the registration day.** Veterans should be sure to obtain the Certificate of Eligibility from the Veterans Administration before the start of the Summer Session. Failure to do so will mean that **the usual fees must be paid by the student at the time of registration.**

It will be necessary for Veterans who have completed the work for either the A.B. or A.M. degree at Montclair to secure and present to the Veteran's Counselor the **Supplemental Certificate of Eligibility** before registering for further work at Montclair. Veterans transferring to Montclair who have previously been training under the G. I. Bill will be required to present a Supplemental Certificate of Eligibility at the time of registration.

Conferences with Advisors

Appointments with the Dean of Instruction, the Chairman of the Graduate Committee, a Department Head, or the Veteran's Counselor may be made by mail or telephone to their respective offices. This should be done at as early a date as possible to avoid delay at the time of registration.

Summer Session Credit Load

The maximum amount of credit which may be earned in the Summer Session is 8 semester-hours, but only 6 s. h. are recommended. There is no provision for a student to audit additional courses; consequently, the total of all courses taken during the Summer Session may not exceed 8 s. h. and students should not enroll for more. Additional credits may be earned by attending one of the sessions at the State School of Conservation that precedes or follows the Summer Session. Attention is called also to the post-Summer Session course in Safety Education and to the Field Studies course in New England and French Canada.

Each Summer Session course is in session at least thirty hours and carries a designated amount of credit. It is not possible to earn three s. h. credit in a two s. h. credit course.

Registration Information

Registration takes place in the College Library, on Monday, June 29, from 9 a.m. to 12 noon, and from 1 to 4 p.m. The Registration form of every student must be signed by a Department Head or his Representative. The student should report to the table of the Department in which he is majoring; or, if not matriculated here for a degree at present, of the Department in which he is taking courses. Signs on the tables indicate the various Departments.

Matriculated students should bring their "Work Programs" when they come to enroll.

The College reserves the right to close any course for which the enrollment is insufficient. The class will meet at least once, however, before this decision is made. Students may then enter another course in place of the one discontinued, by going to the Registrar's Office to re-enroll and to receive the new Class Admission Card in exchange for the card of the discontinued course. Students who decide not to enroll in an alternate course must present the card of the discontinued course at the Registrar's office in order to be eligible for a refund of tuition fees.

If prerequisites are required for a course (see the course description), the student should make certain that he has fulfilled them or their equivalent before enrolling in it.

If no previous work on college level has been taken, the student should consult the Dean of Instruction before enrolling in any course, unless as an Auditor.

A student may not register for credit in any course for which he already holds credit, except by permission of the Dean of Instruction.

Anyone unable to enroll during the hours shown above must register during the regular office hours of the College in the Registrar's Office. The summer office hours are from 8:30 to 3:30 P. M.

No Summer course may be taken for credit after Thursday, July 2.

Withdrawal from a Course

During the registration period of June 29 and 30 and July 1 and 2, students may withdraw from one course and enter another with the consent of their advisors in writing on the registration form. The Class Admission Card from the dropped course must be presented when registering for the new course before the new Class Admission card will be issued. If no new course is being taken, written notice to Miss Favor, Assistant in Graduate Personnel, must be given at once by the student. Miss Favor will notify the teacher of the course from which the student is withdrawing, as well as the Business Office of the College. **Refunds are computed from the date of the receipt of the letter o withdrawal.**

Students who neglect to follow this procedure receive a failing mark fo the course or courses which they cease to attend.

Tuition Fees, Service Charge, and Credit Slips

Check or money-order should be made payable to New Jersey Stat Teachers College.

Tuition fees: to students who are residents of New Jersey, $11.00 pe semester-hour credit carried by the course. Non-residents of New Jersey pa $13.00 per credit. **Courses taken by auditors for no credit cost the same.**

Service charge: $.50 per s. h. point.

Teachers who have supervised Montclair student-teachers and who have i their possession old Montclair credit slips may take them to the Office of th Integration Department, where new ones will be issued. The Business Offic cannot return any unused portion of a credit slip, so it is necessary that th new type credit slip be obtained before presenting it in payment of tuitio fees. Training Teachers may use the credit slips of any one of the six Ne Jersey State Teachers Colleges when taking courses at Montclair, but shoul bring only the new type slip in all cases.

Final Marks

Following are the final marks which may be received for a cours A-Excellent; B-Good; C-Fair; D-Poor; F-Failure; Inc.-Incomplete; Wd-Wit drew; N. C.-No Credit.

The mark of "D" when earned in summer, part-time, or extension cours of this College is not accepted for degree credit at Montclair.

The mark of "F" is given when earned and when the student has failed notify the Assistant in Graduate Personnel promptly of his withdrawal from course.

The mark of "N. C." is given only to auditors.

The mark of "Wd" is given only when prompt notice of withdrawal has been given and when the student's work to that time has been satisfactory to the teacher of the course.

The mark of "Inc." is seldom given. It may, however, be granted to a student whose work is incomplete at the end of the Session and who is eager to finish the work for a higher grade than he could receive otherwise. All responsibility regarding incomplete work rests with the student. He will be notified of a date after which, if the work remains incomplete, the final grade will be recorded without further notice.

Report Cards and Transcripts

An Official Transcript showing the credits earned is sent to the student personally ten days to two weeks following the close of the Session. A report card for each course taken is sent with the transcript. The transcript is sent without cost, but a service charge of $1.00 is made for a duplicate copy.

A student whose college requires that the transcript be mailed directly to the Dean or Registrar should call during the Summer Session at the Registrar's Office to address an envelope for this purpose.

Elementary Education Courses

Courses offered as a part of the curriculum for the graduate major in Educational Administration and Supervision should be carefully distinguished from those offered toward the endorsement in elementary education on the teacher's certificate. The courses in the Administration and Supervision of Elementary Education apply on the Elementary Principal's certificate, but not on the Elementary Teacher's certificate.

Although the New Jersey State Teachers College at Montclair is engaged primarily in preparing secondary school teachers, during the present shortage of teachers in the elementary schools it is deemed expedient to offer courses in the field of elementary education to those students who are eligible to enroll at this College in such courses.

Students eligible to enroll at Montclair in courses leading to certification in elementary education are:

(1) those who already hold a degree from Montclair with a certificate in secondary education; and

(2) those who are now matriculated at Montclair for such a degree.

Montclair cannot accept any other students in these courses.

The eligible students should consult the Registrar's Office for an evaluation of their previous work and a statement concerning the courses to be taken in order to receive the endorsement in elementary education on the secondary certificate already held or to be conferred.

Textbook Exhibit

In the Gymnasium of the Main Building, from July 6 through July 17, there will be an exhibit of high school and elementary school textbooks. While primarily for the benefit of the principals and teachers attending the Summer Session, the exhibit will be open to undergraduate students and to members of the general public who may be interested in seeing the latest textbooks.

Mrs. E. S. Fulcomer will be in charge of the Exhibit.

COURSES OF THE SUMMER SESSION

Descriptions of the courses will be found in the Graduate Bulletin of the College. Courses numbered 500 and above are graduate courses; those numbered 400-499 inclusive are senior-graduate courses and their descriptions in the Graduate Bulletin follow the descriptions of the graduate courses. The description of any entirely new course will be given below because it cannot be found in the Graduate Bulletin.

Art

Art S406—Creative Arts Workshop   **Mr. Vernacchia**
9:30-10:20 A. M.   Credit: 2 semester-hours   Campus Studio Workshop

Art S414—History of Chinese Art   **Mr. Nelson Wu**
See "China Institute of New Jersey" on page 16

Integration S474—Elementary School Arts and Crafts   **Mr. Vernacchia**
See "Elementary Education" on page 19

Business Education

Business Education S404—Business Economics   **Mr. Froehlich**
9:30-10:20 A. M.   Credit: 2 semester-hours   Room 2, Annex No. 2

Business Education S406—Advertising I   **Dr. VanDervee**
10:30-11:20 A. M.   Credit: 2 semester-hours   Room 4, Annex No. 2

**Business Education S504—Improvement of Instruction in
  Business Education**   **Dr. VanDervee**
8:30-9:20 A. M.   Credit: 2 semester-hours   Room 4, Annex No. 2

Business Education S512—Tax Accounting   **Mr. Froehlic**
8:30-9:20 A. M.   Credit: 2 semester-hours   Room 2, Annex No.

Business Education S602—Seminar in Economics
                              Mr. Sheppard and Mr. Froehlic
9:30 A. M.-12:20 P. M.   Credit: 6 semester-hours   Room 5, Annex No.

English

**English S401X—The Teaching of English
  in Secondary Schools**   **Dr. Fulcom**
Students are taught to develop and use materials of the classroom; lesson plans and units of work are prepared and presented for criticism; textbooks are analyzed for training in their use; and bulletin board exhibits and visual education materials are prepared by students for the class.
8:30-9:20 A. M.   Credit: 2 semester-hours   Room

English S431A—Shakespeare I (Tragedies)   **Mr. Bo**
9:30-10:20 A. M.   Credit: 2 semester-hours   Room

English S442A—American Literature I   **Mr. Conr**
9:30-10:20 A. M.   Credit: 2 semester-hours   Room

English S442B—American Literature II   **Mr. Conr**
11:30 A. M.-12:20 P. M.   Credit: 2 semester-hours   Room

English S449—Public Speaking   **Mr. Balla**
8:30-9:20 A. M.   Credit: 2 semester-hours   Room

English S462—Group Discussion and Leadership   **Mr. Balla**
11:30 A. M.-12:20 P. M.   Credit: 2 semester-hours   Room

English S507—Critical Writing   Dr. Fulcomer
10:30-11:20 A. M.   Credit: 2 semester-hours   Room 1

English S528—Perspectives in World Literature   Mr. Bohn
Open to all students, regardless of majors.
10:30-11:20 A. M.   Credit: 2 semester-hours   Room 2

Geography

Geography S413—Economic Geography of South America   Dr. Milstead
10:30-11:20 A. M.   Credit: 2 semester-hours   Room 26

Geography S418—Regional Geography of North America   Dr. Milstead
11:30 A. M.-12:20 P. M.   Credit: 2 semester-hours   Room 26

Geography S504—Economic Geography of Europe   Dr. Milstead
8:30-9:20 A. M.   Credit: 2 semester-hours   Room 26

Health Education

Health Education S407—Prevention and Care of Athletic Injuries   Mr. Coder
11:30 A. M.-12:20 P. M.   Credit: 2 semester-hours   Room D

Health Education S408—Driver Education and Training   Mr. Coder
See "Post-Summer Session Course" on page 22

Health Education S411—School Health Services   Mr. DeRosa
10:30-11:20 A. M.   Credit: 2 semester-hours   Room 7, CHS

Integration S476—Elementary School Health and
    Physical Education   Mr. DeRosa
See "Elementary Education" on page 19

Integration

Integration S400A—Principles and Philosophy   Dr. Stearns
    of Secondary Education
8:30-9:30 A. M.   Credit: 2 semester-hours   Room 2

Integration S407A—Television in Education Workshop:
    Programming and Production   Mr. Sheft

Integration S410—Teaching Materials Workshop   Mr. Forbes
See "Montclair State Teachers College Workshops" on page 16

Integration S500A—Basic Educational Trends   Dr. Fraser
8:30-9:20 A. M.   Credit: 2 semester-hours   Room 24

Integration S500C—Recent Trends in Secondary School
    Methods   Dr. Atkinson
9:30-10:20 A. M.   Credit: 2 semester-hours   Room 28

Integration S500D—School Administration I:
    Functions and Organization   Mr. Morehead
8:30-9:20 A. M.   Credit: 2 semester-hours   Room 27

Integration S500E—School Administration II: Law and
    Finance   Mr. Morehead
9:30-10:20 A. M.   Credit: 2 semester-hours   Room 27

Integration S500F—School Administration III:
    Community Relations   Dr. Atkinson
10:30-11:20 A. M.   Credit: 2 semester-hours   Room 28

11

Integration S502—Organization and Administration of the
Modern High School   Dr. Smit'
8:30-9:20 A. M.   Credit: 2 semestter-hours   Room 2

Integration S503—Methods and Instruments of Research   Dr. Frase
10:30 A. M.-11:20 P. M.   Credit: 2 semester-hours   Room 2

Integration S504A—Curriculum Construction
in the Secondary School   Dr. Smit'
9:30-10:20 A. M.   Credit: 2 semester-hours   Room 2

Integration S505—Organization and Administration of
Extra-Curricular Activities   Mr. Morehea
11:30 A. M.-12:20 P. M.   Credit: 2 semester-hours   Room 2

Integration S508—Supervision of Instruction in
Secondary Schools   Dr. Atkinso
11:30 A. M.-12:20 P. M.   Credit: 2 semester-hours   Room 2

Integration S517—Administration of the Elementary School   Miss Bristc
8:30-9:20 A. M.   Credit: 2 semester-hours   Room 1

Integration S518—Supervision of Instruction in the
Elementary School   Miss Bristc
11:30 A. M.-12:20 P. M.   Credit: 2 semester-hours   Room 1

Integration S520—Principles of Mental Hygiene   Dr. Ingebritse:
11:30 A. M.-12:20 P. M.   Credit: 2 semester-hours   Room 3

Integration S535A—Vocational Guidance   Mr. E. C. Davi
8:30-9:20 A. M.   Credit: 2 semester-hours   Room

Integration S538—Group Guidance and Counseling Activities Mr. Polglaz
9:30-10:20 A. M.   Credit: 2 semester-hours   Room 3

Integration S548—Curriculum Construction in the
Elementary School   Miss Brist
9:30-10:20 A. M.   Credit: 2 semester-hours   Room]

Integration S551—Principles and Techniques of Guidance   Mr. Polgla
8:30-9:20 A. M.   Credit: 2 semester-hours   Room

Integration S602—Seminar in Guidance   Mr. E. C. Dav
10:30 A. M.-12:20 P. M.   Credit: 4 semester-hours   Room

Mathematics

Mathematics S400—Educational Statistics   Mr. Humphre
9:30-10:20 A. M.   Credit: 2 semester-hours   Room 2, Annex No.

Mathematics S410—Mathematics of Finance   Mr. Cliffo
10:30-11:20 A. M.   Credit: 2 semester-hours   Room 3, Annex No.

Integration S477—Elementary School Mathematics   Mr. Humphre
See "Elementary Education" on page 19

Mathematics S504—Modern Algebra   Dr. D. R. Da
8:30-9:20 A. M.   Credit: 2 semester-hours   Room 1, Annex No.

Mathematics S505—Consumer Mathematics: A Background for
Teaching in the Junior High School   Mr. Cliffo
9:30-10:20 A. M.   Credit: 2 semester-hours   Room 3, Annex No.

Mathematics S506—Current Research in
Secondary Mathematics   Dr. D. R. Dav
9:30-10:20 A. M.   Credit: 2 semester-hours   Room 1, Annex No.

Mathematics S523—The Theory of Probability   Mr. Cliffo
11:30 A. M.-12:20 P. M.   Credit: 2 semester-hours   Room 3, Annex No.

12

Music

Integration S475A—Fundamentals of Elementary School Music   Miss Morse
See "Elementary Education" on page 19

New Tools for Learning

**Integration S407A—Television in Education Workshop:
   Programming and Production**   Mr. Sheft

Integration S410—Teaching Materials Workshop   Mr. Forbes
See "Montclair State Teachers College Workshops" on page 16

Social Studies S461—New England and French Canada   Mr. Bye

**Social Studies S468—New Jersey, Lower Hudson Valley, and
   Eastern Pennsylvania**   Mr. Bye

Social Studies S469—Mexico   Mr. Bye
See "Field Studies in American Life" on page 15

Science

Chemistry S408B—Industrial Chemistry, Part II   Dr. Reed
Lectures: 11:30 A. M.-12:20 P. M.; Tues. and Thurs.
Field Trips: Tues. and Thurs. P. M.
                         Credit: 2 semester-hours   Room 22

Chemistry S510—Food Inspection and Analysis   Dr. Reed
Lectures: 10:30-11:20 A. M.
Laboratories: Mon, Wed. and Fri. P. M.
                         Credit: 4 semester-hours   Room 22

Integration S478—Elementary School Science   Mr. Allen
See "Elementary Education" on page 19

Physics S407A & B—Aviation, Parts I and II   Mr. Placek
8:30-10:20 A. M.
Field Trips by Arrangement   Credit: 4 semester-hours   Room 8, CHS

Social Studies

Social Studies S429—Present-Day Social Problems   Dr. Clayton
11:30 A. M.-12:20 P. M.   Credit: 2 semester-hours   Room 21

**Social Studies S446—Current Problems in Economics
   and Government**   Dr. Rellahan
8:30-9:20 A. M.   Credit: 2 semester-hours   Room 20

Social Studies S456—International Economic Relations   Dr. Rellahan
9:30-10:20 A. M.   Credit: 2 semester-hours   Room 20

Social Studies S461—New England and French Canada   Mr. Bye

**Social Studies S468—New Jersey, Lower Hudson Valley, and
   Eastern Pennsylvania**   Mr. Bye

Social Studies S469—Mexico   Mr. Bye
See "Field Studies in American Life" on page 15

**Social Studies S472—Modern Social Studies Instruction
   and Supervision**   Dr. Moffatt
8:30-9:20 A. M.   Credit: 2 semester-hours   Room 21

13

Social Studies S475—History of American Thought   **Dr. Clayton**
9:30-10:20 A. M.   Credit: 2 semester-hours   Room 21

Integration S479—Elementary School Social Studies   **Dr. Moffatt**
See "Elementary Education" on page 19

Social Studies S490A—The United Nations   **Mr. Kops**

Social Studies S490C—The Specialized Agencies of the
   United Nations   **Mr. Kops**
See "United Nations Institute" on page 17

Social Studies S491A and Social Studies S491B— Workshop in
   Citizenship Education, Part I and Part II   **Dr. Clayton**
See "Montclair State Teachers College Workshops" on page 16

Social Studies S496A—The Chinese Society   **Dr. Y. T. Mei**

Social Studies S499—Introduction to Chinese Culture   **Dr. Chih Meng**
See "China Institute of New Jersey" on page 16

Social Studies S518—Recent Trends in American History   **Dr. Moffatt**
10:30-11:20 A. M.   Credit: 2 semester-hours   Room 20

FIELD STUDIES IN AMERICAN LIFE

July 10 through July 26, 1953

Social Studies S469—Mexico   Mr. Bye

This field-study course aims to give a comprehensive view of contemporary Mexican life with its geographic, economic, historic, and cultural setting. Transportation to and from Mexico City is by air and in Mexico by private cars. Overnight stops and meals are at the best hotels. Places visited include Xochimilco, Acolman, Teotihuacan, Fortin, Puebla, Oaxaca, Tehuantepec, Queretero, Guanajuato, Dolores Hidalgo, San Miguel de Allende, San Jose Purua, Morelia, Teluca, Taxco, and Cuernevaca. The itinerary is carefully planned to include all points of major interest and significance. Special studies may be made in the fields of geography, history, art, architecture, archaeology, sociology, economics, and other fields. All expenses: $568.00. Reservations must be made in advance; quota limited.

August 3 through August 14, 1953

Social Studies S468—New Jersey, the Lower Hudson Valley, and Eastern
    Pennsylvania   Mr. Bye

This field study course covers all sections of New Jersey (northeastern, northwestern, central, and southern), the Hudson Valley from Manhattan to Bear Mountain, and southeastern Pennsylvania from Philadelphia to Lancaster and Scranton.

Among the activities and places to be studied are natural resources, conservation, industries, state and national parks, historic sites and buildings, topographic features, and the manners and customs of each section. There are three one-day field trips and a five-day trip by bus with overnight stops at first-class hotels, as well as two days of class work at the College. This course furnishes a series of interesting experiences of special value to teachers of the history and geography of New Jersey, New York, and Pennsylvania. All-expense cost: $99.00

August 17 through August 28, 1953

Social Studies S461—New England and French Canada   Mr. Bye
By chartered bus. All expenses except regular meals (two dinners included in price): $125.00   Credit: 3 semester-hours

See paragraph above for information with regard to registration for this course.

Credit: 2 semester-hours

While the above courses are given as a part of the Summer Session offerings of the State Teachers College at Montclair, registration for them must be made in advance through the Bureau of Field Studies. Likewise, payment is made as requested by the Bureau. Interested students should address Mr. E. C. Bye, Bureau of Field Studies, New Jersey State Teachers College, Upper Montclair, New Jersey. This should be done at once, as the number of students in the courses must be limited to a definite number.

Trenton State Teachers College

June 30 through July 20, 1953

Geography of the Northwest   Dr. Botts
Credit: 5 semester-hours

For further details, write to: Dr. Adelbert K. Botts, Director, College Field Studies, State Teachers College, Trenton, New Jersey.

WORKSHOPS AND INSTITUTES

Montclair State Teachers College Workshops
June 30—August 11, 1953

Integration S407A—Television in Education Workshop:
   Programming and Production   **Mr. Sheft**

Limited to 15 students   Credit: 2 semester-hours
8:30-10:20 A.M., Mon., Wed., Fri., and 8:30-9:20 Tues. and Thurs.   Room A

Integration S410—Teaching Materials Workshop   **Mr. Forbes**
10:30-11:20 A. M.   Credit: 2 semester-hours   Room 4

Social Studies S491A—Workshop in Citizenship Education, I   **Dr. Clayton**

Social Studies S491B—Workshop in Citizenship Education, II   **Dr. Clayton**
Membership in the second part of the workshop is limited to those who have completed Social Studies S491A, and participants in this advanced workshop meet and work with the members of the first part.
10:30-11:20 A. M.   Credit: 2 semester-hours   Room 21

China Institute of New Jersey
June 29—July 11, 1953

China Institute of New Jersey is a permanent year-round organization composed of former students of the "China Workshop" course. The policies and program of the Institute are determined by an elected executive committee, an advisory board of laymen, and representatives from the Faculty of Montclair Teachers College, in consultation with the Chinese Director.

Dr. Chih Meng, Director of the China Institute of America, is Chinese Director of China Institute of New Jersey. The College provides the facilities necessary for the satisfactory completion of the courses offered by the Institute. These are given on the senior-graduate level, so that students may work either for undergraduate or for graduate credit. While the primary and definite purpose of the Institute is to assist the teachers of New Jersey, men and women who desire to take these courses for cultural, vocational, or avocational purposes are welcome also. Students may enroll for college credit if eligible to do so, or simply as Auditors for no credit. The cost is the same in both cases. Those who enroll for credit are expected to complete such notebooks, papers, projects, and examinations as are assigned by the course instructors. The preliminary grading of these papers, projects, and examinations is done by the Chinese teachers, while the final grading and coordinating is done by a representative of the regular Faculty of the College.

Students who enroll for an entire course follow the instructions below:

1. Write to Mrs. Willard Church, State Teachers College, Upper Montclair, N. J. for a set of the registration materials.
2. Return these materials, properly filled in, and accompanied by check or money order made payable to the College.
3. Retain the Class Admission Card which Mrs. Church will send, until the opening of the course on June 29.
4. A student who is planning to take a course of the College that runs from 8:30-9:20 A. M., or the United Nations course, or the post-summer session course in Driver Education, or all of them, should register for these courses at this same time, to obviate a second registration later on.

China Institute Offerings

Art S414—History of Chinese Art   **Mr. Nelson Wu**
Although there is no prerequisite for this course, it is suggested that those who enroll for it should have some knowledge of art or have taken Social Studies S499, Introduction to Chinese Culture. This course was formerly entitled "China Workshop."
9:30 A. M.-4 P.M.   Credit: 3 semester-hours   Room 12, CHS

Social Studies S496A—The Chinese Society   **Dr. Y. T. Mei**
Prerequisite: Social Studies S499, Introduction to Chinese Culture. This course was formerly entitled "China Workshop."
9:30 A. M.-4 P. M.   Credit: 3 semester-hours   Room 4, CHS

Social Studies S499—Introduction to Chinese Culture   **Dr. Chih Meng**
This course was formerly entitled "China Workshop."
9:30 A. M.-4 P. M.   Credit: 3 semester-hours   Auditorium, CHS

United Nations Institute
July 13—July 24, 1953

In the summer of 1951, the College offered the first United Nations Institute, under the co-sponsorship of the Cosmopolitan Club of Montclair and of the New Jersey Chapter, American Association for the United Nations. Last summer, in addition to the beginning course, the College included in this Institute a second course dealing particularly with the United Nations as a basis for the American Foreign Policy. This year, the introductory course will be repeated as usual, and a third course, described below, instead of the second course of last summer.

Social Studies S490A—The United Nations   **Mr. Kops**
Lectures: 9:30 A. M.-12:00 Noon; Workshops: 1:00-3 P. M.
Field Trips to the United Nations by Arrangement
                    Credit: 3 semester-hours   Auditorium, CHS

Social Studies S490C—The Specialized Agencies of the
United Nations   **Mr. Kops**
The purpose of this course is to give the student an opportunity to learn about the various activities of the Specialized Agencies of the United Nations. The course deals with the positive activities of the United Nations in the various areas of human welfare. Visiting lecturers from the agencies themselves and from areas of the world receiving such help are a regular part of the class work. Trips to the New York offices of these agencies and individual research make up the balance of the work for this course. **Social Studies S490A—The United Nations**, or its equivalent is a prerequisite for registration in this course.
Lectures: 9:30 A. M.-12:00 Noon; Workshops 1:00-3 P. M.
Field Trips to the United Nations by Arrangement.
                    Credit: 3 semester-hours   Auditorium, CHS

While the primary and definite purpose of this Institute, like that of the China Institute, is to assist the teachers of New Jersey, men and women who desire to take these courses for other purposes are welcome also. Students may enroll, if eligible to do so, for graduate or for undergraduate credit, or simply as Auditors for no credit. The cost is the same in both cases. Those who enroll for credit are expected to complete such notebooks, papers, projects, and examination as are assigned by the course instructor.

Students who enroll for an entire course follow the instructions below.

    1. Write to Mr. Walter Kops, State Teachers College, Upper Montclair, N. J. for the set of registration materials.

    2. Return the filled in materials, with check made payable to the College. See paragraph on page 8 of this Bulletin for information concerning tuition fees and service charges.

Mr. Castelnueva of Mexico emphasizes a point in an i
group of students at the United Nations Institute.

COURSES FOR THOSE WHO DESIRE TO TEACH IN ELEMENTARY GRADES

These courses are open to the following only:

(1) Those who already hold a degree from Montclair with a Certificate in Secondary Education, and

(2) Those who are now matriculated at Montclair for a degree and the Certificate in Secondary Education.

These courses are offered to assist the Montclair students in attaining provisional and standard certification to teach in elementary grades. Detailed requirements for such certification are listed on pages 14, 15, 16, and 68 of the Eighteenth Edition of the Rules Concerning Teachers' Certificates.

The courses listed below may apply as general electives in undergraduate curriculums, and, **with the Advisor's approval**, as graduate electives for majors in Administration and Supervision.

Integration S474—Elementary School Arts and Crafts   **Mr. Vernacchia**
Section one: 8:30-9:20 A. M.   Campus Studio Workshop
                    Credit: 2 semester-hours
Section two: 10:30-11:20 A. M.   Campus Studio Workshop
                    Credit: 2 semester-hours

Integration S475A—Fundamentals of Elementary School Music   Miss Morse
9:30-10:20 A. M.   Credit: 2 semester-hours   Room 5, CHS

**Integration S476—Elementary School Health and
Physical Education**   **Mr. DeRosa**
Section one: 8:30-9:20 A. M.   Room 7, CHS and Gym, CHS
                    Credit: 2 semester-hours
Section two: 9:30-10:20 A. M.   Room 7, CHS and Gym, CHS
                    Credit: 2 semester-hours

Integration S477—Elementary School Mathematics   Mr. Humphreys
10:30-11:20 A. M.   Credit: 2 semester-hours   Room 2, Annex No. 1

Integration S478—Elementary School Science   Mr. Allen
8:30-9:20 A. M.   Credit: 2 semester-hours   Room 9, Annex No. 3

Integration S479—Elementary School Social Studies   Dr. Moffatt
11:30-12:20 P. M.   Credit: 2 semester-hours   Room 20

In addition to the above courses, **Geography S418, Regional Geography of North America,** applies on the Limited Elementary Certificate. See "Geography" on page 11.

Special Program for Graduates of Liberal Arts Colleges
Part I, 6 semester-hours   Part II, 4 semester-hours
A special program designed to offer a series of experiences leading to certification of liberal arts graduates for teaching in the elementary schools of New Jersey will be offered by the State Teachers Colleges at Glassboro, Jersey City, Newark, Paterson, and Trenton.

The program will consist of two parts comprising a total of 10 semester-hours of credit. The first part will be a unit of six semester-hours offered in the 1953 summer session. This will be followed by a fall session of four semester hours. Complete announcement of this program will be available at any one of the five State Teachers Colleges noted above.

NEW JERSEY STATE SCHOOL OF CONSERVATION
Stokes State Forest, Branchville, N. J.

COURSES IN CONSERVATION, FIELD SCIENCES, CAMPING EDUCATION, SOCIAL STUDIES, AND WATER FRONT SAFETY

Spring and Summer, 1953

The State Department of Education, through the six State Teachers Colleges, offers a wide range of courses at the School of Conservation. Teachers, prospective teachers, camp counselors, nature specialists, and playground directors have an opportunity to combine study and vacation in the beautiful and cool Kittatinny Mountains of northern New Jersey.

Public schools throughout the nation are being charged with the responsibility of teaching conservation education courses. New Jersey teachers have a unique opportunity to become acquainted with the problems and methods of teaching in this fast-growing field. Science, social studies, and elementary school teachers will be particularly interested in the following courses, but all educators should have a basic understanding of conservation if they are to meet the needs of the youngsters in our schools.

Credit for the following courses, offered between June 19 and September 7, may be applied toward graduate or undergraduate degrees at any of the New Jersey State Teachers Colleges, subject to approval in advance by the institution. Credit may be transferred to other institutions where such transfer is permitted toward an undergraduate or graduate degree. Several of the courses may be substituted for courses required for elementary teaching certification.

For additional information write to: Edward J. Ambry, New Jersey State School of Conservation, State Teachers College, Upper Montclair, New Jersey.

1953 SUMMER COURSE OFFERINGS

Integration 440. Camping Education   June 19 through 30
Credit: 2 semester-hours

Integration 441. Conservation Education   June 19 through 30
Credit: 2 semester-hours

Biology 203. Introduction to Field Biology   June 19 through 30
Credit: 2 semester-hours

Physical Education 313. Methods of Teaching Folk and Square Dancing
June 19 through 30
Credit: 2 semester-hours

Physical Education 410. Water Safety and First Aid   June 19 through 30
Credit: 2 semester-hours

Science 412. Field studies in Science: Biological   June 2 through 22
Credit: 2 semester-hours

Integration 441. Conservation Education   June 2 through 22
Credit: 2 semester-hours

Social Studies 494. Social, Economic, and Geographic Implications of Conservation   July 23 through August 12

Everday problems of living as they are related to and affected by the wise use of our natural resources are studied in this course. The student learns about the renewable resources—soil, water, forests, and wildlife—as well as the non-renewable resources— minerals. oils, and coal. Economic, social, community, national, and individual problems are approached by giving the student first-hand experiences gained through extensive field trips in northern New Jersey. This course is of particular interest to social studies and elementary school teachers but also forms an excellent background for all educational fields. Methods of teaching, courses of study, and teaching units are developed.

Credit: 4 semester-hours

Art 415. School Arts and Crafts with Native Materials   August 16 through 27
This course is approved by the State Board of Examiners to meet the art requirement for certification to teach in grades 1-8.

Credit: 2 semester-hours

Integration 480. Field Science for Elementary Teachers August 16 through 27
This course is approved by the State Board of Examiners to meet the science requirement for certification to teach in grades 1-8.

Credit: 2 semester-hours

Social Studies 477. Rural Sociology   August 16 through 27
Credit: 2 semester-hours

Science 416. Problems in Conservation .. Any time between July 2 - August 27
Credit: To be determined by length of stay and nature of problem

Recreational Leadership Institute   August 29 through September 7
This institute is designed for teachers, camp counselors, and other recreational leaders in outdoor education who are interested in folk and square dancing in camping, schools, and community projects. Registrants learn to teach folk and square dancing and to call for such dances. Special emphasis will be given to the function of folk and square dancing as a part of planned recreation in conservation camps and other group projects. Competent instructors will teach the many types of folk dances enjoyed throughout the United States. Registration for this institute is through the American Squares Magazine, 1159 Broad Street, Newark, New Jersey. This institute is not planned for college credit.

POST-SUMMER SESSION COURSE
August 10 through August 21, 1953

To Meet an Urgent Need, the following course is being offered by the State Teachers College at Montclair, with the assistance of the **New Jersey State Safety Council**, the **New Jersey Automobile Club**, the **American Automobile Association**, the **New Jersey State Police**, and the **New Jersey Department of Motor Vehicles.**

This course Offers the Necessary Opportunity for men and women to prepare themselves to teach behind-the-wheel driver education in high schools. Enrollees completing the work of the course are presented with a certificate indicating the work done.

Authorization: In order to teach behind-the-wheel driver education and driver training, a teacher must have his or her certificate endorsed by the Division of Teacher Certification, State Department of Education, for teaching behind-the-wheel automobile driver education and driver training.

The Requirements for such Endorsement on the teacher's certificate are: (18th edition, 1951, "Rules Concerning Teachers Certificates," page 22)

1. A valid New Jersey teacher's certificate.
2. A current New Jersey driver's license.
3. Three years of automobile driving experience.
4. Evidence of satisfactory completion of a course in driver education and driver training approved by the Commissioner of Education.

Veterans may take this course under the G.I. Bill, if they have so arranged with the Veterans' Counselor of the College.

Living Expenses and Traveling Expenses must be paid by the student. Those desiring hotel accommodations should write to Mr. F. K. Schultze, Mgr., New Jersey Auto Club, AAA, 156 Clinton Avenue, Newark 5, New Jersey. The College Residence Halls are closed at this time.

Textbooks and Other Text Materials will be furnished to each enrollee with out charge.

Registration for this course will be accepted up to and including the openin day of the course. However, students should register early if possible, pref erably on the regular registration days for the Summer Session. There is limit to the number of registrations which may be accepted.

Health Education S408—Behind the Wheel Driver Education and Driver Training   **Mr. Code**

*9-12 and 1-4 daily   Credit: 2 semester-hours   Room

*Because Health Education S408 begins on August 10 and the courses of th Summer Session do not end until August 11, Health Education S408 will mee on August 10 and August 11 at the following hours: 1:00-9:00 P. M.

E TEACHERS COLLEGE

SESSION

NEW JERSEY

SUMMER SESSION

Bulletin of

MONTCLAIR
STATE TEACHERS COLLEGE

1 9 5 4
June 28th to August 6th

UPPER MONTCLAIR, NEW JERSEY

OFFICERS OF ADMINISTRATION

State Board of Education

George O. Smalley, *President* .... Bound B
Mrs. Edward L. Katzenbach, *Vice-President* .... Princ
Arthur E. Armitage, Sr. .... Collingsv
Mrs. Margaret T. Armstrong .... Stewarts
Lewis F. Gayner .... S
Phillip R. Gebhardt Cl
John S. Gray .... Ne
James W. Parker, Sr. .... Red]
Mrs. Herbert Reim .... Mayv
Mrs. Frederic H. Sanford .... N
Henry A. Williams .... Pate

Commissioner of Education

Dr. Frederick M. Raubinger

Assistant Commissioner for Higher Education

Dr. Robert H. Morrison

College Administration

E. DeAlton Partridge, Ph.D. .... Pres
Clyde M. Huber, Ph.D. .... Dean of Instru
Bernard Siegel, M.B.A. .... Business Ma
Otis C. Ingebritsen, Ph.D. .... Chairman of the Graduate Comn
Keith W. Atkinson, Ph.D. .... Director of College High S
Earl C. Davis, M.S. .... Director of Personnel and Gui
Margaret A. Sherwin, A.M. .... Dean of W
Mary M. House, B.C.S. .... Reg
Elizabeth S. Favor, A.M. .... Assistant in Graduate Pers
Anne Banks Cridlebaugh, A.M. .... Libr
Otto Cordes, P.E. .... Engineer in Charge, Mainte

Health Services

Charlotte L. Pritchard, R.N. .... College

FACULTY

Summer Session 1954

C. DeAlton Partridge, Ph.D. ....President
Clyde M. Huber, Ph.D. ....Dean of Instruction
Hugh Allen, Jr., M.S. ....Science
Keith W. Atkinson, Ph.D. ....Integration
Edgar C. Bye, A.M. ....Director, New Tools for Learning Bureau
Frank L. Clayton, Ph.D. ....Social Studies
Alden C. Coder, Ed.M. ....Health and Physical Education
Philip S. Cohen, A.M. ....Social Studies
Germaine Poreau Cressey, A.M. ......Acting Chairman of the Dept. of Languages
David R. Davis, Ph.D. ....Acting Head, Department of Mathematics
Earl C. Davis, M.S. ....Personnel and Guidance
Jerome G. DeRosa, A.M. ....Health and Physical Education
Emma Fantone, A.M. ....Director, Audio-Visual Aids Service
L. Howard Fox, A.M. ....Speech
Mowat G. Fraser, Ph.D. ....Head of Department of Integration
Paul E. Froehlich, Ed.D. ....Research
Edwin S. Fulcomer, Ed.D. ....Head of Department of English
V. Paul Hamilton, A.M. ....English
R. Roland Humphreys, A.M. ....Mathematics
Otis C. Ingebritsen, Ph.D. ....Psychology
George W. Kays, A.M. ....Mathematics
Walter E. Kops, A.M. ....Director, United Nations Institute
Russell Krauss, Ph.D. ....English
Chih Meng, Ph.D. ....Director, China Institute
Harley P. Milstead, Ph.D. ....Geography
Allan Morehead, A.M. ....Integration
Filomena Peloro, A.M. ....Spanish
James P. Pettegrove, A.M. ....English
William R. Phipps, Ed.D. ....Integration
John J. Rellahan, Ph.D. ....Acting Head, Department of Social Studies
Thaddeus J. Sheft, A.B. ....Television
Horace J. Sheppard, A.M. ....Head of Department of Business Education
Kenneth O. Smith, Ph.D. ....Physics
V. Scott Smith, Ph.D. ....Integration
Donald O. Thomas, M.B.A. ....Business Education
Elizabeth T. VanDerveer, Ed.D. ....Business Education
Ralph A. Vernacchia, A.M. ....Art
Frederic H. Young, Ph.D ....English

GRADUATE COMMITTEE

Otis C. Ingebritsen, *Chairman*

Clyde M. Huber	Rufus D. Reed
Elizabeth T. VanDerveer	W. Paul Hamilton
David R. Davis	John J. Rellahan

Elizabeth S. Favor, *Secretary*

Montclair
Offers

A Satisfying Social Life

Pioneering Experiences in Education

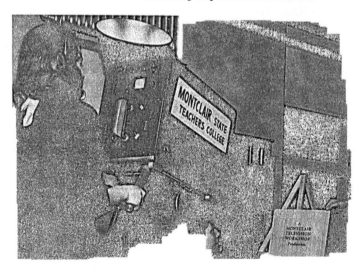

SUMMER SESSION OF THE
NEW JERSEY STATE TEACHERS COLLEGE AT MONTCLAIR
Objectives and Academic Status

The College is a professional school which prepares teachers, supervisors, and principals of high schools, and administrators of public school systems. The degrees offered by this College are those of Bachelor of Arts and Master of Arts. Certificate courses are offered for those who now hold degrees from other colleges.

The New Jersey State Teachers College at Montclair is a fully accredited member of the American Association of Colleges of Teacher Education, the Middle State Association of Colleges and Secondary Schools, and the American Association of University Women.

How to Reach the Campus

The College is located about one mile north of the center of Upper Montclair. Trains of the Greenwood Lake Division, Erie R. R., stop at Montclair Heights, the College Station. Trains of the Lackawanna R. R. connect at Montclair with the following bus lines: Nos. 60, 64, and 76 to the College.

Residence Halls for Men and Women

Edward Russ Hall and Chapin Hall are Montclair College's two well-appointed Residences. The charge for living on campus during the Summer Session is: $14.50 per week; which includes room, breakfast, and dinner. A la carte luncheons are served in the College cafeteria. For one student alone in a double room, an extra charge of $2.00 per week is made. The College provides and launders sheets, pillowcase, and bedpad. Towels, table lamps, blankets, clocks, and similar items must be provided and cared for by the student. The boarding-hall fee must be paid on or before the first day of the Summer Session. No rebate is made for occasional absence or voluntary withdrawal during the session. These prices are subject to change.

For reservations in a College Residence Hall, women address: Dean of Women, State Teachers College, Upper Montclair, N. J. Men address: Dean of Men.

Schedule of the Summer Session

Registration will take place on Monday, June 28. Hours, 9-12 and 1-4. Classes will begin on Tuesday morning, June 29, at 8 A. M. and will continue through Thursday, August 5. All classes meet daily, Monday to Friday, inclusive, at the hours indicated for each, and on the following Saturdays: July 10, July 17, and July 24. Monday, July 5, is a Holiday.

Matriculation for the Master of Arts Degree

Since not more than 8 semester-hours of work taken prior to matriculation re allowed to apply on the Master of Arts degree, the student should take care o complete the matriculation procedure as soon as he has that amount of credit; ooner, if possible. Transfer of graduate credit from other institutions is

5

permitted only to those students who are graduates of New Jersey State Teacher Colleges and the maximum permitted is 8 semester-hours.

Those who desire to become candidates for the degree must request a application form from the Chairman of the Graduate Committee and return i properly filled and accompanied by an Official Transcript of all previous wor on college level. **When such an applicant has been accepted by the Colleg** as a candidate for the degree, a definite statement is furnished to him, showin the requirements which he must fulfill to earn the degree. This sheet of requir ments becomes the student's Work Program and should be brought by th student each time he comes to enroll for courses.

Auditors

Men and women who desire to take courses for cultural, vocational, c avocational purposes without college credits may register as auditors.

A student who desires to enroll in a course for which he already holds cred must register as an auditor in that course.

A student who desires to enroll in a course for which he has not complete the prerequisites must enroll as an auditor in that course.

Change of Status in a Course

If a student desires to change his status in a course from "credit" to "auditor or from "auditor" to "credit," he must make formal application for such chang not later than the middle of the course. Forms for this purpose may be procure from Miss Favor, in the Registrar's Office. Such changes cannot be made afte the midpoint of the course is passed.

Students Matriculated at Montclair for the A.M. Degree

Since September 1, 1952, all students matriculating in the Graduate Divisio have been required to complete at least one full-time summer session, or, in lie thereof, at least one regular semester of full-time graduate attendance.

The selection of courses must be in accordance with the student's Wor Program, and his registration form will be signed by the Head of the Depar ment in which the student is majoring or by a representative of that departmen present in the registration room.

Candidates for a degree must file with the Registrar an application for con ferment of the degree before November 30 of the college year in which the wor is to be completed. Application blanks for this purpose may be secured in th Registrar's Office. The burden of responsibility for the request rests with th candidate. This is of special significance to the teacher-in-service who may hav distributed the work for the degree over several years.

Students Matriculated at Other Colleges

Several years ago, when the State Teachers College at Montclair offere courses to its own accelerated candidates for the Bachelor's degree, it wa possible to accept students from other colleges in freshman, sophomore, an junior year courses, as well as in courses of the senior year. Beginning in th summer of 1950, however, the College returned to its pre-war custom of offerin courses in its Summer Session primarily to teachers-in-service. Since suc teachers already hold the Bachelor's degree, with few exceptions, the course shown in this Bulletin are, for the most part, only Graduate and Senior-Graduat courses.

6

A student who is planning to attend Montclair this summer should take this Bulletin to a conference with the Dean of his own college to arrange a program of work. For the Dean's information: the numbering of courses at Montclair follows this order: 100-399, inclusive, are undergraduate courses: 400-499, inclusive, are senior-college and graduate courses; 500 and above are graduate courses.

At the time of registration, the student should go to the table of the Department in which the courses are listed that he plans to take. The registration form must be signed by the Representative of the Department at that table. The College reserves the right to decide whether the student has fulfilled necessary prerequisites. He should bring with him, however, a letter from his own college. If the student is seeking certification to teach in New Jersey, he must confer with Dr. Fraser, Head of the Department of Integration. Please note paragraph under the Heading: "Certificates."

Certificates

The State Teachers College at Montclair offers work toward the following New Jersey Certificates: Secondary Teaching Certificate; Secondary School Principal's Certificate; Elementary School Principal's Certificate; Subject Supervisor's Certificate; General Supervisor's Certificate; Guidance Certificate; School Administrator's Certificate; Junior College Teacher's Certificate; and the Advanced Professional Certificate.

Those who matriculate at Montclair for a Master of Arts degree will receive information from Dr. Fraser, Head of the Integration Department, as to the requirements for each of these certificates. Students who have not matriculated at Montclair should write to Dr. E. C. Preston, Secretary of the State Board of Examiners, Department of Education, 175 West State Street, Trenton 8, N. J., for information as to the requirements. For an evaluation of work already completed, address Dr. Preston. An official transcript of such previous work should accompany the inquiry, with a statement as to the particular certificate desired.

The student should bring Dr. Preston's reply with him when conferring with Dr. Fraser as to his program of work.

Students who must have this information immediately should go to Trenton to confer with Dr. Preston or his assistant, Miss Smith.

Supervised Student Teaching

The opportunity to do supervised student teaching cannot be offered during the Summer Session. For fall teaching, students confer with Dr. Fraser at the College. Ask his secretary for an appointment.

Veterans

Veteran students taking work under the G. I. Bill and likewise the so-called Korean Veteran must see Mr. Neuner, Veterans' Counselor of the College, before the close of the spring semester on June 10 in order to make certain that when they come to enroll on June 28 their papers will all be in order. Students taking work under the G. I. Bill without having the proper papers must pay the usual tuition fees at the time of registration.

Students who have completed the work of the A.B. or the A.M. degree at Montclair must secure and present to Mr. Neuner the Supplemental Certificate of Eligibility before registering for further work. Veterans transferring to this College who have previously been in training under the G. I. Bill must secure the Supplemental Certificate of Eligibility, and present it to Mr. Neuner at the time of registration.

Conferences with Advisers

Appointments with the Dean of Instruction, the Chairman of the Gradua Committee, a Department Head, or the Veterans' Counselor may be made mail or telephone to their respective offices. This should be done at as early date as possible to avoid delay at the time of registration.

Summer Session Credit Load

The maximum amount of credit which may be earned in the Summer Sessi is 8 semester-hours, but only 6 are recommended. There is no provision for student to audit additional courses; consequently, the total of all courses tak during the Summer Session may not exceed 8 semester-hours and studer should not enroll for more. Additional credits may be earned by attending o of the sessions at the State School of Conservation that precedes or follo the Summer Session. Attention is called also to the Post-Summer Session cour in Behind the Wheel Driver Education and Driver Training and to the Fir Studies course in the Central Eastern Region which begins on August 17.

Each Summer Session course is in session at least thirty hours and carrie designated amount of credit. **It is not possible to earn three s. h. credit in two s. h. credit course.**

Registration Information

Registration takes place in the College Library, on Monday, June 28, fro 9 A. M. to 12 noon, and from 1 to 4 P. M. The Registration form of eve student must be signed by a Department Head or his representative. T student should report to the table of the Department in which he is majorin or, if not matriculated here for a degree at present, of the Department in whi he is taking courses. He may, in some instances, be required to obtain si natures in more than one Department, if he is taking courses in more than of Signs on the tables indicate the various Departments.

Matriculated students should bring their "Work Programs" when they cor to enroll.

The College reserves the right to close any course for which the enrollme is insufficient. The class will meet at least once, however, before this decisi is made. Students may then enter another course in place of the one disco tinued by going to the Registrar's Office to re-enroll and to receive the n Class Admission Card in exchange for the card of the discontinued cour

Students who decide not to enroll in an alternate course must so state, a letter of withdrawal, in order to receive a refund of tuition fees. The ca of the discontinued course should be enclosed in the letter.

If prerequisites are required for a course (see the course description), t student should make certain that he has fulfilled them or their equivalent befo enrolling in it.

If no previous work on college level has been taken, the student must cc sult the Dean of Instruction before enrolling in any course, except as an Audit

A student may not register for credit in any course for which he alrea holds credit, except by permission of the Dean of Instruction.

Anyone unable to enroll during the hours shown above must register duri the regular office hours of the College in the Registrar's office, allowing least 45 minutes for the procedure. The summer office hours are from 8 A. M. to 3:30 P. M.

The final date on which a student may enroll for credit is Thursday, July

Withdrawal from a Course

During the registration period of June 28, and on June 29, June 30, and July 1, a student may, with the advice and consent in writing of his adviser, withdraw from one course and enter another in its place. The Class Admission Card from the dropped course must be presented when registering for the new one in order for the new Class Admission Card to be issued.

If no new course is being taken, written notice to Miss Favor, Assistant in Graduate Personnel, must be given at once by the student. Miss Favor will notify the teacher of the course from which the student is withdrawing, as well as the Business Office of the College. Refunds are computed from the date of the receipt of the letter of withdrawal.

Students who neglect to follow this procedure receive a failing mark for the course or courses which they cease to attend.

Tuition Fees, Service Charge, and Credit Slips

Check or money-order should be made payable to New Jersey State Teachers College.

Tuition Fees: to students who are residents of New Jersey, $11.00 per semester-hour credit carried by the course. Non-residents of New Jersey pay $13.00 per credit. Courses taken by auditors for no credit cost the same.

Service Charge: 50¢ per semester-hour point.

Teachers who have supervised Montclair student-teachers and who have in their possession old Montclair credit slips may take them to the office of the Integration Department, where new ones will be issued. The Business Office cannot return any unused portion of a credit slip, so it is necessary that the new type credit slip be obtained before presenting it in payment of tuition fees. Training Teachers may use the credit slips of any one of the six New Jersey State Teachers Colleges when taking courses at Montclair, but should bring only the new type slip in all cases.

So long as any credit slips remain in a teacher's possession, they will be honored by the College although a new method of remuneration of training teachers is now in effect.

Final Marks

Following are the final marks which may be received for a course: A-Excellent; B-Good; C-Fair; D-Poor; F-Failure; Inc.-Incomplete; Wd-Withdrew; N. C.-No Credit.

The mark of "D" when earned in summer, part-time, or extension courses of this College is not accepted for degree credit at Montclair.

The mark of "F" is given when earned and when the student has failed to notify the Assistant in Graduate Personnel promptly of his withdrawal from a course.

The mark of "N. C." is given only to auditors.

The mark of "Wd" is given only when prompt notice of withdrawal has been given and when the student's work to that time has been satisfactory to the teacher of the course.

The mark of "Inc." is seldom given. It may, however, be granted to a student whose work is incomplete at the end of the Session and who is eager to finish the work for a higher grade than he could otherwise receive. All responsibility regarding incomplete work rests with the student. He will be notified of a date after which, if the work remains incomplete, the final grade will be recorded without further notice.

Report Cards and Transcripts

An Official Transcript showing the credits earned is sent to the studer personally ten days to two weeks following the close of the Session. A repor card for each course taken is sent with the transcript. The transcript is ser without cost, but a service charge of $1.00 is made for a duplicate copy.

A student whose college requires that the transcript be mailed directly t the Dean or Registrar should call, early in the Session, at the Registrar Office to address an envelope for this purpose.

Elementary Education Courses

Courses offered as a part of the curriculum for the graduate major i Educational Administration and Supervision should be carefully distinguishe from those offered toward the endorsement in elementary education on th teacher's certificate. The courses in the Administration and Supervision of El mentary Education apply on the Elementary **Principal's** certificate, but not o the Elementary **Teacher's** certificate.

Although the New Jersey State Teachers College at Montclair is engage primarily in preparing secondary school teachers, during the present shortage c teachers in the elementary schools it is deemed expedient to offer courses in th field of elementary education to those students who are eligible to enroll at thi College in such courses.

Students eligible to enroll at Montclair in courses leading to certification i elementary education are:

(1) those who already hold a degree from Montclair with a certificate i secondary education; and

(2) those who are now matriculated at Montclair for such a degree.

Montclair cannot accept any other students in these courses.

The eligible students should consult Miss House, the College Registrar, fc an evaluation of their previous work and a statement concerning the courses t be taken in order to receive the endorsement in elementary education on th secondary certificate already held or to be conferred.

Textbook Exhibit

In the Gymnasium of the Main Building, from July 7 through July 20, ther will be an exhibit of high school and elementary school textbooks. Whil primarily for the benefit of the principals and teachers attending the Summe Session, the exhibit will be open to undergraduate students and to members c the general public who may be interested in seeing the latest textbooks.

Mrs. E. S. Fulcomer will be in charge of the Exhibit.

COURSES OF THE SUMMER SESSION

Descriptions of the courses will be found in the 1953-55 Graduate Bulletin of the College. Courses numbered 500 and above are graduate courses; those numbered 400-499, inclusive, are senior-graduate courses and their descriptions in the Graduate Bulletin follow the descriptions of the graduate courses. Only entirely new courses are described in the Summer Session Bulletin.

Art

Art S406—Creative Arts Workshop   **Mr. Vernacchia**
9:30-10:20 A. M.   Credit: 2 semester-hours   Campus Studio Workshop

Art S414—History of Chinese Art   **Mr. Na-sun Wu**
See "China Institute of New Jersey" on page 18

Integration S474—Elementary School Arts and Crafts   **Mr. Vernacchia**
See "Elementary Education" on page 21

Business Education

Business Education S405—Marketing   **Mr. Sheppard**
8:30-9:20 A. M.   Credit: 2 semester-hours   Room 5, Annex No. 2

Business Education S408—Business Finance   **Mr. Thomas**
9:30-10:20 A. M.   Credit: 2 semester-hours   Room 2, Annex No. 2

Business Education S409—Money and Banking   **Mr. Thomas**
11:30 A. M.-12:20 P. M.   Credit: 2 semester-hours   Room 2, Annex No. 2

Business Education S411—Retail Store Management   **Dr. VanDerveer**
8:30-9:20 A. M.   Credit: 2 semester-hours   Room 4, Annex No. 2

Business Education S420—Field Studies in Business Education   **Mr. Sheppard**
10:30-11:20 A. M.—Class Sessions
Field Trips by Arrangement   Credit: 2 semester-hours   Room 5, Annex No. 2

Business Education S504—
Improvement of Instruction in Business Education   **Dr. VanDerveer**
9:30-10:20 A. M.   Credit: 2 semester-hours   Room 4, Annex No. 2

English and Speech

English S401X—The Teaching of English in Secondary Schools   **Dr. Fulcomer**
8:30-9:20 A. M.   Credit: 2 semester-hours   Room 1

English S426—The Victorian Novel   **Mr. Pettegrove**
8:30-9:20 A. M.   Credit: 2 semester-hours   Room 3

English S431A—Shakespeare's Major Plays, I: The Tragedies   **Mr. Hamilton**
9:30-10:20 A. M.   Credit: 2 semester-hours   Room 2

English S438—Masters of American Literature   **Dr. Fulcomer**
10:30-11:20 A. M.   Credit: 2 semester-hours   Room 1

English S441—Medieval Epic, Saga, and Romance   **Dr. Krauss**
9:30-10:20 A. M.   Credit: 2 semester-hours   Room 1

English S445—Eighteenth Century Literature   **Mr. Pettegrove**
10:30-11:20 A. M.   Credit: 2 semester-hours   Room 3

English S451—Literature and Art in Western Culture   **Dr. Young**
11:30 A. M.-12:20 P. M.   Credit: 2 semester-hours   Room 2

English S456—Play Direction   **Mr. Fox**
8:30-9:20 A. M.   Credit: 2 semester-hours   Room 2

English S503—Geoffrey Chaucer and His Times   **Dr. Krauss**
11:30 A. M.-12:20 P. M.   Credit: 2 semester-hours   Room 1

English S513—The Renaissance   **Mr. Hamilton**
10:30-11:20 A. M.   Credit: 2 semester-hours   Room 2

Foreign Languages

French S420—French Culture for the Elementary School   **Mrs. Cressey**
This course provides foreign language teachers on the elementary school level with a rich background for the teaching of French in grades one through six. It includes a review of French human geography including the provinces, customs, food, songs, and dances; French history through a study of the great men and women of France; and French holidays and holy days. This course is conducted entirely in French, and the materials are presented with a view toward enabling teachers to present various ·aspects of French culture to elementary school pupils. Prerequisite: At least 18 semester-hours credit in French.
9:30-10:50 A. M.   Credit: 3 semester-hours   Room 9

**Language S420—The Teaching of Foreign Languages in the
Elementary School**   **Mrs. Cressey and Miss Peloro**
This course includes an exploration of the reasons for teaching foreign languages in the elementary schools and a study of appropriate grade levels for beginning foreign languages. Current literature on this subject is used to provide study materials and bases for reports by students. Attention is given to the study and evaluation of the many ·syllabi and guides now available for the teaching of French and Spanish in the elementary school. As an outcome of this course, a syllabus covering grades one through six is produced by the class.
Prerequisite: At least 18 semester-hours credit in French or in Spanish.
11:00 A. M.-12:20 P. M.   Credit: 3 semester-hours   Room 9

Spanish S420—Spanish Culture for the Elementary School   **Miss Peloro**
This course provides foreign language teachers on the elementary school level with a rich background for the teaching of Spanish in grades one through six. It includes a review of Spanish human geography including the provinces, customs, food, songs, and dances; Spanish history through a study of the great men and women of Spain; and Spanish holidays and holy days. This course is conducted entirely in Spanish, and the materials are presented with a view toward enabling teachers to present various aspects of Spanish culture to elementary school pupils. Prerequisite: At least 18 semester-hours credit in Spanish.
9:30-10:50 A. M.   Credit: 3 semester-hours   Room 5, CHS

Geography

Geography S410—Economic Geography of Caribbean America   **Dr. Milstead**
11:30 A. M.-12:20 P. M.   Credit: 2 semester-hours   Room 26

Geography S412—Geography of Africa, Australia,
and New Zealand   **Dr. Milstead**
8:30-9:20 A. M.   Credit: 2 semester-hours   Room 26

Geography S418—Regional Geography of North America   **Dr. Milstead**
9:30-10:20 A. M.   Credit: 2 semester-hours   Room 26

Health Education

Health Education S408—Behind the Wheel Driver Education
and Driver Training   **Mr. Coder**
See "Post-Summer Session Course" on page 24

Health Education S411—School Health Services   **Mr. DeRosa**
10:30-11:20 A. M.   Credit: 2 semester-hours   Room 7, CHS

Integration S476—Elementary School Health and Physical Education
See "Elementary Education" on page 21

Integration

Integration S400A—Principles and Philosophy of
Secondary Education   **Dr. Fraser**
9:30-10:20 A. M.   Credit: 2 semester-hours   Room 24

Integration S407A—Television in Education Workshop   **Mr. Sheft**
See "Montclair State Teachers College Workshops" on page 18

Integration S409—Radio and Sound Equipment in the Classroom   **Mr. Fox**
9:30-10:20 A. M.   Credit: 2 semester-hours   Room A

Integration S410—Teaching Materials Workshop   **Miss Fantone**
See "Montclair State Teachers College Workshops" on page 18

Integration S500A—Basic Educational Trends   **Dr. Fraser**
8:30-9:20A. M.   Credit: 2 semester-hours   Room 24

Integration S500B—Advanced Educational Psychology
Prerequisite: An introductory course in psychology
10:30-11:20 A. M.   Credit: 2 semester-hours   Room 30

Integration S500C—Recent Trends in Secondary School Methods   **Dr. Atkinson**
11:30 A. M.-12:20 P. M.   Credit: 2 semester-hours   Room 29

Integration S500D—School Administration I:
Functions and Organization   **Mr. Morehead**
8:30-9:20 A. M.   Credit: 2 semester-hours   Room 27

Integration S500E—School Administration II:
Law and Finance   **Mr. Morehead**
10:30-11:20 A. M.   Credit: 2 semester-hours   Room 27

Integration S500F—School Administration III:
Community Relations   **Dr. Atkinson**
9:30-10:20 A. M.   Credit: 2 semester-hours   Room 29

Integration S502—Organization and Administration
of the Modern High School   Dr. W. Scott Smith
8:30-9:20 A. M.   Credit: 2 semester-hours   Room 28

Integration S503—Methods and Instruments of Research   Dr. Froehlich
Prerequisite: Mathematics 400 or its equivalent
Section I: 10:30-11:20 A. M.   Credit: 2 semester-hours
              Room 4, Annex No. 2
Section II: 11:30 A. M.-12:20 P. M.   Credit: 2 semester-hours
              Room 4, Annex No. 2

Integration S504A—Curriculum Construction
in the Secondary School   Dr. W. Scott Smith
9:30-10:20 A. M.   Credit: 2 semester-hours   Room 28

Integration S505—Organization and Administration of
Extra-Curricular Activities   Mr. Morehead
11:30 A. M.-12:20 P. M.   Credit: 2 semester-hours   Room 27

Integration S508—Supervision of Instruction in
Secondary Schools   Dr. Atkinson
10:30-11:20 A. M.   Credit: 2 semester-hours   Room 29

Integration S517—Administration of the Elementary School   Dr. Phipps
8:30-9:20 A. M.   Credit: 2 semester-hours   Room 10

Integration S518—Supervision of Instruction
in the Elementary School   Dr. Phipps
11:30 A. M.-12:20 P. M.   Credit: 2 semester-hours   Room 10

Integration S520—Principles of Mental Hygiene   Dr. Ingebritsen
11:30 A. M.-12:20 P. M.   Credit: 2 semester-hours   Room 30

Integration S536—Educational Guidance   Mr. E. C. Davis
8:30-9:20 A. M.   Credit: 2 semester-hours   Room 5

Integration S548—Curriculum Construction
in the Elementary School   Dr. Phipps
9:30-10:20 A. M.   Credit: 2 semester-hours   Room 10

Integration S551—Principles and Techniques of Guidance
This course is prerequisite to all other courses in Guidance.
8:30-9:20 A. M.   Credit: 2 semester-hours   Room 30

Integration S602—Seminar in Guidance   Mr. E. C. Davis
Prerequisites: Integration 551, and have taken (or be taking in conjunction) one
of the following: Int. 535, Int. 536, Int. 537.
10:30 A. M.-12:20 P. M.   Credit: 4 semester-hours   Room

Mathematics

Mathematics S400—Educational Statistics   Mr. Humphrey
This course or its equivalent is prerequisite to Integration 503
10:30-11:20 A. M.   Credit: 2 semester-hours   Room 2, Annex No.

Mathematics S401X—The Teaching of Mathematics
in Secondary Schools   Mr. Humphrey
The student studies the methods of teaching the different units of work in the
junior and senior high school. The student is actively in contact not only with
the theory, but also with the practice of what he studies. He participates,
under the direction of the instructor, in organizing material, in making tests

and in assisting in experimental work. A study of recent trends in the teaching of mathematics, of noteworthy research, of courses in general mathematics, and of modern texts and tests is included.

8:30-9:20 A. M.   Credit: 2 semester-hours   Room 2, Annex No. 1

Mathematics S501A—Administration and Supervision
of Mathematics, I   **Dr. Davis**
8:30-9:20 A. M.   Credit: 2 semester-hours   Room 1, Annex No. 1

Mathematics S509B—A Critical Interpretation of
Mathematics in the Senior H. S., II   **Mr. Kays**
9:30-10:20 A. M.   Credit: 2 semester-hours   Room 3, Annex No. 1

Mathematics S510A—Mathematics in its Relation to Other
Fields of Knowledge: Social Sciences   **Mr. Kays**
11:30 A. M.-12:20 P. M.   Credit: 2 semester-hours   Room 3, Annex No. 1

Mathematics S511B—Non-Euclidean Geometry   **Mr. Kays**
10:30-11:20 A. M.   Credit: 2 semester-hours   Room 3, Annex No. 1

Mathematics S517—The Theory of Numbers   **Dr. Davis**
9:30-10:20 A. M.   Credit: 2 semester-hours   Room 1, Annex No. 1

Integration S477—Elementary School Mathematics   **Mr. Humphreys**
See "Elementary Education" on page 21

New Tools for Learning

Integration S409—Radio and Sound Equipment in the Classroom   **Mr. Fox**
9:30-10:20 A. M.   Credit: 2 semester-hours   Room A

Integration S410—Teaching Materials Workshop   **Miss Fantone**
8:30-9:20 A. M.   Credit: 2 semester-hours   Room 4

For the following courses, see "Field Studies in American Life" on page 17:
Social Studies S460—Central Eastern Region   **Mr. Bye**
Social Studies S469—Mexico   **Mr. Bye**
Social Studies S481—West Indies   **Mr. Bye**

Science

Physics S406—Astronomy   **Mr. Allen**
11:30 A. M.-12:50 P. M., Class Sessions; Evening Sessions and Field Trips by Arrangement.   Credit: 4 semester-hours   Room 9, Annex No. 3

Physics S411A—Photography, I   **Dr. K. O. Smith**
9:30-10:20 A. M.   Credit: 2 semester-hours   Room 25

Physics S512—Modern Physics   **Dr. K. O. Smith**
8:00-9:20 A. M. and Field Trips by Arrangement.
          Credit: 4 semester-hours   Room 25

Integration S478—Elementary School Science   **Mr. Allen**
See "Elementary Education" on page 21

15

Social Studies

Social Studies S434—Contemporary World Affairs		Mr. Cohen
8:30-9:20 A. M.	Credit: 2 semester-hours	Room 21

Social Studies S439—The Family and Its Problems		Dr. Clayton
9:30-10:20 A. M.	Credit: 2 semester-hours	Room 21

Social Studies S443—Youth and the Community		Dr. Clayton
10:30-11:20 A. M.	Credit: 2 semester-hours	Room 21

Social Studies S451—The Middle East		Mr. Cohen
10:30-11:20 A. M.	Credit: 2 semester-hours	Room 20

Social Studies S455—Social Legislation		Dr. Rellahan
8:30-9:20 A. M.	Credit: 2 semester-hours	Room 20

Social Studies S480—Social History of the United States		Mr. Cohen
11:30 A. M.-12:20 P. M.	Credit: 2 semester-hours	Room 20

Social Studies S483—Modern Approaches to Social Problems   Dr. Clayton
This course is designed to acquaint students with techniques and practices developed in recent years for a scientific approach to problems of human relationship. Techniques to be studied include: sampling techiques for testing large groups, questionnaires, interviewing techniques, objective observation of culture patterns, objective observation in controlled laboratory situations, sociometrics, roleplaying techniques, attitude testing, and use of semantic analysis in test construction. Students become acquainted with these techniques through the study of a variety of recent reports. The selection of items to be studied depends on the needs and interests of class members. This course is designed to aid in the development of attitudes and practices which make possible the use of a modern, scientific approach to social problems.
Prerequisite: An introductory course in sociology or special permission of the instructor.

11:30 A. M.-12:20 P. M.	Credit: 2 semester-hours	Room 21

For the following two courses, see "United Nations Institute" on page 19:
Social Studies S490A—The United Nations   Mr. Kops
**Social Studies S490C—The Specialized Agencies of the
    United Nations**   Mr. Kops

For the following two courses, see "China Institute of New Jersey" on page 19:
Social Studies S498—China and the Far East
Social Studies S499—Introduction to Chinese Culture   Dr. Chih Meng

Social Studies S522—The Development of Economic
Institutions and Ideas		Dr. Rellahan
9:30-10:20 A. M.	Credit: 2 semester-hours	Room 20

16

FIELD STUDIES IN AMERICAN LIFE

July 9 through July 18, 1954

Social Studies S481—West Indies   **Mr. Bye**

This course consists of ten days of directed travel in five countries in the Caribbean region. Transportation is by air and private cars, with overnight stops at the best hotels. Opportunities are given for study of geographic, historic, economic, and cultural phenomena in Puerto Rico (one day—see Social Studies 466 for a more thorough study), Santo Domingo (two days), Haiti (two days), Jamaica (one day), Cuba (two days), visiting San Juan, Cuidad Trujillo, San Cristobal, Port au Prince, Kensicoff, Kingston, Havana, and rural areas in all countries.

All expense cost: $395.00   Credit: 2 semester-hours

July 23 through August 8, 1954

Social Studies S469—Mexico   **Mr. Bye**

All expense cost: $618.00   Credit: 3 semester-hours

August 17 through August 30, 1954

Social Studies S460—Central Eastern Region   **Mr. Bye**

All expense cost: $190.00   Credit: 3 semester-hours

While the above courses are given as a part of the Summer Session offerings of the State Teachers College at Montclair, registration for them must be made in advance through the Bureau of Field Studies. Likewise, payment is made as requested by the Bureau. Interested students should address Mr. E. C. Bye, Bureau of Field Studies, New Jersey State Teachers College, Upper Montclair, New Jersey. This should be done at once, as the number of students in the courses must be limited to a definite number.

Courses Offered by New Jersey State Teachers College at Trenton

August 3—August 26, 1954

**Geography 5-511—Geography of the Rocky Mountains,
    the Arid Southwest, and California**   **Dr. Adelbert K. Botts**

$300.00 plus tuition   Credit: 5 semester-hours (graduate or undergraduate)

For further information write to Dr. Adelbert K. Botts, Professor of Geography, State Teachers College, Trenton, New Jersey.

17

WORKSHOPS AND INSTITUTES

Montclair State Teachers College Workshops

June 29—August 6, 1954

Integration S407A—Television in Education Workshop:
    Programming and Production   **Mr. She**

Limited to 20 students   Credit: 2 semester-hours—on a Laboratory basi
10:30 A. M.-12:20 P. M., Monday, Wednesday, Friday, and 10:30-11:20 A. M
Tuesday and Thursday   Room ₄

Integration S410—Teaching Materials Workshop   **Miss Fanton**
8:30-9:20 A. M.   Credit: 2 semester-hours   Room

China Institute of New Jersey

June 28—July 10, 1954

China Institute of New Jersey is a permanent year-round organization com
posed of former students of the Institute. The policies and program of th
Institute are determined by an elected executive committee, an advisory boar
of laymen, and representatives from the Faculty of Montclair State Teacher
College, in consultation with the Chinese Director.

Dr. Chih Meng, Director of the China Institute of America, is also Chines
Director of the China Institute of New Jersey.

Students may enroll for college credit (graduate or undergraduate) if eligibl
to do so, or simply as Auditors for no credit. **The cost is the same in both case**
(See page 8 for information as to fees.) Those who enroll for credit are ex
pected to complete such notebooks, papers, projects, and examinations as ar
assigned by the course instructors. The preliminary grading of these paper
projects, and examinations is done by the Chinese teachers, while the fina
grading and coordinating is done by a representative of the regular Faculty ₀
the College.

Notification of desire to enroll in one of the Institute courses should b
sent on the coupon supplied in the special leaflet published by the Institut
Actual registration and payment of fees will take place in the College Librar
from 8:00-9:00 A. M., on June 28. The Institute will convene in the Auditoriu
of the College High School Building at 9:15. The students taking the A
course and the course in China and the Far East will leave the Auditoriu
later and go to their respective classrooms.

China Institute Offerings

Art S414—History of Chinese Art   **Mr. Na-sun W**
Although there is no prerequisite for this course, it is suggested that those wh
enroll for it should have some knowledge of. art or have taken Social Studi
S499.
9:00 A. M.-4:00 P. M.   Credit: 3 semester-hours   Room 3, CH

Social Studies S498—China and the Far East   Dr. Y. P. Mei
The following course has been given previously, but the following is a revised description:

"This course presents to the student a factual and up-to-date analysis of the forces that are operating in the Far East and shows how these forces may affect future developments in this critical area of the world. China, with its people as a key area in the Far East, is interpreted in terms of current economic, political and cultural developments. Recognized experts from the various countries in the Far East present problems from the standpoint of their experience and background. The course itself is synthesized by a course director who is a serious student of China and its neighbors. There is no prerequisite.
9:00 A. M.-4:00 P. M.   Credit: 3 semester-hours   Room 4, CHS

Social Studies S499—Introduction to Chinese Culture   Dr. Chih Meng
This course was formerly entitled "China Workshop."
9:00 A. M.-4:00 P. M.   Credit: 3 semester-hours   Auditorium, CHS

United Nations Institute

July 12—July 24, 1954

The College offered the first United Nations Institute and Workshop in the summer of 1951 under the co-sponsorship of the Cosmopolitan Club of Montclair and the New Jersey Branch of the American Association for the United Nations. Since then, many other organizations representing leading women's, church, businessmen's, and labor groups have become affiliated as cooperating agencies. As in the past, this year's Institute will again feature participation by members of the United Nations Staff, various national delegations, the Department of State and the United States Delegation.

Course Offerings

Social Studies S490A—The United Nations   Mr. Kops
Lectures: 9:30 A. M.-12 Noon; Workshop: 1:00-3:30 P. M.
                    Credit: 3 semester-hours   Auditorium, CHS

Social Studies S490C—The Specialized Agencies
    of the United Nations   Mr. Kops
Prerequisite: Social Studies 490A or its equivalent.
Workshop: 9:30-12 Noon; Lecture: 1:00-3:30 P. M.
                    Credit: 3 semester-hours   Auditorium, CHS

During the Workshop Sessions, students are asked to select a field for special study within the framework of one of the following areas: A. The United Nations and the Elementary School; B. The United Nations and the Secondary School; C. The United Nations and the Community; D. Basic Facts about the United Nations.

These courses are given on the senior-graduate level, so that students may work either for undergraduate or for graduate credit. Students may enroll for college credit if eligible to do so or simply attend as Auditors for no credit. The cost is the same in both cases. Those who enroll for credit are expected to take

19

part in the Workshop and complete such papers, projects, and examinations are assigned by the course instructor. The Institute will be in session on bo Saturdays, but there will be no required evening meetings.

Students who wish to enroll for either course should write to Mr. Walter Kops, Director, United Nations Institute, State Teachers College, Upper Mor clair, N. J., for a set of the registration materials.

New Jersey State Teachers College at Newark
Announces

Special Features of the 1954 Summer Session

Workshop in International Understanding
A six-point credit, fifty-six day Workshop in International Understanding lea ing on the Queen Mary, July 7, and visiting England, Holland, Belgiu Germany, Switzerland, Austria, Italy, and France, and returning on the Que Elizabeth, August 31. The price of the Workshop depends upon the stear ship class selected. The all-inclusive tourist rate is $1,475.00. For further inform tion, write to Dr. Mary Holman, Director; Workshop in International Unde standing, New Jersey State Teachers College, Newark, New Jersey.

African Institute
A four-point credit, three weeks (June 29-July 21) program designed to gi teachers a background of information about Africa, and to present to teache materials, teaching aids, and methods by means of which Africa can mo effectively be presented in the classroom. For further information, write Dr. David Scanlon, Director; African Institute, New Jersey State Teache College, Newark, New Jersey.

Trenton State Teachers College

July 6-23, 1954

Conservation Education Workshop   **Professor Crow**
Credit: 4 semester-hours
For further details, write to: Professor Victor L. Crowell, Science Departme State Teachers College, Trenton 5, New Jersey.

20

COURSES FOR THOSE WHO DESIRE TO TEACH IN
ELEMENTARY GRADES

These courses are open to the following only:

(1) Those who already hold a degree from Montclair State Teachers College with a Certificate in Secondary Education, and

(2) Those who are now matriculated at Montclair State Teachers College for a degree and the Certificate in Secondary Education.

All other students should apply to one of the following colleges, all of which offer the bachelor's degree in Elementary Education and several of which also offer the master's degree in that field:

New Jersey State Teachers College at Paterson.
New Jersey State Teachers College at Jersey City.
New Jersey State Teachers College at Newark.
New Jersey State Teachers College at Trenton.
New Jersey State Teachers College at Glassboro.

The courses given on this campus are offered to assist the Montclair State Teachers College students in attaining provisional and standard certification to teach in elementary grades. Detailed requirements for such certification are listed on pages 14, 15, 16, and 68 of the Eighteenth Edition of the Rules Concerning Teachers Certificates. Montclair College students should consult Miss House, the College Registrar, for an evaluation of their previous work and a statement concerning their remaining required courses.

The courses listed below may apply as general electives in undergraduate curriculums, and with the Advisor's approval, as graduate electives for majors in Administration and Supervision. The courses with the * do not carry graduate credit, however.

*Integration S474—Elementary School Arts and Crafts   **Mr. Vernacchia**
Section one: 8:30-9:20 A. M.   Credit: 2 semester-hours
         Campus Studio Workshop
Section two: 10:30-11:20 A. M.   Credit: 2 semester-hours
         Campus Studio Workshop

***Integration S476—Elementary School Health and
Physical Education**   **Mr. DeRosa**
9:30-10:20 A. M.   Credit: 2 semester-hours   Room 7, CHS and Gym, CHS

Integration S477—Elementary School Mathematics   **Mr. Humphreys**
11:30 A. M.-12:20 P. M.   Credit: 2 semester-hours   Room 2, Annex No. 1

Integration S478—Elementary School Science   **Mr. Allen**
10:30-11:20 A. M.   Credit: 2 semester-hours   Room 9, Annex No. 3

In addition to the above courses, Geography S418, Regional Geography of North America, applies on the Limited Elementary Certificate. See "Geography" on page 13.

21

NEW JERSEY STATE SCHOOL OF CONSERVATION
Stokes State Forest, Branchville, N. J.

COURSES IN CONSERVATION, FIELD SCIENCES, CAMPING EDUCATION, SOCIAL STUDIES, AND WATER FRONT SAFETY

Spring and Summer, 1954

The State Department of Education, through the six State Teachers Colleges, offers a wide range of courses at the School of Conservation. Teachers, prospective teachers, camp counselors, nature specialists, and playground directors have an opportunity to combine study and vacation in the beautiful and cool Kittatinny Mountains of Northern New Jersey.

Public Schools throughout the nation are being charged with the responsibility of teaching conservation education courses. New Jersey teachers have a unique opportunity to become acquainted with the problems and methods of teaching in this fast-growing field. Science, social studies, and elementary school teachers will be particularly interested in the following courses, but all educators should have a basic understanding of conservation if they are to meet the needs of the youngsters in our schools.

Credit for the following courses, offered between June 16 and August 26, may be applied toward graduate or undergraduate degrees at any of the New Jersey State Teachers Colleges, subject to approval in advance by the institution. Credits may be transferred to other institutions where such transfer is permitted toward an undergraduate or graduate degree. Several of the courses may be substituted for courses required for elementary teaching certification.

For additional information write to: Edward J. Ambry, New Jersey State School of Conservation, Upper Montclair, New Jersey.

1954 SUMMER COURSE OFFERINGS

Integration 441—Conservation Education
    Credit: 2 semester-hours   June 16-26

Biology 203—Introduction to Field Biology
    Credit: 2 semester-hours   June 16-26

Physical Education 410—Water Safety and First Aid
    Credit: 2 semester-hours   June 16-26

Art 415—School Arts and Crafts with Native Materials
    Credit: 2 semester-hours   June 16-26
This course is approved by the State Board of Examiners to meet the art requirement for certification to teach in grades 1-8.

Science 420—Water Supply and Conservation Problems
    Credit: 3 semester-hours   July 6-21

Science 419—Field Science and Conservation
Credit: 2 semester-hours   July 26–August 5
This course is approved by the State Board of Examiners to meet the science
requirement for certification to teach in grades 1-8.

Social Studies 494—Social Studies and Conservation
Credit: 2 semester-hours   August 5–15
This course is approved by the State Board of Examiners to meet the social
studies requirement for certification to teach in grades 1-8.

Art 415—School Arts and Crafts with Native Materials
Credit: 2 semester-hours   August 16–26
This course is approved by the State Board of Examiners to meet the art re-
quirement for certification to teach in grades 1-8.

Social Studies 482—Conservation and Rural Economic Life
Credit: 2 semester-hours   August 16–26

Integration 480—Field Science for Elementary Teachers
Credit: 2 semester-hours   August 16–26
This course is approved by the State Board of Examiners to meet the science
requirement for certification to teach in grades 1-8.

Typical Outdoor Class

23

POST-SUMMER SESSION COURSE

August 9 through August 20, 1954

To Meet an Urgent Need, the following course is being offered by the State Teachers College at Montclair, with the assistance of the New Jersey State Safety Council, the New Jersey Automobile Club, the American Automobile Association, the New Jersey State Police, and the New Jersey Department of Motor Vehicles.

This Course Offers the Necessary Opportunity for men and women to prepare themselves to teach behind-the-wheel driver education in high schools. Enrollees completing the work of the course are presented with a certificate indicating the work done.

Authorization: In order to teach behind-the-wheel driver education and driver training, a teacher must have his or her certificate endorsed by the Division of Teacher Certification, State Department of Education, for teaching behind-the-wheel automobile driver education and driver training.

The Requirements for Such Endorsement on the teacher's certificate are (18th edition, 1951, "Rules Concerning Teachers' Certificates," page 22)

1. A valid New Jersey teacher's certificate.
2. A current New Jersey driver's license.
3. Three years of automobile driving experience.
4. Evidence of satisfactory completion of a course in driver education and driver training approved by the Commissioner of Education.

Veterans may take this course under the G. I. Bill, if they have so arranged with the Veterans' Counselor of the College.

Living Expenses and Traveling Expenses must be paid by the student. Those desiring hotel accommodations should write to Mr. F. K. Schultze, Manager, New Jersey Auto Club, AAA, 156 Clinton Avenue, Newark 5, New Jersey. The College Residence Halls are closed at this time.

Textbooks and Other Text Materials are furnished to each enrollee without charge.

Registration for this course will be accepted up to and including the opening day of the course. However, students should register early if possible, preferably on the regular registration day for the Summer Session. There is a limit to the number of registrations which may be accepted.

Health Education S408—Behind the Wheel Driver Education and Driver Training   Coordinator: Mr. Cod
9:00-12:00 and 1:00-4:00 daily   Credit: 2 semester-hours   Room

1955

Bulletin of
MONTCLAIR STATE TEACHERS COLLEGE
SUMMER SESSION

June 27 to August 5

UPPER MONTCLAIR   NEW JERSEY

SUMMER SESSION

Bulletin of

MONTCLAIR
STATE TEACHERS COLLEGE

1955

June 27th to August 5th

VOLUME 47   NUMBER 2

UPPER MONTCLAIR, NEW JERSEY

OFFICERS OF ADMINISTRATION

STATE BOARD OF EDUCATION

GEORGE O. SMALLEY, *President* ....Bound Brook

MRS. EDWARD L. KATZENBACH, *Vice-President* ....Princeton

ARTHUR E. ARMITAGE, SR. ....Collingswood

MRS. T. B. ARMSTRONG ....Stewartsville

LEWIS F. GAYNER ....Salem

PHILIP R. GEBHARDT ....Clinton

JOHN S. GRAY ....Newton

JOHN F. LYNCH ....Morristown

JAMES W. PARKER, SR. ....Red Bank

MRS. HERBERT REIM ....Maywood

MRS. FREDERIC H. SANFORD ....Nutley

HENRY A. WILLIAMS ....Paterson

COMMISSIONER OF EDUCATION
DR. FREDERICK M. RAUBINGER

ASSISTANT COMMISSIONER FOR HIGHER EDUCATION
DR. ROBERT H. MORRISON

COLLEGE ADMINISTRATION

E. DEALTON PARTRIDGE, Ph.D. ....Presiden

CLYDE M. HUBER, Ph.D. ....Dean of Instructior

BERNARD SIEGEL, M.B.A. ....Business Manage

OTIS C. INGEBRITSEN, Ph.D. ....Chairman of the Graduate Committe

KEITH W. ATKINSON, Ph.D. ....Director of College High Schoc

EARL C. DAVIS, Ph.D. ....Director of Personnel and Guidanc

ELIZABETH S. FAVOR, A.M. ....Assistant in Graduate Personne

MARGARET A. SHERWIN, A.M. ....Dean of Wome

MARY M. HOUSE, B.C.S. ....Registra

ANNE BANKS CRIDLEBAUGH, A.M. ....Libraria

OTTO CORDES, P.E. ....Engineer in Charge, Maintenanc

HEALTH SERVICES

CHARLOTTE L. PRITCHARD, R.N. ....College Nur:

2

FACULTY

Summer Session 1955

E. DeAlton Partridge, Ph.D. ....President
Clyde M. Huber, Ph.D. ....Dean of Instruction
Hugh Allen, Jr., M.S. ....Science
Keith W. Atkinson, Ph.D. ....Integration
William A. Ballare, A.M. ....Speech
Harold C. Bohn, Ed.D. ....English
Edgar C. Bye, A.M. ....Director, New Tools for Learning Bureau
Frank L. Clayton, Ph.D. ....Social Studies
Alden C. Coder, Ed.D. ....Health and Physical Education
Philip S. Cohen, A.M. ....Social Studies
Lawrence H. Conrad, A.M. ....English
David R. Davis, Ph.D. ....Chairman, Department of Mathematics
Earl C. Davis, Ph.D. ....Personnel and Guidance
Jerome G. DeRosa, A.M. ....Health and Physical Education
Emma Fantone, A.M. ....Director, Audio-Visual Aids Service
Paul E. Froehlich, Ed.D. ....Research
Edwin S. Fulcomer, Ed.D. ....Head of Department of English
Charles E. Hadley, Ph.D. ....Biology
W. Paul Hamilton, A.M. ....English
T. Roland Humphreys, A.M. ....Mathematics
Otis C. Ingebritsen, Ph.D. ....Psychology
George W. Kays, A.M. ....Mathematics
Walter E. Kops, A.M. ....Director, Institutes of International Affairs
Chih Meng, Ph.D. ....Director, China Institute
Bruce E. Meserve, Ph.D. ....Mathematics
Harley P. Milstead, Ph.D. ....Geography
Allan Morehead, A.M. ....Integration
Ulrich J. Neuner, A.M. ....Business Education
William R. Phipps, Ed.D. ....Integration
Rufus D. Reed, Ph.D. ....Chairman, Department of Science
John J. Rellahan, Ph.D. ....Acting Head, Department of Social Studies
Horace J. Sheppard, A.M. ....Acting Head, Department of Business Education
W. Scott Smith, Ph.D. ....Acting Head, Department of Integration
Elizabeth T. VanDerveer, Ed.D. ....Business Education
Ralph A. Vernacchia, A.M. ....Art
Richard W. Willing, Ed.D. ....Business Education
Frederic H. Young, Ph.D. ....English

GRADUATE COMMITTEE

Otis C. Ingebritsen, *Chairman*

David R. Davis   William R. Phipps
W. Paul Hamilton   Rufus D. Reed
Clyde M. Huber   John J. Rellahan
Elizabeth S. Favor, *Secretary*   Elizabeth T. VanDerveer

"A Wooded Campus Thirty Minutes from Times Square"

4

SUMMER SESSION OF THE
NEW JERSEY STATE TEACHERS COLLEGE AT MONTCLAIR

Objectives and Academic Status

The College is a professional school which prepares teachers, supervisors, and principals of high schools, and administrators of public school systems. The degrees offered by this College are those of Bachelor of Arts and Master of Arts. Certificate courses are offered for those who now hold degrees from other colleges. See paragraph under "Certificates."

The New Jersey State Teachers College at Montclair is a member of the American Association of Colleges of Teacher Education and fully accredited by the National Council for the Accreditation of Teacher Education, the Middle States Association of Colleges and Secondary Schools, and the American Association of University Women.

How to Reach the Campus

The College is located about one mile north of the center of Upper Montclair. Trains of the Greenwood Lake Division, Erie R. R., stop at Montclair Heights, the College Station. Trains of the Lackawanna R. R. connect at Montclair with the following bus lines: Nos. 60, 64, and 76 to the College.

Residence Halls for Men and Women

Edward Russ Hall and Chapin Hall are Montclair College's two well-appointed Residences. The charge for living on campus during the Summer Session is: $14.50 per week; which includes room, breakfast, and dinner. A la carte luncheons are served in the College cafeteria. For one student alone in a double room, an extra charge of $2.00 per week is made. The College provides and launders sheets, pillowcase, and bedpad. Towels, table lamps, blankets, clocks, and similar items must be provided and cared for by the student. The boarding-hall fee must be paid on or before the first day of the Summer Session. No rebate is made for occasional absence or voluntary withdrawal during the session. These prices are subject to change.

For reservations in a College Residence Hall, women address: Dean of Women, State Teachers College, Upper Montclair, N. J. Men address: Dean of Men.

Schedule of the Summer Session

Registration will take place on Monday, June 27. Hours, 9-12 and 1-3:30. Classes will begin on Tuesday morning, June 28, at 8 A. M. and will continue through Friday, August 5. All classes meet daily, Monday to Friday, inclusive, at the hours indicated for each, and on the following Saturdays: July 9, July 16, and July 30. Monday, July 4, is a Holiday.

Matriculation for the Master of Arts Degree

Since not more than 8 semester-hours of work taken prior to matriculation are allowed to apply on the Master of Arts degree, the student should take care to complete the matriculation procedure as soon as he has that amount of credit; sooner, if possible. Transfer of graduate credit from other institutions is permitted only to those students who are graduates of New Jersey State Teachers Colleges or the State University. The maximum permitted is 8 semester-hours.

Those who desire to become candidates for the degree must request an application form from the Chairman of the Graduate Committee and return it properly filled and accompanied by an Official Transcript of all previous work on college level. **When such an applicant has been accepted by the College** as a candidate for the degree, a definite statement is furnished to him, showing the requirements which he must fulfill to earn the degree. This sheet of requirements becomes the student's Work Program and should be brought by the student each time he comes to enroll for courses.

Students Matriculated at Montclair for the A.M. Degree

Since September 1, 1952, all students matriculating in the Graduate Division have been required to complete at least one full-time summer session, or, in lieu thereof, at least one regular semester of full-time graduate attendance.

The selection of courses must be in accordance with the student's Work Program, and his registration form will be signed by the Head of the Department in which the student is majoring or by a representative of that department present in the registration room.

Candidates for a degree must file with the Registrar an application for conferment of the degree before November 30 of the college year in which the work is to be completed. Application blanks for this purpose may be secured in the Registrar's Office. The burden of responsibility for the request rests with the candidate. This is of special significance to the teacher-in-service who may have distributed the work for the degree over several years.

Students Matriculated at Other Colleges

Several years ago, when the State Teachers College at Montclair offered courses to its own accelerated candidates for the Bachelor's degree, it was possible to accept students from other colleges in freshman, sophomore, and junior year courses, as well as in courses of the senior year. Beginning in the summer of 1950, however, the College returned to its pre-war custom of offering courses in its Summer Session primarily to teachers-in-service. Since such teachers already hold the Bachelor's degree, with few exceptions, the courses shown in this Bulletin are, for the most part, only Graduate and Senior-Graduate courses.

A student who is planning to attend Montclair this summer should take this Bulletin to a conference with the Dean of his own college to arrange a program of work. For the Dean's information: the numbering of courses at Montclair follows this order: 100-399, inclusive, are undergraduate courses: 400-499, inclusive, are senior-college and graduate courses; 500 and above are graduate courses.

At the time of registration, the student should go to the table of the Department in which the courses are listed that he plans to take. The registration form must be signed by the Representative of the Department at that table. The College reserves the right to decide whether the student has fulfilled necessary prerequisites. **He should bring with him, however, a letter from his own college.** If the student is seeking certification to teach in New Jersey, he must confer with the Head of the Department of Integration. Please note paragraph under the Heading: "Certificates."

6

Auditors

Men and women who desire to take courses for cultural, vocational, or avocational purposes without college credits may register as auditors.

A student who desires to enroll in a course for which he already holds credit must register as an auditor in that course.

A student who desires to enroll in a course for which he has not completed the prerequisites must enroll as an auditor in that course.

Change of Status in a Course

If a student desires to change his status in a course from "credit" to "auditor" or from "auditor" to "credit," he must make formal application for such change not later than the middle of the course. Forms for this purpose may be procured from Miss Favor, in the Registrar's Office. Such changes cannot be made after the midpoint of the course is passed.

Certificates

The State Teachers College at Montclair offers work toward the following New Jersey Certificates: Secondary Teaching Certificate; Secondary School Principal's Certificate; Elementary School Principal's Certificate; Subject Supervisor's Certificate; General Supervisor's Certificate; Guidance Certificate; School Administrator's Certificate; Junior College Teacher's Certificate; and the Advanced Professional Certificate.

Those who matriculate at Montclair for a Master of Arts degree will receive information from the Head of the Integration Department, as to the requirements for each of these certificates. Students who have not matriculated at Montclair should write to Dr. E. C. Preston, Secretary of the State Board of Examiners, Department of Education, 175 West State Street, Trenton 8, N. J., for information as to the requirements. **For an evalution of work already completed, address Dr. Preston.** An official transcript of such previous work should accompany the inquiry, with a statement as to the particular certificate desired.

The student should bring Dr. Preston's reply with him when conferring with the Head of the Integration Department as to his program of work

Students who must have this information immediately should go to Trenton to confer with Dr. Preston or his assistant, Miss Smith.

Supervised Student Teaching

The opportunity to do supervised student teaching cannot be offered during the Summer Session. For fall teaching, students confer with the Head of the Integration Department at the College. Ask his secretary for an appointment.

Veterans

Veteran students taking work under the G. I. Bill and likewise the so-called Korean Veteran must see Mr. Neuner, Veterans' Counselor of the College, before the close of the spring semester on June 9 in order to make certain that when they come to enroll on June 27 their papers will all be in order. Students taking work under the G. I. Bill without having the proper papers must pay the usual tuition fees at the time of registration.

Students who have completed the work of the A.B. or the A.M. degree at Montclair must secure and present to Mr. Neuner the Supplemental Certificate of Eligibility before registering for further work. Veterans transferring to this College who have previously been in training under the G. I. Bill must secure the Supplemental Certificate of Eligibility, and present it to Mr. Neuner at the time of registration.

Conferences with Advisers

Appointments with the Dean of Instruction, the Chairman of the Graduate Committee, a Department Head, or the Veterans' Counselor may be made by mail or telephone to their respective offices. This should be done at as early a date as possible to avoid delay at the time of registration; no later than June 9.

Summer Session Credit Load

The maximum amount of credit which may be earned in the Summer Session is 8 semester-hours, but only 6 are recommended. There is no provision for a student to audit additional courses; consequently, the total of all courses taken during the Summer Session may not exceed 8 semester-hours and students should not enroll for more. Additional credits may be earned by attending one of the sessions at the State School of Conservation that precedes or follows the Summer Session. Attention is called also to the Post-Summer Session course in Behind-the-Wheel Driver Education and Driver Training.

Each Summer Session course is in session at least thirty hours and carries a designated amount of credit. It is not possible to earn three s. h. credits in a two s. h. credit course.

Registration Information

Registration takes place in the College Library, on Monday, June 27, from 9 A. M. to 12 Noon, and from 1 to 3:30 P. M. The Registration form of every student must be signed by a Department Head or his representative. The student should report to the table of the Department in which he is majoring; or, if not matriculated here for a degree at present, of the Department in which he is taking courses. He may, in some instances, be required to obtain signatures in more than one Department, if he is taking courses in more than one. Signs on the tables indicate the various Departments.

Matriculated students should bring their "Work Programs" when they come to enroll.

The College reserves the right to close any course for which the enrollment is insufficient. The class will meet at least once, however, before this decision is made. Students may then enter another course in place of the one discontinued by going to the Registrar's Office to re-enroll and to receive the new Class Admission Card in exchange for the card of the discontinued course.

Students who decide not to enroll in an alternate course must so state, in a letter of withdrawal, in order to receive a refund of tuition fees. The card of the discontinued course should be enclosed in the letter.

If prerequisites are required for a course (see the course description), the student should make certain that he has fulfilled them or their equivalent before enrolling in it.

If no previous work on college level has been taken, the student must consult the Dean of Instruction before enrolling in any course, except as an Auditor.

A student may not register for credit in any course for which he already holds credit, except by permission of the Dean of Instruction.

* Anyone unable to enroll during the hours shown above must register during the regular office hours of the College in the Registrar's office, allowing at least 45 minutes for the procedure. The summer office hours are from 8:30 A. M. to 3:30 P. M.

The final date on which a student may enroll for credit is Thursday, June 30.

---

* Late Registration Service Charge added to all late registrations. See paragraph under "Tuition Fees and Service Charges."

Withdrawal from a Course

During the registration period of June 27, and on June 28, June 29, and June 30, a student may, with the advice and consent in writing of his adviser, withdraw from one course and enter another in its place. **The Class Admission Card from the dropped course must be presented when registering for the new one** in order that the new Class Admission Card may be issued.

If no new course is being taken, written notice to Miss Favor, Assistant in Graduate Personnel, must be given at once by the student. Miss Favor will notify the teacher of the course from which the student is withdrawing, as well as the Business Office of the College. Refunds are computed from the date of the receipt of the letter of withdrawal.

The same procedure should be followed by a student who withdraws from a course later in the Summer Session.

Students who neglect to follow this procedure receive a failing mark for the course or courses which they cease to attend.

Tuition Fees, Service Charge, and Credit Slips

Check or money-order should be made payable to New Jersey State Teachers College.

Tuition Fees: to students who are residents of New Jersey, $11.00 per semester-hour credit carried by the course. Non-residents of New Jersey pay $13.00 per credit. **Courses taken by auditors for no credit cost the same.**

Service Charge: 50¢ per semester-hour point.

Late Registration Service Charge: $2.00 will be added to the cost of each late registration; that is, each registration which is not **completed** during the hours set aside for registration on June 27. A registration is complete when it has been duly filled in, signed by the Adviser, and **paid for by the student.** This additional charge will be made in the case of a deferred or a partially deferred payment of the fees and service charges.

Teachers who have supervised Montclair student-teachers and who have in their possession old Montclair credit slips may take them to the office of the Integration Department, where new ones will be issued. The Business Office cannot return any unused portion of a credit slip, so it is necessary that the new type credit slip be obtained before presenting it in payment of tuition fees. Training Teachers may use the credit slips of any one of the six New Jersey State Teachers Colleges when taking courses at Montclair, but should bring only the new type slip in all cases.

So long as any credit slips remain in a teacher's possession, they will be honored by the College although a new method of remuneration of training teachers is now in effect.

Final Marks

Following are the final marks which may be received for a course: A-Excellent; B-Good; C-Fair; D-Poor; F-Failure; Inc.-Incomplete; Wd-Withrew; N. C.-No Credit.

The mark of "D" when earned in summer, part-time, or extension courses of this College is not accepted for degree credit at Montclair.

The mark of "F" is given when earned and when the student has failed to notify the Assistant in Graduate Personnel promptly of his withdrawal from a course.

The mark of "N. C." is given only to auditors.

The mark of "Wd" is given only when prompt notice of withdrawal has been given and when the student's work to that time has been satisfactory to the teacher of the course.

The mark of "Inc." is seldom given. It may, however, be granted to student whose work is incomplete at the end of the Session and who is eager t finish the work for a higher grade than he could otherwise receive. All responsi bility regarding incomplete work rests with the student. He will be notified o a date after which, if the work remains incomplete, the final grade will b recorded without further notice.

Report Cards and Transcripts

An Official Transcript showing the credits earned is sent to the studen personally ten days to two weeks following the close of the Session. A repor card for each course taken is sent with the transcript. The transcript is sen without cost, but a service charge of $1.00 is made for a duplicate copy.

A student whose college requires that the transcript be mailed directly to th Dean or Registrar should call, early in the Session, at the Registrar's Office t address an envelope for this purpose.

Elementary Education Courses

Courses offered as a part of the curriculum for the graduate major ii Educational Administration and Supervision should be carefully distinguishec from those offered toward the endorsement in elementary education on th teacher's certificate. The courses in the Administration and Supervision of Ele mentary Education apply on the Elementary **Principal's** certificate, but not or the Elementary **Teacher's** certificate.

Although the New Jersey State Teachers College at Montclair is engagec primarily in preparing secondary school teachers, during the present shortage o: teachers in the elementary schools it is deemed expedient to offer courses in the field of elementary education to those students who are eligible to enroll at the College in such courses.

Students eligible to enroll at Montclair in courses leading to certification in elementary education are:

(1) those who already hold a degree from Montclair with a certificate ii secondary education; and

(2) those who are now matriculated at Montclair for such a degree.

Montclair cannot accept any other students in these courses.

The eligible students should consult Miss House, the College Registrar, fo an evaluation of their previous work and a statement concerning the courses t be taken in order to receive the endorsement in elementary education on th secondary certificate already held or to be conferred.

Textbook Exhibit

In the Gymnasium of the Main Building, from July 5 through July 15, ther will be an exhibit of high school and elementary school textbooks. Whil primarily for the benefit of the principals and teachers attending the Summe Session, the exhibit will be open to undergraduate students and to members c the general public who may be interested in seeing the latest textbooks.

Mrs. E. S. Fulcomer will be in charge of the Exhibit.

College Book Store

A limited number of books for each course will be on hand in the Book Stor at registration time. It is advantageous to order textbooks immediately upo completion of registration. Store hours: 8 A. M.-12 Noon.

10

COURSES OF THE SUMMER SESSION

Descriptions of the courses will be found in the 1953-55 Graduate Bulletin of the College. Courses numbered 500 and above are graduate courses; those numbered 400-499, inclusive, are senior-graduate courses and their descriptions in the Graduate Bulletin follow the descriptions of the graduate courses. Courses below the 400 number will be found in the Undergraduate Bulletin of the College. Only entirely new courses are described in the Summer Session Bulletin.

Business Education

Business Education S104—Typewriting—Elementary II   **Dr. Willing**
The aim of this course is to increase the typing speed and ability of the student by stressing the need for accuracy in all material typed. Emphasis is placed upon expert proofreading before releasing any papers for approval by the instructor. Advanced letter forms, such as the block, full block, five-indent, and all variations of the modified block, are applied at frequent intervals to insure thorough recall.

Students may be admitted to this course on recommendation of the teacher. Credit for this course may be used by graduate students to meet requirements for certification but not to apply toward requirements for the Master's degree.
8:30 and 11:30 A. M.   Credit: 2 semester-hours   Room 28

Business Education S205—Stenography I   **Dr. Van Derveer**
The theory of Gregg stenography (Simplified) is taught in this beginning course. The student learns to read shorthand fluently and to take dictation on familiar material. Students may be admitted to this course on recommendation of the teacher. Credit for this course may be used by graduate students to meet requirements for certification but not to apply toward requirements for the Master's degree.

9:30 and 10:30 A. M.   Credit: 4 semester-hours   Room 28

Business Education S406—Advertising   **Dr. Willing**
10:30-11:20 A.M.   Credit: 2 semester-hours   Room 2, Annex No. 2

**Business Education S504—Improvement of Instruction in
Business Education**   **Dr. Van Derveer**
8:30-9:20 A. M.   Credit: 2 semester-hours   Room 5, Annex No. 2

Business Education S511—Auditing   **Mr. Neuner**
9:30-10:20 A. M.   Credit: 2 semester-hours   Room 3, Annex No. 2

Business Education S602—Seminar in Economics   **Mr. Sheppard**
9:30 A. M.-12:20 P. M.   Credit: 6 semester-hours   Room 5, Annex No. 2

English and Speech

English S401X—The Teaching of English in Secondary Schools   **Dr. Fulcomer**
8:30-9:20 A. M.   Credit: 2 semester-hours   Room 1

English S431B—Shakespeare's Major Plays II: The Comedies   **Dr. Bohn**
9:30 A. M.-12:20 P. M.   Credit: 2 semester-hours   Room 1

11

English S442A—American Literature I
Not open for credit to students who have credit for English 302.
10:30-11:20 A. M.   Credit: 2 semester-hours

English S442B—American Literature II
Not open for credit to students who have credit for English 302.
11:30 A. M.-12:20 P. M.   Credit: 2 semester-hours

English S449—Public Speaking
Prerequisite: English 204 or the equivalent.
8:30-9:20 A. M.   Credit: 2 semester-hours

English S459—A Survey of Great Chinese Literature
See "Institutes and Workshops" on page 19.

English S462—Group Discussion and Leadership
10:30-11:20 A. M.   Credit: 2 semester-hours

English S505—Philosophy and English Poets
11:30 A. M.-12:20 P. M.   Credit: 2 semester-hours

English S512—Growth and Structure of the English Language
9:30-10:20 A. M.   Credit: 2 semester-hours

English S513—The Renaissance
10:30-11:20 A. M.   Credit: 2 semester-hours

English S539—Theatre and Society
9:30-10:20 A. M.   Credit: 2 semester-hours

Fine Arts

Fine Arts S406—Creative Arts Workshop
9:30-10:20 A. M.   Credit: 2 semester-hours   Campus S

Fine Arts S408—Creative Painting
8:30-9:20 A. M.   Credit: 2 semester-hours   Campus S

Integration S474—Elementary School Arts and Crafts
See "Elementary Education" on page 22.

Geography

Geography S411—Geographic Influences in American History
8:30-9:20 A. M.   Credit: 2 semester-hours

Geography S418—Regional Geography of North America
11:30 A. M.-12:20 P. M.   Credit: 2 semester-hours

Geography S509—Economic Geography of Asia
9:30-10:20 A. M.   Credit: 2 semester-hours

Health Education

Health Education S408—Behind-the-Wheel Driver Education and Driver Training   **Dr. Coder**
See "Post-Summer Session Course" on page 24.

Health Education S411—School Health Services   **Mr. De Rosa**
8:30-9:20 A. M.   Credit: 2 semester-hours   Room 14, CHS

Integration S476—Elementary School Health and Physical Education
See "Elementary Education" on page 22.

Integration

Integration S300B—Principles and Techniques of Teaching in Secondary Schools   **Dr. Atkinson**
10:30 A. M.-12:20 P. M.   Credit: 2 semester-hours   Room 4, CHS
N.B.: The above course meets double periods for the first three weeks of the summer session. Students who desire to obtain further work in the field of teaching techniques may then take Integration S408 for the second three weeks. See below.

Integration S400A—Principles and Philosophy of Secondary Education
9:30-10:20 A. M.   Credit: 2 semester-hours   Room 24

Integration S408—Selection and Utilization of Audio-Visual Materials   **Miss Fantone**
10:30 A. M.-12:20 P. M.   Credit: 2 semester-hours   Room 4
N.B.: The above course meets double periods for the last three weeks of the summer session. See note above.

Integration S500A—Basic Educational Trends
8:30-9:20 A. M.   Credit: 2 semester-hours   Room 24

Integration S500B—Advanced Educational Psychology   **(Visitor)**
Prerequisite: An introductory course in psychology.
9:30-10:20 A. M.   Credit: 2 semester-hours   Room 10

Integration S500D—School Administration I: Functions and Organization   **Mr. Morehead**
9:30-10:20 A. M.   Credit: 2 semester-hours   Room 27

Integration S500E—School Administration II: Law and Finance   **Mr. Morehead**
10:30-11:20 A. M.   Credit: 2 semester-hours   Room 27

Integration S500F—School Administration III: Community Relations   **Dr. Atkinson**
8:30-9:20 A. M.   Credit: 2 semester-hours   Room 4, CHS

Integration S502—Organization and Administration of the Modern High School   **Dr. W. Scott Smith**
11:30 A. M.-12:20 P. M.   Credit: 2 semester-hours   Room 24

Integration S503—Methods and Instruments of Research   Dr. Froehlich
Prerequisite: Mathematics 400 or its equivalent.
Section I: 8:30-9:20 A. M.   Credit: 2 semester-hours   Room 1, Annex No. 2
Section II: 9:30-10:20 A. M.   Credit: 2 semester-hours   Room 1, Annex No. 2

**Integration S504A—Curriculum Construction in the
Secondary School**   Dr. W. Scott Smith
10:30-11:20 A. M.   Credit: 2 semester-hours   Room 24

**Integration S505—Organization and Administration of
Extra-Curricular Activities**   Mr. Morehead
11:30 A. M.-12:20 P. M.   Credit: 2 semester-hours   Room 27

**Integration S508—Supervision of Instruction in
Secondary Schools**   Dr. Atkinson
9:30-10:20 A. M.   Credit: 2 semester-hours   Room 4, CHS

Integration S517—Administration of the Elementary School   Dr. Phipps
8:30-9:20 A. M.   Credit: 2 semester-hours   Room D

**Integration S518—Supervision of Instruction in the
Elementary School**   Dr. Phipps
11:30 A. M.-12:20 P. M.   Credit: 2 semester-hours   Room D

Integration S520—Principles of Mental Hygiene   Dr. Ingebritsen
8:30-9:20 A. M.   Credit: 2 semester-hours   Room 30

**Integration S521A—Educational and Psychological
Measurement in Guidance**   Dr. Ingebritsen
9:30-10:20 A. M.   Credit: 2 semester-hours   Room 30

Integration S537—Social-Moral Guidance   Dr. E. C. Davis
8:30-9:20 A. M.   Credit: 2 semester-hours   Room 5

Integration S538—Group Guidance and Counseling Activities   (Visitor)
10:30-11:20 A. M.   Credit: 2 semester-hours   Room 10

**Integration S548—Curriculum Construction in the
Elementary School**   Dr. Phipps
10:30-11:20 A. M.   Credit: 2 semester-hours   Room D

Integration S551—Principles and Techniques of Guidance   (Visitor)
This course is prerequisite to all other courses in Guidance.
11:30 A. M.-12:20 P. M.   Credit: 2 semester-hours   Room 10

Integration S602—Seminar in Guidance   Dr. E. C. Davis
Prerequisites: Integration 551, and have taken (or be taking in conjunction)
one of the following: Int. 535, Int. 536, Int. 537.
10:30 A. M.-12:20 P. M.   Credit: 4 semester-hours   Room 5

14

Mathematics

Mathematics S300—Social and Commercial Uses of Mathematics   **Mr. Kays**
10:30 A. M.-12:20 P. M.   Credit: 2 semester-hours   Room 3, Annex No. 1
Above course meets double periods the last three weeks of the summer session.

Mathematics S400—Educational Statistics   **Mr. Humphreys**
This course or its equivalent is prerequisite to Integration 503.
11:30 A. M.-12:20 P. M.   Credit: 2 semester-hours   Room 2, Annex No. 1

Mathematics S412—Modern Geometry   **Mr. Kays**
This course presents a treatment of modern synthetic geometry on an advanced level. It is based on a fundamental framework of plane geometry and maturity of teaching in the field of mathematics. Topics treated are loci and geometric constructions; fundamental theorems of Ceva, Menelaus, Stewart, Euler, Ptolemy, etc.; homothetic figures, the harmonic range, noteworthy lines and points, systems of circles, and inversion. This course is not open for credit to students who have received credit for Mathematics 301.
8:30-10:20 A. M.   Credit: 4 semester-hours   Room 3, Annex No. 1

Mathematics S503—Foundations of Algebra   **Dr. D. R. Davis**
9:30-10:20 A. M.   Credit: 2 semester-hours   Room 1, Annex No. 1

Mathematics S505—Consumer Mathematics   **Dr. Meserve**
9:30-10:20 A. M.   Credit: 2 semester-hours   Room 4, Annex No. 1

**Mathematics S509B—A Critical Interpretation of Mathematics
in the Senior High School II**   **Dr. Meserve**
10:30-11:20 A. M.   Credit: 2 semester-hours   Room 4, Annex No. 1

**Mathematics S516A—Theory of Functions of a
Complex Variable**   **Dr. D. R. Davis**
8:30-9:20 A. M.   Credit: 2 semester-hours   Room 1, Annex No. 1

Mathematics S521—Analytical Mechanics   **Dr. Meserve**
11:30 A. M.-12:20 P. M.   Credit: 2 semester-hours   Room 4, Annex No. 1

Integration S477—Elementary School Mathematics   **Mr. Humphreys**
See "Elementary Education" on page 22.

Science

Biology S408—Biological Technique   **Dr. Hadley**
Prerequisites: 8 semester-hours of work in zoology and 4 semester-hours of work in botany.
9:30-10:20 A. M. Lectures daily
M-W-F afternoons Laboratory   Credit: 4 semester-hours   Room 1, Annex No. 3

Chemistry S408A—Industrial Chemistry I   **Dr. Reed**
Prerequisites: General and Organic Chemistry, or special permission of the instructor.
11:30 A. M.-12:20 P. M. Lectures Tuesdays and Thursdays
Tuesday and Thursday afternoons Field Trips
    Credit: 2 semester-hours   Room 9, Annex No. 3

Chemistry S501—The Teaching of Chemistry in Secondary Schools
Prerequisite: 16 semester-hours in Chemistry.
8:00-9:20 A. M.   Credit: 3 semester-hours   Room

Integration S478—Elementary School Science
See "Elementary Education" on page 22.

Social Studies

Social Studies S404—The Philosophy of History
9:30-10:20 A. M.   Credit: 2 semester-hours

Social Studies S446—Problems in Economics and Government
11:30 A. M.-12:20 P. M.   Credit: 2 semester-hours

Social Studies S456—International Economic Relations
10:30-11:20 A. M.   Credit: 2 semester-hours

Social Studies S462—Continental United States
See "New Tools for Learning" on page 17.

Social Studies S475—The History of American Thought
8:30-9:20 A. M.   Credit: 2 semester-hours

Social Studies S479—Education and Intercultural Relationships
11:30 A. M.-12:20 P. M.   Credit: 2 semester-hours

Social Studies S490D—The United States and World Affairs   **Mr. Kop**
See "Institutes and Workshops" on page 19.

Social Studies S490E—Latin America, A Survey   **Mr. Kops**
See "Institutes and Workshops" on page 19.

THE NEW TOOLS FOR LEARNING BUREAU

The New Tools for Learning Bureau coordinates the activities of the Audio-Visual Aids Service, the Audio Aids Laboratory, the Bureau of Field Studies, and the Television Workshop. The Bureau provides all types of services and equipment in the several areas named above. Any summer session student is welcome to avail himself of these services.

Course Offerings

Integration S408—Selection and Utilization of Audio-Materials   **Miss Fantone**

This course meets double periods for the last three weeks of the summer session.

10:30 A. M.-12:20 P. M.   Credit: 2 semester-hours   Room 4

Social Studies S462—Field Studies in American Life: Continental United States   **Mr. Bye and Miss Kuhnen**

This is a sixty-day field study course covering over 12,500 miles by deluxe chartered bus and stopping at first class hotels. A few of the high points en route are: Natural Bridge, Mammoth Cave, Lincoln's New Salem, Dodge City, Denver; Rocky Mountains, Grand Canyon, Bryce, Zion, Sequoia, Yosemite, Mt. Hood, Mt. Ranier, Crater Lake, Yellowstone National Parks; Santa Fe Indian reservation, Petrified Forest; all of California (2 weeks); Oregon, Washington, Montana, Wyoming, Black Hills, Chicago, Niagara Falls.

July 1 to August 29   Credit: 10 semester-hours

Cost: (Not including meals) $650. The quota for this course is already filled, but a waiting list is open. Write, if interested, to Edgar C. Bye, Bureau of Field Studies, New Jersey State Teachers College, Upper Montclair, N. J.

The New Look—Classroom, Laboratory, Studio Building Now Under Construction

18

INSTITUTES AND WORKSHOPS
Institutes on World Affairs

The two Institutes that follow are the first of a series to be offered in this and in future summer sessions.

June 27 through July 16

Social Studies S490D—The United States and

World Affairs   Mr. Kops, Mr. Cohen, Mr. Boucher et al.

The purpose of this course is to give the student an opportunity to make a thorough survey of the leading problems in world affairs. Visiting lecturers from agencies concerned with the problems of today's world supplement the basic information supplied by the regular members of the Institute staff. Included among the subjects studied are: Underdeveloped areas of the world, technical assistance, international trade and cultural interdependence. Special emphasis is placed on the relations of the United States with such areas of the world as the Far East, Eastern Europe, the Middle East, Western Europe, and Latin America. This course is designed primarily for teachers who feel the need for accurate background information and improved teaching materials and techniques for use in their classrooms. In addition to the conventional lectures, this course features the showing of the latest films in the field of world affairs, field trips to the United Nations and to foreign areas of New York, exhibits of teaching materials, demonstrations of teaching techniques and materials, folk singing, and folk dances suitable for classroom use.

9:30 A. M.-12:20 P. M.   Credit: 3 semester-hours   Meets in Dormitory Lounge

Students who wish to enroll for the above Institute should write to Mr. Walter E. Kops, State Teachers College, Upper Montclair, N. J., for preliminary registration. Complete registration and payment of fees will take place in the College Library, from 8:00-9:00 A. M. on June 27. See page 9 of this Bulletin for Fees and Service Charges.

July 18 through August 5

Social Studies S490E—Latin America,

A Survey   Mr. Kops, Mr. Cohen, Mr. Boucher et al.

The purpose of this course is to give the student an opportunity to make a thorough survey of Latin America. Visiting lecturers from agencies concerned with Latin American affairs supplement the basic information supplied by the regular members of the Institute staff. Included among the subjects studied are: Geographic setting and influences, pre-European cultures, exploration and settlement, independence, the Monroe Doctrine, economic colonialism, Pan-Americanism, present-day Latin America, United States relations with Latin America, and Latin America and the United Nations.

This course is designed primarily for teachers who feel the need for accurate background information and improved teaching materials and techniques for use in their classrooms. In addition to conventional lectures, this Institute features the showing of the latest films on Latin America, field trips to the United Nations and Latin American centers of New York, exhibits of materials suitable for teaching, demonstrations of teaching techniques and materials, folk singing, and folk dances suitable for classroom use.

9:30 A. M.-12:20 P. M.   Credit: 3 semester-hours   Meets in Dormitory Lounge

Students taking both the above courses should enroll for them on June 27. Those taking this course only will enroll for it between 8:00 and 9:00 on July 18. Preliminary registration may be made by writing to Mr. Walter E. Kops, State Teachers College, Upper Montclair, New Jersey. See page 9 of this Bulletin for Fees and Service Charges.

FIFTH UNITED NATIONS INSTITUTE
July 28, 29 and 30

A two and one-half day session on the United Nations and its place in today'. world. Program to include a trip to the United Nations, special lectures and demonstrations of special interest to teachers and community leaders. Registra tion fee $2. No credit. Students enrolled in Latin-American Institute described above will be permitted to participate in this program without additional cost

China Institute of New Jersey
June 27—July 9, 1955

China Institute of New Jersey is a permanent year-round organization com posed of former students of the Institute. The policies and program of the Institute are determined by an elected executive committee, an advisory board of laymen, and representatives from the Faculty of Montclair State Teacher: College, in consultation with the Chinese Director.

Dr. Chih Meng, Director of the China Institute of America, is also Chines Director of the China Institute of New Jersey.

Students may enroll for college credit (graduate or undergraduate) if eligible to do so, or simply as Auditors for no credit. **The cost is the same in both cases** (See page 9 for information as to fees.) Those who enroll for credit are ex pected to complete such notebooks, papers, projects, and examinations as are assigned by the course instructors. The preliminary grading of these papers projects, and examinations is done by the Chinese teachers, while the fina grading and coordinating is done by a representative of the regular Faculty of the College.

Notification of desire to enroll in one of the Institute courses should be sent on the coupon supplied in the special leaflet published by the Institute Actual registration and payment of fees will take place in the College Library from 8:00-9:00 A. M., on June 27. The Institute will convene in the Auditoriun of the College High School Building at 9:15. The students taking the Literatur course will leave the Auditorium later and go to their classroom.

China Institute Offerings

English S459—A Survey of Great Chinese Literature
9:30 A. M.-12:20 P. M. and 1-4 P. M.   Credit: 3 semester-hours   Room 3, CH

Social Studies S499—Introduction to Chinese Culture   **Dr. Chih Men**
9:30 A. M.-12:20 P. M. and 1-4 P. M.   Credit: 3 semester-hours   Auditorium, CH
Students enroll for one or the other of the courses of the China Institute o June 27, between 8:00 and 9:00 A. M. in the College Library.

Institutes and Workshops Offered by Rutgers University

250:422. Workshop on Economic Education
A three-week workshop from July 18 to August 5 for administrators, supe visors, curriculum directors, teachers, and others interested in improving the economic understanding.
                    Credit: 3 semester-hours

250:440J. Mathematics Institute

This third Rutgers institute from July 6 to July 15 for teachers of elementary and junior and senior high schools is sponsored jointly by the University and the Association of Mathematics Teachers of New Jersey.

Credit: 2 semester-hours

250:470J   Workshop in Human Relations Education

A six-week workshop from June 27 to August 5 designed to familiarize teachers and administrators, guidance directors, nurses, social workers, policemen, librarians, ministers, personnel directors, industrial workers, and others with the varied problems of intergroup relations.

Credit: 6 semester-hours

250:486J   Science Institute

This second Rutgers institute from July 6 to July 15 is under the joint sponsorship of the University and the New Jersey Science Teachers Association and is designed to bring together teachers of all grades who will live and work together to gain a better understanding of the most recent and effective ideas in the teaching of science.

Credit: 2 semester-hours

250:491-492J   Workshop in Creative Art Education

A three or six-week workshop to work with a wide variety of art materials exploring principles and methods of developing similar activities in elementary and secondary schools.

Credit: 3 or 6 semester-hours

260:526J   School, Business, and Industry: The Work-Study Program for Teachers and Counselors

A cooperative study of school-employment relationships combining eight weeks of paid work-experience with critical consideration of business and industrial practice and job-adjustment problems.

Applications and more detailed information about these institutes and workshops may be obtained from the Director of the Summer Session, Rutgers University, New Brunswick, New Jersey.

New Jersey State Teachers College at Trenton

Summer 1955 Workshops

Workshop	Dates	Points
Conservation Education	July 5-22	4
River Education	June 13-24	2
Elementary School Reading	July 25-August 5	2
Library Science: Instructional Materials	July 5-August 10	6
Music Activities in the Elementary School	June 28-July 8	2
Introduction to Geography for Teachers	July 11-22	2

COURSES FOR THOSE WHO DESIRE TO TEACH IN ELEMENTARY GRADES

These courses are open to the following only:

(1) Those who already hold a degree from Montclair State Teachers College with a Certificate in Secondary Education, and

(2) Those who are now matriculated at Montclair State Teachers College for a degree and the Certificate in Secondary Education.

All other students should apply to one of the following colleges, all of which offer the bachelor's degree in Elementary Education and several of which also offer the master's degree in that field:

New Jersey State Teachers College at Paterson.
New Jersey State Teachers College at Jersey City.
New Jersey State Teachers College at Newark.
New Jersey State Teachers College at Trenton.
New Jersey State Teachers College at Glassboro.

The courses given on this campus are offered to assist the Montclair State Teachers College students in attaining provisional and standard certification to teach in elementary grades. Detailed requirements for such certification are listed on pages 14, 15, 16, and 68 of the Eighteenth Edition of the Rules Concerning Teachers Certificates. Montclair College students should consult Miss House, the College Registrar, for an evaluation of their previous work and a statement concerning their remaining required courses.

The courses listed below may apply as general electives in undergraduate curriculums, and **with the Advisor's approval,** as graduate electives for majors in Administration and Supervision. The courses with the * do not carry graduate credit, however.

*Integration S474—Elementary School Arts and Crafts   Mr. Vernacchia
10:30-11:20 A. M.   Credit: 2 semester-hours   Campus Studio Workshop

***Integration S476—Elementary School Health and
Physical Education   Mr. DeRosa**
9:30-10:20 A. M.   Credit: 2 semester-hours   Room 14, CHS and Gym, CHS

Integration S477—Elementary School Mathematics   Mr. Humphrey
10:30-11:20 A. M.   Credit: 2 semester-hours   Room 2, Annex No.

Integration S478—Elementary School Science   Mr. Alle
8:30-9:20 A. M.   Credit: 2 semester-hours   Room 5, Annex No.

In addition to the above courses, **Geography S418, Regional Geography of Nort America,** applies on the Limited Elementary Certificate. See "Geography" o page 12.

NEW JERSEY STATE SCHOOL OF CONSERVATION

Stokes State Forest, Branchville, N. J.

A New "R" in Education: Resource Education

Teachers across the Nation are becoming aware of the need for greater emphasis in education which deals with the conservation of natural resources.

In New Jersey, teachers have a unique opportunity to acquire first-hand experiences in this area of instruction at the New Jersey State School of Conservation, Stokes State Forest. This school, located in the center of the state's rich dairy country, affords a wide selection of field trip experiences relating conservation to art, science, biology, camping, government, geography, social studies, and economics. The staff is well qualified to assist teachers in planning programs for their respective classes.

In addition to its courses, the Conservation School conducts a Youth Program—Camp Wapalanne—designed for youngsters between the ages of 11 and 18. Teachers interested in counseling may earn up to four college credits during the summer, working as counselors in this Youth Program.

For further details, write to: Edward J. Ambry, Director, New Jersey State School of Conservation, Upper Montclair, N. J. Summer Address: Branchville, N. J.

1955 SUMMER COURSES

Biology 203—Introduction to Field Biology

    Credit: 2 semester-hours   June 16-26

Physical Education 410—Water Safety and First Aid

    Credit: 2 semester-hours   June 16-26

Integration 440—Camping Education

    Credit: 2 semester-hours   June 16-26

Integration 441—Conservation Education

    Credit: 2 semester-hours   June 16-26

Art 415—School Arts and Crafts with Native Materials

    Credit: 2 semester-hours   June 16-26

*Science 419—Field Science and Conservation

    Credit: 2 semester-hours   July 2-11

*Social Studies 494—Social Studies and Conservation

    Credit: 2 semester-hours   July 2-11

Art 415—School Arts and Crafts with Native Materials

    Credit: 2 semester-hours   August 13-23

Integration 480—Field Science for Elementary Teachers

    Credit: 2 semester-hours   August 13-23

Social Studies 477—Rural Sociology

    Credit: 2 semester-hours   August 13-23

Fees: $55.00 for 10-day session. Includes board, room, tuition (2 semester-hours), swimming, boating and other recreation.

Scholarships: Several are available. Write for particulars.

* Courses approved by State Board of Examiners to meet specific requirements for certification in grades one through eight.

POST-SUMMER SESSION COURSE

August 8 through August 19, 1955

To Meet an Urgent Need, the following course is being offered by the State Teachers College at Montclair, with the assistance of the New Jersey State Safety Council, the New Jersey Automobile Club, the American Automobile Association, the New Jersey State Police, and the New Jersey Department of Motor Vehicles.

This Course Offers the Necessary Opportunity for men and women to prepare themselves to teach behind-the-wheel driver education in high schools. Enrollees completing the work of the course are presented with a certificate indicating the work done.

Authorization: In order to teach behind-the-wheel driver education and driver training, a teacher must have his or her certificate endorsed by the Division of Teacher Certification, State Department of Education, for teaching behind-the-wheel automobile driver education and driver training.

The Requirements for Such Endorsement on the teacher's certificate are:

(18th edition, 1951, "Rules Concerning Teachers' Certificates," page 22).

1. A valid New Jersey teacher's certificate.
2. A current New Jersey driver's license.
3. Three years of automobile driving experience.
4. Evidence of satisfactory completion of a course in driver education and driver training approved by the Commissioner of Education.

Veterans may take this course under the G. I. Bill, if they have so arranged with the Veterans' Counselor of the College.

Living Expenses and Traveling Expenses must be paid by the student. Those desiring hotel accommodations should write to Mr. F. K. Schultze, Manager, New Jersey Auto Club, AAA, 156 Clinton Avenue, Newark 5, New Jersey. The College Residence Halls are closed at this time.

Textbooks and Other Text Materials are furnished to each enrollee without charge.

Registration for this course will be accepted up to and including the opening day of the course. However, students should register early if possible, preferably on the regular registration day for the Summer Session. There is a limit to the number of registrations which may be accepted.

**Health Education S408—Behind-the-Wheel Driver
  Education and Driver Training**   Coordinator: Dr. Code

9:00-12:00 and 1:00-4:00 daily   Credit: 2 semester-hours   Room D

24

956
ulletin of
ONTCLAIR STATE TEACHERS COLLEGE

SUMMER SESSION

y 2 to August 10   STATE TEACHERS COLLEGE
Montclair, New Jersey

PER MONTCLAIR   NEW JERSEY

SUMMER SESSION

Bulletin of

MONTCLAIR
STATE TEACHERS COLLEGE

1956

July 2nd to August 10th

VOLUME 48   NUMBER 2

UPPER MONTCLAIR, NEW JERSEY

OFFICERS OF ADMINISTRATION

STATE BOARD OF EDUCATION

MRS. EDWARD L. KATZENBACH, *President* ....Princeto

ARTHUR E. ARMITAGE, SR. ....Collingswoo

MRS. T. B. ARMSTRONG .... Stewartsvill

HARVEY DEMBE ....Bayonn

LEWIS F. GAYNER ....Saler

PHILIP R. GEBHARDT ....Clinto

JOHN S. GRAY ....Newto

JOHN F. LYNCH ....Morristow

JAMES W. PARKER, SR. ....Red Ban

HENRY A. WILLIAMS ....Paterso

MRS. STANLEY C. YORTON ....Nutle

COMMISSIONER OF EDUCATION
DR. FREDERICK M. RAUBINGER

ASSISTANT COMMISSIONER FOR HIGHER EDUCATION
DR. EARL E. MOSIER

COLLEGE ADMINISTRATION

E. DEALTON PARTRIDGE, Ph.D ....Preside

CLYDE M. HUBER, Ph.D. ....Dean of Instructi

EDWARD J. AMBRY, A.M. ..Director, Summer, Part-Time and Extension Divisi

BERNARD SIEGEL, M.B.A. ....Business Manag

OTIS C. INGEBRITSEN, Ph.D. ....Chairman of the Graduate Committ

KEITH W. ATKINSON, Ph.D. ....Director of College High Sch

EARL C. DAVIS, Ph.D. ....Director of Personnel and Guidaɪ

ELIZABETH S. FAVOR, A.M. .... Assistant in Graduate Person

MARGARET A. SHERWIN, A.M. ....Dean of Worɪ

MARY M. HOUSE, B.C.S. ....Regist

ANNE BANKS CRIDLEBAUGH, A.M. ....Librarɪ

OTTO CORDES, P.E. ....Engineer in Charge, Maintena

HEALTH SERVICES

CHARLOTTE L. PRITCHARD, R.N. ....College Nu

2

FACULTY
Summer Session 1956

E. DeAlton Partridge, Ph.D. ....President
Clyde M. Huber, Ph.D. ....Dean of Instruction
Edward J. Ambry, A.M. ....Director, Summer, Part-Time and Extension
Keith W. Atkinson, Ph.D. ....Integration
LeRoy Booth, Ed.D. ....Integration
Bertrand P. Boucher, A.M. ....Geography
Milton W. Brown, Ph.D. ....Integration
Leonard Buchner, A.M. ....Integration
Edgar C. Bye, A.M. ....Director, Bureau of Field Studies
Frank L. Clayton, Ph.D. ....Social Studies
Alden C. Coder, Ed.D. ....Driver Education
Philip S. Cohen, A.M. ....Social Studies
David R. Davis, Ph.D. ....Chairman, Department of Mathematics
Earl C. Davis, Ph.D. ....Personnel and Guidance
Jerome G. DeRosa, A.M. ....Health and Physical Education
James E. Downes, A.M. ....Economics
Emma Fantone, A.M. ....Director, Audio-Visual Center
L. Howard Fox, A.M. ....Speech
Carl E. Frankson, Ph.D. ....Head of the Department of Industrial Arts
Paul E. Froehlich, Ed.D. ....Research
Edwin S. Fulcomer, Ed.D. ....Head of the Department of English
W. Paul Hamilton, A.M. ....English
Clarence Hinchey, Ed.D. ....Integration
T. Roland Humphreys, A.M. ....Mathematics
Emil Kahn, A.M. ....Music
Walter E. Kops, A.M. ....Director, Institutes of World Affairs
Russell Krauss, Ph.D. ....English
Orpha M. L. Lutz, Ph.D. ....Psychology
Chih Meng, Ph.D. ....Director, China Institute
Bruce E. Meserve, Ph.D. ....Mathematics
Harley P. Milstead, Ph.D. ....Geography
Allan Morehead, A.M. ....Integration
James P. Pettegrove, A.M. ....English
William R. Phipps, Ed.D. ....Integration
George F. Placek, A.M. ....Science
John J. Rellahan, Ph.D. ....Acting Head, Department of Social Studies
Jerome Seidman, Ph.D. ....Integration
Thaddeus J. Sheft, A.B. ....Audio-Visual Aids
Horace J. Sheppard, A.M. ....Acting Head, Department of Business Education
Kenneth O. Smith, Ph.D. ....Physics
W. Scott Smith, Ph.D. ....Acting Head, Department of Integration
Elizabeth T. VanDerveer, E.D. ....Business Education
Ralph A. Vernacchia, A.M. ....Art
Richard W. Willing, Ed.D. ....Business Education
Frederic H. Young, Ph.D. ....English

GRADUATE COMMITTEE

Otis C. Ingebritsen, *Chairman*   Elizabeth S. Favor, *Secretary*
Edward J. Ambry   W. Paul Hamilton   William R. Phipps
David R. Davis   Clyde M. Huber   Rufus D. Reed
John J. Rellahan   Elizabeth T. VanDerveer

3

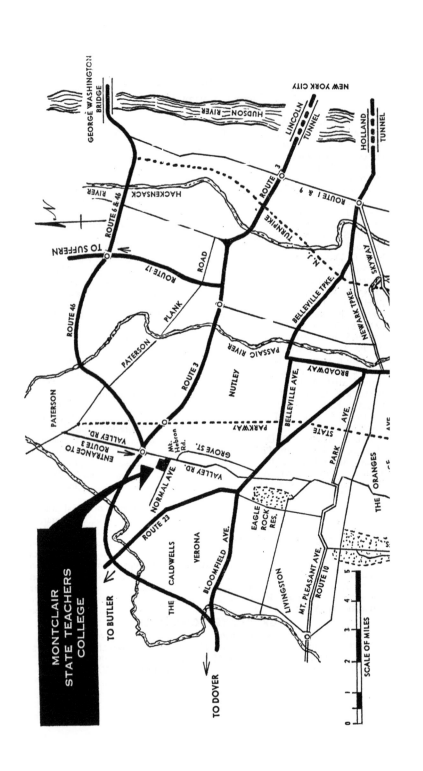

SUMMER SESSION OF THE
NEW JERSEY STATE TEACHERS COLLEGE AT MONTCLAIR

Objectives and Academic Status

The College is a professional school which prepares teachers, supervisors, and principals of high schools, and administrators of public school systems. The degrees offered by this College are those of Bachelor of Arts and Master of Arts. Certificate courses are offered for those who now hold degrees from other colleges. See paragraph under "Certificates."

The New Jersey State Teachers College at Montclair is a member of the American Association of Colleges of Teacher Education and fully accredited by the National Council for the Accreditation of Teacher Education, the Middle States Association of Colleges and Secondary Schools, and the American Association of University Women.

How to Reach the Campus

The College is located about one mile north of the center of Upper Montclair. Trains of the Greenwood Lake Division, Erie R.R., stop at Montclair Heights, the College Station. Trains of the Lackawanna R.R. connect at Montclair with the following bus lines: Nos. 60, 64, and 76 to the College.

Residence Halls for Men and Women

Edward Russ Hall, Chapin Hall, and the new Dormitory for Men provide excellent living quarters for summer school students. The charge for living on campus during the Summer Session is: $14.50 per week; which includes room, breakfast, and dinner. A la carte luncheons are served in the College cafeteria. For one student alone in a double room, an extra charge of $2.00 per week is made. The College provides and launders sheets, pillowcase, and bedpad. Towels, blankets, clocks and similar items must be provided and cared for by the student. The boarding-hall fee must be paid on or before the first day of the Summer Session. No rebate is made for occasional absence or voluntary withdrawal during the session. These prices are subject to change.

For reservations in a College Residence Hall, women address: Dean of Women, State Teachers College, Upper Montclair, N. J. Men address: Dean of Men.

Schedule of the Summer Session

Registration will take place on Monday, July 2. Hours, 9-12 and 1-3:30. Classes will begin on Tuesday morning, July 3, at 8 A.M. and will continue through Friday, August 10. All classes meet daily, Monday to Friday, inclusive, at the hours indicated for each, and on the following Saturdays: July 7, July 14, and July 28. Wednesday, July 4, is a Holiday.

Matriculation for the Master of Arts Degree

Since not more than 8 semester-hours of work taken prior to matriculation re allowed to apply on the Master of Arts degree, the student should take care complete the matriculation procedure as soon as he has that amount of credit; oner, if possible. Transfer of graduate credit from other institutions is permitted ly to those students who are graduates of New Jersey State Teachers Colleges

5

or the State University of New Jersey. The maximum permitted is 8 semest hours. .

Those who desire to become candidates for the degree must request application form from the Chairman of the Graduate Committee and return properly filled and accompanied by an Official Transcript of all previous wi on college level. **When such an applicant has been accepted by the College** a candidate for the degree, a definite statement is furnished by the Chairm of the Graduate Committee, showing the requirements which he must fulfill earn the degree. This sheet of requirements becomes the student's Work P gram and should be brought by the student each time he comes to enroll . courses.

The completion of the above procedure constitutes matriculation. Sim registration for courses does not.

Students Matriculated at Montclair for the A.M. Degree

Since September 1, 1952, all students matriculating in the Graduate Divis: have been required to complete at least one full-time (6 s.h.) Summer Sessi or, in lieu thereof, at least one regular semester of full-time graduate attendan

The selection of courses must be in accordance with the student's Wc Program, and his registration form will be signed by the Head of the Departme in which the student is majoring or by a representative of that departme present in the registration room. .

Candidates for a degree must file with the Registrar an application ì conferment of the degree before November 30 of the college year in which t work is to be completed. Application blanks for this purpose may be secured the Registrar's Office. The burden of responsibility for the request rests w. the candidate. This is of special significance to the teacher-in-service who m have distributed the work for the degree over several years.

Students Matriculated at Other Colleges

Several years ago, when the State Teachers College at Montclair offe courses to its own accelerated candidates for the Bachelor's degree, it was possi to accept students from other colleges in freshman, sophomore, and junior y courses, as well as in courses of the senior year. Beginning in the summer 1950, however, the College returned to its pre-war custom of offering courses its Summer Session primarily to teachers-in-service. As such teachers, few exceptions, already hold the Bachelor's degree, the courses shown in Bulletin are, for the most part, only Graduate and Senior-Graduate co carrying graduate credit.

A student who is planning to attend Montclair this summer should take Bulletin to a conference with the Dean of his own college to arrange a pro of work. For the Dean's information: the numbering of courses at Mont follows this order: 100-399, inclusive, are undergraduate courses; 400-499, clusive, are senior-college and graduate courses; 500 and above are grad courses.

At the time of registration, **the student from another college should b with him a letter from his own Dean showing the courses which will be acce for credit there and which he has been advised to take.** He should go to table of the Department in which the courses are listed. The registration i must be signed by the Representative of the Department at that table. College reserves the right to decide whether the student has fulfilled nece prerequisites. If the student is seeking certification to teach in New Jersey must confer with the Head of the Department of Integration. Please note p graph under the heading: "Certificates."

Auditors

Men and women who desire to take courses for cultural, vocational, or avocational purposes without college credits may register as auditors.

A student who desires to enroll in a course for which he already holds credit must register as an auditor in that particular course.

A student who desires to enroll in a course for which he has not completed the prerequisites must enroll as an auditor in that particular course.

Change of Status in a Course

If a student desires to change his status in a course from "credit" to "auditor" or from "auditor" to "credit," he must make formal application for such change not later than the middle of the course. Forms for this purpose may be procured in the Registrar's office. Such changes cannot be made after the midpoint of the course is passed.

Certificates

The State Teachers College at Montclair offers work toward the following New Jersey Certificates: Secondary Teaching Certificate; Secondary School Principal's Certificate; Subject Supervisor's Certificate; General Supervisor's Certificate; Guidance Certificate; School Administrator's Certificate; Junior College Teacher's Certificate; and the Advanced Professional Certificate.

Those who matriculate at Montclair for a Master of Arts degree will receive information from the Head of the Integration Department as to the requirements for each of these certificates. Students who have not matriculated at Montclair should write to the Secretary of the State Board of Examiners, Department of Education, 175 West State Street, Trenton 25, N. J., for information as to the requirements. For an evaluation of work already completed, address the Secretary also. An official transcript of such previous work should accompany the inquiry, with a statement as to the particular certificate desired.

The student should bring the reply from the State Board of Examiners with him when conferring with the Head of the Integration Department as to his program of work.

Supervised Student Teaching

The opportunity to do supervised student teaching cannot be offered during the Summer Session. For fall teaching, students confer with the Head of the Integration Department at the College. Ask his secretary for an appointment.

Veterans

Veteran students taking work under the G.I. Bill and likewise the so-called Korean Veteran must see the Veterans' Counselor of the College, before the close of the spring semester on June 14 in order to make certain that when they come to enroll on July 2 their papers will all be in order. Students taking work without the papers necessary must pay the usual tuition fees at the time of registration.

Veterans who have completed the work of the A.B. or the A.M. degree at Montclair must secure and present to the Veterans' Counselor the Supplemental Certificate of Eligibility before registering for further work. Veterans transferring to this College who have previously been in training under one of the Veterans' Bills must secure the Supplemental Certificate of Eligibility and present it to the Veterans' Counselor at the time of registration.

Conferences with Advisers

Appointments with the Dean of Instruction, the Chairman of the Gradu Committee, a Department Head, or the Veterans' Counselor may be made mail or telephone to their respective offices. This should be done at as ea a date as possible to avoid delay at the time of registration on July 2 and later than the end of the spring semester on June 14. After that date, it m not be possible to see these officials until the Summer Session opens.

Summer Session Credit Load

The maximum amount of credit which may be earned in the Summer S sion is 8 semester-hours, but only 6 are recommended. There is no provisi for a student to audit additional courses; consequently, the total of all cour taken during the Summer Session may not exceed 8 semester-hours and stude may not enroll for more. Additional credits may be earned by attending o of the sessions of the State School of Conservation at the Stokes State For that precedes or follows the Summer Session at Montclair. Attention is call also to the Post-Summer Session course in "Behind-the-Wheel Driver Educ tion and Driver Training."

Each Summer Session course is in session at least thirty hours and carr a designated amount of credit. **It is not possible to earn 3 semester-hours cre in a course designated to carry 2 semester-hours.**

Registration Information

Registration takes place in the College Library, on Monday, July 2, fr 9 A.M. to 12 Noon, and from 1 to 3:30 P.M. Anyone unable to enroll during t hours shown must register during the regular office hours of the College the Registrar's office, and the last date on which he may enroll for credit July 6.

Because the registration form must be signed by a Department Head or representative, must be inspected at the checking table, and paid for at t Business Manager's desk, before the student may receive his Class Admissi Cards, the procedure is time consuming and the student should allow at le 45 minutes. The student should report to the Head of the Department in wh he is majoring, or, if not matriculated for a degree here, to the Head of Department offering the courses in which he is interested.

On Monday, July 2, the Department Heads, Director of the Summer S sion, and the Business Manager are assembled in the College Library, but July 3, 5, and 6 they will be in their individual offices and the student m seek them there. Late students, registering on July 3, 5, and 6 should allow e more time, should come during the morning hours, and will be charged the l service charge of $2.00 in addition to the regular fees and service charges.

Students may, in some instances, be required to obtain signatures in m than one Department, if taking courses in more than one.

Matriculated students should bring their Work Programs when they c to enroll.

The College reserves the right to close any course for which the enrollm is insufficient. The class will meet at least once, however, before this decis is made. Students may then enter another course in place of the one discontin by going to the Registrar's Office to re-enroll and to receive the new C Admission Card in exchange for the card of the discontinued course.

Students who decide not to enroll in an alternate course must so state, letter of withdrawal, in order to receive a refund of tuition fees. The car the discontinued course should be enclosed in the letter.

If prerequisites are required for a course (see the course description), student should make certain that he has fulfilled them or their equivalent be enrolling in it.

If no previous work on college level has been taken, the student must consult the Dean of Instruction before enrolling in any course, except as an Auditor.

A student may not register for credit in any course for which he already holds credit, except by permission of the Dean of Instruction.

Withdrawal from a Course

During the registration day of July 2, and on July 3, July 5, and July 6, a student may, with the advice and consent in writing of his adviser, withdraw from one course and enter another in its place. The Class Admission Card from the dropped course must be presented in order to obtain the one for the new course.

A student who withdraws from a course without entering an alternate one, or who withdraws later in the session, must write a formal notice of withdrawal to the Director of the Summer Session. He, in turn, will notify the teacher of the course from which the student is withdrawing, as well as the Business Manager of the College. Refunds are computed from the date of the receipt of the letter of withdrawal.

Students who neglect to follow this procedure receive a failing mark for the course or courses which they cease to attend.

Tuition Fees, Service Charge, and Credit Slips

Check or money-order should be made payable to New Jersey State Teachers College.

Tuition Fees: to students who are residents of New Jersey, $11.00 per semester-hour credit carried by the course. Non-residents of New Jersey pay $13.00 per credit. Courses taken by auditors for no credit cost the same.

Service Charge: 50¢ per semester-hour point.

Late Registration Service Charge: $2.00 will be added to the cost of each late registration; that is, each registration which is not completed during the hours set aside for registration on July 2. A registration is complete when it has been duly filled in, signed by the Adviser, and paid for by the student. This additional charge will be made in the case of a deferred or a partially deferred payment of the fees and service charges.

Teachers who have supervised Montclair student-teachers and who have in their possession old Montclair credit slips may take them to the office of the Integration Department, where new ones will be issued. The Business Office cannot return any unused portion of a credit slip, so it is necessary that the new type credit slip be obtained before presenting it in payment of tuition fees. Training Teachers may use the credit slips of any one of the six New Jersey State Teachers Colleges when taking courses at Montclair, but should bring only the new type slip in all cases.

So long as any credit slips remain in a teacher's possession, they will be honored by the College although a new method of remuneration of training teachers is now in effect.

Final Marks

Following are the final marks which may be received for a course: A—Excellent; B—Good; C—Fair; D—Poor; F—Failure; Inc—Incomplete; Wd—Withdrew; N.C.—No Credit.

The mark of "D" when earned in summer, part-time, or extension courses of this College is not accepted for degree credit at Montclair.

The mark of "F" is given when earned and when the student has failed to notify the Director of the Summer Session promptly of his withdrawal from a course.

9

The mark of "N.C." is given only to those enrolled as Auditors.

The mark of "Wd" is given only when prompt notice of withdrawal has been given and when the student's work until that time has been satisfactory to the teacher of the course.

The mark of "Inc." is seldom given. It may, however, be granted to a student whose work is incomplete at the end of the Session and who is eager to finish the work for a higher grade than he could otherwise receive. **All responsibility regarding the incomplete work rests with the student.** He will be notified of a date after which, if the work remains incomplete, the final grade will be recorded without further notice.

Report Cards and Transcripts

An Official Transcript showing the credits earned is sent to the student personally ten days to two weeks following the close of the Session. A report card for each course taken is sent with this transcript, which is sent without cost. **A service charge of $1.00 is made for a duplicate copy of the transcript.**

A student whose college requires that the transcript be mailed directly to it should call, early in the Session, at the Registrar's Office to address an envelope for this purpose.

Elementary Education Courses

Courses offered as a part of the curriculum for the graduate major in Educational Administration and Supervision should be carefully distinguished from those offered toward the endorsement in elementary education on the teacher's certificate. Although the College at Montclair is engaged primarily in preparing secondary school teachers, it has been deemed expedient during the shortage of teachers in the elementary schools to assist our students to procure the elementary endorsement on their secondary teacher's certificates.

Students eligible to enroll at Montclair in courses leading to this endorsement in elementary education are:

(1) those who already hold a degree from Montclair with a certificate secondary education; and

(2) those who are now matriculated at Montclair for such a degree.

Montclair cannot accept any other students in these courses.

The eligible students should consult Miss House, the College Registrar, for an evaluation of their previous work and a statement covering the courses to be taken in order to receive the endorsement in elementary education on the secondary certificate already held or to be conferred.

Textbook Exhibit

In the Gymnasium of the Main Building, from July 16 through July 27, there will be an exhibit of high school and elementary school textbooks. While primarily for the benefit of the principals and teachers attending the Summer Session, the exhibit will be open to undergraduate students and to members of the general public who may be interested in seeing the latest textbooks.

Mrs. Bertrand P. Boucher will be in charge of the Exhibit.

College Book Store

A limited number of books for each course will be on hand in the Book Store at registration time. It is advantageous to order textbooks immediate upon completion of registration. Store hours: 8 A.M. - 12 Noon.

COURSES OF THE SUMMER SESSION

Descriptions of the courses will be found in the 1955-57 Graduate Bulletin of the College. Courses numbered 500 and above are graduate courses; those numbered 400-499, inclusive, are senior-graduate courses and their descriptions in the Graduate Bulletin follow the descriptions of the graduate courses. Courses below the 400 number will be found in the Undergraduate Bulletin of the College. Only entirely new courses are described in the Summer Session Bulletin.

Business Education

Business Education S503—The Business Education Curriculum   Dr. Van Derveer
8:30-9:20 A.M.   Credit: 2 semester-hours   Room 5, Annex No. 2

Business Education S520A—Improvement of Instruction in
   Business Education: General Business Subjects   Dr. Willing
9:30-10:20 A.M.   Credit: 2 semester-hours   Room 2, Annex No. 2

Business Education S520C—Improvement of Instruction in
   Business Education: Secretarial Subjects   Dr. Van Derveer
9:30-10:20 A.M.   Credit: 2 semester-hours   Room 28

Business Education S532—Field Studies and Audio-Visual Aids in
   Business Education   Mr. Sheppard
10:30 A.M.-12:20 P.M.   Credit: 4 semester-hours   Room 5, Annex No. 2

Business Education S533—Supervised Work Experience and
   Seminar   Dr. Van Derveer and Dr. Willing
Full-time work for six weeks under College Supervision. Evening conference:
7-9 P.M. each Wed. evening   Credit: 4 semester-hours   Room 5, Annex No. 2

Business Education S542A—Advanced Business Law Cases I   Dr. Willing
8:30-9:20 A.M.   Credit: 2 semester-hours   Room 2, Annex No. 2

English and Speech

English S409—The Teaching and Appreciation of Poetry   Mr. Pettegrove
10:30-11:20 A.M.   Credit: 2 semester-hours   Room 2

English S431A—Shakespeare: Tragedies   Mr. Hamilton
10:30-11:20 A.M.   Credit: 2 semester-hours   Room 1

English S443—Modern Drama   Dr. Fulcomer
9:30-10:20 A.M.   Credit: 2 semester-hours   Room 1

English S454—Training the Speaking Voice   Mr. Fox
11:30 A.M.-12:20 P.M.   Credit: 2 semester-hours   Room A

English S465—Speech Arts Activity   Mr. Fox
10:50-11:20 A.M.   Credit: 1 semester-hour   Room A

English S503—Geoffrey Chaucer and His Times   Dr. Krauss
11:30 A.M.-12:20 P.M.   Credit: 2 semester-hours   Room 1

English S519—English in the Modern High School   Dr. Fulcomer
8:30-9:20 A.M.   Credit: 2 semester-hours   Room 1

English S520A—Great Books on Education: Plato to Rousseau   **Dr. Kraus**
This course is acceptable as an Integration elective for all graduate majors.
9:30-10:20 A.M.   Credit: 2 semester-hours   Room

English S521—English Literature of Social Problems   **Mr. Pettegrov**
This course is recommended as an elective for Social Studies graduate students
9:30-10:20 A.M.   Credit: 2 semester-hours   Room

English S531—Seventeenth Century Literature   **Mr. Hamilton**
8:30-9:20 A.M.   Credit: 2 semester-hours   Room

English S536—Philosophy of Great Literature   **Dr. Youn**
This course is recommended as an elective for all graduate students.
11:30 A.M.-12:20 P.M.   Credit: 2 semester-hours   Room

Fine Arts

Fine Arts S210—Experiencing Art   **Mr. Vernacchi**
This course is designed to give the student the experience of art through creating
selecting, arranging, contemplating, and reading. Emphasis is placed on th
development of an understanding of the nature of art and the experience o
art, and their significance to the individual and their role in a culture. Th
course content is selected from all art forms and is related to student need
and interests. Personal exploration of materials, tools and processes of ar
readings in contemporary and historical art forms and art philosophy, trips t
appropriate sources, and contacts with producing artists are procedural method
of the course.
9:30-10:20 A.M.   Credit: 2 semester-hours   Campus Studio Worksho

Fine Arts S406A—Art Workshop I   **Mr. Vernacchi**
The workshop is designed to allow the student to have a concentrated experienc
in an art form of his choice. Each student projects his own problem in con
sultation with, and under the direction of, a faculty member. In addition, th
student is expected to set up an exhibit of the work he has accomplished durin
his four years.
10:30-11:20 A.M.   Credit: 2 semester-hours   Campus Studio Worksho

Fine Arts S416—Appreciation of Chinese Art
See Institutes and Workshops on Page 19.

Integration S474—Elementary School Arts and Crafts   **Mr. Vernacchi**
See "Elementary Education" on page 22.

Geography

**Geography S412—Geography of Africa, Australia, and
   New Zealand**   **Dr. Milstea**
8:30-9:20 A.M.   Credit: 2 semester-hours   Room

Geography S413—Economic Geography of South America   **Dr. Milstea**
10:30-11:20 A.M.   Credit: 2 semester-hours   Room

Geography S504—Economic Geography of Europe   **Dr. Milstea**
11:30 A.M.-12:20 P.M.   Credit: 2 semester-hours   Room

Health Education

Health Education S408—Behind-the-Wheel Driver   Dr. Coder
8:30 A.M.-12:20 P.M.; 1:00-2:30 P.M.;
July 2-20   Credit: 3 semester-hours   Room 3, College HS
See also the Post-Summer-Session section of this course on page 24.

Health Education S411—School Health Services   Mr. DeRosa
9:30-10:20 A.M.   Credit: 2 semester-hours   Room 13, CHS

**Integration S476—Elementary School Health and
Physical Education**   Mr. DeRosa
See "Elementary Education" on page 22.

Integration

Integration S300A—Aims and Organization of Secondary Education   Dr. Seidman
8:30-9:20 A.M.   Credit: 2 semester-hours   Room 9

**Integration S300B—Principles and Techniques of Teaching
in the Secondary School**   Dr. Atkinson
10:30-11:20 A.M.   Credit: 2 semester-hours   Room 4, CHS

**Integration S400A—Principles and Philosophy
of Secondary Education**   Dr. Seidman
11:30 A.M.-12:20 P.M.   Credit: 2 semester-hours   Room 9

Integration S407A—Television in Education Workshop I
See "Audio-Visual Center" on page 16.

**Integration S408—Selection and Utilization of
Audio-Visual Materials**   Miss Fantone
See "Audio-Visual Center" on page 16.

**Integration S409—Radio and Sound Equipment in
the Classroom**   Mr. Fox
See "Audio-Visual Center" on page 16.

Integration S500A—Basic Educational Trends   Dr. Hinchey
8:30-9:20 A.M.   Credit: 2 semester-hours   Room 29

**Integration S500D—School Administration I:
Functions and Organization**   Mr. Morehead
9:30-10:20 A.M.   Credit: 2 semester-hours   Room 27

**Integration S500E—School Administration II:
Law and Finance**   Mr. Morehead
10:30-11:20 A.M.   Credit: 2 semester-hours   Room 27

**Integration S500F—School Administration III:
Community Relations**   Dr. Atkinson
3:30-9:20 A.M.   Credit: 2 semester-hours   Room 4, CHS

13

**Integration S502—Organization and Administration
of the Modern High School**   **Dr. W. Scott Smith**
10:30-11:20 A.M.   Credit: 2 semester-hours   Room 29

Integration S503—Methods and Instruments of Research   **Dr. Froehlich**
Prerequisite: Mathematics 400 or an equivalent course in Statistics.
Section I: 8:30-9:20 A.M.   Credit: 2 semester-hours   Room 1, Annex No. 2
Section II: 9:30-10:20 A.M.   Credit: 2 semester-hours   Room 1, Annex No. 2
Section III: 10:30-11:20 A.M.   Credit: 2 semester-hours   Room 1, Annex No. 2

**Integration S504A—Curriculum Construction in the
Secondary School**   **Dr. Hinchey**
9:30-10:20 A.M.   Credit: 2 semester-hours   Room 29

**Integration S505—Organization and Administration of
Extra-Curricular Activities**   **Mr. Morehead**
11:30 A.M.-12:20 P.M.   Credit: 2 semester-hours   Room 27

**Integration S508—Supervision of Instruction in
Secondary Schools**   **Dr. Atkinson**
11:30 A.M.-12:20 P.M.   Credit: 2 semester-hours   Room 4, CHS

Integration S517—Administration of the Elementary School   **Dr. Milton Brown**
8:30-9:20 A.M.   Credit: 2 semester-hours   Room 10

**Integration S518—Supervision of Instruction in the
Elementary School**   **Dr. Phipps**
11:30 A.M.-12:20 P.M.   Credit: 2 semester-hours   Room 21

Integration S520—Principles of Mental Hygiene   **Dr. Lutz**
11:30 A.M.-12:20 P.M.   Credit: 2 semester-hours   Room 30

Integration S521B—Psychological Tests in Guidance Programs   **Dr. Seidman**
9:30-10:20 A.M.   Credit: 2 semester-hours   Room 9

**Integration S530A—Corrective and Remedial Reading in
Secondary Schools**   **Mr. Leonard J. Buchner**
9:30-10.20 A.M.   Credit: 2 semester-hours   Room 21

Integration S535—Vocational Guidance   **Dr. E. C. Davis**
Prerequisite: Integration 551.
8:30-9:20 A.M.   Credit: 2 semester-hours   Room 5

Integration S536—Educational Guidance   **Dr. LeRoy Booth**
Prerequisite: Integration 551.
9:30-10:20 A.M.   Credit: 2 semester-hours   Room 30

**Integration S548—Curriculum Construction in the
Elementary School**   **Dr. Phipps**
9:30-10:20 A.M.   Credit: 2 semester-hours   Room 10

Integration S551—Principles and Techniques of Guidance   **Dr. LeRoy Booth**
This course is prerequisite to all other courses in Guidance.
8:30-9:20 A.M.   Credit: 2 semester-hours   Room 30

**Integration S556—Improvement of the Teaching of Reading
in the Secondary School**   **Dr. Phipps**
This course is planned to present a complete picture of the reading process in
its general and specialized aspects as it functions in the various subject-matter
fields of the secondary school. Problems in reading are examined and procedures
for the development of growth in personality, interests, understandings, insights,
critical thinking, tastes, and appreciations are studied through an examination
of the results of recent research.
10:30-11:20 A.M.   Credit: 2 semester-hours   Room 10

Integration S602—Seminar in Guidance   Dr. E. C. Davis
Prerequisites: Integration 551, and have taken (or be taking in conjunction) one
of the following: Int. 535, Int. 536, Int. 537.
10:30 A.M.-12:20 P.M.   Credit: 4 semester-hours   Room 6

Mathematics

Mathematics S300—Social and Commercial Uses of Mathematics Mr. Humphreys
9:30-10:20 A.M.   Credit: 2 semester-hours   Room 3, Annex No. 1

Mathematics S400—Educational Statistics   Dr. Meserve
This course or its equivalent is prerequisite to Integration 503.
9:30-10:20 A.M.   Credit: 2 semester-hours   Room 4, Annex No. 1

Mathematics S407—Advanced Calculus   Dr. D. R. Davis
8:30-9:20 A.M.   Credit: 2 semester-hours   Room 1, Annex No. 1

Mathematics S509A—A Critical Interpretation of Mathematics
  in the Senior High School I   Dr. D. R. Davis
9:30-10:20 A.M.   Credit: 2 semester-hours   Room 1, Annex No. 1

Mathematics S511A—Foundations of Geometry   Dr. Meserve
11:30 A.M.-12:20 P.M.   Credit: 2 semester-hours   Room 4, Annex No. 1

Integration S477—Elementary School Mathematics   Mr. Humphreys
See "Elementary Education" on page 22.

Science

Physics S407—Aviation, Parts I and II   Mr. Placek
10:30 A.M.-12:20 P.M. and Field Trips by Arrangement
                Credit: 4 semester-hours   Room 8, College HS

Physics S409A—Introduction to Radio Communication I   Dr. K. O. Smith
Prerequisite: General College Physics.
9:30-10:20 A.M.   Credit: 2 semester-hours   Room 25

Physics S512—Modern Physics   Dr. K. O. Smith
Prerequisites: General college physics, general college chemistry, and a course
in electrical measurements.
8:00-9:20 A.M. and Field Trips by Arrangement
                Credit: 4 semester-hours   Room 25

Integration S478—Elementary School Science   Mr. Placek
See "Elementary Education" on page 22.

Social Studies

Social Studies S413—Economic History of the United States   Dr. Rellahan
8:30-9:20 A.M.   Credit: 2 semester-hours   Room 20

Social Studies S429—Present-Day Social Problems   Dr. Clayton
11:30 A.M.-12:20 P.M.   Credit: 2 semester-hours   Room 20

Social Studies S439—The Family and its Problems   Dr. Clayton
10:30-11:20 A.M.   Credit: 2 semester-hours   Room 20

Social Studies S461—New England and French Canada   Mr. Bye
See "Bureau of Field Studies" on page 17

Social Studies S469—Mexico   **Mr. Bye**
See "Bureau of Field Studies" on page 17

Social Studies S472—Modern Social Studies Instruction and
    Supervision   **Dr. Clayton**
8:30-9:20 A.M.   Credit: 2 semester-hours   Room 21

Social Studies S481—The West Indies   **Mr. Bye**
See "Bureau of Field Studies" on page 17

Social Studies S490D—The United States and World
    Affairs   **Mr. Kops, Mr. Cohen and Mr. Boucher**
See "Institutes and Workshops" on page 19

Social Studies S490F—Russia in the Modern World
                    Mr. Kops, Mr. Cohen and Mr. Boucher
See "Institutes and Workshops" on page 19

Social Studies S497—Chinese Philosophy   **Dr. Mei**
See "Institutes and Workshops" on page 19

Social Studies S522—Development of Economic Institutions
    and Ideas   **Dr. Rellahan**
9:30-10:20 A.M.   Credit: 2 semester-hours   Room 20

Audio-Visual Center

Integration S407A—Television in Education Workshop:
    Programming and Production   **Mr. Sheft**
11:30 A.M.-12:20 P.M.   Credit: 2 semester-hours   TV Studio

Integration S408—Selection and Utilization of Audio-Visual
    Materials   **Miss Fantone**
10:30-11:20 A.M.   Credit: 2 semester-hours   Room 4

Integration S409—Radio and Sound Equipment in the
    Classroom   **Mr. Fox**
8:30-9:30 A.M.   Credit: 2 semester-hours   Room A

BUREAU OF FIELD STUDIES

July and August, 1956

Music S460—Musical Studies in Europe   **Mr. Kahn**

This field-study course gives an opportunity to study by direct observation major European musical events of the summer season together with visits to famous places in the history of music. Beginning on July 2nd, the tour extends to September 3rd, covering the countries of France, Germany, Austria, Switzerland, the Netherlands, and Italy. Among other things, opportunities are provided to attend the Richard Wagner Festival in Bayreuth and the Salzburg Musical Festival and to visit the musical shrines and museums in Vienna and the LaScala Opera House and museum in Milan. Famous places, such as London, Paris, Rome, Florence, Venice, Amsterdam, Frankfurt, Stuttgart, and Lucerne are included in the itinerary. Students who are registered for credit are required to present a written report at the end of the trip.

Credit: 6 semester-hours

Two months cost: $930.00 plus tuition fees.

For further information and registration forms, address Mr. Emil Kahn, care the Bureau of Field Studies, State Teachers College, Upper Montclair, N. J.

August 13-23

Social Studies S461—New England and French Canada   **Mr. Bye**

This field-study course gives an opportunity to study by direct observation the historical and geographical features of New England and the Province of Quebec. The trip, occupying the twelve days immediately following the Summer Session, is made in a modern chartered motor coach with overnight stops at first-class hotels. It is an indispensable background for an understanding of Colonial and Revolutionary life and history in this region. All expenses, except meals, $135.00.

Credit: 3 semester-hours

July 3 - July 24

Social Studies S469—Mexico   **Mr. Bye**

This field-study course aims to give a comprehensive view of contemporary Mexican life with its geographic, economic, historic, and cultural setting. Transportation to and from Mexico City is by air and in Mexico by private cars. Overnight stops and meals are at the best hotels. All expenses, except tuition and 1/3 of the meals, $535.00. Sponsored by N.J.E.A. and N.E.A.

Credit: 3 semester-hours

July 27 - August 5

Social Studies S481—West Indies.   **Mr. Bye**

This course consists of ten days of directed travel in five countries in the Caribbean region. Transportation is by air and private cars with overnight stops at the best hotels. Opportunities are given for study of geographic, historic, economic, and cultural phenomena in Puerto Rico, Santo Domingo, Haiti, Jamaica, and Cuba. All expenses, including meals, $435.00.

Credit: 2 semester-hours

If interested in any of the above courses taught by Mr. Bye, address him, care of the Bureau of Field Studies, State Teachers College, Upper Montclair, New Jersey.

Dormitory — first of four new buildings to be completed in the expansion program. Overlooking the New York skyline, this up-to-date two-story structure contains single and double rooms for 102 students.

18

INSTITUTES AND WORKSHOPS

Institutes on World Affairs

July 2 through July 20

Social Studies S490D—The United States and World Affairs
Mr. Kops, Mr. Cohen, Mr. Boucher et al.

9:30 A.M.-12:20 P.M.   Credit: 3 semester-hours   Chapin Hall Lounge

July 23 through August 10

Social Studies S490F—Russia in the Modern World
Mr. Kops, Mr. Cohen, Mr. Boucher et al.

The purpose of this course is to give the students an opportunity to study the development of modern Russia and the impact of its emergence as a world power. Particular attention is devoted to the role played by the geographical and historical forces that influenced Soviet foreign policy. The course meets three hours a day for each of fifteen days. Visiting lecturers from agencies concerned with Russian affairs supplement the basic information supplied by the regular members of the Institute staff. Included among the topics studied are: The nature and source of Soviet power, land and people of the Soviet Union, the role of the Communist Party, United States relations with Russia, Russia in the United Nations, Russian interest in the Far East and the Middle East, and the Cold War.

This course is designed primarily for teachers who feel the need for accurate background information and improved teaching materials and techniques for use in their classrooms. In addition to conventional lectures, this course features the showing of the latest films on the Soviet Union, field trips to New York City, exhibits of materials suitable for classroom use, and demonstrations of teaching techniques.

9:30 A.M.-12:20 P.M.   Credit: 3 semester-hours   Chapin Hall Lounge

China Institute of New Jersey

July 2 through July 14

China Institute of New Jersey is a permanent year-round organization composed of former students of the Institute. The policies and program of the Institute are determined by an elected executive committee, an advisory board of laymen, and representatives from the Faculty of Montclair State Teachers College, in consultation with the Chinese Director.

Dr. Chih Meng, Director of the China Institute of America, is also Chinese Director of the China Institute of New Jersey.

Students may enroll for college credit (graduate or undergraduate) if eligible to do so, or simply as Auditors for no credit. **The cost is the same in both cases.** (See page 9 for information as to fees.) Those who enroll for credit are expected to complete such notebooks, papers, projects, and examinations as are assigned by the course instructors. The preliminary grading of these papers, projects, and examinations is done by the Chinese teachers, while the final grading and coordinating is done by a representative of the regular Faculty of the College.

Notification of desire to enroll in one of the Institute courses should be sent on the coupon supplied in the special leaflet published by the Institute. Actual registration and payment of fees will take place in the College Library, from 8:30-9:00 A.M. on July 2. The Institute will convene in the Auditorium of the College High School Building at 9:15. Later, the students will go to the individual classrooms assigned to their courses.

China Institute Offerings

Fine Arts S416—Appreciation of Chinese Art   **Mr. Wang and Mr. Chiang-Yee**

This is an introductory course on Chinese art in its various aspects; its historical development, aesthetic principles, and various forms, such as: calligraphy, painting, sculpture, bronze and jade, pottery and porcelain, architecture, etc. Topics include "The Philosophical Basis of Chinese Art," "Nature in Chinese Art," and "Symbolism in Chinese Art." Each lecture is illustrated by photographs and lantern slides, as well as demonstrations. Students have an opportunity to learn the elements of Chinese painting, from widely recognized Chinese artists.

9:30 A.M.-12:20 P.M. and 1-4 P.M.   Credit: 3 semester-hours   Room 14, CHS

Social Studies S497—Chinese Philosophy   **Dr. Mei**

Prerequisite: Social Studies 499, Introduction to Chinese Culture, or, an equivalent course in Philosophy.

9:30 A.M.-12:20 P.M. and 1-4 P.M.   Credit: 3 semester-hours   Room 5, CHS

SIXTH UNITED NATIONS INSTITUTE

July 12, 13, and 14

A two and one-half day session on the United Nations and its place in today's world. Program to include a trip to the United Nations, special lectures and demonstrations of special interest to teachers and community leaders. Registration fee $2.00. **No credit.** Students enrolled in the "United States and World Affairs" course described on the previous page will be permitted to participate in this program without additional cost. Those interested should notify Mr. Walter Kops, care of the College.

WORKSHOP ON ECONOMIC EDUCATION

July 2 - July 20

Social Studies S525—Workshop on Economic Education   Mr. James E. Downes

This workshop is designed to provide teachers, supervisors, and administrators with a better understanding of the American economy and its operation. Instruction is given by a staff of economists and curriculum specialists, supplemented by business men, labor leaders, and representatives of agricultural groups. Workshop committees, with the help of specialists, prepare syllabi and teaching materials. Special library facilities are provided as well as selected teaching aids and field trips.

Registration 9:00 A.M., July 2   Credit: 3 semester-hours   Mens Dormitory
Meeting hours to be announced

THE NEW JERSEY STATE TEACHERS COLLEGE AT NEWARK

Announces

Workshop for Teachers of Non-English Speaking Children

This four semester-hour workshop, during a three-week period (July 23-August 10) will consider the background materials and techniques by means of which the classroom teacher can best meet the needs of non-English speaking children.

For further information, please address Dr. David Scanlon, New Jersey State Teachers College, Newark, New Jersey.

The Amphitheatre provides a natural setting for quiet study. Located to the north of the Administration Building, it also is used for outdoor classes, assemblies and graduation exercises.

One of three new curriculums, Fine Arts features a number of creative workshop programs suitable for either elementary or secondary teachers. Ceramics is illustrated in the above photograph.

21

COURSES FOR THOSE WHO DESIRE TO TEACH IN
ELEMENTARY GRADES

These courses are open to the following only:

(1) Those who already hold a degree from Montclair State Teachers College with a Certificate in Secondary Education, and

(2) Those who are now matriculated at Montclair State Teachers College for a degree and the Certificate in Secondary Education.

All other students should apply to one of the following colleges, all of which offer the bachelor's degree in Elementary Education and several of which also offer the master's degree in that field:

New Jersey State Teachers College at Paterson.
New Jersey State Teachers College at Jersey City.
New Jersey State Teachers College at Newark.
New Jersey State Teachers College at Trenton.
New Jersey State Teachers College at Glassboro.

The courses given on this campus are offered to assist the Montclair State Teachers College students in attaining provisional and standard certification to teach in elementary grades. Detailed requirements for such certification are listed on pages 14, 15, 16, and 68 of the Eighteenth Edition of the Rules Concerning Teachers Certificates. Montclair College students should consult Miss House, the College Registrar, for an evaluation of their previous work and a statement concerning their remaining required courses.

The courses listed below may apply as general electives in undergraduate curriculums, and **with the Advisor's approval**, as graduate electives for majors Administration and Supervision. The courses with the * do not carry graduate credit, however.

*Integration S474—Elementary School Arts and Crafts   **Mr. Vernacchi**
11:30-12:20 A.M.   Credit: 2 semester-hours   Campus Studio Worksho

*Integration S476—Elementary School Health and
    Physical Education   **Mr. DeRos**
8:30-9:20 A.M.   Credit: 2 semester-hours   Room 13, CHS and Gym, CH

Integration S477—Elementary School Mathematics   **Mr. Humphrey**
10:30-11:20 A.M.   Credit: 2 semester-hours   Room 2, Annex No.

Integration S478—Elementary School Science   **Mr. Place**
9:30-10:20 A.M.   Credit: 2 semester-hours   Room 5, Annex No.

22

NEW JERSEY STATE SCHOOL OF CONSERVATION

Stokes State Forest, Branchville, N. J.

Courses in Conservation, Field Science, Camping and Outdoor Education, Social Studies, and Waterfront Safety

Spring and Summer, 1956

The State Department of Education, through the six State Teachers Colleges, offers a wide range of courses at the School of Conservation. Teachers, prospective teachers, camp counselors, nature specialists, and playground directors have an opportunity to combine study and vacation in the beautiful and cool Kittatinny Mountains of Northern New Jersey.

Public Schools throughout the nation are being charged with the responsibility to teach conservation education courses. New Jersey teachers have a unique opportunity to become acquainted with the problems and methods of teaching in this fast-growing field. Science, social studies, and elementary school teachers will be particularly interested in the following courses, but all educators should have a basic understanding of conservation and outdoor education if they are to meet the needs of the youngsters in our schools.

Credit for the following courses, offered between June 14 and August 24, may be applied toward graduate or undergraduate degrees at any of the New Jersey State Teachers Colleges, subject to approval in advance by the institution. Credits may be transferred to other institutions where such transfer is permitted toward an undergraduate or graduate degree. Several of the courses may be substituted for courses required for elementary teaching certification.

For additional information write to: Edward J. Ambry, or Benton P. Cummings, New Jersey State School of Conservation, Upper Montclair, New Jersey.

1956 SUMMER COURSE OFFERINGS

Biology 203—Introduction to Field Biology
　　Credit: 2 semester-hours　　　　　　　　　　　　　　June 14-24

Physical Education 410—Water Safety and First Aid
　　Credit: 2 semester-hours　　　　　　　　　　　　　　June 14-24

Integration 440—Camping and Outdoor Education
　　Credit: 2 semester-hours　　　　　　　　　　　　　　June 14-24

Industrial Arts 443—The Use of Basic Industrial Materials in Industry
　　Credit: 2 semester-hours　　　　　　　　　　　　　　June 14-24

Art 415—School Arts and Crafts with Native Materials
　　Credit: 2 semester-hours　　　　　　　　　　　　　　August 13-24

Integration 480—Field Science for Elementary Teachers
　　Credit: 2 semester-hours　　　　　　　　　　　　　　August 13-24

Social Studies 494—Social Studies and Conservation
　　Credit: 2 semester-hours　　　　　　　　　　　　　　August 13-24

Social Studies 477—Rural Sociology
　　Credit: 2 semester-hours　　　　　　　　　　　　　　August 13-24

---

* Courses approved by State Board of Examiners to meet specific requirements for certification grades one through eight.

POST-SUMMER SESSION COURSE

August 13 through August 24, 1955

To Meet an Urgent Need, the following course is being offered by the State Teachers College at Montclair, with the assistance of the New Jersey State Safety Council, the New Jersey Automobile Club, the American Automobile Association, the New Jersey State Police, and the New Jersey Department of Motor Vehicles.

This Course Offers the Necessary Opportunity for men and women to prepare themselves to teach behind-the-wheel driver education in high schools. Enrollees completing the work of the course are presented with a certificate indicating the work done.

Authorization: In order to teach behind-the-wheel driver education and driver training, a teacher must have his or her certificate endorsed by the Division of Teacher Certification, State Department of Education, for teaching behind-the-wheel automobile driver education and driver training.

The Requirements for Such Endorsement on the teacher's certificate are: (18th edition, 1951, "Rules Concerning Teachers' Certificates," pages 22).

1. A valid New Jersey teacher's certificate.
2. A current New Jersey driver's license.
3. Three years of automobile driving experience.
4. Evidence of satisfactory completion of a course in driver education and driver training approved by the Commissioner of Education.

Veterans may take this course under the G. I. Bill, if they have so arranged with the Veterans' Counselor of the College.

Living Expenses and Training Expenses must be paid by the student. Those desiring hotel accommodations should write to Mr. F. K. Schultze, Manager, New Jersey Auto Club, AAA, 156 Clinton Avenue, Newark 5, New Jersey. The College Residence Halls are closed at this time.

Extra Charges are made for textbooks and other text materials. Some materials are furnished free.

Registration for this course will be accepted up to and including the opening day of the course. However, students should register early if possible, preferably on the regular registration day for the Summer Session. There is a limit to the number of registrations which may be accepted.

Health Education S408—Behind-the-Wheel Driver Education and Driver Training

9:00-12:00 and 1:00-4:00 daily   Credit: 3 semester-hours

Dr. Coder

Room 3, CHS

1957

Bulletin of
MONTCLAIR STATE TEACHERS COLLEGE

SUMMER SESSION

July 1 to August 9

UPPER MONTCLAIR • NEW JERSEY

SUMMER SESSION

Bulletin of
MONTCLAIR
STATE TEACHERS COLLEGE

1957.
July 1st to August 9th

VOLUME 49   NUMBER 1

UPPER MONTCLAIR, NEW JERSEY

OFFICERS OF ADMINISTRATION

STATE BOARD OF EDUCATION

MRS. EDWARD L. KATZENBACH, *President* .... Princeton
ARTHUR E. ARMITAGE, SR. .... Collingswood
MRS. T. B. ARMSTRONG .... Stewartsville
HARVEY DEMBE .... Bayonne
LEWIS F. GAYNER .... Salem
PHILIP R. GEBHARDT .... Clinton
MRS. R. ADAM JOHNSTONE .... Ho-ho-kus
JOHN F. LYNCH .... Morristown
JAMES W. PARKER, SR. .... Red Bank
WILLIAM A. SUTHERLAND .... Liberty Corner
HENRY A. WILLIAMS .... Paterson
MRS. STANLEY C. YORTON .... Nutley

COMMISSIONER OF EDUCATION
DR. FREDERICK M. RAUBINGER

ASSISTANT COMMISSIONER FOR HIGHER EDUCATION
DR. EARL E. MOSIER

DIRECTOR OF TEACHER EDUCATION AND CERTIFICATION
DR. ALLAN F. ROSEBROCK

COLLEGE ADMINISTRATION

E. DEALTON PARTRIDGE, Ph.D. .... President
CLYDE M. HUBER, Ph.D. .... Dean of Instruction
EDWARD J. AMBRY, A.M.
　　　　　　　　Director, Summer, Part-Time and Extension Division
JOHN J. RELLAHAN, Ph.D. .... Chairman, Graduate Council
KEITH W. ATKINSON, Ph.D. .... Director, College High School
EARL C. DAVIS, Ph.D. .... Director, Personnel and Guidance
MARGARET A. SHERWIN, A.M. .... Dean of Women
MARY M. HOUSE, A.M. .... Registrar
ANNE BANKS CRIDLEBAUGH, A.M. .... Librarian
BERNARD SIEGEL, M.B.A. .... Business Manager
OTTO CORDES, P.E. .... Engineer in Charge, Maintenance

HEALTH SERVICES

CHARLOTTE L. PRITCHARD, R.N. .... College Nurse

2

FACULTY
Summer Session 1957

E. DeALTON PARTRIDGE, Ph.D. .... President
CLYDE M. HUBER, Ph.D. .... Dean of Instruction
EDWARD J. AMBRY, A.M. .... Director, Summer, Part-Time and Extension
KEITH W. ATKINSON, Ph. D. .... Integration
WILLIAM A. BALLARE, A.M. .... Speech
ROBERT BECKWITH, A.M. .... Director, Institute of World Affairs
HAROLD C. BOHN, Ed.D. .... English
BERTRAND P. BOUCHER, A.M. .... Geography
LEONARD BUCHNER, A.M. .... Integration
EDGAR C. BYE, A.M. .... Director, Bureau of Field Studies
FRANK L. CLAYTON, Ph.D. .... Social Studies
ALDEN C. CODER, Ed.D. .... Driver Education
PHILIP S. COHEN, A.M. .... Social Studies
LAWRENCE H. CONRAD, A.M. .... English
EARL C. DAVIS, Ph.D. .... Personnel and Guidance
JEROME G. DeROSA, A.M. .... Health and Physical Education
ARTHUR W. EARL, Ed.D. .... Industrial Arts
EMMA FANTONE, A.M. .... Director, Audio-Visual Center
CARL E. FRANKSON, Ph.D. .... Head, Department of Industrial Arts
MOWAT G. FRASER, Ph.D. .... Head, Department of Integration
M. HERBERT FREEMAN, Ph.D. .... Head, Department of Business Education
PAUL E. FROEHLICH, Ed.D. .... Business Education
EDWIN S. FULCOMER, Ed.D. .... Head, Department of English
IRWIN H. GAWLEY, JR., Ed.D. .... Science
ABRAHAM GELFOND, Ph.D. .... Integration
HOWARD L. HAAS, M.Ed. .... Business Education
CHARLES E. HADLEY, Ph.D. .... Biology
W. PAUL HAMILTON, A.M. .... English
T. ROLAND HUMPHREYS, A.M. .... Mathematics
DANIEL JACOBSON, Ph.D. .... Geography
EMIL KAHN, A.M. .... Music
WALTER E. KOPS, A.M. .... Director, Economic Education Workshop
CHIH MENG, Ph.D. .... Director, China Institute
BRUCE E. MESERVE, Ph.D. .... Chairman. Department of Mathematics
MAURICE P. MOFFATT. Ph.D. .... Chairman, Department of Social Studies
ALLAN MOREHEAD, A.M. .... Integration
LOUIS C. NANASSY. Ed.D. .... Business Education
RUFUS D. REED. Ph.D. .... Chairman. Department of Science
JOHN J. RELLAHAN. Ph.D. .... Chairman, Graduate Council: Social Studies
GEORGE E. SALT, A.M. .... Education and English
JEROME SEIDMAN, Ph.D. .... Integration
HORACE J. SHEPPARD. A.M. .... Business Education
RAMON F. STEINEN, A.M. .... Mathematics
RALPH A. VERNACCHIA. A.M. .... Art
FREDERIC H. YOUNG, Ph.D. .... English

GRADUATE COUNCIL

JOHN J. RELLAHAN, *Chairman*	ESTELLE F. MARSAND. *Secretary*	
EDWARD J. AMBRY	M. HERBERT FREEMAN	ORPHA M. LUTZ
L. HOWARD FOX	W. PAUL HAMILTON	BRUCE E. MESERVE
CARL E. FRANKSON	CLYDE M. HUBER	E. DeALTON PARTRIDGE
WILLIAM R. PHIPPS		RUFUS D. REED

3

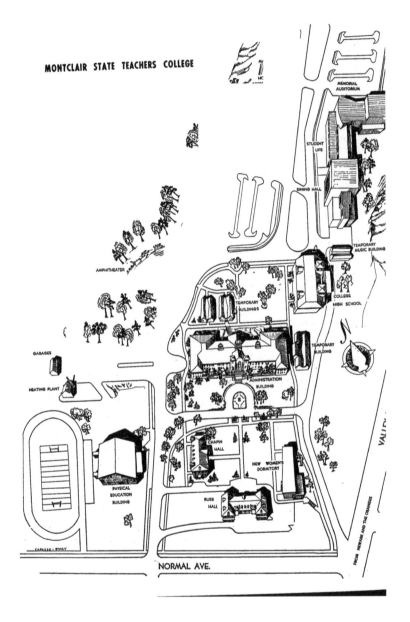

MONTCLAIR STATE TEACHERS COLLEGE

LODGE

MEMORIAL
AUDITORIUM

STUDENT
LIFE

DINING HALL

TEMPORARY
MUSIC BUILDING

AMPHITHEATER

TEMPORARY
BUILDINGS

COLLEGE
HIGH SCHOOL

TEMPORARY
BUILDING

GARAGES

HEATING PLANT

ADMINISTRATION
BUILDING

CHAPIN
HALL

NEW WOMEN'S
DORMITORY

PHYSICAL
EDUCATION
BUILDING

RUSS
HALL

FROM NEWARK AND THE ORANGES

VALLE

NORMAL AVE.

SUMMER SESSION OF THE
NEW JERSEY STATE TEACHERS COLLEGE AT MONTCLAIR

Objectives and Academic Status

The College is a professional school which prepares teachers, supervisors, and principals of high schools, and administrators of public school systems. The degrees offered by this College are those of Bachelor of Arts and Master of Arts. Certificate courses are offered for those who now hold degrees from other colleges. See paragraph under "Certificates."

The New Jersey State Teachers College at Montclair is a member of the American Association of Colleges of Teacher Education and fully accredited by the National Council for the Accreditation of Teacher Education, the Middle States Association of Colleges and Secondary Schools, and the American Association of University Women.

How to Reach the Campus

The College is located about one mile north of the center of Upper Montclair. Trains of the Greenwood Lake Division, Erie R.R., stop at Montclair Heights, the College Station. Trains of the Lackawanna R.R. connect at Montclair with the following bus lines: Nos. 60, 64, and 76 to the College.

Residence Halls for Men and Women

Edward Russ Hall, Chapin Hall, and the new Dormitory for Men provide excellent living quarters for summer school students. The charge for living on campus during the Summer Session is: $14.50 per week; which includes room, breakfast, and dinner. A la carte luncheons are served in the College cafeteria. The College provides and launders sheets, pillowcase, and bedpad. Towels, blankets, clocks and similar items must be provided and cared for by student. The boarding-hall fee must be paid on or before the first day of the Summer Session. No rebate is made for occasional absence during the session. These fees are subject to change.

For reservations in a College Residence Hall, women address: Dean of Women, State Teachers College, Upper Montclair, N. J. Men address: Dean of Men.

Schedule of the Summer Session

Registration will take place on Monday, July 1. Hours, 9-12 and 1-3:30. Classes will begin on Tuesday morning, July 2 at 8 A. M. and will continue through Friday, August 9. All classes meet daily, Monday to Friday, inclusive, at the hours indicated for each, and on the following Saturdays: July 6, July 13, and July 27. Thursday, July 4, is a Holiday.

Matriculation for the Master of Arts Degree

Since not more than 8 semester-hours of work taken prior to matriculation are allowed to apply on the Master of Arts degree, the student should take care to complete the matriculation procedure as soon as he has that amount of credit; sooner if possible. Transfer of graduate credit from other institutions is permitted only to those students who are graduates of New Jersey State Teachers Colleges or the State University of New Jersey. The maximum permitted is 8 semester hours.

5

Those who desire to become candidates for the degree must request an application form from the Chairman of the Graduate Council and return it, properly filled and accompanied by an Official Transcript of all previous work on college level. **When such an applicant has been accepted by the College** as a candidate for the degree, a definite statement is furnished by the Chairman of the Graduate Council, showing the requirements which he must fulfill to earn the degree. This sheet of requirements becomes the student's Work Program and should be brought by the student each time he comes to enroll for courses.

The completion of the above procedure constitutes matriculation. Simple registration for courses does not.

Students Matriculated at Montclair for the A.M. Degree

Since September 1, 1952, all students matriculating in the Graduate Division have been required to complete at least one full-time (6 s.h.) Summer Session, or, in lieu thereof, at least one regular semester of full-time graduate attendance.

The selection of courses must be in accordance with the student's Work Program, and his registration form will be signed by the Head of the Department in which the student is majoring or by a representative of that department present in the registration room.

Candidates for a degree must file with the Registrar an application for conferment of the degree before November 30 of the college year in which the work is to be completed. Application blanks for this purpose may be secured in the Registrar's Office. The burden of responsibility for the request rests with the candidate. This is of special significance to the teacher-in-service who may have distributed the work for the degree over several years.

Students Matriculated at Other Colleges

Several years ago, when the State Teachers College at Montclair offered courses to its own accelerated candidates for the Bachelor's degree, it was possible to accept students from other colleges in freshman, sophomore, and junior year courses, as well as in courses of the senior year. Beginning in the summer of 1950, however, the College returned to its pre-war custom of offering courses in its Summer Session primarily to teachers-in-service. As such teachers, with few exceptions, already hold the Bachelor's degree, the courses shown in this Bulletin are, for the most part, only Graduate and Senior-Graduate courses carrying graduate credit.

A student who is planning to attend Montclair this summer should take this Bulletin to a conference with the Dean of his own college to arrange a program of work. For the Dean's information: the numbering of courses at Montclair follows this order: 100-399, inclusive, are undergraduate courses; 400-499, inclusive, are senior-college and graduate courses; 500 and above are graduate courses.

At the time of registration, the student from another college should bring with him a letter from his own Dean showing the courses which will be accepted for credit there and which he has been advised to take. He should go to the table of the Department in which the courses are listed. The registration form must be signed by the Representative of the Department at that table. The College reserves the right to decide whether the student has fulfilled necessary prerequisites. If the student is seeking certification to teach in New Jersey, he must confer with the Head of the Department of Integration. Please note paragraph under the heading: "Certificates."

6

Auditors

Men and women who desire to take courses for cultural, vocational, or avocational purposes without college credits may register as auditors.

A student who desires to enroll in a course for which he already holds credit must register as an auditor in that particular course.

A student who desires to enroll in a course for which he has not completed the prerequisites must enroll as an auditor in that particular course.

Change of Status in a Course

If a student desires to change his status in a course from "credit" to "auditor" or from "auditor" to "credit," he must make formal application for such change not later than the middle of the course. Forms for this purpose may be procured in the Registrar's office. Such changes cannot be made after the midpoint of the course is passed.

Certificates

The State Teachers College at Monclair offers work toward the following New Jersey Certificates: Secondary Teaching Certificate; Secondary School Principal's Certificate; Subject Supervisor's Certificate; General Supervisor's Certificate; Guidance Certificate; School Administrator's Certificate; Junior College Teacher's Certificate; and the Advanced Professional Certificate.

Those who matriculate at Montclair for a Master of Arts degree will receive information from the Head of the Integration Department as to the requirements for each of these certificates. Students who have not matriculated at Montclair should write to the **Secretary of the State Board of Examiners, Department of Education, 175 West State Street, Trenton 25, N. J.,** for information as to the requirements. For an evaluation of work already completed, address the Secretary also. An official transcript of such previous work should accompany the inquiry, with a statement as to the particular certificate desired.

The student should bring the reply from the State Board of Examiners with him when conferring with the Head of the Integration Department as to his program of work.

Supervised Student Teaching

The opportunity to do supervised student teaching cannot be offered during the Summer Session. For fall teaching, students confer with the Head of the Integration Department at the College. Ask his secretary for an appointment.

Veterans

Veteran students taking work under the G.I. Bill and likewise the so-called Korean Veteran must see the Veterans' Counselor of the College before the close of the spring semester on June 14 in order to make certain that when they come to enroll on July 1 their papers will all be in order. Students taking work without the necessary papers must pay the usual tuition fees at the time of registration.

Veterans who have completed the work of the A.B. or the A.M. degree at Montclair must secure and present to the Veterans' Counselor the Supplemental Certificate of Eligibility before registering for further work. Veterans transferring to this College who have previously been in training under one of the Veterans' Bills must secure the Supplemental Certificate of Eligibility and present it to the Veterans' Counselor at the time of registration.

7

Conferences with Advisers

Appointments with the Dean of Instruction, the Chairman of the Graduate Council, a Department Head, or the Veterans' Counselor may be made by mail or telephone to their respective offices. This should be done at as early a date as possible to avoid delay at the time of registration on July 1 and no later than the end of the spring semester on June 14. After that date, it may not be possible to see these officials until the Summer Session opens.

Summer Session Credit Load

The maximum amount of credit which may be earned in the Summer Session is 8 semester-hours, but only 6 are recommended. There is no provision for a student to audit additional courses; consequently, the total of all courses taken during the Summer Session may not exceed 8 semester-hours and students may not enroll for more. Additional credits may be earned by attending one of the sessions of the State School of Conservation at the Stokes State Forest that precedes or follows the Summer Session at Montclair. Attention is called also to the Post-Summer Session course in "Behind-the-Wheel Driver Education and Driver Training."

Each Summer Session course is in session at least thirty hours and carries a designated amount of credit. **It is not possible to earn 3 semester-hours credit in a course designated to carry 2 semester-hours.**

Registration Information

Registration takes place in the College Library, on Monday, July 1, from 9 A. M. to 12 Noon, and from 1 to 3:30 P. M. Anyone unable to enroll during the hours shown must register during the regular office hours of the College in the Registrar's office, and the last date on which he may enroll for credit is July 5.

Because the registration form must be signed by a Department Head or his representative, must be inspected at the checking table, and paid for at the Business Manager's desk, before the student may receive his Class Admission Cards, the procedure is time consuming and the student should allow at least 45 minutes. The student should report to the Head of the Department in which he is majoring, or, if not matriculated for a degree here, to the Head of the Department offering the courses in which he is interested.

On Monday, July 1, the Department Heads, Director of the Summer Session, and the Business Manager are assembled in the College Library, but on July 2, 3, and 5 they will be in their individual offices and the student must seek them there. Late students, registering on July 2, 3, and 5 should allow even more time, should come during the morning hours, and will be charged the late service charge of $2.00 in addition to the regular fees and service charges.

Students may, in some instances, be required to obtain signatures in more than one Department, if taking courses in more than one.

Matriculated students should bring their Work Programs when they come to enroll.

The College reserves the right to close any course for which the enrollment is insufficient. The class will meet at least once, however, before this decision is made. Students may then enter another course in place of the one discontinued by going to the Registrar's Office to re-enroll and to receive the new Class Admission Card in exchange for the card of the discontinued course.

Students who decide not to enroll in an alternate course must so state, in a letter of withdrawal, in order to receive a refund of tuition fees. The card of the discontinued course should be enclosed in the letter.

If prerequisites are required for a course (see the course description), the student should make certain that he has fulfilled them or their equivalent before enrolling in it.

8

If no previous work on college level has been taken, the student must consult the Dean of Instruction before enrolling in any course, except as an Auditor.

A student may not register for credit in any course for which he already holds credit, except by permission of the Dean of Instruction.

Withdrawal from a Course

During the registration day of July 1, and on July 2, July 3, and July 5, a student may, with the advice and consent in writing of his adviser, withdraw from one course and enter another in its place. The Class Admission Card from the dropped course must be presented in order to obtain the one for the new course.

A student who withdraws from a course without entering an alternate one, or who withdraws later in the session, must write a formal notice of withdrawal to the Director of the Summer Session. He, in turn, will notify the teacher of the course from which the student is withdrawing, as well as the Business Manager of the College. Refunds are computed from the date of the receipt of the letter of withdrawal.

Students who neglect to follow this procedure receive a failing mark for the course or courses which they cease to attend.

Tuition Fees, Service Charge, and Credit Slips

Check or money-order should be made payable to New Jersey State Teachers College.

Tuition Fees: to students who are residents of New Jersey, $11.00 per semester-hour credit carried by the course. Non-residents of New Jersey pay $13.00 per credit. Courses taken by auditors for no credit cost the same.

Service Charge: 50¢ per semester-hour point.

Late Registration Service Charge: $2.00 will be added to the cost of each late registration; that is, each registration which is not completed during the hours set aside for registration on July 1. A registration is complete when it has been duly filled in, signed by the Adviser, and paid for by the student. This additional charge will be made in the case of a deferred or a partially deferred payment of the fees and service charges.

Teachers who have supervised Montclair student-teachers and who have in their possession old Montclair credit slips may take them to the office of the Integration Department, where new ones will be issued. The Business Office cannot return any unused portion of a credit slip, so it is necessary that the new type credit slip be obtained before presenting it in payment of tuition fees. Training Teachers may use the credit slips of any one of the six New Jersey State Teachers Colleges when taking courses at Montclair, but should bring only the new type slip in all cases.

So long as any credit slips remain in a teacher's possession, they will be honored by the College although a new method of remuneration of training teachers is now in effect.

Final Marks

Following are the final marks which may be received for a course: A—Excellent; B—Good; C—Fair; D—Poor; F—Failure; Inc—Incomplete; Wd—Withdrew; N.C.—No Credit.

The mark of "D" when earned in summer, part-time, or extension courses of this College is not accepted for degree credit at Montclair.

The mark of "F" is given when earned and when the student has failed to notify the Director of the Summer Session promptly of his withdrawal from a course.

The mark of "N.C." is given only to those enrolled as Auditors.

The mark of "Wd" is given only when prompt notice of withdrawal has been given and when the student's work until that time has been satisfactory to the teacher of the course.

The mark of "Inc." is seldom given. It may, however, be granted to a student whose work is incomplete at the end of the Session and who is eager to finish the work for a higher grade than he could otherwise receive. **All responsibility regarding the incomplete work rests with the student.** He will be notified of a date after which, if the work remains incomplete, the final grade will be recorded without further notice.

Report Cards and Transcripts

An **Official Transcript** showing the credits earned is sent to the student personally ten days to two weeks following the close of the Session. A report card for each course taken is sent with this transcript, which is sent without cost. **A service charge of $1.00 is made for a duplicate copy of the transcript.**

A student whose college requires that the transcript be mailed directly to it should call, early in the Session, at the Registrar's Office to address an envelope for this purpose.

Elementary Education Courses

Courses offered as a part of the curriculum for the graduate major in Educational Administration and Supervision should be carefully distinguished from those offered toward the endorsement in elementary education on the teacher's certificate. Although the College at Montclair is engaged primarily in preparing secondary school teachers, it has been deemed expedient during the shortage of teachers in the elementary schools to assist our students to procure the elementary endorsement on their secondary teacher's certificates.

Students eligible to enroll at Montclair in courses leading to this endorsement in elementary education are:

(1) those who already hold a degree from Montclair with a certificate in secondary education; and

(2) those who are now matriculated at Montclair for such a degree.

Montclair cannot accept any other students in these courses.

The eligible students should consult Miss House, the College Registrar, for an evaluation of their previous work and a statement covering the courses to be taken in order to receive the endorsement in elementary education on the secondary certificate already held or to be conferred.

College Book Store

A limited number of books for each course will be on hand in the Book Store at registration time. It is advantageous to order textbooks immediately upon completion of registration. Store hours: 8 A. M. - 12 Noon.

COURSES OF THE SUMMER SESSION

Descriptions of the courses will be found in the 1955-57 Graduate Bulletin of the College. Courses numbered 500 and above are graduate courses; those numbered 400-499, inclusive, are senior-graduate courses and their descriptions in the Graduate Bulletin follow the descriptions of the graduate courses. Courses below the 400 number will be found in the Undergraduate Bulletin of the College. Only entirely new courses are described in the Summer Session Bulletin.

Business Education

Business Education S501A—Research Seminar in
    Business Education   Dr. Nanassy
8:30-9:20 A. M.   Credit: 2 semester-hours   Room 1, Annex 2

Business Education S505—Tests and Measurements in
    Business Education   Mr. Haas
9:30-10:20 A. M.   Credit: 2 semester-hours   Room 1, Annex 2

Business Education S520A—Improvement of Instruction in
    Business Education   Dr. Nanassy
9:30-10:20 A. M.   Credit: 2 semester hours   Room 5, Annex 2

Business Education S532—Field Studies and Audio-Visual Aids
    in Business Education   Mr. Sheppard
10:30-12:20 P. M.   Credit: 4 semester-hours   Room 5, Annex 2

Business Education S533—Supervised Work Experience
    and Seminar   Dr. Freeman and Mr. Haas
Wednesday Evenings
7:00-9:00 P. M.   Credit: 4 semester-hours   Room 5, Annex 2

English and Speech

English S200A—Composition   Dr. Young
8:30-10 A. M.   Credit: 3 semester-hours   Room 2

English S449—Public Speaking   Mr. Ballare
11:30-12:20 P. M.   Credit: 2 semester-hours   Room 3

English S467—Oral Interpretation for the Teacher   Mr. Ballare
10:30-11:20 A. M.   Credit: 2 semester-hours   Room 3

English S507—Critical Writing   Dr. Fulcomer
9:30-10:20 A. M.   Credit: 2 semester-hours   Room 1

English S519—English in the Modern High School   Dr. Fulcomer
8:30-9:20 A. M.   Credit: 2 semester-hours   Room 1

English S524—Five Great Books   Dr. Young
11:30-12:20 P. M.   Credit: 2 semester-hours   Room 2

English S532—The Victorian Novel   Mr. Hamilton
10:30-11:20 A. M.   Credit: 2 semester-hours   Room 1

English S539—Theatre and Society   Dr. Bohn
10:30-11:20 A. M.   Credit: 2 semester-hours   Room 2

English S544B—Shakespeare - The Comedies   Dr. Bohn
8:30-9:20 A. M.   Credit: 2 semester-hours   Room 3

This course presents all of Shakespeare's plays as opposed to those taught only in high school, which is the chief concern of English 301B. Here the poet's full development can be seen, providing a complete critical experience. Critical analysis, contentual evaluation, and textual problems are the main areas of concern. This course deals with the comedies. The chronicle plays are woven into the discussion.

English S545A—American Literature   Mr. Conrad
9:30-10:20 A. M.   Credit: 2 semester-hours   Room 2

English S545B—American Literature   Mr. Conrad
11:30 A. M. - 12:20 P. M.   Credit: 2 semester-hours   Room 1

This chronological survey reflects the interplay of life and letters in the American scene, examining the political, social, and ethical motivations of the great movements in literature, and reading the separate works in the light of the influences that brought them into being. Part A commences with the Puritan Tradition and ends just as the Civil War is beginning. Part B traces, in life and in literature, the growth of the great democratic tradition in America.

Fine Arts

Fine Arts S406A or B—Art Workshop, I or II   Mr. Vernacchia
10:30 A. M. - 11:20 A. M.   Credit: 2 semester-hours each
                    New Classroom Bldg. Rm.221
Students who have taken Fine Arts S406A may enroll in S406B, Part II.

Fine Arts S474A—Arts and Crafts in Education, I   Mr. Vernacchia
11:30 A. M. - 12:20 P. M.   Credit: 2 semester-hours
                    New Classroom Bldg. Rm.221

Included in this course are workshop activities in the arts and crafts of the elementary and secondary school program. Painting, drawing, modeling, pottery, weaving, papier-mache, paper sculpture, school display techniques and lettering, wood, leather, plastics, metal work, and puppetry, are materials and processes which are explored.

Fine Arts S500—Contemporary Art   Mr. Vernacchia
8:30-10:00 A. M.   Credit: 3 semester-hours
                    New Classroom Bldg. Rm.221

This course presents a survey of the major influences and trends in the development of painting, sculpture, and architecture of this century. The use of visual materials such as slides, art films, and reproductions supplement discussion and studio participation. This course is planned for students who wish to enlarge their general education in art and requires no technical competency.

Geography

Geography S410—Economic Geography of Caribbean America   Dr. Jacobson
10:30-11:20 A. M.   Credit: 2 semester-hours   Room 26

Geography S418—Regional Geography of North America   Dr. Jacobson
8:30-9:20 A. M.   .   Credit: 2-semester-hours   Room 26
See "Elementary Education" on page 22.

Geography S509—Economic Geography of Asia   .   Dr. Jacobson
11:30 A. M. - 12:20 P. M.   Credit: 2-semester-hours   Room 26

Health Education

Health Education S408—Driver Education   Dr. Coder
11:00 A. M. - 5:00 P. M. — 3 weeks
July 1-19   Credit: 3 semester-hours   Room A
See also the Post-Summer-Session section of this course on page 24.

Health Education S411—School Health Services   Mr. DeRosa
9:30 to 10:20 A. M.   Credit: 2 semester-hours   Room 13, CHS

Integration S476—Elementary School Health and
    Physical Education   Mr. DeRosa
See "Elementary Education" on page 22.

Industrial Arts

Industrial Arts S402—Comprehensive General Shop   Dr. Earl
11:30 A. M. - 12:20 P. M.   New Classroom Bldg.
1:00 P. M. - 2:40 P. M.   Credit: 4 semester-hours   General Shop

Students from all college departments are now offered the opportunity to
gain shop experiences in the new Industrial Arts laboratory. No previous experience is necessary.

The following partial list gives an idea of the type of work which may be
done: Art Metal, Basketry, Bookbinding, Candlemaking, Ceramics, Home Repairs, Jewelry, Leather, Metal, Photography, Plastics, Printing, Rubber Stamp
Making, Silk Screening, Wood and Textiles.

Industrial Arts S501—Curriculum Construction and Course
    Organization in Industrial Arts Education   Dr. Frankson
                                                                 New Classroom Bldg.
8:30-10:00 A. M.   Credit: 3 semester-hours   Seminar Room

This course presents a study of curriculum construction techniques used
in developing a program of industrial arts. How to make a course of study and
how to develop instructional materials are given special attention. The evaluation of pupil progress based on tests and other evaluative criteria are studied.

Industrial Arts S521—Seminar in Vocational Education
    in New Jersey   Dr. Frankson
                                                                 New Classroom Bldg.
10:00-11:30 A. M.   Credit: 3 semester-hours   Seminar Room

The industrial development of the United States is studied as a background for the development of vocational schools. Emphasis is placed on trade,
industrial, and distributive education programs in New Jersey, State and Federal legislation, teacher training, and occupational efficiency resulting from the
program.

Integration

Integration S200A—Child Growth and Development
11:30 A. M. - 12:20 P. M.   Credit: 2 semester-hours   Room 10

Integration S200B—Adolescent Psychology and Mental Hygiene   Dr. Seidman
10:30-11:20 A. M.   Credit: 2 semester-hours   Room 22

Integration S300A—Aims and Organization of
    Secondary Education   Mr. Salt
9:30-10:20 A. M.   Credit: 2 semester-hours   Room 30

Integration S300B—Principles and Techniques of Teaching
    in the Secondary School   Mr. Salt
11:30 A. M. - 12:20 P. M.   Credit: 2 semester-hours   Room 30

Integration S400A—Principles and Philosophy of
Secondary Education   Dr. Fraser
8:30-9:20 A. M.   Credit: 2 semester-hours   Room 29

Integration S408—Selection and Utilization of
Audio-Visual Materials   Miss Fantone
10:30-11:20 A. M.   Credit: 2 semester-hours   Audio-Vis. Aids Lab.

Integration S500A—Basic Educational Trends   Dr. Fraser
9:30-10:20 A. M.   Credit: 2 semester-hours   Room 29

Integration S500B—Advanced Educational Psychology   Dr. Seidman
8:30-9:20 A. M.   Credit: 2 semester-hours   Room 22

Integration S500D—School Administration I:
Functions and Organization
11:30 A. M. - 12:20 P. M.   Credit: 2 semester-hours   Room 29

Integration S500E—School Administration II:
Law and Finance   Mr. Morehead
8:30-9:20 A. M.   Credit: 2 semester-hours   Room 25

Integration S500F—School Administration III:
Community Relations   Dr. Atkinson
10:30-11:20 A. M.   Credit: 2 semester-hours   Room 4, CHS

Integration S502—Organization and Administration
of the Modern High School   Dr. Atkinson
8:30-9:20 A. M.   Credit: 2 semester-hours   Room 4, CHS

Integration S503—Methods and Instruments of Research   Dr. Froehlich
Prerequisite: Mathematics 400 or an equivalent course in Statistics.
Section I: 8:30-9:20 A. M.   Credit: 2 semester-hours   Room 2, Annex No. 2
Section II: 9:30-10:20 A. M.
                             Credit: 2 semester-hours   Room 2, Annex No. 2
Section III: 11:30 A. M. - 12:20 P. M.
                             Credit: 2 semester-hours   Room 2, Annex No. 2

Integration S504A—Curriculum Construction in the
Secondary School   Mr. Salt
10:30-11:20 A. M.   Credit: 2 semester-hours   Room 30

Integration S505—Organization and Administration of
Extra-Curricular Activities   Mr. Morehead
9:30-10:20 A. M.   Credit: 2 semester-hours   Room 24

Integration S508—Supervision of Instruction in
Secondary Schools   Dr. Atkinson
11:30 A. M. - 12:20 P. M.   Credit: 2 semester-hours   Room 4, CHS

Integration S521A—Educational and Psychological
Measurement in Guidance   Dr. Seidman
Prerequisite: This course is open only to those with teaching experience.
11:30 A. M. - 12:20 P. M.   Credit: 2 semester-hours   Room 22

Integration S530A—Corrective and Remedial Reading
in Secondary Schools   Mr. Buchner
10:30-11:20 A. M.   Credit: 2 semester-hours   Room 9

Integration S535—Vocational Guidance   Dr. Gelfond
11:30 A. M. - 12:20 P. M.   Credit: 2 semester-hours   Room 24

Integration S536—Educational Guidance   Dr. Davis
8:30-9:20 A. M.   Credit: 2 semester-hours   Room 24

Integration S538—Group Guidance and Counseling Activities   Mr. Haas
10:30-11:20 A. M.   Credit: 2 semester-hours   Room 29

Integration S539—Elementary School Guidance Services   Dr. Gelfond
10:30-11:20 A. M.   Credit: 2 semester-hours   Room 27

14

Integration S548—Curriculum Construction in the
Elementary School
9:30-10:20 A. M.   Credit: 2 semester-hours   Room 10

Integration S551—Principles and Techniques of Guidance   Dr. Gelfond
9:30-10:20 A. M.   Credit: 2 semester-hours   Room 27
This course is prerequisite to all other courses in Guidance

Integration S556—Improvement of the Teaching of Reading
in the Secondary School   Mr. Buchner
8:30-9:20 A. M.   Credit: 2 semester-hours   Room 10

Integration S602—Seminar in Guidance   Dr. Davis
Prerequisites: Integration 551, and have taken (or be taking in conjunction) one of the following: Int. 535, Int. 536, Int. 537.
10:30 A. M. - 12:20 P. M.   Credit: 4 semester-hours   Room 25

Mathematics

Mathematics S300—Social and Commercial Uses of Mathematics   Mr. Steinen
9:30-10:20 A. M.   Credit: 2 semester-hours   New Bldg., Room 104

Mathematics S400—Educational Statistics   Mr. Humphreys
11:30 A. M. - 12:20 P. M.   Credit: 2 semester-hours   New Bldg., Room 106

Mathematics S410—Mathematics of Finance   Mr. Steinen
11:30 A. M. - 12:20 P. M.   Credit: 2 semester-hours   New Bldg., Room 104

Mathematics S501C—Teaching of Advanced
Secondary School Mathematics   Dr. Meserve
9:30-10:20 A. M.   Credit: 2 semester-hours   New Bldg., Room 108

Mathematics S510B—Applications of Mathematics:
Science, Art and Music   Mr. Humphreys
10:30-11:20 A. M.   Credit: 2 semester-hours   New Bldg., Room 106

Mathematics S515—Differential Equations   Mr. Steinen
8:30-9:20 A. M.   Credit: 2 semester-hours   New Bldg., Room 108

Music

Music S460—Musical Studies in Europe   Mr. Kahn
See "Bureau of Field Studies" on page 17

Science

Biology S407—Comparative Embryology   Dr. Hadley
9:30-10:20 A. M.   New Bldg., Room 217
Laboratory: Mon., Wed., Fri. — 1:00-5:00 P. M.
Prerequisite: 8 semester-hours of work in zoology.
Credit: 4 semester-hours

Chemistry S408B—Industrial Chemistry, Part II   Dr. Reed
11:30 A. M. - 12:20 P. M.   Credit: 2 semester-hours   Annex 3, Rooms 1 & 4
Trips: Tues., Thurs.—P. M.

Chemistry S510—Food Inspection and Analysis   Dr. Gawley
10:30-11:20 A. M.   Credit: 4 semester-hours   Room 23
Laboratory: Mon., Wed., Fri. — 1:00-5:00 P. M.
Prerequisites: Organic chemistry and quantitative analysis.

Integration S478—Elementary School Science   Dr. Reed
See "Elementary Education" page 22.   Annex 3, Rooms 1 & 4

Social Studies

Social Studies S408—A History of New Jersey   Dr. Moffatt
8:30-9:20 A. M.   Credit: 2 semester-hours   Room 20

Social Studies S446—Current Problems in Economics
and Government   Dr. Rellahan
9:30-10:20 A. M.   Credit: 2 semester-hours   Room 21

Social Studies S456—International Economic Relations   Dr. Rellahan
10:30-11:20 A. M.   Credit: 2 semester-hours   Room 21

Social Studies S460—Central Eastern Region   Mr. Bye

Social Studies S466—Puerto Rico and The Virgin Islands   Mr. Bye
See "Bureau of Field Studies" on page 17

Social Studies S475—The History of American Thought   Dr. Clayton
9:30-10:20 A. M.   Credit: 2 semester-hours   Room 23

Social Studies S476—Personality Development and
Group Relations   Dr. Clayton
8:30-9:20 A. M.   Credit: 2 semester-hours   Room 23

Social Studies S479—Education and Intercultural Relationships   Dr. Clayton
11:30 A. M. - 12:20 P. M.   Credit: 2 semester-hours   Room 23

Social Studies S481—The West Indies   Mr. Bye
See "Bureau of Field Studies" on page 17

Social Studies S525—Workshop on Economic Education   Mr. Kops
See "Workshop on Economic Education" on page 20

Integration S479—Elementary School Social Studies   Dr. Moffatt
See "Elementary Education" on page 22.

BUREAU OF FIELD STUDIES
July 8 - August 25, 1957

Music S460—Musical Studies in Europe   Mr. Kahn

This field study course gives an opportunity to study by direct observation major European musical events of the summer season together with visits to famous places in the history of music. Beginning on July 8th, the tour extends to August 25th, covering the countries of England, Scotland, France, Germany, Austria, Switzerland, the Netherlands, and Italy. Among other things, opportunities are provided to attend the Richard Wagner Festival in Bayreuth, the Holland Music Festival, the Edinburgh Festival and the Salzburg Musical Festival, and to visit the LaScala Opera House and Museum in Milan. Famous places such as London, Paris, Rome, Florence, Venice, Pisa, Amsterdam, Frankfurt, Stuttgart, Munich and Lucerne are included in the itinerary. Lectures on Art and Architecture will be an added feature of this trip. This course may be taken for credit or non-credit.

Credit: 6 semester-hours

Cost for Air Travel and all European expenses: $1,213.00, plus tuition fees. For further information and registration forms, address Mr. Emil Kahn, care of the Bureau of Field Studies, State Teachers College, Upper Montclair, N. J.

July 7 - 26

Social Studies S466—Puerto Rico and the Virgin Islands   Mr. Bye

This is a nine-day field study course devoted to a survey of our nearest island possession. It includes a rather thorough exploration of San Juan and its vicinity, including the University, the rain forests and the submarine gardens, a trip through the island visiting pineapple, coffee, sugar, textile, and rum producing areas, churches, homes, and historic places. One day is spent in St. Thomas, largest of the Virgin Islands. The trip to and from the islands is made by air.

Credit: 2 semester-hours

Social Studies S481—West Indies   Mr. Bye

This course consists of directed travel in five countries in the Caribbean region. Transportation is by air and private cars with overnight stops at the best hotels. Opportunities are given for study of geographic, historic, economic and cultural phenomena in Puerto Rico, Santo Domingo, Haiti, Jamaica and Cuba.

Credit: 2 semester-hours

The above two courses extend through July 7-26 inclusive. Students must sign up for the entire trip, but may enroll in either Social Studies S466 or Social Studies S481, or both courses, for a total of 4 semester-hours. Students may take this trip on a non-credit basis if they desire.

August 12 - 25

Social Studies S460—Central Eastern Region   Mr. Bye

This fifteen-day tour of Pennsylvania, Maryland, Virginia, West Virginia, North Carolina and Tennessee covers the major points of historic interest associated with the Colonial Period, the American Revolution and the Civil War, and the geographic features of the coastal plain, the Piedmont, the Great Valley and the Appalachian Mountains in these states. Travel is by modern chartered motor coach and overnight stops are made at first-class hotels. Among the places visited are: Valley Forge, Philadelphia, Baltimore, Annapolis, Washington, Arlington, Alexandria, Mt. Vernon, Fredricksburg, Richmond, Washington's birthplace at Wakefield, Lee's plantation at Stratford, Yorktown, Williamsburg, Jamestown, Raleigh, Chattanooga, Asheville, Great Smoky Mountains, Norris Dam, Jefferson's Monticello at Charlottesville, Natural Bridge, Skyline Drive in the Shenandoah National Park, Luray Caverns, Winchester, Harper's Ferry, Frederick, Gettysburg, and the Pennsylvania Dutch area around Lancaster and Ephrata.

Credit: 3 semester-hours

If interested in any of the above courses taught by Mr. Bye, address him, care of the Bureau of Field Studies, State Teachers College, Upper Montclair, New Jersey.

INSTITUTES AND WORKSHOPS

Institutes on World Affairs

July 1 through July 19

Social Studies S490G—Western Europe at Mid-Century
Mr. Beckwith, Mr. Cohen, Mr. Boucher, et al.

The free nations of Western Europe are examined for their influence upon world affairs as well as for the ways in which they are affected by developments on the international scene. They are studies as the point of East-West contact and as a center of East-West rivalry. Particular attention is paid to the changing status of Western European powers and to the geographical, economic, and historical forces which are bringing about this change. Included among the areas studied are: political and governmental institutions; geographic influences; intra-European cooperation; economic bases of politics and history; pertinent historical trends and developments; social and intellectual developments; and, the role of tradition and provincialism. Among the nations considered are: the United Kingdom, France, the Benelux countries, West Germany, the Scandinavian countries, Italy, Portugal, Spain, and Ireland.

This course is designed primarily for teachers who feel the need for up-to-date background information and improved teaching materials and techniques for use in their classes. All teachers interested in world affairs are given the opportunity to build up a personal background of information and understanding. Background lectures, small study groups, field trips to New York City, films and exhibits of materials suitable for classroom use are included in the program. Spokesmen for the various national points of view supplement the basic information presented by the regular members of the Institute staff.
9:30 A. M. - 12:20 P. M.   Credit: 3 semester-hours   Chapin Hall Lounge

July 22 through August 9

Social Studies S490D—The United States and World Affairs
Mr. Beckwith, Mr. Cohen, Mr. Boucher, et al.

9:30 A. M. - 12:20 P. M.   Credit: 3 semester-hours   Chapin Hall Launge

China Institute of New Jersey

July 1 through July 13

China Institute of New Jersey is a permanent year-round organization composed of former students of the Institute. The policies and program of the Institute are determined by an elected executive committee, an advisory board of laymen, and representatives from the Faculty of Montclair State Teachers College, in consultation with the Chinese Director.

Dr. Chih Meng, Director of the China Institute of America, is also Chinese Director of the China Institute of New Jersey.

Students may enroll for college credit (graduate or undergraduate) if eligible to do so, or simply as Auditors for no credit. **The cost is the same in both cases.** (See page 9 for information as to fees.) Those who enroll for credit are expected to complete such notebooks, papers, projects, and examinations as are assigned by the course instructor. The preliminary grading of these papers, projects, and examinations is done by the Chinese teachers, while the final grading and coordinating is done by a representative of the regular Faculty of the College.

Notification of desire to enroll in one of the Institute courses should be sent on the coupon supplied in the special leaflet published by the Institute. Actual registration and payment of fees will take place in the College Library, from 8:30-9:00 A. M. on July 1. The Institute will convene in the Auditorium of the College High School Building at 9:15. Later, the students will go to the Individual classroom assigned to their courses.

China Institute Offerings

Fine Arts S416—Appreciation of Chinese Art

Mrs. Pearl Hsu and Mr. Y. C. Wang

9:30 A. M. - 12:20 P. M. and 1-4 P. M.

Credit: 3 semester-hours Room 14, CHS

Social Studies S499—Introduction to Chinese Culture Dr. Wu-chi Liu

9:30 A. M. - 12:20 P. M and 1-4 P. M.

Credit: 3 semester-hours Room 5, CHS

Seventh United Nations Institute
July 24, 25, and 26

A two and one-half day session on the United Nations and its place in today's world. Program to include a trip to the United Nations, special lectures and demonstrations of special interest to teachers and community leaders. Registration fee $2.00. **No credit.** Students enrolled in the "United States and World Affairs" course described on the previous page will be permitted to participate in this program without additional cost. Those interested should notify Mr. Robert Beckwith, care of the College.

Workshop on Economic Education
July 1 - July 19

Social Studies S525—Workshop on Economic Education Mr. Kops

This workshop is designed to provide teachers, supervisors, and administrators with a better understanding of the American economy and its operation. Instruction is given by a staff of economists and curriculum specialists, supplemented by business men, labor leaders, and representatives of agricultural groups. Workshop committees, with the help of specialists, prepare syllabi and teaching materials. Special library facilities are provided as well as selected teaching aids and field trips.

Registration 9:00 A. M. - July 1 Credit: 3 semester-hours Men's Dormitory
Meeting hours to be announced.

COURSES FOR THOSE WHO DESIRE TO TEACH IN ELEMENTARY GRADES

These courses are open to the following only:

(1) Those who already hold a degree from Montclair State Teachers College with a Certificate in Secondary Education, and

(2) Those who are now matriculated at Montclair State Teachers College for a degree and the Certificate in Secondary Education.

All other students should apply to one of the following colleges, all of which offer the bachelor's degrees in Elementary Education and several of which also offer the master's degree in that field.

New Jersey State Teachers College at Paterson.

New Jersey State Teachers College at Jersey City.

New Jersey State Teachers College at Newark.

New Jersey State Teachers College at Trenton.

New Jersey State Teachers College at Glassboro.

The courses given on this campus are offered to assist the Montclair State Teachers College students in attaining provisional and standard certification to teach in elementary grades. Detailed requirements for such certification are listed on pages 14, 15, 16 and 68 of the Eighteenth Edition of the Rules Concerning Teachers Certificates. Montclair College students should consult Miss House, Registrar, for an evaluation of their previous work and a statement concerning their remaining required courses.

The courses listed below may apply as general electives in undergraduate curriculums, and with the Advisor's approval, as graduate electives for majors in Administration and Supervision. The course with the * does not carry graduate credit.

*Integration S476—Elementary School Health and Physical Education Mr. De Rosa
8:30-9:20 A. M.   Credit: 2 semester-hours   Room 13 & Gym, CHS

Integration S478—Elementary School Science Dr. Reed
10:30-11:20 A. M.   Credit: 2 semester-hours   Rooms 1 & 4, Annex 3

Integration S479—Elementary School Social Studies Dr. Moffatt
9:30-10:20 A. M.   Credit: 2 semester-hours   Room 20

Geography S418—Regional Geography of North America See page 12

The following course is open to all students and may be taken by those who desire to teach in the Elementary grades.

Fine Arts S474A—Arts and Crafts in Education, I
See Page 12 for course description, hours, credits, etc.

NEW JERSEY STATE SCHOOL OF CONSERVATION
Stokes State Forest, Branchville, N. J.

Courses in Conservation, Field Science, Camping and Outdoor Education, Social Studies, and Waterfront Safety

Spring and Summer, 1957

WORKSHOP IN OUTDOOR EDUCATION

"Today's Stewardship Provides for Tomorrow."

The State Departments of Education and Conservation, through the six State Teachers Colleges, sponsor the N. J. State School of Conservation. In 1957, it offers a summer-long workshop in areas related to conservation and outdoor education. From June 13 to August 24, a continuous series of opportunities is offered to teachers and teachers-in-training.

While specific courses, listed below, for which credit is given, are offered, the living experience in the out-of-doors provides a major part of the value of the workshop. Special events of a camping nature include: cook-outs, barbecues and campfires. Outstanding leaders in out-of-door fields are regular participants in the program. This year special arrangements for week-end study and combinations of instructional times offer opportunities to many who were previously unable to enroll.

Credit for the following courses, may be applied toward graduate or undergraduate degrees at any of the N. J. State Teachers Colleges, subject to approval in advance by the institution. Credits may be transferred to other institutions where such transfer is permitted toward an undergraduate or graduate degree. Some of the courses may be substituted for courses required for elementary teaching certification (* marked thus below).

For additional information write to: N. J. State School of Conservation, Upper Montclair, New Jersey.

COURSES	1	2	3	4
Biology 203—Introduction to Field Biology	X			
Physical Education 410—Water Safety and First Aid	X		X	
Industrial Arts 442—Conservation of Basic Industrial Materials	X			
Integration 442—Practicum in Camp Leadership	X			
*Art 415—School Arts and Crafts with Native Materials		X	X	X
*Social Studies 494—Social Studies and Conservation		X	X	X
Integration 440—Camping Education		X	X	
Integration 441—Conservation Education				X
*Integration 480—Field Science for Elementary Teachers				X
Integration 539—Elementary School Guidance Services				X

All of the above courses carry two credits.
Sessions: 1. June 15-27; 2. June 24 - July 21; 3. July 6 - August 11; 4. August 12-24.
(Sessions longer than two weeks are week-end combinations).

POST-SUMMER SESSION COURSE

August 12 through August 23, 1957

To Meet an Urgent Need, the following course is being offered by the State Teachers College at Montclair, with the assistance of the New Jersey State Safety Council, the New Jersey Automobile Club, the American Automobile Association, the New Jersey State Police, and the New Jersey Department of Motor Vehicles.

This Course Offers the Necessary Opportunity for men and women to prepare themselves to teach behind-the-wheel driver education in high schools. Enrollees completing the work of the course are presented with a certificate indicating the work done.

Authorization: In order to teach behind-the-wheel driver education and driver training, a teacher must have his or her certificate endorsed by the Division of Teacher Certification, State Department of Education, for teaching behind-the-wheel automobile driver education and driver training.

The Requirements for Such Endorsement on the teacher's certificate are: (18th edition, 1951, "Rules Concerning Teachers' Certificates," page 22).

1. A valid New Jersey teacher's certificate.
2. A current New Jersey driver's license.
3. Three years of automobile driving experience.
4. Evidence of satisfactory completion of a course in driver education and driver training approved by the Commissioner of Education.

Veterans may take this course under the G. I. Bill, if they have so arranged with the Veterans' Counselor of the College.

Living Expenses and Training Expenses must be paid by the student. Those desiring hotel accommodations should write to Mr. F. K. Schultze, Manager, New Jersey Auto Club, AAA, 156 Clinton Avenue, Newark 5, New Jersey. The College Residence Halls are closed at this time.

Extra Charges are made for textbooks and other text materials. Some materials are furnished free.

Registration for this course will be accepted up to and including the opening day of the course. However, students should register early if possible, preferably on the regular registration day for the Summer Session. There is a limit to the number of registrations which may be accepted.

Health Education S408—Driver Education	Dr. Coder
9:00-12:00 and 1:00-4:00 daily Credit: 3 semester-hours	Room A

SUMMER SESSION

MONTCLAIR STATE TEACHERS COLLEGE
UPPER MONTCLAIR • NEW JERSEY

June 30 to August 8

1918—FIFTIETH ANNIVERSARY—1958

SUMMER SESSION

MONTCLAIR

STATE TEACHERS COLLEGE

UPPER MONTCLAIR, NEW JERSEY

1958

June 30th to August 8th

VOLUME 50   NUMBER 2

SUMMER SESSION CALENDAR

Registration

Classes Begin — Late Registration Period

End of Late Registration Period

No Classes

Classes This Saturday

Classes This Saturday

Classes This Saturday

Grades Due For All August Master's Degree Candidates

Classes End — Commencement 2:00 P. M.

SPECIAL EVENTS

Assembly — 9:30 A. M. — 9:30

Book Exhibit

Book Exhibit

Book Exhibit

Assembly — 10:30 A. M.

Evening China Institute Program

Assembly — 11:30 A.M.

SPECIAL FEATURES
TOURS — WORKSHOPS

Field Studies—Music Department   July 9 — August 27, 1958
Music S460—Musical Studies in Europe   Mr. Kahn

This field study course gives an opportunity to study by direct observation major European
musical events of the summer season together with visits to famous places in the history of
music. Beginning on July 9th, the tour extends to August 27th, covering the countries of
England, Scotland, France, Germany, Austria, Switzerland, the Netherlands, and Italy.
Among other things, opportunities are provided to attend the Richard Wagner Festival in
Bayreuth, the Holland Music Festival, the Edinburgh Festival and the Salzburg Musica
Festival, and to visit the LaScala Opera House and Museum in Milan. Famous places such
as London, Paris, Rome, Florence, Venice, Pisa, Amsterdam, Frankfurt, Stuttgart, Munich
and Lucerne are included in the itinerary. Lectures on Art and Architecture will be an
added feature of this trip. This course may be taken for credit or non-credit.

Credit: 6 semester-hours

Cost for Air Travel and all European expenses: Approximately $1,300.
For further information and registration forms, address Mr. Emil Kahn, care of the Bureau
of Field Studies.

Field Studies—Social Studies Department
Social Studies—S462—Continental United States   Mr. Bye

This is a sixty-day study course covering over 12,500 miles by deluxe chartered bus and
stopping at first class hotels. A few of the high points en route are: Natural Bridge, Mam-
moth Cave, Lincoln's New Salem, Dodge City, Denver; Rocky Mountains, Grand Canyon,
Bryce, Zion, Sequoia, Yosemite, Mt. Hood, Mt. Ranier, Crater Lake, Yellowstone National
Parks; Santa Fe Indian reservation, Petrified Forest; all of California (2 weeks); Oregon,
Washington, Montana, Wyoming, Black Hills, Chicago, Niagara Falls.
June 27 — August 26

Credit : 10 semester-hours

Cost: (Not including meals) $775.
Write to Edgar C. Bye, Director, Bureau of Field Studies.

Social Studies S491A—Workshop in Citizenship Education, Part I   Dr. Clayton

The purpose of this workshop is to present a study of what has been done in some of the
many projects in citizenship education throughout the country. Consultants are invited in
needed. Attention is given to programs and practices already in use in the schools. New
means for citizenship education are sought, and methods of evaluation are reviewed. Experience in the group processes essential to democratic action is provided. Principals and
administrators who want to join with others in learning how to make more effective the
citizenship education in the schools with which they are connected are invited to participate.
Each participant in the workshop works on actual plans for carrying out such education in
the school and the classroom. For additional information write to Dr. Frank Clayton, Social
Studies Department.
11:30 — 12:20 P. M.   Room

Credit: 2 semester-hours

N. J. CONGRESS OF PARENTS AND TEACHERS
PARENT-TEACHER WORKSHOP

July 14—18, inclusive

The New Jersey Congress, in cooperation with this State Teachers College, will offer a 5-day
workshop for parent-teacher officers and members and for teachers and future teachers.

PURPOSES:

1. To increase understanding of P.T.A. philosophy and objectives.
2. To stimulate and direct the planning for effective parent-teacher meetings.
3. To activate planning for action programs with the help of resource people
   and materials.
4. To suggest opportunities for new and different community activities of local
   parent-teacher associations.
5. To offer experience in gaining group leadership skills and help in the
   development of plans for parent-teacher study groups.

Write to Director, Summer Session, for additional information.

OFFICERS OF ADMINISTRATION
State Board of Education

MRS. EDWARD L. KATZENBACH, *President* .... Princeton

ARTHUR E. ARMITAGE, Sr. .... Collingswood

MRS. T. B. ARMSTRONG .... Stewartsville

HARVEY DEMBE .... Bayonne

PHILIP R. GEBHARDT .... Clinton

MRS. R. ADAM JOHNSTONE .... Ho-ho-kus

FRANCIS KNOWLES .... Penns Grove

JOHN F. LYNCH .... Morristown

JAMES W. PARKER, Sr. .... Red Bank

WILLIAM A. SUTHERLAND .... Liberty Corner

HENRY A. WILLIANS .... Paterson

MRS. STANLEY C. YORTON .... Nutley

Commissioner of Education
DR. FREDERICK M. RAUBINGER

Assistant Commissioner for Higher Education
DR. EARL E. MOSIER

Director of Teacher Education and Certification
DR. ALLAN F. ROSEBROCK

COLLEGE ADMINISTRATION

E. DeALTON PARTRIDGE, Ph.D .... President

CLYDE M. HUBER, Ph.D. .... Dean of the College

EDWARD J. AMBRY, A.M. .... Director, Summer Session

JOHN J. RELLAHAN, Ph.D. .... Chairman, Graduate Council

KEITH W. ATKINSON, Ph.D. .... Director, College High School

NED S. SCHROM, Ed.D. .... Dean of Students

LAWTON W. BLANTON, A.M. .... Director, Admissions

MARGARET A. SHERWIN, A.M. .... Assistant, Student Personnel

RUTH FREEMAN .... Recorder

ANNE BANKS CRIDLEBAUGH, A.M. .... Librarian

BERNARD SIEGEL, M.B.A. .... Business Manager

OTTO CORDES, P.E. .... Engineer in Charge, Maintenance

HEALTH SERVICES

CHARLOTTE L. PRITCHARD. R.N. .... College Nurse

F A C U L T Y
Summer Session 1958

E. DeALTON PARTRIDGE, Ph.D. .... Presiden

CLYDE M. HUBER, Ph.D. .... Dean of the Colleg

EDWARD J. AMBRY, A.M. .... Director, Summer Sessio

HUGH ALLEN, JR., A.M. .... Scienc

KEITH W. ATKINSON, Ph.D. .... Educatio

LeROY J. BOOTH, Ed.D. .... Educatio

LEONARD BUCHNER, A.M. .... Educatio

EDGAR C. BYE, A.M. .... Director, Bureau of Field Studie

FRANK L. CLAYTON, Ph.D .... Social Studie

ALDEN C. CODER, Ed.D. .... Driver Educatio

EARL C. DAVIS, Ph.D. .... Educatio

JEROME G. DeROSA, A.M. .... Health and Physical Educatio

ARTHUR W. EARL, Ed.D. .... Industrial Art

STEVEN C. L. EARLEY, Ph.D. .... Englis

EMMA FANTONE, A.M. .... Director, Audio-Visual Cente

L. HOWARD FOX, A.M. .... Speecl

CARL E. FRANKSON, Ph.D. .... Head, Department of Industrial Art

PAUL E. FROEHLICH, Ed.D. .... Business Educatio

EDWIN S. FULCOMER, Ed.D. .... Head, Department of Englisl

NORMAN A. GATHANY, Ed.D. .... Educatio

IRWIN H. GAWLEY, JR., Ed.D. .... Scienc

ABRAHAM GELFOND, Ph.D. .... Educatio

HOWARD L. HAAS, Ed.D. .... Business Educatio

W. PAUL HAMILTON, A.M. .... Englisl

T. ROLAND HUMPHREYS, A.M. .... Mathematic

DANIEL JACOBSON, Ph.D. .... Geograph

EMIL KAHN, A.M. .... Mus'

STEELE M. KENNEDY, Ph.D. .... Educatio

RUSSELL KRAUSS, Ph.D. .... Englis

Y. P. MEI, Ph.D. .... Visiting Lecturer, Chi

MAURICE P. MOFFATT, Ph.D. .... Chairman, Department of Social Studi

ALLAN MOREHEAD, Ed.D. .... Educati

JAMES P. PETTEGROVE, A.M. .... Engli

LAWRENCE J. REED, M.S. .... Mathemati

JOHN J. RELLAHAN, Ph.D. .... Chairman, Graduate Council: Social Studi

GEORGE E. SALT, A.M. .... Education and Engli

HAROLD M. SCHOLL, A.M. .... Engli

JEROME SEIDMAN, Ph.D. .... Educati

HORACE J. SHEPPARD, A.M. .... Business Educati

KENNETH O. SMITH, Ph.D. .... Phys

MAX A. SOBEL, Ph.D. .... Mathemat

ELIZABETH T. VAN DERVEER, Ed.D. .... Business Educati

RALPH A. VERNACCHIA, A.M. ....

RALPH WALTER, Ed.D. .... Educati

GRADUATE COUNCIL

JOHN J. RELLAHAN, *Chairman* ROSE METZ, *Secretary*

EDWARD J. AMBRY	M. HERBERT FREEMAN	MAURICE P. MOFFATT
EARL C. DAVIS	W. PAUL HAMILTON	ALLAN MOREHEAD
L. HOWARD FOX	CLYDE M. HUBER	E. DeALTON PARTRID
CARL E. FRANKSON	ORPHA M. LUTZ	RUFUS D. REED
	BRUCE E. MESERVE	

6

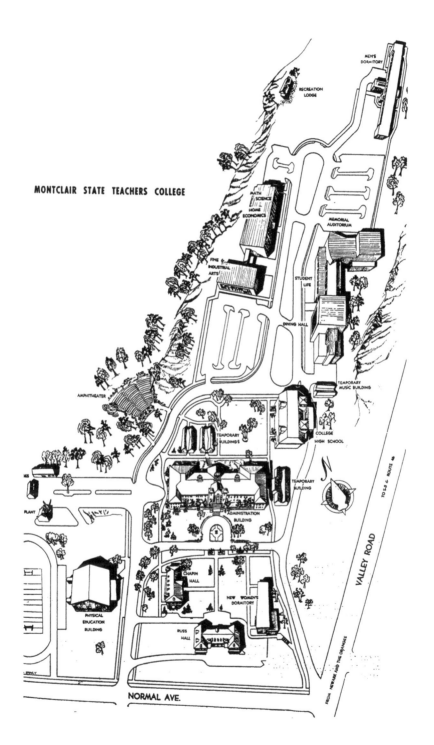

MONTCLAIR STATE TEACHERS COLLEGE

AIMS AND OBJECTIVES

The Summer School is designed specifically to meet the needs of

1. Students enrolled in graduate programs who wish to meet requirements [the Master of Arts Degree,

2. Teachers-in-service who desire to complete degree requirements, to impro their professional standing, or to take courses for state certification purpos

3. Graduates and upperclassmen from liberal arts colleges seeking provisior or limited certification to teach in the New Jersey public schools,

4. Persons interested in pursuing college work, whether or not they desi credit,

5. Persons interested in special workshops, institutes, and seminars.

The New Jersey State Teachers College at Montclair, a member of the Americ Association of Colleges of Teacher Education, is fully accredited by the Middle States Ass ciation of Colleges and Secondary Schools, the National Council for the Accreditation Teacher Education, and the American Association of University Women.

ADMISSION REGULATIONS

Persons interested in attending the New Jersey State Teachers College at Montcla may enter in one of two categories: students seeking a degree (degree candidates), or studer not seeking a degree (auditors, special students, and certification students).

Degree Candidates

Applicants for admission must hold the bachelor's degree from an institution of cepted standing. Selection is based on evidence that the applicant is able to pursue credita a program of graduate study in his chosen field. His scholastic record must therefore sh distinction, and his undergraduate program must show adequate preparation.

Application for admission must be made upon a form which may be obtained fr the Chairman of the Graduate Council. This form when submitted should be accompan by an official transcript of the student's undergraduate record, and of his graduate record he has done advanced work elsewhere. It is to the student's advantage to complete his plication at the earliest possible date. The latest date on which a completed application be accepted is two weeks in advance of the scheduled registration date.

Transfer of graduate credit will be accepted for graduates only from the St University of New Jersey and from the other New Jersey State Teachers Colleges. maximum permitted is eight (8) semester hours.

Once an applicant has been accepted by the College, a definite statement is furnis showing the requirements he must fulfill to earn the degree. This statement, known a *Work Program*, must be shown each time the applicant registers.

All students matriculating in the Graduate Division are required to complete least one full-time (6 s.h.) Summer Session, or one regular semester of fulltime gradu work.

A candidate for the degree must file with the Registrar an application for con ment of the degree before November 30 of the college year in which he expects to comp his work. Application blanks for this purpose may be secured in the Registrar's Office. *responsibility for making said application rests with the candidate.*

8

1. AUDITORS. Persons who desire to take courses for cultural, vocational, professional, or avocational purposes but who do not wish college credit may register as auditors. All persons auditing a course must register, and the tuition fee for auditors is the same as for other students.

2. SPECIAL STUDENTS. Persons who wish to enroll in courses for the purpose of having credit transferred to another institution may be admitted by submitting to the Director of Summer Session an official letter from the Dean of the Graduate School in which they are earning the degree. This letter must contain a statement that the student is in good standing and should indicate the courses, or kind of courses, for which the student may register. The College reserves the right to decide whether or not the student has fulfilled necessary prerequisites.

3. CERTIFICATION STUDENTS. Inquiries regarding certification requirements in New Jersey should be addressed to:

> Secretary, State Board of Examiners
> State Department of Education
> 175 West State Street
> Trenton, New Jersey

Enclose an official transcript of previous college work.

Make an appointment with the Chairman of the Education Department at Montclair State Teachers College. At the time of the interview, bring reply from the State Board of Examiners. Students desiring information concerning supervised student teaching should ask for written instructions at the Education Department of this College. As a prerequisite, students must have an above average undergraduate scholastic record and must take a minimum of six semester hours at this College.

GENERAL INFORMATION

LOCATION OF CAMPUS: Situated on the northern boundary of Upper Montclair, the College is approximately three miles north of the center of the town of Montclair and twelve miles east of New York City. The main entrance is at the intersection of Valley Road and Normal Avenue. Public transportation is available on the Greenwood Lake Division of the Erie Railroad and on Public Service bus routes (Nos. 60, 64, and 76 connect with the Lackawanna Railroad in the town of Montclair). Other bus lines serve the campus from New York, Newark, the Oranges, and Paterson. The junction of Highways No. 46 and 3 is located about one mile north of the campus.

Living Accommodations

1. Housing. Three College dormitories (Russ, Chapin, and Stone Halls) will be available for the accommodation of men and women registrants during the Summer Session. Applications for room reservations should be submitted prior to June 1, 1958; to Dean of Students, State Teachers College, Upper Montclair, New Jersey.

2. Rates. Room and board is $14.50 a week. This fee includes breakfast and dinner; also bed linen and the laundry of sheets. Students must provide blankets and spreads. The $14.50 fee, which must be paid on or before the first day of the Summer Session, is subject to change.

3. Meals. The Dining Hall will be open during the entire Summer Session.

LIBRARY FACILITIES. The main library, located in the Admistration Building will be open during the Summer Session to accommodate all students. All books, including the reference collection, are on open shelves. Hours will be posted.

OFFICE OF THE SUMMER SESSION. Located at the eastern end of the Administration Building, it is open from 8:30-4:30 weekdays and 9:00-12:00 on Saturdays.

Extra Curricular Activities

Recreational Facilities. The College Gymnasium contains basketball, volleyball, squash, and badminton courts. Located on the campus are softball fields and recreation areas. Municipal golf courses are within commuting distance, as are public swimming pools.

9

ACADEMIC REGULATIONS AND PROCEDURES

STUDENT RESPONSIBILITY. During the Summer Session the principles and regulation: governing course work and credit which appear in the regular College Catalog remain ir force. The College expects those who are admitted to assume responsibility for knowing and meeting the various regulations and procedures set forth. The College also expects those who are admitted to carry out their responsibilities so that their work is a credit to themselves and to the College. Hence, the College reserves the right to terminate the enrollment of any student whose conduct, class attendance, or academic record should prove un satisfactory.

CREDIT LOADS. Courses in the Summer Session are of the same quality and carry the same credit as those offered during the academic year. The maximum amount of credit which may be earned in the Summer Session is eight (8) semester hours; however, the College recommends that a student register for no more than six (6 s.h.). Additional credits may be earned in the Post-Summer Session at the New Jersey State School of Con servation, Stokes State Forest, Branchville, New Jersey.

CHANGE OF PROGRAM. No student will be allowed to make changes in his schedule without the approval of the Chairman of the Graduate Council or the Director of Summer Session. The deadline for making changes is July 2. If a student desires to change his status from that of *auditor* to *credit* or vice versa, he must make formal application for such change not later than the third week of the course. Forms for this purpose may be procured in the Registrar's office.

WITHDRAWAL FROM A COURSE. From the date of registration until July 2, a student may, with the written consent of his adviser, withdraw from one course and register for another. He must present his class admission card for the course he is dropping in order to obtain one for the new course. A student who withdraws from a course without enrolling in another, or who withdraws entirely from the Summer Session, must write a formal notice of withdrawal to the Director of the Summer Session. Refunds are based o the date the letter of withdrawal is received. Those who do not follow this procedure wil receive the mark of F for the course or courses from which they withdraw. Students ma) not withdraw from a course after the third week of the Summer Session.

GRADES AND TRANSCRIPTS. Only a student taking a course for credit receives grade. The grade given represents the quality of work done in a given course. The followin are the final marks which may be received

A—Excellent; B—Good; C—Fair; D—Poor; F—Failure;

Inc.—Incomplete; Wd—Withdrawn; N.C.—No Credits

The mark D earned in summer, part-time or extension courses at this College is not ac cepted for degree credit at Montclair. The mark F signifies failure or that the student h failed to submit a written notice of his withdrawal from a course. The mark N.C. is give to those enrolled as auditors. The mark Wd is given to those who submit in writing the intention of withdrawing from a course before the end of the third week.

The mark INC. is given a student whose work is incomplete at the end of the Summer Se sion. All responsibility regarding finishing incomplete work rests with the student. He wi be notified of a date on which the incomplete work is due; if said work is not finished o the prescribed date, a final grade of F will be recorded.

An official transcript showing credits and grades earned will be mailed to the student to days to two weeks following the close of the Summer Session. A report card for eac course will also be mailed. A service charge of $1.00 is made for duplicate copies of eac transcript.

REGISTRATION

All students who wish to enroll in the Summer Session must register in person on Monday, June 30. Procedures for registration will be posted on a bulletin board in the center hall of the Administration Building. No student may register for credit after July 2. A student has completed his registration when

1. His program has been approved by the Chairman of his Department

2. His registration forms have been properly and completely filled out

3. His fees have been paid

4. He receives his class cards

Students registering on July 1 and 2 will be charged a late registration fee of $2.00 Matriculated students should bring their Work Programs to the place of registration. The College reserves the right to close any course for which the enrollment is insufficient. The class will meet at least once, however, bfore such a decision is made. Students may then register in another course. If prerequisites are required (see course description), the student must be sure he has fulfilled them or their equivalent.

A student from another college should bring with him a letter from his Dean showing the courses which he has been advised to take and which will be accepted for credit. The numbering of courses at Montclair is as follows: 100-399, inclusive, undergraduate courses; 400-499, inclusive, senior class and graduate courses; 500 and above, graduate courses.

TUITION, FEES, AND EXPENSES

TUITION. For residents of New Jersey, $11.00 per semester-hour credit; for out-of-state residents, $13.00 per credit.

SERVICE CHARGE. For all students, fifty cents (50c) per semester-hour credit.

LATE REGISTRATION FEE. For all students, $2.00. Date after which this additional fee will be charged is June 30.

REFUNDING OF FEES. When the Director of the Summer Session receives written notice for withdrawal prior to the first meeting of the course, all fees are refunded in full. Other refunds are prorated from the day on which the Director of the Summer Session receives written notification of the student's desire to withdraw. Withdrawal before July 11 — 60% refund; before July 25 — 30%. No refunds are allowed after July 25. Refund policy is subject to change.

WORK SCHOLARSHIP. Tuition and dormitory fee scholarships are available. Students are assigned work in the various college departments. Write to Dean of Students, for information.

CERTIFICATION

Certificates to teach in New Jersey Public Schools are issued by the State Board of Examiners, Department of Education, 175 West State Street, Trenton 25, New Jersey.

Courses leading to certification to teach in the secondary schools are offered at this College and at Trenton State Teachers College. Courses required for certification to teach in the elementary schools are offered at Glassboro, Jersey City, Newark, Paterson, and Trenton State Teachers Colleges.

11

Special certification programs have been designed to meet the needs of persons seeking certification to teach Industrial Arts and Fine Arts — write to the Director of Summer Session for complete information.

Graduates from liberal arts colleges who wish to meet the professional education requirements for certification should select courses from the following list:

Education 200A — Child Growth and Development
Education 200B — Adolescent Psychology and Mental Hygiene
Education 300A — Aims and Organization of Secondary Education
Education 300B — Principles and Techniques of Teaching in the Secondary School
Education 400A — Principles and Philosophy of Secondary Education
Education 408 — Selection and Utilization of Audio-Visual Materials
Education 410 — Teaching Materials Workshop
Health Ed. 411 — School Health Services

All general questions regarding certification should be addressed to the Chairman, Education Department at this College.

SPECIAL SERVICES

ACADEMIC ADVISERS. Appointments with the Dean of the College, the Chairman of the Graduate Council, the Director of the Summer Session, or a Department Chairman, may be made by mail or telephone. Appointments should be made as early as possible prior to the date of registration.

BOOKSTORE. Located adjacent to the main lobby of the Student Life Building, this on-campus facility will be open from 8:00 a.m. to noon daily. A limited number of books for each course will be available. Textbook orders should be placed immediately upon completion of registration.

HEALTH SERVICE. A full-time registered nurse is on duty in the medical offices located in Russ Hall. Emergency medical care is available, as is infirmary care, for minor illnesses. Treatment by the College Medical Department includes simple medicinals, but not expensive prescription drugs.

INFORMATION OFFICE. An office is maintained at the College switchboard in the center hall of the Administration Building where information may be obtained regarding the location of various College personnel and services. A bulletin board on which important announcements are displayed is situated opposite this informational office. The telephone number of the College is PIlgrim 6-9500.

VETERANS' COUNSELOR. Veterans seeking admission to the Summer Session should apply well in advance of the registration date (June 30) to the Veterans' Counselor. The veteran should apply for a certificate of eligibility and entitlement at the nearest regional office of the Veterans Administration. In requesting this certificate, the veteran is advised to indicate clearly his educational objective. The Veterans Administration has established certain limitations, especially with regard to change of course. In order that a veteran may be assured that his certificate is in order and that he has taken the proper steps to expedite his training under the G.I. Bill, veterans enrolling for the first time at this College should report upon arrival to the Veterans' Counselor. His office is located adjacent to the cente hall in the Administration Building.

AUDIO-VISUAL AIDS CENTER. This center has a complete set of Coronet and othe selected films. Students may use materials and films available on a free-loan basis for clas presentation while enrolled in the Summer Session. For use away from the campus, film are available on a rental basis. Send for a descriptive catalog and additional information.

READING IMPROVEMENT LABORATORY. Enrollment in this laboratory, located i Room 5, Administration Building, is limited to junior and senior high school age pupil. Because the laboratory is used for demonstration purposes, enrollment is small (usually 10-1 pupils); all of the modern techniques are used. Persons interested should write to Director Reading Improvement Laboratory.

Students seeking additional courses and courses in specific subject matter fields to complete certification requirements should consult department chairman.

SPEECH IMPROVEMENT LABORATORY. The Speech and Hearing Center will offer an intensive remedial speech program. It will accommodate a maximum of thirty-five children between 5 and 18 years of age. The program is designed to provide therapy for children with the usual types of speech problems, as well as those who have major problems of voice, articulation, and rhythm (stuttering). Children with retarded language development or loss of language are also eligible. Persons who are interested in enrolling a child in this program are requested to write to Dr. Harold Scholl, Director of the Speech and Hearing Center.

TEXT BOOK EXHIBIT. On July 17, 18 and 19, there will be an exhibit of high school and elementary school textbooks. The exhibit is primarily for teachers and administrators attending the Summer Session, but will be open to undergraduate students and the general public. The location of the exhibit will be announced during the Summer Session.

COURSES OF THE SUMMER SESSION

Descriptions of the courses will be found in the 1957-59 Graduate Bulletin of the College. Courses numbered 500 and above are graduate courses; those numbered 400-499, inclusive, are senior-graduate courses and their descriptions in the Graduate Bulletin follow the descriptions of the graduate courses. Courses below the 400 number will be found in the Undergraduate Bulletin of the College. Only entirely new courses are described in the Summer Session Bulletin.

All rooms listed are in the Administration Building unless specified otherwise.

Business Education

Business Education S421—Finance and Investments for Families   **Dr. Haas**
11:30-12:20 P.M.   Credit: 2 semester-hours   Room 1, Annex 2

**Business Education S501A—Research Seminar in Business
Education I**   **Dr. Van Derveer**
9:30-10:20 A.M.   Credit: 2 semester hours   Room 1, Annex 2

**Business Education S502—Principles and Problems of
Business Education**   **Dr. Haas**
9:30-10:20 A.M.   Credit: 2 semester-hours   Room 5, Annex 2

**Business Education S505—Tests and Measurements in
Business Education**   **Dr. Haas**
8:30-9:20 A.M.   Credit: 2 semester-hours   Room 5, Annex 2

**Business Education S520B—Improvement of Instruction in
Business Education—Bookkeeping, Accounting and
Business Arithmetic**   **Dr. Van Derveer**
8:30-9:20 A.M.   Credit: 2 semester-hours   Room 1, Annex 2

**Business Education—S532—Field Studies and Audio-Visual Aids
in Business Education**   **Mr. Sheppard**
10:30-12-20 P.M.   Credit: 4 semester-hours   Room 5, Annex 2

**Business Education S533—Supervised Work Experience and
Seminar**   **Dr. Van Derveer**
7:00-9:00 P.M. Wednesdays   Credit: 4 semester-hours   Room 5, Annex 2

EDUCATION

Education S200A—Child Growth and Development   **Dr. Walter**
11:30-12:20 P.M.   Credit: 2 semester-hours   Room 21

Education S200B—Adolescent Psychology and Mental Hygiene   **Dr. Walter**
8:30-9:20 Section I   Credit: 2 semester-hours   Room 21
10:30-11:20 A.M. Section II   Credit: 2 semester-hours   **Dr. Seidman**
                                                                          Room 22

Education S300A—Aims and Organization of Secondary Education   **Dr. Kennedy**
8:30-9:20 A.M.   Credit: 2 semester-hours   Room 10

15

Education S300B—Principles and Techniques of Teaching in the Secondary School — **Dr. Kennedy**
9:30-10:20 Section I Credit: S semester-hours — Room 10
11:30-12:20 P.M. Section II Credit: S semester-hours — Room 10

Education S400A—Principles and Philosophy of Secondary Education — **Mr. Salt**
8:30-9:20 A.M. Section I Credit: 2 semester-hours — Room 30
— **Dr. Gathany**
9:30-10:20 A.M. Section II Credit: 2 semester-hours — Room 9

Education S408—Selection and Utilization of Audio-Visual Materials — **Miss Fantone**
10:30-11:20 A.M. Credit: 2 semester-hours — Audio-Vis. Aids Lab.

Education S410—Teaching Materials Workshop — **Miss Fantone**
8:30-9:20 A.M. Credit: 2 semester-hours — Audio-Vis. Aids Lab.

Education S476—Elementary School Health and Physical Education — **Mr. DeRosa**
8:30-9:20 A.M. Credit: 2 semester-hours — Room 13, CHS
See announcement on page 23

Education S478—Elementary School Science — **Mr. Allen**
10:30-11:20 A.M. Credit: 2 semester-hours — Room 207, Finley
See announcement on page 23

Education S479—Elementary School Social Studies — **Dr. Moffatt**
9:30-10:20 A.M. Credit: 2 semester-hours — Room 20
See announcement on page 23

Education S500A—Basic Educational Trends — **Dr. Walter**
9:30-10:20 A.M. Credit: 2 semester-hours — Room 24

Education S500C—Recent Trends in Secondary School Methods — **Mr. Salt**
9:30-10:20 A.M. Credit: 2 semester-hours — Room 30

Education S500D—School Administration I: Functions and Organization — **Dr. Gathany**
10:30-11:20 A.M. Credit: 2 semester hours — Room 25

Education S500E—School Administration II: Law and Finance — **Dr. Morehead**
9:30-10:20 A.M. Credit: 2 semester-hours — Room 22

Education S500F—School Administration III: Community Relations — **Dr. Atkinson**
11:30-12:20 P.M. Credit: 2 semester hours — Room 4, CHS

Education S502—Organization and Administration of the Modern High School — **Dr. Atkinson**
10:30-11:20 A.M. Credit: 2 semester-hours — Room 4, CHS

Education S503—Methods and Instruments of Research — **Dr. Froehlich**
Prerequisite: Mathematics 400 or an equivalent course in Statistics.
8:30-9:20: A.M. Section I Credit: 2 semester-hours — Room 2, Annex No. 2
9:30-10:20 A.M. Section II Credit: 2 semester-hours — Room 2, Annex No. 2
10:30-11:20 A.M. Section III Credit: 2 semester-hours — Room 2, Annex No. 2

Education S504A—Curriculum Construction in the Secondary School **Mr. Salt**
11:30-12:20 P.M.   Credit: 2 semester-hours   Room 30

Education S505—Organization and Administration of Extra-Curricular Activities
8:30-9:20 A.M.   Credit: 2 semester-hours   Room 9

Education S508—Supervision of Instruction in the Secondary Schools **Dr. Atkinson**
8:30-9:20 A.M.   Credit: 2 semester-hours   Room 4, CHS

Education S520—Principles of Mental Hygiene **Dr. Seidman**
8:30-9:20 A.M.   Credit: 2 semester-hours   Room 22

Education S521A—Educational and Psychological Measurement in Guidance **Dr. Seidman**
Prerequisite: Teaching experience
11:30-12:20 P.M.   Credit: 2 semester-hours   Room 22

Education S530A—Corrective and Remedial Reading in Secondary Schools **Mr. Buchner**
10:30-11:20 A.M.   Credit: 2 semester-hours   Room 3

Education S535—Vocational Guidance **Dr. Gelfond**
Prerequisite: Education 551
9:30-10:20 A.M.   Credit: 2 semester-hours   Room 25

Education S536—Educational Guidance **Dr. Davis**
Prerequisite: Education 551
8:30-9:20 A.M.   Credit: 2 semester-hours   Room 25

Education S538—Group Guidance and Counseling Activities **Dr. Booth**
Prerequisite: Education 551
9:30-10:20 A.M.   Credit: 2 semester-hours   Room 29

Education S539—Elementary School Guidance Services **Dr. Gelfond**
Prerequisite: Education 551
11:30-12:20 P.M.   Credit: 2 semester-hours   Room 25

Education S551—Principles and Techniques of Guidance **Dr. Gelfond**
This course is a prerequisite for most courses in guidance—See Adviser
8:30-9:20 A.M.   Credit: 2 semester-hours   Room 24

Education S554—Psychology and Education of Exceptional Children **Dr. Booth**
10:30-11:20 A.M.   Credit: 2 semester-hours   Room 30

Education S556—Improvement of Reading in the Secondary School **Mr. Buchner**
8:30-9:20 A.M.   Credit: 2 semester-hours   Room 3

Education S602—Seminar in Guidance **Dr. Davis**
Prerequisite: Education 551, and have taken (or be taking in conjunction) one of the following: Ed. 535, Ed. 536, Ed. 537
10:30-12:20 P.M.   Credit: 4 semester-hours   Room 9

English and Speech

English S100C—Fundamentals of Writing   **Dr. Earley**
8:30-9:50 A.M.   Credit: 3 semester-hours   Room 1, Annex 1

English S435—Stagecraft   **Mr. Fox**
11:30-12:20 P.M.   Credit: 2 semester-hours   Stagecraft Lab, Memorial Aud.

English S446—The One-Act Play   **Mr. Fox**
10:30-11:20 A.M.   Credit: 2 semester-hours   Memorial Aud., Room 4

English S454—Training the Speaking Voice   **Dr. Scholl**
9:30-10:20 A.M.   Credit: 2 semester-hours   Memorial Aud., Room 4

English S459X—A Survey of Great Chinese Literature   **Dr. Mei**
8:30-9:20 A.M.   Credit: 2 semester-hours   Room 5 CHS

English S503—Geoffrey Chaucer and His Times   **Dr. Krauss**
10:30-11:20 A.M.   Credit: 2 semester-hours   Room 1

English S514—Origin and Development of the Arthurian Legend   **Dr. Krauss**
11:30-12:20 P.M.   Credit: 2 semester-hours   Room 1

English S518—The Major Romantic Poets   **Mr. Pettegrove**
9:30-10:20 A.M.   Credit: 2 semester-hours   Room 2

English S519—English in the Modern High School   **Dr. Fulcomer**
8:30-9:20 A.M.   Credit: 2 semester-hours   Room 1

English S521—English Literature of Social Problems   **Mr. Pettegrove**
11:30-12:20 P.M.   Credit: 2 semester-hours   Room 2

English S531—Seventeenth Century Literature   **Mr. Hamilton**
10:30-11:20 A.M.   Credit: 2 semester-hours   Room 2

English S533—Masters of American Literature   **Dr. Fulcomer**
9:30-10:20 A.M.   Credit: 2 semester-hours   Room 1

English S544A—Shakespeare—The Tragedies   **Mr. Hamilton**
8:30-9:20 A.M.   Credit: 2 semester-hours   Room 2

Fine Arts

Fine Arts S402A—Textile and Costume Arts
8:30-9:20 A.M.   Credit: 2 semester-hours   Room 223 Finley

Fine Arts S403A—Print Making   **Mr. Vernacchia**
10:30-11:20 A.M.   Credit: 2 semester-hours   Room 221 Finley

Fine Arts S406A or S406B—Art Workshop I or II
9:30-10:20 A.M.   Credit: 2 semester-hours   Room 223 Finley
Students who have taken Fine Arts S406A may enroll in S406B, Part II.

Fine Arts S474A or S474B—Arts and Crafts in Education, I or II   **Mr Vernacchia**
11:30-12:20 P.M.   Credit: 2 semester-hours   Room 221 Finle

Included in this course are workshop activities in the arts and crafts of the elementary an secondary school program. Painting, drawing, modeling, pottery, weaving, papier-mache paper sculpture, school display techniques and lettering, wood, leather, plastics, metal work and puppetry, are materials and processes which are explored. See announcement on page 23

Geography

Geography S406—Geology   **Dr. Jacobson**
8:30-9:20 A.M.   Credit: 2 semester-hours   Room 26

Geography S414A—Advanced Economic Geography   **Dr. Jacobson**
9:30-10:20 A.M.   Credit: 2 semester-hours   Room 26

Geography S418—Regional Geography of North America   **Dr. Jacobson**
10:30-11:20 A.M.   Credit: 2 semester-hours   Room 26
See announcement on page 23

Health Education

Education S476—Elementary School Health and Physical Education   **Mr. DeRosa**
8:30-9:20 A.M.   Credit: 2 semester-hours   Room 13 CHS
See announcement on page 23.

Health Education S408—Driver Education   **Dr. Coder**
Credit: 3 semester-hours   Room A
See the Pre-Summer and Post-Summer Session announcement on page 24

Health Education S411—School Health Services   **Mr. DeRosa**
9:30-10:20 A.M.   Credit: 2 semester-hours   Room 13 CHS

Industrial Arts

**Industrial Arts S201A, S201B, or S301A—Wood and Crafts,
I, II, or III**   **Dr. Earl**
8:00-11:40 A.M.   Credit: 4 semester-hours   General Shop, Finley

Industrial Arts S402—Comprehensive General Shop   **Dr. Earl**
12:00-3:40 P.M.   Credit: 4 semester-hours   General Shop, Finley

The following partial list gives an idea of the type of work which may be done: Art Metal, Basketry, Bookbinding, Candlemaking, Ceramics, Home Repairs, Jewelry, Leather, Metal, Photography, Plastics, Printing, Rubber Stamp Making, Silk Screening, Wood and Textiles.

**Industrial Arts S501—Curriculum Construction and Course
Organization in Industrial Arts Education**   **Dr. Frankson**
8:30-9:50 A.M.   Credit: 3 semester-hours   Seminar Room, Finley

Industrial Arts S503—Problems in Teaching Industrial Arts   **Dr. Frankson**
10:00-11:30 A.M.   Credit: 3 semester-hours   Seminar Room, Finley

Mathematics

**Mathematics S300—The Social and Commercial Uses of
Mathematics**   **Mr. Reed**
11:30-12:20 P.M.   Credit: 2 semester-hours   Room 105, Finley

Mathematics S400—Educational Statistics
Section I: 10:30-11:20 A.M.   Credit: 2 semester-hours

Section II: 9:30-10:20 A.M.   Credit: 2 semester-hours

Mathematics S503—Foundations of Algebra
8:30-9:20 A.M.   Credit: 2 semester-hours

Mathematics S507—The Teaching of General Mathematics
9:30-10:20 A.M.   Credit: 2 semester-hours

Mathematics S509C—A Critical Interpretation of Mathematics in the Junior High School
8:30-9:20 A.M.   Credit: 2 semester-hours

Mathematics S510C—Applications of Mathematics: Geography, Astronomy, and Navigation
10:30-11:20 A.M.   Credit: 2 semester-hours

Mathematics S521—Analytical Mechanics
11:30-12:20 P.M.   Credit: 2 semester-hours

Music

Music S460—Musical Studies in Europe
   See "Special Features" on page 4.

Science

Chemistry S408A—Industrial Chemistry, Part I
11:30-12:20 P.M.,   Credit: 2 semester-hours
   Tues. and Thurs. and afternoons

Chemistry S501—The Teaching of Chemistry in Secondary Scho
Prerequisite: 16 semester-hours in Chemistry.
10:30-11:20 A.M.   Credit: 3 semester-hours
   with laboratory 1:00-4:30 P.M. on Wednesdays

Education S478—Elementary School Science
10:30-11:20 A.M.   Credit: 2 semester-hours
   See announcement on page 23

Physics S406A—Astronomy
8:30-9:20 A.M.   Credit: 2 semester-hours

Physics S411A—Photography
11:30-12:20 P.M.,   Credit: 2 semester-hours
         Monday, Wednesday, Friday and afternoons

Physics S512—Modern Physics
8:30-10:20 A.M. ,   Credit: 4 semester-hours
   and afternoons

Social Studies

Education S479—Elementary School Social Studies   **Dr. Moffatt**
9:30-10:20 A.M.   Credit: 2 semester-hours   Room 20
See announcement on page 23

Social Studies S408—A History of New Jersey   **Dr. Moffatt**
8:30-9:20 A.M.   Credit: 2 semester-hours   Room 20

Social Studies S439—The Family and Its Problems   **Dr. Clayton**
10:30-11:20 A.M.   Credit: 2 semester-hours   Room 20

**Social Studies S446—Current Problems in Economics and
Government**   **Dr. Rellahan**
10:30-11:20 A.M.   Credit: 2 semester-hours   Room 21

Social Studies S455—Social Legislation   **Dr. Rellahan**
9:30-10:20 A.M.   Credit: 2 semester-hours   Room 21

Social Studies S462—Continental United States   **Mr. Bye**
See "Special Features" on page 4

Social Studies S491A—Workshop in Citizenship Education, Part I   **Dr. Clayton**
11:30-12:20 P.M.   Credit: 2 semester-hours   Room 20
See "Special Features" on page 4

Social Studes S498X—China and the Far East   **Dr. Mei**
9:30-10:30 P.M.   Credit: 2 semester-hours   Room 5, CHS

COURSES FOR THOSE WHO DESIRE TO TEACH IN
ELEMENTARY GRADES

These courses are open to the following only:

(1) Those who already hold a degree from Montclair State Teachers College with a Certificate in Secondary Education, and

(2) Those who are now matriculated at Montclair State Teachers College for a degree and the Certificate in Secondary Education.

All other students should apply to one of the following colleges, all of which offer the bachelor's degree in Elementary Education and several of which also offer the master's degree in that field.

New Jersey State Teachers College at Paterson.

New Jersey State Teachers College at Jersey City.

New Jersey State Teachers College at Newark.

New Jersey State Teachers College at Trenton.

New Jersey State Teachers College at Glassboro.

The courses given on this campus are offered to assist the Montclair State Teachers College students in attaining provisional and standard certification to teach in elementary grades. Detailed requirements for such certification are listed on pages 14, 15, 16 and 68 of the Eighteenth Edition of the Rules Concerning Teachers Certificates. Montclair College students should consult the College Registrar, for an evaluation of their previous work and a statement concerning their remaining required courses.

The courses listed below may apply as general electives in undergraduate curriculums. They do not carry graduate credit.

Integration S476—Elementary School Health and
Physical Education **Mr. DeRosa**
8:30-9:20 A.M. Credit: 2 semester-hours Room 13 & Gym, CHS

Integration S478—Elementary School Science **Mr. Allen**
10:30-11:20 A.M. Credit: 2 semester-hours Room 207, Finley

Integration S479—Elementary School Social Studies **Dr. Moffatt**
9:30-10:20 A.M. Credit: 2 semester-hours Room 20

Geography S418—Regional Geography of North America **Dr. Jacobson**
10:30-11:20 A.M. Credit: 2 semester-hours Room 26

The following course is open to all students and may be taken by those who desire to teach in the Elementary grades.

Fine Arts S474 or S474B—Arts and Crafts in Education, I or II **Mr. Vernacchia**
11:30-12:20 P.M. Credit: 2 semester-hours Room 221, Finley

DRIVER EDUCATION COURSES

PRE-SUMMER SESSION COURSE

Health Education S408—Driver Education   **Dr. Coder**

June 23 — June 28   9:00 A.M. — 4:00 P.M. and
June 30 — July 3   1:00 P.M. — 8:00 P.M.   Room A
                      Credit: 3 semester-hours

POST-SUMMER SESSION COURSE

Health Education S408—Driver Education   **Dr. Coder**

August 11 — August 22   9:00 A.M. — 5:00 P.M.   Room A
                      Credit: 3 semester-hours

AUTHORIZATION TO TEACH BEHIND-THE-WHEEL DRIVER EDUCATION AND DRIVER TRAINING: A teacher must have his or her certificate endorsed by the Division of Teacher Certification, State Department of Education. The requirements for such endorsement are: ("Rules Concerning Teachers' Certificates" — 18th edition — revised 1956)

1. A valid New Jersey teacher's certificate.

2. A current New Jersey driver's license.

3. Three years of automobile driving experience.

4. Evidence of satisfactory completion of a course in driver education and driver training approved by the Commissioner of Education.

Secondary schools in New Jersey are increasing their offerings in Driver Education. This increase has resulted in a demand for more Driver Education teachers. To meet this demand, Montclair State Teachers College is increasing the number of courses being conducted in this field. Assistance is given by the New Jersey State Safety Council, the New Jersey Automobile Club, the American Automobile Association, the New Jersey State Police, and the New Jersey Department of Motor Vehicles.

LIVING EXPENSES AND TRAINING EXPENSES must be paid by the student. Those desiring hotel accommodations should write to Mr. F. K. Schultze, Manager, New Jersey Auto Club, AAA, 156 Clinton Avenue, Newark 5, New Jersey. The College Residence Halls are closed during the pre and post-summer session periods.

EXTRA CHARGES are made for textbooks and other text materials. Some materials are furnished free.

Registration for these courses is limited. Students must be approved by Dr. Alden Coder prior to registration. Write to Dr. Coder for complete information. Fees are to be paid on first day class meets.

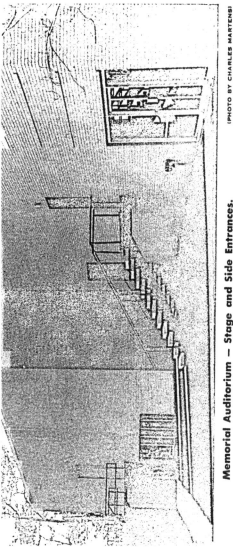

Memorial Auditorium — Stage and Side Entrances.

Memorial Auditorium.

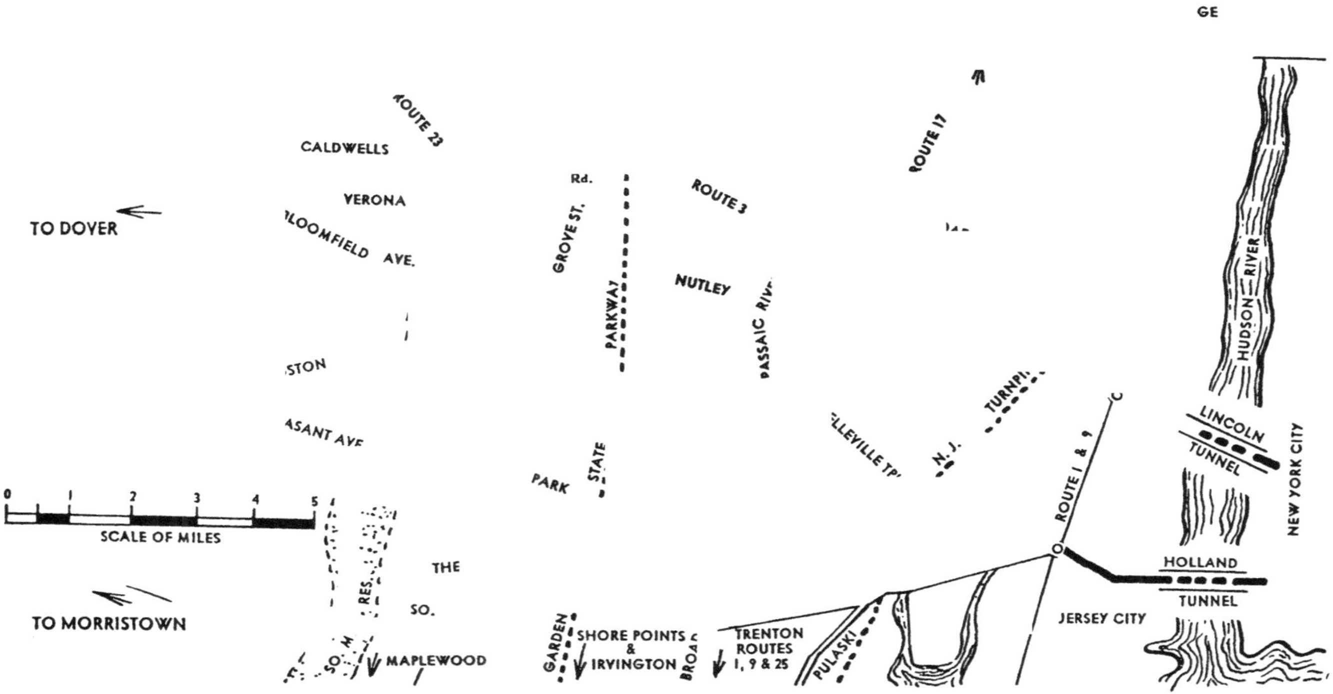

GE

HUDSON RIVER

LINCOLN TUNNEL

NEW YORK CITY

HOLLAND TUNNEL

JERSEY CITY

ROUTE 1 & 9

N.J. TURNPIKE

ROUTE 17

BELLEVILLE TPKE

PULASKI

PASSAIC RIVER

TRENTON ROUTES 1, 9 & 25

ROUTE 3

NUTLEY

BROAD

SHORE POINTS & IRVINGTON

GARDEN

PARKWAY

STATE

PARK

GROVE ST.

Rd.

ROUTE 23

CALDWELLS

VERONA

BLOOMFIELD AVE.

STON

PLEASANT AVE.

THE

SO.

MAPLEWOOD

RES.

SO.

TO DOVER

0 1 2 3 4 5

SCALE OF MILES

TO MORRISTOWN

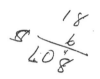

SUMMER SESSION

MONTCLAIR STATE COLLEGE
UPPER MONTCLAIR, NEW JERSEY

1959
June 29th to August 7th

VOLUME No. 51   NUMBER 4

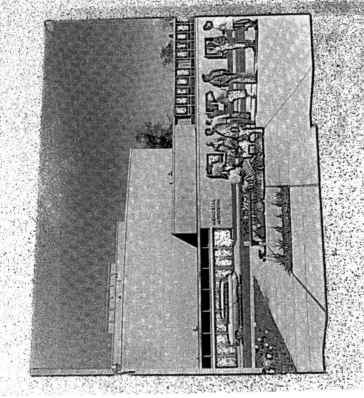

June 29	Registration
June 30	Classes Begin -— Late Registration Period
July 1	End of Late Registration Period
July 4	No Classes
July 11	Classes This Saturday
July 18	Classes This Saturday
July 20	Mid-point in Summer Session
	(withdrawals not permitted after this date)
July 31	Grades Due For All August Master's Degree Candidates
August 7	Classes End — Commencement 2:00 P. M.

SPECIAL EVENTS

July 14	Assembly — 10:30 A. M.
July 16	Book Exhibit
July 17	Book Exhibit
July 18	Book Exhibit
July 28	Assembly — 9:30 A. M.

**N. J. CONGRESS OF PARENTS AND TEACHERS
PARENT-TEACHER WORKSHOP**
July 6 - 10, inclusive

The New Jersey Congress, in cooperation with this State College, will offer a 5-day workshop for parent-teacher officers and members and for teachers and future teachers.

PURPOSES:
1. To increase understanding of P.T.A. philosophy and objectives.
2. To stimulate and direct the planning for effective parent-teacher meetings.
3. To activate planning for action programs with the help of resource people and materials.
4. To suggest opportunities for new and different community activities of local parent-teacher associations.
5. To offer experience in gaining group leadership skills and help in the development of plans for parent-teacher study groups.

Write to Director, Summer Session, for additional information.

SPECIAL FEATURES
TOURS — WORKSHOPS

Field Studies - Music Department   **July 11 - August 26, 1959**
Music S460 - Music Tour of Europe   **Mr. Kahn**

This field study course gives an opportunity to study by direct observation major European musical events of the summer season together with visits to famous places in the history of architecture and art. Beginning on July 11th, the tour extends to August 26th, covering the countries of France, Switzerland, Monaco, Italy, Austria, Germany, Holland, England and Scotland. Among other things, opportunities are provided to attend the Richard Wagner Festival in Bayreuth, the Music Festival in Aix-en-Provence, France, the Edinburgh Festival, and the Salzburg Musical Festival.

Famous places such as London, Paris, Rome, Florence, Venice, Pisa, Amsterdam, Frankfurt, Stuttgart, Munich, and Geneva are included in the itinerary. Lectures on art and architecture will be an added feature of this trip. This course may be taken for credit or non-credit.

Credit: 6 semester-hours
Cost for Air Travel and all expenses, including tuition: Approximately $1,300.
For further information and registration forms, address:
Mr. Emil Kahn, care of the Bureau of Field Studies.

Field Studies - Social Studies Department   **July 10 - August 4, 1959**
Social Studies - S469 — Mexico   **Mr. Bye**
In Cooperation with NEA and NJEA
This field study course aims to give a comprehensive view of contemporary Mexican life with its geographic, economic, historic, and cultural setting. Transportation to and from Mexico City is by air and in Mexico by private cars. Overnight stops and meals are at the best hotels. Places visited include Xochimilco, Acolman, Teotilhucán, Fortin, Puebla, Oaxaca, Guadalajaro, Queretero, Guanajuato, San Miguel de Allende, San Jose Purua, Morelia, Toluca, Taxco, and Cuernevaca. The itinerary is carefully planned to include all points of major interest and significance. Special studies may be made in the fields of geography, history, art, architecture, archaeology, sociology, economics, and other fields.

Credit: 3 semester hours
Cost from New York (Includes certain designated meals) $596. (Subject to changes in tariffs and rates.)

Field Studies — Social Studies Department   **August 10 - August 21, 1959**
Social Studies — S461 New England and French Canada   **Mr. Bye**

This field study course gives an opportunity to study by direct observation the historical and geographical features of New England and the Province of Quebec. The trip, occupying the twelve days immediately following the summer session, is made in a modern chartered motor coach with overnight stops at first-class hotels. The route covers the lower Connecticut Valley, including Hartford, Springfield, Northampton, and Deerfield; the Rhode Island cities of Providence and Newport; historic Massachusetts towns such as Plymouth, Boston, Lexington, Concord, Salem, and Marblehead; the coast of New Hampshire and southern Maine; the White Mountains in the Mt. Washington and Franconia Notch area; the Canadian Province of Quebec, including the ancient French city of Quebec, Montgomery Falls, St. Anne de Beaupre, Montreal; the western shores of Lake Champlain, Lake George, and the Hudson River. It is an indispensable background for an understanding of Colonial and Revolutionary life and history of this region.

Credit: 3 semester hours
Cost: (Plus meals) $150. (Subject to changes in tariffs and rates)
Write to: Mr. Edgar C. Bye, Director, Bureau of Field Studies.

4

OFFICERS OF ADMINISTRATION
State Board of Education

MRS. EDWARD L. KATZENBACH, President ———————————— Princeton
MRS. T. B. ARMSTRONG ———————————————— Stewartsville
HARVEY DEMBE ————————————————————————— Bayonne
PHILIP R. GEBHARDT ————————————————————— Clinton
MRS. R. ADAM JOHNSTONE ——————————————— Ho-Ho-Kus
JOHN F. LYNCH ————————————————————————— Morristown
JAMES W. PARKER, SR. ——————————————————— Red Bank
JACK SLATER ——————————————————————————— Paterson
GEORGE F. SMITH ———————————————————————— Metuchen
WILLIAM A. SUTHERLAND ————————————— Liberty Corner
MRS. STANLEY C. YORTON ————————————————— Nutley

Commissioner of Education
Dr. FREDERICK M. RAUBINGER

Assistant Commissioner for Higher Education
Dr. EARL E. MOSIER

Director of Teacher Education and Certification
Dr. ALLAN F. ROSEBROCK

COLLEGE ADMINISTRATION

E. DeALTON PARTRIDGE, Ph. D. ——————————————— President
CLYDE M. HUBER, Ph. D. ————————————— Dean of the College
EDWARD J. AMBRY, A.M. ————Director, Field Services and Summer Session
JOHN J. RELLAHAN, Ph. D. ————————— Chairman, Graduate Council
KEITH W. ATKINSON, Ph. D. ————————— Director, College High School
NED S. SCHROM, Ed.D ————————————————— Dean of Students
LAWTON W. BLANTON, A.M. ————————————— Director, Admissions
NORMAN LANGE, Ed.D. ——————— Director, Student Teaching and Placement
MARGARET A. SHERWIN A.M. ——————— Assistant Director of Students
PETER P. STAPAY, Ed.M. ———————————————————— Registrar
ANNE BANKS CRIDLEBAUGH, A.M. ——————————————— Librarian
BERNARD SIEGEL, M.B.A. ————————————— Business Manager
OTTO CORDES, P.E. ——————— Engineer in Charge, Maintenance

HEALTH SERVICES
CHARLOTTE L. PRITCHARD, R.N. —————————— College Nurse

GRADUATE COUNCIL

JOHN J. RELLAHAN, Chairman		ROSE METZ, Secretary
EDWARD J. AMBRY	M. HERBERT FREEMAN	BRUCE E. MESERVE
EARL C. DAVIS	W. PAUL HAMILTON	MAURICE P. MOFFATT
ARTHUR W. EARL	CLYDE M. HUBER	ALLAN MOREHEAD
L. HOWARD FOX	ORPHA M. LUTZ	E. DeALTON PARTRIDGE
	RUFUS D. REED	

5

FACULTY
SUMMER SESSION 1959

E. DeALTON PARTRIDGE, Ph.D. — President
CLYDE M. HUBER, Ph.D. — Dean of the College
EDWARD J. AMBRY, A.M. — Director, Summer Session
KEITH W. ATKINSON, Ph.D. — Education
HAROLD C. BOHN, Ed.D. — English
LeROY J. BOOTH, Ed.D. — Education
LEONARD BUCHNER, A.M. — Education
EDGAR C. BYE, A.M. — Coordinator, Bureau of Field Studies
FRANK L. CLAYTON, Ph.D. — Social Studies
PAUL C. CLIFFORD, A.M. — Mathematics
ALDEN C. CODER, Ed.D. — Driver Education
LAWRENCE H. CONRAD, A.M. — English
EARL C. DAVIS, Ph. D. — Education
JEROME G. DeROSA, A.M. — Health and Physical Education
JOSEPH W. DUFFY, Ed.D. — Industrial Arts
ARTHUR W. EARL, Ed.D. — Acting Chairman, Department of Industrial Arts
EMMA FANTONE, A.M. — Coordinator, Audio-Visual Center
JACOB J. FISHER, A.M. — Science
L. HOWARD FOX, A.M. — Speech
PAUL E. FROEHLICH, Ed.D. — Education
EDWIN S. FULCOMER, Ed.D. — Chairman, Department of English
IRWIN H. GAWLEY, Jr., Ed.D. — Science
ABRAHAM GELFOND, Ph.D. — Education
HOWARD L. HASS, Ed.D. — Business Education
JANE M. HILL, A.M. — Mathematics
EVA HUBSCHMAN, A.M. — Speech
T. ROLAND HUMPHREYS, A.M. — Mathematics
EMIL KAHN, A.M. — Music
STEELE M. KENNEDY, Ph.D. — Education
EDITH G. H. LENEL, Ph.D. — Order Librarian
RAYMOND C. LEWIN, A. M. — Education
ORPHA M. LUTZ, Ph.D. — Education
EVAN M. MALETSKY, A.M. — Mathematics
JEROME H. MANHEIM, M.S. — Mathematics
ROBERT W. McLACHLAN, Ph.D. — Chemistry
CLAIRE M. MERLEHAN, A.M. — Reference Librarian
BRUCE E. MESERVE, Ph.D. — Chairman, Department of Mathematics
MAURICE P. MOFFATT, Ph.D. — Chairman, Department of Social Studies
ALLAN MOREHEAD, Ed.D. — Chairman, Department of Education
ROBERT Z. NORMAN, Ph.D. — Mathematics
JAMES P. PETTEGROVE, A. M. — English
LAWRENCE J. REED, M.S. — Mathematics
RUFUS D. REED, Ph.D. — Chairman, Department of Science
JOHN J. RELLAHAN, Ph.D. — Chairman, Graduate Council: Social Studies
GEORGE E. SALT, A.M. — Education
HAROLD M. SCHOLL, Ed.D. — Acting Chairman, Department of Speech
JOHN A. SCHUMAKER, A.M. — Mathematics
JEROME SEIDMAN, Ph.D. — Education
THADDEUS J. SHEFT, A.M. — Associate Coordinator, Audio-Visual Center
HORACE J. SHEPPARD, A.M. — Acting Chairman, Dept. of Business Education
KENNETH O. SMITH, Ph.D. — Physics
MAX A. SOBEL, Ph.D. — Director, National Science Foundation Program
— Mathematics
ADRIAN STRUYK, A.M. — Mathematics
RICHARD W. TEWS, Ph.D. — Director, Panzer School of Physical Education and Hygiene
CHARLES E. TRESSLER, A.M. — Industrial Arts
RALPH A. VERNACCHIA, A.M. — Fine Arts
RALPH WALTER, Ed.D. — Education
FREDERICK H. YOUNG, Ph.D. — English

Montclair State College

AIMS AND OBJECTIVES

The Summer School is designed specifically to meet the needs of:

1. Students enrolled in graduate programs who wish to meet requirements for the Master of Arts Degree.

2. Teachers-in-service who desire to complete degree requirements, to improve their professional standing, or to take courses for state certification purposes.

3. Graduates and upperclassmen from liberal arts colleges seeking provisional or limited certification to teach in the New Jersey public schools.

4. Persons interested in pursuing college work, whether or not they desire credit.

5. Persons interested in special workshops, institutes, and seminars.

Montclair State College, a member of the American Association of Colleges of Teacher Education, is fully accredited by the Middle States Association of Colleges and Secondary Schools, and the American Association of University Women. Also fully accredited by the National Council for Accreditation of Teacher Education for the preparation of Elementary and Secondary School teachers, and provisionally accredited for the preparation of School Service Personnel, with the Master's Degree as the highest degree approved.

ADMISSION REGULATIONS

Persons interested in attending Montclair State College may enter in one of two categories: students seeking a degree (degree candidates), or students not seeking a degree (auditors, special students, and certification students). Students registering for the first time must pay a $5.00 Admission fee (see "Fees" page 11).

Degree Candidates

Applicants for admission must hold the bachelor's degree from an institution of accepted standing. Selection is based on evidence that the applicant is able to pursue creditably a program of graduate study in his chosen field. His scholastic record must therefore show distinction, and his undergraduate program must show adequate preparation.

Application for admission must be made upon a form which may be obtained from the Graduate office. When this form is submitted, students should request colleges previously attended to forward official transcripts to: Chairman, Graduate Council. It is to the student's advantage to complete his application at the earliest possible date. The latest date on which a completed application can be accepted is two weeks in advance of the scheduled registration date.

Transfer of graduate credit will be accepted for graduates only from the State University of New Jersey and from the other New Jersey State Colleges. The maximum permitted is eight (8) semester hours.

Once an applicant has been accepted by the College, a definite statement is furnished showing the requirements he must fulfill to earn the degree. This statement, known as a **Work Program**, must be shown each time the applicant registers.

All students matriculating in the Graduate Division are required to complete at least one full-time (6 s.h.) Summer Session, or one regular semester of full-time graduate work.

A candidate for the degree must file with the Registrar an application for conferment of the degree before November 30 of the college year in which he expects to complete his work. Application blanks for this purpose may be secured in the Registrar's Office. **The responsibility for making said application rests with the candidate.**

8

1. AUDITORS. Persons who desire to take courses for cultural, vocational, professional, or avocational purposes but who do not wish college credit may register as auditors. All persons auditing a course must register, and the tuition fee for auditors is the same as for other students.

2. SPECIAL STUDENTS. Persons who wish to enroll in courses for the purpose of having credit transferred to another institution may be admitted by submitting to the Director of Summer Sessions an official letter from the Dean of the University or College in which they are earning the degree. This letter must contain a statement that the student is in good standing and should indicate the courses, or kind of courses, for which the student may register. The College reserves the right to decide whether or not the student has fulfilled necessary prerequisites.

3. CERTIFICATION STUDENTS. Inquiries regarding certification requirements in New Jersey should be addressed to:

> Secretary, State Board of Examiners
> State Department of Education
> 175 West State Street
> Trenton 25, New Jersey

Request your college to send an official transcript of previous college work to the same address.
Make an appointment with the Certification Advisor at Montclair State College. At the time of the interview, bring reply from the State Board of Examiners. Students desiring information concerning supervised student teaching should ask for written instructions at the Education Department of this College. As a prerequisite, students must have an above average undergraduate scholastic record and must take a minimum of six semester hours at this College.

GENERAL INFORMATION

LOCATION OF CAMPUS: Situated on the northern boundary of Upper Montclair, the College is approximately three miles north of the center of the town of Montclair and twelve miles east of New York City. The main entrance is at the intersection of Valley Road and Normal Avenue. Public transportation is available on the Greenwood Lake Division of the Erie Railroad and on Public Service bus routes. (Nos. 60, 64, and 76 connect with the Lackawannna Railroad in the town of Montclair). Other bus lines serve the campus from New York, Newark, the Oranges, and Paterson. The junction of Highways No. 46 and 3 is located about one mile north of the campus.

Living Accommodations

1. Housing. Three College dormitories (Russ, Chapin, and Stone Halls) will be available for the accommodation of men and women registrants during the Summer Session. Applications for room reservations should be submitted prior to June 1, 1959, to: Dean of Students, Montclair State College, Upper Montclair, New Jersey.

2. Rates. Room and board is $18.00 a week. This fee includes breakfast and dinner; also bed linen and the laundry of sheets. Students must provide blankets and spreads. The $18.00 fee, which must be paid on or before the first day of the Summer Session, is subject to change.

3. Meals. The Dining Hall will be open during the entire Summer Session.

LIBRARY FACILITIES. The main library, located in the Administration Building will be open during the Summer Session to accommodate all students. All books, including the reference collection, are on open shelves. Hours will be posted. Library cards will be issued upon presentation of tuition receipt.

OFFICE OF THE SUMMER SESSION. Located at the eastern end of the Administration Building, it is open from 8:30-4:00 weekdays and 8:30-12:00 on July 11 and July 18.

Extra Curricular Activities
Recreational Facilities. The College Gymnasium contains basketball, volleyball, squash, and badminton courts. Located on the campus are softball fields and recreation areas. Municipal golf courses are within commuting distance, as are public swimming pools.

ACADEMIC REGULATIONS AND PROCEDURES

STUDENT RESPONSIBILITY. During the Summer Session the principles and regulations governing course work and credit which appear in the regular College Catalog remain in force. The College expects those who are admitted to assume responsibility for knowing and meeting the various regulations and procedures set forth. The College also expects those who are admitted to carry out their responsibilities so that their work is a credit to themselves and to the College. Hence, the College reserves the right to terminate the enrollment of any student whose conduct, class attendance, or academic record should prove unsatisfactory.

CREDIT LOADS. Courses in the Summer Session are of the same quality and carry the same credit as those offered during the academic year. The maximum amount of credit which may be earned in the Summer Session is eight (8) semester hours; however, the College recommends that a student register for no more than six (6 s.h.). Additional credits may be earned in the Post-Summer Session at the New Jersey State School of Conservation, Stokes State Forest, Branchville, New Jersey.

CHANGE OF PROGRAM. No student will be allowed to make changes in his schedule without the approval of the Chairman of the Graduate Council or the Director of Summer Session. The deadline for making changes is July 1. If a student desires to change his status from that of **auditor** to **credit** or vice versa, he must make formal application for such change not later than the third week of the course. Forms for this purpose may be procured in the Registrar's office.

WITHDRAWAL FROM A COURSE. From the date of registration until July 1, a student may, with the written consent of his advisor, withdraw from one course and register for another. He must present his class admission card for the course he is dropping in order to obtain one for the new course. A student who withdraws from a course without enrolling in another, or who withdraws entirely from the Summer Session, must write a formal notice of withdrawal to the Director of the Summer Session. Refunds are based on the date the letter of withdrawal is received. Those who do not follow this procedure will receive the mark of F for the course or courses from which they withdraw. Students may not withdraw from a course after the third week of the Summer Session.

GRADES AND TRANSCRIPTS. Only a student taking a course for the credit receives a grade. The grade given represents the quality of work done in a given course. The following are the final marks which may be received:

A—Excellent   B—Good   C—Fair   D—Poor   F—Failure

Inc.—Incomplete   WP—Withdrawn, Passing   N.C.—No Credits

WF—Withdrawn, Failing

10

The mark D earned in summer, part-time or extension courses at this College is not accepted for degree credit at Montclair. The mark F signifies failure or that the student has failed to submit a written notice of his withdrawal from a course. The mark N.C. is given to those enrolled as auditors. The mark WP is given to those who submit in writing their intention of withdrawing from a course before the end of the third week, and are doing passing work in the course involved. WF is assigned to students who withdraw before the end of the third week and are doing failing work at the time of withdrawal.

The mark INC. is given a student whose work is incomplete at the end of the Summer Session. All responsibility regarding finishing incomplete work rests with the student. He will be notified of date on which the incomplete work is due; if said work is not finished on the prescribed date, a final grade of F will be recorded.

An official transcript showing credits and grades earned will be mailed to the student ten days to two weeks following the close of the Summer Session. A report card for each course will also be mailed. A service charge of $1.00 is made for duplicate copies of each transcript.

REGISTRATION

All students who wish to enroll in the Summer Session must register in person on Monday, June 29. Procedures for registration will be posted on a bulletin board in the center hall of the Administration Building. No student may register for credit after July 1. A student has completed his registration when,

1. His program has been approved by the Chairman of his Department.

2. His registration forms have been properly and completely filled out.

3. His fees have been paid.

4. He receives his class cards.

Students registering on June 30 and July 1 will be charged a late registration fee of $5.00. Matriculated students should bring their Work Programs to the place of registration.

The College reserves the right to close any course for which the enrollment is insufficient. The class will meet at least once, however, before such a decision is made. Students may then register in another course. If prerequisites are required (See course description), the student must be sure he has fulfilled them or their equivalent.

A student from another college should bring with him a letter from his Dean showing the courses which he has been advised to take and which will be accepted for credit. The numbering of courses at Montclair is as follows: 100-399, inclusive, undergraduate courses; 400-499 inclusive, senior class and graduate courses; 500 and above, graduate courses.

TUITION, FEES AND EXPENSES

ADMISSION FEE. $5.00 to be paid the first time student is admitted to the Summer or Part-Time and Extension Division of the College. Fee must accompany Admission Form.

TUITION. For residents of New Jersey, $13.00 per semester-hour credit; for out-of-state residents, $15.00 per credit.

SERVICE CHARGE. For all students, fifty cents (50c) per semester-hour credit.

LATE REGISTRATION FEE. For all students, $5.00. Date after which this additional fee will be charged is June 29.

PROGRAM CHANGE FEE. $2.00.

11

REFUNDING OF FEES. When the Director of the Summer Session receives written notice of withdrawal prior to the first meeting of the course, all fees are refunded in full. Other refunds are prorated from the day on which the Director of the Summer Session receives written notification of the student's desire to withdraw. Withdrawal before July 11 — 60% refund; before July 20 — 30%. No refunds are allowed after July 20. Refund policy is subject to change.

WORK SCHOLARSHIP. Tuition and dormitory fee scholarships are available. Students are assigned work in the various college departments. Write to Dean of Students for information.

CERTIFICATION

Certificates to teach in New Jersey Public Schools are issued by State Board of Examiners, Department of Education, 175 West State Street, Trenton 25, New Jersey.

Courses leading to certification to teach in the secondary schools are offered at this College and at Trenton State College. Courses required for certification to teach in the elementary schools are offered at Glassboro, Jersey City, Newark, Paterson and Trenton State Colleges.

Special certification programs have been designed to meet the needs of persons seeking certification to teach Industrial Arts and Fine Arts — write to the Director of Summer Session for complete information.
Graduates and Upperclassmen from liberal arts colleges who wish to meet the professional education requirements for certification should select courses from the following list:

Education 200A–Child Growth and Development
Education 200B–Adolescent Psychology and Mental Hygiene
Education 201—Human Development and Behavior, Part I
Education 202—Human Development and Behavior, Part II
Education 300A–Aims and Organizations of Secondary Education
Education 300B–Principles and Techniques of Teaching in the Secondary School
Education 303—The Teacher in School and Community
Education 304—Principles and Techniques of Secondary Education
Education 400A–Principles and Philosophy of Secondary Education
Education 408—Selection and Utilization of Audio-Visual Materials
Education 410—Teaching Materials Workshop
Health Ed. 411–School Health Services

Subject matter methods courses are offered by Departments listed under Departmental Headings.
All general questions regarding certification should be addressed to the Certification Officer at this College.

SPECIAL SERVICES

ACADEMIC ADVISERS. Appointments with the Dean of the College, the Chairman of the Graduate Council, the Director of the Summer Session, or a Department Chairman, may be made by mail or telephone. Appointments should be made as early as possible prior to the date of registration.

BOOKSTORE. Located adjacent to the main lobby of the Student Life Building, this on-campus facility will be open from 8:00 a.m. to noon daily. A limited number of books for each course will be available. Textbook orders should be placed immediately upon completion of registration.

HEALTH SERVICE. A full-time registered nurse is on duty in the medical offices located in Russ Hall. Emergency medical care is available, as is infirmary care, for minor illnesses. Treatment by the College Medical Department includes simple medicinals, but not expensive prescription drugs.

INFORMATION OFFICE. An office is maintained at the College switchboard in the center hall of the Administration Building where information may be obtained regarding the location of various College personnel and services. A bulletin board on which important announcements are displayed is situated opposite this informational office. The telephone number of the College is PIlgrim 6-9500.

VETERANS' COUNSELOR. Veterans seeking admission to the Summer Session should apply well in advance of the registration date (June 29) to the Veterans' Counselor. The Veteran should apply for a certificate of eligibility and entitlement at the nearest regional office of the Veterans Administration. In requesting this certificate, the veteran is advised to indicate clearly his educational objective. The Veterans Administration has established certain limitations, especially with regard to change of course. In order that a veteran may be assured that his certificate is in order and that he has taken the proper steps to expedite his training under the G. I. Bill, veterans enrolling for the first time at this College should report upon arrival to the Veterans' Counselor. His office is located adjacent to the center hall in the Administration Building.

AUDIO-VISUAL AIDS CENTER. This center has a complete set of Coronet and other selected films. Students may use materials and films available on a free-loan basis for class presentation while enrolled in the Summer Session. For use away from the campus, films are available on a rental basis. Send for a descriptive catalog and additional information.

READING IMPROVEMENT LABORATORY. Enrollment in this laboratory, located in the Administration Building, is limited to junior and senior high school pupils. Because the laboratory is used for demonstration purposes, enrollment is small (usually 10-12 pupils); all of the modern techniques are used. Persons interested should write to Coordinator, Reading Improvement Laboratory, at this College.

SPEECH AND HEARING CENTER. The Speech and Hearing Center will offer an intensive remedial speech program. It will accommodate a maximum of sixty children between 4 and 18 years of age. The program is designed to provide therapy for children with the usual types of speech problems, as well as those who have major problems of voice, articulation, and rhythm (stuttering). Children with retarded language development or loss of language are also eligible. Persons who are interested in enrolling a child in this program are requested to write to: Coordinator, Speech and Hearing Center.

TEXT BOOK EXHIBIT. On July 16, 17, and 18, there will be an exhibit of high school and elementary school textbooks. The exhibit is primarily for teachers and administrators attending the Summer Session, but will be open to undergraduate students and the general public. The location of the exhibit will be announced during the Summer Session.

MONTCLAIR STATE COLLEGE
COURSES OF THE SUMMER SESSION

Descriptions of the courses will be found in the 1957-59 Graduate Bulletin of the College. Courses numbered 500 and above are graduate courses; those numbered 400-499, inclusive, are senior-graudate courses and their descriptions in the Graduate Bulletin follow the descriptions of the graduate courses. Courses below the 400 number will be found in the Undergraduate Bulletin of the College. Only entirely new courses are described in the Summer Session Bulletin.

All rooms listed are in the Administration Building unless specified otherwise.

* Courses listed with this mark indicate they may not be used for graduate credit. These are teacher-certification or pre-requisite courses.

Business Education Department

**Business Education S520A-Improvement of Instruction in
Business Education: General Business Subjects   Dr. Haas**
8:30-9:20 A. M.   Credit: 2 semester hours   Room 1, Annex 2

**Business Education S520B-Improvement of Instruction in
Business Education: Bookkeeping, Accounting, and
Business Arithmetic   Dr. Haas**
9:30-10:20 A.M.   Credit: 2 semester hours   Room 1, Annex 2

**Business Education S532-Field Studies and Audio-Visual
Aids in Business Education   Mr. Sheppard**
10:30-12:20 P.M.   Credit: 4 semester hours   Room 5, Annex 2

Business Education S542A-Advanced Business Law Cases I   Dr. Hass
11:30-12:20 P.M.   Credit: 2 semester hours   Room 1, Annex 2

Education Department

*Education S200A-Child Growth and Development   Dr. Walter
11:30-12:20 P.M.   Credit: 2 semester hours   Room 22

*Education S200B-Adolescent Psychology and Mental Hygiene .Dr. Lutz
9:30-10:20 A.M.   Credit: 2 semester hours   Room 29

***Education S201-Human Development and Behavior,
Part I   Dr. Seidman**
11:30-12:50   Credit: 3 semester hours   Room 30

15

***Education S202-Human Development and Behavior,
Part II**   **Dr. Seidman**
Pre-requisite: Education 200A, Education 201, or equivalent
8:30-9:50 A.M.   Credit: 3 semester hours   Room 30

***Education S300A-Aims and Organization of Secondary
Education**   **Mr. Lewin**
10:30-11:20 A.M.   Credit: 2 semester hours   Room 10

***Education S300B-Principles and Techniques of Teaching in
the Secondary School**   **Mr. Lewin**
9:30-10:20 A.M.   Credit: 2 semester hours   Room 10

*Education S303-The Teacher in School and Community   **Dr. Kennedy**
10:00-11:20 A.M.   Credit: 3 semester hours   Room 30

***Education S304-Principles and Techniques of Secondary
Education**   **Dr. Kennedy**
11:30-12:50 P.M.   Credit: 3 semester hours   Room 24

***Education S400A-Principles and Philosophy of Secondary
Education**   **Mr. Lewin**
8:30-9:20 A.M. Section I   Credit: 2 semester hours   Room 24
10:30-11:20 A.M. Section II Credit: 2 semester hours   **Mr. Salt**
                                                          Room 29

Education S406-Educational Sociology   **Dr. Davis**
Pre-requisite: General Sociology or equivalent
9:30-10:20 A.M.   Credit: 2 semester hours   Room 7 CHS

**Education S408-Selection and Utilization of Audio-Visual
Materials**   **Miss Fantone**
8:30-9:20 A.M.   Credit: 2 semester hours   Audio-Vis Aids Lab.

Education S409-Radio and Sound Equipment in the Classroom **Mr. Sheft**
11:30-12:20 P.M.   Credit: 2 semester hours   Audio-Vis. Aids Lab.

Education S461-The Junior High School Curriculum   **Dr. Gelfond**
9:30-10:20 A.M.   Credit: 2 semester hours   Room 24

Education S500A-Basic Educational Trends   **Dr. Walte**
Pre-requisite: Teaching Experience
9:30-10:20 A.M.   Credit: 2 semester hours   Room 2:

Education S500C-Recent Trends in Secondary School Methods **Mr. Sal**
Pre-requisite: Teaching Experience
11:30-12:20 P.M.   Credit: 2 semester hours   Room 2

16

Education S500D-School Administration I: Functions and Organizations   **Dr. Walter**

Pre-requisite: Teaching Experience

10:30-11:20 A.M.   Credit: 2 semester hours   Room 22

Education S500E-School Administration II: Law and Finance   **Dr. Morehead**

Pre-requisite: Teaching Experience

9:30-10:20 A.M.   Credit: 2 semester hours   Room 25

Education S500F-School Administration III: Community Relations   **Dr. Atkinson**

Pre-requisite: Teaching Experience

8:30-9:20 A.M.   Credit: 2 semester hours   Room 4, CHS

Education S502-Organization and Administration of the Modern High School   **Dr. Atkinson**

Pre-requisite: Teaching Experience

9:30-10:20 A.M.   Credit: 2 semester hours   Room 4, CHS

Education S503-Methods and Instruments of Research   **Dr. Froehlich**

Pre-requisite: Mathematics 400 or an equivalent course as determined by the Chairman of the Graduate Council

8:30-9:20 A.M. Section I   Credit: 2 semester hours   Room 2, Annex No. 2

9:30-10:20 A.M. Section II   Credit: 2 semester hours   Room 2, Annex No. 2

Education S505-Organization and Administration of Extra-Curricular Activities   **Dr. Morehead**

10:30-11:20 A.M.   Credit: 2 semester hours   Room 24

Education S508-Supervision of Instruction in the Secondary Schools   **Dr. Atkinson**

Pre-requisite: Teaching Experience

11:30-12:20 P.M.   Credit: 2 semester hours   Room 4, CHS

Education S530B-Workshop in Corrective and Remedial Reading in Secondary Schools   **Mr. Buchner**

Pre-requisite: Education 530A, Education 556 or equivalent course

10:30-11:20 A.M.   Credit: 2 semester hours   Room 26

Education S534-Community Resources for Guidance   **Dr. Gelfond**

Pre-requisite: Education 551

10:30-11:20 A.M.   Credit: 2 semester hours   Room 25

Education S536-Educational Guidance   **Dr. Booth**

Pre-requisite: Education 551

11:30-12:20 P.M.   Credit: 2 semester hours   Room 9

Education S550-Child and Adolescent Development
Pre-requisite: Child Development and Psychology courses
9:30-10:20 A.M.   Credit: 2 semester hours

Dr. Booth
Room 9

Education S551-Principles and Techniques of Guidance
(Note: This course is pre-requisite for most guidance courses
offered in this Division of the College)
8:30-9:20 A.M.   Credit: 2 semester hours

Dr. Gelfond
Room 25

**Education S553-Core-Curriculum and Life Adjustments
Programs in High Schools**
Pre-requisite: Teaching Experience
8:30-9:20 A.M.   Credit: 2 semester hours

Mr. Salt
Room 29

**Education S554A-Psychology and Education of Exceptional
Children**
8:30-9:20 A.M.   Credit: 2 semester hours

Dr. Booth
Room 9

**Education S556-Improvement of Reading in the Secondary
School**
11:30-12:20 P.M.   Credit: 2 semester hours

Mr. Buchner
Room 26

Education S602-Seminar in Guidance
Pre-requisite: Education 551, and at least one other guidance course
10:30-12:20 P.M.   Credit: 4 semester hours

Dr. Davis
Room 2

English Department

*English S100C-Fundamentals of Writing
8:30-9:50 A.M.   Credit: 3 semester hours

Mr. Pettegrove
Room 13, CHS

***English S401X-The Teaching of English in Secondary
Schools**
8:30-9:20 A.M.   Credit: 2 semester hours

Dr. Fulcomer
Room 1

English S536-Philosophy of Great Literature
11:30-12:20 P.M.   Credit: 2 semester hours

Dr. Young
Room 1

English S544B-Shakespeare (Comedies)
8:30-9:20 A.M.   Credit: 2 semester hours

Dr. Bohn
Room 3

18

English S545A-American Literature Part I   Mr. Conrad
9:30-10:20 A.M.   Credit: 2 semester hours   Room 3

English S545B-American Literature Part II   Mr. Conrad
11:30-12:20 P.M.   Credit: 2 semester hours   Room 3

English S546-Modern Drama   Dr. Bohn
9:30-10:20 A.M.   Credit: 2 semester hours   Room 1

English S548-Fiction as Image of World History   Dr. Young
10:30-11:30 A.M.   Credit: 2 semester hours   Room 1

Fine Arts Department

Fine Arts S406A or S406B-Art Workshop I or II   Mr. Vernacchia
June 30 - July 17
8:30-10:20 A.M.   Credit: 2 semester hours   Room 221, Finley

Fine Arts S474A or S474B-Arts and Crafts in Education
     I or II   Mr. Vernacchia
July 18 - August 7
8:30-10:20 A.M.   Credit: 2 semester hours   Room 221, Finley

Fine Arts S500X-Contemporary Art   Mr. Vernacchia
10:30-11:20 A.M.   Credit: 2 semester hours   Room 221, Finley

Industrial Arts Department

Industrial Arts S401 or S402-Comprehensive General Shop
     For Elementary and Junior High School or Comprehensive
     General Shop for Senior High School   Mr. Tressler
2:00-3:40 P.M.   Credit: 4 semester hours   General Shop, Finley

Industrial Arts S502-Shop Planning and Equipment Selection
     in Industrial Arts Education   Dr. Duffy
8:30-9:50 A.M.   Credit: 3 semester hours   Seminar Room, Finley

Industrial Arts S511-Supervision of Industrial Arts   Dr. Earl
10:00-11:20 A.M.   Credit: 3 semester hours   Seminar Room, Finley

Mathematics Department

Mathematics S300-The Social Uses of Mathematics   Mr. L. Reed
11:30-12:20 P.M.   Credit: 2 semester hours   Room 106, Finley

*Mathematics S400-Educational Statistics
Section: I: 9:30-10:20   Credit: 2 semester hours ·   Mr. Humphreys
    Room 106, Finley
    Mr. L. Reed
Secton 11: 10:30-11:20 A.M. Credit: 2 semester hours   Room 209, Finley

*Mathematics S401X-The Teaching of Mathematics in
    Secondary Schools   Mr. Humphreys
10:30-11:20 A.M.   Credit: 2 semester hours   Room 106, Finley

Mathematics S405-History of Mathematics   Mr. Struyk
10:30-11:20 A.M.   Credit: 2 semester hours   Room 104, Finley

Mathematics S407-Advanced Calculus   Mr. Manheim
10:30-11:20 A.M.   Credit: 2 semester hours   Room 107, Finley

Mathematics S506-Current Research in Secondary
    Mathematics   Mr. Manheim
11:30-12:20 P.M.   Credit: 2 semester hours   Room 107, Finley

Mathematics S508-Elements of Geometry   Mr. Schumaker
8:30-9:20 A.M.   Credit: 2 semester hours   Room 107, Finley

The elements of geometry include the logical foundations of geometry, finite projective geometries, construction of rational points on a line and a plane, and topology. The emphasis is on the mathematical pre-requisites for understanding contemporary proposals for secondary-school geometry.

Mathematics S510B-Applications of Mathematics: Science
    Art and Music   Mr. L. Reed
9:30-10:20 A.M.   Credit: 2 semester hours   Room 104, Finley

Mathematics S517-The Theory of Numbers   Mr. Schumaker
9:30-10:20 A.M.   Credit: 2 semester hours   Room 107, Finley

Mathematics S525-Curriculum and Teaching of Junior
    High School Mathematics   Mr. Humphreys
8:30-9:20 A.M.   Credit: 2 semester hours   Room 106, Finley

This course is intended to give teachers a deeper insight into the mathematical subject matter and the methods of teaching in grades seven and eight. The structure of the curriculum is studied with an emphasis upon the usual subject matter with provisions for individual differences. Patterns in arithmetic are stressed as an introduction for algebra. Experimental approaches to the study of statistics and geometry are also included.

Mathematics S530-Mathematical Materials and Their
    Applications in the Teaching of Mathematics   Mr. Struyk
11:30-12:20 P.M.   Credit: 2 semester hours   Room 104, Finley

Mr. Humphreys
Room 106, Finley
Mr. L. Reed
Room 209, Finley

The following courses are open only to National Science Foundation participants. Students were selected in March 1959, and registrations were closed. **These courses are listed for record purposes only.**

Mr. Humphreys
Room 106, Finley

Mr. Struyk
Room 104, Finley

Mr. Manheim
Room 107, Finley

Mr. Manheim
Room 107, Finley

Mr. Schumaker
Room 107, Finley

Mr. L. Reed
Room 104, Finley

Mr. Schumaker
Room 107, Finley

Mr. Humphreys
Room 106, Finley

Mr. Struyk
Room 104, Finley

Mathematics S503-Foundations of Algebra — Dr. Norman
11:00-12:00 Noon   Credit: 2 semester hours   Room 108, Finley

Mathematics S508-Foundations of Geometry — Dr. Meserve
June 30 - July 17
8:30-10:30 A.M.   Credit: 2 semester hours   Room 108, Finley

Mathematics S522-Introduction to Probability and Statistics — Mr. Clifford
July 20 - August 7
8:30-10:30 A.M.   Credit: 2 semester hours   Room 108, Finley

The primary objective of the course is to give at least a minimum preparation in probability and statistics for the topics that are included in the newer high school program. Topics include: the summarization of data, intuitive probability, axiomatic development of probability, the Binomial and Poisson distributions and the normal curve distribution, elements of sampling and elements of testing hypotheses. Both the experimental and the axiomatic approach to this material are studied. An examination of currently available material is included.

This course may be used in place of Mathematics 408 as a pre-requisite for Mathematics 523 - 524.

Mathematics S525-Curriculum and Teaching of Junior High School Mathematics — Miss Hill
9:30-10:30 A.M.   Credit: 2 semester hours   Room 105, Finley

Mathematics S601X-Workshop: Curriculum Problems in The Mathematics Field — Mr. Maletsky
1:30-3:00 P.M.   Credit: 2 semester hours   Room 105, Finley
(3 days each week - days to be arranged)

Music Department

Music S460-Music Studies in Europe — Mr. Kahn
For Details, write to Mr. Kahn - See "Special Features" on page 4
Credit: 6 semester hours.

Panzer School of Physical Education and Hygiene

Health Education S408-Driver Education — Dr. Coder
Credit: 3 semester hours   Room A
Pre-requisite: Approval by Instructor prior to registration.
For Details: write to Dr. Coder - See page 24

Health Education S411-School Health Services — Mr. De Rosa
8:0-9:20 A.M.   Credit: 2 semester hours   Room 7, CHS

***Physical Education S404-Tests and Measurements in
Physical Education** **Dr. Tews**
7:00-8:00 P.M. Credit: 2 semester hours Gym No. 4, College Gymnasium

This course is designed to acquaint students majoring in physical education with the history of measurement and evaluation in this field and to understand current trends and practices. Various tests in general qualities and traits relating to motor performance and tests relating to sports skills are presented to, and administered by, the students. Test evaluation and construction of written test questions are discussed. Methods of treating statistical data relating to physical education are presented.

***Physical Education S409-Organization and Administration
of Physical Education** **Dr. Tews**
8:00-9:00 P.M. Credit: 2 semester hours Gym No. 4, College Gymnasium

Science Department

Biology S407-Comparative Embryology **(to be announced)**
Pre-requisite: 8 semester-hours of work in zoology
8:30-9:20 A.M. Credit: 4 semester hours Room 217, Finley

 With laboratory 1:00-4:45 P.M. Monday, Wednesday
 and Friday afternoons.

Biology S501-The Teaching of Biology in Secondary Schools
(to be announced)
Pre-requisites: 16 semester-hours of work in biology
9:30-10:50 A.M. Credit: 3 semester hours Room 217, Finley

Chemistry S408B-Industrial Chemistry, Part II **Dr. Gawley**
Pre-requisites: General and organic chemistry, or special
 permission of the instructor.
11:30-12:20 P.M. Credit: 2 semester hours Room 204, Finley

Meets Tues. and Thurs. Afternoons.

Chemistry S411-Physical Chemistry, Part I **Dr. McLachlan**
Pre-requisites: Chemistry 101 and 102, general college chemistry,
 Chemistry 202, analytical chemistry, and Physics 101 and 102,
 general college physics.
10:30-11:20 A.M. Credit: 4 semester hours Room 206, Finley

 With laboratory 1:00-4:45 P.M. Monday, Wednesday and
 Friday afternoons.

Physics S512-Modern Physics **Dr. Smith**
Pre-requisites: General college physics, general college chemistry,
 and a course in electrical measurements.
8:30-10:20 A.M. Credit: 4 semester hours Room 201, Finley

***Science S401X-The Teaching of Science in the Secondary
Schools** **Dr. R. Reed**
9:30-10:20 A.M. Credit: 2 semester hours Room 209, Finley

Science S418-Three Centuries of Science Progress **Dr. R. Reed**
8:30-9:20 A.M. Credit: 2 semester hours Room 209, Finley

22

Social Studies Department

*Social Studies S202X-The Development of the United States
(1865 - Present)   **Dr. Clayton**
9:30-10:20 A.M.   Credit: 2 semester hours   Room 21

*Social Studies S401X-The Teaching of Social Studies in the
Secondary Schools   **(to be announced)**
8:30-9:20 A.M.   Credit: 2 semester hours   Room 22

Social Studies S408-A History of New Jersey   **Dr. Moffatt**
9:30-10:20 A.M.   Credit: 2 semester hours   Room 20

Social Studies S419-American Political Biography   **Dr. Moffatt**
8:30-9:20 A.M.   Credit: 2 semester hours   Room 20

Social Studies S461-New England and French Canada   **Mr. Bye**
August 10 - 21
For details, write to Mr. Edgar Bye - See "Special Features" on page 4
Credit: 3 semester hours

Social Studies S469-Mexico (In Cooperation with NEA and
NJEA)   **Mr. Bye**
July 10 - August 4
For details, write to Mr. Edgar Bye - See "Special Features" on page 4
Credit: 3 semester hours

Social Studies S475-The History of American Thought   **Dr. Clayton**
11:30-12:20 P.M.   Credit: 2 semester hours   Room 21

Social Studies S476-Personality Development and Group
Relations   **Dr. Clayton**
8:30-9:20 A.M.   Credit: 2 semester hours   Room 21

Social Studies S522-The Development of Economic Institutions
and Ideas   **Dr. Rellahan**
10:30-11:20 A.M.   Credit: 2 semester hours   Room 9

Speech Department ·

Speech S100D-Fundamentals of Speech   **Mr. Fox**
.1:30-12:50 P.M.   Credit: 3 semester hours   Room 4 Memorial Auditorium

23

AUTHORIZATION TO TEACH BEHIND-THE-WHEEL DRIVER EDUCATION AND DRIVER TRAINING: A teacher must have his or her certificate endorsed by the Division of Teacher Certification, State Department of Education. The requirements for such endorsement are: (Rules Concerning Teachers' Certificates" — 18th edition — revised 1956)

1. A valid New Jersey teacher's certificate.

2. A current New Jersey drivers license.

3. Three years of automobile driving experience.

4. Evidence of satisfactory completion of a course in driver education and driver training approved by the Commissioner of Education.

Secondary schools in New Jersey are increasing their offerings in Driver Education. This increase has resulted in a demand for more Driver Education teachers. To meet this demand, Montclair State College is increasing the number of courses being conducted in this field. Assistance is given by the New Jersey State Safety Council, the New Jersey Automobile Club, the American Automobile Association, the New Jersey State Police, and the New Jersey Department of Motor Vehicles.

LIVING EXPENSES AND TRAINING EXPENSES must be paid by the student. Those desiring hotel accommodations should write to Mr. F. K. Schultze, Manager, New Jersey Auto Club, AAA, 156 Clinton Avenue, Newark 5, New Jersey. The College Residence Halls are closed during the pre and post-summer session periods.

EXTRA CHARGES are made for textbooks and other text materials. Some materials are furnished free.
Registration for these courses is limited. Students must be approved by Dr. Alden Coder prior to registration. Write to Dr. Coder for complete information. Fees are to be paid on first day class meets.

PRE-SUMMER SESSION   POST-SUMMER SESSION

DRIVER EDUCATION COURSES

PRE-SUMMER SESSION COURSE

Health Education S408-Driver Education   **Dr. Coder**
June 17-June 19 — 7:00 P.M. - 10:00 P.M. and
June 22 - June 27 — 9:00 P.M. - 4:00 P.M. and
June 29 - July 3 — 1:00 P.M. - 4:00 P.M.   Room A
        Credit: 3 semester hours

POST-SUMMER SESSION COURSE

Health Education S408-Driver Education   **Dr. Coder**
August 5 - August 7 — 1:00 P.M. - 4:30 P.M. and
August 10 - August 14 — 9:00 A.M. - 3:00 P. M. and
August 17 - August 21 — 9:00 A.M. - 3:00 P.M.   Room A
        Credit: 3 semester hours

24

Speech S411-Advanced Speech Pathology   Dr. Scholl

Pre-requisite: Speech 410 or equivalent
9:30-9:20 A.M.   Credit: 3 semester hours   Room 1 Memorial Auditorium

Additional hours to be arranged by Instructor)
The purpose of the course is to provide further study and evaluation of modern techniques of speech rehabilitation, and to review research findings in the areas of voice, articulation, rhythm, and symbolization disorders. Consideration is given to the ways in which speech rehabilitation may be integrated with related health services and educational services in schools and special centers. In addition to one hour of class lecture each day, students are expected to spend four hours a week participating in speech therapy sessions at the Montclair State College Speech and Hearing Center and at other selected hospitals and institutions.

Speech S436-Fundamentals of Stage Lighting   Mr. Fox

Pre-requisite: Speech 105A or Speech 435, or permission
     of the instructor.
10:00-11:20 A.M.   Credit: 3 semester hours   Stage Memorial Auditorium

The purpose of the course is to analyze the functions of light on a stage and to study and use the instruments available to achieve desired effects. Optimum and minimum equipment are studied. The laboratory work is done in the Memorial Auditorium at the College, which houses modern and flexible stage lighting equipment, and in a small auditorium with limited facilities. Students are encouraged to apply the principles of stage lighting to the specific auditoriums in which they may work. Appropriateness of lighting for different types of stage activities is fundamental consideration in the course.

Speech S454-Training the Speaking Voice   Mrs. Hubschman

9:30-10:20 A.M.   Credit: 2 semester hours   Room 2 Memorial Auditorium

Summer Session
Montclair State College
Upper Montclair, N. J.

FORM 3547 REQUESTED

960

ulletin of

ontclair State College

SUMMER SESSION

MONTCLAIR STATE COLLEGE
UPPER MONTCLAIR, NEW JERSEY

1 9 6 0
JUNE 27 TO AUGUST 5

olume 52   Number 3

June 27	Registration
June 28	Classes Begin — Late Registration Period
June 29	End of Late Registration Period (No Registration Accepted After 4:00 P.M.)
July 4	No Classes
July 9	Saturday Classes
July 16	Saturday Classes
July 18	Mid-point in Summer Session (withdrawals not permitted after this date)
July 23	Saturday Classes
July 29	Grades Due For All August Master's Degree Candidates
August 5	Classes End — Commencement 2:00 P.M.

SPECIAL EVENTS

July 12	Assembly — 10:30 A.M.
July 14	Book Exhibit — 8:00 - 3:00 P.M.
July 15	Book Exhibit — 8:00 - 3:00 P.M.
July 26	Assembly — 9:30 A.M.

OFFICERS OF ADMINISTRATION

State Board of Education

MRS. EDWARD L. KATZENBACH, President .... Princeton
MRS. T. B. ARMSTRONG .... Stewartsville
HARVEY DEMBE .... Bayonne
PHILIP R. GEBHARDT .... Clinton
MRS. R. ADAM JOHNSTONE .... Ho-Ho-Kus
JOHN F. LYNCH .... Morristown
JAMES W. PARKER, SR. .... Red Bank
JACK SLATER .... Paterson
GEORGE F. SMITH .... Metuchen
WILLIAM A. SUTHERLAND .... Liberty Corner
MRS. STANLEY C. YORTON .... Nutley

Commissioner of Education
DR. FREDERICK M. RAUBINGER

Assistant Commissioner for Higher Education
DR. EARL E. MOSIER

Director of Teacher Education and Certification
DR. ALLAN F. ROSEBROCK

COLLEGE ADMINISTRATION

E. DeALTON PARTRIDGE, Ph.D. .... President
CLYDE M. HUBER, Ph.D. .... Dean of the College
EDWARD J. AMBRY, A.M. .... Director, Field Services and Summer Session
JOHN J. RELLAHAN, Ph.D. .... Chairman, Graduate Council
KEITH W. ATKINSON, Ph.D. .... Director, College High School
LEO G. FUCHS, Ed.M. .... Dean of Students
LAWTON W. BLANTON, A.M. .... Director, Admissions
NORMAN LANGE, Ed.D. .... Director, Student Teaching and Placement
PETER P. STAPAY, Ed.M. .... Registrar
ANNE BANKS CRIDLEBAUGH, A.M. .... Librarian
BERNARD SIEGEL, M.B.A. .... Business Manager
OTTO CORDES, P.E. .... Engineer in Charge, Maintenance

HEALTH SERVICES

CHARLOTTE L. PRITCHARD, R.N. .... College Nurse

GRADUATE COUNCIL

JOHN J. RELLAHAN, Chairman   ROSE METZ, Secretary

EDWARD J. AMBRY	M. HERBERT FREEMAN	BRUCE E. MESERVE
CAROLYN E. BOCK	W. PAUL HAMILTON	MAURICE P. MOFFATT
EARL C. DAVIS	CLYDE M. HUBER	ALLAN MOREHEAD
ARTHUR W. EARL	ORPHA M. LUTZ	E. DeALTON PARTRIDGE
L. HOWARD FOX		

4

FACULTY
SUMMER SESSION 1960

E. DeALTON PARTRIDGE, Ph.D. .... President
CLYDE M. HUBER, Ph.D. .... Dean of the College
EDWARD J. AMBRY, A.M. .... Director, Summer Session
HUGH ALLEN, JR., Ed.D. .... Science
KEITH W. ATKINSON, Ph.D. .... Education
WILLIAM A. BALLARE, A.M. .... English
LeROY J. BOOTH, Ed.D. .... Education
DANIEL BROWER, Ph.D. .... Education
LEONARD BUCHNER, A.M. .... Education
EDGAR C. BYE, A.M. .... Coordinator, Bureau of Field Studies
PAUL C. CLIFFORD, A.M. .... Mathematics
ALDEN C. CODER, Ed.D. .... Driver Education
LAWRENCE H. CONRAD, A.M. .... English
MARGARET COTTER, A.M. .... Associate Director, National Science
Foundation Program: Mathematics
ANNE BANKS CRIDLEBAUGH, A.M. .... Librarian
EARL C. DAVIS, Ph.D. .... Education
JOSEPH W. DUFFY, Ed.D. .... Industrial Arts
CARYL DUNAVAN, A.M. .... Education
ARTHUR W. EARL, Ed.D. .... Acting Chairman, Department of Industrial Arts
STEVEN C. L. EARLEY, Ph.D. .... English
EMMA FANTONE, A.M. .... Coordinator, Audio-Visual Center
E. B. FINCHER, Ph.D. .... Social Studies
L. HOWARD FOX, A.M. .... Speech
PAUL E. FROEHLICH, Ed.D. .... Business Education
EDWIN S. FULCOMER, Ed.D. .... Chairman, Department of English
IRWIN H. GAWLEY, JR., Ed.D. .... Science
HAROLD A. GOUSS, A.M. .... Mathematics
HOWARD L. HAAS, Ed.D. .... Business Education
W. PAUL HAMILTON, A.M. .... English
EVA HUBSCHMAN, A.M. .... Speech
T. ROLAND HUMPHREYS, A.M. .... Mathematics
EMIL KAHN, A.M. .... Music
ELLEN KAUFFMAN, A.M. .... Speech
FRANK S. KELLAND, A.M. .... Geography
WALTER E. KOPS, A.M. .... Social Studies
STEPHEN W. KOWALSKI, A.M. .... Science
RUSSELL KRAUSS, Ph.D. .... English
EDITH G. H. LENEL, Ph.D. .... Catalog Librarian
RAYMOND C. LEWIN, M.A. .... Education
ORPHA M. LUTZ, Ph.D. .... Education
EVAN M. MALETSKY, A.M. .... Mathematics
CLYDE W. McELROY, Ed.D. .... Speech
ROBERT W. McLACHLAN, Ph.D. .... Science
CLAIRE M. MERLEHAN, A.M. .... Reference Librarian
BRUCE E. MESERVE, Ph.D. .... Chairman, Department of Mathematics
MAURICE P. MOFFATT, Ph.D. .... Chairman, Department of Social Studies
ALLAN MOREHEAD, Ed.D. .... Chairman, Department of Education
EARL K. PECKMAN, Ed.D. .... Education

5

JAMES P. PETTEGROVE, A.M. .... English
ANTHONY PETTOFREZZO, Ph.D. .... Mathematics
JOHN J. RELLAHAN, Ph.D. .... Chairman, Graduate Council: Social Studies
ELOISA RIVERA-RIVERA, Ph.D. .... Foreign Language
CHARITY EVA RUNDEN, Ph.D. .... Education
GEORGE E. SALT, A.M. .... Education
HAROLD M. SCHOLL, Ed.D. .... Acting Chairman, Department of Speech
NORMAN SCHAUMBERGER, A.M. .... Mathematics
JEROME SEIDMAN, Ph.D. .... Education
THADDEUS J. SHEFT, A.M. .... Associate Coordinator, Audio-Visual Center
HORACE T. SHEPPARD, A.M. .... Business Education
B. ERNEST SHORE, A.M. .... Foreign Language
KENNETH O. SMITH, Ph.D. .... Science
MAX A. SOBEL, Ph.D. ....Director, National Science Foundation Program:
Mathematics
HENRY SYER, Ph.D. .... Mathematics
LILLIAN SZKLARCZYK, A.M. .... Foreign Language
RICHARD W. TEWS, Ph.D. .... Director, Panzer School of Physical Education
and Hygiene
CHARLES E. TRESSLER, A.M. .... Industrial Arts
RALPH A. VERNACCHIA, A.M. .... Fine Arts
HAZEL WACKER, Ed.D. .... Physical Education
RALPH WALTER, Ed.D. .... Education
REINHOLD WALTER, Ed.D. .... Mathematics
FOSTER L. WYGANT, Ed.D. .... Fine Arts
FREDERICK H. YOUNG, Ph.D. .... English

6

SPECIAL FEATURES — TOURS
FIELD STUDIES — SOCIAL STUDIES DEPARTMENT

Social Studies — S460 — Central Eastern Region   August 15-29, 1960
                                                                          Mr. Bye
This fifteen-day tour of Pennsylvania, Maryland, Virginia, West Virginia, North Carolina, and Tennessee covers the major points of historic interest associated with the Colonial Period, the American Revolution, and the Civil War, and the geographic features of the coastal plain, the Piedmont, the Great Valley, and the Appalachian Mountains in these states. Travel is by modern chartered motor coach, and overnight stops are made at first-class hotels. Among the places visited are: Valley Forge, Philadelphia, Baltimore, Annapolis, Washington, Arlington, Alexandria, Mt. Vernon, Fredericksburg, Richmond, Washington's birthplace at Wakefield, Lee's plantation at Stratford, Yorktown, Williamsburg, Jamestown, Raleigh, Chattanooga, Asheville, Great Smoky Mountains, Norris Dam, Jefferson's Monticello at Charlottesville, Natural Bridge, Skyline Drive in the Shenandoah National Park, Luray Caverns, Winchester, Harper's Ferry, Frederick, Gettysburg, and the Pennsylvania Dutch area around Lancaster and Ephrata.
                              Credit: 3 semester hours
Cost: $175 includes tuition and all expenses except meals. (Subject to changes in tariffs and rates.)
Write to: Mr. Edgar Bye, Coordinator, Bureau of Field Studies.

Social Studies S485 — Maritime Provinces of Canada   July 6-26, 1960
                                                                          Mr. Bye
This is a twenty-one day field study course covering Nova Scotia, Cape Breton Island, New Brunswick, and the Gaspe. The route runs through Vermont and Quebec to the Gaspe. It covers Nova Scotia and Cape Breton Island thoroughly, including the spectacular Cabot Trail, and returns through Maine, New Hampshire, Massachusetts, and Connecticut. Among the places visited and topics studied are: Riviere du Loup; picturesque fishing villages along the river and Gulf of St. Lawrence; lumbering and pulp-wood operations; Gaspe; Perce with its bird sanctuary; Moncton, New Brunswick, with its tidal bore; St. John, New Brunswick, with its reversing falls; Truro; Digby; Grand Pre; Annapolis Royal; Lunenburg; Halifax; Sydney; Louisburg; Cape Breton Highlands National Park. The history of the conflicts between the French and the English for this territory, the varied geographical and scenic phenomena, and the customs and daily life of the French Canadian and English-speaking people of the region are observed.
                              Credit: 3 semester hours
Cost from New York, $395, includes tuition and all expenses except breakfasts and lunches. (Subject to changes in tariffs and rates.)
Write to: Mr. Edgar Bye, Coordinator, Bureau of Field Studies

Social Studies S487 — Field Studies in the Arts: European Civilization
                                                              July 9-August 26, 1960
                                                                         Mr. Kahn
This field study course gives an opportunity to study by direct observation the development of European culture from ancient Greco-Roman civilization to modern times. It deals with Byzantine, Romanesque, Gothic, Renaissance, Baroque, and Rococo architecture and art and changes in art forms to modern times. The spectacular rise of European music since the Renaissance forms an important part of this study. The close relationship between the arts and historical and social changes in European civilization is examined. Many of the greatest examples of European culture are examined, and some of the finest music is heard in original settings. (Richard Wagner Festival in Bayreuth; Netherlands, Edinburgh, and Salzburg Music Festivals; and various opera and concert performances.) Master works of art and architecture are viewed in Rome, London, Paris, Amsterdam, Cologne, Munich, Florence, Siena, Venice, Assisi, Milan, etc., also the chateaux of the Loire Valley and the Bavarian Royal Castles. In 1960, the Passion Play at Oberammergau is included.
                              Credit: 6 semester hours
Cost from New York, $1,385, includes tuition and all expenses except 12 lunches. (Subject to changes in tarriffs and rates.)
Write to: Mr. Emil Kahn, Bureau of Field Studies.

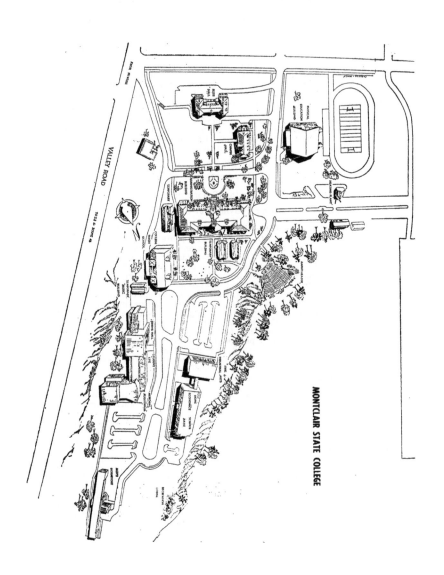

MONTCLAIR STATE COLLEGE

SPECIAL YOUTH ACTIVITIES

June 27-August 5

Reading Improvement Laboratory: Available to all New Jersey students in grades 7-12; small groups are formed according to age and achievement levels and meet daily 10:00 A.M. to 12:00 Noon. The latest in equipment, films, and workshop materials are used to demonstrate speed of comprehension, study skills, and vocabulary growth. Enrollment is limited. Apply at least three months in advance of each term.

Fee: $40.00   Write to: Coordinator, Reading Improvement Laboratory

Speech and Hearing Center: The Speech and Hearing Center will offer an intensive remedial speech program. It will accommodate a maximum of sixty children between 4 and 18 years of age. The program, offered 10:15 A.M. to 12:15 P.M. daily, is designed to provide therapy for children with the usual types of speech problems, as well as those who have major problems of voice, articulation, and rhythm (stuttering). Children with retarded language development or loss of language are also eligible.

Fee: $60.00   Write to: Coordinator, Speech and Hearing Center

Workshop for Apprentices in Dramatic Production: The Speech Department is pleased to announce a new summer program in theater for pre-college students. High school students and recent graduates between the ages of 16 and 19 years are eligible. Activities include the study of voice and diction, acting, scenery design and construction, lighting, and make-up. Following a 1:30 P.M. daily seminar, students will participate as actors and crew members in the preparation and presentation of at least two major dramatic productions. Full use will be made of the extensive facilities in the air-conditioned Memorial Auditorium — one of the most modern and beautiful college theaters in the East.

Registration is limited to 30 students. Applications must be made in advance and must be accompanied by a letter of recommendation from the applicant's high school Dramatics or English teacher. A personal interview will also be arranged.

Fee: $60.00   Write to: Coordinator, Summer Theater Programs

Montclair State College Day Camp: A general program of games, relays, story-telling, rhythms, nature walks, and crafts will be presented for children in the 6-12 year age range. The dates will coincide with those of the regular summer session, June 27 to August 5, and the time of day will be 8:30 A.M. to 12:30 P.M. The fee will include some arts and crafts supplies and light refreshments.

Fee: $8.00 per week   Write to: Director, Panzer School of Physical Education and Hygiene, c/o this College

Montclair State College Day Camp: Art for High School Students Program — This studio program emphasizes painting, with opportunities to work in related contemporary media as individual interests develop, such as collage, mosaic, and two-dimensional casting. An exhibit of student work will be organized at the end of the Summer Session.

Enrollment is limited to 20 students. Some materials will be supplied. Studio sessions meet Monday through Thursday, 10:00 A.M. to 12:00 Noon. Advance registration will take place on June 20, 9:00 A.M. to 12:00 Noon, in the Art Library, Finley Hall.

Fee $48.00   Write to: Coordinator, Youth Art Program

Montclair State College Day Camp: Arts and Crafts Activity Program — This is a planned program in art and craft activities for children in grades 5 through 8. Drawing, painting, ceramics, and enamelling on metal, are typical activities. The group will meet Monday through Thursday from 1:15 P.M. to 2:30 P.M. Materials are included in the fee.

Fee: $24.00   Write to: Coordinator, Youth Art Program

9

AIMS AND OBJECTIVES

The Summer School is designed specifically to meet the needs of:

1. Students enrolled in graduate programs who wish to meet requirements for the Master of Arts Degree.
2. Teachers-in-service who desire to complete degree requirements, to improve their professional standing, or to take courses for state certification purposes.
3. Graduates and upperclassmen from liberal arts colleges seeking provisional or limited certification to teach in the New Jersey public secondary schools.
4. Persons interested in pursuing college work, whether or not they desire credit.
5. Persons interested in special workshops, institutes, and seminars.

Montclair State College, a member of the American Association of Colleges of Teacher Education, is fully accredited by the Middle States Association of Colleges and Secondary Schools, and the American Association of University Women. Also fully accredited by the National Council for Accreditation of Teacher Education for the preparation of Elementary and Secondary School teachers and School Service Personnel, with the Master's Degree as the highest degree approved.

ADMISSION REGULATIONS

Students may enter in one of two categories: Students seeking a Master's Degree (degree candidates), or students not seeking a degree (auditors, certification students, and special students).

Degree Candidates — MATRICULATION FOR THE MASTER OF ARTS DEGREE

Persons Eligible — Teachers-in-service, as well as those interested in personal and professional growth who hold a bachelor's degree from an accredited college, have a high scholastic average and hold a N. J. Teacher's certificate.

Procedure

1. File an application with the Chairman of the Graduate Council and pay a $5.00 application for admission to Master's Degree Program fee (see "Tuition, Fees and Expenses" pages 13-14).

2. Have forwarded to the Graduate Office official transcripts of all previous college work. (Upon acceptance, a student will be furnished a definite statement of requirements, entitled a Work Program. The Work Program must be presented each time a student registers.)

3. Obtain approval of courses from the Chairman of your department prior to registration. (Advisors may be consulted during the hours of registration.)

Transfer of Credits — Not more than 8 semester-hours of work taken prior to matriculation are accepted for credit toward the A.M. degree. Transfer of graduate credit from other institutions — up to 8-semester hours — is allowed only to those students who are graduates of either a New Jersey State College or the State University.

Master's Thesis — Students writing a thesis must register for the course in thesis writing (Graduate A-500), which carries 4 semester-hours of credit.

Students who fail to complete the thesis in one calendar year must re-register for this course. For further information regarding the thesis, see the Graduate Bulletin

Basic Requirement — All students in the Graduate Division will be required to complete at least one full-time (6 s.h.) summer session or at least one regular semester.

Application for degree conferment — A candidate for degree must file with the Registrar an application for conferment of the degree before November 30 of the college year in which he expects to complete his work. Application blanks for this purpose may be secured in the Registrar's Office. The responsibility for making said application rests with the candidate.

Non-Degree Students

1. AUDITORS. Persons who desire to take courses for cultural, vocational, professional, or avocational purposes, but who do not wish college credit may register as auditors. All persons auditing a course must register, and the tuition fee for auditors is the same as for other students.

2. SPECIAL STUDENTS. (Non-matriculated students and students working beyond the Master's Degree or for advanced certificates.) Persons who wish to enroll in courses for the purpose of having credit transferred to another institution may be admitted by submitting to the Director of Summer Session an official letter from the Dean of the University or College in which they are earning the degree. This letter must contain a statement that the student is in good standing and should indicate the courses, or kind of courses, for which the student may register. The College reserves the right to decide whether or not the student has fulfilled necessary prerequisites.

3. CERTIFICATION STUDENTS. (Students seeking initial teaching certificates — emergency, provisional or limited.) Before registration will be accepted students should follow instructions listed under the heading, "Certification for Teaching" page 14.

STUDENT SNACK BAR PATIO

11

GENERAL INFORMATION

Location of Campus: Situated on the northern boundary of Upper Montclair, the College is approximately three miles north of the center of the town of Montclair and twelve miles west of New York City. The main entrance is at the intersection of Valley Road and Normal Avenue. Public transportation is available on the Greenwood Lake Division of the Erie Railroad and on Public Service bus routes. (Nos. 60 and 76 connect with the Lackawanna Railroad in the town of Montclair.) Other bus lines serve the campus from New York, Newark, the Oranges, and Paterson. The junction of Highways Nos. 46 and 3 is located about one mile north of the campus.

1. Housing. Three College dormitories (Russ, Chapin, and Stone Halls) will be available for the accommodation of men and women registrants during the Summer Session. Applications for room reservations should be submitted prior to June 1, 1960 to: Dean of Students, Montclair State College, Upper Montclair, New Jersey.

2. Rates. Room and board is $18.00 a week. This fee includes breakfast and dinner Monday through Friday and all three meals Saturday and Sunday. The College supplies and launders sheets, pillow case and bed pad. Students must supply their own blankets, spreads, towels, etc. The $18.00 fee, which must be paid on or before the first day of the summer session, is subject to change.

3. Meals. The Dining Hall will be open during the entire Summer Session.

LIBRARY FACILITIES. The main library, located in the Administration Building, will be open during the Summer Session to accommodate all students. All books, including the reference collection, are on open shelves.. Hours will be posted. Each student is entitled to one library card free of charge. New entrants may obtain their cards at the library loan desk upon presentation of a paid tuition receipt. Library cards issued at any time since September 1958 are still valid. All library cards should be retained and may be used during subsequent summer, fall, or spring sessions.

OFFICE OF THE SUMMER SESSION. Located at the eastern end of the Administration Building, it is open from 8:30-4:00 weekdays and 8:30-12:00 on July 9, 16 and 23.

Extra Curricular Activities

Recreational Facilities. The College gymnasium contains basketball, volleyball, squash, and badminton courts. Located on the campus are softball fields and recreation areas. Municipal golf courses are within commuting distance, as are public swimming pools.

ACADEMIC REGULATIONS AND PROCEDURES

STUDENT RESPONSIBILITY — The College expects those who are admitted to assume responsibility for knowing and meeting the various regulations and procedures set forth in the College catalog. The College reserves the right to terminate the enrollment of any student whose conduct, class attendance, or academic record should prove unsatisfactory.

CREDIT LOADS — Students may not register for more than eight (8) semester-hours in the Summer Session. Six (6) semester-hours, as a maximum, is strongly recommended.

CHANGE OF SCHEDULE — No student will be permitted to change his scheduled courses without approval of his advisor and the Director of the Summer Session. **The deadline for making changes is the last day of the late registration period** (June 29). To change from "auditor" to "credit", or vice-versa, a student must make formal application not later than the mid-point in the Summer Session. Forms are available in the Registrar's Office.

12

WITHDRAWAL FROM A COURSE — A written notice to the Director of the Summer Session is required. Refunds are computed from the date of receipt of such written notice. Students who do not submit a written notice will receive the mark of "F" in those courses which they cease to attend. Students who withdraw after the mid-point in the Summer Session will receive an automatic grade of "F".

GRADES — Only students enrolled for credit receive grades. The following final grades may be received:

A — Excellent   B — Good   C — Fair   D — Poor   F — Failure

Inc. — Incomplete   WP — Withdrawn, Passing   N.C. — No Credit

WF — Withdrawn, Failing

The mark "D" is not accepted for master's degree credit at Montclair State College. The mark "WP" is given to those who submit, in writing, their intention of withdrawing from a course before the mid-point in a summer session and are doing passing work in the course involved. "WF" is assigned to students who withdraw before the mid-point and are doing failing work at the time of withdrawal. The mark "F" signifies (1) failure (2) the student has failed to submit written notice of his withdrawal (3) has requested withdrawal after the mid-point in the summer session. The mark "Inc" is given to a student who, because of illness, is unable to complete his work at the end of a summer session. He will be notified when the work is due; if said work is not finished on the prescribed date, a final grade of "F" is recorded.

An official record showing credits and grades earned will be mailed to the student three weeks following the close of the summer session.

REGISTRATION

All students who wish to enroll in the Summer Session must register in person on Monday, June 27. Procedures for registration will be posted on a bulletin board in the center hall of the Administration Building. No student may register for credit after June 29. A student has completed his registration when:

1. His program has been approved by the Chairman of his Department.
2. His registration forms have been properly and completely filled out.
3. His fees have been paid.
4. He receives his class cards.

Students registering on June 28 and June 29 will be charged a late registration fee of $5.00. Matriculated students should bring their Work Programs to the place of registration.

The College reserves the right to close any course for which the enrollment is insufficient. Students may then register in another course. If prerequisites are required (See course description), the student must be sure he has fulfilled them or their equivalent.

A student from another college should bring with him a letter from his Dean showing the courses which he has been advised to take and which will be accepted for credit. The numbering of courses at Montclair is as follows: 100-399 inclusive, undergraduate courses; 400-499 inclusive, senior class and graduate courses; 500 and above, graduate courses.

TUITION, FEES AND EXPENSES

All checks should be made out to Montclair State College.

TUITION. For residents of New Jersey, $13.00 per semester-hour credit; for out-of-state residents, $15.00 per credit.

SERVICE CHARGE. For all students, fifty cents (50¢) per semester-hour credit.

REGISTRATION FEE. For all students, $2.00: to be paid each time a student registers.

LATE REGISTRATION FEE. For all students, $5.00. This additional fee will be charged students registering on June 28 and June 29.

APPLICATION FOR ADMISSION FEE. $5.00 to be paid whenever student files application for Matriculation for the Master's Degree. Fee must accompany the application form and is not refundable.

LABORATORY AND STUDIO FEES. Certain course fees may be announced at the first meeting of the classes.

TRANSCRIPT FEE. $1.00 for single copy. (Special rates for multiple copies; inquire at Registrar's Office).

REFUNDING OF FEES. When the Director of the Summer Session receives written notice of withdrawal prior to the first meeting of the course, all fees are refunded in full. Other refunds are prorated from the day on which the Director of the Summer Session receives written notification. Withdrawal before the end of the first third of the Summer Session — 60% refund; during the middle third — 30%; during the last third — no refund. Withdrawals after the mid-point in the Summer Session, July 18, will result in an automatic grade of F.

WORK SCHOLARSHIP. Tuition and dormitory fee scholarships are available. Students are assigned work in the various college departments. Write to Dean of Students for information.

CERTIFICATION FOR TEACHING

Certificates to teach in New Jersey Public Schools are issued by: State Board of Examiners, Department of Education, 175 West State Street, Trenton 25, New Jersey. Address all inquiries regarding requirements and have your college send an official transcript of all previous work to the above.

ENROLLING AT MONTCLAIR. At registration bring reply received from the State Board of Examiners and transcripts of all previous academic work. All general questions regarding certification and student-teaching should be addressed to the Certification Advisor at this college.

COURSE OFFERINGS. The following **Professional Education** courses are approved by the State Board of Examiners for certification to teach in New Jersey Secondary Schools. Courses should be selected from the following:

Education	S201	Human Development and Behavior I
Education	S202	Human Development and Behavior II
Education	S303	The Teacher in School and Community
Education	S304	Principles and Techniques of Secondary Education
Education	S401	The Development of Educational Thought
Education	S406	Educational Sociology
Education	S407A	Television in Education Workshop: Programming and Production
Education	S410	Teaching Materials Workshop
Education	S500B	Advanced Educational Psychology
Health Education	S411	School Health Services
Science	S401X	The Teaching of Science in Secondary Schools
English	S401X	The Teaching of English in Secondary Schools
Social Studies	S401X	The Teaching of Social Studies in Secondary Schools
Mathematics	S401X	The Teaching of Mathematics in Secondary Schools
Fine Arts	S401	Art Curriculum of Elementary and Secondary Schools

Supervised Student Teaching. Students desiring information concerning this requirement should ask for written instructions from the Director of Student Teaching.

SERVICES

ACADEMIC ADVISORS. Appointments with the Dean of the College, the Chairman of the Graduate Council, the Director of the Summer Session, or a Department Chairman, may be made by mail or telephone. Appointments should be made as early as possible prior to the date of registration.

BOOKSTORE. Located adjacent to the main lobby of the Student Life Building, this on-campus facility will be open from 8:00 A.M. to Noon daily. A limited number of books for each course will be available. Textbook orders should be placed immediately upon completion of registration.

HEALTH SERVICE. A full-time registered nurse is on duty in the medical offices located in Russ Hall. Emergency medical care is available.

INFORMATION OFFICE. An office is maintained at the College switchboard in the center hall of the Administration Building where information may be obtained regarding the location of various College personnel and services. The telephone number of the College is PIlgrim 6-9500.

VETERANS' COUNSELOR. Veterans seeking admission to the Summer Session should apply well in advance of the registration date (June 27) to the Veterans' Counselor. The veteran should apply for a certificate of eligibility and entitlement at the nearest regional office of the Veterans Administration. In requesting this certificate, the veteran is advised to indicate clearly his educational objective. The Veterans Administration has established certain limitations, especially with regard to change of course. In order that a veteran may be assured that his certificate is in order and that he has taken the proper steps to expedite his training under the G.I. Bill, veterans enrolling for the first time at this College should report upon arrival to the Veterans' Counselor. His office is located adjacent to the center hall in the Administration Building.

AUDIO-VISUAL CENTER. This Center provides audio-visual materials, equipment, and services for use by faculty and students for classroom instruction and presentation. The staff of the Center is available for special consultation on audio-visual problems, for demonstrations of audio-visual materials and methods, and for special teaching and training in the area of audio-visual education. The Center handles the scheduling of all films for the College, as well as their ordering, mailing, and rentals. Student assistants are provided whenever

TEXTBOOK EXHIBIT. On July 14 and 15 from 8:00 A.M. to 3:00 P.M. there will be an exhibit of high school and elementary school textbooks. The exhibit is primarily for teachers and administrators attending the Summer Session, but will be open to undergraduate students and the general public. The location of the exhibit will be announced during the Summer Session.

MONTCLAIR STATE COLLEGE
COURSES OF THE SUMMER SESSION

Descriptions of the courses will be found in the 1959-61 Graduate Bulletin of the College. Courses numbered 500 and above are graduate courses; those numbered 400-499, inclusive, are senior-graduate courses and their descriptions in the Graduate Bulletin follow the descriptions of the graduate courses. Courses below the 400 number will be found in the Undergraduate Bulletin of the College. Only entirely new courses are described in the Summer Session Bulletin.

All rooms listed are in the Administration Building unless specified otherwise.

*Courses listed with this mark (*) indicate that they may not be used for graduate credit. These are teacher-certification or prerequisite courses.

BUSINESS EDUCATION DEPARTMENT

EVENING COURSES

* Business Education S201 — Accounting I
6:15-7:30 P.M.   Credit: 3 semester hours
Dr. Froehlich
Room 2, Annex 2

* Business Education S305 — Business Law I
7:45-9:00 P.M.   Credit: 3 semester hours
Dr. Haas
Room 1, Annex 2

Business Education S408 — Business Finance
6:15-7:30 P.M.   Credit: 3 semester hours
Dr. Haas
Room 1, Annex 2

Business Education S410 — Advanced Accounting
7:45-9:00 P.M.   Credit: 3 semester hours
Dr. Froehlich
Room 2, Annex 2
Prerequisite: Business Education 201, 202, 301 and 302

DAYTIME COURSES

Business Education S503 — The Business Education Curriculum
Mr. Sheppard
9:30-10:20 A.M.   Credit: 2 semester hours   Room 1, Annex 2

Business Education S532 — Field Studies and Audio-Visual Aids
in Business Education   Mr. Sheppard
10:30-12:20   Credit: 4 semester hours   Room 1, Annex 2

EDUCATION DEPARTMENT

* Education S201 — Human Development and Behavior, Part I   Dr. Brower
10:00-11:20 A.M. Section I   Credit: 3 semester hours   Room 2, Annex 1
11:30-12:50 P.M. Section II   Credit: 3 semester hours   Room 2, Annex 1

* Education S202 — Human Development and Behavior, Part II   Dr. Lutz
10:00-11:20 A.M. Section I   Credit: 3 semester hours   Room 30
11:30-12:50 P.M. Section II   Credit: 3 semester hours   Room 30
Prerequisite: Education 200A, Educaton 201, or equivalent

* Education S303 — The Teacher in School and Community   Dr. Morehead
8:30-9:50 A.M. Section I   Credit: 3 semester hours   Room 10
10:00-11:20 A.M. Section II   Credit: 3 semester hours   Dr. Seidman
Room 1, Annex 1

* Education S304 — Principles and Techniques of Secondary
Education   Dr. Seidman
8:30-9:50 A.M. Section I   Credit: 3 semester hours   Room 1, Annex 1
11:30-12:50 P.M. Section II   Credit: 3 semester hours   Dr. Runden
Room 5, Annex 1

* Education S401 — The Development of Educational Thought
8:30-9:50 A.M. Section I   Credit: 3 semester hours   Mr. Kops
Room 30
10:00-11:20 A.M. Section II   Credit: 3 semester hours   Mr. Lewin
Room 10
11:30-12:50 P.M. Section III   Credit: 3 semester hours   Mr. Lewin
Room 10

17

Education S406 — Educational Sociology — Dr. Peckham
11:30-12:20 P.M.   Credit: 2 semester hours   Room3
     Prerequisite: General Sociology or equivalent

Education S407A — Television in Education Workshop: Programming
     and Production   **Mr. Sheft**
10:30-11:20 A.M.   Credit: 2 semester hours   Audio-Vis. Aids. Lab.

Education S410 — Teaching Materials Workshop   **Mr. Dunavan**
8:30-9:20 A.M.   Credit: 2 semester hours   Audio-Vis. Aids Lab.

Education S440 — Camping and Outdoor Education   **Dr. Wacker**
10:30-11:20 A.M.   Credit: 2 semester hours   Room A

Education S500A — Basic Educational Trends   **Dr. Walter**
11:30-12:20 P.M.   Credit: 2 semester hours   Room 3, Annex 2
     Prerequisite: Teaching Experience

Education S500B — Advanced Educational Psychology   **Dr. Booth**
11:30-12:20 P.M.   Credit: 2 semester hours   Room 3, Annex 1
     Prerequisite: An introductory course in psychology

Education S500C — Recent Trends in Secondary School Methods   **Mr. Salt**
8:30-9:20 A.M.   Credit: 2 semester hours   Room 25
     Prerequisite: Teaching Experience

Education S500D — School Administration I: Functions and
     Organization   **Dr. Peckham**
8:30-9:20 A.M.   Credit: 2 semester hours   Room 22
     Prerequisite: Teaching Experience

Education S500F — School Administration III: Community
     Relations   **Dr. Atkinson**
9:30-10:20 A.M.   Credit: 2 semester hours   Room 2, Annex 2
     Prerequisite: Teaching Experience

Education S502 — Organization and Administration of the
     Modern High School   **Dr. Peckham**
9:30-10:20 A.M.   Credit: 2 semester hours   Room 3
     Prerequisite: Education 500D or equivalent or Teaching Experience

Education S503 — Methods and Instruments of Research   **Dr. Walter**
9:30-10:20 A.M. Section I   Credit: 2 semester hours   Room 3, Annex 2
11:30-12:20 P.M. Section III   Credit: 2 semester hours   Room 3, Annex 2
10:30-11:20 A.M. Section II   Credit: 2 semester hours   **Mr. Kops**
     Prerequisite: Mathematics 400 or equivalent as   Room 9
                 determined by Chairman of Graduate Council

Education S504B — Seminar in Curriculum Organization   **Mr. Salt**
10:30-11:20 A.M.   Credit: 2 semester hours   Room 25
     Prerequisite: Education 504A, Education 548, or Education 553

Education S505 — Organization and Administration of
     Extra-Curricular Activities   **Mr. Salt**
11:30-12:20 P.M.   Credit: 2 semester hours   Room 25

Education S506 — School Law   **Dr. Morehead**
10:30-11:20 A.M.   Credit: 2 semester hours   Room 9

Education S508 — Supervision of Instruction in
     Secondary Schools   **Dr. Atkinson**
11:30-12:20 P.M.   Credit: 2 semester hours   Room 2, Annex 2
     Prerequisite: Teaching Experience

Education S521B — Psychological Tests in Guidance Programs   Dr. Booth
10:30-11:20 A.M.   Credit: 2 semester hours   Room 3, Annex 1
    Prerequisite: Education 521A

Education S530A — Corrective and Remedial Reading in
   Secondary Schools   Mr. Buchner
11:30-12:20 P.M.   Credit: 2 semester hours   Room 26

Education S537 — Social-Moral Guidance   Dr. Davis
8:30-9:20 A.M.   Credit: 2 semester hours   Room 4, Annex 1

Education S538 — Group Guidance and Counseling Activities   Dr. Runden
9:30-10:20 A.M.   Credit: 2 semester hours   Room 4, Annex 1

Education S540 — Recreational and Activity Leadership   Dr. Tews
8:30-9:20 A.M.   Credit: 2 semester hours   Room A

Education S550 — Child and Adolescent Development   Dr. Booth
8:30-9:20 A.M.   Credit: 2 semester hours   Room 3, Annex 1
    Prerequisite: Child Development and Psychology Courses

Education S551 — Principles and Techniques of Guidance   Dr. Atkinson
8:30-9:20 A.M.   Credit: 2 semester hours   Room 2, Annex 2
    Note: This course is prerequisite to most guidance courses offered
       in this Division of the College

Education S556 — Improvement of Reading in the
   Secondary School   Mr. Buchner
8:30-9:20 A.M.   Credit: 2 semester hours   Room 26

Education S602 — Seminar in Guidance   Dr. Davis
10:30-12:20 P.M.   Credit: 4 semester hours   Room 4, Annex 1
    Prerequisite: Education 551 and at least one other guidance course.

ENGLISH DEPARTMENT

English S100C — Fundamentals of Writing   Dr. Fulcomer
8:30-9:50 A.M.   Credit: 3 semester hours   Room 1

English S100G — Western World Literature   Dr. Earley
10:00-11:20 A.M.   Credit: 3 semester hours   Room 5, Annex 1

English S201A — American Literature I   Mr. Conrad
10:00-11:20 A.M.   Credit: 3 semester hours   Room 1

English S401X — The Teaching of English in Secondary
   Schools   Mr. Hamilton
8:30-9:20 A.M.   Credit: 2 semester hours   Room 3

English S451 — Literature and Art in Western Culture   Dr. Young
11:30-12:20 P.M.   Credit: 2 semester hours   Room 1

English S502 — Victorian Poetry   Mr. Pettegrove
11:30-12:20 P.M.   Credit: 2 semester hours   Room 2

English S503 — Geoffrey Chaucer and His Times   Dr. Krauss
9:30-10:20 A.M.   Credit: 2 semester hours   Room 2

English S511 — The History of Literary Criticism   Dr. Krauss
10:30-11:20 A.M.   Credit: 2 semester hours   Room 2

English S512 — The Growth and Structure of the English
    Language   Mr. Pettegrove
8:30-9:20 A.M.   Credit: 2 semester hours   Room 2

English S544A — Shakespeare (Tragedies)   Mr. Hamilton
10:30-11:20 A.M.   Credit: 2 semester hours   Room 3

FINE ARTS DEPARTMENT

Fine Arts S401 — Art Curriculum of Elementary and
    Secondary Schools   Dr. Wygant
8:30-9:20 A.M.   Credit: 2 semester hours   Room 221, Finley

Fine Arts S403A or S403B — Print Making I or II   Mr. Vernacchia
10:30-11:20 A.M.   Credit: 2 semester hours each   Room 219, Finley

Fine Arts S406A or S406B — Art Workshop I or II   Mr. Vernacchia
11:30-12:20 P.M.   Credit: 2 semester hours each   Room 219, Finley

Fine Arts S500X — Contemporary Art   Mr. Vernacchia
9:30-10:20 A.M.   Credit: 2 semester hours   Room 219, Finley

FOREIGN LANGUAGE DEPARTMENT

French S406 — Contemporary French Novel   Mrs. Szklarczyk
9:30-10:20 A.M.   Credit: 2 semester hours   Room 9

Language S300 — Foundations of Language   Mr. Shore
8:30-9:20 A.M.   Credit: 2 semester hours   Room 29

Language S402 — Phonetics: Spanish   Dr. Rivera-Rivera
10:30-11:20 A.M.   Credit: 2 semester hours   Room 29
    Prerequisite: Three years of college level Spanish,
          interview with professor

Language S408 — Introduction to Language Laboratory   Miss Fantone
8:30-9:20 A.M.   Credit: 2 semester hours   Language Lab.

Spanish S415 — Projects in Spanish and Latin American Folklore
                                    Dr. Rivera-Rivera
9:30-10:20 A.M.   Credit: 2 semester hours   Room 29
    Prerequisite: Three years of college level Spanish

GEOGRAPHY DEPARTMENT

Geography S414A — Advanced Economic Geography   Mr. Kelland
8:30-9:20 A.M.   Credit: 2 semester hours   Room 4, Annex D

Geography S418 — Regional Geography of North America   Mr. Kelland
11:30-12:20 P.M.   Credit: 2 semester hours   Room 4, Annex D

Geography S419X — Geography of the Soviet Union   Mr. Kelland
9:30-10:20 A.M.   Credit: 2 semester hours   Room 4, Annex D

INDUSTRIAL ARTS DEPARTMENT

Industrial Arts S201A or S201B or 301A — Wood and
    Crafts I or II or III   Mr. Tressler
12:00 Noon-3:40 P.M.   Credit: 4 semester hours each   General Shop, Finley

Industrial Arts S503 — Problems in Teaching Industrial Arts   Dr. Duffy
10:00-11:20 A.M.   Credit: 3 semester hours   Seminar Room, Finley

Industrial Arts S511 — Supervision of Industrial Arts   Dr. Earl
8:30-9:50 A.M.   Credit: 3 semester hours   Seminar Room, Finley

MATHEMATICS DEPARTMENT

Mathematics S300 — The Social Uses of Mathematics   Mr. Humphreys
10:30-11:20 A.M.   Credit: 2 semester hours   Room 114, Finley

Mathematics S400 — Educational Statistics   Mr. Humphreys
9:30-10:20 A.M. Section I   Credit: 2 semester hours   Room 114, Finley
11:30-12:20 P.M. Section II   Room 114, Finley

Mathematics S401X — The Teaching of Mathematics in
     Secondary Schools   Mr. Gouss
8:30-9:20 A.M.   Credit: 2 semester hours   Room 114, Finley

Mathematics S406 — Solid Analytic Geometry   Dr. Pettofrezzo
8:30-9:20 A.M.   Credit: 2 semester hours   Room 106, Finley

Mathematics S409 — Introduction to Contemporary
     Mathematics   Dr. Sobel
8:30-9:20 A.M.   Credit: 2 semester hours   Room 104, Finley

Mathematics S501 — Administration and Supervision of
     Mathematics   Mr. Gouss
11:30-12:20 P.M.   Credit: 2 semester hours   Room 104, Finley

Mathematics S503 — Foundations of Algebra   Dr. Pettofrezzo
9:30-10:20 A.M.   Credit: 2 semester hours   Room 106, Finley

Mathematics S512 — Numerical Analysis   Dr. Pettofrezzo
10:30-11:20 A.M.   Credit: 2 semester hours   Room 106, Finley

Mathematics S522 — Introduction to Probability and
     Statistics   Mr. Gouss
9:30-10:20 A.M.   Credit: 2 semester hours   Room 104, Finley

Mathematics S525 — Curriculum and Teaching of Junior High
     School Mathematics   Mr. Maletsky
10:30-11:20 A.M.   Credit: 2 semester hours   Room 104, Finley

FINLEY HALL

The following courses are open only to National Science Foundation participants. Students were selected in March 1960, and registrations are closed. These courses are listed for record purposes only.

- **Mathematics S302X — Higher Algebra**   **Dr. Reinhold Walter**
  10:30-12:00 Noon   Credit: 2 semester hours   Room 105, Finley

  Mathematics S453 — Differential Calculus   **Mr. Maletsky**
  8:30-10:00 A.M.   Credit: 3 semester hours   Room 107, Finley
  Prerequisites: At least one year each of college mathematics, college physics, and college chemistry, or permission of the instructor.

  Mathematics S480 — Elements of Logic   **Mr. Schaumberger**
  11:00-12:00 Noon   Credit: 2 semester hours   Room 105, Finley

  Mathematics S535 — Professionalized Subject Matter:
  Algebra   **Dr. Meserve**
  8:30-10:30 A.M.   Credit: 2 semester hours   Room 105, Finley
  First three weeks — June 27 through July 16

  Mathematics S536 — Professionalized Subject Matter:
  Analysis   **Mr. Clifford**
  8:30-10:30 A.M.   Credit: 2 semester hours   Room 105, Finley
  Last three weeks — July 18 through August 5

  Mathematics S603A and S603B — Workshop on Junior High
  School Mathematics I and II   **Dr. Syer**
  8:30-10:30 A.M.   Credit: 2 semester hours each   Room 108, Finley

  Mathematics S603C — Workshop on Junior High School
  Mathematics III   **Dr. Sobel**
  11:00-12:00 Noon   Credit: 2 semester hours   Room 108, Finley

The above courses: S603A, S603B, and S603C will provide the necessary mathematical backgrounds to understand and interpret current curriculum recommendations in the junior high school. Areas to be covered include: structure of the number system, probability, foundations of algebra and foundations of geometry — each oriented for junior high school teachers. Current curriculum recommendations will be examined.

PANZER SCHOOL OF PHYSICAL EDUCATION AND HYGIENE

Health Education S408 — Driver Education   **Dr. Coder**
          Credit: 3 semester hours   Room A
Prerequisite: Approval by Instructor prior to registration.
          For details: write to Dr. Coder — see page 26.

Health Education S411 — School Health Services   **Dr. Tews**
9:30-10:20 A.M.   Credit: 2 semester hours   Room A

Health Education S412 — Alcohol Education Workshop   **Dr. Tews**
          Credit: 2 semester hours   Room 1
Pre-Summer Session — June 23 through July 7
          See page 26 for details

Education S440 — Camping and Outdoor Education   **Dr. Wacker**
10:30-11:20 A.M.   Credit: 2 semester hours   Room A

Education S540 — Recreational and Activity Leadership   **Dr. Tews**
8:30-9:20 A.M.   Credit: 2 semester hours   Room A

SCIENCE DEPARTMENT

Chemistry S101 — General College Chemistry   Mr. Kowalski
10:30-11:20 A.M.   Credit: 4 semester hours   Room 204, Finley
1:00-4:45 P.M. laboratory on Monday, Wednesday and Friday

Chemistry S408A — Industrial Chemistry, Part I   Dr. Gawley
11:30-12:20 P.M. and afternoons (Meets only on Tuesday
    and Thursday)   Room 204, Finley
              Credit: 2 semester hours
    Prerequisite: General and organic chemistry, or special permission of
       the instructor

Chemistry S412 — Physical Chemistry, Part II   Dr. McLachlan
10:30-11:20 A.M.   Credit: 4 semester hours   Room 206, Finley
1:00-4:45 P.M. laboratory on Monday, Wednesday and Friday
    Prerequisite: General college chemistry and analytical chemistry and
       general college physics

Physics S406A — Astronomy, Part I   Dr. Allen
10:30-11:20 A.M.   Credit: 2 semester hours   Room 207, Finley
    Prerequisite: General college physics and chemistry

Physics S411A — Photography, Part I   Dr. Smith
11:30-12:20 P.M.   Credit: 2 semester hours   Room 201, Finley
1:00-3:00 P.M. laboratory on Monday, Wednesday and Friday
    Prerequisite: General physics and general chemistry, or special
       permisson of the instructor

Physics S513 — Nuclear Radiation   Dr. Smith
8:30-9:20 A.M.   Credit: 2 semester hours   Room 201, Finley
    Prerequisite: General college physics, general college chemistry and a
       course in electrical measurements

Science S401X — The Teaching of Science in Secondary
    Schools   Dr. Gawley
8:30-9:20 A.M.   Credit: 2 semester hours   Room 204, Finley

Science S409 — Senior High School Physical Science
    Demonstrations   Dr. Smith and Dr. Gawley
9:30-10:20 A.M.   Credit: 2 semester hours   Room 201, Finley

Science S418 — Three Centuries of Science Progress   Dr. Allen
9:30-10:20 A.M.   Credit: 2 semester hours   Room 207, Finley

Science S422 — Consumer Science   Mr. Kowalski
11:30-12:20 P.M. (Meets only on Tuesday, Thursday and Saturday)
           Credit: 2 semester hours   Room 207, Finley
1:00-3:00 P.M. laboratory: Tuesday, Thursday and Saturday

The purpose and organization of this course is to acquaint the consumer with the aspects of science in everyday life. Basic scientific principles are developed in the process of testing and evaluating consumer products. Field trips are taken to local industries and public utilities to evaluate processes as well as products. A laboratory testing program deals with such commercial products as household appliances to foodstuffs and fertilizers. A testing and instruction program is also developed with a local industry. This course is designed as a general education elective for non-science majors and minors.

SOCIAL STUDIES DEPARTMENT

* Social Studies S100A — The Development of World Civilization
                                                    (to be announced)
10:00-11:20 A.M.   Credit: 3 semester hours   Room 21

* Social Studies S200A — Contemporary American Life
                                                    (to be announced)
8:30-9:50 A.M.   Credit: 3 semester hours   Room 21

* Social Studies S401X — The Teaching of Social Studies in
      Secondary Schools   Dr. Moffatt and Dr. Fincher
  8:30-9:20 A.M.   Credit: 2 semester hours   Room 20

Social Studies S408 — History of New Jersey   Dr. Moffatt
9:30-11:20 A.M.   Credit: 2 semester hours   Room 20
   (First three weeks— June 27 through July 16)

Social Studies S435B — The Americas: A Contemporary Political,
    Economic, and Cultural Survey, Part II   Dr. Fincher
9:30-11:20 A.M.   Credit: 2 semester hours   Room 20
   (Last three weeks — July 18 through August 5)

Social Studies S456 — International Economic Relations   Dr. Rellahan
8:30-9:20 A.M.   Credit: 2 semester hours   Room 9

Social Studies S460 — Central Eastern Region   Mr. Bye
   August 15-29   Credit: 3 semester hours
For details, write to Mr. Edgar Bye — See "Special Features" on page 7.

Social Studies S485 — Maritime Provinces of Canada   Mr. Bye
   July 6-26   Credit: 3 semester hours
For details, write to Mr. Edgar.Bye — See "Special Features" on page 7.

Social Studies S487 — Field Studies in the Arts: European
    Civilization   Mr. Kahn
   July 9 — August 26   Credit: 6 semester hours
For details, write to Mr. Emil Kahn — See "Special Features" on page 7.

SPEECH DEPARTMENT

* Speech S100D — Fundamentals of Speech   Dr. McElroy
11:30-12:50 P.M.   Credit: 3 semester hours   Room 20

Speech S437 — Dramatic Production Workshop   Dr. McElroy
1:30-4:00 P.M.   Credit: 4 semester hours   Room 2
   60 hours of practicum to be arranged   Memorial Auditorium

Speech S439 — Workshop in Speech Correction
Credit: 3 to 8 semester hours

This course is especially designed for students who wish to fulfill certification requirements to teach children with speech disorders or for graduate students needing to fulfill prerequisites for matriculation for the Master's degree in Speech. Four areas in the Speech sciences are offered on a workshop basis requiring attendance during all or part of the six-week summer session, depending upon the number of units elected.

Speech S439A, Part I — Phonetics   Mrs. Hubschman
8:30-10:20 A.M.   Credit: 2 semester hours   Room 1
First three weeks — June 27 through July 16   Memorial Auditorium

An intensive study is made of the manner and place of articulation of sounds heard in American English. Skill is developed in using the International Phonetic Alphabet to transcribe speech both prescriptively and descriptively, from live and recorded voices. Consideration is also given to the intonation and stress patterns of spoken English.

Speech S439B, Part II — Anatomy and Physiology of the Auditory and
Vocal Mechanisms   Miss Kauffman
8:30-10:20 A.M.   Credit: 2 semester hours   Room 1
Last three weeks — July 18 through August 5   Memorial Auditorium

The work of this course entails a detailed study of the larynx and ear as they function in the production and reception of speech. Consideration is also given to the physics of sound and to the structure and functioning of the nervous system.

Speech S439C, Part III — Speech Pathology   Miss Kauffman
1:30-2:50 P.M.   Credit: 3 semester hours   Room 1
Memorial Auditorium
The purpose of this course is to present a comprehensive analysis of the major pathologies of articulation, voice, rhythm, and symbolization. The etiology and treatment of severe stuttering, aphasia, cerebral palsy, and the dysphonias are discussed.

Speech S439D, Part IV — Practicum in Speech Correction   Dr. Scholl
10:15-12:15 P.M.   Credit: 1 semester hour   Room 4
Memorial Auditorium

Speech S439E, Part V — Advanced Practicum in Speech
Correction   Dr. Scholl
10:15-12:15 P.M.   Credit: 1 semester hour   Room 4
Memorial Auditorium

Students are required to spend forty-five clock hours in the Speech and Hearing Center for each semester-hour of credit in order to gain experience in planning and carrying out programs in therapy with children who have speech and hearing problems. Written observation reports, lesson plans, and progress reports are required. Students also participate in staff conferences and meetings with parents of children enrolled for speech therapy. Practicum hours may also be arranged at local speech centers and hospital units.

Speech S535 — Seminar in Speech and Language
Rehabilitation and Practicum   Dr. Scholl
8:30-9:50 A.M.   Credit: 6 semester hours   Room 4
10:15-12:15 P.M. (Practicum)   Memorial Auditorium

Speech S567 — Seminar in Dramatic Production   Mr. Fox
12:30-4:30 P.M.   Credit: 6 semester hours   Room 4
(60 hours of Practicum to be arranged)   Memorial Auditorium

DRIVER EDUCATION COURSES

PRE-SUMMER SESSION COURSE

Health Education S408 — Driver Education   Dr. Coder
June 15-16-17 — 7:00 P.M.-10:00 P.M. and   Room A
June 20 through June 25 — 9:00 A.M.-4:00 P.M. and
June 27 through July 1 — 1:00 P.M.-4:00 P.M.
Credit: 3 semester hours

POST-SUMMER SESSION COURSE

Health Education S408 — Driver Education   Dr. Coder
August 3-4-5 — 1:00 P.M.-4:30 P.M. and   Room A
August 8 through August 12 — 9:00 A.M.-3:00 P.M. and
August 15 through August 19 — 9:00 A.M.-3:00 P.M.
Credit: 3 semester hours

Authorization to Teach Behind-the-Wheel Driver Education and Driver Training:
A teacher must have his or her certificate endorsed by the Division of Teacher
Certification, State Department of Education. The requirements for such endorsement are: ("Rules Concerning Teachers' Certificates" — 18th edition — revised
1956)

1. A valid New Jersey teacher's certificate.
   A current New Jersey driver's license.
   Three years of automobile driving experience.
2.
4: Evidence of satisfactory completion of a course in driver education and
   driver training approved by the Commissioner of Education.
5. A good driving record.

Secondary schools in New Jersey are increasing their offerings in Driver Education. This increase has resulted in a demand for more Driver Education teachers.
To meet this demand, Montclair State College is increasing the number of courses
being conducted in this field. Assistance is given by the New Jersey State Safety
Council, the New Jersey Automobile Club, the American Automobile Association,
the New Jersey State Police, and the New Jersey Department of Motor Vehicles.

EXTRA CHARGES are made for textbooks and other materials. Some materials
are furnished free.

Registration for these courses is limited. Students must be approved by Dr.
Alden Coder prior to registration. Write to Dr. Coder for complete information.
Fees are to be paid on first day class meets.

ALCOHOL EDUCATION WORKSHOP
June 23 through July 7

Health Education S412 — Alcohol Education Workshop   Dr. Tews
June 23 and June 24 — 7:00-10:00 P.M.   Room 1
June 27 through July 7 — 1:30-4:30 P.M.
Credit: 2 semester hours

    A workshop offered with the cooperation of the State Department of Health
and aimed at preparing teachers of health, school nurse teachers, guidance personnel, and others, for more understanding service in this special area of education. The workshop will concentrate on a careful study of the physiological,
sociological, and psychological problems involved in the use of beverage alcohol
and on the materials, techniques, etc., found to be most useful in alcohol
education programs.

    A limited number of Tuition Scholorships are available. For full details
regarding this workshop, write to: Director, Field Services.

NEW JERSEY STATE SCHOOL OF CONSERVATION
BRANCHVILLE, NEW JERSEY

The six State Colleges, the State Department of Education, and the State Department of Conservation and Economic Development, jointly operate the New Jersey State School of Conservation at Lake Wapalanne in Stokes State Forest, Sussex County. Credit for the courses given at the New Jersey State School of Conservation may be applied toward the Bachelor's or Master's degrees at the New Jersey State Colleges, subject to approval in advance by the institution concerned. Students are advised to check with their advisors relative to the application of these credits toward degrees.

Courses in Camping, Conservation, Education, Field Biology, Field Science, Fine Arts, Geography, Industrial Arts, and Outdoor Education, are offered at the New Jersey State School of Conservation. Special descriptive announcements may also be had by writing to the New Jersey State School of Conservation, Branchville, New Jersey.

STUDENT LIFE BUILDING

27

BULLETIN OF

ℝ

SUMMER
SESSION

JUNE 22 TO AUGUST 4

UPPER MONTCLAIR, NEW JERSEY

SUMMER SESSION

MONTCLAIR STATE COLLEGE

UPPER MONTCLAIR, NEW JERSEY

1961

JUNE 22 to AUGUST 4

Volume 53   Number 4

FINLEY HALL — CLASSROOM BUILDING

une 22	Registration	See page 11 for complete registration information and priority schedule
une 23	Registration	
une 26	Classes begin	Late registration period
une 27	End of late registration period No registrations accepted after 3:00 P. M.	
uly 3	Recess - no classes	
uly 4	No classes	
uly 8	Saturday classes	
uly 15	Saturday classes Mid-point in semester	No withdrawals permitted after this date
uly 22	Saturday classes	
uly 28	Grades due for all August Degree candidates	
.ugust 4	Classes end	Commencement - 2:00 P. M.

SPECIAL EVENTS AND FEATURES

uly 10-14	New Jersey Congress of Parents and Teachers Parent-Teacher Workshop	9:00 A. M. - 12:30 P. M. Life Hall
uly 13-14	Book Exhibit	8:00 A. M. - 3:00 P. M. - Life Hall

SPECIAL TOURS*

uly 1-25	Mexico	Social Studies S469
uly 9- ugust 24	European Civilization	Social Studies S487
ugust 1-18	Hawaii	Social Studies S488
une 30- ugust 21	Roman Roads	Latin S406

*Write to Bureau of Field Studies for further details.
Courses are listed in Bulletin under departmental headings.

3

OFFICERS OF ADMINISTRATION

State Board of Education

MRS. EDWARD L. KATZENBACH, *President* .... Princeton
HARVEY DEMBE .... Bayonne
MRS. R. ADAM JOHNSTONE .... Ho-Ho-Kus
JOHN F. LYNCH .... Morristown
JAMES W. PARKER, SR. .... Red Bank
JOSEPH L. RICHMOND .... Woodstown
HARRY M. SEALS .... Annandale
JACK SLATER .... Paterson
GEORGE F. SMITH .... Metuchen
WILLIAM A. SUTHERLAND .... Liberty Corner
MRS. STANLEY C. YORTON .... Nutley

Commissioner of Education

DR. FREDERICK M. RAUBINGER

Assistant Commissioner for Higher Education

DR. EARL E. MOSIER

Director of Teacher Education and Certification

DR. ALLAN F. ROSEBROCK

COLLEGE ADMINISTRATION

E. DeALTON PARTRIDGE, Ph.D. .... *President*
CLYDE M. HUBER, Ph.D. .... *Dean of the College*
LEO G. FUCHS, Ed.M. .... *Dean of Students*
JOHN J. RELLAHAN, Ph.D. .... *Chairman of the Graduate Council*
EDWARD J. AMBRY, A.M. .... *Director of Field Services and Summer Session*
IONA S. HENRY, Ed.D. .... *Assistant Director of Students — Women*
NORMAN E. LANGE, Ed.D. .... *Director of Student Teaching and Placement*
PETER P. STAPAY, Ed.M. .... *Registrar*
ANNE BANKS CRIDLEBAUGH, A.M. .... *Librarian*
BERNARD SIEGEL, M.B.A. .... *Business Manager*

HEALTH SERVICES

CHARLOTTE L. PRITCHARD, R.N., A.M. .... *College Nurs*

GRADUATE COUNCIL

John J. Rellahan, *Chairman*

Edward J. Ambry	M. Herbert Freeman	Rose G. Metz, *Secretary*
Carolyn E. Bock	Irwin H. Gawley	Maurice P. Moffatt
Earl C. Davis	W. Paul Hamilton	Allan Morehead
L. Howard Fox	Clyde M. Huber	E. DeAlton Partridge
Carl E. Frankson	Orpha M. Lutz	John A. Schumaker

FACULTY
SUMMER SESSION 1961

E. DeALTON PARTRIDGE, Ph.D. .... President

CLYDE M. HUBER, Ph.D. .... Dean of the College

EDWARD J. AMBRY, A.M. .... Director, Summer Session

KEITH W. ATKINSON, Ph.D. .... Education

WILLIAM A. BALLARE, A.M. .... Speech

JOSEPH F. BECKER, A.M. .... Science

CATHERINE V. BIEBER, A.M. .... Home Economics

CAROLYN E. BOCK, Ph.D. .... Chairman, Department of Foreign Languages

HAROLD C. BOHN, Ed.D. .... English

DANIEL BROWER, Ph.D. .... Education

LEONARD J. BUCHNER, A.M. .... Coordinator, Reading Laboratory

EDGAR C. BYE, A.M. .... Coordinator, Bureau of Field Studies

PAUL C. CLIFFORD, A.M. .... Assoc. Dir., N. S. F. Program: Mathematics

ALDEN C. CODER, Ed.D. .... Driver Education

EDWARD COGAN, Ph.D. .... N. S. F. Program: Mathematics

PHILIP S. COHEN, A.M. .... Social Studies

LAWRENCE H. CONRAD, A.M. .... English

ANNE BANKS CRIDLEBAUGH, A.M. .... Librarian

EARL C. DAVIS, Ph.D. .... Education

NANCY A. deGROFF, M.S. .... New Jersey State School of Conservation

JOSEPH W. DUFFY, Ed.D. .... Industrial Arts

ARTHUR W. EARL, Ed.D. .... Industrial Arts

GERALD EDWARDS, Ed.D. .... Physical Education

CLIFFORD E. EMANUELSON, Ed.M. .... Dir., N. J. State School of Conservation

EMMA FANTONE, A.M. .... Coordinator, Audio-Visual Center

ERNEST B. FINCHER, Ph.D. .... Social Studies

L. HOWARD FOX, Ph.D. .... Speech

CARL E. FRANKSON, Ph.D. .... Chairman, Department of Industrial Arts

MARIE M. FRAZEE, A.M. .... Academic Counselor

PAUL E. FROEHLICH, Ed.D. .... Business Education

EDWIN S. FULCOMER, Ed.D. .... Chairman, Department of English

IRWIN H. GAWLEY, JR., Ed.D. .... Science

HAROLD A. GOUSS, A.M. .... Mathematics

HOWARD L. HAAS, Ed.D. .... Business Education

KATHARINE B. HALL, Ph.D. .... Home Economics

DUANE M. HARMON, M.S. .... Education

RUSSELL HAYTON, M.Sac.M. .... Music

CLYDE W. HIBBS, Ph.D. .... New Jersey State School of Conservation

JANE M. HILL, A.M. .... N.S.F. Program: Mathematics

HILDEGARDE HOWDEN, A.M. .... Mathematics
EVA HUBSCHMAN, A.M. .... Speech
T. ROLAND HUMPHREYS, A.M. .... Mathematics
EMIL KAHN, A.M. .... Music
FRANK S. KELLAND, A.M. .... Geography
GEORGE G. KING, A.M. .... Education
WALTER E. KOPS, A.M. .... Social Studies
RUSSELL KRAUSS, Ph.D. .... English
EDITH G. H. LENEL, Ph.D. .... Catalog Librarian
RAYMOND C. LEWIN, A.M. .... Education
ORPHA M. LUTZ, Ph.D. .... Education
EVAN M. MALETSKY, Ph.D. .... Mathematics
CLYDE W. McELROY, Ed.D. .... Speech
CLAIRE M. MERLEHAN, A.M. .... Reference Librarian
BRUCE E. MESERVE, Ph.D. .... Chairman, Department of Mathematics
BEN MINOR, M.E.E. .... Science
MAURICE P. MOFFATT, Ph.D. .... Chairman, Department of Social Studies
KARL R. MOLL, A.M. .... Speech
ALLAN MOREHEAD, Ed.D. .... Chairman, Department of Education
ROBERT Z. NORMAN, Ph.D. .... N. S. F. Program: Mathematics
EARL K. PECKHAM, Ed.D. .... Education
ANTHONY J. PETTOFREZZO, Ph.D. .... Mathematics
GEORGE F. PLACEK, A.M. .... Science
FLORENCE M. REIFF, M.S. .... Home Economics
JOHN J. RELLAHAN, Ph.D. .... Chairman, Graduate Council: Social Studies
GEORGE E. SALT, A.M. .... Education
HAROLD M. SCHOLL, Ed.D. .... Chairman, Department of Speech
JOHN A. SCHUMAKER, Ph.D. .... Mathematics
HORACE J. SHEPPARD, A.M. .... Business Education
THADDEUS J. SHEFT, A.M. .... Associate Coordinator, Audio-Visual Center
KENNETH O. SMITH, Ph.D. .... Science
MAX A. SOBEL, Ph.D. .... Director, N.S.F. Program: Mathematics
JEROME STREICHLER, A.M. .... Industrial Arts
RICHARD W. TEWS, Ph.D. .... Director, Panzer School of
Physical Education and Hygiene
CHARLES E. TRESSLER, A.M. .... Industrial Arts
RALPH A. VERNACCHIA, A.M. .... Fine Arts
HAZEL M. WACKER, Ed.D. .... Physical Education
RALPH WALTER, Ed.D. .... Education
FOSTER L. WYGANT, Ed.D. .... Fine Arts
FREDERIC H. YOUNG, Ph.D. .... English

6

SPECIAL YOUTH ACTIVITIES

JUNE 26 — AUGUST 4

READING IMPROVEMENT LABORATORY: Available to New Jersey students in grades 7-12; small groups are formed according to age and achievement levels and meet daily, 10:00 A. M. to 12:00 Noon. The latest in equipment, films, and workshop materials are used to demonstrate speed of comprehension, study skills, and vocabulary growth. Enrollment is limited. Apply at least three months in advance of each term.

Fee: $50.00   Write to: Coordinator, Reading Improvement Laboratory

SPEECH AND HEARING CENTER: The Speech and Hearing Center will offer an intensive remedial speech program. It will accommodate a maximum of sixty children between 4 and 18 years of age. The program, offered 10:30-12:20 P. M. daily, is designed to provide therapy for children with the usual types of speech problems, as well as those who have major problems of voice, articulation, and rhythm (stuttering). Children with retarded language development or loss of language are also eligible.

A special class for adults who have: (1) language impairments due to brain injury, (2) voice problems due to laryngeal pathologies, or (3) stuttering speech will also be arranged.

Fee: $60.00   Write to: Coordinator, Speech and Hearing Center

MONTCLAIR STATE COLLEGE DAY CAMP: A general program of games, relays, storytelling, rhythms, and nature walks will be presented for children in the 6-12 year age range. In cooperation with the College Art Department, youngsters will enjoy approximately one hour of Arts and Crafts activities. The dates will coincide with those of the regular summer session, June 26 to August 4, and the hours will be 8:30 A. M. to 12:30 P. M. The fee will include some arts and crafts supplies and light refreshments.

Fee: $8.00 per week   Write to: Director, Panzer School of Physical Education and Hygiene, c/o this College

WORKSHOP FOR APPRENTICES IN DRAMATIC PRODUCTION: The Speech Department is pleased to announce that it will expand its summer program in theater for pre-college students. Secondary school students and recent graduates are eligible. Activities include the study of acting, scenery design and construction, lighting, make-up, and voice and diction. Following a 1:30 P. M. daily seminar, students will participate as actors and crew members in the preparation and presentation of at least three major dramatic productions. Full use will be made of the extensive facilities in the air-conditioned Memorial Auditorium — one of the most modern and beautiful college theaters in the East.

Registration is limited. Applications must be made in advance and must be accompanied by a letter of recommendation from the applicant's school Dramatics or English teacher. A personal interview will also be arranged.

Fee: $60.00   Write to: Coordinator, Summer Theater Programs

AIMS AND OBJECTIVES

The Summer School is designed specifically to meet the needs of:
1. Students enrolled in graduate programs who wish to meet requirements for the Master of Arts degree.
2. Teachers-in-service who desire to complete degree requirements, to improve their professional standing, or to take courses for state certification purposes.
3. Graduates and upperclassmen from liberal arts colleges seeking provisional or limited certification to teach in the New Jersey public secondary schools.
4. Persons interested in pursuing college work, whether or not they desire credit.
5. Persons interested in special workshops, institutes, and seminars.

Montclair State College, a member of the American Association of Colleges of Teacher Education, is fully accredited by the Middle States Association of Colleges and Secondary Schools, and the American Association of University Women. Also fully accredited by the National Council for Accreditation of Teacher Education for the preparation of Elementary and Secondary School teachers and School Service Personnel, with the Master's Degree as the highest degree approved.

ADMISSION REGULATIONS

Students may enter in one of two categories: Students seeking a Master's Degree (degree candidates), or students not seeking a degree (auditors, certification students, and special students).

Degree Candidates — MATRICULATION FOR THE MASTER OF ARTS DEGREE

Persons Eligible — Teachers-in-service, as well as those interested in personal and professional growth who hold a bachelor's degree from an accredited college, have a high scholastic average and hold a N. J. teacher's certificate.
Procedure
1. File an application with the Chairman of the Graduate Council and pay a $5.00 application for admission fee (see "Tuition, Fees and Expenses").
2. Have forwarded to the Graduate Office official transcripts of all previous college work. (Upon acceptance, a student will be furnished a definite statement of requirements, entitled a Work Program. This Work Program must be presented each time a student registers.)
3. Obtain approval of courses from your Department Chairman or Advisor during the hours of registration.
Note: 1 and 2 above should be completed at least one month prior to registration for the Summer Session.
Transfer of Credits — Not more than 8 semester-hours of work taken prior to matriculation are accepted for credit toward the A. M. degree. Transfer of graduate credit from other institutions — up to 8 semester-hours — is allowed only to those students who are graduates of either a New Jersey State College or the State University.
Research Requirement — Education 503, Methods and Instruments of Research, followed by a Departmental Research Seminar or Education 603B, Principles and Practices of Research. Students are advised to schedule Education 503 early in their program of studies.
Master's Thesis — Students writing a thesis must register for the course in thesis writing (Graduate A-500), which carries 4 semester-hours of credit. For further information regarding the thesis, see the Graduate Bulletin.
Residence Requirement — All matriculated students in the Graduate Division will be required to complete at least one full-time (6 s. h.) summer session or at least one regular semester.

Application for degree conferment — A candidate for a degree must file with the Registrar an application for conferment of the degree before November 30 of the college year in which he expects to complete his work. Application blanks for this purpose may be secured in the Registrar's Office. The responsibility for making said application rests with the candidate. Students should check with advisors concerning final examination dates and other details involved in the graduation procedure.

Non-Degree Students

1. AUDITORS. Persons who desire to take courses for cultural, vocational, professional, or avocational purposes, but who do not wish college credit, may register as auditors. All persons auditing a course must establish eligibility, register, and pay the same tuition fees as other students.

2. SPECIAL STUDENTS. (Non-matriculated students and students working beyond the Master's degree or for advanced certificates.) Persons who wish to enroll in courses for the purpose of having credit transferred to another institution may be admitted by submitting to the Director of Summer Session an official letter from the Dean of the University or College in which they are earning the degree. This letter must contain: a statement that the student is in good standing, his accumulative average, and the courses or kind of courses for which the student may register. The College reserves the right to decide whether or not the student has fulfilled necessary prerequisites. Certain 400-numbered courses and all 500 and 600-numbered courses are open only to graduate students. College Deans should inquire about students' eligibility if interested in 400-level courses.

3. CERTIFICATION STUDENTS. (Students seeking initial teaching certificates — emergency, provisional or limited.) Before registration will be accepted, students should follow instructions listed under the heading "Certification for Teaching" page 13.

GENERAL INFORMATION

LOCATION OF CAMPUS. Situated on the northern boundary of Upper Montclair, the College is approximately three miles north of the center of the town of Montclair and twelve miles west of New York City. The main entrance is at the intersection of Valley Road and Normal Avenue. Public transportation is available on the Greenwood Lake Division of the Erie Railroad and on Public Service bus routes. (Nos. 60 and 76 connect with the Lackawanna Railroad in the town of Montclair.) Other bus lines serve the campus from New York, Newark, the Oranges, and Paterson. The junction of Highways Nos. 46 and 3 is located about one mile north of the campus.

HOUSING: Three College dormitories (Russ, Chapin, and Stone Halls) will be available for the accommodation of men and women registrants during the Summer Session. Applications for room reservations should be submitted prior to June 1, 1961 to: Dean of Students, Montclair State College, Upper Montclair, New Jersey.

RATES: Room and board is $18.00 a week. This fee includes breakfast and dinner Monday through Friday and all three meals Saturday and Sunday. The College supplies and launders sheets, pillow case and bed pad. Students must supply their own blankets, spreads, towels, etc. The $18.00 fee, which must be paid on or before the first day of the summer session, is subject to change.

MEALS: The Dining Hall will be open during the entire Summer Session. Rates are: Breakfast, $.50; Lunch, $.75 (also served a la carte); Dinner, $1.25.

LIBRARY FACILITIES. The main library, located in the Administration Building, will be open during the Summer Session to accommodate all students. All books, including the reference collection, are on open shelves. Hours will be posted. Each student is entitled to one library card free of charge. New students may obtain their cards at the library loan desk upon presentation of a paid tuition receipt. Library cards issued at any time since September 1958 are still valid. All library cards should be retained and may be used during subsequent summer, fall, or spring sessions.

OFFICE OF THE SUMMER SESSION. Located at the eastern end of the Administration Building, it is open from 8:30 A. M. to 4:00 P. M. weekdays, and 8:30 A. M. to 12:00 Noon on July 8, 15 and 22. Telephone number is PIlgrim 6-9500, Extension 201.

RECREATIONAL FACILITIES. The College gymnasium contains basketball, volleyball, squash, and badminton courts. Located on the campus are softball fields and recreational areas. Municipal golf courses are within commuting distance, as are public swimming pools.

ACADEMIC REGULATIONS
AND PROCEDURES

STUDENT RESPONSIBILITY. The College expects those who are admitted to assume responsibility for knowing and meeting the various regulations and procedures set forth in the College catalogs. The College reserves the right to terminate the enrollment of any student whose conduct, class attendance, or academic record should prove unsatisfactory.

CREDIT LOADS. Students may not register for more than eight (8) semester-hours in the Summer Session. Six (6) semester-hours, as a maximum, is strongly recommended.

COURSE NUMBERING. A course numbering system has been developed for all courses in the various departments and curricula. Courses are numbered in the following manner.

100-199	Freshman
200-299	Sophomore
300-399	Junior
400-499	Senior-Graduate
500-699	Graduate

WITHDRAWAL FROM A COURSE. A written notice to the Director of the Summer Session is required. Refunds are computed from the date of receipt of such written notice. Students who do not submit a written notice will receive the mark of "F" in those courses which they cease to attend. Students who withdraw after the mid-point in the Summer Session will receive an automatic grade of "F".

GRADES. Only students enrolled for credit receive grades. The following final grades may be received:

A	Excellent	B	Good
C	Fair	D	Poor
F	Failure	Inc.	Incomplete
WP	Withdrawn, Passing	WF	Withdrawn, Failing
	N. C.	No Credit	

The mark "D" is not accepted for Master's degree credit at Montclair State College. The mark "WP" is given to those who submit in writing their intention of withdrawing from a course before the mid-point in the summer session and are doing passing work in the course involved. "WF" is assigned to students who withdraw before the mid-point and are doing failing work at the time of withdrawal. The mark "F" signifies: (1) failure, (2) the student has failed to submit written notice of his withdrawal, (3) the student has requested withdrawal after the midpoint in the Summer Session. The mark "Inc." is given to a student who, because of illness, is unable to complete his work at the end of a summer session. He will be notified when the work is due; if said work is not finished on the prescribed date, a final grade of "F" is recorded.

An official record showing credits and grades earned will be mailed to the student three weeks following the close of the summer session.

10

REGISTRATION

PROCEDURE. All students must register in person. Details for registration will be posted on a bulletin board in the center hall of the Administration Building. Students must bring records of previous college work in order to establish priority registration. In addition, matriculated students must present their Work Program to advisors.

A student has completed his registration when:

1. His program has been approved by his Departmental advisor and by advisors in other departments in which he selects courses.
2. His registration forms have been properly and completely filled out.
3. His fees have been paid.
4. He receives his class admission cards

PLACE. Administration Building.

TIME AND PRIORITY SCHEDULE

Thursday, June 22 — 2:00 P. M. to 5:00 P. M. Matriculated Graduate Students

6:00 P. M. to 9:00 P. M. Certification students previously registered at M. S. C. (Liberal Arts graduates and others working on an initial provisional or limited teaching certificate.)

Friday, June 23 — 1:30 P. M. to 4:00 P. M. Certification students registering for the first time at M. S. C. All students must attend a registration meeting which will be held promptly at 1:30 P. M. in Room 24, Administration Building. Registration procedures follow this meeting and should be concluded by 4:00 P. M.

4:00 P. M. to 5:00 P. M. Special Students (Undergraduates matriculated at colleges other than M. S. C. seeking courses at M. S. C. to be transferred to their respective colleges.)

6:00 P. M. to 9:00 P. M. Special Students (Beyond A. M., non-matriculated students, special interest, auditors, and advanced certification, such as guidance, secondary school principal, etc.)

Students unable to take advantage of the above priority arrangement may register with other groups provided they arrive AFTER their priority schedule. Students MAY NOT register ahead of their priority listing.

LATE REGISTRATION

Monday, June 26, 1:00 P. M. to 3:00 P. M.
Tuesday, June 27, 1:00 P. M. to 3:00 P. M.
Students registering on June 26 and June 27 will be charged a $5.00 late registration fee.
No registrations will be accepted after 3:00 P. M., June 27.
Classes begin on June 26.

M. S. C. UNDERGRADUATE REGISTRATION PROCEDURE. Students should check with the College Registrar for "permission to take summer work" forms and registration details.

UNDERGRADUATES MATRICULATED AT COLLEGES OTHER THAN M. S. C. Follow procedures outlined under heading, "Admission Regulations, Special Students" and register at time specified.

CHANGE OF SCHEDULE. No student will be permitted to change his schedule without approval of his advisor and the Director of the Summer Session. Changes may be made between 1:00 P. M. and 3:00 P. M. on June 26 and June 27. No changes will be permitted after 3:00 P. M. on June 27. To change from "auditor" to "credit", or vice versa, a student must make formal application not later than the mid-point (July 15) in the Summer Session. Forms are available in the Summer Session office.

CANCELLATION OF COURSES. The College reserves the right to close any course for which the enrollment is insufficient. Students may then register in another course or receive a refund of tuition. If prerequisites are required (see course listings), the student must be sure he has fulfilled them or their equivalents

TUITION, FEES AND EXPENSES
(Subject to change at any time by action of the State Board of Education)

All checks should be made out to **Montclair State College.**

TUITION. For residents of New Jersey, $13.00 per semester hour credit; for out-of-state residents, $15.00 per credit.

SERVICE CHARGE. For all students, fifty cents ($.50) per semester hour credit.

REGISTRATION FEE. For all students, $2.00: to be paid each time a student registers.

LATE REGISTRATION FEE. For all students, $5.00. This additional fee will be charged students registering on June 26 and June 27.

APPLICATION FOR ADMISSION FEE. $5.00 to be paid whenever student files an application for admission to a degree granting program. This fee must accompany the application form and is not refundable.

LABORATORY AND STUDIO FEES. Certain course fees may be announced at the first meeting of the classes.

TRANSCRIPT FEE. $1.00 for single copy. (Special rates for multiple copies. Inquire at Registrar's Office.)

REFUNDING OF FEES. When the Director of the Summer Session receives written notice of withdrawal prior to the first meeting of the course, all fees are refunded in full. Other refunds are pro-rated from the day on which the Director of the Summer Session receives written notification. Withdrawal before the end of the first third of the Summer Session — 60% refund; during the middle third — 30%; during the last third — no refund. Withdrawals after the mid-point (July 15) will result in an automatic grade of "F".

WORK SCHOLARSHIP. Tuition and room fee scholarships are available. Students are assigned work in the various College departments. Write to Dean of Students for information.

CERTIFICATION FOR TEACHING

Certificates to teach in New Jersey Public Schools are issued by: State Board of Examiners, Department of Education, 175 West State Street, Trenton 25, New Jersey. Address all inquiries regarding requirements and have college transcript sent by your college to the above.

ENROLLING AT MONTCLAIR. At registration bring reply received from the State Board of Examiners and transcripts of all previous academic work. All general questions regarding certification should be addressed to the Certification Advisor at this College.

COURSE OFFERINGS. The following **Professional Education** courses are approved by the State Board of Examiners for certification to teach in New Jersey Secondary Schools. Courses should be selected from the following (indicated in the suggested sequence in which they should be taken.)

Education	S201	Human Development and Behavior I
Education	S202	Human Development and Behavior II
Education	S303	The Teacher in School and Community
Education	S304	Principles and Techniques of Secondary Education
Education	S401	The Development of Educational Thought
Education	S406	Educational Sociology
Education	S407A	Television in Education Workshop: Programming and Production
Education	S409	Radio and Sound Equipment in the Classroom
Health Educ.	S100	Healthful Living
Health Educ.	S411	School Health Services
English	S401X	The Teaching of English in Secondary Schools
Mathematics	S401X	The Teaching of Mathematics in Secondary Schools
Science	S401X	The Teaching of Science in Secondary Schools
Social Studies	S401X	The Teaching of Social Studies in Secondary Schools

Supervised Student Teaching. Students desiring information concerning this requirement should ask for written instructions from the Director of Student Teaching.

SERVICES

ACADEMIC ADVISORS. Appointments with the Dean of the College, the Chairman of the Graduate Council, the Director of the Summer Session, or a Department Chairman, may be made by mail or telephone. Appointments should be made as early as possible prior to the end of the spring semester (June 8). Advisors are available during all hours of registration.

BOOKSTORE. Located adjacent to the main lobby of the Student Life Building, this on-campus facility will be open from 8:00 A. M. to Noon daily. A limited number of books for each course will be available. Textbook orders should be placed immediately upon completion of registration. Telephone PI 6-4184

HEALTH SERVICE. A full-time registered nurse is on duty in the medical offices located in Russ Hall. Emergency medical care is available.

INFORMATION OFFICE. An office is maintained at the College switchboard in the center hall of the Administration Building where information may be obtained regarding the location of various College personnel and services. The telephone number of the College is PIlgrim 6-9500.

VETERANS' COUNSELOR. Veterans seeking admission to the Summer Session should apply well in advance of the registration date (June 22 and 23) for a certificate of eligibility and entitlement at the Newark, New Jersey office (20 Washington Place) of the Veterans Administration. In requesting this certificate, the veteran is advised to indicate clearly his educational objective. The Veterans Administration has established certain limitations, especially with regard to change of course. In order that a veteran may be assured that his certificate is in order and that he has taken the proper steps to expedite his training under the G. I. Bill, he should report at registration time to the Veterans' Counselor, whose office is located adjacent to the center hall in the Administration Building.

AUDIO-VISUAL CENTER. This Center provides audio-visual materials, equipment and services for use by faculty and students for classroom instruction and presentation. The staff of the Center is available for special consultation on audio-visual problems, for demonstrations of audio-visual materials and methods, and for special teaching and training in the area of audio-visual education. The Center handles the scheduling of all films for the College, as well as their ordering, mailing, and rentals. Student assistants are provided whenever the use of equipment is requested but are also available for other services.

TEXTBOOK EXHIBIT. On July 13 and July 14 from 8:00 A. M. to 3:00 P. M. there will be an exhibit of high school and elementary school textbooks. The exhibit is primarily for teachers and administrators attending the Summer Session, but will be open to undergraduate students and the general public. The exhibit will be located in Life Hall.

NEW JERSEY STATE SCHOOL OF CONSERVATION
BRANCHVILLE, NEW JERSEY

The six State Colleges, the State Department of Education, and the State Department of Conservation and Economic Development, jointly operate the New Jersey State School of Conservation at Lake Wapalanne in Stokes State Forest, Sussex County. Credit for the courses given at the New Jersey State School of Conservation may be applied toward the bachelor's or master's degrees at the New Jersey State Colleges, subject to approval in advance by the institution concerned. Students are advised to check with their advisors relative to the application of these credits toward degrees.

Courses in Camping, Conservation, Education, Field Biology, Field Science, Fine Arts, Geography, Industrial Arts and Outdoor Education, are offered a the New Jersey State School of Conservation. Special descriptive announce ments may also be had by writing to the New Jersey State School of Conser vation, Branchville, New Jersey.

SUMMER SESSION

MONTCLAIR STATE COLLEGE

UPPER MONTCLAIR, NEW JERSEY

1962

JUNE 21 to AUGUST 3

Volume 54   Number 3

June 21	Registration	See page 10 for complete registration information and priority schedule
June 22	Registration	
June 25	Classes begin	Late registration period
June 26	End of late registration	No registrations accepted after 3:00 P. M.
July 4	No classes	
July 7	Saturday classes	
July 12	Special Registration for 2nd series of three-week courses	
July 13	Mid-point in semester	No withdrawals or change of status after this date
August 3	Classes end	

SPECIAL EVENTS AND FEATURES

July 9-13	New Jersey Congress of Parents and Teachers Workshop:	9:00 A. M. - 12:30 P. M. Life Hall
July 12	Book Exhibit	Life Hall: 8:00 A. M. - 3:00 P. M.
July 13	Book Exhibit	Life Hall: 8:00 A. M. - 3:00 P. M.

SPECIAL TOURS*

July 1 August 15	Recent Trends in European Education	Education S463
July 5 August 27	World Survey	Social Studies S486X
July 9 August 25	Cultural Tour of Europe	Social Studies S487

*Write to Bureau of Field Studies for further details.
Courses are listed in bulletin under departmental headings.

COLLEGE ADMINISTRATION

E. DeALTON PARTRIDGE, Ph.D. .... *President*
CLYDE M. HUBER, Ph.D. .... *Dean of the College*
LAWTON W. BLANTON, A.M. .... *Dean of Students*
JOHN J. RELLAHAN, Ph.D. .... *Chairman of Graduate Council*
EDWARD J. AMBRY, A.M. .... *Director of Field Services
and Summer Session (on leave)*
RAYMOND C. LEWIN, A.M. .... *Acting Director of Field Services
and Summer Session*
ROBERT E. MacVANE, Ed.M. .... *Assistant Director of Field Services
and Summer Session*
IONA S. HENRY, Ed.D. .... *Assistant Director of Students — Women*
NORMAN E. LANGE, Ed.D. .... *Director of Student Teaching and Placement*
PETER P. STAPAY, Ed.M. .... *Registrar*
MARIE M. FRAZEE, A.M. .... *Academic Counselor*
CLAIRE M. MERLEHAN, A.M. .... *Acting Head Librarian*
BERNARD SIEGEL, M.B.A. .... *Business Manager*

HEALTH SERVICES

CHARLOTTE L. PRITCHARD, R.N., A.M. .... *College Nurse*

GRADUATE COUNCIL

John J. Rellahan, *Chairman*
Carolyn E. Bock
Harold C. Bohn
Earl C. Davis
L. Howard Fox
Carl E. Frankson

M. Herbert Freeman
Irwin H. Gawley
Clyde M. Huber
Raymond C. Lewin
Orpha M. Lutz

Rose Metz, *Secretary*
Maurice P. Moffatt
Allan Morehead
E. DeAlton Partridge
Anthony J. Pettofrezzo

FACULTY

SUMMER SESSION 1962

E. DeALTON PARTRIDGE, Ph.D. .... *President*
CLYDE M. HUBER, Ph.D. .... *Dean of the College*
EDWARD J. AMBRY, A.M. .... *Director, Summer Session (on leave)*
RAYMOND C. LEWIN, A.M. .... *Acting Director, Summer Session*
HUGH ALLEN JR., Ed.D. .... *Chairman, Department of Science*
KEITH W. ATKINSON, Ph.D. .... *Education*
WILLIAM A. BALLARE, A.M. .... *Speech*
HAROLD C. BOHN, Ed.D. .... *Chairman, Department of English*
DANIEL BROWER, Ph.D. .... *Education*
LEONARD J. BUCHNER, A.M. .... *Coordinator, Reading Laboratory*
EDGAR C. BYE, A.M. .... *Coordinator, Bureau of Field Studies*
PAUL C. CLIFFORD, A.M. .... *National Science Foundation
Program: Mathematics*
ALDEN C. CODER, Ed.D. .... *Driver Education*
LAWRENCE H. CONRAD, A.M. .... *English*
MARGARET J. COTTER, A.M. .... *National Science Foundation
Program: Mathematics*
EARL C. DAVIS, Ph.D. .... *Education*
NANCY A. deGROFF, M.S. .... *New Jersey State School of Conservation*
JOHN F. DEVLIN, A.M. .... *National Science Foundation
Program: Mathematics*
JOSEPH W. DUFFY, Ed.D. .... *Industrial Arts*
GERALD EDWARDS, Ed.D. .... *Mathematics*
CLIFFORD E. EMANUELSON, Ed.M. .... *Dir., N. J. State School of Conservation*
CARL E. FRANKSON, Ph.D. .... *Chairman, Department of Industrial Arts*
EMMA FANTONE, A.M. .... *Coordinator, Audio-Visual Center*

3

AIMS AND OBJECTIVES

The Summer School is designed specifically to meet the needs of:
1. Matriculated students enrolled in graduate programs who wish to meet requirements for the Master of Arts degree.
2. Teachers-in-service who desire to complete degree requirements, to improve their professional standing, or to take courses for state certification purposes.
3. Graduates from liberal arts colleges seeking provisional or limited certification to teach in the New Jersey public secondary schools.
4. Undergraduates from Montclair and other colleges desiring to continue college programs over the summer.
5. Persons interested in pursuing college work for cultural or avocational purposes whether or not they desire credit.
6. Persons interested in special workshops, institutes, and seminars.

ADMISSION REGULATIONS

Students may enter in one of two categories: Students seeking a Master's Degree (degree candidates), or students not seeking a degree.

Degree Candidates — MATRICULATION FOR THE MASTER OF ARTS DEGREE

Persons Eligible — Teachers-in-service, as well as those interested in personal and professional growth who hold a bachelor's degree from an accredited college, have a high scholastic average and hold a New Jersey teacher's certificate.

Procedure
1. File an application with the Chairman of the Graduate Council and pay a $5.00 application for admission fee (see "Tuition, Fees and Expenses").
2. Have forwarded to the Graduate Office official transcripts of all previous college work. (Upon acceptance, a student will be furnished a definite statement of requirements, entitled a Work Program. This Work Program must be presented each time a student registers.)
3. Obtain approval of courses from your Department Chairman or Advisor during the hours of registration.

Note: 1 and 2 above should be completed at least one month prior to registration for the Summer Session.

Transfer of Credits — Not more than 8 semester hours of work taken prior to matriculation are accepted for credit toward the A.M. degree. Transfer of graduate credit from other institutions — up to 8 semester hours — is allowed only to those students who are graduates of either a New Jersey State College or the State University of New Jersey.

Research Requirement — Education 503, Methods and Instruments of Research, and Education 603, Principles and Practices of Research, or a departmental research seminar. Education 503 should be taken rather early in the program and precedes work in more advanced research courses.

Master's Thesis — Students writing a thesis must register for the course in thesis writing (Graduate A600) which carries 4 semester hours of credit. For further information regarding the thesis, see the Graduate Bulletin.

Residence Requirement — All matriculated students in the Graduate Division will be required to complete at least one full-time (6 s. h.) summer session or at least one regular semester to fulfill this requirement.

Application for degree conferment — A candidate for a degree must file with the Registrar an application for conferment of the degree before November 30 of the college year in which he expects to complete his work. Application blanks for this purpose may be secured in the Registrar's Office. The responsibility for making said application rests with the candidate. Students should check with advisors concerning final examination dates and other details involved in the graduation procedure.

5

STUDENTS NOT SEEKING A DEGREE, but

1. **Desiring to Transfer Credit.** Persons who wish to enroll in courses for the purpose of having credit transferred to another institution may be admitted by submitting to the Director of Summer Session an official letter from the Dean of the University or College in which they are earning the degree. This letter must contain a statement that the student is in good standing, his accumulative average, and the courses or kind of courses for which the student may register. Special transfer of credit forms must be completed in the Part-Time and Extension Office. The College reserves the right to decide whether or not the student has fulfilled necessary prerequisites. Certain 400-numbered courses and all 500 and 600-numbered courses are open only to graduate students. College Deans should inquire about students' eligibility if interested in 400-level courses.

2. **Desiring to Audit.** Persons who desire to take courses for cultural, vocational, professional, or avocational purposes, but who do not wish college credit, may register as auditors. All persons auditing a course must establish eligibility, register, and pay the same tuition fees as other students.

3. Desiring initial teaching certificates, (emergency, provisional or limited). Before registration will be accepted, students should follow instructions listed under the heading, "Certification for Teaching". (See Below)

4. **Desiring work beyond A.M. or for advanced certificates.**

CERTIFICATION FOR TEACHING

Certificates to teach in New Jersey Public Schools are issued by: the State Board of Examiners, Department of Education, 175 West State Street, Trenton 25, New Jersey. Address all inquiries to them regarding certification requirements.

ENROLLING AT MONTCLAIR. At registration time bring correspondence received from the State Board of Examiners as well as transcripts of all previous academic work. All general questions regarding certification should be addressed to the Certification Advisor at this College.

COURSE OFFERINGS. The following professional Education courses offered this summer are approved by the State Board of Examiners for certification to teach in New Jersey Secondary Schools. Courses should be selected from the following (indicated in the suggested sequence in which they should be taken):

Education	S201	Human Development and Behavior I
Education	S202	Human Development and Behavior II
Education	S303	The Teacher in School and Community
Education	S304	Principles and Techniques of Secondary Education
Education	S401	The Development of Educational Thought
*Education	S406	Educational Sociology
*Education	S408	Selection and Utilization of Audio-Visual Materials
*Education	S410	Teaching Materials Workshop
*Education	S492	Comparative Education
Health Ed.	S100	Healthful Living
English	S401X	The Teaching of English in Secondary Schools
Mathematics	S401X	The Teaching of Mathematics in Secondary Schools
Science	S401X	The Teaching of Science in Secondary Schools
Social Studies	S401X	The Teaching of Social Studies in Secondary Schools

* Under certain conditions, Ed. 406, 408, 410 and 492 may carry graduate credit.

Supervised Student Teaching. Students desiring information concerning this requirement should ask for written instructions from the Director of Student Teaching.

6

NEW JERSEY CONGRESS OF PARENTS AND TEACHERS
PARENT-TEACHER WORKSHOP

July 10-14
9:00 A. M. - 12:30 P. M.

The New Jersey Congress, in cooperation with Montclair State College, will offer a five day workshop for parent-teacher officers and members, and for teachers and future teachers.

The purposes of this Workshop are:

1. To increase understanding of P. T. A. philosophy and objectives.

2. To stimulate and direct the planning for effective parent-teacher meetings.

3. To activate planning for action programs with the help of resource people and materials.

4. To suggest opportunities for new and different community activities of local parent-teacher associations.

5. To offer experience in gaining group leadership skills and help in the development of plans for parent-teacher study groups.

Write to: Mrs. Joseph Schultz, P. T. A. Coordinator, 122 Gordon Street, Ridgefield Park, New Jersey. Telephone: HU 8-9307

NEW ADDITION TO FINLEY HALL

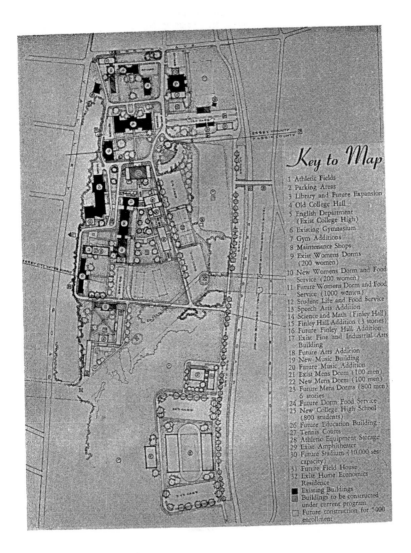

Key to Map

1 Athletic Fields
2 Parking Areas
3 Library and Future Expansion
4 Old College Hall
5 English Department
   (Exist College High)
6 Existing Gymnasium
7 Gym Additions
8 Maintenance Shops
9 Exist Womens Dorms
   (200 women)
10 New Womens Dorm and Food
   Service (200 women)
11 Future Womens Dorm and Food
   Service (1000 women)
12 Student Life and Food Service
13 Speech Arts Addition
14 Science and Math (Finley Hall)
15 Finley Hall Addition (3 stories)
16 Future Finley Hall Addition
17 Exist Fine and Industrial Arts
   Building
18 Future Arts Addition
19 New Music Building
20 Future Music Addition
21 Exist Mens Dorm (100 men)
22 New Mens Dorm (100 men)
23 Future Mens Dorms (800 men)
   6 stories
24 Future Dorm Food Service
25 New College High School
   (800 students)
26 Future Education Building
27 Tennis Courts
28 Athletic Equipment Storage
29 Exist Amphitheater
30 Future Stadium (10,000 seat
   capacity)
31 Future Field House
32 Exist Home Economics
   Residence
■ Existing Buildings
▨ Buildings to be constructed
   under current program
□ Future construction for 5000
   enrollment

COURSES OF THE SUMMER SESSION

Descriptions of the graduate courses will be found in the 1959-1961 Graduate Bulletin of the College. Courses numbered 500 and above are open only to graduate students; those numbered 400-499, inclusive, are senior-graduate courses and their descriptions in the Graduate Bulletin follow the descriptions of the graduate courses. Courses below the 400 number will be found in the Undergraduate Bulletin of the College. Only entirely new courses are described in the Summer Session Bulletin.

All rooms listed are in the Administration Building unless specified otherwise.
*Courses listed with this mark (*) indicate that they may not be used for graduate credit.

BUSINESS EDUCATION DEPARTMENT

*Business Education S103 — Typewriting I   Dr. Haas
1:00-2:30 P. M.   Credit: 0 semester hours   Room 27
      This basic course in typewriting is not offered for credit. The fee charged is equivalent to a course offered for 3 semester hours. (See "Tuition, Fees and Expenses.")

*Business Education S201 — Accounting I   Dr. Froehlich
10:05-11:20 A. M.   Credit: 3 semester hours   Room 2, Annex 2

Business Education S404 — Business Economics   Dr. Froehlich
11:30-12:20 P. M.   Credit: 2 semester hours   Room 2, Annex 2

Business Education S421 — Finance and Investments for Families   Dr. Haas
10:30-11:20 A. M.   Credit: 2 semester hours   Room 5, Annex 2

Business Education S502 — Principles and Problems of Business Education
                                               Mr. Sheppard
8:30-9:20 A. M.   Credit: 2 semester hours   Room 5, Annex 2

Business Education S518 — Advertising II   Mr. Sheppard
9:30-10:20 A. M.   Credit: 2 semester hours   Room 5, Annex 2

EDUCATION DEPARTMENT

*Education S201 — Human Development and Behavior I   Mr. Harmon
8:05-9:20 A. M. Sec. I   Credit: 3 semester hours   Room 22
11:30-12:45 P. M. Sec. II   Credit: 3 semester hours   Room 22

*Education S202 — Human Development and Behavior II   Dr. Lutz
8:05-9:20 A. M.   Credit: 3 semester hours   Room 30
      Prerequisite: Education 200A, Education 201, or equivalent

*Education S303 — The Teacher in School and Community   To be announced
8:05-9:20 A. M. Sec. I   Credit: 3 semester hours   Room 25
                                               To be announced
11:30-12:45 P. M. Sec. II   Credit: 3 semester hours   Room 10

*Education S304 — Principles and Techniques of Secondary
                 Education   Mr. Lewin
11:30-12:45 P. M.   Credit: 3 semester hours   Room 1

17

*Education S401 — The Development of Educational Thought Mr. Lewin
8:05-9:20 A. M. Sec. I   Credit: 3 semester hours   Room 29
                                                                  Mr. Kops
11:30-12:45 P. M. Sec. II   Credit: 3 semester hours   Room 24

Education S406 — Educational Sociology   Mr. Kops
8:05-9:20 A. M.   Credit: 3 semester hours   Room 24

Education S407A — Television in Education Workshop: Miss Fantone
                  Programming and Production
9:30-10:20 A. M.   Credit: 2 semester hours   A-V Lab

Education S409 — Radio and Sound Equipment in the Classroom   Mr. Sheft
10:30-11:20 A. M.   Credit: 2 semester hours   A-V Lab

Education S452 — Psychology and Education of the Handicapped Dr. Brower
11:30-12:45 P. M.   Credit: 3 semester hours   Room 30
     This course is designed for the preparation of teachers of handicapped
children and youth. It also serves to orient prospective teachers of regular
classes to the needs of those with handicaps of sensory, motor, intellectual,
emotional and neurological origin.

Education S500A — Basic Educational Trends   Dr. Peckham
9:30-10:20 A. M.   Credit: 2 semester hours   Room 25
     Prerequisite: Teaching experience

Education S500C — Recent Trends in Secondary School Methods   Mr. Salt
8:30-9:20 A. M.   Credit: 2 semester hours   Room 1, Annex 2
     Prerequisite: Teaching experience

Education S500D — School Administration I: Dr. Morehead
                  Functions and Organization
8:30-9:20 A. M.   Credit: 2 semester hours   Room 10
     Prerequisite: Teaching experience

Education S500F — School Administration III   Dr. Atkinson
                  Community Relations
8:30-9:20 A. M.   Credit: 2 semester hours   Room 4, CHS

Education S501 — Tests and Measurements in Secondary   Mr. Sheppard
                 Education
11:30-12:20 P. M.   Credit: 2 semester hours   Room 5, Annex 2
     The purpose of this course is to develop an appreciation of the meaning
and importance of measurement in education, and to give a working knowledge
of instruments of measurement.

Education S502 — Organization and Administration of the   Dr. Peckham
                 Modern High School
11:30-12:20 P. M.   Credit: 2 semester hours   Room 25
     Prerequisite: Education 500D or equivalent

Education S503 — Methods and Instruments of Research   Dr. Walter
10:30-11:20 A. M. Sec. I   Credit: 2 semester hours   Room 5, CHS
                                                                 Dr. Peckham
10:30-11:20 A. M. Sec. II   Credit: 2 semester hours   Room 25
     Prerequisite: Mathematics 400 or equivalent

18

Education S504A — Curriculum Construction in the   Mr. Salt
                     Secondary School
11:30-12:20 P. M.   Credit: 2 semester hours   Room 1, Annex 2
    Prerequisite: Teaching experience

Education S505 — Organization and Administration of   Dr. Morehead
                    Extra-Curricular Activities
9:30-10:20 A. M.   Credit: 2 semester hours   Room 10

Education S507 — School Finance   Dr. Morehead
10:30-11:20 A. M.   Credit: 2 semester hours   Room 10
    Students who have taken Education 500E for credit are not permitted to
    take Education 507

Education S508 — Supervision of Instruction in Secondary   Dr. Atkinson
                    Schools
10:30-11:20 A. M.   Credit: 2 semester hours   Room 4, CHS
    Prerequisite: Teaching experience

Education S520 — Principles of Mental Hygiene   To be announced
9:30-10:20 A. M.   Credit: 2 semester hours   Room 30
    Prerequisite: Introductory Psychology

Education S535 — Vocational Guidance   Mr. King
11:30-12:20 P. M.   Credit: 2 semester hours   Room 2, Annex 1
    Prerequisite: Education 551

Education S536 — Educational Guidance   Mr. King
8:30-9:20 A. M.   Credit: 2 semester hours   Room 2, Annex 1
    Prerequisite: Education 551

Education S539 — Elementary School Guidance Services   Dr. Davis
8:30-9:20 A. M.   Credit: 2 semester hours   Room 9
    Prerequisite: Education 551

Education S550 — Child and Adolescent Development   Dr. Walter
11:30-12:20 P. M.   Credit: 2 semester hours   Room 5, CHS
    Prerequisite: Child Development and Psychology courses

Education S551 — Principles and Techniques of Guidance   Mr. King
9:30-10:20 A. M. Sec. I   Credit: 2 semester hours   Room 2, Annex 1
11:30-12:20 P. M. Sec. II   Credit: 2 semester hours   Dr. Atkinson
                                                                 Room 4, CHS
    This course is prerequisite for most guidance courses offered in this Divi-
    sion of the College.

Education S553 — Core-Curriculum and Life-Adjustment
                    Programs in High Schools   Mr. Salt
9:30-10:20 A. M.   Credit: 2 semester hours   Room 1, Annex 2
    Prerequisite· Teaching experience

Education S554A — Psychology and Education of
                     Exceptional Children   Dr. Brower
10:30-11:20 A. M.   Credit: 2 semester hours   Room 30
    Prerequisite: Introductory Psychology

19

Education S556 — Principles of Reading Improvement
in the Secondary School   **Mr. Buchner**
8:30-9:20 A. M.   Credit: 2 semester hours   Room 26

Education S558 — Corrective and Remedial Reading
in the Secondary School   **Mr. Buchner**
11:30-12:20 P. M.   Credit: 2 semester hours   Room 26
    Prerequisite: Education 556 or Education 557

Education S560A — Laboratory Course in the Production of   **Dr. Duffy**
Audio-Visual Instructional Materials:
Non-Projected Materials I
11:30-12:45 P. M.   Credit: 2 semester hours   A-V Lab
    Prerequisite: Education 408

This complete course combines laboratory and seminar experiences in the organization and preparation of instructional materials for classroom use. It is intended for teachers, administrators, and audio-visual specialists who wish to develop ability to plan and produce audio-visual materials for instructional purposes. Students will have opportunities to prepare pictures, slides, transparencies, displays, models, graphs, magnetic tapes, motion picture segments, and instructional television programs, according to their interests and needs.

It is offered in two parts. Part I deals with non-projected audio-visual instructional materials, such as drawings, charts and graphs, bulletin boards, feltboards, maps, demonstrations, exhibits and displays, dioramas, etc. Part II includes production of projected and audio materials, such as slides, filmstrips, opaques, transparencies, magnetic tapes, motion pictures, television programs, etc.

Education S602 — Seminar in Guidance   **Dr. Davis**
10:30-12:20 P. M.   Credit: 4 semester hours   Room 9
    Prerequisites: Education 551, Education 503 and approval of instructor.

Education S603B — Principles and Practices of Research   **Dr. Walter**
9:30-10:20 A. M.   Credit: 2 semester hours   Room 5, CHS
    Prerequisite: Education 503

ENGLISH DEPARTMENT

*English S100C — Fundamentals of Writing   **Dr. Young**
8:30-9:45 A. M.   Credit: 3 semester hours   Room 3

*English S100G — Western World Literature   **Dr. Fulcomer**
10:05-11:20 A. M.   Credit: 3 semester hours   Room 1

*English S202 — American Literature II   **Mr. Conrad**
10:05-11:20 A. M.   Credit: 3 semester hours   Room 3

*English S410X — The Teaching of English in Secondary Schools   **Dr. Fulcomer**
8:30-9:20 A. M.   Credit: 2 semester hours   Room 1

English S505 — Philosophy and British Poetry
of the Nineteenth Century   **Dr. Young**
10:30-11:20 A. M.   Credit: 2 semester hours   Room 1, Annex 1

English S530 — Dante and His Influence in England and America   **Dr. Krauss**
11:30-12:20 P. M.   Credit: 2 semester hours   Room 1, Annex 1

English S534 — Medieval Epic, Saga and Romance   Dr. Krauss
9:30-10:20 A. M.   Credit: 2 semester hours   Room 1, Annex 1

English S535 — Eighteenth Century Literature   Dr. Bohn
10:30-11:20 A. M.   Credit: 2 semester hours   Room 2

English S543 — Contemporary American Literature   Mr. Conrad
8:30-9:20 A. M.   Credit: 2 semester hours   Room 2

English S544B — Shakespeare (Comedies)   Dr. Bohn
9:30-10:20 A. M.   Credit: 2 semester hours   Room 2

FINE ARTS DEPARTMENT

*Fine Arts S302 — Foundations of Art Education   Mr. Vernacchia
8:30-9:20 A. M.   Credit: 2 semester hours   Room 219, Finley

Fine Arts S403A or S403B — Print Making I and II   Mr. Vernacchia
10:30-11:20 A. M.   Credit: 2 semester hours   Room 219, Finley

Fine Arts S408A or S408B — Painting Laboratory I and II   Dr. Wygant
8:30-9:20 A. M.   Credit: 2 semester hours   Room 221, Finley

Fine Arts S491X — Art of the Twentieth Century   Mr. Vernacchia
11:30-12:20 P. M.   Credit: 2 semester hours   Room 219, Finley

FOREIGN LANGUAGE DEPARTMENT

Latin S406 — Field Studies in Roman Civilization   Dr. Bock
June 30-August 21   Credit: 6 semester hours   Field Trip

The course is designed to acquaint students and teachers of Latin, history, and languages with the Roman Conquest of Europe, specifically in Britain, France, Belgium, Switzerland, and Germany by studying and visiting Roman ruins and monuments in these countries, thus providing historical and archaeological background for the enrichment of their classes. Military invasions followed by colonization and the planting of Roman culture and civilization are an object of investigation, and remains "in situ" and in the museums are viewed. Art and archaeology are reinforced by readings related to paralleling the site from the Latin authors: Caesar and Tacitus. Readings and a term paper due three months after the end of the tour are under the supervision of the instructor. Lectures on and tours of the sites are given by historians, archaeologists, and military personnel, authorities on the area, secured from the universities, archaeological societies, museums and cultural commissions.

For further details write to Dr. Carolyn E. Bock, Bureau of Field Studies.

GEOGRAPHY DEPARTMENT

*Science S100C — The Earth Sciences   Mr. Kelland
9:30-10:20 A. M.   Credit: 2 semester hours   Room 4, Annex D

Geography S414A — Advanced Economic Geography   Mr. Kelland
10:30-11:20 A. M.   Credit: 2 semester hours   Room 4, Annex D

Geography S419X — Geography of the Soviet Union   Mr. Kelland
11:30-12:20 P. M.   Credit: 2 semester hours   Room 4, Annex D

HOME ECONOMICS DEPARTMENT

Home Economics S423 — Seminar in the Supervision   **Mrs. Bieber**
of Home Economics
9:30-12:00 Noon   Credit: 2 semester hours   Room 114, Finley
(July 24-August 4)

This course is designed for cooperating teachers planning to work with home economics student teachers in the pre-service program at Montclair State College. The course deals with principles, methods and techniques of leadership in improving the programs of home economic education.

Home Economics S424 — Workshop in Home Economics Education: **Dr. Hall**
9:30-11:20 A. M.   Educables — Retarded Children   **Miss Reiff**
1:00-3:00 P. M.   Credit: 3 semester hours   Room 114, Finley
(July 5-July 22)

This course includes a study of the general characteristics of the educable retarded child, teaching for individual differences, development of methods and specific techniques, and materials for this child in home economics. Suitable evaluation instruments are considered. Opportunity is provided for observing and working with children in a classroom situation.

TO BE CONSTRUCTED — GRACE FREEMAN HALL
WOMEN'S DORMITORY

INDUSTRIAL ARTS DEPARTMENT

Industrial Arts S402 — Comprehensive General Shop
for Senior High School
12:30-4:10 P. M. Sec. I   Credit: 4 semester hours   Mr. Tressler
6:30-10:10 P. M. Sec. II   Credit: 4 semester hours   Mr. Streichler
General Shop, Finley

Industrial Arts S501 — Curriculum Construction and Course   Dr. Frankson
Organization in Industrial Arts Education
8:30-9:45 A. M.   Credit: 3 semester hours   Seminar Room, Finley

Industrial Arts S502 — Shop Planning and Equipment Selection   Dr. Earl
in Industrial Arts Education
10:05-11:20 A. M.   Credit: 3 semester hours   Seminar Room, Finley

MATHEMATICS DEPARTMENT

*Mathematics S300 — Social Uses of Mathematics   Mr. Humphreys
9:30-10:20 A. M. Sec. I   Credit: 2 semester hours   Room, 3, CHS
11:30-12:20 P. M. Sec. II   Credit: 2 semester hours   Room 3, CHS

*Mathematics S310 — An Introduction to Mathematics   Mr. Gouss
11:30-12:20 P. M.   Room 104, Finley

*Mathematics S400 — Educational Statistics   Mr. Humphreys
8:30-9:20 A. M. Sec. I   Credit: 2 semester hours   Room 3, CHS
Mr. Gouss
9:30-10:20 A. M. Sec. II   Credit: 2 semester hours   Room 106, Finley

*Mathematics S401X — Teaching of Mathematics in
Secondary Schools   Mr. Gouss
8:30-9:20 A. M.   Credit: 2 semester hours   Room 106, Finley

Mathematics S405 — History of Mathematics   Mrs. Howden
10:30-11:20 A. M.   Credit: 2 semester hours   Room 106, Finley

Mathematics S415 — Differential Equations   Mrs. Howden
8:30-9:20 A. M.   Credit: 2 semester hours   Room 104, Finley

Mathematics S504 — Modern Algebra   Dr. Schumaker
10:30-11:20 A. M.   Credit: 2 semester hours   Room 104, Finley
Prerequisite: Mathematics 503 or permission of instructor

Mathematics S524 — Statistical Inference and
Sampling Theory   Dr. Pettofrezzo
11:30-12:20 P. M.   Credit: 2 semester hours   Room 108, Finley
Prerequisite: Mathematics 408 or Mathematics 522

Mathematics S529 — Curriculum Construction in Mathematics   Dr. Maletsky
9:30-10:20 A. M.   Credit: 2 semester hours   Room 104, Finley

Mathematics S551 — Mathematics of Social Sciences   Mrs. Howden
11:30-12:20 P. M.   Credit: 2 semester hours   Room 106, Finley

The following courses are open only to National Science Foundation participants. Students were selected in March 1961 and registrations are closed. These courses are listed for record purposes only.

*Mathematics S102 — Mathematical Analysis II   Dr. Pettofrezzo
8:30-10:20 A. M.   Credit: 4 semester hours   Room 108, Finley

Mathematics S407 — Advanced Calculus   Dr. Schumaker
8:30-9:20 A. M.   Credit: 2 semester hours   Room 105, Finley

Mathematics S409 — Introduction to Contemporary
      Mathematics   Mr. Clifford, Dr. Sobel
9:30-10:20 A. M.   Credit: 2 semester hours   Room 105, Finley

Mathematics S503 — Foundations of Algebra   Dr. Maletsky
8:30-9:20 A. M.   Credit: 2 semester hours   Room 107, Finley

Mathematics S508 — Foundations of Geometry   Dr. Meserve
9:30-10:20 A. M.   Credit: 2 semester hours   Room 107, Finley

Mathematics S602A — Workshop on Contemporary
      Mathematics   Mr. Clifford, Dr.Sobel
11:00-12:00 Noon   Credit: 2 semester hours   Room 105, Finley

Mathematics S603A — Workshop on Junior High School
      Mathematics   Miss Hill
11:00-12:00 Noon   Credit: 2 semester hours   Room 107, Finley

SPECIAL ANNOUNCEMENT

With the aid of a special grant from the National Science Foundation, this college will offer an opportunity for thirty college professors of prospective teachers of mathematics to devote four weeks to a study of the recommendations of the Mathematical Association of America for the training of secondary school teachers of mathematics. There will be a detailed orientation program in the areas of algebra, geometry, analysis, and probability and statistics. There will also be an opportunity to participate in a daily workshop for high school (or junior high school) teachers in the N.S.F. Institute to be held simultaneously on campus. In addition, it will be possible to make an intensive study of a geometry program, and attend frequent seminars.

Dates for this program: July 11 to August 3

Write to Dr. Max Sobel, Director, N.S.F. Institute, for details. Closing date April 28, 1961.

MUSIC DEPARTMENT

*Music S100 — Music Appreciation   Mr. Hayton
9:30-10:20 A. M.   Credit: 2 semester hours   Room 13, Music Building

PANZER SCHOOL OF PHYSICAL EDUCATION AND HYGIENE

*Health Education S100 — Healthful Living   Dr. Wacker
9:30-10:20 A. M.   Credit: 2 semester hours   Room 5, Gym

*Physical Education S202 — History and Principles
      of Physical Education   Dr. Wacker
8:05-9:20 A. M.   Credit: 3 semester hours   Room 5, Gym

Health Education S408 — Driver Education   Dr. Coder
              Credit: 3 semester hours   Room A
        Prerequisite: Approval by instructor prior to registration
        For details write to Dr. Coder - see page 28.

Health Education S411 — School Health Services   Dr. Tews
10:30-11:20 A. M.   Credit: 2 semester hours   Room 1

Health Education S412 — Alcohol Education Workshop   Dr. Tews
              Credit: 2 semester hours   Room 1
        Pre-summer session - June 22 through July 7 - see page 28 for details.

SCIENCE DEPARTMENT

Biology S407 — Comparative Embryology   To be announced
0:30-11:20 A. M.   Credit: 4 semester hours   Room 217, Finley
        1:00-4:45 P. M. laboratory on Monday, Wednesday and Friday
        Prerequisite: 8 semester hours work in zoology

Chemistry S408B — Industrial Chemistry, Part II   Dr. Gawley
1:30-12:20 P. M. and   Credit: 2 semester hours   Room 204, Finley
        afternoons (Meets only on Tuesday and Thursday)
        Prerequisite: General and organic chemistry, or special permission of
        instructor.

Physics S407 — Aviation   Mr. Placek
:30-10:20 A. M.   Credit: 4 semester hours   Room 8, CHS
        Students who took Physics 307 not eligible to take this course.

Physics S410 — Meteorology   Mr. Minor
0:30-11:20 A. M.   Credit: 2 semester hours   Room 201, Finley

Physics S411B — Photography II   Dr. Smith
1:30-12:20 P. M. and   Credit: 2 semester hours   Room 201, Finley
:00-3:00 P. M. (Meets only on Monday, Wednesday and Friday)
        Prerequisite: General physics and general chemistry or permission of
        instructor.

Physics S512 — Modern Physics   Dr. Smith
:30-10:20 A. M.   Credit: 4 semester hours   Room 201, Finley
        Prerequisite: General college physics, general college chemistry and a
        course in electrical measurement

Science S100C — The Earth Sciences   Mr. Kelland
:30-10:20 A. M.   Credit: 2 semester hours   Room 4, Annex D

Science S401X — Teaching of Science in Secondary Schools   Dr. Gawley
8:30-9:20 A. M.   Credit: 2 semester hours   Room 204, Finley

Science S413 — Field Studies in Science: Physical   Mr. Minor
11:30-12:20 P. M. and   Credit: 2 semester hours   Room 207, Finley
        afternoon field trips to be arranged (Meets on Monday, Wednesday and
        Friday only)

†Science S418 — Three Centuries of Science Progress   Mr. Becker
9:30-10:20 A. M.   Credit: 2 semester hours   Room 23

†Science S422 — Consumer Science   Mr. Becker
11:30-12:20 P. M. (Tues. Th. & Sat.)   Credit: 2 semester hours   Room 23
11:30-1:20 P. M. (Lab.) (Mon. Wed. Fri.)

SOCIAL STUDIES

*Social Studies S200A — Contemporary American Life   Mr. Cohen
8:30-9:45 A. M.   Credit: 3 semester hours   Room 21

*Social Studies S401X — Teaching of the Social Studies in
        Secondary Schools   Dr. Moffatt
        Dr. Fincher
8:30-9:20 A. M.   Credit: 2 semester hours   Room 20

Social Studies S419 — American Political Biography   Dr. Moffatt
9:30-11:20 A. M.   Credit: 2 semester hours   Room 20
    (First three weeks — June 26 through July 15)

Social Studies S434 — Contemporary World Affairs   Dr. Fincher
9:30-11:20 A. M.   Credit: 2 semester hours   Room 20
    (Last three weeks — July 17 through August 4)

Social Studies S450A — Modern Economic Problems and Policies   Dr. Rellahan
9:30-10:20 A. M.   Credit: 2 semester hours   Room 9

Social Studies S451 — The Middle East   Mr. Cohen
11:30-12:45 P. M.   Credit: 3 semester hours   Room 21

Social Studies S469 — Mexico   Mr. Bye
July 1-25   Credit: 3 semester hours   Field Study

Social Studies S487 — Field Studies in the Arts: Mr. Kahn
        European Civilization
July 9-August 24   Credit: 6 semester hours   Field Study

Social Studies S488 — Hawaii   Mr. Bye
August 1-18   Credit: 3 semester hours   Field Study

    This is a twenty-day field-study course devoted to a study of our fiftieth state. It covers the islands of Oahu, Hawaii, Maui, and Kauai and investigates all of the major geographic, historic, economic, and cultural features of the islands. Among the high points are the city of Honolulu and its environs including Pearl Harbor; the pineapple, sugar cane, and papaya plantations of Oahu as well as the villages, mountain terrain, architecture, and historic spots; the Kona coast of Hawaii, the city of Hilo, the Kileuea crater and lava flows, the steam vents and sulpher banks, and the tree fern forests; the volcanic phenomena of the island of Maui and the canyons, caves, and geysers of Kauai as well as the rice paddies. There are visits to schools and public buildings and opportunities to meet Hawaiian people of all classes.

    For additional information about Social Studies S469, S487, S488, write to: Bureau of Field Studies.

†These courses meet requirements for electives in Science required for MSC undergraduates.

26

SPEECH

*Speech 100D — Fundamentals of Speech   Mr. Moll
11:30-12:45 P. M.   Credit: 3 semester hours   Room 3

*Speech S106 — Introduction to Oral Interpretation   Mr. Ballare
11:30-12:20 P. M.   Credit: 2 semester hours   Room 2

Speech S437A — Dramatic Production Workshop I   Dr. McElroy
1:30-4:20 P. M.   Credit: 2 semester hours   Room 2, Aud.
     (First three weeks — June 26 through July 15)
     (Some evening rehearsals and crew calls to be arranged)

Speech S437B — Dramatic Production Workshop II   Dr. McElroy
1:30-4:20 P. M.   Credit: 2 semester hours   Room 2, Aud.
     (Second three weeks — July 17 through August 4)
     (Some evening rehearsals and crew calls to be arranged)

Speech S439 — Workshop in Speech Correction
     Credit: 3 to 8 semester hours

Speech S439A — Phonetics   To be announced
2:30-3:20 P. M.   Credit: 2 semester hours   Room 1, Aud.

Speech S439D — Practicum in Speech Correction   Mrs. Hubschman
10:30-11:20 A. M.   Credit: 1 semester hour   Room 4, Aud.

Speech S439E — Advanced Practicum in Speech Correction   Mrs. Hubschman
11:30-12:20 P. M.   Credit: 1 semester hour   Room 4, Aud.

Speech S439F — Voice Disorders   Mrs. Hubschman
1:30-2:20 P. M   Credit: 2 semester hours   Room 2, Aud.

The purpose of the course is to study selected disorders of voice production. Consideration is given to etiology, pathology, and therapy related to vocal nodules, contact ulcers, paralysis of the vocal cords, and other organic voice problems. Speech rehabilitation techniques for the laryngectomized and persons with cleft palate conditions are also discussed.

Speech S468 — Measurement of Hearing   Dr. Scholl
9:00-10:15 A. M.   Credit: 3 semester hours   Room 2, Aud.

Speech S532 — Practicum in Speech Rehabilitation   Dr. Scholl
10:30-12:20 P. M   Credit: 2 semester hours   Room 2, Aud.

Speech S535 — Seminar in Speech and Language Rehabilitation
     With Practicum   To be announced
9:00-12:20 P. M.   Credit: 6 semester hours   Room 1, Aud.

Speech S567 — Seminar in Dramatic Production   Dr. Fox
1:30-3:10 P. M.   Credit: 6 semester hours   Room 4, Aud.
     (60 hours of practicum to be arranged)

DRIVER EDUCATION COURSES

PRE-SUMMER SESSION COURSE
Health Education S408 — Driver Education   Dr. Coder
    June 14-15-16 — 7:00-10:00 P. M. and   Room A
    June 19 through June 24 — 3:00-10:00 P. M. and
    June 26 through June 30 — 1:00-4:00 P. M.
            Credit: 3 semester hours

POST-SUMMER SESSION COURSE
Health Education S408 — Driver Education   Dr. Coder
    August 2-3-4 — 1:00-4:30 P. M. and   Room A
    August 7 through August 11 — 9:00 A. M.-3:00 P. M. and
    August 14 through August 18 — 9:00 A. M.-3:00 P. M.
            Credit: 3 semester hours

Authorization to Teach Behind-the-Wheel Driver Education and Driver Training:
A teacher must have his or her certificate endorsed by the Division of Teacher
Certification, State Department of Education. The requirements for such endorsement are: ("Rules Concerning Teachers' Certificates" — 18th edition —
revised 1956)

1. A valid New Jersey teacher's certificate.
2. A current New Jersey driver's license.
3. Three years of automobile driving experience.
4. Evidence of satisfactory completion of a course in driver education and
   driver training approved by the Commissioner of Education.
5. A good driving record.
6. A standard sized car is required for road and skills test.

Secondary schools in New Jersey are increasing their offerings in Driver Education. This increase has resulted in a demand for more Driver Education teachers.
To meet this demand, Montclair State College is increasing the number of courses
being conducted in this field. Assistance is given by the New Jersey State Safety
Council, the New Jersey Automobile Club, the American Automobile Association,
the New Jersey State Police, and the New Jersey Department of Motor Vehicles.

EXTRA CHARGES are made for textbooks and other materials. Some materials
are furnished free.

Registration for these courses is limited. Students must be approved by Dr.
Alden Coder prior to registration. Write to Dr. Coder for complete information.
Fees are to be paid on first day class meets.

ALCOHOL EDUCATION WORKSHOP
June 22 through July 7

Health Education S412 — Alcohol Education Workshop   Dr. Tews
    June 22 and June 23 — 7:00-10:00 P. M. and   Room 1
    June 26 through June 30 — 1:30-4:30 P. M. and
    July 5 through July 7 — 1:30-4:30 P. M.
            Credit: 2 semester hours

    A workshop offered with the cooperation of the State Department of
Health and aimed at preparing teachers of health, school nurse teachers, guidance personnel, and others, for more understanding service in this special area
of education. The workshop will concentrate on a careful study of the physiological, sociological, and psychological problems involved in the use of beverage
alcohol and on the materials, techniques, etc., found to be most useful in alcohol
education programs.

    A limited number of Tuition Scholarships are available. For full details
regarding this workshop, write to: Director, Field Services.

1962

BULLETIN OF

MONTCLAIR STATE COLLEGE

SUMMER
SESSION

JUNE 21 to AUGUST 3

UPPER MONTCLAIR, NEW JERSEY

Montclair State College, a member of the American Association of Colleges of Teacher Education, is fully accredited by the Middle States Association of Colleges and Secondary Schools. Montclair State is also fully accredited by the National Council for Accreditation of Teacher Education for the preparation of Elementary and Secondary School Teachers and School Service Personnel, with the Master's Degree as the highest degree approved.

State Board of Education

Mrs. Edward L. Katzenbach, President .... Princeton

Harvey Dembe .... Bayonne

Martin Fox .... Millburn

Mrs. R. Adam Johnstone .... Ho-Ho-Kus

John F. Lynch .... Morristown

James W. Parker, Sr. .... Red Bank

Joseph L. Richmond .... Woodstown

Harry M. Seals .... Annandale

Jack Slater .... Paterson

George F. Smith .... Metuchen

William A. Sutherland .... Liberty Corner

Commissioner of Education
DR. FREDERICK M. RAUBINGER

Assistant Commissioner for Higher Education
DR. EARL E. MOSIER

Director of Teacher Education and Certification
DR. ALLAN F. ROSEBROCK

GENERAL INFORMATION

LOCATION OF CAMPUS. Situated on the northern boundary of Upper Montclair, the College is approximately three miles north of the center of the town of Montclair and twelve miles west of New York City. The main entrance is at the intersection of Valley Road and Normal Avenue. Public transportation is available on the Greenwood Lake Division of the Erie Railroad and on Public Service bus routes, (Nos. 60 and 76 connect with the Lackawanna Railroad in the town of Montclair.) Other bus lines serve, the campus from New York, Newark, the Oranges, and Paterson. The junction of Highways Nos. 46 and 3 is located about one mile north of the campus.

Housing: Three College dormitories (Russ, Chapin, and Stone Halls) will be available for the accommodation of men and women registrants during the Summer Session. Applications for room reservations should be sent to: Dean of Students, Montclair State College, Upper Montclair, New Jersey.

Rates: Room and board is $18.00 a week. This fee includes breakfast and dinner Monday through Friday and all three meals Saturday and Sunday. The College supplies and launders sheets, pillow case and bed pad. Students must supply their own blankets, spreads, towels, etc. The $18.00 fee which must be paid on or before the first day of the Summer Session, is subject to change.

Meals: The Dining Hall will be open during the entire Summer Session. Rates are: Breakfast, $.50; Lunch, a la carte; Dinner, $1.25.

LIBRARY FACILITIES. The main library, located in College Hall, will be open during the Summer Session to accommodate all students. All books, including the reference, collection, are on open shelves. Hours will be posted. Each student is entitled to one library card free of charge. New students may obtain their cards at the library loan desk upon presentation of a paid tuition receipt. Library cards issued at any time since September 1958 are still valid. All library cards should be retained and. may be used during subsequent summer, fall, or spring sessions.

OFFICE OF THE SUMMER SESSION. Located at the eastern end of College Hall, it is open from 8:30 A. M. to 4:00 P. M. weekdays, and 8:30 A. M. to 12:00 Noon on July 7. Telephone number is PIlgrim 6-9500, Extension 201.

EXTRA-CURRICULAR ACTIVITIES
Recreational Facilities. The College gymnasium contains basketball, volleyball, squash, and badminton courts. Located on campus are softball fields and recreational areas. Municipal golf courses are within commuting distance, as are public swimming pools.

SERVICES

ACADEMIC ADVISORS. Appointments with the Dean of the College, the Chairman of the Graduate Council, the Director of the, Summer Session, or Department Chairman, may be made by mail or telephone. Appointments should be made as early as possible prior to the end of the spring semester (June 7). Advisors are available during hours of registration.

BOOKSTORE. Located adjacent to the main lobby of the Student Life Building, this on-campus facility will be open from 8:00 A. M. to Noon daily. A limited number of books for each course will be available. Textbook orders should be placed immediately upon completion of registration.

HEALTH SERVICE. A full-time registered nurse is on duty in the medical offices located in Russ Hall. Emergency medical care is available.

INFORMATION OFFICE. An office is maintained at the College switchboard in the center hall of College Hall where information may be obtained regarding the location of various College personnel and services. The telephone number of the College is PIlgrim 6-9500.

VETERANS' COUNSELOR. Veterans seeking admission to the Summer Session should apply well in advance of the registration dates (June 21 and June 22) for a certificate of eligibility and entitlement at the Newark, New Jersey office (20 Washington Place) of the Veterans Administration. In requesting this certificate, the veteran is advised to indicate clearly his educational objective. The Veterans Administration has established certain limitations, especially with regard to change of course. In order that a veteran may be assured that his certificate is in order and that he has taken the proper steps to expedite his training under the G. I. Bill, he should report at registration time to the Veterans' Counselor whose office is located adjacent to the center hall in College Hall.

AUDIO-VISUAL CENTER. This Center provides audio-visual materials, equipment and services for use by faculty and students for classroom instruction and presentation. The staff of the Center is available for special consultation on audio-visual problems, for demonstrations of audio-visual materials and methods, and for special teaching and training in the area of audio-visual education. The Center handles the scheduling of all films for the College, as well as their ordering, mailing, and rentals. Student assistants are provided whenever the use of equipment is requested but are also available for other services.

MONTCLAIR COOPERATIVE FILM LIBRARY
Coronet and other selected films
available on rental basis

Send for descriptive catalog to
MONTCLAIR COOPERATIVE FILM LIBRARY
Montclair State College
Upper Montclair, New Jersey

Gymnasium — Montclair State College

8

ACADEMIC REGULATIONS
AND PROCEDURES

STUDENT RESPONSIBILITY. The College expects those who are admitted to assume responsibility for knowing and meeting the various regulations and procedures set forth in the College catalogs. The College reserves the right to terminate the enrollment of any student whose conduct, class attendance, or academic record should prove unsatisfactory.

CREDIT LOADS. Students may not register for more than eight (8) semester hours in the Summer Session. Six (6) semester hours, as a maximum, is strongly recommended.

COURSE NUMBERING. A course numbering system has been developed for all courses in the various departments and curricula. Courses are numbered in the following manner:

100-199	Freshman
200-299	Sophomore
300-399	Junior
400-499	Senior-Graduate
500-699	Graduate

WITHDRAWAL FROM A COURSE. A written notice to the Director of the Summer Session is required. Refunds are computed from the date of receipt of such written notice. Students who do not submit a written notice will receive the mark of "F" in those courses which they cease to attend. Students who withdraw after the mid-point (July 13) in the Summer Session will receive an automatic grade of "F".

GRADES. Only students enrolled for credit receive grades. The following final grades may be received:

A	Excellent	B	Good
C	Fair	D	Poor
F	Failure	Inc.	Incomplete
WP	Withdrawn, Passing	WF	Withdrawn, Failing
	NC	No Credit	

The mark "D" is not accepted for Master's degree credit at Montclair State College. The mark "WP" is given to those who submit in writing their intention of withdrawing from a course before the mid-point in the Summer Session and are doing passing work in the courses involved. "WF" is assigned to students who withdraw before the mid-point and are doing failing work at the time of withdrawal. The mark "F" signifies: (1) failure, (2) the student has failed to submit written notice of his withdrawal, (3) the student has requested withdrawal after the mid-point in the Summer Session. The mark "Inc." is given to a student who, because of illness, is unable to complete his work at the end of a Summer Session. He will be notified when the work is due; if said work is not finished on the prescribed date, a final grade of "F" is recorded.

For three-week courses the above information applies but is geared to the three weeks' duration of the course.

An official record showing credits and grades earned will be mailed to the student three weeks following the close of the Summer Session.

REGISTRATION

PROCEDURE. All students must register in person. Details for registration will be posted on a bulletin board in the center hall of College Hall.
Students must bring records of previous college work in order to establish priority registration. In addition, matriculated students must present their Work Program to advisors.
A student has completed his registration when:

1. His program has been approved by his departmental advisor and by advisors in other departments in which he selects courses.

2. His registration forms have been properly and completely filled out.

3. He pays his tuition and fees.

4. He receives his class admission cards.

PLACE. College Hall

TIME AND PRIORITY SCHEDULE

Thursday, June 21 — 2:00 P. M. to 5.00 P. M. Matriculated graduate students
6:00 P. M. to 9:00 P. M. Certification students previously registered at MSC (Liberal arts graduates and others working on an initial provisional or limited teaching certificate).

Friday, June 22 — 1.30 P. M. to 5.00 P. M. Certification students registering for the first time at MSC. All students must attend a registration meeting which will be held promptly at 1:30 P. M. in the College auditorium. Registration procedures follow this meeting.

1:30 P. M. to 5:00 P. M. Special undergraduate students (undergraduates matriculated at colleges other than MSC seeking courses at MSC to be transferred to their respectiv colleges.) Students should se Dean Huber prior to complet ing registration.

6:00 P. M. to 9:00 P. M. Special students (beyond A.M. non-matriculated students special interest, auditors, an advanced certification, such a guidance, secondary school prin cipal, etc).

Students unable to take advantage of the above priority arrangement ma register with other groups provided they arrive **after their priority schedul**
Students MAY NOT register ahead of their priority listing.

LATE REGISTRATION
Monday, June 25, 1:00 P. M. to 3.00 P. M.
Tuesday, June 26, 1:00 P. M. to 3:00 P. M.
Students registering on June 25 and 26 will be charged a $5.00 lat registration fee.
No registrations will be accepted after 3:00 P. M., June 26.
Classes begin on June 25. Late registrants must meet the first schedule class after completing registration or be charged with an unexcuse absence.
Special three week course registration - July 12 - only for those exclusiv ly taking last sections of three week courses.

M.S.C. UNDERGRADUATE REGISTRATION PROCEDURE. Students should check with the College Registrar for "permission to take summer work" forms and registration details.

UNDERGRADUATES MATRICULATED AT COLLEGES OTHER THAN M.S.C. Follow procedures outlined above and register at time specified.

CHANGE OF SCHEDULE. No student will be permitted to change his schedule without approval of his advisor and the Director of the Summer Session. Changes may be made between 1:00 P. M. and 3:00 P. M. on June 25 and 26. No changes will be permitted after 3:00 P. M. on June 26. To change from "auditor" to "credit", or vice versa, a student must make formal application not later than the mid-point (July 13) in the Summer Session. Forms are available in the Summer Session office.

CANCELLATION OF COURSES. The College reserves the right to close any course for which the enrollment is insufficient. Students may then register in another course or receive a refund of tuition. If prerequisites are required (see course listings) the student must be sure he has fulfilled them or their equivalents.

*TUITION FEES AND EXPENSES

All checks should be made out to Montclair State College.

TUITION. For residents of New Jersey, $13.00 per semester hour credit; for out-of-state residents, $15.00 per credit.

SERVICE CHARGE. Fifty cents ($.50) per semester hour credit.

REGISTRATION FEE. $2.00 to be paid each time a student registers.

LATE REGISTRATION FEE. $5.00. This additional fee will be charged students registering on June 25 and June 26.

APPLICATION FOR ADMISSION FEE. $5.00 to be paid when student files an application for admission to a degree-granting program. This fee must accompany the application form and is not refundable.

TRANSCRIPT FEE. $1.00 for single copy. Inquire at Registrar's Office.

REFUNDING OF FEES. When the Director of the Summer Session receives written notice of withdrawal prior to the first meeting of the course, all tuition fees are refunded in full. Other refunds are pro-rated from the day on which the Director of the Summer Session receives written notification. Withdrawal before the end of the first third of the Summer Session — 60% tuition refund; during the middle third — 30%; during the last third — no refund. Withdrawals after the mid-point (July 13) will result in an automatic grade of "F".

WORK SCHOLARSHIPS. A limited number of tuition and room-fee scholarships are available. Students are assigned work in the various College departments. Write to Dean of Students for information.

* Subject to change any time by action of the State Board of Education.

SPECIAL ACTIVITIES
JUNE 25 – AUGUST 3

READING IMPROVEMENT LABORATORY: Available to New Jersey students in grades 7-12; small groups are formed according to age and achievement levels and meet daily, 10:00 A. M. to 12:00 Noon. The latest in equipment, films, and workshop materials are used to demonstrate speed of comprehension, study skills, and vocabulary growth. Enrollment is limited. Apply at least three months in advance of each term.

Fee: $50.00   Write to: Coordinator, Reading Improvement Laboratory

SPEECH AND HEARING CENTER: The Speech and Hearing Center will offer an intensive remedial speech program. It will accommodate a maximum of sixty children between 4 and 18 years of age. The program, offered at 10:45 A. M. to 12:30 P. M. daily, is designed to provide therapy for children with the usual types of speech problems, as well as for those who have major problems of voice, articulation, and rhythm (stuttering). Children with retarded language development or loss of language are also eligible. Therapy is also provided for children who have speech problems associated with tongue thrusting, malocclusion, and cleft palate.

Fee: $60.00   Write to: Coordinator, Speech and Hearing Center

MONTCLAIR STATE COLLEGE DAY CAMP: A general program of games, relays, story-telling, rhythms, and nature walks will be presented for children in the 6-12 year age range. The youngsters also will enjoy approximately one hour of arts and crafts activities. The dates will coincide with those of the regular summer session, June 25 to August 3, and the hours will be 8:30 A. M. to 12:30 P. M. The fee will include some arts and crafts supplies and light refreshments.

Fee: $8.00 per week   Write to: Director, Panzer School of Physical
Education and Hygiene, c/o this College

WORKSHOP FOR APPRENTICES IN DRAMATIC PRODUCTION: The Speech Department is pleased to announce that it will continue its summer program in theater for pre-college students. Secondary school students and recent graduates are eligible. Activities include the study of acting, scenery design and construction, lighting, make-up, and voice and diction. Following a 1:30 P. M. daily seminar, students will participate as actors and crew members in the preparation and presentation of major dramatic productions. Full use will be made of the extensive facilities in the air-conditioned Memorial Auditorium — one of the most modern and beautiful college theaters in the East.

Registration is limited. Application must be made in advance and should be accompanied by a letter of recommendation from the applicant's school Dramatics or English teacher. A personal interview will also be arranged.

Fee: $60.00   Write to: Coordinator, Summer Theater Programs

MONTCLAIR TO THE ARCTIC: For the month of July, 1962, a touring group of Players, the undergraduate dramatics organization on the Montclair campus, will tour a play to defense stations in Labrador, Newfoundland, Greenland, and Iceland for the USO. This honor came to Montclair when Players was selected as one of nine such groups from throughout the United States for the year 1962. The play will be LIGHT UP THE SKY, as requested by the touring selection committee of the USO and the American Educational Theater Association, joint sponsors of the tours.

TEXTBOOK EXHIBIT

On July 12 and July 13 from 8:00 A. M. to 3:00 P. M. there will be an exhibit of high school and elementary school textbooks. The exhibit is primarily for teachers and administrators attending the Summer Session, but will be open to undergraduate students and the general public. The exhibit will be located in Life Hall.

NEW JERSEY CONGRESS OF PARENTS AND TEACHERS
PARENT-TEACHER WORKSHOP
July 9-13

The New Jersey Congress, in cooperation with Montclair State College, will offer a five day workshop for parent-teacher officers and members, and for teachers and future teachers.

The purposes of this Workshop are:

1. To increase understanding of P. T. A. philosophy and objectives.
2. To stimulate and direct the planning for effective parent-teacher meetings.
3. To activate planning for action programs with the help of resource people and materials.
4. To suggest opportunities for new and different community activities of local parent-teacher associations.
5. To offer experience in gaining group leadership skills and help in the development of plans for parent-teacher study groups.

Write to: Mrs. Thomas C. Jones, P. T. A. Coordinator, State Chairman — Cooperation with Colleges, 1270 Wood Valley Road, Mountainside, New Jersey.

NEW JERSEY STATE SCHOOL OF CONSERVATION
BRANCHVILLE, NEW JERSEY

The six State Colleges, the State Department of Education, and the State Department of Conservation and Economic Development, jointly operate the New Jersey State School of Conservation at Lake Wapalanne in Stokes State Forest, Sussex County. Credit for the courses given at the New Jersey State School of Conservation may be applied toward the bachelor's or master's degrees at the New Jersey State Colleges, subject to approval in advance by the institution concerned. Students are advised to check with their advisors relative to the application of these credits toward degrees.

Courses in Camping, Conservation, Education, Field Biology, Field Science, Fine Arts, Geography, Industrial Arts, and Outdoor Education, are offered at the New Jersey State School of Conservation. Special descriptive announcements may also be had by writing to the New Jersey State School of Conservation, Branchville, New Jersey.

ALCOHOL EDUCATION WORKSHOP
June 21 through July 5

Health Education S412 — Alcohol Education Workshop	Dr. Tews
June 21 and June 22 — 7:00 to 10:00 P. M. and	Room 5-G
June 25 through June 29 — 1:30 to 4:30 P. M. and	
July 2, 3, 5 — 1:30 to 4:30 P. M.	

Credit: 2 semester hours

A workshop offered with the cooperation of the State Department of Health and aimed at preparing teachers of health, school nurse teachers, guidance personnel, and others, for more understanding service in this special area of education. The workshop will concentrate on a careful study of the physiological, sociological, and psychological problems involved in the use of beverage alcohol and on the materials, techniques, etc., found to be most useful in alcohol education programs.

A limited number of Tuition Scholarships are available. For full details regarding this workshop, write to: Director, Field Services.

DRIVER EDUCATION COURSES

PRE-SUMMER SESSION COURSE

Health Education S408 — Driver Education	Dr. Coder
June 13, 14, 15 — 7:00 to 10:00 P. M. and	Room A-A
June 18 through June 23 — 3:00 to 10:00 P. M. and	
June 25 through June 29 — 1:00 to 4:00 P. M.	

Credit: 3 semester hours

POST-SUMMER SESSION COURSE

Health Education S408 — Driver Education	**Dr. Coder**
August 1, 2, 3 — 1:00 to 4:30 P. M. and	Room A-A

August 6 through August 10 — 9:00 A. M. to 3:00 P. M. and
August 13 through August 17 — 9:00 A. M. to 3:00 P. M.

Credit: 3 semester hours

Authorization to Teach Behind-the-Wheel Driver Education and Driver Training:
A teacher must have his or her certificate endorsed by the Division of Teacher
Certification, State Department of Education. The requirements for such endorsement are: ("Rules Concerning Teachers' Certificates" — 18th edition —
revised 1956).

1. A valid New Jersey teacher's certificate.
2. A current New Jersey driver's license.
3. Three years' of automobile driving experience.
4. Evidence of satisfactory completion of a course in driver education and
   driver training approved by the Commissioner of Education.
5. A good driving record.
6. A standard sized car is required for road and skills test.

Secondary schools in New Jersey are increasing their offerings in Driver Educa-
tion. This increase has resulted in a demand for more Driver Education teachers.
To meet this demand, Montclair State College is increasing the number of
courses being conducted in this field. Assistance is given by the New Jersey
State Safety Council, the New Jersey Automobile Club, and American Automobile
Association, the New Jersey State Police, and the New Jersey Department of
Motor Vehicles.

EXTRA CHARGES are made for textbooks and other materials. Some materials
are furnished free.

Registration for these courses is limited. Students must be approved by Dr.
Coder prior to registration. Write to Dr. Coder for complete information. Fees
are to be paid on first day class meets.

PRE-SUMMER SESSION COURSE

Phys. Ed. S415 — Movement Techniques and Rhythmic	**Mrs. Sommer**
Accompaniment	Room 4-G

June 11 thru 15 — 4:30 to 6:30 P. M.
June 18 thru 22 — 4:15 to 6:30 P. M.
June 25 thru 30 — 9:00 to 1:00 P. M.

Credit: 2 semester hours

Registration at the first meeting of the class.

POST-SUMMER SESSION COURSE

Industrial Arts S407 — Field Study of the Practical Arts	**Dr. Duffy**
August 6-29 (18 days) 8:05 A. M. — 3:30 P. M.	**Mr. Streichler**

Registration — June 21 and June 22

Credit: 4 semester hours

Registration for this course is limited. Students must be approved b
Dr. Duffy prior to or at the time of registration.

THREE WEEK COURSES

First three weeks — June 25 through July 13

Education S504A	Curriculum Construction in Secondary School
Education S521A	Educational and Psychological Measurement in Guidance
Education S554A	Psychology and Education of Exceptional Children, I
Social Studies S471	The United States since World War I
Speech S105A	Introduction to Dramatic Production, I
Speech S437A	Dramatic Production Workshop

Last three weeks — July 16 through August 3

Education S504B	Seminar in Curriculum Organization
Education S521B	Psychological Tests in Guidance Programs
Education S554B	Psychology and Education of Exceptional Children, II
Social Studies S493A	Western Europe since World War I
Speech S105B	Introduction to Dramatic Production, II
Speech S437B	Advanced Dramatic Production Workshop

Student Life Building Lounge

COURSES OF THE SUMMER SESSION

Descriptions of the graduate courses will be found in the Graduate Bulletin of the College. Courses numbered 500 and above are open only to graduate students; those numbered 400-499, inclusive, are senior-graduate courses and their descriptions in the Graduate Bulletin follow the descriptions of the graduate courses. Courses below the 400 number will be found in the Undergraduate Bulletin of the College. Only entirely new courses are described in the Summer Session Bulletin.

CODE FOR BUILDINGS

Building	Code	Building	Code
College Hall (formerly		College High School	F
Administration Building)	A	Gymnasium	G
Annex #1	B	Finley Hall	H
Annex #2	C	Auditorium	J
Annex #3	D	Recreation Building	R
Annex #4	E		

BUSINESS EDUCATION DEPARTMENT

Business Education S411 — Tax Accounting
10:30-11:20 A. M.　　　　　Credit: 2 semester hours
Dr. Froehlich
Room 4-C

Business Education S501B — Research Seminar in Business Education
9:30-10:20 A. M.　　　　　Credit: 2 semester hours
Prerequisite: A.M. candidate
Dr. Froehlich
Room 1-C

Business Education S503 — The Business Education Curriculum
8:30-9:20 A. M.　　　　　Credit: 2 semester hours
Prerequisite: Business Education 502
Mr. Sheppard
Room 1-C

Business Education S516 — Business Organization and Management II
11:30-12:20 P. M.　　　　　Credit: 2 semester hours
Dr. Froehlich
Room 2-C

Business Education S532 — Field Studies and Audio-Visual Aids in Business Education
10:30-12:20 P. M.　　　　　Credit: 4 semester hours
Field trips to be scheduled
Mr. Sheppard
Room 1-C

EDUCATION DEPARTMENT

Education S201 — Human Development and Behavior I
11:30-12:45 P. M. Sec. I　　　Credit: 3 semester hours
8:05- 9:20 A. M. Sec. II　　　Credit: 3 semester hours
Dr. Seidman
Room 22-A
Mr. Fuchs
Room 22-A

Education S202 — Human Development and Behavior II
8:05-9:20 A. M.　　　　　Credit: 3 semester hours
Prerequisite: Education 201 or equivalent
Dr. Lutz
Room 30-A

Education S303 — The Teacher in School and Community
8:05- 9:20 A. M. Sec. I　　　Credit: 3 semester hours
11:30-12:45 P. M. Sec. II　　　Credit: 3 semester hours
Dr. Gorman
Room 25-A
Mr. Fuchs
Room 25-A

Education S304 — Principles and Techniques of Secondary Education
11:30-12:45 P. M.　　　　　Credit: 3 semester hours
Mr. Jump
Room 9-A

16

Education S401 — The Development of Educational Thought   Mr. Jump
8:05- 9:20 A. M. Sec. I   Credit: 3 semester hours   Room 9-A
11:30-12:45 P. M. Sec. II   Credit: 3 semester hours   Dr. Richardson
    Room 24-A

Education S406 — Educational Sociology   Dr. Gorman
11:30-12:45 P. M.   Credit: 3 semester hours   Room 30-A

Education S408 — Selection and Utilization of A-V Materials   Mr. Sheft
9:30-10:20 A. M.   Credit: 2 semester hours   Room D-A

Education S410 — Teaching Materials Workshop   Miss Fantone
10:30-11:20 A. M.   Credit: 2 semester hours   Room D-A

Education S462 — Survey of Reading Methods in   Mr. Buchner
    Secondary School Subjects
8:05-9:20 A. M.   Credit: 3 semester hours   Rooms 26 & 29-A

Education S463 — Recent Trends in European Education   Dr. Lange
July 1-August 15   Credit: 6 semester hours   Field Study
    Present educational policies and procedures in selected countries of Europe are investigated. A survey is made of present educational systems and a study is made of recent changes in selected European educational systems. This course is a field-study course covering a period of six weeks of intensive study and visitation to school systems in Europe.

Education S492 — Comparative Education   Dr. Richardson
8:05-9:20 A. M.   Credit: 3 semester hours   Room 24-A

Education S500A — Basic Educational Trends   Dr. Walter
11:30-12:20 P. M.   Credit: 2 semester hours   Room 5-F
    Prerequisite: Teaching Experience

Education S500C — Recent Trends in Secondary School Methods   Mr. Salt
8:30-9:20 P. M.   Credit: 2 semester hours   Room 10-A
    Prerequisite: Teaching Experience

Education S500D — School Administration I: Dr. Morehead
    Functions and Organization
9:30-10:20 A. M.   Credit: 2 semester hours   Room 10-A
    Prerequisite: Teaching Experience

Education S500F — School Administration III: Dr. Atkinson
    Community Relations
10:30-11:20 A. M.   Credit: 2 semester hours   Room 4-F
    Prerequisite: Teaching Experience

Education S501 — Tests and Measurements in   Dr. Walter
    Secondary Education
8:30-9:20 A. M.   Credit: 2 semester hours   Room 5-F

Education S502 — Organization and Administration of the   Dr. Peckham
    Modern High School
11:30-12:20 P. M.   Credit: 2 semester hours   Room 4-C
    Prerequisite: Education 500D or equivalent

Education S503 — Methods and Instruments of Research   Dr. Walter
10:30-11:20 A. M. Sec. I   Credit: 2 semester hours   Room 5-F
8:30-9:20 A. M. Sec. II   Credit: 2 semester hours   Dr. Peckham
    Room 3-F
    Prerequisite: Math. 400 or Educ. 501, or equivalent

Education S504A — Curriculum Construction in the Secondary School   Mr. Salt
10:30-12:20 P. M.   Credit: 2 semester hours   Room 7-F
    Prerequisite: Teaching Experience
    (First three weeks — June 25 through July 13)

17

Education S504B — Seminar in Curriculum Organization
10:30-12:20 P. M.   Credit: 2 semester hours
    Prerequisite: Educ. 504A or equivalent
    (Last three weeks — July 16 through August 3)

Education S505 — Organization and Administration of
                Extra-Curricular Activities
11:30-12:20 P. M.   Credit: 2 semester hours

Education S506 — School Law
10:30-11:20 A. M.   Credit: 2 semester hours
    (Not open to students who have had Educ. 500E)
    Prerequisite: Education 500D or equivalent

Education S508 — Supervision of Instruction in
                Secondary Schools
11:30-12:20 P. M.   Credit: 2 semester hours
    Prerequisite: Education 500D or equivalent

Education S510 — Seminar in Secondary Administration
                and Supervision
9:30-10:20 A. M.   Credit: 2 semester hours
    Prerequisite: Educ. 502 or 601A, and 508 or 601B

Education S521A — Educational and Psychological
                Measurement in Guidance
8:30-10:20 A. M.   Credit: 2 semester hours
    Prerequisite: Teaching Experience
    (First three weeks — June 25 through July 13)

Education S521B — Psychological Tests in Guidance Programs
8:30-10:20 A. M.   Credit: 2 semester hours
    Prerequisite: Education 521A
    (Last three weeks — July 16 through August 3)

Education S535 — Vocational Guidance
11:30-12:20 P. M.   Credit: 2 semester hours
    Prerequisite: Education 551

Education S551 — Principles and Techniques of Guidance
9:30-10:20 A. M. Sec. I   Credit: 2 semester hours
8:30-9:20 A. M. Sec. II   Credit: 2 semester hours
    Prerequisite: Teaching Experience
    This course is a prerequisite for most guidance cours
division of the college.

Education S554A — Psychology and Education of
                Exceptional Children, I
10:30-12:20 P. M.   Credit: 2 semester hours
    Prerequisite: Introductory Psychology
    (First three weeks — June 25 through July 13)

Education S554B — Psychology and Education of
                Exceptional Children, II
10:30-12:20 P. M.   Credit: 2 semester hours
    Prerequisite: Education 554A
    (Last three weeks — July 16 through August 3)

Education S558 — Corrective and Remedial Reading
                in Secondary School
11:30-12:20 P. M.   Credit: 2 semester hours   Ro

Education S587 — Administration and Supervision of
                Guidance Programs
8:30-9:20 A. M.   Credit: 2 semester hours
    Prerequisite: Education 551 and 6 S .H. in Area 3 of P

Education S588 — Techniques of Interviewing and Counseling   Dr. Brower
9:30-10:20 A. M.   Credit: 2 semester hours   Room 5-F
   Prerequisite: 12 S. H. in Personnel and Guidance

Education S602 — Seminar in Guidance   Dr. Davis
10:30-12:20 P. M.   Credit: 4 semester hours   Room 3-F
   Prerequisite: Educ. 551, 503, and A.M. Candidate

ENGLISH DEPARTMENT

English S100C — Fundamentals of Writing   Mrs. Meiers
11:30-12:45 P. M.   Credit: 3 semester hours   Room 1-B

English S100G — Western World Literature   Dr. Leavitt
8:05-9:20 A. M.   Credit: 3 semester hours   Room 1-B

English S201 — American Literature I   Mr. Conrad
8:05-9:20 A. M.   Credit: 3 semester hours   Room 2-B

English S202 — American Literature II   Mr. Conrad
11:30-12:45 P. M.   Credit: 3 semester hours   Room 2-B

English S352 — Language, Thought and Behavior   Mrs. Meiers
9:30-10:20 A. M.   Credit: 2 semester hours   Room 1-B

English S401X — The Teaching of English in Secondary Schools   Dr. Bohn
8:30-9:20 A. M.   Credit: 2 semester hours   Room 1-A

English S503 — Geoffrey Chaucer and His Times   Dr. Krauss
9:30-10:20 A. M.   Credit: 2 semester hours   Room 1-A

English S513 — The Renaissance   Dr. Krauss
11:30-12:20 P. M.   Credit: 2 semester hours   Room 1-A

English S531 — Seventeenth Century Literature   Mr. Pettegrove
8:30-9:20 A. M.   Credit: 2 semester hours   Room 2-A

English S532 — The Victorian Novel   Mr. Pettegrove
11:30-12:20 P. M.   Credit: 2 semester hours   Room 2-A

English S533 — Masters of American Literature   Dr. Leavitt
10:30-11:20 A. M.   Credit: 2 semester hours   Room 2-A

English S544B — Shakespeare (Comedies)   Dr. Bohn
10:30-11:20 A. M.   Credit: 2 semester hours   Room 1-A

FINE ARTS DEPARTMENT

Fine Arts S401 — Art Curriculum of Elementary   Mr. Vernacchia
     and Secondary Schools
8:30-9:20 A. M.   Credit: 2 semester hours   Room AL-H

Fine Arts S403A — Print Making I or II   Mr. Vernacchia
   or S403B
11:30-12:45 P. M.   Credit: 2 semester hours   Room 219-H

Fine Arts S440A — Home Design and Community Planning I   Dr. Wygant
9:30-10:20 A. M.   Credit: 2 semester hours   Room 221-H

Fine Arts S445 — Life Drawing   Dr. Wygant
8:30-9:20 A. M.   Credit: 2 semester hours   Room 221-H

Fine Arts S490 — Art of the Nineteenth Century   Mr. Vernacchia
10:30-11:20 A. M.   Credit: 2 semester hours   Room 221-H

19

FOREIGN LANGUAGE DEPARTMENT

French S407 — Modern French Theater   Dr. Szklarczyk
9:30-10:20 A. M.   Credit: 2 semester hours   Room 4-D
    The purpose of this course is to acquaint students with the history and development of the French theater since 1920. Major currents and trends in contemporary drama will be analyzed. Authors studied will include Jules Romains, Paul Claudel, Henri de Montherlant, Jean Girardoux, Jean-Paul Sartre, Albert Camus and other dramatists representative of each major trend of the modern French theater.

French S421 — French Language Seminar   Dr. Szklarczyk
8:30- 9:20 A. M.   Credit: 2 semester hours   Language Lab-A

Spanish S505 — Spanish Literary Expression and Style   Dr. Prieto
11:30-12:20 P. M.   Credit: 2 semester hours   Room 4-D

Spanish S521 — Contemporary Spanish Drama   Dr. Prieto
10:30-11:20 A. M.   Credit: 2 semester hours   Room 4-D
    This course includes an analysis of characters, space, and time in contemporary Spanish plays and their relationship to Spanish life. Works of Benavente, Casona, Garcia Lorca, Lopez Rubio, Buero Vallejo, and Sastre are studied.
(N,te: The above courses may be taken with the permission of the instructor.)

GEOGRAPHY DEPARTMENT

Science S100C — Earth Science   Mr. Kelland
10:30-11:20 A. M.   Credit: 2 semester hours   Room 5-D

Geography S414A — Advanced Economic Geography   Mr. Kelland
11:30-12:20 P. M.   Credit: 2 semester hours   Room 5-D

Geography S419X — Geography of the Soviet Union   Mr. Kelland
9:30-10:20 A. M.   Credit: 2 semester hours   Room 5-D

HOME ECONOMICS DEPARTMENT

Home Economics S424 — Workshop in Home Economics   Miss Reiff
Education: Educables — Retarded Children
July 5-July 21, including Saturdays
9:30-11:30 A. M.   Credit: 3 semester hours   Room 114-H
1:00-3:00 P. M.
Sats. 1:00-3:00 P. M.

INDUSTRIAL ARTS DEPARTMENT

Ind. Arts S101 — Introduction to Industrial Arts   Mr. Streichler
8:05-9:20 A. M.   Credit: 2 semester hours   Room 117-H

Ind. Arts S401 — Comprehensive General Shop for
     Elementary and Junior High School   To be announced
12:30-4:10 P. M. Sec. I   Credit: 4 semester hours   Room 116-H
6:00-9:40 P. M. Sec. II   Mr. Tressler
     Room 116-H

Ind. Arts S407 — Field Study of the Practical Arts   Dr. Duffy
     Mr. Streichler
8:05-3:30 P. M.   Credit: 4 semester hours   Room 117-H
August 6-29, (18 Days — Post Session)
     Open to undergraduates with approval of instructor.

Ind. Arts S421 — Jewelry Making and Lapidary   Dr. Duffy
9:30-11:00 A. M.   Credit: 2 semester hours   Room 116-H

Ind. Arts S503 — Problems in Teaching Industrial Arts   To be announced
8:05-9:20 A. M.   Credit: 3 semester hours   Room 114-H

Ind. Arts S511 — Supervision of Industrial Arts   To be announced
11:30-12:45 P. M.   Credit: 3 semester hours   Room 117-H
     Prerequisite: 4 S. H. credit in Ind. Arts and approval of instructor

MATHEMATICS DEPARTMENT

Mathematics S300 — Social Uses of Mathematics   Mr. Humphreys
8:30-9:20 A. M.   Credit: 2 semester hours   Room 108-H

Mathematics S310 — An Introduction to Mathematics   Mr. Humphreys
10:30-11:20 A. M.   Credit: 2 semester hours   Room 108-H
     May be substituted for Math. 300

Mathematics S400 — Educational Statistics   Dr. Edwards
8:30- 9:20 A. M. Sec. I   Credit: 2 semester hours   Room 7-F
9:30-10:20 A. M. Sec. II   Credit: 2 semester hours   Mr. Humphreys
     Prerequisite for Education 503   Room 108-H

Mathematics S401X — The Teaching of Mathematics   Mr. Gouss
     in Secondary Schools
8:30-9:20 A. M.   Credit: 2 semester hours   Room 104-H

Mathematics S407 — Advanced Calculus   Mr. Williams
8:30-9:20 A. M.   Credit: 2 semester hours   Room 106-H

Mathematics S409 — Introduction to Contemporary Mathematics   Mr. Gouss
11:30-12:20 P. M.   Credit: 2 semester hours   Room 104-H

Mathematics S501 — Administration and Supervision of Mathematics   Mr. Gouss
10:30-11:20 A. M.   Credit: 2 semester hours   Room 104-H

Mathematics S503 — Foundations of Algebra   Mr. Williams
10:30-11:20 A. M.   Credit: 2 semester hours   Room 106-H

Mathematics S508 — Foundations of Geometry   Mr. Devlin
9:30-10:20 A. M.   Credit: 2 semester hours   Room 104-H

Mathematics S552 — Mathematics of Physical Sciences   Mr. Williams
11:30-12:20 P. M.   Credit: 2 semester hours   Room 106-H

The following courses are open only to National Science Foundation participants. Students were selected in March 1962 and registrations are closed. These courses are listed for record purposes only.

Mathematics S201 — Calculus I   Dr. Pettofrezzo
8:30-10:20 A. M.   Credit: 4 semester hours   Room 14-F

Mathematics S504 — Modern Algebra   Dr. Meserve
8:30-9:20 A. M.   Credit: 2 semester hours   Room 105-H

Mathematics S517 — The Theory of Numbers   Mr. Devlin
8:30-9:20 A. M.   Credit: 2 semester hours   Room 107-H

Mathematics S480 — Elements of Logic   Dr. Maletsky
9:30-10:20 A. M.   Credit: 2 semester hours   Room 105-H

Science S418 — Three Centuries of Science Progress   Dr. Allen
9:30-10:20 A. M.   Credit: 2 semester hours   Room 107-H

Mathematics S405 — History of Mathematics   Miss Cotter
11:00-12:00 Noon   Credit: 2 semester hours   Room 14-F

Mathematics S522 — Introduction to Probability and Statistics   Mr. Rourke
11:00-12:00 Noon   Credit: 2 semester hours   Room 105-H

Mathematics S529 — Curriculum Construction in Mathematics   Dr. Syer
11:00-12:00 Noon   Credit: 2 semester hours   Room 107-H

MUSIC DEPARTMENT

Music S100 — Music Appreciation   Mr. Hayto
9:30-10:20 A. M.   Credit: 2 semester hours   Room 13-

PANZER SCHOOL OF PHYSICAL EDUCATION AND HYGIEN

Health Education S100 — Healthful Living   Dr. Tew
11:30-12:20 P. M.   Credit: 2 semester hours   Room 5-

Phys. Ed. S415 — Movement Techniques and   Mrs. Somme
                 Rhythmic Accompaniment
June 11-15 4:30-6:30 P. M.   Credit: 2 semester hours   Room 4-
June 18-22 4:15-6:30 P. M.
June 25-30 9:00-1:00 P. M.
        This course is designed to develop skill and understanding of body move
ment techniques and the rhythmic accompaniment of such techniques. Lecture
reading assignments, demonstrations, and participation will be utilized to relat
anatomical structure and functions to these movement techniques and to develo
teaching skills.

Health Education S408 — Driver Education   Dr. Cod
                        Credit: 3 semester hours   Room A-
        Prerequisite: Approval of instructor prior to registration.
        For details, see pages 13-14 and write to Dr. Coder.

Health Education S412 — Alcohol Education Workshop   Dr. Te
                        Credit: 2 semester hours   Room 5-
        Pre-Summer Session — June 21 through July 5.
        See page 13 for details.

SCIENCE DEPARTMENT

Biology S407 — Comparative Embryology   Dr. McDowell
10:30-11:20 A. M.   Credit: 4 semester hours   Room 217-H
1:00-5:00 P. M. Laboratory on Monday, Wednesday and Friday
      Prerequisite: 8 semester hours work in Zoology

Biology S412 — Genetics   Dr. McDowell
11:30-12:20 P. M.   Credit: 2 semester hours   Room 217-H
      Prerequisite: Elementary Biology

Chemistry S413 — Atomic Structure and Atomic Energy   Dr. Gawley
9:30-10:20 A. M.   Credit: 2 semester hours   Room 204-H
      Prerequisites: General Chemistry, General Physics and permission of
      the instructor.

Physics S411A — Photography I   Dr. Smith
Meets Monday, Wednesday and Friday only
11:30-12:20 P. M.   Credit: 2 semester hours   Room 201-H
1:00-3:00 P. M. Laboratory   and 214-H
      Prerequisites: General Physics, General Chemistry and permission of
      instructor.

Physics S513 — Nuclear Radiation   Dr. Smith
8:30-9:20 A. M.   Credit: 2 semester hours   Room 201-H
      Prerequisites: General Physics, General Chemistry and permission of
      instructor.

Science S100C — Earth Science   Mr. Kelland
10:30-11:20 A. M   Credit: 2 semester hours   Room 5-D

Science S401X — The Teaching of Science in Secondary Schools   Dr. Gawley
8:30-9:20 A. M.   Credit: 2 semester hours   Room 204-H

Science S409 — Senior High School Physical   Dr. Gawley
      Science Demonstrations
10:30-11:20 A. M.   Credit: 2 semester hours   Room 204-H

Science S418 — Three Centuries of Science Progress   Dr. Smith
9:30-10:20 A. M.   Credit: 2 semester hours   Room 201-H

SOCIAL STUDIES DEPARTMENT

Social Studies S200A — Contemporary American Life   Mr. Johnson
11:30-12:45 P. M.   Credit: 3 semester hours   Room 21-A

Social Studies S202X — The Development of the   To be announced
      United States
11:30-12:20 P. M.   Credit: 2 semester hours   Room 5-C

Social Studies S401X — The Teaching of Social Studies   Dr. Moffatt
      in Secondary Schools   Dr. Royer
8:30-9:20 A. M.   Credit: 2 semester hours   Room 20-A

Social Studies S412 — International Government   Mr. Johnson
8:05-9:20 A. M.   Credit: 3 semester hours   Room 21-A

Social Studies S456 — International Economic Relations   Dr. Rellahan
10:30-11:20 A. M.   Credit: 2 semester hours   Room 9-A

Social Studies S471 — The United States since World War I   Dr. Moffatt
9:30-11:10 A. M.   Credit: 2 semester hours   Room 20-A
      (First three weeks — June 25 through July 13)

Social Studies S480 — Social History of the United States — **Dr. Royer**
11:30-12:20 P. M.   Credit: 2 semester hours   Room 20-A

Social Studies S486X — World Survey   **Mr. Bye**
July 5-August 27   Credit: 6 semester hours   Field Study

Social Studies S487 — Field Studies in the   **Mr. Kahn**
          Arts: European Civilization
July 9-August 25   Credit: 6 semester hours   Field Study

Social Studies S493A — Western Europe since World War I   **Dr. Royer**
9:30-11:10 A. M.   Credit: 2 semester hours   Room 20-A
          (Last three weeks — July 16 through August 3)

SPEECH DEPARTMENT

Speech S100D — Fundamentals of Speech   **Mr. Moll**
11:30-12:45 P. M.   Credit: 3 semester hours   Room 108-H

Speech S105A — Introduction to Dramatic Production I   **Dr. McElroy**
1:30-4:30 P. M.   Credit: 2 semester hours   Room Aud.-J
          (First three weeks — June 25 through July 13)

Speech S105B — Introduction to Dramatic Production II   **Dr. McElroy**
1:30-4:30 P. M.   Credit: 2 semester hours   Room Aud.-J
          (Last three weeks — July 16 through August 3)

Speech S204 — Introduction to Public Speaking   **Mr. Moll**
9:30-10:20 A. M.   Credit: 2 semester hours   Room 106-H

Speech S435 — Stagecraft   **To be announced**
1:30-2:45 P. M.   Credit: 2 semester hours   Room Aud.-J

Speech S437A — Dramatic Production Workship   **To be announced**
1:30-4:30 P. M.   Credit: 2 semester hours   Room Aud.-J
          (First three weeks — June 25 through July 13)

Speech S437B — Advanced Dramatic Production Workshop   **Mr. Ballare**
1:30-4:30 P. M.   Credit: 2 semester hours   Room Aud.-J
          (Last three weeks — July 16 through August 3)

Speech S439B — Anatomy and Physiology of the   **Miss Kauffman**
          Auditory and Vocal Mechanisms
9:30-10:20 A. M.   Credit: 2 semester hours   Room 2-J

Speech S439D — Practicum in Speech Correction   **Mrs. Hubschman**
10:30-11:20 A. M.   Credit: 1 semester hour   Room 1-J

Speech S439E — Advanced Practicum in Speech Correction   **Mrs. Hubschman**
11:30-12:20 P. M.   Credit: 1 semester hour   Room 2-J

Speech S439G — Principles of Speech Therapy   **Mrs. Hubschman**
1:30-2:20 P. M.   Credit: 2 semester hours   Room 2-J
This course presents the basic theories and practices of speech correction which
the speech therapist can apply in programs of re-education and rehabilitation.
Emphasis is placed on speech development in the individual, and on the voice
and speech problems commonly found in grades K through 12. Speech screening
and speech practice materials are developed. Demonstrations with children
enrolled in the Speech and Hearing Center on campus are arranged.

Speech S468 — Measurement of Hearing   **Dr. Leight**
8:05-9:20 A. M.   Credit: 3 semester hours   Room 2-J

Speech S532 — Practicum in Speech Rehabilitation   **Dr. Leight**
10:30-11:20 A. M.   Credit: 2 semester hours   Room 2-J

Speech S535 — Seminar in Speech and Language Rehabilitation   **Dr. Scholl**
9:00-12:30 P. M.   Credit: 6 semester hours   Room 4-J

Speech S567 — Seminar in Dramatic Production   **Dr. McElroy and Staff**
1:30-5:00 P. M.   Credit: 6 semester hours   Room Aud.-J

24

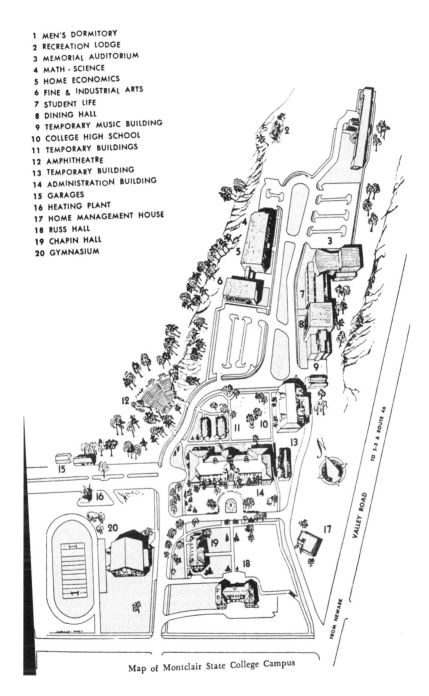

1 MEN'S DORMITORY
2 RECREATION LODGE
3 MEMORIAL AUDITORIUM
4 MATH - SCIENCE
5 HOME ECONOMICS
6 FINE & INDUSTRIAL ARTS
7 STUDENT LIFE
8 DINING HALL
9 TEMPORARY MUSIC BUILDING
10 COLLEGE HIGH SCHOOL
11 TEMPORARY BUILDINGS
12 AMPHITHEATRE
13 TEMPORARY BUILDING
14 ADMINISTRATION BUILDING
15 GARAGES
16 HEATING PLANT
17 HOME MANAGEMENT HOUSE
18 RUSS HALL
19 CHAPIN HALL
20 GYMNASIUM

Map of Montclair State College Campus

Summer Session
MONTCLAIR STATE COLLEGE
UPPER MONTCLAIR, N. J.

Sec. 34
U

Upper
Pe

1963 SUMMER SESSION
JUNE 25 to AUGUST 9

MONTCLAIR STATE COLLEGE
UPPER MONTCLAIR, NEW JERSEY

SUMMER SESSION

MONTCLAIR STATE COLLEGE

UPPER MONTCLAIR, NEW JERSEY

JUNE 25 to AUGUST 9

1963

Volume 55   Number 5

June 25	Registration	See page 12 for complete registration information and priority schedule
June 26	Registration	
June 27	Classes begin	Late Registration period
June 28	End of late registration	No registrations accepted after 3:00 P. M.
July 4 & 5	No classes	
July 18	Special Registration for 2nd series of three-week courses	
July 19	Mid-point in semester	No withdrawals or change of status after this date
August 9	Classes end	

SPECIAL EVENTS AND FEATURES·

July 8-12	New Jersey Congress of Parents and Teachers Workshop:	Life Hall: 9:00 A. M. - 12:30 P. M.
July 11	Book Exhibit	Life Hall: 8:30 A. M. - 2:30 P. M.
July 12	Book Exhibit	Life Hall: 8:30 A. M. - 2:30 P. M.

SPECIAL TOURS*

July 9 August 19	Recent Trends in European Education	Education S493
July 5 August 22	South Pacific	Social Studies S489

*Write to Bureau of Field Studies for further details.
Courses are listed in bulletin under departmental headings.

Montclair State College, a member of the American Association of Colleges of Teacher Education, is fully accredited by the Middle States Association of Colleges and Secondary Schools. Montclair State is also fully accredited by the National Council for Accreditation of Teacher Education for the preparation of Elementary and Secondary School Teachers and School Service Personnel, with the Master's Degree as the highest degree approved.

State Board of Education

Commissioner of Education
DR. FREDERICK M. RAUBINGER

Assistant Commissioner for Higher Education
DR. EARL E. MOSIER

Director of Teacher Education and Certification
DR. ALLAN F. ROSEBROCK

Director of Field Services for High Education
MR. STEPHEN POLIACIK

COLLEGE ADMINISTRATION

E. DeALTON PARTRIDGE, Ph.D. .... *President*
CLYDE M. HUBER, Ph.D. .... *Dean of the College*
LAWTON W. BLANTON, A.M. .... *Dean of Students*
JOHN J. RELLAHAN, Ph.D. .... *Chairman of Graduate Council*
EDWARD J. AMBRY, A.M. .... *Director of Field Services and Summer Session*
ROBERT E. MacVANE, Ed.M. .... *Asst. Director of Field Services and Summer Session*
IONA S. HENRY, Ed.D. .... *Assistant Director of Students—Women*
NORMAN E. LANGE, Ed.D. .... *Director of Student Teaching and Placement*
PETER P. STAPAY, Ed.M. .... *Registrar*
MARIE M. FRAZEE, A.M. .... *Academic Counselor*
CLAIRE M. MERLEHAN A.M. .... *Head Librarian*
BERNARD SIEGEL, M.B.A. .... *Business Manager*

HEALTH SERVICES

CHARLOTTE L. PRITCHARD, R.N., A.M. .... *College Nurse*

GRADUATE COUNCIL

John J. Rellahan, *Chairman*
Edward J. Ambry
Harold C. Bohn
Delvin L. Covey
Earl C. Davis
L. Howard Fox

Carl E. Frankson
M. Herbert Freeman
Irwin H. Gawley
Clyde M. Huber
Walter E. Kops

Rose Metz, *Secretary*
Orpha M. Lutz
Allan Morehead
E. DeAlton Partridge
Anthony J. Pettofrezzo

FACULTY

SUMMER SESSION 1963

E. DeALTON PARTRIDGE, Ph.D. .... President
CLYDE M. HUBER, Ph.D. .... Dean of the College
EDWARD J. AMBRY, A.M. .... Director, Summer Session
HUGH ALLEN, Jr., Ed.D. .... Chairman, Department of Science
DAVID N. ALLOWAY, A.M. .... Social Studies
PHILIP H. ANDERSON, A.M. .... Mathematics
KEITH W. ATKINSON, Ph.D. .... Education
WILLIAM A. BALLARE, A.M. .... Speech
JOSEPH F. BECKER, Ph.D. .... Science
DANIEL BROWER, Ph.D. .... Education
LEONARD J. BUCHNER, A.M. .... Coordinator, Reading Laboratory
MARSHALL BUTLER, A.M. .... Industrial Arts
EDGAR C. BYE., A.M. .... Coordinator, Bureau of Field Studies
ALDEN C. CODER, Ed.D. .... Driver Education
DELVIN L. COVEY, Ph.D. .... Chairman, Department of Foreign Languages
EARL C. DAVIS, Ph.D. .... Education
JOHN F. DEVLIN, A.M. .... Mathematics
JOSEPH W. DUFFY, Ed.D. .... Industrial Arts

ARTHUR W. EARL, Ed.D. .... Industrial Arts
CLIFFORD E. EMANUELSON, Ed.M. .. Dir., N. J. State School of Conservation
EMMA FANTONE, A.M. .... Coordinator, Audio-Visual Center
MARGARET P. FEIERABEND, A.M. .... English
L. HOWARD FOX, Ph.D. .... Chairman, Department of Speech
CARL E. FRANKSON, Ph.D. .... Chairman, Department of Industrial Arts
MARIE M. FRAZEE, A.M. .... Academic Counselor
PAUL E. FROEHLICH, Ed.D. .... Business Education
LEO G. FUCHS, Ed.M. .... Education
RICHARD J. GALLIEN, A.M. .... New Jersey State School of Conservation
VLADIMIR L. GARICK, Ph.D. .... Science
IRWIN H. GAWLEY, JR., Ed.D. .... Science
ABRAHAM GELFOND, Ph.D. .... Education
ALFRED H. GORMAN, Ed.D. .... Education
DONALD B. GREGG, A.M. .... Education
RUSSELL HAYTON, M. SAC.M. .... Music
RICHARD H. HODSON, A.M. .... Science
EVA HUBSCHMAN, A.M. .... Speech
EDWARD W. JOHNSON, A.M. .... Science
RAYMOND JUMP, A.M. .... Education
ELLEN KAUFFMAN, A.M. .... Speech
FRANK S. KELLAND, A.M. .... Geography
RUSSELL KRAUSS, Ph.D. .... English
NORMAN E. LANGE, Ed.D. .... Education
CHARLES L. LEAVITT, Ph.D. .... English
GILBERT LEIGHT, Ph.D. .... Speech
RAYMOND C. LEWIN, A.M. .... Education
ORPHA M. LUTZ, Ph.D. .... N.S.F. Program: Education
EVAN M. MALETSKY, Ph.D. .... N.S.F. Program: Mathematics
CLYDE W. McELROY, A.M. .... Speech
BRUCE E. MESERVE, Ph.D. .... Chairman, Department of Mathematics
KARL R. MOLL, A.M. .... Speech
CLAIRE M. MERLEHAN, A.M. .... Head Librarian
ALLAN MOREHEAD, Ed.D. .... Chairman, Department of Education
JAMES B. NORRIS, A.M. .... New Jersey State School of Conservation
GEORGE A. OLSEN, A.M. .... Industrial Arts
RICHARD PASVOLSKY, A.M. .... New Jersey State School of Conservation
EARL K. PECKHAM, Ed.D. .... Education
JEANETTE T. POORE B.S. in L.S. .... Librarian
SARA M. PRIETO, Ph.D. .... Foreign Language
HERBERT E. REASKE, A.M. .... English
THOMAS H. RICHARDSON, Ed.D. .... Education
HERMAN ROSENBERG, Ph.D. .... N.S.F. Program: Mathematics
HELEN E. ROYER, Ph.D. .... Social Studies
GEORGE E. SALT, A.M. .... Education
HAROLD M. SCHOLL, Ed.D. .... Speech
JEROME M. SEIDMAN, Ph.D. .... Education
THADDEUS J. SHEFT, A.M. .... Associate Coordinator, Audio-Visual Center
MARION SIEGELTUCH, M.L.S. .... Librarian
BURTON B. SILVER, A.M. .... Science
MAX A. SOBEL, Ph.D. .... Director N.S.F. Program: Mathematics
BETTY K. SOMMER .... Physical Education
JERRY STREICHLER, Ed.D. .... Industrial Arts
ADRIAN STRUYK, A.M. .... Mathematics
LILLIAN SZKLARCZYK, Ph.D. .... Foreign Language
RICHARD W. TEWS, Ph.D. .... Director, Panzer School of Physical
Education and Hygiene
RALPH A. VERNACCHIA, A.M. .... Fine Arts
HAZEL M. WACKER, Ed.D. .... Health and Physical Education
RALPH WALTER, Ed.D. .... Education
VERNON WILLIAMS, A.M. .... Mathematics
FOSTER L. WYGANT, Ed.D. .... Fine Arts
FREDERIC H. YOUNG, Ph.D. .... English

AIMS AND OBJECTIVES

The Summer School is designed specifically to meet the needs of:

1. Matriculated students enrolled in graduate programs who wish to meet requirements for the Master of Arts degree.
2. Teachers-in-service who desire to complete degree requirements, to improve their professional standing, or to take courses for state certification purposes.
3. Graduates from liberal arts colleges seeking provisional or limited certification to teach in the New Jersey public secondary schools.
4. Undergraduates from Montclair and other colleges desiring to continue college programs over the summer.
5. Persons interested in pursuing college work for cultural or avocational purposes whether or not they desire credit.
6. Persons interested in special workshops, institutes, and seminars.

. ADMISSION REGULATIONS

Students may enter in one of two categories: Students seeking a Master's Degree (degree candidates), or students not seeking a degree.

Degree Candidates — MATRICULATION FOR THE MASTER OF ARTS DEGREE

Persons Eligible — Teachers-in-service, as well as those interested in personal and professional growth who hold a bachelor's degree from an accredited college, have a high scholastic average and hold a New Jersey teacher's certificate.

Procedure

1. File an application with the Chairman of the Graduate Council and pay a $5.00 application for admission fee (see "Tuition, Fees and Expenses").

2. Have forwarded to the Graduate Office official transcripts of all previous college work. (Upon acceptance, a student will be furnished a definite statement of requirements, entitled a Work Program. This Work Program must be presented each time a student registers.)

3. Obtain approval of courses from your Department Chairman or Advisor during the hours of registration.

Note: 1 and 2 above should be completed at least one month prior to registration for the Summer Session.

Transfer of Credits — Not more than 8 semester-hours of work taken prior to matriculation are accepted for credit toward the A.M. degree. Transfer of graduate credit from other institutions — up to 8 semester hours — may be granted graduates of accredited institutions who matriculate on or after April 12, 1962.

Research Requirement — Education 503, Methods and Instruments of Research, and Education 603, Principles and Practices of Research, or a departmental research seminar. Education 503 should be taken rather early in the program and precedes work in more advanced research courses.

Master's Thesis — Students writing a thesis must register for the course in thesis writing (Graduate A600) which carries 4 semester hours of credit. For further information regarding the thesis, see the Graduate Bulletin

Residence Requirement — All matriculated students in the Graduate Division will be required to complete at least one full-time (6 s. h.) summer session or at least one regular semester to fulfill this requirement.

Application for degree conferment — A candidate for a degree must file with the Registrar an application for conferment of the degree before November 30 of the college year in which he expects to complete his work. Application blanks for this purpose may be secured in the Registrar's Office. The responsibility for making said application rests with the candidate. Students should check with advisors concerning final examination dates and other details involved in the graduation procedure.

STUDENTS NOT SEEKING A DEGREE, but

1. **Desiring to Transfer Credit.** Persons who wish to enroll in courses for the purpose of having credit transferred to another institution may be admitted by submitting to the Director of Summer Session an official letter from the Dean of the University or College in which they are earning the degree. This letter must contain a statement that the student is in good standing, his accumulative average, and the courses or kind of courses for which the student may register. Special transfer of credit forms must be completed in the Part-Time and Extension Office. The College reserves the right to decide whether or not the student has fulfilled necessary prerequisites. Certain 400-numbered courses and all 500 and 600-numbered courses are open only to graduate students. College Deans should inquire about students' eligibility if interested in 400-level courses.

2. **Desiring to Audit.** Persons who desire to take courses for cultural, vocational, professional, or avocational purposes, but who do not wish college credit, may register as auditors. All persons auditing a course must establish eligibility, register, and pay the same tuition fees as other students.

3. **Desiring initial teaching certificates,** (emergency, provisional or limited). Before registration will be accepted, students should follow instructions listed under the heading, "Certification for Teaching". (See Below)

4. **Desiring work beyond A.M. or for advanced certificates.**

CERTIFICATION FOR TEACHING

Certificates to teach in New Jersey Public Schools are issued by: the State Board of Examiners, Department of Education, 175 West State Street, Trenton 25, New Jersey. Address all inquiries to them regarding certification requirements.

ENROLLING AT MONTCLAIR. At registration time bring correspondence received from the State Board of Examiners as well as transcripts of all previous academic work. All general questions regarding certification should be addressed to the Certification Advisor at this College.

COURSE OFFERINGS. The following professional Education courses offered this summer are approved by the State Board of Examiners for certification to teach in New Jersey Secondary Schools. Courses should be selected from the following (indicated in the suggested sequence in which they should be taken):

Education	S201	Human Development and Behavior I
Education	S202	Human Development and Behavior II
Education	S303	The Teacher in School and Community
Education	S304	Principles and Techniques of Secondary Education
Education	S401	The Development of Educational Thought
Education	S406	Educational Sociology
Education	S408	Selection and Utilization of Audio-Visual Materials
Education	S409	Radio and Sound Equipment in the Classroom
Education	S492	Comparative Education
English	S519	English in the Modern High School
Fine Arts	S302	Foundations of Art Education
Health Ed.	S100	Healthful Living
Mathematics	S401X	The Teaching of Mathematics in Secondary Schools
Science	S401X	The Teaching of Science in Secondary Schools

Supervised Student Teaching. Students desiring information concerning this requirement should ask for written instructions from the Director of Student Teaching.

8

GENERAL INFORMATION

LOCATION OF CAMPUS. Situated on the northern boundary of Upper Montclair, the College is approximately three miles north of the center of the town of Montclair and twelve miles west of New York City. The main entrance is at the intersection of Valley Road and Normal Avenue. Public transportation is available on the Greenwood Lake Division of the Erie Railroad and on Public Service bus routes, (Nos. 60 and 76 connect with the Lackawanna Railroad in the town of Montclair.) Other bus lines serve the campus from New York, Newark, the Oranges, and Paterson. The junction of Highways Nos. 46 and 3 is located about one mile north of the campus.

Housing: Four College dormitories (Russ, Chapin, North Hall and Stone Hall) will be available for the accommodation of men and women registrants during the Summer Session. Applications for room reservations should be sent to: Dean of Students, Montclair State College, Upper Montclair, New Jersey.

*Rates: Room and board is $18.00 a week. This fee includes breakfast and dinner Monday through Friday and all three meals Saturday and Sunday. The College supplies and launders sheets, pillow case and bed pad. Students must supply their own blankets, spreads, towels, etc. The $18.00 fee must be paid on or before the first day of the Summer Session.

*Meals: The Dining Hall will be open during the entire Summer Session. Rates are: Breakfast, $.50; Lunch, a la carte; Dinner, $1.25.
* Subject to change any time by action of the State Board of Education

LIBRARY FACILITIES. The Harry A. Sprague Library was opened in the Spring of 1963. Funds of over $1,000,000 for this building were provided for in the New Jersey Bond Issue of 1959. The library is of modern construction using brick, glass and aluminum facings. It is completely air conditioned. It has three floors, and is planned to accommodate 800 students and an eventual collection of 200,000 volumes.

The main floor includes the Circulation Area, the Technical Processes Area, and the Reference and Bibliography Center. Here, also, is the Humanities Center, which includes books and periodicals in the fields of Philosophy, Religion, Literature, Languages, Music, Fine Arts, History. Biography and Fiction.

The second floor has three main subject areas. The Science and Mathematics Center includes books and periodicals in the fields of Physics. Chemistry. Astronomy, Geology, Biology, Botany. Zoology and in the various branches of Mathematics. The Social Science Center contains books and periodicals in the fields of Sociology, Political Science and Government, Economics, International Relations, Anthropology and Geography. The Education Center contains books in Education, Psychology, Physical Education, Health, Industrial Arts and Business Education. Near the Education area is a curriculum laboratory. On the lower level there is an Art Gallery, a Reserve Book Room, lounge and storage areas.

Special collections are located in a separate room on the second floor. These collections include the China Institute Library, the Lincoln Collection, the Alumni Memorial Library, the Webster Collection, the Finley Collection and the College Archives.

Two classrooms are located outside the main area of the library but are an integral part of the building. Faculty carrels, individual study desks. typing areas and conference rooms are also provided.

OFFICE OF THE SUMMER SESSION. Located at the eastern end of College Hall, it is open from 8:30 A.M. to 4:00 P.M. weekdays. Telephone number is Pilgrim 6-9500, Extension 201.

EXTRA-CURRICULAR ACTIVITIES
Recreational Facilities. The College gymnasium contains basketball, volleyball, squash, and badminton courts. Located on campus are softball fields and recreational areas. Municipal golf courses are within commuting distance, as are public swimming pools.

SERVICES

ACADEMIC ADVISORS. Appointments with the Dean of the College, the Chairman of the Graduate Council, the Director of the Summer Session, or Department Chairmen, may be made by mail or telephone. Appointments should be made as early as possible prior to the end of the spring semester (June 7). Advisors are available during hours of registration.

BOOKSTORE. Located adjacent to the main lobby of the Student Life Building, this on-campus facility will be open from 8:00 A.M. to Noon daily. A limited number of books for each course will be available. Textbook orders should be placed immediately upon completion of registration.

HEALTH SERVICE. A full-time registered nurse is on duty in the medical offices located in Russ Hall. Emergency medical care is available.

VETERANS' COUNSELOR. Veterans seeking admission to the Summer Session should apply well in advance of the registration dates (June 25 and June 26) for a certificate of eligibility and entitlement at the Newark, New Jersey office (20 Washington Place) of the Veterans Administration. In requesting this certificate, the veteran is advised to indicate clearly his educational objective. The Veterans Administration has established certain limitations, especially with regard to change of course. In order that a veteran may be assured that his certificate is in order and that he has taken the proper steps to expedite his training under the G. I. Bill, he should report at registration time to the Veterans' Counselor whose office is located adjacent to the center hall in College Hall.

AUDIO-VISUAL CENTER. This Center provides audio-visual materials, equipment and services for use by faculty and students for classroom instruction and presentation. The staff of the Center is available for special consultation on audio-visual problems, for demonstrations of audio-visual materials and methods, and for special teaching and training in the area of audio-visual education. The Center handles the scheduling of all films for the College, as well as their ordering, mailing, and rentals. Student assistants are provided whenever the use of equipment is requested but are also available for other services.

ACADEMIC REGULATIONS
AND PROCEDURES

STUDENT RESPONSIBILITY. The College expects those who are admitted to assume responsibility for knowing and meeting the various regulations and procedures set forth in the College catalogs. The College reserves the right to terminate the enrollment of any student whose conduct, class attendance, or academic record should prove unsatisfactory.

CREDIT LOADS. Students may not register for more than eight (8) semester hours in the Summer Session. Six (6) semester hours, as a maximum, is strongly recommended.

COURSE NUMBERING. A course numbering system has been developed for all courses in the various departments and curricula. Courses are numbered in the following manner:

100-199	Freshman
200-299	Sophomore
300-399	Junior
400-499	Senior-Graduate
500-699	Graduate

WITHDRAWAL FROM A COURSE. A written notice to the Director. of the Summer Session is required. Refunds are computed from the date of receipt of such written notice. Students who do not submit a written notice will receive the. mark of "F" in those courses which they cease to attend. Students who withdraw after the mid-point (July 19) in the Summer Session will receive an automatic grade of "F".
Withdrawal from a three-week course is allowed up to the mid-point of the course.

GRADES. Only students enrolled for credit receive grades. The following final grades may be received:

A	Excellent	B	Good
C	Fair	D	Poor
F	Failure	Inc.	Incomplete
WP	Withdrawn, Passing	WF	Withdrawn, Failing
	NC	No Credit	

The mark "D" is not accepted for Master's degree credit at Montclair State College. The mark "WP" is given to those who submit in writing their intention of withdrawing from a course before the mid-point in the Summer Session and are doing passing work in the courses involved. "WF" is assigned to students who withdraw before the mid-point and are doing failing work at the time of withdrawal. The mark "F" signifies: (1) failure, (2) the student has failed to submit written notice of his withdrawal, (3) the student has requested withdrawal after the mid-point in the Summer Session. The mark "Inc." is given to a student who, because of illness, is unable to complete his work at the end of a Summer Session. He will be notified when the work is due; if said work is not finished on the prescribed date, a final grade of "F" is recorded.
For three-week courses the above information applies but is geared to the three weeks' duration of the course.
An official record showing credits and grades earned will be mailed to the student three weeks following the close of the Summer Session.

REGISTRATION

PROCEDURE. All students must register in person. Details for registration will be posted on a bulletin board in the lobby of Panzer Gymnasium.

Students must bring records of previous college work in order to establish priority registration. In addition, matriculated students must present their Work Program to advisors.

A student has completed his registration when:

1. His program has been approved by his departmental advisor and by advisors in other departments in which he selects courses.
2. His registration forms have been properly and completely filled out.
3. He pays his tuition and fees.
4. He receives his class admission cards.

PLACE. Panzer Gymnasium.

TIME AND PRIORITY SCHEDULE

Tuesday, June 25 — 9:00 a. m. - 12:00 noon. Matriculated graduate students

1:00 p. m. - 4:00 p. m. Certification students previously registered at MSC (Liberal arts graduates and others working on an initial provisional or limited teaching certificate).

Wednesday, June 26 — 9:00 a. m. - 12:00 noon Certification students registering for the first time at MSC. All students must attend a registration meeting which will be held promptly at 9:00 A. M. in the College High School auditorium. Registration procedures follow this meeting.

9:00 a. m. - 12:00 noon Special undergraduate students (undergraduates matriculated at colleges other than MSC seeking courses at MSC to be transferred to their respective colleges.) Students should see Dean Huber prior to completing registration.

1:00 p. m. - 4:00 p. m. Special students (beyond A. M., non-matriculated students, special interest, auditors, and advanced certification, such as guidance, secondary school principal, etc)

Students unable to take advantage of the above priority arrangement may register with other groups provided they arrive **after their priority schedule**. Students MAY NOT register ahead of their priority listing.

LATE REGISTRATION

Thursday, June 27, 1:00 P. M. to 3:00 P. M.

Friday, June 28, 1:00 P. M. to 3:00 P. M.

Students registering on June 27 and 28 will be charged a $5.00 late registration fee.

No registrations will be accepted after 3:00 p. m., June 28.

Classes begin on June 27. Late registrants must meet the first scheduled class after completing registration or be charged with an unexcused absence.

Special three week course registration — July 18 — for those exclusively taking last sections of three week courses.

12

M. S. C. UNDERGRADUATE REGISTRATION PROCEDURE. Students should check with the College Registrar for "permission to take summer work" forms and registration details.

UNDERGRADUATES MATRICULATED AT COLLEGES OTHER THAN M. S. C. Follow procedures outlined above and register at time specified.

CHANGE OF SCHEDULE. No student will be permitted to change his schedule without approval of his advisor and the Director of Summer Session. Changes may be made between 1:00 P. M. and 3:00 P. M. on June 27 and 28. No changes will be permitted after 3:00 P. M. on June 28. To change from "auditor" to "credit," or vice versa, a student must make formal application not later than the mid-point (July 19) in the Summer Session. Forms are available in the Summer Session office.

CANCELLATION OF COURSES. The College reserves the right to close any course for which the enrollment is insufficient. Students may then register in another course or receive a refund of tuition. If prerequisites are required (see course listings) the student must be sure he has fulfilled them or their equivalents.

*TUITION FEES AND EXPENSES

All checks should be made out to Montclair State College.

TUITION. For residents of New Jersey, $13.00 per semester hour credit; for out-of-state residents, $15.00 per credit.

SERVICE CHARGE. Fifty cents ($.50) per semester hour credit.

REGISTRATION FEE. $2.00 to be paid each time a student registers.

LATE REGISTRATION FEE. $5.00. This additional fee will be charged students registering on June 27 and June 28.

APPLICATION FOR ADMISSION FEE. $5.00 to be paid when student files an application for admission to a degree-granting program. This fee must accompany the application form and is not refundable.

TRANSCRIPT FEE. $1.00 for single copy. Inquire at Registrar's Office.

REFUNDING OF FEES. When the Director of Summer Session receives a written notice of withdrawal prior to the first meeting of courses, all fees are refunded in full. Other refunds are pro-rated from the day on which the Director receives written notification. Withdrawal before the end of the first third of the semester — 60% refund; between the first third and mid-point of the semester — 30% refund; no refunds after the mid-point of the semester. Withdrawals after the mid-point (July 19) in the semester will result in an automatic grade of F.

WORK SCHOLARSHIPS. A limited number of tuition and room-fee scholarships are available. Students are assigned work in the various College departments. Write to Dean of Students for information.

---

* Subject to change any time by action of the State Board of Education.

SPECIAL ACTIVITIES
JUNE 27 – AUGUST 9

READING IMPROVEMENT LABORATORY: Available to New Jersey students in grades 7-12; small groups are formed according to age and achievement levels and meet daily, 10:00 A. M. to 12:00 Noon. The latest in equipment, films, and workshop materials are used to demonstrate speed of comprehension, study skills, and vocabulary growth. Enrollment is limited. Apply at least three months in advance of each term.

Fee: $50.00   Write to: Coordinator, Reading Improvement Laboratory

SPEECH AND HEARING CENTER: The Speech and Hearing Center will offer an intensive remedial speech program. It will accommodate a maximum of sixty children between 4 and 18 years of age. The program, offered at 10:45 A. M. to 12:30 P.M. daily, is designed to provide therapy for children with the usual types of speech problems, as well as for those who have major problems of voice, articulation, and rhythm (stuttering). Children with retarded language development or loss of language are also eligible. Therapy is also provided for children who have speech problems associated with tongue thrusting, malocclusion, and cleft palate.

Fee: $60.00   Write to: Coordinator, Speech and Hearing Center

MONTCLAIR STATE COLLEGE DAY CAMP: A general program of games, relays, story-telling, rhythms, and nature walks will be presented for children in the 6-12 year age range. The youngsters also enjoy approximately one hour of arts and crafts activities. The dates will coincide with those of the regular summer session, June 27 to August 9, and the hours will be 8:30 A. M. to 12:30 P.M. The fee will include some arts and crafts supplies and light refreshments.

Fee: $10:00 per week   Write to: Director, Panzer School of Physical
                              Education and Hygiene, c/o this College

WORKSHOP FOR APPRENTICES IN DRAMATIC PRODUCTION: The Speech Department is pleased to announce that it will continue its summer program in theater for pre-college students. Secondary school students and recent graduates are eligible. Activities include the study of acting, scenery design and construction, lighting, make-up, and voice and diction. Following a 1:30 P. M. daily seminar, students will participate as actors and crew members in the preparation and presentation of major dramatic productions. Full use will be made of the extensive facilities in the air-conditioned Memorial Auditorium — one of the most modern and beautiful college theaters in the East.

Registration is limited. Application must be made in advance and should be accompanied by a letter of recommendation from the applicant's school Dramatics or English teacher. A personal interview will also be arranged.

Fee: $60.00   Write to: Coordinator, Summer Theater Programs

TEXTBOOK EXHIBIT

On July 11 and July 12 from 8:30 A.M. to 2:30 P.M. there will be an exhibit of high school and elementary school textbooks. The exhibit is primarily for teachers and administrators attending the Summer Session, but will be open to undergraduate students and the general public. The exhibit will be located in Life Hall.

NEW JERSEY CONGRESS OF PARENTS AND TEACHERS
PARENT-TEACHER WORKSHOP
July 8-12

The New Jersey Congress, in cooperation with Montclair State College, will offer a five day workshop for parent-teacher officers and members, and for teachers and future teachers.

The purposes of this Workshop are:
1. To increase understanding of P. T. A. philosophy and objectives.
2. To stimulate and direct the planning for effective parent-teacher meetings.
3. To activate planning for action programs with the help of resource people and materials.
4. To suggest opportunities for new and different community activities of local parent-teacher associations.
5. To offer experience in gaining group leadership skills and help in the development of plans for parent-teacher study groups.

Write to: Dr. Clyde Slocum, P. T.A. Coordinator, State Chairman — Cooperation with Colleges, Monmouth College, Long Branch, New Jersey.

NEW JERSEY STATE SCHOOL OF CONSERVATION
BRANCHVILLE, NEW JERSEY

The six State Colleges, the State Department of Education, and the State Department of Conservation and Economic Development, jointly operate the New Jersey State School of Conservation at Lake Wapalanne in Stokes State Forest, Sussex County. Credit for the courses given at the New Jersey State School of Conservation may be applied toward the bachelor's or master's degrees at the New Jersey State Colleges, subject to approval in advance by the institution concerned. Students are advised to check with their advisors relative to the application of these credits toward degrees.

Courses in Camping, Conservation, Education, Field Biology, Field Science, Fine Arts, Geography, Industrial Arts, and Outdoor Education, are offered at the New Jersey State School of Conservation. Special descriptive announcements may be had by writing to the New Jersey State School of Conservation, Branchville, New Jersey.

ALCOHOL EDUCATION WORKSHOP
June 24 through July 9

Health Education S412 — Alcohol Education Workshop   Dr. Tews
     June 24, 25, 26 — 7:00 to 10:00 P. M. and   Room 5-G
     June 27, 28   — 1:30 to 4:30 P. M.
     July 1, 2, 3, 8, 9 — 1:30 to 4:30 P. M.
                 Credit: 2 semester hours

A workshop offered with the cooperation of the State Department of Health and aimed at preparing teachers of health, school nurse teachers, guidance personnel, and others, for more understanding service in this special area of education. The workshop will concentrate on a careful study of the physiological, sociological and psychological problems involved in the use of beverage alcohol and on the materials, techniques, etc., found to be most useful in alcohol education programs.

A limited number of Tuition Scholarships are available. For full details regarding this workshop, write to: Director, Field Services.

DRIVER EDUCATION COURSES

PRE-SUMMER SESSION COURSE

Health Education S408 — Driver Education   **Dr. Coder**
    June 17 through June 26 — 7:00 - 10:00 P. M. and   Rooms 1 & 9-D
    June 27 through July 3 — 1:00 - 6:00 P. M. and
                    7:00 - 9:30 P. M.
             Credit: 3 semester hours

SUMMER SESSION COURSE

Health Education S408 — Driver Education   **Dr. Coder**
    July 22 through August 9 — 1:00 - 5:00 P. M.   Rooms 1 & 9-D
             Credit: 3 semester hours

Authorization to Teach Behind-the-Wheel Driver Education and Driver Training:
A teacher must have his or her certificate endorsed by the Division of Teacher
Certification, State Department of Education. The requirements for such endorsement are: ("Rules Concerning Teachers' Certificates" — 18th edition —
revised 1956).

    1. A valid New Jersey teacher's certificate.
    2. A current New Jersey driver's license.
    3. Three years of automobile driving experience.
    4. Evidence of satisfactory completion of a course in driver education and
        driver training approved by the Commissioner of Education.
    5. A good driving record.
    6. A standard sized car is required for road and skills test.

Secondary schools in New Jersey are increasing their offerings in Driver Educa-
tion. This increase has resulted in a demand for more Driver Education teachers.
To meet this demand, Montclair State College is increasing the number of
courses being conducted in this field. Assistance is given by the New Jersey
State Safety Council, the New Jersey Automobile Club, the American Automobile
Association, the New Jersey State Police, and the New Jersey Department of
Motor Vehicles.

EXTRA CHARGES are made for textbooks and other materials. Some materials
are furnished free.

Registration for these courses is limited. Students must be approved by Dr.
Coder prior to registration. Write to Dr. Coder for complete information. Fees
are to be paid on first day class meets.

PRE-SUMMER SESSION COURSE

Phys. Ed. S415 — Movement Techniques and Rhythmic   **Mrs. Sommer**
    Accompaniment   Room 4-P
    June 13 through June 21 — 4:15 P. M. to 6:15 P. M.
    June 24 through July 3 — 1:00 P. M. to 5:00 P. M.
             Credit: 2 semester hours
Registration at the first meeting of the class.

POST-SUMMER SESSION COURSE

Industrial Arts S407 — Field Study of Industry
    July 29 through August 9 — 1:00 P. M. to 4:00 P. M.
    August 12 through August 23 — 8:00 A. M. to 3:30 P. M.
             Credit: 4 semester hours
Registration for this course is limited. Students must be approved by the
instructor prior to or at the time of registration (June 25 and 26).

THREE WEEK COURSES

First three weeks — June 27 through July 19.

Chemistry S101 — General College Chemistry I

Education S530 — Curriculum Construction in Secondary School

Education S567 — Education and Psychological Measurement in Guidance

Speech S437A — Dramatic Production Workshop

Last three weeks — July 22 through August 9

Chemistry S102 — General College Chemistry II

Education S539 — Seminar in Curriculum Organization

Education S568 — Psychological Tests in Guidance Programs

Health Education S408 — Driver Education

Speech S437B — Advanced Dramatic Production Workshop

OUTDOOR STUDENT CONFERENCE

COURSES OF THE SUMMER SESSION

Descriptions of the graduate courses will be found in the Graduate Bulletin of the College. Courses numbered 500 and above are open only to graduate students; those numbered 400-499, inclusive, are senior-graduate courses and their descriptions follow the descriptions of the graduate courses. Courses below the 400 number will be found in the Undergraduate Bulletin of the College. Only entirely new courses are described in the Summer Session Bulletin.

CODE FOR BUILDINGS

Auditorium	A	Music Building	M
Annex 2	B	Panzer Gymnasium	P
College Hall	C	Recreation Building	R
Annex 3	D	Sprague Library	S
Annex 4	E	Chapin Hall	T
Finley Hall	F	Mallory Hall	V
College High School	H		

BUSINESS EDUCATION DEPARTMENT

Business Education S520B — Improvement of Instruction in Business
8:30 - 9:20 A. M.   Education: Bookkeeping, Accounting,   Dr. Froehlich
                          and Business Arithmetic   Room 1-B
                          Credit: 2 semester hours

Business Education S533 — Supervised Work Experience and
                          Seminar   Dr. Froehlich
Seminar 7:00 - 9:00 P. M. Wed.   Credit: 4 semester hours   Room 1-B

EDUCATION DEPARTMENT

Education S201 — Human Development and Behavior I   Mr. Harmon
8:05 - 9:20 A. M. Sec. I   Credit: 3 semester hours   Room 15-M
11:30 - 12:45 P. M. Sec. II   Credit: 3 semester hours   Mr. Fuchs
                                                            Room 15-M

Education S202 — Human Development and Behavior II   Dr. Seidman
11:30 - 12:45 P.M.   Credit: 3 semester hours   Room 111-V

Education S303 — The Teacher in School and Community   To be announced
8:05 - 9:20 A. M. Sec. 1   Credit: 3 semester hours   Room 13-M
11:30 - 12:45 P. M. Sec. II   Credit: 3 semester hours   Dr. Gorman
                                                            Room 13-M

Education S304 — Principles and Techniques of
                Secondary Education   Mr. Lewin
8:05 - 9:20 A. M. Sec. I   Credit: 3 semester hours   Room 4-H
11:30 - 12:45 P. M. Sec. II   Credit: 3 semester hours   Mr. Jump
                                                            Room 104-S

Education S401 — Development of Educational Thought   Mr. Jump
8:05 - 9:20 A. M. Sec. I   Credit: 3 semester hours   Room 104-S
8:05 - 9:20 A. M. Sec. II   Credit: 3 semester hours   Dr. Richardson
                                                            Lounge-T
11:30 - 12:45 P. M. Sec. III Credit: 3 semester hours   Mr. Lewin
                                                            Lounge-T

Education S406 — Educational Sociology   Dr. Gorman
8:05 - 9:20 A. M   Credit: 3 semester hours   Room 13-H

Education S408 — Selection and Utilization of A-V Materials   Miss Fantone
10:30 - 11:20 A. M.   Credit: 2 semester hours   Aud.-H

Education S409 — Radio and Sound Equipment in the Class Room   Mr. Sheft
11:30 - 12:20 P. M.   Credit: 2 semester hours   Aud.-H

Education S463 — Reading and the Improvement of Study Skills   Mr. Gregg
8:05 - 9:20 A. M.   Credit: 3 semester hours   Room 13-E

Education S492 — Comparative Education   Dr. Richardson
11:30 - 12:45 P. M.   Credit: 3 semester hours   Room 103-S

Education S493 — Recent Trends in European Education   Dr. Lange
July 9 - August 19   Credit: 6 semester hours   Field Study
    Present educational policies and procedures in selected countries of
Europe are investigated. A survey is made of present educational systems
and a study is made of recent changes in selected European educational
systems. This course is a field-study course covering a period of six weeks
of intensive study and visitation to school systems in Europe.

Education S501 — Tests and Measurements in Secondary Education   Dr. Walter
9:30 - 10:20 A. M.   Credit: 2 semester hours   Room 5-H

Education S502 — Teaching the Block-of-Time Curriculum in the
                Junior and Senior High School   Mr. Salt
8:30 - 9:20 A. M.   Credit: 2 semester hours   Room 103-S

Education S503 — Methods and Instruments of Research   Dr. Peckham
8:30 - 9:20 A. M. Sec. 1   Credit: 2 semester hours   Room 104-F
11:30 - 12:20 P. M. Sec. II   Credit: 2 semester hours   Dr. Walter
        Prerequisite: Math 400 or Educ. 501 or equivalent   Room 5-H

Education S510 — Introduction to Educational Administration   Dr. Morehead
11:30 - 12:20 P. M.   Credit: 2 semester hours   Room 7-H
              Prerequisite: Teaching Experience

Education S512 — School-Community Relations   Dr. Atkinson
11:30 - 12:20 P. M.   Credit: 2 semester hours   Room 4-H
              Prerequisite: Teaching Experience

Education S514 — School Law   Dr. Morehead
10:30 - 11:20 A. M.   Credit: 2 semester hours   Room 7-H
              Prerequisite: Educ. 510 or equivalent

Education S516 — School Finance   Dr. Morehead
8:30 - 9:20 A. M.   Credit: 2 semester hours   Room 7-H
              Prerequisite: Educ. 510 or equivalent

Education S520 — Organization and Administration of the
                Modern High School   Dr. Peckham
11:30 - 12:20 P. M.   Credit: 2 semester hours   Room 13-H
              Prerequisite: Educ. 510 or equivalent

Education S529 — Seminar in Secondary Administration
and Supervision   **Dr. Peckham**
9:30 - 10:20 A. M.   Credit: 2 semester hours   Room 13-H
Prerequisite: Educ. 503, 520 and 540 or equiv.

Education S530 — Curriculum Construction in Secondary School   **Mr. Salt**
10:30 - 12:20 P. M.   Credit: 2 semester hours   Room 106-F
Prerequisite: Educ. 510 or equivalent
(First three weeks — June 27 through July 19)

Education S535 — Organization and Administration of Extra-
Curricular Activities   **To be announced**
9:30 - 10:20 A. M.   Credit: 2 semester hours   Room 7-H
Prerequisite: Education 580

Education S539 — Seminar in Curriculum Organization   **Mr. Salt**
10:30 - 12:20 P. M.   Credit: 2 semester hours   Room 106-F
Prerequisite: Education 530
(Last three weeks — July 22 through August 9)

Education S540 — Supervision in Secondary School, Part I   **Dr. Atkinson**
9:30 - 10:20 A. M.   Credit: 2 semester hours   Room 4-H
Prerequisite: Educ. 510 or equivalent

Education S556N — Corrective and Remedial Reading,
Part I: Causation   **Mr. Buchner**
11:30 - 12:20 P. M.   Credit: 2 semester hours   Rooms 1 & 13-E
Prerequisite: Permission of Instructor

Education S560 — Advanced Educational Psychology   **Dr. Brower**
8:30 - 9:20 A. M.   Credit: 2 semester hours   Room 15-E
Prerequsite: An Introductory Course in Psychology

Education S566 — Psychology and Education of the Gifted   **Dr. Brower**
9:30 - 10:20 A. M.   Credit: 2 semester hours   Room 14-H

Education S567 — Educational and Psychological Measurement
in Guidance   **Dr. Seidman**
8:30 - 10:20 A. M.   Credit: 2 semester hours   Room 12-H
Prerequisite: Teaching Experience
(First three weeks — June 27 through July 19)

Education S568 — Psychological Tests in Guidance Programs   **Dr. Davis**
8:30 - 10:20 A. M.   Credit: 2 semester hours   Room 12-H
Prerequisite: Education 567
(Last three weeks — July 22 through August 9)

Education S573 — Production of A-V Instructional Materials:
Part I, Non-Projected Materials   **Dr. Duffy**
9:30 - 10:20 A. M.   Credit: 2 semester hours   Aud.-H
Prerequisite: Education 408

Education S580 — Principles and Techniques of Guidance   **Dr. Atkinson**
10:30 - 11:20 A. M. Sec. I   Credit: 2 semester hours   Room 4-H
11:30 - 12:20 P.M. Sec. II   Credit: 2 semester hours   **Mr. Gregg**
Prerequisite: Teaching Experience   Room 106-V
This course is a prerequisite for most guidance courses offered
in this division of the college.

Education S581 — Community Resources for Guidance   Mr. Fuchs
9:30 - 10:20 A. M.   Credit: 2 semester hours   Room 13-M
                               Prerequisite: Education 580

Education S583 — Educational Guidance   Dr. Gelfond
10:30 - 11:20 A. M.   Credit: 2 semester hours   Room 104-F
                               Prerequisite: Education 580

Education S585 — Group Guidance and Counseling Activities   Dr. Gelfond
11:30 - 12:20 P. M.   Credit: 2 semester hours   Room 104-F
                               Prerequisite: Education 580

Education S588 — Techniques of Interviewing and Counseling Dr. Brower
11:30 - 12:20 P. M.   Credit: 2 semester hours   Room 15-E
                       Prerequisite: 12 s. h. in Personnel and Guidance

Education S602 — Seminar in Guidance   Dr. Davis
10:30 - 12:20 P. M.   Credit: 4 semester hours   Room 12-H
                    Prerequisite: Educ. 580, Educ. 503 and A. M. Candidate

Education S603 — Principles and Practices of Research   Dr. Walter
8:30 - 9:20 A. M.   Credit: 2 semester hours   Room 5-H
                               Prerequisite: Education 503

ENGLISH DEPARTMENT

English S100C — Fundamentals of Writing   Mrs. Feierabend
8:05 - 9:20 A. M.   Credit: 3 semester hours   Room 3-B

English S100G — Western World Literature   Mr. Reaske
11:30 - 12:45 P. M.   Credit: 3 semester hours   Room 4-B

English S301 — Shakespeare's Major Plays   Mrs. Feierabend
11:30-12:45 P. M.   Credit: 3 semester hours   Room 3-B

English S413 — Modern Poetry   Dr. Krauss
10:30 - 11:20 A. M.   Credit: 2 semester hours   Room 5-B

English S419 — Theories and Teaching of Grammar   Dr. Leavitt
11:30 - 12:20 P. M.   Credit: 2 semester hours   Room 2-B

English S512 — The Growth and Structure of the
               English Language   Dr. Leavitt
8:30 - 9:20 A. M.   Credit: 2 semester hours   Room 2-B

English S514 — Origin and Development of the
               Arthurian Legend   Dr. Krauss
8:30 - 9:20 A. M.   Credit: 2 semester hours   Room 5-B

English S515 — Robert Browning   Dr. Young
8:30 - 9:20 A. M.   Credit: 2 semester hours   Room 4-B

English S519 — English in the Modern High School   Dr. Young
9:30 - 10:20 A. M.   Credit: 2 semester hours   Room 2-B
             (Accepted by State Department of Education for Certification)

English S534 — Medieval Epic, Saga, and Romance   **Dr. Krauss**
11:30 - 12:20 P. M.   Credit: 2 semester hours   Room 5-B

English S536 — Philosophy of Great Literature   **Dr. Young**
11:30 - 12:20 P. M.   Credit: 2 semester hours   Room 1-B

English S543 — Contemporary American Literature   **Dr. Leavitt**
10:30 - 11:20 A. M.   Credit: 2 semester hours   Room 2-B

FINE ARTS DEPARTMENT

Fine Arts S302 — Foundations of Art Education   **Mr. Vernacchia**
                    (Methods of Teaching Fine Arts)
9:30 - 10:20 A. M.   Credit: 2 semester hours   Art Lib.-F

Fine Arts S403A or S403B — Print Making I or II   **Mr. Vernacchia**
11:30 - 12:45 P. M.   Credit: 2 semester hours each   Room 219-F

Fine Arts S408A or S408B — Painting Laboratory I or II   **Dr. Wygant**
10:30 - 11:20 A. M.   Credit: 2 semester hours each   Room 221-F
(2 hrs. weekly additional laboratory assignment to be made by instructor)

Fine Arts S490 — Art of the Nineteenth Century   **Dr. Wygant**
9:30 - 10:20 A. M.   Credit: 2 semester hours   Room 221-F

Fine Arts S491 — Art of the Twentieth Century   **Mr. Vernacchia**
8:30 - 9:20 A. M.   Credit: 2 semester hours   Room 219-F

FOREIGN LANGUAGE DEPARTMENT

French S406 — The Contemporary French Novel   **Dr. Szklarczyk**
8:30 - 9:20 A. M.   Credit: 2 semester hours   Room 4-D

Language S515 — The History of the French Language   **Dr. Szklarczyk**
9:30 - 10:20 A. M.   Credit: 2 semester hours   Room 4-D

Spanish S415 — Projects in Spanish and
                    Spanish American Folklore   **Dr. Prieto**
10:30 - 11:20 A. M.   Credit: 2 semester hours   Room 4-D

Spanish S506 — Spanish American Novel   **Dr. Prieto**
11:30 - 12:20 P. M.   Credit: 2 semester hours   Room 4-D

GEOGRAPHY DEPARTMENT

Science S100C — The Earth Sciences   **Mr. Kelland**
9:30 - 10:20 A. M.   Credit: 2 semester hours   Room 5-D

Geography S418 — Regional Geography of North America   **Mr. Kelland**
11:30 - 12:20 P. M.   Credit: 2 semester hours   Room 5-D

22

INDUSTRIAL ARTS DEPARTMENT

Ind. Arts S221 — Woods and Crafts I   Mr. Olsen
6:00 - 9:40 P. M.   Credit: 4 semester hours   Room 118-F

Ind. Arts S232 — Metals and Power II   Mr. Butler
6:00 - 9:40 P. M.   Credit: 4 semester hours   Room 119-F

Ind. Arts S313 — Graphic Arts and Drawing III   Dr. Earl
6:00 - 9:40 P. M.   Credit: 4 semester hours   Room 117-F

Ind. Arts S407 — Field Studies of Industry   Dr. Streichler
July 29 - August 9 — 1:00 P. M. to 4:00 P. M.
August 12 - August 23 — 8:00 A. M. to 3:30 P. M.
                        Credit: 4 semester hours   Room 116-F

Ind. Arts S431 — Advanced Electronics   Dr. Duffy
11:30 - 12:20 P. M.   Credit: 2 semester hours   Room 119-F

Ind. Arts S511 — Supervision of Industrial Arts   Dr. Frankson
10:30 - 11:20 A. M.   Credit: 2 semester hours   Room 116-F

Ind. Arts S601 — Seminar in Industrial Arts Problem —
                  Solving Approach to Teaching   Dr. Frankson
8:05 - 9:45 A. M.   Credit: 4 semester hours   Room 116-F

MATHEMATICS DEPARTMENT

Mathematics S300 — The Social Uses of Mathematics   To be Announced
11:30 - 12:20 P. M.   Credit: 2 semester hours   Room 107-F

Mathematics S310 — An Introduction to Mathematics   To be Announced
9:30 - 10:20 A. M.   Credit: 2 semester hours   Room 110-V
                        May be substituted for Math. 300

Mathematics S400 — Educational Statistics   To be Announced
8:30 - 9:20 A. M. Sec. I   Credit: 2 semester hours   Room 109-V
10:30 - 11:20 A. M. Sec. II   Credit: 2 semester hours   Mr. Anderson
                                                                   Room 109-V
11:30 - 12:20 P. M. Sec. III   Credit: 2 semester hours   To be Announced
                        Prerequisite for Education 503   Room 110-V

Mathematics S401X — The Teaching of Mathematics
                     in Secondary Schools   Mr. Anderson
9:30 - 10:20 A. M.   Credit: 2 semester hours   Room 109-V

Mathematics S415 — Differential Equations   To be Announced
10:30 - 11:20 A. M.   Credit: 2 semester hours   Room 110-V

Mathematics S480 — Elements of Logic   Mr. Anderson
11:30 - 12:20 P. M.   Credit: 2 semester hours   Room 109-V

Mathematics S518 — The Theory of Functions of Real Variables   Mr. Williams
10:30 - 11:20 A. M.   Credit: 2 semester hours   Room 107-F

23

Mathematics S530 — Mathematics Materials for the
                     Teacher of Mathematics   Mr. Struyk
9:30 - 10:20 A. M.   Credit: 2 semester hours   Room 108-F

Mathematics S533 — Non-Euclidean Geometry   To be Announced
8:30 - 9:20 A. M.   Credit: 2 semester hours   Room 110-V

Mathematics S552 — Mathematics of Physical Sciences   Mr. Devlin
8:30 - 9:20 A. M.   Credit: 2 semester hours   Room 108-F

The following courses are open only to National Science Foundation participants. Students were selected in March 1963 and registrations are closed. These courses are listed for record purposes only.

Mathematics S101 — Mathematical Analysis   Dr. Rosenberg
8:30 - 10:30 A. M.   Credit: 4 semester hours   Room 106-F

Mathematics S407 — Advanced Calculus   To be Announced
8:30 - 9:20 A. M.   Credit: 2 semester hours   Room 105-F

Mathematics S508 — Foundations of Geometry   Dr. Meserve
9:30 - 10:20 A. M.   Credit: 2 semester hours   Room 107-F

Mathematics S518 — The Theory of Functions of Real Variables
                                            Mr. Williams
8:30 - 9:20 A. M.   Credit: 2 semester hours   Room 107-F

Mathematics S523 — The Theory of Probability   Dr. Maletsky
9:30 - 10:20 A. M.   Credit: 2 semester hours   Room 105-F

Mathematics S529 — Curriculum Construction in Mathematics   Dr. Sobel
11:00 - 12:00 Noon   Credit: 2 semester hours   Room 105-F

Mathematics S552 — Mathematics of Physical Sciences   Mr. Devlin
11:00 - 12:00 Noon   Credit: 2 semester hours   Room 108-F

Education S503 — Methods and Instruments of Research   Dr. Lutz
11:00 - 12:00 Noon   Credit: 2 semester hours   Room SL-V

MUSIC DEPARTMENT

Music S100 — Music Appreciation   Mr. Hayton
9:30 - 10:20 A. M.   Credit: 2 semester hours   Room 15-M

Music S426 — Survey of Music Literature   Mr. Hayton
10:30 - 11:20 A. M.   Credit: 2 semester hours   Room 15-M

PANZER SCHOOL OF PHYSICAL EDUCATION
AND HYGIENE

Health Education S100 — Healthful Living   Dr. Tews
10:30 - 11:20 A. M.   Credit: 2 semester hours   Room 5-P

Physical Education S101 — Activities and Methods
                     for the Elementary Grades   Dr. Wacker
8:05 - 9:45 A. M.   Credit: 3 semester hours   Room 4-P

Health Education S408 — Driver Education   Dr. Coder
                    Credit: 3 semester hours   Room 1 & 9-D
        Prerequisite: Approval of instructor prior to registration
        For details, see page 16 and write to Dr. Coder.

Health Education S412 — Alcohol Education Workshop   Dr. Tews
                    Credit: 2 semester hours   Room 5-P
          Pre-Summer Session — June 24 through July 9
          See page 15 for details

Phys. Education S413 — Social Recreation   Dr. Wacker
10:30 - 11:20 A. M.   Credit: 2 semester hours   Room 4-P

Phys. Education S415 — Movement Techniques and
                       Rhythmic Accompaniment   Mrs. Sommer
                    Credit: 2 semester hours   Room 4-P
June 13-21, 4:15 - 6:15 P. M.
June 24 - July 3, 1:00 - 5:00 P. M.

SCIENCE DEPARTMENT

Biology S408 — Biological Techniques   Mr. Silver
12:30 - 2:20 P.M.   Credit: 4 semester hours   Room 209-F
          Prerequisite: 8 s.h. Zoology; 4 s.h. Botany

*Biology S412 — Genetics   Mr. Silver
10:30 - 11:20 A. M.   Credit: 2 semester hours   Room 209-F
          Prerequisite: Elementary course in General Biology

Chemistry S101 — General College Chemistry I   Dr. Becker
9:30 - 11:20 A. M. and
12:30 - 4:20 P. M.   Credit: 4 semester hours   Room 204-F
          (First three weeks — June 27 through July 19)

Chemistry S102 — General College Chemistry II   Dr. Gawley
9:30 - 11:20 A. M. and
12:30 - 4:20 P. M.   Credit: 4 semester hours   Room 204-F
          (Last three weeks — July 22 through August 9)

Chemistry S412 — Physical Chemistry II   Dr. Garik
10:30 - 11:20 A. M.   Credit: 4 semester hours   Room 206-F
12:30 - 4:20 P.M. — Laboratory on Monday, Wednesday and Friday
          Prerequisite: Permission of Instructor

Physics S512 — Modern Physics   Mr. Hodson
8:30 - 10:20 A. M.   Credit: 4 semester hours   Room 201-F
          Prerequisite: General College Physics and Electrical Measurements

Science S100C — The Earth Sciences   Mr. Kelland
9:30 - 10:20 A. M.   Credit: 2 semester hours   Room 5-D

Science S401X — The Teaching òf Science in Secondary Schools   Dr. Gawley
8:30 - 9:20 A. M.   Credit: 2 semester hours   Room 204-F

*Science S418 — Three Centuries of Science Progress   Mr. Hodson
10:30 - 11:20 A .M.   Credit: 2 semester hours   Room 201-F

*These courses are acceptable for undergraduate general education science and
mathematics electives.

The following program is designed to meet the needs of Earth Science Teachers. However, students may register for these courses **separately.**

Physics S406X — Astronomy   Dr. Allen
8:30 - 9:20 A. M. Daily   Credit: 2 semester hours   Room 207-F
and 12:30 - 3:20 P. M. Laboratory on Mondays
   Prerequisite: General College Physics and Chemistry

Physics S410 — Meteorology   Dr. Allen
9:30 - 10:20 A. M. Daily   Credit: 2 semester hours   Room 207-F
and 12:30 - 3:20 P. M. Laboratory on Wednesdays
   Prerequisite: General College Physics

Science S413 — Field Studies in Science: Physical   Mr. Kelland
10:30 - 11:20 A. M. Daily   Credit: 2 semester hours   Room 207-F
and 12:30 - 3:20 P. M. Laboratory on Fridays

SOCIAL STUDIES DEPARTMENT

Social Studies S200A — Contemporary American Life   Mr. Johnson
11:30 - 12:45 P. M.   Credit: 3 semester hours   Room 11-M

Social Studies S201 — The Development of the
                      United States (To 1865)   Mr. Alloway
8:05 - 9:20 A. M.   Credit: 3 semester hours   Room 114-F

Social Studies S425X — Medieval Civilization   Mr. Alloway
10:30 - 11:20 A. M.   Credit: 2 semester hours   Room 114-F

Social Studies S449 — South Asia   Mr. Johnson
10:30 - 11:20 A. M   Credit: 2 semester hours   Room 5-D

Social Studies S474 — America in Transition   Dr. Royer
11:30 - 12:20 P. M.   Credit: 2 semester hours   Room 114-F

Social Studies S489 — South Pacific   Mr. Bye
July 5 - August 22   Credit: 6 semester hours   Field Study
        This is a seven week field study course covering the islands of the
South Pacific region, Australia and New Zealand. The purpose of this course
is (1) to study the various culture patterns of these islands, (2) to appreciate their significance in recent history and in the future history of the
twentieth century, (3) to understand the importance of Australia and New
Zealand in the modern world. Among the places to be visited are Tahiti,
Fiji, Tonga, New Zealand, Australia, Tasmania, East New Guinea, Papua,
New Caledonia, the Isle of Pines, Samoa, Hawaii, and other islands. The geographic, historical, economic and anthropological patterns of the region are
studied. There are visits to farms, mines, schools, public buildings and native
villages, and opportunities to meet people in all sorts and conditions of life.

Social Studies S515 — History of Political Thought   Dr. Royer
9:30 - 10:20 A. M.   Credit: 2 semester hours   Room 114-F

26

SPEECH DEPARTMENT

Speech S100D — Fundamentals of Speech   Mr. Moll
8:05 - 9:20 A. M.   Credit: 3 semester hours   Room 11-M

Speech S204 — Introduction to Public Speaking   Mr. Moll
10:30 - 11:20 A. M.   Credit: 2 semester hours   Room 11-M

Speech S435 — Stagecraft   Dr. McElroy
1:30 - 2:45 P. M.   Credit: 2 semester hours   Room Aud-A

Speech S437A — Dramatic Production Workshop   Dr. McElroy
1:30 - 4:30 P. M.   Credit: 2 semester hours   Room Aud-A
     (First three weeks — June 27 through July 19)

Speech S437B — Advanced Dramatic Production Workshop   Mr. Ballare
1:30 - 4:30 P. M.   Credit: 2 semester hours   Room 4-A
     (Last three weeks — July 22 through August 9)

**Speech S439B — Anatomy and Physiology of the
         Audio and Vocal Mechanisms**   Miss Kauffman
8:00 - 8:50 A. M.   Credit: 2 semester hours   Room 1-A

Speech S439C — Speech Pathology   Dr. Scholl
9:30 - 10:20 A. M.   Credit: 2 semester hours   Room 2-A

Speech S439D — Practicum in Speech Correction   Mrs. Hubschman
10:30 - 11:20 A. M.   Credit: 1 semester hour   Room 1-A

Speech S439E — Advanced Practicum in Speech Correction   Mrs. Hubschman
11:30 - 12:20 P. M.   Credit: 1 semester hour   Room 1-A

Speech S456 — Play Direction   Dr. Fox
1:30 - 3:00 P. M.   Credit: 2 semester hours   Room Aud-A

Speech S468 — Measurement of Hearing   Dr. Leight
9:05 - 10:20 A. M.   Credit: 3 semester hours   Room 1-A

Speech S532 — Practicum in Speech Rehabilitation   Dr. Scholl
10:30 - 12:20 P. M.   Credit: 2 semester hours   Room 2-A

Speech S535 — Seminar in Speech Rehabilitation   Dr. Scholl
9:30 - 12:30 P. M.   Credit: 6 semester hours   Room 2-A

Speech S567 — Seminar in Dramatic Production   Dr. Fox
1:30 - 5:00 P. M.   Credit: 6 semester hours   Room Aud-A

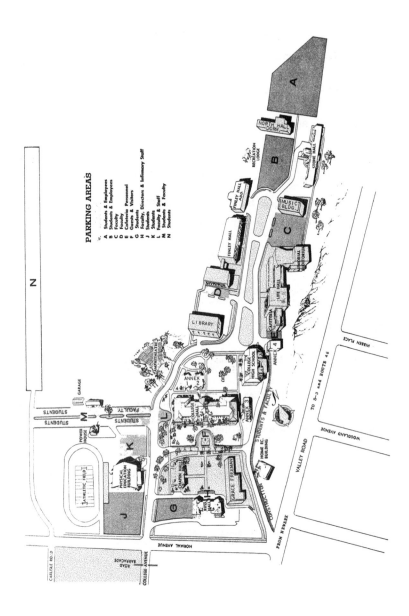

PARKING AREAS

A Students & Employees
B Students & Employees
C Faculty
D Faculty
E Cafeteria Personnel
F Guests & Visitors
G Students
H Faculty, Directors & Infirmary Staff
J Students
K Students
L Faculty & Staff
M Students & Faculty
N Students

MONTCLAIR STATE COLLEGE
UPPER MONTCLAIR, N. J.

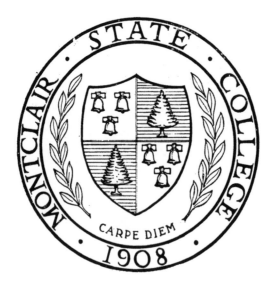

Non Profit Organizati
U. S. Postage
P A I D
Upper Montclair, N.
Permit No. 102

Lightning Source UK Ltd.
Milton Keynes UK
UKHW010623030119
334852UK00010B/907/P